The Scotch Irish—Rough-tongued, hard-fighting, defiant, tens of thousands of them fled oppression and poverty in Northern Ireland in the 18th century to come to America and settle a frontier nation. . .

Their Women—Courageous, passionate—with their men, they walked the roads to the virgin lands on paths marked by hard times and Indian troubles. Their whole generation became. . .

The Movers

The Destination?—Wherever the corn grew eight feet tall and opportunity waited. Pennsylvania, Kentucky, Indiana, and all the Midwest and South beckoned. Shapers of the heartland, fighters of the Indian wars and the Revolution in the West, the Scotch-Irish epitomize the restless independence of the American spirit.

Also by Nancy Niblack Baxter

GALLANT FOURTEENTH:
THE STORY OF AN INDIANA CIVIL WAR REGIMENT 1980

THE MOVERS

A Saga of the Scotch-Irish

Nancy N. Baxter

The Heartland Chronicles

Guild Press
Austin, Texas

Copyright © 1987 by Nancy N. Baxter
Published by Guild Press, Austin Texas
Library of Congress Catalog Card Number: 86-22859
ISBN: 0-9617367-1-2

This book was produced by Wordware Publishing, Inc.

For information and distribution information contact
Guild Press c/o Wordware Publishing
1506 Capital Avenue, Plano Texas 75074

This book is dedicated to the memory of William Hunter (1908-1985), for many years Chief Historian at the Pennsylvania Historical and Museum Commission, who believed the story of the Scotch-Irish should be told and did so much to make the telling of this part of it possible.

Historical Note

When James I of England (1603-1625) came to the throne, the last of the traditional Irish chieftains surrendered to him after bitter warfare. James allowed the clan chiefs to kiss his ring at Whitehall, thus ending a conquest of Ireland which had lasted four hundred years. The outraged Irish people retreated to the hills and refused to submit willingly to British rule. James I hit upon a scheme to subdue the defiant, Catholic population. He sent Protestants into the North of Ireland to settle and subdue it and gave them the Irishmen's land. Most of the new settlers were Scotch Presbyterians.

"The Scotch in northern Ireland will be God's bulldogs," he told one of his ministers. "We shall let them bite the wild Irish into submission."

The decision of James I to settle Catholic Ireland with Scotch Protestants was not only to change British history to this day, but also to have a major impact upon American history.

Although many of the events of this book are based on historical fact, and some of the characters in this book were living people, the story is fiction.

NOTE: Some old spelling forms have been retained in *The Movers*.

Acknowledgments

I would like to thank these people for the long hours and patience spent in helping assemble the material for this book: J. Martin West, Director of Old Fort Ligonier museum, and one of the consultants for the George Washington mini-series, who served as historical editor of the book; Tom Shaw, Assistant Site manager at Historic Fort Snelling in St. Paul, whose wide, practical experience with the history of agriculture was invaluable; Richard Day, the expert on everything to do with Vincennes, Indiana; Robert Stevens and Donna Beeson of the Lewis Historical Collections Library at Vincennes University; Robert Holden, Historian at the George Rogers Clark National Historical Park in Vincennes and an expert on the Battle of Tippecanoe; Jean Jose, Assistant Director at the Indiana State Library and Marybelle Burch of the Manuscripts Division of that library; Liliane Krasean, who did the excellent translation of the Lasselle Papers; John Martin Smith of Auburn, Indiana's resident Shaker historian; Cheryl Hartman of "Indians of Indiana," Irving Stultz of Plymouth, Indiana, and Al Pifer of the Michigan Metis.

I should also thank Kentuckians Sylvia Brown of Asbury Theological Seminary, Wilmore, Kentucky, which specializes in collections on Methodist history; James R. Bentley and the staff of the Filson Club in Louisville; the archivists at the Pleasant Hill Shaker community; and Dixie Hibbs, historian of Bardstown.

For necessary advice and encouragement I owe sincere thanks to my cousins Thornton and Evelyn McClure and Tom Emison, keepers of the ancestral flame in southern Indiana; Phillip Leininger, a former Hoosier who is now a New York editor; Mrs. William Hunter of Mechanicsburg; my husband and children; my mother-in-law Mrs. Jane Baxter and my father, the late Judge John L. Niblack. I am especially grateful to the late William A. Hunter, a walking encyclopaedia of the history of the Scotch-Irish, to whom the book is dedicated.

GLOSSARY OF MIAMI INDIAN TERMS

A-ká-wi-ta	Porcupine
A-ki-má-wi-ta	Band chief
A-lan-ya	Brave, young man
A-son-da-ki	Shining sun
A-la-mé-lon-da	Wounded
Cai-ip-a-wa	Morning
Ci-ci-kwi-a	Rattlesnake
Ke-ki-on-ga	Miami home Village near Ft. Wayne, Indiana. Means "blackberry patch" or perhaps "place of haircuts" (for war)
Kin-ok-ca	Otter
Ki-no-zá-wia	Hidden Panther, uncle of Asondaki
Ki-ol-ia (moon)	Late autumn
Kin-nik-in-nick	Aromatic smoking herbs
Ki-tchi-man-it-o-wa	Great Serpent god
Ko-Ká	Frog
Len-ni-Pin-ja	Fire Tiger supposed to dwell in rivers like Mississinewa
Ma-kon-sa (moon)	March, spring time
Man-it-to (Manitou, Mannito)	God or gods, spirits of things
Má-qua	Bear
Mi-a-la-ná-qua	Catfish, cousin of Asondaki
Mi-shi-kin-mó-qua	Little Turtle, great Indian chief
Mock-kó-sa	Fawns
Mock-sin-kic-kee	"Lake of Boulders" where Potawatomis camped. Lake Maxinkuckee at Culver, Indiana
Mos-wa	Deer
M'tá-kwa-pi-min-ji	Mulberry Blossom, Asondaki's mother
Na-na-mam-kic-kee	Earthquake
Ni-ka	Friend
Peorias	An Indian tribe; "Old ones" whom the Miamis regarded as ancestors
Sá-kia	Heron
Tan-dak-sa	Bluejay
Tcing-wi-a	Lightning god
Te-cum-seh	Shawnee leader, head of confederation; killed in the War of 1812
Tens-kwat-a-wa	The Prophet, Tecumseh's brother
We-mi-am-iki	"The people"; Miamis; "All-beavers" or good folk
Wi-pi-mi	Arrow; manhood's arrow

—McClure Family—

Dr. Alexander McClure
Dunleigh, Northern Ireland

Archibald McClure
b. 1695

Rev. George McClure
b. 1700
married Moira O'Donnell

John McClure
b. 1718
married Jane Andrews

John McClure b. 1745 *married* Janie McGuire	**William McClure** b. 1749 *married* Margaret Baird Mossman	**Daniel McClure** b. 1754 *married* Martha Baird	**George McClure** b. 1757 *married* Jean Jordan	**Jenny McClure** b. 1759 *married* James Scott
James (Jim) b. 1786	John b. 1788	John (Jack) b. 1787	Catherine b. 1787	Ismael b. 1788
Mary b. 1790	Elizabeth b. 1790	Thomas b. 1789	Polly 1789	John Robert b. 1801
Margaret b. 1792	Archibald b. 1792	Charles b. 1790	Margaret b. 1790	
Elizabeth b. 1794	Charles b. 1793	Joseph b. 1791	Robert b. 1792	
John Wedge b. 1797	Mary b. 1795	Mary b. 1793	Cynthia b. 1793	
	Will, Jr. b. 1796	Martha b. 1795	William b. 1795	
	Louisa b. 1798	Daniel b. 1797	George, Jr. b. 1796	
	Malinda b. 1800	Elizabeth b. 1798	Matilda b. 1797	
	Caroline Jean b. 1803	Esther b. 1800	James b. 1800	
		James b. 1802	John b. 1802	
		Jane b. 1804		

—Baird Family—

Thomas Baird (Bard)
Chambersburg, Pa.
m. Mary Douglas
|

James
Elizabeth   m. A. Mossman —— Margaret m. William McClure
Mary   m. Hugh Emison —— Samuel   Thomas
Thomas   m. Esther Kilgore   m.
Charles | Mary McClure
John   Mary
Samuel   m.
William   Samuel Thompson
Robert
Joseph
Martha b. 1766   m. Dan'l McClure

Possible GENEALOGY

—Emison Family—

Sir Samuel Emison
Dublin, Ireland

Sir Thomas Emison   **Barclay Ash Emison**

James Emison   **Hugh Emison**   **Young Ash Emison**   **Rafe Emison**   others
                      b. 1744
                   married   *married*   *married*
                   Mary Baird   Mary Mitchell   Alice Rogers
                 James   b. 1773   various children   Old Ash Emison
                 Thomas b. 1776
                 others
                 Samuel b. 1788   m. Mary McClure   Twins Ashley, Sara
                 others

THE
Movers
Frontier
(1751-1760)

OTTAWA

HURON

Michelimackinac

Detroit

MAUMEE RIVER

Kekioqa

WYANDOT

WABASH RIVER

Weas

TWIGHTWEES
(MIAMI)

MIAMI RIVER

Pickawillany

SCIOTO RIVER

MIN

SHAWNE

Vincennes

OHIO   RIVER

MISSISSIPPI
RIVER

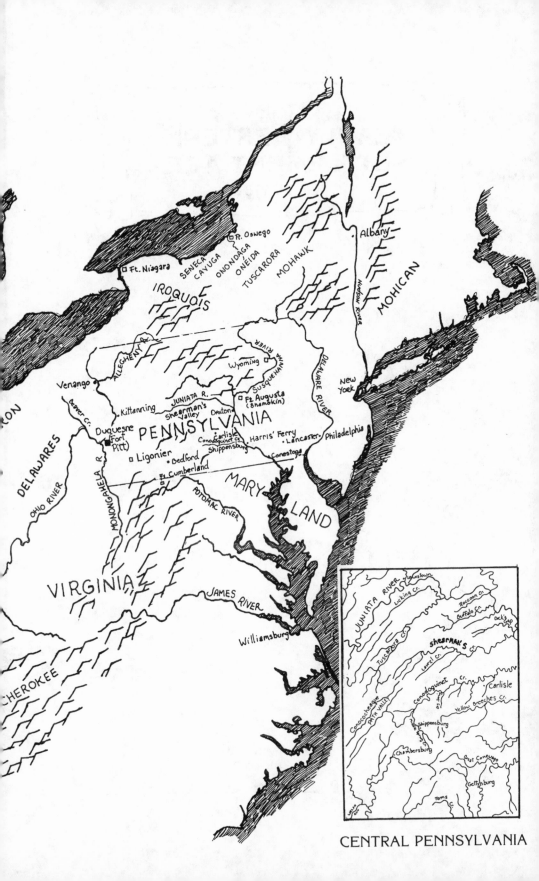

Ft. Niagara

SENECA
CAYUGA
Ft. Oswego
ONONDAGA
ONEIDA
TUSCARORA
MOHAWK
Albany

IROQUOIS

MOHICAN

Venango
ALLEGHENY R.
Wyoming
SUSQUEHANNA RIVER
Susquehanna
Ft. Augusta
(Shamokin)

Kittanning
JUNIATA R.
Shearman's
Valley
Duncans
New
York

DELAWARE RIVER

Beaver Cr.
Duquesne
(Fort
Pitt)
PENNSYLVANIA
Carlisle
Conodoguinet Cr.
Harris' Ferry
Lancaster
Philadelphia

DELAWARES
Ligonier
Bedford
Shippensburg
Conestoga

MONONGAHELA R.
Ft. Cumberland
MARY
LAND

OHIO RIVER
POTOMAC RIVER

VIRGINIA
JAMES RIVER

Williamsburg

CHEROKEE

JUNIATA RIVER
Johnstown
Licking Cr.
Raccoon Cr.
Buffalo Cr.
Jack's Gap
SHEARMAN'S
Cr.
Tuscarora Cr.
Laurel Cr.
Conococheague
PATH VALLEY
Conodoguinet Cr.
Carlisle
Yellow Breeches Cr.
Shippensburg
Chambersburg
Gt. Conewago
Gettysburg
Toms
Cr.

CENTRAL PENNSYLVANIA

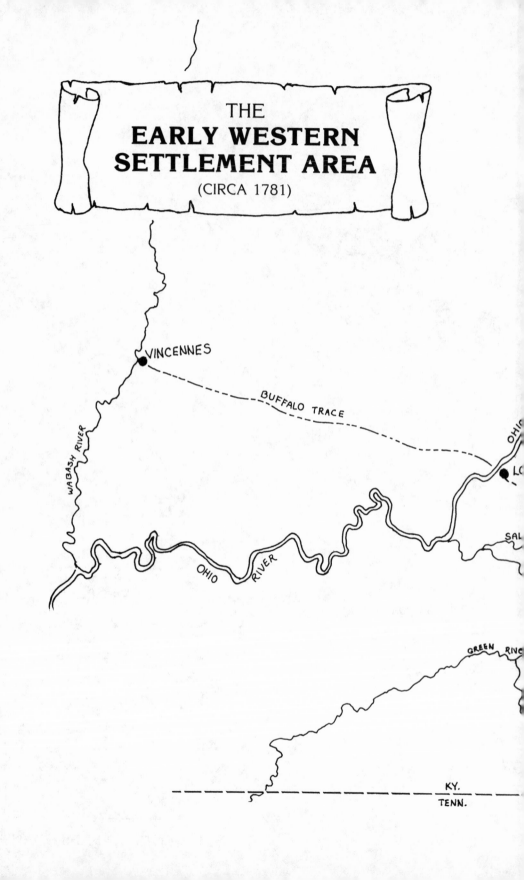

THE
EARLY WESTERN SETTLEMENT AREA
(CIRCA 1781)

VINCENNES

BUFFALO TRACE

WABASH RIVER

OHIO

OHIO RIVER

LO

SAL

GREEN RIV

KY.

TENN.

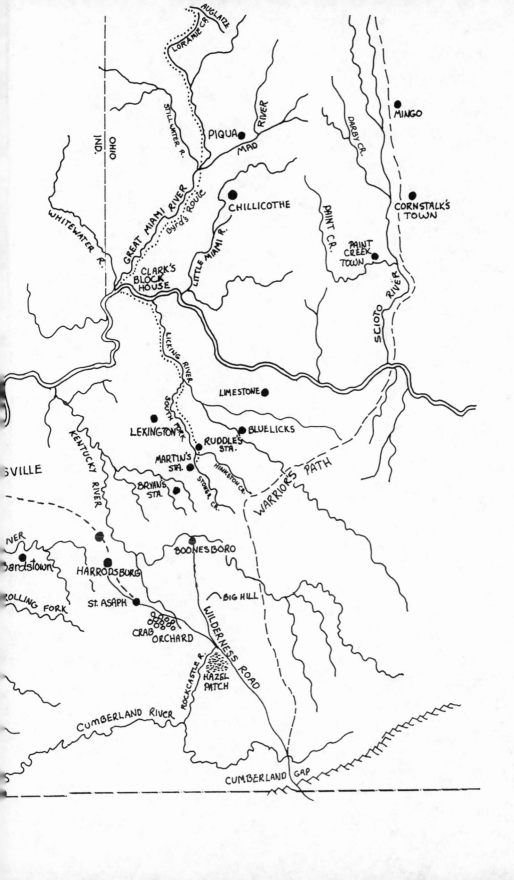

PART I

IRELAND
1736-1751

Bring to me the King's harp
And I will forget my grief
By the notes of that sweet sounding harpwood
The woe-begone find relief
The youth who owned this harpwood
Played with exquisite tune
The songs of the vanished race of Conn
Beneath green Ireland's moon

Beloved to me the woods of home
And lakes of Scotland drear
But the thing I love most in all the world
Is this harp of Ireland dear.

Chapter I

It was a misty morning in July of 1736 outside Londonderry, Ireland. A young man of eighteen strode down a narrow country lane every bit as confidently as if he owned the road.

The sun was up, but its wan, slanting light was just beginning to pierce the early morning dampness. The young Scotch-Irishman, whose name was John McClure, whistled a tune through his teeth and put his hand inside the pocket of his baggy linen breeches. Without touching the small Bible, or the piece of folded parchment within the pocket, he drew out a raisin bun and began to chew on it.

From the corner of his eye John McClure could see the western mountains. Clouds of mist still obscured their peaks and drifted down in great, gossamer loops over the green slopes. Picking up his pace, he passed without notice one of the great bawns, or defense towers of northern Ireland, which the Scots had put up a hundred years ago when King James had sent them to settle and subdue the Irish.

After a while he turned at a weatherbeaten crossroads sign that marked the Lough Swilly road into the city. Traffic was already heavy. Farm carts loaded with green apples, hogs, bins of eggs and tubs of butter jostled along, driven by farmers eager to get into town before market day reached its height. Women with bushels of blackberry tarts or pork pies picked their way along the muddy roadside, their ruffled skirts shuffling around bare legs and ankles. John cast a scornful glance at them. Mere Irish they were, a beaten race after they lost the Battle of the Boyne in his grandfather's time. He had no patience with the Mere Irish, even if some in the village, like his minister uncle, visited them out of Christian charity.

Still, these were women and some of them bonny, and John combed his dark hair with his fingers, hoping they liked the way he looked as he quickly brushed past them. He was dressed in his best linen shirt and jacket and dyed brown breeches. Good leather shoes were on the feet that usually went unshod in the wood shavings and sawdust of the cooperage shop where he labored. He was, after all, coming to see a government agent, to confirm ownership of a valuable piece of land at Barnstead Hollow which had belonged to his father. The pounds he would realize from the sale of this land would enable him, when the moment was ripe, to set up his own shop making hogsheads for liquids and ship supplies. Without the field at Barnstead Hollow, John's shop would be an impossible dream.

As he arrived at the outskirts of Derry, John's curious mind began to whir with the sights and sounds of the city. A brisk wind from the Atlantic blew down Lough Foyle and touseled his hair and wet his eyebrows. He went through the gate and beneath the city wall, where the guns from the war with the Irish still stood and passed the buildings of an older time, the cathedral with its fairy spire pushing at the sky and the guild hall of the founding London companies. Finally he passed into the newer mercantile wharf area.

"Dinna linger," he told himself sternly. "You must be to the land office before noon." He went up the steps of a new English building with sash windows and the Lion of King George II displayed above the door. The Scots might now inhabit Northern Ireland, but it was the English who ruled.

John's stiff shoes clattered across the wooden planks of the hall. A sign above the door indicated that the "Clerk of the Records" conducted business within. He entered a high-ceilinged room with blue wainscoting around the walls and huge dog andirons in a formal fireplace at the end.

A man in a tied-back wig sat at the desk, scratching in a record book. Although he must have heard John McClure enter, he did not look up. John waited patiently for a full two minutes, looking at his back. Finally John cleared his throat. "If I could be so bold, sir, could I trouble you for assistance?"

The back answered. "As you can see, sir, I am engaged in a business matter here. I shall be at your disposal presently."

John emitted a slow, controlled breath. He was used to contemptuous treatment from the English. Landlords from Kent visited their absentee holdings in his neighborhood once a year and drove through the village in creaking carriages with handkerchiefs to their noses "against the smell of Scottish swine." Their ladies in lawn dresses chatted about the inconveniences of "Irish Holiday" without any care for who heard them.

But that this third son or nephew of some minor secretary to Lord Who-You-Will should sneer at him—John's hand tightened into a fist and then slowly relaxed. Finally the clerk rose, with studied indifference, as John saw it, and placed his pen in a pewter inkpot. He sauntered to the huge table which served as an official desk and faced the young man. "Now may I be of service to you?" he asked, looking with icy eyes past John at a horsefly walking on the cornice above the door. His ruffled shirt smelled of snuff.

John took out the piece of parchment. "I wish to register this. I know my father intended to register it, but he died suddenly. Now I wish to confirm it before I enter man's estate. To rest my mind, you understand. There was no will."

"Yes, of course." The clerk picked up the paper absently, allowing his eyes to go out the window, obviously not concentrating. "What is he a-thinkin' of?" John asked himself. Possibly some decadent pleasure. The English were wastrels, everyone knew that. There was a broadside sheet from a racetrack on the desk. He probably had a mistress.

John told the details of his father's death. "Wheels of a cart. . . ill and had a spell." He finished the explanation and fixed his eye on the clerk, who evaded it.

"Oh, yes. Well, I'll just take this deed and have a look at the records. I should have some report on it by, say, four o'clock."

Four o'clock! John had hoped to be halfway to the village by then. "I thank you, sir," the young Scotch-Irishman said and left to buy a pie from a seller's stand and watch life among the counting houses and herring factories near the quay. Finally, when the sun blazed like a firebrand in the sky, he decided to return to sit in the relatively cool and silent records hall.

Nowhere in the several rooms which stretched down the hall were there sounds or evidence of any sort of work being done. After about half an hour the clerk came down an elaborate flight of stairs. John immediately approached him. "Is all in order?" he asked tensely.

The clerk carried a huge leather-bound ledger, and he put it down with a resounding "whump" on the table. John looked down at the writing which flowed across the pages, straight, neat and unfeeling.

"It appears you do not hold clear title to the land. In fact, you do not hold title at all."

"What can you mean?" John asked blankly.

"What I mean, young swain, is that this document book, records of eighteenth of February, 17 and 32, show a piece of land exact in nature as your deed describes it, transferred by one Archibald McClure to one Elvin Baker for the sum of twenty-five pounds sterling. Legally drafted, the signature, as you see, unsteady 'but true."

John could not contain himself. "Elvin Baker is an English tavern keeper in the village next ours. He is a rascal and a skinflint. He must have got Father drunk and had him sign a piece of paper."

"Your family's scapegrace habits do not concern me," the clerk retorted cooly. "The deed was properly drawn and, as you can see, properly recorded as stipulated in Act Six Anne, C 2. That is a new law, my young ignoramus, which specifies that recorded deeds have precedence over unrecorded." He shut the book with finality and stood frigidly beside it.

John was beside himself. His plans were flying away like woodsprites at the crow of the cock. "Isn't there something about being under force—this man knew my father's weakness, extended credit when he shouldn't have—stole his land while he wasn't himself. 'Tis fraud! I shall go to the law!" He stood defiantly before the clerk.

"You could do that if you could properly read the solicitor's shingle." Loathing stood thick between them.

McClure told himself that he could probably read far better than this pock-faced scribe whose "advancement" had carried him to an unimportant job in the backwaters of rural Ireland, in Derry. Not even Belfast or Dublin. "No matter," McClure spat out. "If I got a solicitor, English law would support the English tradesman. Not the Scot."

The clerk stepped forward suddenly and collared John, placing his long, bony hands around John's neck. He pulled him up short to deliver the full impact of what he had to say. "You Scottish curs seem devoid of even the basic understanding of that law, which operates for you too. You came here hoping to profit from the land English armies helped subdue for you. Then you tried to corner the markets in wool and livestock and now linen and bankrupt the merchants in the Mother Country. We had to pass laws against you. With your snivelling Presbyterian prayers and preachers you mock the King's church. Uncouth and unkempt. Get away from me."

John's thoughts raged, and his hands ached to throttle the fop on the spot; but he managed to control himself. Wrenching himself free just as the clerk pushed him away, he strode out of the building and went to the waterfront to try to collect his wits.

It was too late to return home. Night-time was no time for a man with several shillings in his pocket to be abroad; there could be highwaymen even on the remote Derry road. John's uncle, with whom he lived, had given him money to take cheap lodgings, and he'd just as well do it.

He was in no mood to return to the village anyway just yet, to walk by the cooperage shop and look at its profitable kegs and tuns neatly stacked out back, its piles of covered oak and ash, now mockingly unattainable. He didn't want to tell his uncle of his blasted hopes. And he had been fool enough to tell others. Off he had gone, whistling his tune—he had not calculated on the power of the English. Much land in Ireland today was probably passing into English hands because of this new law directed against the poor and illiterate. Again, his hand formed a fist.

Yet it was too early to seek a bed and fish chowder, all he wanted to eat. He sat on the quay for about an hour, then walked through the streets until he found a small inn with a wilted-looking flower for its sign—The Primrose.

He engaged a bed upstairs in the "Green Hills" room. That probably meant he would sleep beneath a green coverlet between the hills of a lumpy feather bed with two other men and an unknown quantity of vermin.

He sighed. The down-at-the-heels feeling of the place suited him quite well. His eyes roved about the taproom, noting the painted black tables with tops that were not even clean when they were new and which were now inch-thick in the smell and seasoning of fermented spirits. The middle-aged barmaid wore an apron which actually had handprints in black on it.

He ordered supper, watching the murky daylight die. The barmaid brought blue bottles and put tallow tapers in them. Sailors at tables passed rum around freely, their faces smirking out of the small islands of pulsating light created by the candles. John watched them scornfully. To him, all drunks had one face, the face of blasted hope, of wasted opportunity. One night four years ago, after dragging his father in from the road and wiping vomit off his face for the third time that month, John had vowed never to taste a drop of strong liquor. It was an odd vow in a land where whiskey oiled every activity for both Irishman and Scot. But he had kept it, especially after the way Archibald McClure had died.

John dozed at the table for a long while, and when he awoke, his smoke-filled lungs yearned for fresh air. Pushing through the door, he came out into the moon-flooded street and wandered his way down a series of small, crooked lanes. It must have been near eleven o'clock. The wind blew smartly off the sea, bringing with it the brackish smells of rotting clamshells. Having breathed his fill, he was about to turn again to the inn. Suddenly he was startled by the opening of the door of a rickety two-story dwelling directly in front of him. Fearful of thieves, he darted into the small space between the house and its equally shabby neighbor and stood in the refuse-laden shadows.

A man and a woman burst into the street arguing in loud, drunken voices. He could not see their faces. "I tol' you I does it for money, not for love, and that's that." The woman turned toward the spot where John stood for a moment, showing a pasty, painted face and a tightly-drawn bodice. "Pay up or get nothing from me. I don't care if you are a gent'man," she cried.

The man said something harsh to her and grabbed her roughly in his arms, putting his hand over her mouth and attempting to take her into the house.

"No!" she screamed. "I'll not be forced. 'Tis all I have to me pride."

"Pride, have you?" the man slurred . "No gutter jade is going to minx me." He cursed her again and with the back of his hand began to deliver rhythmic blows to her face. She whimpered and struggled, but he was intent on beating her insensible. John could take no more. He stepped from the shadows and, grabbing the man's shoulders, wheeled him about. Still holding on to the crying woman with one arm, her assailant looked up with clouded eyes.

"Ah yes, the Scottish clod," he mumbled. God damn it, John thought, it was the government records clerk, drunk and beating up a Mere Irish whore.

"Let her go, you beast," John said, trying to extricate himself and the woman at the same time. The clerk resisted and before John knew it, the man slipped and pulled him down. The three of them were wrestling on the filthy path, the girl trapped underneath.

"Y' swine, I shall give you a carving," the clerk mumbled, pinning John on the ground on top of the girl. Then he reached into his waistcoat and pulled out a Chinese ornamental knife. Suddenly John McClure was afraid for his life.

John was able to move his arm a little, although it was held by the other man. He bent it and seized the knife. With a supreme effort then, John swung himself over and on top. The girl was screaming below them; he ignored her. He looked directly in the face of his opponent, smelled his foul, yeasty breath. Suddenly John's anger snapped like an unbound leather thong. He said quietly, through his teeth, "God damn you forever, you servants of the King. You don't deserve to live." Rage gave him strength and he plunged the knife firmly down, stabbing as hard as he could.

In a sudden death-fearing moment of sobriety, the government clerk lunged aside. John McClure's knife found not the man, but the woman below, and in an instant, by mistake, he rid the King of one woman of the night and source of venereal disease in Ireland.

The government clerk sat up, sputtering incoherently. John shook his head in anguished disbelief at what he had wrought. He managed to free himself, and fled down the street, the sound of his brogues echoing on the cobblestones.

In his haste, he did not notice something had fallen out of his pocket, something the magistrate picked up the next morning.

"Why," the magistrate asked his stolid assistant, "would this be under that whore?"

The assistant ran his forefinger over the little book's fine leather cover and traced the gold-leaf title: *New Testament and Presbyterian Catechism.*

"Ain't got th' owner's name in it, though, so it don't matter," the assistant said disappointedly.

Reverend George McClure listened quietly to the story his nephew told him the next morning in Dunleigh. He sighed a long sigh. "Let's not talk now. You need food and rest," he said. This nephew of his had run halfway home through the midnight darkness, then thrown himself on the hay of a deserted farm in exhaustion for a few hours' sleep last night before proceeding disconsolately home.

John looked at the minister and said, "But I must talk. God will never, should never forgive me. I have blood on my hands. Surely I have lost my eternal soul among the Chosen." Then he put his head in his hands and gave way to despair. His uncle led him to the chair before the hearth. "Uncle, what hope has such a wretch as I?" John asked in a muffled voice.

"What hope, indeed?" But as Uncle George said it, he smiled and patted John's shoulder rather absently. "I promise you we will talk this evening, after you have slept and supped. Feed the body, then the soul, is a good old Scottish proverb."

It was after five when John rose, cleaned his face and body at the big wash basin, and sat down to eat. He looked across the table at the homely, concerned face of his uncle. Love for the good man who had cared for him since his father's death trickled through the numb despair he felt.

"In the time it took the sun to set and rise," George McClure said musingly to his nephew after a while, "the boy has gone from me." The smile that shone on his face was wistful and kind.

"The horse races we have had, galloping down the country roads, the suppers shared by candlelight—all of these are fled away like wisps of smoke in the wind. The man who has returned has travelled in such a distant land I do not know him."

John McClure nodded. The two men had lived like brothers in this parsonage at the top of the hill. They agreed on everything, except his uncle's frequent visits of Christian comfort to the Mere Irish homes down the lane.

"About your temporal future, John. I have considered long and deeply this afternoon. The law is often confused on these points, and it is possible your crime would be viewed as an accident occurring while you attempted defense of a fellow human, a commendable act in the eyes of the law."

The minister rose from the chair and began striding around the room, as he often did when composing a sermon in his mind. "Practically speaking, the young records man was probably too intoxicated to be able to recall anything.

If he should remember your part, there is small chance he would pursue the matter. Questions could be asked that could ruin him. No, I do not think he will follow you to Dunleigh."

"Even if he is too ashamed to pursue me, the magistrate will know I'm Scotch. I left my Presbyterian Bible. . ."

"And that is as far as they will get. Your Bible." The word rang hollowly in the air, and was followed by a sad silence.

"John," his uncle said, "Should they ever come for you, you would have to go. But your real sin is against God, not man. It is God's price, really, that you must pay. You wished your enemy to die, and in your wrath you tried to kill him. A deep sin according to Christ's word. And you killed—murdered—"the word seared John like a hot knife—"a woman no longer innocent, but like the one the Lord pardoned."

George McClure seemed to be growing more agitated. "You have asked me if there is hope for you in Heaven after you have done this terrible sin, and I will answer you with a question. Is not God infinite tenderness and mercy, giving all things justly to His children and asking only love and obedience in return? Is his love not like that of a human father who wishes to give only good to his children?"

John, thoughtful, nodded.

"But if one of those children should prove reprobate, disobey and steal a portion of his father's substance—what then?" Without waiting for an answer, the minister went on. "Will not the human father whip the child? Why should He leave unpunished him who disobeys?" George McClure sat down again and gave John a stricken look.

"But we all have sinned and fallen short," John ventured.

"True—even the founder of our faith, John Calvin, knew the awful reality of original sin. He was guilty of condemning a Spanish monk to the stake. Was he for that one great sin condemned for all eternity? We do not know. He did not forgive himself."

"But if I am to die eternally, why should I even live now?" the young man implored his uncle.

"Do not look at me that way, John. I must be strong. Truly God is no respecter of persons, not even my own nephew's." George McClure lowered his voice, turned his face into the shadows. "God is a God of justice. The Presbyterian faith teaches the soul that sins must die. . ."

Stricken by the awful implications of Calvinism towards one he loved, his Uncle threw himself down heavily into the wooden chair, with his head on his arms across its back. Finally, he raised his face to John. "I know all this doctrine, and yet I also know the nature of the love that welcomed the prodigal son home. Surely in that is some hope for you."

Young John shook his head numbly, and they both sat down again at the table. Outside the crickets hummed. The village was hushed; tomorrow would be the Sabbath. John broke the silence. "Uncle, play for me on the Irish harp." He did not know why he asked. Usually he left the house when his uncle took out the barbaric instrument of the Mere Irish, but there was something about its inexpressibly sad tone that answered his need tonight.

The harp hung on the wall. His uncle took it down, put it to his ear, and plunked its strings to tune it. Then he began to play a five-hundred-year-old tune:

Bring to me the King's harp
And I will forget my grief
By the notes of that sweet sounding harpwood
The woe-begone find relief
The youth who owned this harpwood
Played with exquisite tune
The songs of the vanished race of Conn
Beneath green Ireland's moon

Beloved to me the woods of home
And lakes of Scotland drear
But the thing I love most in all the world
Is this harp of Ireland dear.

As the strains died, John said calmly, "You say you believe the law will not act against me and I think you are right. We shall see. I will continue to work at the shop to learn my trade in the best way I can. Perhaps if I am expert at all I do, I will find the favor of the Lord and be confirmed, after all, among the ranks of the Saved. And when the time comes. . ." His voice trailed off.

His uncle sat next to him and looked intently at him. "When the time comes?"

"I shall go to America." His uncle's mouth moved almost imperceptibly, but he did not speak. John went on. "When I was on the quay in Derry, I watched a hundred-ton ship loadin' immigrants, crammin' fathers, mothers, droolin' grandfathers and babes into the cabins to brave the ocean perils to go to a new land." His voice grew bitter. "There is nothin' now in this land for me. I do not wish to live where agents of the King take the hope from my life, and the lives of all of us Scots. But I shall not go until all is in readiness. If I am to find a fresh start in a world where I am a stranger, I must have money for proper passage, outfittin' for the trade when I arrive. And truly it will be cheaper and take less time than waitin' twenty years to buy a business here. I will not come as our fathers did to Ireland as paupers. I shall be able to live with the Church then, as a givin' member. How I shall live with God, He alone knows. I will never give up hope."

His voice was again a muted whisper. "But how I shall live with myself. . ." He buried his head in his hands as he pictured something he had not told his uncle, had not even allowed himself to recall. At the moment he first stabbed, blindly, hatefully, and the knife mistakenly found the woman's breast, her eyes rested on his for a split second. In that time he had watched her expression pass through fear, surprise, and pain to something else. In that instant all of her hope for life, her vital energy, her blasted future, rose accusingly out of those wide, surprised eyes and entered into his own soul.

"How can I live my life knowing what my anger has done?" he asked in a whisper.

His uncle looked at him for a long moment. "My grandfather had a piece of advice. He got it from his own grandfather, who lived through the wars of religion in Scotland, when the babes died of starvation and men were tortured on the rack. 'Do the very best ye can each day, and things will generally swing 'round better than ye reckon,' was what he said.'' The minister stood and, taking the harp, crossed the room to hang it up.

John stared out the window, which was open to get the night air. They had not lit the candle, and it was dark enough in the room to see the stars. His uncle stopped and, turning with the greatest tenderness in his look, said, "Perhaps, John, you can claim redemption even with this sin. But if you do, you will know your salvation when it comes to you through some transfiguring act of grace. In the meantime, you've got to get through from first light until sunset." He put the harp back on the wall and climbed the loft to sleep.

John McClure sat for a long time at the window, staring through the empty darkness of the night toward the far-away lights at the end of the village. Then he rose and went to the sugar box on the dry sink and put in the two small coins left from what his uncle had given him. It was a small gesture of hope, the beginning of affirmation that life must, and would, begin again for him. There would be a future, however bitter.

The village of Dunleigh changed little outwardly in the seven years that passed. Two new homes now stood in the lane the villagers called Gentry Row. Their tall, many-paned windows and square, carefully-tended gardens reflected a change in architecture that had reached even the remotest parts of the British Empire. Rob Rogers, the apothecary and Mr. Stark, owner of the William and Mary Inn now resided in "Georgian" homes of two stories. The pewter on the mantels and the well-equipped outkitchens behind the house proclaimed the prosperity of a few in northern Ireland.

For most, however in that tormented land, life grew only worse. The Established Church grew stronger, England passed even stricter laws than in the past prohibiting trade, and "rackrent" landlords raised the rents again and again, forcing folk off the land.

Two years of recent famine in Dunleigh caused many to eat the seed corn and oats they should have sown. There was nothing to do but sell what little they had and "ship out." These new, poor immigrants, however, could not pay. They must go as "redemptioners," working for their passage by their own sweat as bound servants when they arrived in port. But the choice was to starve.

Abandoning hearth and home, these castaways became part of the mass of five to six thousand Scotch-Irish a year in the 1740's who shipped to the Colonies, a tide of human misery and hope that swelled from the ports, from Belfast, Londonderry, Newry and Larne in Ireland across the Atlantic and into Philadelphia, New Castle, and Chester and from there into the bays and river valleys of the West with the odd Indian names—the Chesapeake, the Susquehanna, the Shenandoah.

And in the villages the Scotch-Irish left, small farm plots and cottages which were not reoccupied stood forlorn, their weedy gardens and rotting roofs mutely testifying to the failure of the British government to find an answer for "The Irish Question."

On a vibrant May afternoon in 1742, a young girl of eighteen who lived down the hill from Reverend McClure had her own concerns to worry about. She stood before a small quicksilver mirror and tried to make her too-curly, red-brown hair behave as she forced a comb through it. I canna be spending time on my person, she thought. There is the packing'-up to do. She went about the small, comfortable house with loving attention, separating small, personal possessions she needed to carry in a valise with her, grouping other items with the bed, wardrobe, and table which had already been put together near the door for the pickup wagon.

She took up a leather-bound Bible, and opening its pages, surveyed the handwriting. "This Bible was given to Ruth Anderson by her loving husband in the year of our marriage 1715." Then, in newer handwriting the proud notation under the numeral 1: "Birth of a daughter, Jane Margaret, September 9, 1724."

There were other numbers, written with a round hand consecutively down the page on specified lines after that, "2, 3, 4." But there was nothing beside them, and finally in fresh ink and Jane's own hand was the notation, "Died this first day of April, 1742, John Anderson. He goes above." Directly under it, "April 15, Mother died also today of flux and fever."

The girl, whose long-lashed, beautiful eyes seemed starkly blue against her pale skin, sighed and closed the Bible, placing it on a small table with French legs. Her anger flared briefly. What she should have written in the Bible for her father's cause of death was the truth: he had died from grief, looking at his promising business flicker and die, smothered by the laws forbidding the linen trade. Day after day, his mind and hands idle, he had looked out of his window at Irishmen who were more like skeletons than men walking the road, with no work, no land, and no hope. And eventually he had become like them.

To divert her mind from her still-fresh grief, she took inventory of what she had assembled to keep besides the Bible and furniture: spoons, a set of china plates, imported from London in the prosperous days, a small leather trunk of her own clothing, and a wool spinning wheel. And, of course, her mother's four-foot treadle loom. If she could choose to take only one thing it would be this loom of her mother's, made of brightly-burnished cherry wood. The loom had, as a matter of fact, made the very dress she was wearing.

Jane looked down, smoothing the skirt. 'Twas linen so fine you could barely see the threads, made by one of the finest craftsmen in northern Ireland—her own mother. She clenched her fist (she would not cry, she was determined to cry no more) and remembered her lovely mother sitting at the loom not long ago. Her eyes were strained by overwork, her health was failing, yet she said, "Lass, this will be your wedding dress. The yarn has been bleached; we will bleach it again. For the pure, all things must be pure."

Ruth Anderson had smiled a little and taken Jane's hand and put it to her own face. "I will embroider it with scenes of our life here so that when I am gone"—here Jane had protested—"you can remember me and your Dada and Kitty and Byblow. He was a good hound, now wasn't he?" They talked of trifles in the last days, ignoring the illness and bad fortune that had descended on the happiness of the home. Soon, however, Jane's father's sickness demanded all of her mother's time. Because the completion of the wedding dress had become almost an obsession with her mother (although there was no wedding in sight, and no one Jane cared for), Jane worked the embroidery on the bodice and on a wide band three inches up from the hem.

As the minister, Reverend McClure, came into the house to pray for the family, as the apothecary's boy arrived with new herbs to try to stall the flux and fever, as she washed her father's linen and brought beef tea and steeped pear leaves and administered spoons of rum and tried to get her mother to rest, she lowered her head over her hoop and needle, putting all of her love into the work. She designed in her mind the scenes of her childhood, the loved church on the hill where she had listened to sermons and been catechized, the fields of gillyflowers and primroses behind the cottage, the lough where she and her friend Sarah had played. Her needle outlined the looms at work by sunlight and candlelight, the table with its puddings and joints, in the days when times were good.

And, holding hands in the middle of the skirt stood her mother and father, no longer young but ever loving. Their marriage had been a bond of unusual joy and affection which had surrounded her with a security and serenity that she instinctively realized were pearls of great price. Now gone. (Sure, she would not cry. A Christian, Reverend McClure said, must not cry for the advancement to Glory of the just.)

The intense feeling passed. Just the barest hint of a smile passed her lips as she looked at the fine French knots and daisy loops of pink, blue, and gold on her wedding dress. Her mother had seen it so. As Ruth Anderson lay on her bed on the morning of her death, sweating and not always aware of her surroundings, Jane showed it to her. Her mother had raised a shaking, weak hand and scanned the stitches. " 'Tis fine work. You will wear it and my grandchildren and their grandchildren will see it and know of us. I die content. Take care of my loom, dearing."

And she had said nor known no more, not even when Reverend McClure, kneeling by the bedside softly prayed the Lord's prayer with her. He reached the culminating words of affirmation so dear to her mother, "Thine is the kingdom, and the power, and the glory forever." As Jane tried with a dry, tightened throat to join in for her mother's sake, she heard a low voice from the shadows in the back of the room speaking the words of the prayer. And when Reverend McClure ceased speaking, the voice said clearly, almost defiantly, "Amen."

Distracted, Jane had not thought to wonder who it was, but later she was told it was Reverend McClure's nephew, who sometimes came with him on his ministerial calls of comfort to the sick and dying. She knew him, but not well. He was very short, but very handsome, a cooper's assistant who walked through town without seeing the faces of those he passed. If he came to church at all, he sat in the back row, taciturn and unparticipating, and he did not come to many village festivals.

The next week, as Reverend McClure, acting as the relative Jane did not have in the parish, assisted her in the details of settling her parents' meager estate, John McClure stayed about in the shadows. He served whiskey at the wake, he sold the thin cow in another village, he disposed of the furniture her father had willed to cover debts. She wondered at this silent young man's presence and tried to fathom him. She found him looking at her, and as he spoke of the details of the settling up, something about him was reassuring.

Three nights after her mother's wake, Jane had eaten her little meal of barley soup, wheat bread, and butter, and tea. She was washing her china dish and teacup teacup and saucer in a bucket when she heard a rap at the door. "Jane, may I speak with you for a moment?"

She opened the door and the Reverend's long, anxious face peered in. She smiled because she sincerely liked this man of faith who had been a part of her life since she was a little girl, who had taught her the beliefs of her religion and confirmed her faith, as well as acting as a kind friend in her recent trouble.

She asked him to sit down and then began to speak before he could. "Mr. McClure, I know what you are goin' to say. You're goin' to tell me as a woman alone I must plan for my future. I want you to know I have been thinkin' on it, and I believe I have an answer. I wish to take up my parents' trade. I believe that although times are difficult now for weavers, they will surely soon be better. There have been cycles before, as my father has told me."

Reverend McClure was looking at her with astonishment, but before he could answer she rattled on. "I love this village. I could go to live with my aunt in Derry, but I wish to remain here, where I had my childhood. Now you will say that I may not live alone, and you are, of course, right. So I think I will become a companion to some older lady in the church who needs a thoughtful young girl to care for her. I can bring her tea and take care of the garden and give her medicine, and when she naps, I can do my linen work. We should get along well. Of course you would need to find me some suitable. . ." George McClure interrupted her.

"Jane, you have no money. The money from the sale of your father's possessions did not even pay his debts—let that go. Times are wretched, people starve all over Ulster, and a woman without means or relatives has no future. You canna hope to make a life as a lady's companion—the ladies here canna even feed themselves now, let alone a strapping young girl."

Her face fell. This was the final straw. Through all the crumbling of her world in the last month she had kept her control and faced her troubles like the Scotswoman that her father always told her to be. But now. . . she began to weep.

She would not go to Aunt Hepzibah's. She was a brittle old woman who painted and smelled of spirits. She was considered reprobate by the Church because she played whist with the soldiers of the king. And anyway, she lived in Derry, and Jane hated Derry. She twisted her handkerchief and paced about the cottage. She needed to blow her nose, but it would not be discreet.

"Jane, this is not the time to speak of it, but my nephew wishes to talk to you. He is waiting on the path outside the house. Perhaps you could walk with him for a wee bit.''

Uncomprehending, Jane looked at the minister, and then, wiping her nose, went to the door. Her color was high and her eyes flashed as she saw the young man on the path. His hands were in his pockets and his back to the door, in an attitude of studied, or was it nervous, casualness. "What is it, Mr. McClure?" Jane demanded as she came out the door.

John McClure turned and faced her. Even with her swollen eyes, he thought she was as fine a woman as he had ever seen. But she was a proud woman, and now she was angry. In her grief and confusion she must view him as an intruder. She came up to him and stood looking at him with defiance. She was exactly his height, and her eyes flashed. "What is it you want with me?" she demanded.

"Miss Anderson—it would please me very much if you would walk with me. I promise you I will take only a few minutes of your evening, and I will soon be done with what I have to say. I respect your grief and would not intrude on it, except that my need is great.''

His need? He was a strange one. Her curiosity was piqued. They walked side by side, in a strained silence down the lane in front of the house until they came to open fields. The air was balmy and sweet. Month-old lambs bleated at their mothers' sides in the crofts, and every flower of the field was about to bloom. The pastoral scene irritated her. She had no use for violets and greening trees at the moment. What was it this gloomy young man wanted? She dared not guess. She had no wish to be pitied.

"Miss, I am a man with a future I have made with my own hands. I have saved every penny I made for the past seven years and I have known nothing but my work. I am one of the finest coopers in all Ireland. Someday I will have my own shop. I am going to America as soon as I have the money, and I need a woman to be my wife. You are young and strong and will be a good mother. . .'' He paused, embarrassed.

She was outraged. This awkward, callous young man was offering for her as if she were a mare! Next he would be examining her teeth. She was tempted to whinny and bare them.

Instead she looked into his eyes, trying to find the right words to refuse him. Her mother had always told Jane she had the second sight, and it flowed through her eyes. She could see things that happened afar off and read anyone by the "lights of the body,'' servile or double-faced, lying or sincere. So Jane Anderson looked in John McClure's eyes and saw in this young man she hardly knew, character, sincere concern for her, and beyond that a veil which hid a world of pain and meaning too deep to be plumbed with casual looking.

And, in addition, as she looked into his eyes she was grabbed by a spark, a blaze of animal power and passion which lit a fire in her that was very strange indeed. She heard herself saying with wonder, "Yes, I will marry you.''

So now the embroidered wedding dress would be worn, and as she awaited the arrival of her new uncle, Reverend McClure, with a cart to take her belongings to her new home at the parsonage, she thought of what she had done. She tried to piece together memories of the man she would spend the rest of her life with. She could recall him walking to church alone, talking, even laughing at the Derry fair once or twice with rough, older men like Sam Bard.

He had been in the boxing matches at the fair. "McClure the Fist," they called him. She remembered him standing nose to nose with a challenger from Raphoe, grimly pounding that ruffian to the ground. There was determination, even in his fighting. If he had impressed her at all, it would have been as a fighting terrier sort of a man, hanging on grimly, against high odds. A fine match, Jane smiled to herself ruefully. She was known in the village as the "Bountiful Soul" for the high-kicking steps she joyfully invented at village dances.

Her heart fell. She had been sold like a piece of furniture. Too soon after her parents' death, she was marrying a stranger in a muted marriage in the midst of a year of famine. There would be no celebration, no bridal maids or men to come for them, only Sarah McCord, her friend from childhood, to walk with her, carrying May flowers, and only the Reverend to accompany John. Her mother had been buried less than a month; celebration would not be fitting. What in the world had she done?

And what did he say about America? She would change that idea. She had no intention of leaving this village whose very church bells and cow moos she loved. She had been to many a wedding in the village. She knew what they said. She would be told to honor her husband, to submit to his will, for the husband is the head of the wife as Christ is the head of the Church. There was room in all that, she told herself defiantly, for her to keep her own spirit free.

She jumped up and threw open the door on the fine May day. "As I promise to love, honor, and obey John McClure, whatever he may be, I also promise to love, honor, and obey my own self, too," she cried aloud to whoever was in the road. In this case, three boys pushing wood blocks with sticks and old Mr. Davey and his bedraggled poodle dog. If they heard her, they didn't give much sign.

She shrugged her shoulders, staring down the road to the parsonage, where a horse and wagon, with two shapes above it, was materializing. It wasn't as if she had had much choice in all this. It was either the McClure or Aunt Hepzibah's high screeching voice and walk-up lodgings which smelled like cooking pigs feet. Jane Margaret Andrews, soon to be Jane Andrews McClure, threw back her head and laughed a raucous, rolling laugh. Life, apparently, was not over. She dipped a mincing curtsey to the fates and rose to prepare to meet her mysterious bridegroom and new uncle, endure the ceremony, and begin her life as "wyfe not maide."

They were married at her friend Sarah McCord's house, ate a brief wedding supper there, and returned to the parsonage early in the evening. Uncle, as he told Jane to call him, tactfully inquired about her wishes, then set up the Anderson bed by the fire and went to bed in the loft. And so they lay, two embarrassed people in long nightgowns side by side, wondering how to proceed. There had been none of the usual male attendants to give them lewd, reassuring instructions and tuck them in the marriage bed, no discreet parental suggestions. And these were, after all, the reserved Scots, not the sensual English Puritans with their bundling boards.

Well, Jane thought, we have been thrown into the river; now we had better swim. She spoke into the darkness. "I hope we will be havin' many little ones. I ha' always dreamt of teachin' a child as I was taught, to love the goodness of the livin' things of the earth. If you will turn over the soil for me, I'll put in thyme and parsley and June peas. And Sweet William, too."

He said nothing. She thought for a moment and then told him of the family of dogs she had known as a child, all of them named Byblow, all with small brains and large loyalties, and the injured ravens and bluebirds she had nurtured, then set free. Her new husband seemed to listen politely and after a while he too spoke, hesitantly, about his work. He had come to it because of his love of wood, and his desire to hold wood in his hands all the days of his life, he told her.

"There is almost no wood at all in Ireland," he said a little sadly. "They cut it down so the English King Henry could build his navy. And now the wind sweeps over the hills like a scouring broom, and we must haul the oak for our barrels from the boglands to the east. Pity it is." He ceased speaking and silence settled around them.

"I dinna know what the future will bring, but this I will tell you," John finally said. "I will try to be a fittin' husband. And I have known no woman but you."

So, Jane thought, he had paid her the ultimate tribute a man can give the woman he marries. And as he turned to her to finally perform the ancient rites of marriage consummation, he was tender and solicitious. When he was finished and one tear stood on her eyelashes, he wiped it gently away.

The next morning, as the sun streamed through the window of the cottage she now called home, Jane McClure sang as she started the fire to make tea and toast for breakfast.

"When June comes, I will go a-berryin'," she said to John as he returned from the necessary out back. "I can make strawberry conserve and blackberry preserves. And perhaps I can find. . ." He interrupted her. "Woman, stay your chatter. My spirits are down today. You will find that is part of what you bought in the bargain you made."

Stung, she drew back from the fire to cover her confusion, and unclamped the iron toaster band, shaking out the slices of bread that had browned. She reached for the plate with its pat of butter. Her parents in all of their days had never spoken to her harshly. She knew that many Scots were dour, but that was not her nature. Still, she could learn to prattle less. That would probably be the least of her lessons.

"Is there somethin' to know?" she asked, placing the slices of buttered toast before him.

"Nothin' I care to tell," he said with finality.

Later she hesitantly mentioned the incident to the Reverend and he nodded sadly. "He is sometimes so. Disremember it. Today he is grieved because I told him his boyhood friend, Samuel Bard, has shipped for America. Bard goes to make his fortune in a land far from famine and hopelessness. Many of his cousins are already there. And John would go with him, but he canna. Some years of work and saving remain yet in his plan. He is a proud man and will take his family like 'better people.' And I think he is right. Sam has borrowed from his kin, and God only knows when he can pay them back.'' He looked searchingly at her. "You know of his plan to go abroad in a few years. What think you of it?''

"I would stay here,'' she said slowly, and then looked at him. "But if I must go, I will make the best of it.'' He nodded and went out to saddle his mare Dainty. He needed to call on an aging parishioner who must be provided for by the church. There were many these days who needed relief.

Jane busied herself making a wonderful supper. There had not been many good suppers in Dunleigh lately; this one would be a marriage celebration given by the bride herself. John had given her money to buy food at the market, and she intended to show her skill at cookery with a rabbit and onion pie. She made a flaky crust and fricasseed the tender meat in a rich, buttery gravy with carrots and turnips from the garden. She had asked Uncle to set and rake out the coals for her in the unfamiliar oven. Cautiously she opened the door, and the savory aroma of succulent meat floated through the cottage. She set the table with her mother's china dishes and picked a bouquet of tulips.

When the men seated themselves and began to eat, Uncle praised her pie profusely and sincerely. The bachelor meals he and John had shared had been simple soups with bread made by the old parishioner who did up for them.

Good things were ahead for this house, George McClure thought. Perhaps John might even change his mind about shipping out. Perhaps George would live to see grandnephews playing before the fire. Since it appeared he would never see his own children. A shadow descended over his exuberant spirits and he put his head down, applying himself to the food.

It was a disappointment that was on his mind every day, try as he would to resign himself to God's will. He had waited to marry through ten years of caring for aged parents, then recovering from a broken engagement only to have his orphaned nephew put under his care. He had prayed for God to send a helpmate to him, too, but no suitable yet pious maiden a minister could marry had appeared. Until. . . against his will, Moira O'Donnell came into his mind.

He realized it was over a month since he had visited the O'Donnell's. Patrick O'Donnell had been his gardener until he grew too ill to dig in the roses. For years Reverend George had travelled down the crooked lane to the cottage to bring potions for the old man's heart, to see the old Irishwoman hobble geese the English landlord demanded as his due. Lately he had been going to see their daughter. Moira O'Donnell had returned last year to the village after being a seamstress for a wealthy family near Dublin. Her loving nature had brought the cottage to life for both her parents and Reverend George. He visited frequently now, and when he did, Moira would stand at the gate, having heard his horse. She would welcome him in the way of the Irish, with a warm touch on the arm which he would pretend not to notice and which would melt his heart and will.

Who could help but admire Moira O'Donnell, George McClure asked himself? This radiant girl should have married long ago and had children of her own, but instead she worked to take care of her parents, making the sod fire, sweeping the floor with the rude broom, trying to scrub soot from the blackened walls. Those who believed the Mere Irish slovenly and uncaring did not know Moira, whose tin pots and prized copper kettle shone brighter than anyone else's in the county.

He long since ceased to wonder how she felt about his continued visits—visits her church disapproved of, her cousins scorned. It bothered him that the visits had gone beyond his Christian duty. He knew he was drawn not only to the helpless parents, the victims of a ruthless land system, but to her, to her goodness, her quiet patience as she fussed with the coverlet on the white-haired man's bed and said loudly in his ear, "Dada, the Reverend is here to pay you a visit."

And she would show him in to administer the medicine he brought. It was an infusion of foxglove from the medicine garden he kept, made according to a recipe given him by his father Alexander McClure, the physician whose healing talents the village remembered even now.

Long ago Patrick O'Donnell had taught the Reverend to play the Irish harp. Now Moira would sing for him about the lordly Irish clans and the vanished "Donegal castle on the far crags of the sea," the home of her father's own clan, now humbled and dispersed by both the Irish and the Scots.

George prayed each day that he would value Moira's virtues ever more deeply, even though she was a Roman Catholic, a Papist; that he would not feel his heart rise when he saw the translucent quality of her skin in the sunlight outside the cottage or wish to touch her hair, the color of wheat. Most of all, he fervently prayed that she, for whom he had come to care so deeply, would turn from the folly of Rome and find the true way of salvation planned in Heaven for the Elect.

George McClure had finished his pie and he saw Jane watching him. She asked curiously if he would have something else. No, no, he assured her and then went off to walk in the still night air. He needed to think about his sermons for the coming Sabbath.

Quiet did not come to the house until about midnight. Reverend George had returned late from his walk, after stopping off at one of the houses down the lane to inquire after an older woman in his congregation. She had suddenly begun speaking in tongues in the middle of the afternoon service last Sunday. He had found her unable to explain how "the fits" sent by the Devil's hand hit her right in a Presbyterian church.

Wrapped in thought, the Reverend sat before the fire, hardly noticing the newly married couple. Jane was setting up her spinning wheel, while John cleaned the smooth-bore Dublin musket he purchased a week ago. She was set on making a marriage coverlet of the dyed blue wool she had saved from her parents' last lot, and she was not expert at spinning. Now she cleaned the parts of the wheel that had been her grandmother Anderson's. The large, old-fashioned wool wheel stood as tall as she did and had a delicate, finely-made spindle.

They sat, separated by their own thoughts, three people of the same household but not yet a family, until the embers of the fire which had cooked their supper flickered. Then Reverend George mumbled his goodnights and made his way up the stairs to the loft, and Jane was alone again with her husband in the stillness of the night.

A cool wind had blown down from the hills, and leaves rustled on the branches of the two elder trees in the yard. Perhaps there would be rain soon. The promise of it had drifted in the air for days. Jane wondered what their bedding would bring this night. Probably nothing. Her new husband had scarcely spoken a word to her all evening. All his attention had gone into the muzzle of the musket.

Jane attempted conversation more than once, asking questions about the day he had spent at the shop, mentioning her own ramblings in the market. He grunted and finally looked up at her sharply, and the words died on her lips. What in the world would they have to say to each other, she and this man who locked himself away from her?

She entered the bed and lay, rigidly, waiting for John McClure to do something, anything. What he did was to come quickly to her, take her in his arms again and put his lips on hers. It was the first time in her life anyone had kissed her lips that way. His breath was sweet, and he parted his lips and kissed her again, then pulled back a little and breathed slowly beside her. She wondered what he was thinking, this man who acted as if she were a block of wood all day and now was kissing her tenderly.

Were all men so? Did they not know that women needed gentling, that they were not objects of possession, like andirons or horse bridles? Well, she could endure whatever she must. After all, the kiss was not bad; in fact, it felt unexpectedly warming. She could see her husband's face in the last flashes of the fireplace embers and was drawn to the strong, honest lines of his profile. Mentally she ran a finger over his nose and chin, feeling terribly tempted to do it in reality. Her mother would have said he was bonny. She would also have thought him a good man. Something about him inspired trust, in spite of his silent ways.

His arm was around her and she began to be aware of his flesh on hers through the nightgowns they both wore. She was curious about his body and was glad when he sat up and took off the garment. Hestitantly, she too sat up and pulled the gown over her head. She had not looked at him the night before; indeed, the only man she had seen without clothes was Crazy Willie, who had run down the street naked one Midsummer Night's Eve crying that the spirits of the cairns were after him. It was dark that night, and all she could see in her startled state was a flash of dark hair at the poor looney man's crotch.

Of course she had noticed animals' parts. She wondered when she first thought about the wedding night, if men were like horses. Boldly she raised her hand to his chest. Her fingertip touched one nipple, then another, then shaped his shoulder. He seemed to enjoy her touch and kissed her again, with what seemed to be tender encouragement. Sensations became difficult to sort out; at the same moment she was aware of his maleness rising against her thigh she felt his hands touch her breasts.

For a moment time stood still and she was conscious of life beyond the bed, of the fecund vitality of the sleeping village, of the pulsatingly fertile life of the world beyond, of the thousands of men and women and creatures coupling in all the teeming cities and seas of this ebony night. Then all consciousness passed except that of the moment she was experiencing, composed all of feeling and of fire. The man had became one with her senses and will, melded with her as hot metal melts into metal, filling her with intense feelings which amazed her.

The man groaned, then fell gently back. Slowly, coming back from what was almost unconsciousness, she realized the moment was over. She rose to close the window against the rising wind and looked out a moment to see the rain pelting in slanting drops. When she returned to the bed, her husband's even breathing showed that he had gone to sleep. He hadn't said a word. Ah, well, she thought, as she crawled into her nightdress and under the covers. No matter. She had heard it said that any two young people in good health could marry and be content enough if they were buxom in bed. It seemed to be true. Even though she and John had been uncommunicative strangers, love, it seemed, had a distinct tongue all its own. As long as they could talk this way, they would always have an understanding that did not depend on words. And maybe later on the other would come.

Chapter II

John McClure recorded in the big Anderson Bible this entry: Born this day, October 15, 1745, John McClure, Jr. (The entry didn't say that the birth was after twenty-two hours of labor which left Jane exhausted, vowing never to have another child.)

As she recovered from the birth, Jane wondered about the new baby's future. Would he grow up in Ireland? John had not spoken of America lately. Perhaps the increased work load at the shop and the prospect of larger family responsibility had driven it from his mind. Or had he decided to stay? Pray God so. And what of Uncle? Was he glad a baby had come to the tiny house?

That very day, as a matter of fact, Reverend George was making a momentous decision, as he rode horseback out of the village. Since as a Presbyterian he believed that he spoke directly with his God, the minister was explaining himself to that most important Being. This was the gist of the conversation: "Father, it is obvious that I must move from the cottage. Much as I wish to be about the house to see this new babe eat his gruel and sit on my lap and pull at my spectacles, as he will, my nephew and dear Jane will be needing stretching room. And I, dear Father, need a bed of my own and a place to think when I plan my sermons to Your Elect.

"Forgive me, Father, I am such a distractible man, I hear the scraping of the ashshovel, the clanging of the iron lid on the spider pot, the very bubbling of the oatmeal as I sit at my desk. Not to mention the creakings of the ropes on the bed below, the arguings, even, at times, the muted, loving sighs." (It struck him that the last thought was not appropriate reportage to the Most High, so he withdrew it.)

He thanked Divine Providence that his parishoners were now able to afford a small but neat new parsonage for him. (The town had always called his cottage the parsonage, but he had personally owned title to it.) He cleared his throat mentally, and went on. "And so, dear Father, I ask for courage and direction in what I am about to do. As You tell us, truly, all things work together for good for those who have a holy purpose. . ."

And surely it is a holy purpose, not a human one, he thought. He had talked on that subject again today with his nephew. As he had prepared to make his ministerial visits, John had demanded, "Tell me why, against the village's wishes, you continue to visit the Papists?''

George McClure simply pulled out his Bible and read from it. '' 'And now abideth faith, hope, charity, these three; but the greatest of these is charity. For now we see through a glass darkly, but then face to face,' '' he read. ''And John, when I see my God face to face I want to be able to say I had charity to all men, even the Mere Irish.''

And if there was a reason beyond that, God would forgive, he thought, as he reined Dainty at a familiar thorn tree down a long lane. The door of the little cottage behind the tree opened to the luminous face of Moira O'Donnell.

''Welcome, Reverend. It is always a good day when you come. And will you be taking a bit of tay with me?'' What he wished to say was that he adored her more than he could put in words, that he had lived through the last two days to see her, that he was only a poor preacher with no material hopes on earth and small hope of Heaven, but that when he was with her he was as rich and kingly as any of the ancient, vanished clans of Irish chieftains. What he did say was ''Good morning, Miss O'Donnell. I am happy to come by to give you spiritual comfort. I would be happy for a cup of tea.''

The cottage shone inside. Moira's mother had died last year, following her husband to the small Irish cemetery with its celtic crosses out on the windswept hill looking toward the sea. Since that time, Moira spent her time polishing the little house so it would be presentable to the ladies who now came bringing their needlework to her. They kept her so busy that she even travelled out of the country to do seasonal wardrobes.

Still, she spoke sometimes to her friend the Reverend of her loneliness now in her childhood home, and of her love of God, which comforted her. Now, she bustled about at the mud and wattle fireplace, blowing on coals and setting a teakettle on the rude hook which hung out from the masonry. George watched her.

Tea was an innovation he had introduced into the family; the Irish did not take it, drinking instead milk, ale, whiskey, or sometimes the native raisin brew usquebagh. He had changed her ways, and it wasn't just the few tea leaves she was measuring into the little pot she had been given in exchange for embroidery. The presumptuousness of it all frightened him. Ah, well, once having ventured upon the waters. . .

''Moira, we have spoken often of your faith. I know it is deep and that the Christ you love is the one I love.'' He knew Presbytery would not understand, let alone forgive such talk to a Papist, but it was the way he felt. The problem was not with Moira but with her heathenish Church.

''I have told you that God has a plan for us all, and that it is through reading His word directly and praying to Him as our Father and friend that we find Him. I have prayed that you will desire to'' (here he paused) ''leave the past behind and find your salvation as one of the Elect of God.'' She set her teacup down and looked at him.

''Reverend, my friend,'' she said emphatically, ''you know I ha' listened to your talkin' and seremonizin' here for the old uns. You are a man of honor and a man of God, and my heart warms to what you say when you talk of the love God sheds directly on us." He nodded, encouraged.

"What are you askin' of me?" She turned her face a little on the side, quizzically, and he thought, What am I asking you? What have I wanted to ask you, lo these many months, or is it years? I have no right to ask you anything but what concerns your immortal soul.

He said, "Moira, I believe you are ready to come out from the Church you were baptized in and to join the Presbyterian way. I promise you Christ will welcome you and you will find spiritual satisfaction you have never dreamed of."

She was silent for a long minute, looking at the floor, thoughtful to the point of sadness. "I knew someday you would ask me this. Part of my heart flies away to do it. I believe my faith will save me and I want to know the Father of all face to face, as you have said He speaks. I ask myself what of the Church, and I answer that the priests did little enough for the old uns. They turned their backs on us after you came t' call. I have lost my love, or call it better, fear, of them. So much for that." She tossed her head defiantly.

Thank God, he thought. Never had she committed so much in their religious discussions. Few Mere Irish in all the Isle converted, even though English laws encouraged it by giving a father's land to any younger son who did so.

"No, it is not the priests I fear, but my cousins." She bit her lip. They had spoken of the O'Donnell clan before, and he knew it was a painful subject. "They are not bad men. On the contrary, they are decent. Just wild. After the Scots and English sent the lord of Donegal running, my cousins took to the mountains. They have their cattle, they need do little else but raise their corn, run the cattle into the woods and"—her eyes fell—"defy the Scots they hate, in the north of Ireland."

"And because of them you cannot convert?" he asked, his hopes fading.

"I should be so alone against them all. None leave Mither Church, no, not any of the families. No O'Neills, O'Boyles, MacGuires or McGuinesses. And certainly not the O'Donnells. They know I am of my own mind, but how could I leave the Church?"

"I have thought of that, Moira." He moved to the bench beside her, then took her hand. "God, grant me courage," he prayed, "to proceed in justice to her."

"Now that I know you wish to come to the true faith, I must tell you the full truth. I could not speak all these years until I knew your heart toward God. Now I may say it. I will protect you from your cousins, take you into my own family, help you find your way to Christ myself. Although I am a poor suitor, could you care for me, I would give my life for you."

She turned away, obviously disturbed. "You know not what you ask. Our people do not mix in religion, let alone marry. Although I am different in my heart from most, I am of that race you and your village call the Mere Irish. Will you separate me from mine and yourself from your own?"

"I know there will be difficulty, even danger. But now I know your faith is strong, I ask about your love. Can you love me?" He looked, long and searchingly, into her eyes. Slowly her fear, anger, and outrage ebbed away, to be replaced by a wispy, fay smile.

"How could I help but love you," she asked, putting her arm through his in that intimate, affectionate way she had. "You helped me nurse my father and then my mother, with your father's ash-bark concoctions and your kindly words. You saw us all through the worst, secured the lease to my little cot for me when the landlord would have taken it away—I think I owe everything to you, in spite of the differences between us, of religion, of background. . ." she put her hand over his mouth, lest he should deny those differences.

He took the small, very white hand, tentatively. He must step gingerly. "I would know what you think of me," he ventured.

"I am thinkin' you are the Good Samaritan among these Levites. That you have bound up Irish wounds and cared for us from your own sustenance. Sure that is what you are."

"Anything more?"

"Yes, more, but I will not tell you now. It is too thorny a field for me to walk through yet. If—we were to marry," (his heart leapt) "where would it be? This is not a good place."

"Of course not. We should go to Enniskillen, I think. A brother minister who was with me in school at Glasgow will understand our pickle of affairs. You could stay with him and his wife. First, he would instruct you in the Confession of Faith and catechize you so that you could prepare to join the congregation. Then, after we felt you confirmed in the faith, in a reasonable amount of time, we could be married and return. The congregation here will question, but they will accept." She nodded, knowing the respect and veneration Reverend George commanded in the village.

Moira took the teacups to the washbucket and clattered them there to hide her thoughts. She felt so many ways at once, and had for many weeks, as she thought about Reverend George McClure. Pride, that he had honored her family and seemed to enjoy her company, shame, that she had shattered the O'Donnell loyalty by admitting a Protestant to her hearth, and anger at the stupidity of a system that judged people by whether they stood or sat when they prayed, whether their priests wore white or black robes.

She returned to where he sat, still by the little table, patiently waiting while she sorted out her tumultuous thoughts. "One step at a time is enough. I will go to visit your friend's family in Enniskillen and we will discuss the faith a Christian should have. Then we shall see whether and whither. Be pickin' me up, if you will, tomorrow in the wagon. Now, my friend, you must go. If we are talkin' of marryin' it is not seemly you should be alone here with me."

He nodded mutely. His happiness was fuller than he could have ever thought possible. Not only was there the likelihood that he had won a soul for Christ, but possibly also a bride. And at home waiting, he had a new grandnephew in the bargain.

But as he left the cottage and looked toward the mountains, now almost vanished behind the cloak of drizzling rain that was falling, he felt a pang. The O'Donnells were a tough tribe, as pugnacious as fighting cocks and twice as touchy. They had not adopted the habits of the English; they still drank the usquebagh and ale and skimmed their pots of beef broth and milk with straw.

They would not take kindly to the news filtering into their woodland crofts from others of the kin, and the threat of some sort of quick, retaliatory vengeance was real. A wagon overturned by horsemen who pounded by too quickly to be recognized, outbuildings burned. Such things had happened. Well, come cousin or church covenanter, he would be ready. He had the sword of salvation and the breastplate of righteousness. And now, it seemed at this late date and after so many lonely nights, he had Moira too.

Jane observed the changes in George McClure after he came in that afternoon, and wondered about them. He was as bounding as a boy of fifteen who has won the horserace. He had joyfully announced he was moving. He would be willing to sell them the house reasonably if they wished it. And as the days passed and he moved his possessions down the lane, he was uncommonly cheerful, whistling "Lord Lovett," "Barbry Allen," and some of the low Irish tunes he seemed to enjoy. He brought her presents from his trips to Presbytery and Synod meetings and when he visited he chucked Johnny on the chin in an altogether uncharacteristic manner, and she wondered at him.

"If I dinna know better," she said to John over supper of rarebit and bread pudding one night in early December, "I would say that Uncle is courtin'." She was nursing Johnny unobtrusively across the table.

"Courtin'?" John snorted as he buttered a hot scone. "Uncle is forty-five years old and can barely support himself from the generosity of the parish." Still, he grew thoughtful, "Every dog must have his day."

"He has been journeyin' to Enniskillen a good bit lately," John went on. His wife watched him and wondered what he would think if his uncle were to marry. She could never be sure of her husband's reaction, although she could anticipate his moods a good sight better than she had been able to when she married him.

Mostly the marriage was better than she had anticipated, she thought, as she reached over the sleepy, sucking baby to nibble her food with a fork. John was hard-working in the extreme, often rising at six to make the fire, take a slice of bread and a piece of cheese and head for the cooper's shop. If other businesses in northern Ireland had not prospered, the cooperage business had, and Sandy Craig had grudgingly raised John's wages not once but twice in the years they had been married.

Well he should, Jane told herself, John was at least as good a cooper as he was. Jane suspected her husband was having faint hopes that now that the business was so prosperous, Sandy might change his mind about selling him a partnership. When wages were paid, John still carefully salted away half in the wooden sugar casket with the small lock on the side. The pile of coins and bills had been depleted by the purchase of the house and land, but it was growing again, slowly. She suspected that even though he never spoke of the past, particularly his own, the future was still on his mind. She dare not ask about anything but the day-to-day business of running the home. John was not one to share his plans about the future or anything else; he kept the depths of his heart locked as tight as the money chest.

Still, Jane was growing genuinely fond of her husband, in spite of his taciturn nature. He was gentle to the baby, and if he was sharp sometimes to her when she pried or asked too many questions, he made it up to her with tender, if unspoken solicitousness, in the long, sharing nights they continued to enjoy when the fire burned low.

A week later, John roared into the cottage, slamming down the leather lunch pouch he carried to work with him on days he did not come home for dinner. Jane ran to him. "It's Uncle," he said, before she could ask. "He's goin' to hell in a handcart and taking us along with him in the bargain." He took off his hat and flung it toward the peg on the wall, then, missing, stooped to pick it up. "Innkeeper Stark's wife came by the shop today to pick up some cider barrels for the inn. She mentioned she had heard that Uncle was reprimanded formally by the Belfast Presbytery." Mrs. Stark had a brother who lived in Enniskillen; the folk in that large town made it a point to know about Church affairs.

"Uncle reprimanded by Presbytery? Whatever for?" Jane looked at her husband in astonishment.

"For, you cannot conceive of it—posting the banns to marry a Papist!"

But Jane was not as surprised as he expected. "Ah, now I see. He should have confided in his kin. But I reckon I know who. Miss O'Donnell from down the lane outside of town."

"Patrick O'Donnell's—the gardener's—girl? Well, of course, he has been visitin' all of them for these many years, but how could he possibly think of considerin' a low Irish wench? Uck. I canna dream of it. These people don't wash for weeks and leave hair in their butter. Their homes are frightful pigsties. . .''

"Not Moira O'Donnell's. She keeps a better house than I do. She scrubs her fireplace and airs her bed twice a week."

"And how do you know that, woman?" John roared. The baby, startled by the noise, awoke in his cradle and began to cry. Jane, walking over to pick him up said, calmly, "Because I once went to visit the family when the mother was dyin'. I helped Uncle look to things. She is a lovely woman," she sighed. "But he is stirrin' up a hornet's nest."

"More than hornets! The O'Donnells are wild men when it comes to their kin. And what are the parishoners goin' to say?"

"What they have been sayin' for ten years. Some, that he is misguided in his zeal. Some, that he is foolish to throw his pearls before the swine. Some, even, that he neglects the Elect for the Fallen. But most will say what is true, that he is a real Christian to seek out the lost sheep."

"Must he marry to do it?"

"Marriage among us is so rare that it is probably her only protection. Besides, I think he loves her."

"Well, I fear for him, and for us for that matter. I don't like havin' Mrs. Stark chatter about us."

Carrying the baby, Jane walked towards him. "We must think of Uncle. How alone he must feel, that he couldn't even tell his kith and kin." She was thoughtful for a moment. "I would be with him when he marries. I wish to go."

"Are you mad, woman? Go traipsin' out through the countryside to see our foolish uncle humiliate us marryin' a wench from a servile race?"

"However you say it, John, I will go."

"Then you will hire a wagoner and go by yourself. I willna' be made a fool of in public."

"Although you love Uncle?"

"Although I love him."

And so it was that the week before Christmas, George Nehemiah McClure, son of Doctor Alexander McClure, who had lost two fingers in the siege of Derry, married Moira O'Donnell, whose father, one of the Popish troops of the Lord of Donegal, had helped to press that siege. And the only witness to the joining of the two was Reverend George's niece, Jane McClure, who had come with her baby at the breast, from far-away Dunleigh, so that her husband's uncle would not celebrate this sacred moment without kin.

Jane's thoughts, try as she would to concentrate on the service and people before her, were not on the present but on the future. That evening, Dainty would bring Reverend and Mrs. McClure to their parsonage home and test the faith and will of both the Scots and native Irish, when it came to the mixing of the unmixable, the joining of the oil and the water.

The word of rumor, however, swifter by far than the feet of George McClure's mare, raced back to the village before the couple and set snares for their return. Perhaps the rumor was carried once more by Mrs. Stark, who just happened again to be visiting her brother and started off for her home village just as the bride was being escorted by her maids down the street.

It might have been carried by the carter bringing Christmas whiskey and hams from village to village, or even by the young Mere Irish boy lurking about the horse trough with his fat pony for who-knows-what purpose. However it was carried, the word that Reverend McClure had married a Papist came to Dunleigh late that afternoon and brought consternation with it.

Mrs. Stark, whose bosom was so large that John McClure always wondered why she didn't sink through the floor with it, marched into the cooper's shop. John was finishing work on the last of the barrels for the herring fishery in Lough Swilly; they were of fir and therefore not very interesting to him. "What is it, Madame?" he asked, looking up, startled, from his staves.

"Sir, has it come to this? That the bells are ringin' in Enniskillen for the weddin' of a minister of the Gospel and a haythen?" She snapped her parasol shut and pointed it at him.

Sandy Craig, his face as stony as always, gestured with a nod of the head that McClure should take the discussion outside, and John ushered the woman, fluffed up as an angry goose, out the door.

"Mrs. Stark, I know the situation and I don't like it myself, but we must try to make the best of it." He noticed the woman had a new emerald collar brooch hiding in the fat folds of her lower neck.

"Best of it? Are we to go to the communion table side by side with the dowaughter of one of the traitors from the Battle of the Boyne? There's some around here who don't disremember that. And I suppose she'll be sitting in the best pew, with her chapped hands and bare feet."

You ought to know, John thought. Mrs. Stark, in an earlier, merely plump state, had improved her position in the village by marrying the portly keeper of the William and Mary Inn. Her own feet had been regularly shod for the first time the week she married Bratton Stark.

John believed he was doing a good job of remaining patient. He was nearly as angry at Uncle as this shrew of a woman was. He managed to murmur some soothing injunctions about Christian forbearance and she went on, somewhat mollified.

The outlying farms had heard of the odd marriage by evening. Even Crazy Willie seemed to know, John noted, as he approached (today, thank heaven, clothed but not, one could say, in his right mind,) making the sign of the cross and talking over imaginary rosary beads as his eyes rolled in his head.

By this time, however, the news of the wedding at Enniskillen was heading for the ears of those who could stand it the least. In the mountains northwest of Lough Swilly, in a clay and straw cottage, where thatched roof hung so deeply over the eaves that it almost touched the ground, Brian O'Donnell and his brother Shawn waited for the return of their cousin Joseph from Enniskillen.

Brian's wife Margaret, a silent woman whose thin shoulder bones stood out sharply in the coarse brown bag of a dress she wore, kneeled by a smoky turf fire in the center of the cottage. Over the fire was suspended a kettle of bones and milk on a tripod. The tripod shifted as she added more turf and blew on the fire, and scalding soup splashed on her arm. She cursed and whimpered. Brian scarcely noted her. With a primitive chisel he was hollowing out a piece of ash to make a manger for two new cows that had just been given him.

The mood in the room was tense, but Brian seemed determinedly unconcerned as he went about the work. As the tool bit and shaved the wood, he brushed shavings out of the manger with a large, hairy hand. They accumulated on the dirty rushes of the floor, along with fur and leavings from the assortment of animals who stayed inside these cold December evenings and the potato skins and pork bones that went unnoticed when meals were finished.

Shawn, a curly-headed boy of eighteen with a muscular build and intelligent eyes, sat in the corner, working over the harnesses. "Then when shall he be a-comin'?" he asked in a low voice. Just as he said it the door burst open and the youth who was seen earlier at the watering trough at Enniskillen appeared. The wind was bitter in the mountains; young Joseph O'Donnell approached the fire to warm his hands. No one spoke.

"It's done," Joseph said finally, taking a tin cup of broth the woman Margaret handed him.

"Knot's tied?" Brian asked his cousin, still not looking up from the chiselling.

"Tied in a pretty bow, pretty as the bride. One more knot in the rope about our necks, if you ask me."

"P'r'aps so, p'r'aps so," Brian said, walking around the manger to see how even his work was.

"You know so, brother," said Shawn, walking to him and turning him around to face him. "Another back of the hand from the people who took the land what belongs to us. Who tills our plots and tithes us blue and keeps us from even ruling over our own byres."

"Be so good as to speak truth, brother," Brian said, looking squarely at him. "It is the English that took our land and tithes us and keeps us from having our own priests and schoolmasters, lest we should learn enough to make a coin or two that was theirs."

Shawn's voice grew louder. "But it is the Scots who fought us like tigers for land that had been taken from us, land our chieftains held on these green shores a thousand yayrs or more." His eyes flashed. "'Tis the Scots who brought their husbandman ways into Ireland and planted gardens and sowed their flax and drained the fields. And nicely, then, out of the goodness of their Protestant hearts, offered to hire the poor paddies to build their homes. There they sit now, drinkin' tay and eatin' their shortbread and watchin' us from their glass windows carry firewood and wheelbarrows of manure about. They hate our Irish crucifixes. They spit upon our Gaelic tongue."

"Some do. The rest be poor as we," his brother Brian said quietly. "What would you have us do to this McClure who has taken our cousin from the arms of Church to his bed?"

"All their clergy are lechers, worse than the village priests of yore," Margaret put in from across the room.

"I do not know what we are to do," Shawn said. "We are not few, but we lack spirit. Soon, I think, we will all know what must happen."

His cousin Joseph looked up with interest from the soup he was drinking with the woman. "In the South," Joseph said, "already the boys talk. They talk of laws which keep all landownin' from the Irish, of our churches closed down, of our women taken like whores from their cottages for the 'use' of the landlords. They say the time will come when we will rise from our ditches. . ."

"Shut your face, Joseph," Brian commanded sharply. The day which might come was not now, and the arm of the magistrate could be heavy. Besides, what was there to do? Strangle a man because he won and wed a maid? In a warped way, it was like the olden tales, of Deirdre of the sorrows, stolen away by lovers against all the fates. Still, it rankled deeply.

"We shall act," Brian finally said to his two younger brothers. "In a way that fits and that will show us men. And then we shall sit, wait and see. Shawn, saddle the horses. We leave in an hour for Dunleigh."

John and Jane McClure lay beneath three blankets and a quilt that same cold December evening. Little Johnnie was also in the bed, having a late-night feeding. His mother hoped it would last him until morning, so she would not have to tread across freezing floorboards to feed him in the night.

Most of the last two days Jane had been in the coach to and from Enniskillen. Now she yearned to sleep. The wind had died, and the village was still with a hush only the cold could bring. She rose, sighing, and put the baby, warmly swaddled, in his crib. Finally John spoke. "And so, they are man and wife."

"She is a good woman, John."

"About that I do not know. I know though, that he is a good man. The village has resigned itself to Uncle's 'Christian duty.' " Unspoken questions were in his mind too: is this night going to pass without a barn or even house burning? Will Irishmen ride through town dumping tar over doorsteps? Will they knock fences down and scuffle with our youths in the streets?

Just then a strange, mournful noise started outside. Like the wailing of a Banshee, it began on one long note. Then a chorus of other moans began, soon mounting in intensity until they sounded over the whole village.

"What is it?" Jane asked, astonished. "It sounds like a huge herd of cows mooin'."

"Ah," John said softly. "That is it. It is the Mere Irish, the O'Donnells. They have come."

"What are they doin'?" his wife wanted to know. The moos grew in cadence and ranged through a variety of notes from low, death-like moans to high, bleating yelps which sounded almost like mocking laughs.

"They are blowin' the wedding. You wouldn't know it, I have not heard it done in the village. But in the South it is done when the Irish wish to show their scorn of a marriage. They have rams' horns, big whistles, even bottles whose ends are out. They sit about a fire, out of sight, yet near. They could carry on for an hour or more."

"It is so obvious. No one can help but know their anger. They are mockin' us. Yet. . ." she listened to the mournful notes tremulously hanging on the crisp air, "it is so sad."

All night long the blowing continued, the entire village lying awake and silent under its eerie assault. Finally, just before the dreary dawn, the sounds all stopped at once. In a moment, far away, the sounds of horses' hoofs were heard, diminishing gradually toward the mountains until there was again silence.

As Jane McClure lay in bed, wondering if the baby, silent through all the noise, would now cry, she heard something she had never heard in all her married life—her husband's laughter. Beginning as a tired chuckle, it grew into a barking round of sharp, rolling laughs. He laughed on and off for a full moment, then turned over to go to sleep, saying with finality, "A fine weddin' night for Uncle." But Jane knew that the laughter in this house and probably several others in the village had come not out of amusement. No, the laughter came from relief, joy that they had to endure nothing more than the blowing of bottles from a people whose real power for anger and destruction was unknown and whose cause for anger was far greater than any lying in the beds would dare admit.

Chapter III

Jane would always remember the year 1749. It was made memorable by two events: the birth of William McClure in July and Uncle's November announcement to the Presbytery in Belfast that he would start an evangelical mission to the Mere Irish in Ulster. After praying on this subject for days, George proposed to travel around like the Englishman George Whitefield was doing. He would consciously bring to the lost souls of the Roman Catholic Church the message that God's redeeming love could be salvation for them.

"John," Reverend George said, "this is the calling of the Lord. The gospel goes to the reprobate, even to those who seem lost." John gave him a sharp look and his uncle, conscious of having inadvertently said a wounding thing, cleared his throat and gave up trying to explain his mission.

And so George McClure made his plans, undaunted by the knowledge that there had been other missions to the Irish, and all of them had failed.

After Christmas, Reverend George rode out into the countryside in earnest, taking his Bible with him, knocking on the doors of cottages to talk to the people. He began with Moira's past friends. Most often, he exited soon after a frigid reception, and the words "God be with ye, sir," a tipping of the cap and a shutting of the door. Occasionally someone listened and the prospect of a convert excited him. By spring the family of farmers who rented Moira's cottage began attending Presbyterian services. This caused a new wave of mutterings, which only seemed to make his purpose stronger.

In the Dunleigh congregation, the minister began to urge a new sense of the brotherhood of man. "Reach out to those we call the Mere Irish. Open your hearts and even your homes. Show how a Christian loves, as Christ loved."

Parishioners emerged from the morning and afternoon services shaking their heads. "Enough is enough, Reverend," Mrs. Stark remonstrated as they stood outside the church.

"Enough is never enough for a disciple of the Lord as long as there is one act of intolerance in this world," he said, trying not to sound sharp to the stout woman before him.

The innkeeper's wife looked at him a moment and then bustled stolidly off, rather like the queen on a chessboard moving from one square to another. He watched her puffing down the lane, and thought of the beautiful new home her husband built, the furniture from London he had brought over. Now she sat in it alone. He had died of apoplexy in the streets of Dunleigh. John McClure had helped carry the body home.

George McClure mopped his brow. It was unusually warm for a May afternoon. "What will they all think next week," he asked himself, as he turned to look back at the deserted church on the hill, "when I talk about opening up occupations to the Irish and revising the land laws so they may earn an honest living?"

Then cold, blustery weather blew in from the sea. Cloaks, scarves, and caps could not keep it out. One day John returned home from the shop for dinner to find Moira speaking to Jane in low tones in the windy garden. The two little boys, Johnny, five, and William, a crawling baby, were playing in their worsted jackets among the stubs of last year's cabbages and sprouting parsley as their mother spaded a plot for carrot seeds.

Moira looked at John with concerned eyes. She told him that her cousins Brian and Shawn O'Donnell were at the parsonage. They had waited until George McClure left on his parish visiting, then had accosted her about the "preaching to the Irish." She was afraid, particularly of Shawn.

"Are they yet there?" John asked.

"Yes. They're a-wantin' to get a message to your uncle. 'Stay away from the Celtic cross,' they say."

John turned abruptly from the women, and before they could protest, headed toward the parsonage.

The two Irishmen were in the cottage, sitting before the fire, when John shoved open the door and strode in. "So the nephew is here, it seems," Brian O'Donnell said, without looking at the Scot.

"To tell you to get out of the village before there's trouble," John said. They rose and faced him, their faces white and implacable. John McClure felt, as always, small before the Mere Irish. Brian O'Donnell was only two inches taller than he, but the Irishman's chest was thick and muscular and his arms were like bags of oats. He seemed to dwarf John, although Shawn stood at his eye level.

"The only trouble will come if the Reverend Father continues his mission to the haythen." Brian's tone was even.

Anger made John mount a more vehement defense of his uncle than he might otherwise have done. "My Uncle takes his instructions from God, not the Irish."

"And the heavenly Father tells him to go out in Christian sheepfolds not his own to stayl the sheep," Shawn O'Donnell spoke stridently. "I thought all the wolves in Ireland were gone after the last famine."

In a flash John made a fist at the younger brother. "Go in peace, man, before you rouse my anger."

"And, sure we would not be wantin' to do that," Shawn said, the mockery in his voice as thick as honey on bread. "It might cause the earth to shake and my cousin's new London china plates to fall off the shelf and smash to smithereens. But come now, show us what you've got in those Scotch hands." He began to feint at John, pushing his fists in John's face, until the Scotch-

Irishman closed on him.

"Now we won't play the fool, men," said Brian O'Donnell, with growing alarm. He attempted to separate the two as they scuffled and snorted; he had no wish to witness a fight in the house of the Presbyterian minister, no matter what his sins toward the Irish were.

"He's had too much whiskey, and he's strutting like a fightin' cock," Brian shouted at McClure just as the Scot landed a strong right to his brother's jaw. John felt a flash of red anger; naturally it would be whiskey. He surged forward with renewed energy to the fight.

At that moment Moira, Jane, and the boys pushed through the door. Horror registered on the women's faces as Shawn O'Donnell and John McClure continued their fistfighting. The scene became a confusion of attempts to pull the combatants apart, babies crying, and women's voices shouting, "Shame, shame, stop the brawling." Finally Brian O'Donnell succeeded in pulling his brother back and holding his arms. Jane and Moira pushed John back onto the settee before the fireplace, where he slumped, panting like an animal.

"This has gone beyond where it ought," Brian O'Donnell glowered at the women. "But mark me: let your people meddle not in the religion of the Irish. The English and Scotch have taken our land and even our daily bread from us. But they could not take our masses. Mass houses spring up and priests pray in them in spite of the law and none of you can do anything about it."

He gave Moira a slighting look. "Your husband could no more take our faith from us than the waves can take the cliffs at Donegal, beat how they may. A few grains of sand slide into the water; they are nothing. Anyway, the issue is lucre, filthy lucre, not the cross of Christ, say what they will. Still, this religious squabblin' breeds bad blood, and 'tis this I fayre." He pushed his brother toward the door, but Shawn managed to turn and spit out one last imprecation before he was forced to leave.

"You," he cried at Moira in a hate-filled voice. "Named for the blessed Virgin. Tell your husband I curse him in the name of the dark ones of the cairns. And tell him to watch the steps he takes lest he stumble over an Irishman." Then they were gone.

But that night, when Moira, still ashen from the conflict of the afternoon, told her husband the story, he shook his head. "Brian O'Donnell and I do not disagree. What has been done to the Mere Irish is awful sowing. And it will reap a harvest of blood, that is sure. But what I am trying to do is to heal that, not make it worse. If we Scots reach out to the Irish, both with the Lord and even more with our common human love, we can cause a change. We must try, for our children's sake."

There was a wistfulness in his voice. His wife reached for his hand. Perhaps God, who had blessed them richly so far, would send a child to seal His pleasure at the marriage. If He did, what a blessing it would be to have an Ireland at peace for the child. Many felt it was a hopeless dream; she did not.

"Nevertheless," George McClure added soberly, "if blood comes, it will not be over the religions but over the pence and pounds, as Brian O'Donnell said. We put our feet on their necks so we can raise ourselves up."

Summer and fall, with the fields ripe with grain, brought a brief period of respite from the tensions in the village, a patch of blue sky between clusters of ominous, black clouds for the two McClure families. There was time for morning devotions together by the fire and evening suppers spread on the hill. Afterward, as the sun set amidst long fiery bands of ochre and mauve, Moira, whom John had learned to accept and even admire, would laughingly teach Irish dances to Jane. Or Uncle would play the harp. Sometimes he read *Pilgrim's Progress*, his tones properly solemn and admonitory as he described for the wide-eyed Johnny and baby William the sinful worldliness of Vanity Fair.

Then in September of 1750, with harvest largely in, George McClure began again in earnest to ride the rounds of the three villages he now served. He held services, baptized babies, catechized, and prayed for the sick and dying. Then, when the sun set on his regular ministerial day, he held extra services in the countryside for the "awakening" of both Scots and Irish. His text was always the same. "Come unto me, all ye that labor and are heavy laden, and I will give you rest. . . For I am humble and lowly of heart. And ye shall find rest unto your souls." And, on the hillsides or in the barns where he preached, these words always brought grunts of affirmation from those whose yoke was truly heavy and whose burden was grievous.

One Sunday in November, Reverend George announced a season of holy communion that would welcome for the first time two new Irish communicants from near the crossroads of the Derry road. For two days running, in the drizzling, late fall rain which continued for the best part of a week, Shawn O'Donnell was seen in Dunleigh. Once he bought leather at the wainwright's cot, another time he simply stood with his pony under the sole great oak remaining in the village, sharpening a stick with his Irish knife, a look of arrogant unconcern on his face.

Toward the end of the workday on Friday, John McClure found the younger O'Donnell leaving the blacksmith's shop. He exchanged defiant words with him for a moment, then beat him savagely, and left him in the manure behind the smith's. But not before O'Donnell inflicted two black eyes and a deep gash wound on John's face. The scar from this would be visible for the rest of his life.

He dragged home, where his concerned wife washed his wounds. Then, head throbbing with pain, he stood by the window just before the last light, determined to read over for the second time a letter which had arrived last month. It said:

Dear Friend: You have expressed interest in life here in Pennsylvania and what it would be if you was to come out. We have been here just a few months, but allready air on our path to riches. We are here with some of our relatives near a town called Chambersburg. There is talk of starting up a new town on the Great Road near the Susquehanny River, and if they do it, we will settle there because there will be lots of work for a wheelwright. I got me a loan to pay back, and I intend to do it in no time atall.

Every week more settlers is coming out to take all the land from Harris's Ferry to the mountains. We was down by the Delaware River, but we left to git farther out. I married me a fine wife name of Sally Strong and we now have two children, a boy and a girl.

There is enough land for every mother's son in Ulster here, and it is water off a duck's back to become a laird. Some people resents us Scotch-Irish out here spreading all through the colonies, coming in on ever boat. They won't let us land in Connecticut now and some of the other New England states is talking of banning us. But what I say is we ere building a country! Jest like we did for the English in Ulster. The savages are about, but they don't bother people much.

Some folks takes "cabbin rights" and squats, but they ben gettin' put off the land. We'll see to yours four square since you have the money to put into the best land. I know the deputy land commissioner. Lots of folks sells out after ten years to the Germans, you can aluz do that.

Well, anyways; we will help you build a cabbin—they put them up in a few days from logs of huge oaks that grow everywhere pushing out the light, as it were. Nobody here hires hands, everbody does for all. To grow crops, we girdle the trees, like the savages do. We burn them in a circle around the trunk till they die and then plant. You will find, after you arrive, that this plant Indian corn will be your sustenance. They grinds it, chunks it and eats it young with the milk in it, cooked in the coals of the fireplace like a potato. Wheat don't grow good until a field is a bit wore out. Shoots up five foot tall and falls over.

You say that you have got a gun. Good. Learn to shoot straight and fast. There are animals of all sorts here. Some of them walks on two legs and I don't mean the bars.

Now as to what you must bring with you.

Tools are like gold here. You work wood; bring your best tools with you: good quality planes, braces, broadaxes, felling axes, saws, grindstone and so forth. But take as little as possible on the sea trip; sell what you have and bring currency; you can buy here. There are as many Presbyterians as there are squirrels and not nearly as many Papists as there are skunks.

Should you come, you and your family can stay with my cousin Isaac in Philadelphia, efn you can abide the silly Quakers who runs things there. There is nothing in the way of common sense under those big hats they ware. Should you come to Cumberland County, Sally and I will help you begin life in the woods. It seems as if half Ulster has come out and when you come you will not find strangers but friends.

Yours etc
Sam Bard

Carefully John touched the gash on his face, which his wife had washed out and drenched in spirits. He placed Bard's letter in the will drawer of the desk. Yes, my friend, he thought, but when I come, it will not be to sell. It seems I will be a farmer as well as a cooper. So be it. But when I build, I will build large, for the future, and once I light, I will stay. I know now that the time will come soon, and I will know it when it does.

That night McClure's pained sleep was troubled by a series of fitful dreams.

He saw in his mind the ghost, Brohgan the Dispossessed, who the Irish believed rose to punish the usurpers of his land, expanding his giant spectral shape like molten glass on a pipe to hover over his stolen castle.

At first McClure sensed he was in the ancient Irish fortress that the Irish described, and the ghost's presence lurked somewhere amid the cold, barren rooms. Then as he turned a corner, a castle wall with a tapestry on it suddenly became the wall of Moira's family cottage. He was in bed in the Old Un's bed, which looked just as John had remembered it, with an embroidered bedquilt over a feather bed, at the moving sale he had helped Uncle with. He was alone in that dream house in the darkest night he had ever known.

The ghost of Brohgan was up in the loft. It uttered sad, unearthly moanings that shook the rafters, and he sensed it was coming down the notched steps that descended from the loft. Almost simultaneously, as the time goes in dreams, the ghost lurked by the fireplace, looking like a mountain mist. Its two giant bug's eyes glowed red and faintly illuminated the room, like a holy light in one of the Papist churches. Oddly, on what should have been its trunk, it wore a little purple waistcoat with silver buttons. Its bottom half looked like a dragon's. "Oooh, give to me me due," it said, in the quivery brogue of an old Mere Irishman.

Its "tail" knocked Moira's polished copper teapot from the fire and then John could see its eyes turning toward him, boring holes into his quivering form under the quilted bedcovers. Bolting from the bed, he streaked to the door while the ghost had stopped in his tracks. He stepped outside. Now the eerie red glow which pulsated in the dreamscape of the cottage was gone and he stood again in pitch blackness. A candle appeared suddenly in his hands but it was almost too hot to handle, so he dropped it into what seemed to be sand. It went out, but miraculously relit itself and moved away from him.

All around him stretched the undulating, lifeless hills of a desert like the ones in Uncle's Araby books. He began to walk and found his feet mired and slowed by the sand, which seemed to cling about his feet, almost as if each grain were alive and willing him to fall back. He advanced slowly, and after a while he turned to look back. The cottage was gone; darkness had swallowed it up. Before him the light of the candle was a pulsating series of circles of light. Something was ahead, up there far in the distance on one of the rises of this desert. Little shapes were standing by the side of this "road." He sensed he needed to travel on, but the sand continued to pull at his feet.

Something was also behind him; it made the hackles on the back of his neck stand up. Dread overtook him as he realized the ghost of Brohgan was indeed still with him. Its cold, fetid breath was about him and he felt a hand on his shoulder. He fought to bridge the void between waking and sleeping, trying to give voice to his terror as the beast-ghost pulled him backwards to what he thought must be certain death. He managed to utter the cry "Murderer." Then he awoke to find the white faces of Jane and Moira, in the place of the ghost of Brohgan, floating above him.

"John, It's Uncle," Jane said, as her husband painfully pulled himself back to the world and sat up.

"What of Uncle?" John's thoughts were soggy, his body prickled and torn with a hundred aches. Uncle had ridden out through the rain to a barn meeting northwest of town. But it was two in the morning. . .

"He's been found at the crossroads on the Derry road." John could see the tears brimming in Moira's large eyes. "Dainty slipped her girth and threw him. He is yet alive, the man says, but they would not move him until we got to the spot."

"I will borrow Sandy's horse," he said, reaching for his shirt and breeches and glancing at his uncle's wife. "Moira, do you want to stay with Mrs. McClure or ride behind?"

"Be it his life or death, I would be there," she said, and turned so he could quickly dress.

The Reverend George McClure lay on his back, his head cradled in the dark blue skirt of an Irishwoman. " 'Twere about a half an hour ago he went, with a little sigh," she said, staring straight ahead. "I couldna' put him down until his kin came for him. Next Sunday he would have admitted me to communion."

Moira, her face shrouded in the hood of the full, woolen cap she wore, stood by the horse, sobbing, as John knelt beside his uncle's body. George McClure's face, drained of color, was composed and life-like.

"Uncle, Uncle," John shook his head, as if to negate both the death and all the pain and despair in this beautiful, tormented land.

"For now we see through a glass, darkly," he murmured. Tenderly, as he lifted the body to strap it on to the waiting horse, he added, "then, face to face." The Irishwoman began a keening wail as she walked back to the cottage by the road.

"The saddle girth was snapped right in two," Moira said from behind him as they rode home. The wind buffeted her voice so John could barely hear. What she did not say was that she could not rid herself of the picture of an Irish boy outside her parents' cottage in a happier day, proudly saddling his pony and saying, "My brother Brian says I shall be his keeper of the leather. There's naught of horseflesh I don't know." Tears were drying into hard, dirty streaks on her face. She put her head down, into John McClure's back and prayed the hour trip would pass quickly for the living and dead.

John McClure had but one thought: Now, indeed, ready or no, we shall go from here. For if I stay in this land, I shall end up killin' again. And this time my knife will not waste itself upon the innocent.

PART II

PENNSYLVANIA 1751-1780

SONG FOR THE VOYAGE TO AMERICEY
To be sung to fiddle and zither

What shall we take, my pretty babes, for a trip across the sea
What shall we take, my little ones, for a trek to Americey?
Take the harp from the cottage wall
Take the harness from the horses' stall
Take the quilt from the trundle bed and
The marriage dress, the marriage dress, the pretty little marriage dress.

What shall we take to the forest woods in the land across the waves
What shall we take to the savage fort from the shop with the barrel staves
The maul, the awl, the plane of steel
The froe, the adze, and the grinding wheel
The musket made in Dublin town and
The marriage dress, the marriage dress, the pretty little marriage dress.

What shall we take from our little home, the home we love so dear?
What shall we bear to the seaside town for the voyage gray and drear?
Grandfather's Bible, old and worn
From the garden, the hoe for the Indian corn
China dishes, our friends' best wishes and
The marriage dress, the very pretty dress her dying mother sewed.

Chapter IV

"Is it time to come out of your nest, Mr. Smythe?" Johnny McClure shouted up at the top of his voice to the crows'-nest. The boy was carefully observing the change of watches, as he had every day for six weeks on this Alantic crossing.

Up above, the foretopman watched clouds chased by the noon-day sun scramble after each other to disappear across the horizon. The air was hot and still, as if earth's dome covered a giant, heated forge. In a moment, the foretopman descended the ropes like a spider scuttling down a web.

"What made ye fly off your feet up there, sir?" Johnny asked as the seaman put first one foot, then another on the deck. "Seems like a fair enough day."

"We calls it a cross-swell, Johnny Irish, and I don't like it. Man and boy I ben doin' this a long time, and I never got caught like that." Twenty years he had been at sea. Johnny knew this and a good deal more. As Smythe swabbed the deck, or sat picking hemp bits into oakum for cauking, he had told Johnny of his life, of his boyhood home in the south of England. John felt as if he had been there himself to see the gorse, the lush grass, the rains at Christmas, the autumn nights when Smythe had come back into his mother's cottage after a tramp with the dog. It did not sound too different from being a boy in Ireland. He tried not to stare at the stubs of two fingers which were missing from the foretopman's left hand.

The old sailor had told him frankly the first week, " 'Twere the price I paid for changing my life, lad. Left the stinks of my uncle's tannery and shipped on a German schooner out of Hamburg. But 'twere on a passage round the Cape of Good Hope, and I too green to know the ropes. Lost the pegs," he held them before his face and peered through them like a criminal looking through bars, "in a storm."

" 'Tis an odd day, Johnny Irish," Smythe continued now. "Too bright. Mid-June ain't the time for brightness on the Atlantic. Did ye notice what happened at four bells?"

"The fog left?" The sailor was teaching him to watch the time and weather, to link their fine, small changes together into patterns.

"An' since the fog lifted," Smythe told him, "the mist's ben rising from the ocean. But look. . ." he pointed, "just see the porpoises." The man and boy ran toward the bow of the ship and joined other passengers. They watched the gray-black animals breech the water, arch gracefully, and dive with barely a splash.

Smythe put his arm around the boy's shoulders as they gazed at the hot sky. Suddenly another cross-swell hit the boat, and the fortetopman held John against the gunwales to steady him. John was luckier than the other Scotch-Irish immigrants on the deck. Ladies taking the air were swept off their feet. They screamed as they tumbled with their parasols amidst ropes, giant cleats, and the portable cooking stoves on which they'd earlier cooked lunch.

As Johnny righted himself, he asked, "You say the weather always means somethin', that we can read it like a cipher book, Mr. Smythe. So what does this weather mean?"

"It means, young Scotch-Irishman, that we may be in for a wind change. And that I am goin' below for some sleep." He winked at Johnny and headed below.

Johnny stayed on deck, even though the wind began to freshen and many of the passengers went into the cabin. His father and mother were busy and had told him to stay on deck, and Johnny McClure was a staunch and dutiful boy.

In about an hour the ship began to pitch erratically, and Smythe's head appeared out of the hold in the fo'c'sle. Johnny McClure made his way to him. "M' bunk in the fo'c'sle is foremost on the port side," the seaman told him, "so the lurching didn't really bother me, boy. But when she heeled on that starboard tack, I was flung out of m' bunk. You'd better go below. It could be rough for. . ." A call of "all hands" cut him short and seemed to drive all thoughts except shortening the sail from his mind.

But Johnny did not go below. Instead, he hid behind a huge pile of rope and watched the weather come in slowly off the horizon. As sunset approached, he noticed a line of salmon-colored clouds surge rapidly forward. He heard Smythe call to the others, "Wind from the southwest." Suddenly the crew scurried to wrest the reefing lines through the salt-encrusted canvas, and to slide down the ratlines to the now-lurching deck. Johnny wondered, as he held onto his perch, if his friend Smythe missed his two fingers when he roved the lines. He took a biscuit from his pocket and ate it, precariously holding onto a stay with one hand.

His father appeared from the cabin to check his son, who begged to stay on deck. John McClure, hesitating, scanned the horizon. He saw only a freshening wind and nodded. His hands were full belowdecks with little Will, who had been seasick almost the whole voyage.

The stars appeared, and then, one by one, blinked out during the next hour or so. Johnny dug in behind his rope pile and held on, as the rising pitch of the wind through the wet rigging became a raucous whine. Glancing at the helm Johnny saw pink water surging up the neck of the barometer glass. Captain Benmans, a dapper man in a tie-wig, had come on deck now, and Johnny noticed his stern, searching gaze.

About nine o'clock the ship's rigging sighed, and the *Indian Princess* stood up straight, as the wind quieted down. Is the hard weather over? John wondered in his hiding place. But no, the ship had just worn around, as Mr. Smythe would say. Almost immediately moist air from the southwest blasted the sails. The underlying swell increased to monstrous waves. Smythe and the others on his watch pitched in immediately, even before Captain Benmans shouted for the wheel to be put hard down. Almost like a human thing sensing danger and rising to the occasion, The *Indian Princess* put its starboard shoulder into the sea and began to move off rapidly. Johnny's father felt the change and with difficulty pulled himself out of the area belowdecks. "For God's sake, Johnny, are you daft? Come in. It's startin' to blow fierce."

As he took his son below, John McClure shouted at Smythe, who was hurrying by, "Seaman, canna we get the ship to steady?"

Smythe paused a moment before racing to his position, to shoot the elder McClure a scornful look. "A real storm is heading at us and 'tis due to get worse. You'd better get below."

McClure's desparing cry was borne on the wind. "My uncle's wife is having her lyin' in. She is in agony with this pitchin'. I dinna suppose there is anything. . ."

"I'm sorry, Sir, 'tis no time for a babe to be coming into this dark and stormy world."

The cabin seemed no safer to young Johnny McClure than the deck. Sure, he thought, he'd rather be above, where the air was fresh, even if the deck was bucking like an Irishman's wild pony. Down here the lurching was making folk ill, and all the puke and chamber pot stuff were mixing in that stinking barrel, spilling over the top with every wave. His father put him in his bunk and Johnny lay there, thinking of the rope swing at the cottage in Ireland. And he thought of his friend on deck, climbing into the sky on icy ropes in a tunnel of roaring wind and hissing water, that before midnight grew into the worst strom any on the boat, including the captain, had ever seen. It was a rare June hurricane in the paths of the Southerlies.

Holding on with white knuckles to his children's bunk, John McClure cursed with every oath he had ever heard the day he had taken his family from Ulster. Forward, his wife fought to keep Moira McClure, now in the last stage of a premature labor, in her bunk. The ship would swiftly ride to the top of a wave, be blown nearly on its side, and then be slammed to the bottom of a watery trough fifty feet down, moving unsecured debris out of every corner, bunk, and bin, to quickly mix with the drenching salt water that was everywhere.

All the cabin lamps had long ago been drowned as sheets of water were driven through the battened-down hatches and the dried-out topsides. Like Guy Fawkes dolls, men, women, and children were tossed about the cabin until most finally tied themselves into the bunks in the frightening darkness.

Tom Barlow, a neighbor from Raphoe, near Dunleigh, had helped Jane tie Moira into the starboard bunk. "We'll keep the slops and tin cups off her with some tied-off blankets," he had shouted above the tumult that filled the gloomy cabin.

An hour passed, somehow. Jane had managed to wet a cloth before the bucket spilled, and now, as she tenderly mopped the perspiration off Moira's forehead, the Irishwoman's eyes opened. When she tried to speak only a rasping whisper emerged. She had lain like this for ten hours, screaming in fear, as both the storm and her labor inched forward. Her strength was ebbing.

The boat lurched sharply. Jane tied her lashings to the edge of the bunk and dug her feet in. "Moira, you must try. Remember Uncle—George, canna come to the new land, and this child is his future." Moira seemed to understand. With effort she put her hand under her pillow. She brought up a book, and tremblingly gave it to Jane just as a racking pain began. Jane understood. It was the dead minister's copy of *Pilgrim's Progress*. For an instant, in her mind, they were all together again on the hill near Dunleigh. But how could she read a book in this fetid darkness, she wondered? Then she remembered she knew a passage by heart, Uncle's favorite one it was. In a moment she was shouting it. "*And Pliable said to Christian, 'Now that we two are alone, tell me what things are in the place the pilgrims are going and how we will enjoy them.' And Christian said, 'There are crowns of glory and garments that will makes us shine like the sun in the firmament of Heaven and there shall be no more crying or sorrow.'*" (What else was it?) She paused, and Moira moaned with another deep pain. Oh, yes, "*'We shall see the elders with their golden crowns and the holy virgins with the golden harps, and men that for the word were cut in pieces, eaten of Beasts, drowned in the Seas.'*"

She was almost screaming at Moira: "*Christian said, 'There are crowns of glory and garments that will make us shine like the sun and there shall be no more crying or sorrow. All will be well then, and clothed and wearing Immortality as with a garment'*—I canna remember more, Moira."

Then finding her voice again, Moira cried out strongly, and Jane called for the taper that someone was hoarding at the other end of the cabin so she could see the progress of the labor. Surely it would not be long now.

The sharp cry from belowdecks had come through the hatch to the second foretopman, and he thought, numbly, that it sounded like the cry of a rabbit he heard once in the woods near his home, facing a snarling bulldog. Jamie Smythe could see neither the bow nor the stern. The fury of the wind drove shafts of torrential rain horizontally to mingle with the spume from the wave tops into his face. For the eight of them on this last watch on the *Indian Princess* tied to the base of the main mast, the entire world was a maelstrom of heaving motion and raging water, a world where breathing was searing agony. Even hope was a luxury: hope that the tangled mess of the top mast would not stove the side of the ship in before tearing loose from the shredded rigging, hope the harness would hold from the bottom of the fifty-foot wave troughs to the next wrenching crest, hope they would live one more moment. Or die quickly.

Belowdecks, only prayer remained to the wretched Irish. Their whole energy went into holding on. John McClure had lashed both his sons to a bunk as firmly as the mariners above bound their lives to the ship. Through long hours in the gloom, in air more foul than a cesspool, all below waited in the anteroom of death, yet all were still living. All, that is, except one.

At the height of the hurricane of June 12, 1751, Moira McClure breathed her last from a massive loss of blood after her dead child was born, afterbirth first, in a bed that lurched like a leaping horse. Jane McClure folded Moira's hands, which were wet from her own tears, wrapped the dead babe in a towel and laid it beside her. Then she tightened her own lacings and sank on her knees by the bunk.

And John McClure, unknowing of the sorrow forward of him, listened to the eerie sounds of children whose cries were rythmic sobs they could not stop. They sang a rueful chorus through the gloom, "Dada, Dada, Dada, make it stop, make it stop, make it stop." And as his sons sobbed themselves into exhausted sleep, John McClure shouted something into the wind. "If you want a Jonah, take me, but save the ship. I am lost anyway. Save us, if You have a care about anything down here." Perhaps it was a prayer.

The storm continued blowing, and yet not increasing. All anyone above or belowdecks knew was that life was given for that moment and that the ship still held together. Hours passed; most, their minds dulled, drained, and unable to suffer any more, slept. When Jane McClure awoke to the same listing, she found a few men and women were out of their lacings, hanging on by the bunk where the dead woman lay covered with a blanket. Their haggard faces looked at her ominously. A hollow female voice rose above the howl of the wind. "The woman must be buried at sea."

Jane looked into the coldness of their stares. "What do you mean? We canna have a burial on that deck. 'Tis a question whether any will survive. Why do you talk of services at such a time?"

"It is such a time we talk of," the wrung-out woman who seemed to speak for the crowd said. "The dead are ill luck aboard a vessel in smooth seas; they are killin' omens for us all aboard a ship distressed unto sinkin'. The woman and the babe must go."

Weary voices from all over the cabin shouted, "Aye."

John McClure left his bunk and staggered forward, grasping whatever support he could find. "What? You sound like the Mere Irish talkin' about the spirits of the cairns. It is a desecration to my uncle's wife to speak so. If we all die, she goes down with us. If we live we shall give her Christian burial in a day or two. I say no buryin'."

Strong arms bound him. "We say yes!" a score of voices cried. "Her ghost may yet be hoverin'; it will prolong the storm."

"Think of it this way, man," the voice of Tom was calm and reasonable. "A woman in her birth blood is nothing to have in a closed cabin. We must try to cleanse these quarters or pestilence will finish off what the storm began."

Hands took the dead baby and, wrenching the rope off the cleat that held the porthole fast, waited for a starboard lurch and tossed the bundle into the darkness.

Then they reached for the woman's body to shove it forcibly through the same hole.

"Animals, animals!" Jane McClure began to scream and covered her eyes with her hands. When she took them away, the bunk, free of its linen, was being sloshed and cleansed. Some way the slop buckets had been filled with seawater and the porthole closed. As the lurching had decreased to a degree, women were wiping the floor with soiled linen from someone's bed. The only emotion their faces registered was the determination to survive.

"What direction does the wind blow from now?" Jane asked, as if in a dream.

"It is yet furious but seems to have switched to the west," Tom answered compassionately.

"Who knows but that her body may float home. The sand may bury it by the cliffs near Donegal," she said "Perhaps, after all, she may finally be accepted by her own." With that thought she touched her own bosom, where she had put the copy of the book she had read to Moira. It would go to the New World too, if on this Pilgrim's Progress they should by God's mercy ever get there. Then she fell onto the wet bunk. Just before she sank in exhausted sleep she said aloud, "Mother, you were right. You were always sayin,' 'He who chooses to walk the new road must be willin' to pay many tolls.' And so we have paid the first."

Chapter V

Philadelphia lay before the eyes of the weary immigrants like a huge jewel in the ring of the Delaware River basin. The battered *Indian Princess* was preparing to dock. All along the quay, one and two hundred tonners, coasters, fishing vessels, and merchant rowboats bobbed on the tide. Above them the city rose, not unlike Derry above the basin of the River Foyle, with church spires lifting skyward against a background of hills.

The *Indian Princess* was only one of three ships which tied up and disgorged human cargo that day in July. The docks swarmed with people: redemptioners selling themselves to men who would be their masters for the next four years, boys dragging luggage handcarts, weeping women who had come to meet people who died on the voyage.

Jane McClure's two boys scampered off and on the gangplank. They chattered their goodbyes to Jamie Smythe and the other seamen and chased the seabirds about. Jane watched them with dull eyes. Tom Barlow and his wife left to go directly to Shearman's valley not far from where the McClures would settle, but Jane hardly noticed the goodbye.

At a time when her spirits should have been reviving, Jane was deeply distressed. Her mind seemed trapped somewhere in the hurricane. She heard, over and over, as in a dream, the deafening wail of the wind and Moira's cries. She saw the stone-like face of the baby who looked so much like Uncle and who had never breathed. Her lurching stomach would not hold down the corn pudding and cider her husband brought from the stands near the quay. And so she drifted that first morning, caring for her children somehow, looking through her trunks on the dock to see what was water-ruined and what would keep.

After all accounts were settled, John and Jane McClure gathered their bundles out of the hold and hired a handcart to follow them with the load of possessions from Dunleigh. Each held a child by the hand as they bade goodbye to the shattered hulk that was the *Indian Princess*.

"You must try to be civil," her husband warned her. Coming toward them was a man with an embroidered silk waistcoat buttoned across an expansive, prosperous stomach. Isaac Bard, Sam's older brother and a successful lumber merchant in Philadelphia, would be taking them under his wing for a week's stay in the brick home he and his wife had built near the docks.

"This City of Brotherly Love is a fine place, except for the Quakers," Isaac said with a sharp glint in his eye as they walked from the harbor.

"But didn't they build Pennsylvania?"

"Yes, and now they're a workin' just as hard to tear it down. They rule us all with an iron glove. There's trouble here because of their Indian and land policies."

Indifferently, Jane McClure watched young girls with wide petticoats carry baskets of eggs down the lane to market. Men in covered, two-wheeled carts delivered kegs and tables into the frame houses which crowded against each other to the very edges of the streets. The town was cleaner than Derry, cleaner by far than Dublin, which she had seen once on a linen-selling expedition with her father. There were, of course, bloated cat carcasses, swarming with blue flies by the side of the road on this hot morning. Horse offal was everywhere and ridges of slimy mud from recent downpours covered the road. But these were to be expected.

"Black man," two-year-old Will McClure remarked, pointing with his chubby finger at a man riding atop a carriage coming toward them. They shifted to the side of the road as the high-wheeled carriage creaked by. The driver, dressed in livery and holding a gold-embellished whip, could not even spare a glance. Inside the carriage a handsome woman rode, holding a handkerchief to her nose against the sewage smells which drifted up from the river. Behind her, twin girls with little mob caps and pert faces danced china dolls on their knees.

"Shipping fortune," Bard observed matter-of-factly.

The Bard house was a three-story Georgian mansion with a huge, snarling Prussian soldier's face as its door knocker. Inside Angelica Bard welcomed Jane and the little boys and showed them to roomy bedrooms upstairs, while Isaac Bard took John McClure to his counting-house office.

The women and children soon clustered around the table in the summer kitchen, where a black freewoman was taking biscuits out of a tall-footed spider oven sitting in hot coals.

"Dorcas learned to make beaten biscuits in Maryland," Angelica said, taking Will on her knee. "Beat one hundred strokes and they are light as air." Angelica's skin is translucent, like Moira's, Jane thought sadly. She must have the blood of the Norsemen in her too, as Moira did. She put her hand to the dark line of her own eyebrows, which met in the middle of her forehead.

Angelica pulled out pats of butter stamped with a flower crest and strawberry preserves, which she spread on biscuits for the boys. She had no children of her own.

Soon she was telling Jane how to grind corn at the handgrinder with two gray, revolving stones, which stood in the corner of this summer kitchen.

"Tonight Dorcas will help me make lemon poundcake," Angelica Bard said, then, seeing that Jane was not listening. . . "You are not happy, dearing," she said and put her arm on Jane's shoulder.

Jane began to describe the melancholy mood she had been in since the ship docked, and finished by saying, "My mother always said a sour woman is worse than a sour pickle. Then she would put me to work scrubbing something, anything, so the foul humors would bubble out with the soap suds."

"Your mother sounds like a rare Scotswoman," Angelica smiled, letting Will off her lap to chase a brown setter which was careening its way through the kitchen.

"Was. She and my father were master weavers. I was their only child. We had good times in our house until the starvin' times came ten years ago." Then she spoke with longing of her life in Ireland, of her untrammeled childhood and her cozy marriage cottage, until the embers of the cooking fire died. The black woman's stiff broom swept across the hearth with a comfortable, scratching sound. The boys were outside, their happy yelps and the dog's barks mingling joyously under the window. But Jane seemed transported to another time.

Angelica looked at her with genuine sympathy, and Jane realized she was spilling her thoughts like a bucket of hazelnuts to this new friend. Somehow, since the voyage had ended, all the feelings she'd ever owned had made their way to the surface of her life and lay like scabs on the skin, ready to be picked off to reveal the pain beneath.

Angelica Bard reached over to pat her hand and they went to find the boys, who were dragging the suffering setter into the carriage house.

That evening the two couples left the children behind with the black woman Dorcas, and walked the streets of Philadelphia to "take the air." John McClure seemed to come alive in the frenetic atmosphere of the new land. He listened to the bells of scores of churches and watched wide-eyed as a procession of new immigrants hurried down the streets from the harbor, barefoot, wearing homespun.

"Like the man going to St. Ives—kits, cats, bags, wives," John murmured. "Half of Ulster has been set down in America."

"Even England has seen it and debated the flight of the Scotch-Irish in Parliament," Isaac told him. "There are ten thousand of us in an area shaped like a turk's cap all the way from the mountains in Virginia to where a man named Harris has a ferry on the Susquehanna. The Scots from the North of Ireland have poured into this land as no other nation has."

Jane McClure was not listening. Her eyes were fixed apprehensively on what she saw ahead of her—a Quaker talking earnestly with an Indian with blue leggings and two feathers in his coal-black hair.

"That's a Delaware from the village of Shamokin," Isaac told them.

"His head is shaved except for that clump of hair along the middle," John commented.

"That's a scalplock."

That night, as Jane lay in the curtained cherry bed in the bedroom of the new house beside her already-sleeping husband, her mood was blacker than ever. For John, this new land was wildly exciting, a new start. Why not for her? Would she dwell forever in the hold of that awful ship with nothing but echoing screams in her mind? She turned over again, pulling down her linen night shift so it did not twist about her legs, and sighed gently. Dunleigh, with its loved hills and cottages, her very childhood, had been lopped off like a limb, and the stump hurt sorely.

Lancaster, Pennsylvania, was a bustling western city enjoying a bubble of economic prosperity built on selling hardware, foodstuffs, and outfits for the wilderness. The McClures spent more than a week looking it over, after Isaac Bard's wagon brought them there from Philadelphia. Isaac believed they should take advantage of Lancaster's good prices for horse teams and basic supplies as they prepared to start up the Susquehanna River and into the forests of Pennsylvania, to meet Sam Bard in Cumberland County.

Quakers, nattily dressed in waistcoats and frilly linen shirts smiled patronizingly at the customers heading into the frontier areas. They ran the branch offices of Philadelphia concerns whose owners were getting richer than Midas.

Enormous Cumberland County, which lay further north and west of Lancaster, had been open only a year. Thousands of people, many of them squatters, had rushed into its rich river valleys even before it was officially offered to the public.

"Pa, this is the horsiest country in the world," Johnny said with excitement as he watched scores of horses being bought and sold.

"They don't seem to use oxen so much, or sleds here, Johnny," his father told him. "They go sensibly, on the backs of good, solid mounts. The distances are great." John bought a team of enormous chestnut horses for ten pounds each, a fortune, he thought, and a second-hand farm wagon that looked like a shoe. He bargained for other necessities: flax, corn and garden seeds, precious sugar, flour, bacon, frying pans, spider ovens to put in the coals of a fire, a plow, and spades. Any more was impossible to carry with the load they brought from Ireland. Of course it was too much.

They lingered a day in a pillared inn named the Sweet Briar. Little William coughed with croup and Jane could not bring herself to begin the trip. The inn, run by Deutsch, or Germans, was cleaner than anything either John or Jane had ever seen. Its floors were sanded and scrubbed and waxed until they shone. And this was not even for kin. Out back was a stone-bottomed barn, almost as big as the inn itself.

Finally, just after sunrise on a clear day, they took to the road northwest. The Lancaster Road ran like a ribbon between mountain ranges. Beautiful farms lined it, each with its neat, two-story stone house and garden, each with miniature stone pig houses and chicken coops. "I shall have a planned home like that, an estate, and a barn, one of those big barns, where I can have my shop. These farms are dripping prosperity," John McClure said emphatically.

"Prosperity shows grace," Johnny said clearly, repeating one of Calvin's teachings he had been taught to say without much understanding of its meaning.

Jane nodded wordlessly. Truly Calvin, and his disciple John Knox who founded the Scottish Presbyterian church, taught that business was God's work.

She wondered if the Germans who built these farms were Calvinists too. John Calvin's teachings had spawned so many denominations.

"There is not much money in our purse," her husband said. "If we could just have saved for one more year, another six months. But the times would not wait." He spoke often of money these days. Jane turned to look dully at him.

But then, possibly to brighten her spirits, he said: "While we waited for parcels to be packed in Lancaster, a Deutschman who spoke English told me a good deal about the countryside roundabout. This good soil grows twenty bushels of wheat, much more than in Ireland, and fifty to seventy-five bushels per acre of Indian corn. And whilst in Ulster some farmers specialize in flax, everyone here has his own five-acre flax plot. Why, after you go through the fourteen steps, after you soak and break and hackle the fibers, you end up with enough linen yarn to make breeches and shirts for a family's summer out o' your own field."

"Apples," Will said from his mother's arms, pointing at the trees. "Pears," he said, bouncing up and down. "Need pear."

"They're green, Will. 'Tis only July," his brother told him, looking wonderingly at the orchards. In Derry, as in the rest of Ireland, fruit trees were largely for the estates of the rich.

John McClure continued to rattle on with uncharacteristic enthusiasm. "I asked the German where all the turnip fields were. He had to have someone tell him the word in Deutsch, and then laughed. 'Turnips, in this dirt, they do not grow well,' he said."

"Dada, every farm has sheeps and whole famblies of pigs," Johnny noticed.

"Merino sheep, they're called, Johnny, so the man said. Surely it is an earthly paradise, with so many rich people about," his father marvelled.

By early afternoon the houses were fewer and farther between, and the wagon went through great, silent areas of forest from time to time. They pulled to the side of the road to water the horses and let them rest. Isaac had told John that frontier people practiced the ancient laws of hospitality in remote places: they welcomed strangers. John decided to test the theory by asking a farmer hoeing corn at a neat log cabin for water from his well.

"Certainly I will let thee have water for thy beasts," he said. A Quaker, John thought.

He was a man of about thirty, with protruding teeth and a left eye that wandered around as he talked. "You be on the way to Carlisle?" he asked, and John McClure nodded over his shoulder as he took the water from the well. A well was a luxury out here, he had been told. Most people settled on streams, but some of the best land was in valleys like this one, the valley of the Susquehanna, a rich stretch of farmland framed on two sides by hazy blue mountains.

"We go just beyond Carlisle. We have come from near Derry, Ireland and go to the area nigh to Blue Mountain," John said, as he had so often in the last two weeks. "We have land waitin' for us, already surveyed."

"There be many of thy persuasion out there," the farmer said. "Most all are Scotch, although some there be from England. Not many have title to the land, as you do."

There was no affront intended in the man's words, and yet John felt one. "Is squattin' really a crime? The land is out there. The government of the Penns is far away, from what I hear. It seems natural to improve it and then go to buy it, after it is one's own."

"So the Scotch from Ireland reason," said the man calmly. He offered McClure a drink from a wooden noggin, and they sat together on the grass by the well.

"And I cannot deny it is all God's bounty and that the Scotch-Irish are the ones who have come to claim it. We Quakers who farm have no fights with other farmers like the fights the proprietors dream up in Philadelphia. But it is a question of scripture and its interpretation. We seem to emphasize a different part of the Holy Writ than thou. 'That he who loveth God love his brother also' is our favorite text."

"But who will deny that?" John looked at him searchingly.

"It is the practice, man, the practice of the Lord's revelation we differ from you Presbyterians on. We have seen too many Scotch-Irish go into the valleys and deal harshly with their fellow beings."

"You mean the savages?"

"Call them Indians, fellow creatures, yellow men, as most of the folk out here do, but call them not savages. They love this land which was their fathers', and part of which was bought honestly from them by William Penn. They ask only to hunt and fish in peace. Yet you Scotch-Irish petition the proprietors to take the new land from them by force."

John sighed. It seemed that even here in the New World there were to be different opinions, ideas battling. He might have left the Irish and English behind, but not the kinds of arguments that made them his enemies. Why should he not answer? "I hear tell that in the mountain valleys out there". . . he gestured to the west toward where a large peak could barely be seen in the distance. . ."Indians brood over their lost land and have been known to kill white men."

"We are told to give up our cloak to him that needs it and to walk the extra mile with him that would compel us. Thy kind do not talk, do not reason as Christians with our Indian brethren, but instead take the musket to them."

"Who can reason with a bunch of savages? 'Twould be folly to try to. It is destined that the white man will rule the earth. These savages are fallen children, perhaps the children of the Evil One."

The Quaker remained calm but his voice took on a stronger note. "That is the Old Theology—a belief in the blot of original sin, man's hopelessness before an avenging God. We pray for the yellow men's redemption, for their coming to Christ. In the meantime, we must treat them with human dignity and show them the way, as loving disciples of the Lord."

"And if they cut off thy arm? Burn thy house? Take thy children into slavery?" John could not help being sarcastic. No wonder Bard scorned the Quakers. This philosophy could not help but sow trouble.

"It need not happen." The Quaker's left eye was wandering so fast now it seemed to be rolling. He had picked up a piece of weed grass and was spinning it between the palms of his hands agitatedly. "There is room enough for colonist and Indian, Quaker and Presbyterian, to dwell in these valleys. This land is a rich garden; here the lion should lie down with the lamb and a little child lead them."

John looked off to where white clouds formed over the Susquehanna, a few miles to the west. Ulstermen already crowded the banks on the east side of the river, Bard had said, thirty miles up to Paxtang, the site of the Harris ferry and supply store. They spilled across the river westward all the way to the high mountain chain that marked the beginning of the true wilderness.

"God knows I hope all can live here, as you say, my friend. Thank you for the cool drink," John said, picking up his buckets and taking the water to the horses and his waiting family.

He climbed into the wagon and sat beside his remote and distracted wife. Almost to himself, he said, "I dinna want to go to war against the Quakers, or Indians, or anyone anymore. All I came for is a little peace. And seeing these mountains and valleys, I can't help but feel hope. Of course, if a savage appeared on the doorstep, threatening the family. . ."

"They seem to me to be but men, frightening as they are," Jane said.

"Well, I have small need to kill anyone, I suppose," John said bitterly, turning his face away from her. "I shall avoid it. But instinctively I'm repulsed by even the few Indians I've seen. Some say the first thing you have to know to live out here is who your enemies are. You have to know who to hate to survive on the frontier." Jane shrugged.

He snapped the lines and started up. He was not probing deeply into speculative thought now. His mind was set on reaching the cluster of five or six cabins known as Carlisle, Pennsylvania, thirty miles down this road and virtually at the end of civilization. There, or near there in the wilderness beyond, were plenty of people ready to hate and to be hated and provide sufficient test for any religious or philosophical theories anyone could come up with.

It was late afternoon when John stopped the horses for the last rest. By nightfall they should reach the raw, new town where Sam Bard and his wife Sally had just finished building a log home. The woods around them was a deep, breathing entity, exuding a stillness that was palpable and overpowering to a man who had grown up in a land swept bare of timber, where wind could rush uninhibited from sea to mountain. "Mrs. McClure, let the boys stretch their legs a mite. Perhaps a walk through these tall trees would do us both good."

His wife nodded mutely. William was asleep; he lay limply across her lap. A slight flush colored his cheek, the remnant of the fever that had plagued him for the last week. She laid him down carefully on a woven blanket on the floor of the shoe-shaped wagon. "He will sleep and we will walk only a short way in," she said. John McClure helped Johnny down from the back of the wagon and, taking the boy by the hand, led him into the woods.

"Why are there so many trees, Dada? They frighten me."

"You'll get used to it. Y' know, trees are beautiful things, John. 'Tis the reason I became a cooper. Why, wood is almost human. Each type of wood has to be known, its personality sounded, like your own friends' or relatives', so that you can suit the barrel to the need. To carry molasses, from the West Indies, for instance you have to find beech saplings with the bark left on, and the staves should be of maple, just like those trees over there, to blend with the sweet taste of the sugar syrup."

Father and son walked ahead, through rows of oaks, chestnuts, and ashes which shot sixty feet in the air and whose lowest branches were far above the touch of reaching fingertips. As they drew away, Jane could hear little Johnny's voice chirping questions and his father's lower tones answering him patiently. John is a good father, she thought. And I am no longer a good mother, let alone a "Bountiful Soul." "Get hold of yourself," her mother used to say when Jane let some trivial event grow into a storm of tears or a pout. But how did she do that now?

She looked about her at the long rows of tall trunks with leafy canopies overhead and suddenly decided not to follow her husband and son. Instead she diverged into a patch of pine to the right. Oddly, there was no underbrush where she had been walking, but now she had to pick her way through bushes almost as tall as she was, with thick bunches of flat leaves and clusters of green seeds. Perhaps they bloom in the spring, she thought. That would be lovely. At least there would be something in this overgrown land to make up for the loss of the green fields of Ireland.

The light of the August afternoon was declining as she entered the pine grove. Needles at least six inches thick carpeted the floor of the forest. They felt slick beneath the soles of her feet and stuck onto her stockings. She stopped and looked around. The silence of the forest troubled her, driving out other thoughts. Where were the birds? The air felt close, and not a breeze stirred.

She was conscious that she was out of sight of the wagon, and that she did not really know her way back. A feeling close to fear began to prickle at her back. She wheeled about, this way and that, looking for her bearings and finding only pines, which pointed toward the sky each looking just like the other. She called her husband in a hoarse voice, but the sound came back to her, "John, John, Johhhn" bouncing off hills out of her sight.

Thoughts of Druid offerings and tales of living, moving trees flashed through her mind as she began to run frantically. Like an animal, she darted this way, that way through the pines, retracing her steps. Where was she? She would never find her way out, would circle far from John and little John, and die under some tree from starvation and grief. William would never remember his mother—she covered her mouth with her hands as she began to sob and then, blindly rushing through some younger pines, she caught her dress on a lower stickly branch and she fell to the ground.

There she lay, pounding on the detestable needles, screaming with anger and fright at this silent place of giant trees and Indians, so unlike the comfortable villages of home. It was an endless sea like the one of the storm; she was a lost mortal in the midst of it.

Floods of tears poured from her eyes to mingle with the acrid, prickly pine needles beneath her face and hands.

She did not know how long she lay there, but after a time she felt a hand on her arm and rose to see the startled faces of her husband and son. "Ma, whatever is the matter?" Johnny asked, looking at her quizzically. His face, usually serious, looked like an old man's, and she could almost imagine that his forehead was wrinkled, as he tried to puzzle out why his mother was lying on the floor of a forest screaming and pounding her fists. The thought of how it all must look awakened her sense of humor and she began to laugh, first timidly, surprised at herself, then bellowingly. She stood beneath the pine trees, making the forest ring with raucous Irish whoops. Tears of laughter now replaced the tears of anger and fright, and she stood against her husband, helpless.

Finally, she could talk again. She motioned that they should get started back out of the woods. "I—was—lost," she said, gasping for breath. "But I guess I'm not any more. We must—hurry. Sally will have a hot supper ready for us in Carlisle and we don't want to make her wait. And. . ." she scanned the sky, "it's getting cloudy." John nodded. Whatever happened in the woods had released the pain she had carried about.

But for him, he thought as they returned to the wagon, for him the woods meant something else. Hundreds of thousands of feet of planks, puncheons, logs to make the most beautiful things of wood. The variety! He did not even know the names of all these trees. The huge, smooth, gray-barked ones with almond-shaped leaves and green kernels on them, they must be a form of beech. The shaggy ones with bark like the skin on an old black man's face, hickories. Then there were the several kinds of sugar tree he had heard about but never seen. All were the raw material of the very stuff of living—useful hoes and flails for wheat, polished bowls and burnished trenchers for folks' eating tables, cradles where babies rocked, and church rafters and pews.

No, the woods were not a thing of fear, but of promise. His step lightened as he emerged, batting his eyes, into the light at the road. For at that moment, John McClure decided that he would no longer be a wet cooper, but a dry barrel craftsman, that he would make beautiful or useful household items for himself and others. Now that he had his choice, he would produce things for folk to live by, and not the stuff to hold their dead fish and the whiskey to make their behavior crazed, and the gunpowder to blow themselves up. Woodworking and dry barrelling. It would be a good way to occupy himself in the new, clean land.

Chapter VI

At the door of the brand new log house in Carlisle, Sam Bard's jovial face greeted them. John had not seen Bard in eleven years, but the stubbed nose, large brown eyes, and hint of a limp in his walk were immediately familiar. John flashed back to a bareback horserace between Dunleigh and Raphoe, when the wildly shouting Bard skidded into a ditch, was thrown and brought up with the injury to his leg he would carry the rest of his life. We all bear our injuries, friend, John thought.

"Bring these younguns and Jane here in and we'll settle you," Bard said, clapping John on the shoulder. Jane thought those might have been the sweetest words she had heard in quite a while. The cotton clouds that were on the horizon earlier in the day had turned to thunderheads, and it had rained the last few miles of the trip. Jane could see a bright fire burning in the fireplace within. Exhausted, she herded the little boys through the door.

The dusky, candlelit interior smelled damp but not unpleasant. A pot of stew bubbled over the fire in the corner, and the smell of onion and herb gravy made the little boys' mouths water. "Eat," said Will and toddled toward the hearth.

A small woman with black loops of hair escaping from beneath a blue cap, bustled out to greet them and drew them to the fire. "I'm Sally Bard. I am glad you're safely with us. Sam has been a-worryin'." Her voice doesn't really have the sound of Ulster in it, Jane thought. Sam's Irish accents had altered in some way, too. They were shorter, rougher, mixed up with touches of spice from somewhere else, like the stew in the pot, Jane thought. She had heard that within a year it happened to all who came, that their children would forget they ever knew King's English.

"Where is it you've come from, Sally?" asked Jane, taking off her cloak and bonnet and spreading them on the back of a chair to dry.

"From around Baltimore. There be many of us folk now from Maryland." Her smile was honest and warm. Jane took an instant liking to her. "Come younguns, your clothes must be wet. Some mulled cider will warm y' up," Sally urged.

Another man sat by the fireside. Jane noticed his breeches—they were made out of the skins of deer. She'd seen these skin pants in Lancaster also. The man also wore a sleeved linen jacket. His hair was long and dank, and although he seemed younger than they, his face was weathered. He stood to offer John his hand, saying, "Will Lytle, sir, at your service."

Gratefully the McClures seated themselves by the fire. Sally and her daughter Caroline, a thin nine-year-old, busied themselves with supper details in the keeping room across the hall, where the cider was mulling with spices, and other good things were cooking in a second fireplace. John and Johnny sat on the floor with steaming mugs of cider in their hands. There were questions about the trip, but they barely began to answer them before supper was called.

The large table in the keeping room was spread with food before the fire, and the group "set themselves" and began talking in low, friendly tones. Sam Bard came in from the horse shed just as Sally ladled the stew and apples onto wooden plates. "Your horses are bedded down all right," he said. "I have plenty of oats—enough to give you some as a settlin'-in gift. Save you lookin' for 'em."

Johnny and Will McClure and the Bard's young son Ardry were seated at a small chair-table which had been taken down from the wall and set up for them. Jane had never seen a piece of furniture like it; it was a true changeling with its large, round back which slipped into a flat surface so easily when the need came.

John McClure helped himself to bread baked that morning, soft of crust, hard to cut, and perfectly delicious. "Tell us about the trip," Sam Bard demanded. John swallowed a bite of bread and began to detail the ordeals of the trip, just as they had done for Isaac Bard's relatives and friends in Philadelphia. There seemed to be a thirst in the Colonies for the poignant, even tragic details of sea trips like the McClures', almost as if those who were settled could draw comfort from the fact that others, too, suffered to get to the frontier.

"Very well, m' friends," Sam said when John finished his story. "Now for some acclimatin' advice from a expert of almost ten years' experience. First, get seasoned. Don't eat unripe fruits. Avoid changes in wind and don't stay out in the evenin' breezes. Keep kivvered up at night even in summer. For the stitch take boiled crab claws." With each piece of advice, he pointed the tines of his fork at the group. "Now, you are bound to lose your teeth, like so many others, from drinkin' hot soup and eatin' frozen apples. Finally, leave the Injeeans alone and they will leave you alone."

John asked the question that had been on his mind all day, ever since he talked to the Quaker. "Will the Indians ever rise up against the white folk?"

"Will, mebbe you can tell him about 'em," Bard said, looking at the muscular woodsman. "Lytle's lived with the Injeeans and fought with 'em and I think he knows 'em about as well as anybody in these yere parts."

"Well, I have done a little tradin' with the Indians here and there. New York, Forks of the Ohio, even Pickawillany in the Ohio country." Alternating great gulps of cider with mouthfuls of bread, Lytle went on, "Acorse they can kill settlers and many of them have done a deal of murderin' and hackin' to pieces, in Virginia, Massachusetts—hundreds killed. But I opine that there are ways to deal with 'em and I have seen that you must gain their friendship and yet let them know jes' where the line must be drawn. Fair treatment is best because it works. Jes' lately I been up at Johnson's Hill in the Iroquois country and

I've seen it work.''

"Johnson's hill? Johnson, the white brother of the Indians?'' Johnny's voice piped excitedly from the children's table. He had heard of him in Philadelphia.

"Hush, John,'' his mother said. "Go on, sir.''

"You've heard tell of William Johnson, I reckon. In Europe he's known as a miracle worker because he alwuz finagles the Injeeans into His Majesty's corner against the French. He don't attack 'em, he talks to 'em.''

"Oh, sir, tell us about him,'' Johnny said, rising from his chair and coming to stand by the trader's chair.

"All right, lad. Bring yer stew plate and sit here at the corner of the table and I'll tell you about Warraghiyagey.'' He winked at the others. "That was the name given Mr. Johnson when he was adopted into the Mohawk tribe eight years ago.''

He looked directly into Johnny's eyes, but what he said was for all the newcomers. "The Mohawks took William in their tribe, they told him all their tales of Hiawather and how he united the five Injeean nations. The Cayugas, Onondagas, Oneidas, Mohawks and Senecas.''

"Did they tattoo him?'' Johnny asked, his eyes wide.

"No, but they painted him with red paint, dumped him into a river and scraped his skin almost off with sand. Then they declared that he had passed the test and was a blood brother. Injeean friend.''

"You mean Injeean laird,'' Sam Bard said. He was picking his teeth with his knife. His wife shot him a look and he quickly put the knife down.

"Well, he waren't opposed to making a few pounds. He ran a grist mill that he designed himself, bought land, built his store into a huge tradin' post,'' Lytle said.

"He plays the part of king and all the Injeeans and white folk kiss his foot,'' Bard added.

"I saw his house just after he rebuilt it—Mount Johnson. Two floors, servants' quarters in a huge attic and a lead roof imported from London.'' Sally Bard and her daughter Caroline, starved for elegance in this log-box society, listened attentively, and this seemed to make Lytle expansive. "He had all kinds of fancy plate and dishware in the house, but I don't think he ever used it.''

"That was cause he were too busy dancin' nekkid with the savages in the firelight.''

"Naked?'' Jane asked boldly. "I've wondered—I mean, the few we saw in Philadelphia and Lancaster were clothed.'' Her husband frowned at her.

"The Ottawas, I know, wear only a breech cloth most of the year, Ma'm,'' Lytle said rather primly. "Their women wear blankets below and nothing up above. . .''

"Was this man born to the nobility?'' Sally Bard asked quickly. Naked Indian women were not a suppertime subject for good Presbyterians.

Lytle leaned back and laughed an enormous laugh. "No, he's new rich. Typical of a good many in these colonies. He were born a miller's son in County Meath.''

"He keeps a Injeean paramour,'' Bard again grumbled, "ensconced like the

Queen of Sheba.''

"She is French, I believe, Mr. Bard. May I give you some puddin'?" Sally Bard said firmly.

Later, as the group retired to the other room, Johnny followed William Lytle adoringly and listened to him telling John McClure that "only the Lord of the Injeeans could enjoy a paramour in a satin bed on a cold night in Mohawk country."

William, who had been sucking his thumb most of the evening toddled after him. "Paramour, paramour," he mimicked, savoring the sound of the word.

"Umm. Maybe it's some sort of a dog, Will," Johnny said. He thought more about it later, as his father tucked him under a quilt in the loft with the other children. Dada, Ma, and Lytle would soon be pulling out pallets before the fire. Perhaps a paramour was a hot brick, a bed warmer. He had enjoyed a hot brick sometimes at his feet in bed on a chilly night in Ireland. Just before he drifted into sleep, he thought of the Irish miller's son who danced Indian dances and lived like a rich man in the wilderness. "I will be a laird someday myself, yes, and Will too," he promised himself.

Even Jane McClure felt a sense of the future. Tomorrow they would meet the people of Carlisle and then set up to go out to the land, their land. For the first time in many days Jane fell asleep happy, as the sound of rain pattered on the clapboard roof and the wind blew over the little settlement.

John McClure's dream of a permanent stone house like the ones he had seen outside of Lancaster would have to wait. On a swath of creek bottom land Bard had reserved for him a few miles outside Carlisle, Bard told him he would be building a cabin "improvement" made of logs, with a cat-and-clay chimney and girdling trees in one small field for corn. He and a few neighbors would put up the cabin, while his wife and sons lived in the wagon near the creek. The land's only advantage in the beginning would be a view of the misty mountains to the west.

A friend of Bard's, a neighbor named Rafe Emison, offered to help clear. He brought a team of oxen and they toiled through the cool, bright days of early September with felling axes, chains, saws, hooks, and sledges to make a huge pile of brush and staked logs.

When they cleared the twenty-by-thirty-foot site for the cabin, John begged for a few more days' help to clear a cornfield. "I don't want to girdle trees," he said. "I wish to do all things seemly." Bard and Emison looked at him hard, wiped the perspiration from their brows, and finally agreed.

Now, late in the month, they were pulling stumps. Emison cursed the hard, dry ground, mumbling that spring was a better time to do this sort of work. He eased the team forward, taking the stumps to the edge of the clearing to make a fence for the cows McClure had contracted to buy with nearly the last of his money.

"You can't burn these damn things," Emison grumbled as they sat by the pile of twisted roots.

McClure looked at the man he had sweated and strained with for the past two days. Emison's looks and manner were deceptive. He was handsome almost to the point of being pretty, with bronze curls all over his forehead. With his formal, reserved speech pattern, he might have been taken for an English drawing room dandy. But his arms were as strong as McClure's and his experience with the wilderness first-hand. His father, a schoolmaster from the Pale around Dublin, came to Pennsylvania in the first settlement wave thirty years before. Emison had "settled in" three times in his thirty-five years before coming to the Cumberland Valley. Well, McClure told himself, he had better get to know Emison. He would owe him a season of stump-pulling in return for the work done here.

"The Scotch-Irish seem to be as appreciated in Pennsylvania as last week's catch of fish," John mused, leaning against the thickest of the roots.

"So you have taken note of that."

"And yet I was not fully prepared for it. Why are we so scorned in Philadelphia and the eastern colonies?"

"What are ever the reasons that bigotry is practiced? We're new. We're as poor as chipmunks. There are a deal of us and more coming. Our religion is different. We believe that we are the Elect of God, that all are predestined before the world was born for either salvation or damnation—and of course, those in the church are the Saved. No one wants to hear that any group claims special favor from God. That's why the Jews have been so hated for so many years."

"Then it's all unfair."

"No." Emison was still breathing heavily from exertion as he took off his hat and put in a new linen sweatband from his pocket. "We deserve some of the scorn. Too many from northern Ireland have taken squatter's land and gone to seed themselves on it. Pigs in the woods, stumps in the yards, squalor and laziness inside the cabin. Get a crop or two and move on. Or sell out in ten years to the Germans."

"In Ireland the Scotch were frugal, neat, hardworking."

"Not all were. But here life is too easy. Corn shoots up eight feet tall, pigs fatten on acorn mast from oak trees. Livin' too easy is never good for folk."

John nodded and looked at the ground.

"Yes, surviving in the woods is easy. But getting rich is quite another thing," Emison said, looking into the thick stand of trees.

"I'm just beginning to see how right you are," McClure said, and forced himself to return to the backbreaking work of stumping his only field.

By the first week in October a cabin began to take shape on the cleared ground, slowly, painfully, by the effort of men and beasts. John McClure's next neighbor, Walter Cherry, also came to help, bringing his team of horses. John rushed about in a storm of determination as he always did, insisting over the protests of his neighbors that what he really needed was a small double cabin with four window holes, made of hewn logs. Bard, Emison, and Walt Cherry insisted that a simple one-room shelter made of round logs was all that anyone ever built, that windows were expensive, that they needed to return to harvest.

All to no avail. John McClure was hanging on with his teeth to his lordly ideas. Even if he couldn't have a stone house right away, he could have a comfortable double cabin. "Better folk" didn't live in windowless boxes. And so they went on, Bard and McClure dragging the fallen trees with the oxen and bringing the logs to be hewn by Cherry. Cherry used his short broadaxe on them; it took huge notches out of the prostrate log and then went between each notch and hacked out the wood, so instead of ending up with a round log, there was a smooth, squared-up one. As soon as Cherry tired, John McClure relieved him while the other two men worked on fitting and hoisting these smooth, square oak logs into the skeleton of a log home.

It took a day or two to finish the frame and get the joists up, then they hewed and fit the house's side logs. When the sides were up, Cherry, who had a reputation as a good axeman, split trees the diameter of a man's body in two with a steel wedge and a huge wooden glut spike. Each half log would be a floor puncheon board. The flat side of these boards would eventually wear into a fairly smooth floor for the cabin. The last task was putting on a roof of three-foot clapboards which John McClure, as an expert cooper, expected to split out from the logs with maul and froe in "no time atall."

As they neared this stage, John negotiated with Emison for winter supplies. He must be canny, he knew. He would barter his skill at making light furniture, flour barrels, cake boxes and all the variety of baskets and boxes a household needed, for the necessary items of living. Emison had ample corn; the harvest had been good and cribs all over the valley were bursting with the yellow gold everyone made into pone, mush, hotcakes, and fritters. "I can spare, let me see, sixty bushels, along with the cabbages and apples, which I will throw in *gratis*." John nodded to thank him, smiling slightly. Where, in the middle of the wilderness, did Emison get these Latin expessions he occasionally sprinkled into his conversation?

"I can only spare a few bags of flour," Emison told him. "It's dear. But you can get some at Hunter's Mill on the river. It's an overnight trip. If they have grain, they will sell. For a price." His voice had an odd edge, which John was too busy to ask about.

And so, after they had worked two weeks at cabin-building, the roof was finally ready to put on. Two more days of work, Jane thought, as she scrubbed linens at the stream which flowed in back of the cabin site. Soon, she thought, the time would come when John would make a proper scrubbing board and get a wash pot in which she could boil the clothing with the lye soap she had learned to make. She spread shirts on the bushes which seemed to be everywhere—laurel they were called—and went to see if Will, sleeping in the wagon under a canvas, was awake from his morning nap.

It was October, but it was close and overly warm, she noticed, pushing her wavy hair back from her damp forehead. She had been told summers in Pennsylvania were hotter and heavier-feeling than those in Ulster, but no one said summer lasted until the leaves fell. By now in Dunleigh, housewives would be closing their shutters at teatime against the cool mist from the lough, and from the wind which blew hard, plastering the skirts of the women against their legs as they walked the country lanes near. . . Moira's parents' house.

She shook her head against the memory that threatened to disturb her peace and picked up little Will, who was rocking on his knees under his blanket, rythmically grunting, just beginning to awake. She took down his napkin and noticed that his "loose dirties" continued, causing his little bottom to be the color of a ripe apple. Was it the water? She wiped him clean with the old napkin and drew a clean square of linen from the huge pocket of her apron. Putting it around his waist, she tied it at the corners. She drew him to her and patted him as he toddled off, saying, "I go see Johnny." He would not need napkins much longer, she thought, thanking heaven that she would soon be moving from the camping wagon, where a call of nature was answered with a hole and spade in the woods.

Keep to a household schedule, she told herself, even in a wagon. She took out her grandmother's wool wheel and began spinning the Merino wool that had been given her by Sally Bard in Carlisle. She did not spin her own wool much in Ulster; that was usually done by spinning girls. But it was easy enough for all that. She stood beside the giant wheel and turned it a little at a time, pulling and drawing out the thread to "give it the spin" and winding it on the spindle. There were, of course, two kinds of wheels, but she had no small linen wheel here. So she would spin the wool and trust to God to provide the linen wheel. And the flax also. She had better include that in her prayer if she was to have a linsey coverlet, half-linen, half-wool, as they did it in Pennsylvania.

Soon the men would be wanting a noon dinner in a basket, Jane mused as she watched Will and Johnny play by the creek. There were so many mouths to feed. Bard had come for these last two days to help and Emison and Walter Cherry had brought their two sons also. Cold meat, cornbread (which she was getting passing good at making in the iron spider pot in the coals) and peaches Sally Bard sent. That should satisfy 'em. She didn't need to start quite yet.

After she had fixed the dinner, as she was walking out with the basket, she wondered where her monthly cycle was. She had weaned Will early, at seventeen months, so he would not nurse on the sea voyage. The old women said worry and body-wearying work could cause delays and even stop a woman's bleeding. Well, if that was the case, she might not have a cycle until Christmas. Or. . . she did not allow the words too dreadful to consider to form in her mind.

The next morning, when Jane arose from her pallet she found the "monthly" had come. She fell on her knees with a gratitude that chagrined her. "Thank you, God. I know it isn't right for an obedient Christian wife to do so, but I thank you that I am not with child. Not here, not now."

Johnny McClure woke early, ready for his part in this last day of the cabin-rearing. His mother handed him a trencher of bacon, fried mush, and molasses. He sat next to the cooking fire scooping it up, beside Abijah Cherry. This twelve-year-old, whom everyone called "Bige," had decided Johnny McClure was his bondservant.

"Now youngun," he said, "My pa and Mr. Emison and Ash will be puttin' up that there chimbly on the big fireplace. T' other one in the extry room your

Pa nagged 'bout is done. You'll be carryin' mud in buckets from the mortar hole near the crick to make the "mud cats" we air goin' to use as bricks. We'll make the bricks and hand 'em to the men. Then we both hafta daub the crevices between the logs in the house and smooth 'em with a wooden trowel. I'll show ye how."

Johnny was tired of fetching for Bige. "I know how, Bige. Pa showed me a'ready. And even if I didn't know, I wouldn't be lookin' t' you to be my schoolmaster," Johnny said.

Bige looked at him for a moment with his mouth open, then said, scornfully, "Prob'ly bein' so smart you'll be directin' your Pa when he and Mr. Bard put up the roof. Why, mebbe you'll be tellin' 'em how to raise the end gables at the proper angle, how to set on the roofin' clapboards jes' so."

Johnny ignored him. "Ma, will you cook in the cabin tonight?"

"No, not yet." She was cleaning bacon grease from a frying pan with creek sand and maple leaves. "The mortar in the fireplace has to season. But we can sleep in the cabin tonight." Tonight. . . she could hardly allow herself to think of it. Tonight, after six weeks of mildewed cloaks, fires put out by hail and undercooked dinners, poison oak that blistered the arms, children crying as wolves howled, visits from prowling skunks and once a bobcat, cold wind from Blue mountain which crept under the coverlets— after all of that, they would be, bless God, under roof.

Later in the day she suspended the tripod over the fire for the last time and set it to stewing a small turkey John shot last night. Into the pot went wild onions, salt, and a bay leaf from her cooking basket. Rice would be good with it, she told herself, but a little corn would work almost as well. Her grandmother's Cock-a-Leekie soup.

She was also making a cake to celebrate the home-raising. She had brought special things from a shop in Philadelphia. Taking out a bowl, she mixed one pound of flour and one pound of sugar (maple) a pound of butter kept cool at the creek, a pound of chopped black walnuts and a bit of the rind of the last of the lemons. She greased the spider with bacon fat, rolled coals under its spiney legs, put some maple leaves in the bottom, and poured in the cake batter. Then she covered the spider, put coals on the lid and said a prayer that the bottom wouldn't burn. John loved the pound cake Angelica Bard baked; she would make it for him now.

As the late October sun slanted low over the new cabin, the men fixed long poles down in rows to hold the overlapping clapboards on the roof and came into the cabin. Johnny and little Will checked the baking spider, which was emitting wonderful odors of lemon and nuts, and then went inside. The men were pulling off moccasins and shoes and sharing a whiskey jug as a reward for the day's labors.

"I saw three savages on the road the other day as I went to contract for the cows," McClure told the other men, shaking his head to the jug as it came to him. "Naked from the waist up. Made my heart jump although I dinna want it to. They wore leggin's, necklaces around their necks. Their skin was the color of dark copper and their hair oily black with the tuft—the scalplock. Dinna look at me, just passed on in single file along the road. Were they Delawares?''

"Yes, Delawares," Emison said, as he lit an Indian pipe of his own tobacco and passed it to his son Ash to puff. "Generally they avoid the settlements. I suppose they were on the way to visit relatives at one of the local harvest festivals. The bottomland paths could be rutted from settlers' wagons and hard to walk on. They know the best ways to get through the mountains and the river valleys, and they're on the move a lot lately." He scratched his chin thoughtfully. "You could call them vagrants—rackrent vagrants of a different sort, dispossessed of the land."

"Was it theirs?"

"In a way of speaking. When the English and Dutch came here one hundred and some years ago, they drove the Leni Lenapi tribes, the Delawares we call them, out of the coastal area. They are trying to live now at the crossroads of the mountains in Pennsylvania, at Kittanning and Shamokin up north. Mostly they're friendly—some of 'em even go hunting and fishing with settlers. They carry on their old clan activities and worship the Great Spirit in the Twelfth Heaven in a big house they built up there, and at harvest they eat venison and corn and pray for continued good harvests."

"I hear they'd just as soon eat a man as a deer steak," John said darkly. From across the room Bard turned around and shot a look of agreement at him.

"That's a popular myth," Emison countered. "Very few Indians involve themselves in cannibalism. The Delawares are civilized, peaceful people. They're not bloodthirsty, but they believe in vengeance and punishment for insult. And they have been insulted, you know, by the walkers. . .''

Bard, still listening from the other side of the room, hooted, but Emison refused to acknowledge the affront.

"A few years ago some of Indians agreed to give up all the land out here that was within one day's walk, and the two walkers from the proprietors raced until they dropped and took far more land than the Indians bargained for."

"I heard tell the Indians have never forgotten it," John said. Emison nodded, twirling his pipe in his hands thoughtfully.

"But isn't there room enough for 'em—out there?" John spread his hand broadly toward the west. His sense of geography wasn't very clear yet. This place was so much larger than Ulster.

"No, because no matter how far west they go, we'll follow and turn their hunting lands into farmland. Across the mountains, English traders are picking up thousands of fur pelts at a post in the Ohio land the Indians call Pickawillany, a big Indian village." John told him that Lytle had mentioned it to them in Carlisle.

"Lytle. Yes, he and his kind are scurrying out of the settlements and into the wilderness and its riches faster than spiders out of the woodpile. And they're just the first. Settlers with women and babies and garden hoes will follow. And someday there will be no place left to push the Indians."

Finally Bard, who had been listening to snitches of what was being said, could restrain himself no longer. He rose, left the coversation by the new, empty fireplace and came over to where John and Emison sat near the window hole.

"The land in Pennsylvania should belong to the white race, no matter what all the Injeean lovers think." He said each word deliberately, as if it were law. The others in the room picked up their stools and came over to join in, just as Jane McClure came through the door opening and began making final supper preparations on a small, folding table in the corner.

"Our part in God's eternal plan is t' bring the Bible and plow to these heathen lands; their part is t' retreat," said Walter Cherry, who folded his long legs like a Delaware on the new puncheon floor. It was the first thing he had said all afternoon. The McClures were coming to know him as a taciturn, honest man, a strict Calvinist who lived with a wife and six children a mile down the path.

His son Bige, near him, was speechless for once, watching Jane mix a sugar and lemon glaze to pour over the walnut cake. Rich sweets were not an everyday occurrence in the woods, and his mother kept house only when the notion took her. Corn meal mush was breakfast, dinner and supper at the Cherry cabin on more than one day.

Jane handed out the soup and then, assured that her boys were eating quietly in the corner and playing with wood shavings and scraps from the building, she ventured, "Mr. Bard, what are the Indians like as men? Do they have feelin's common to us all? How do they treat their wives?"

"They are savages, Ma'm. They love their wives, I reckon, in their own way, but they are naturally debauched. There are eight thousand of 'em out there worshippin' trees and the spirits of dogs. When I see 'em in town or on a road I declare to you it makes my flesh creep. Hairless on their faces and chests and greased. Smell like dog shit—pardon—I hate to see 'em. They're an insult to a Christian with their heathen ways." Emison grunted and dumped his pipe ashes onto the floor. Obviously he did not agree.

The room grew quiet and even Jane sat back on her heels for a moment as the men ate their soup in silence. Then, finally, Emison spoke from his seat by the window, his strong profile outlined by the last glow of the receding sun behind him. "Why is it these Indians seem to dominate all we talk and even think about? There's a shadow over us in the Cumberland Valley. Not a supper, not a conversation can be carried on without their silent presence in our midst. And I think that is as much their fault as it is ours. They sit in their longhouses and camps and talk constantly of us, what blankets or needles or guns we will trade them, how much land we will want, how we will ruin the hunting grounds. We are each other's obsession."

Bard's voice was gritty, his eyes bright with fanaticism. "They ain't even a part of the human race, man. Once on a tradin' trip beyond the mountains I come upon a summer camp of Shawnees. They were dancin' a war dance, throwin' their heads back, screamin' bloody oaths. Each Injeean pretending he was already murderin' a victim, plantin' the axe over and over in his brains, rippin' women's bellies up with knives sharp as a razor. I tell you we fled."

"That's an isolated incident. Massacres are rare here," Emison put in.

Bard turned and gave Emison a long, hostile look, as if he must take the responsibility for what was to follow: "The next week we heerd that a party of three English traders was set upon in a pass. Their skulls was crushed in and scalps took." His voice was almost a whisper. "They cut off their hands and feet and et 'em. They kill babies at the breast, women. They deserve vengeance from the arm o' the Lord."

John McClure sat stock-still, looking at the floor. Jane moved quietly among the men, collecting the bowls.

Walter Cherry said, "Mebbe our fellow Christians, the Quakers and Moravians will be able to make Christian gentlemen out of 'em yet. They ere tryin'."

Bige Cherry chimed in, "Like sewin' a silk purse out of a porker's ear."

Jane McClure looked at the gawky boy, wondering what qualified him to speak in a gathering of men. His teeth stuck out and so did his ideas. In Ulster boys did not venture into men's conversations. Maybe it was cheekiness, but maybe it was something else. Twelve-year-olds who shouldered guns for food and protection could have opinions that adults listened to, if only for fairness's sake.

"The Moravians over east o' here baptize the savages, but then they're daft anyways. They preach separate to the men and women, so some says. I for one, was never there," Bard opined.

"And the Injeeans fall on their knees for 'em and get baptized and take names like ours. John or Matthew Big Foot." Bige leaned his head back and brayed laughter.

His father added, " 'Tis true. Last year they baptized a old degenerate named Taddyuscung. Took away his feathers, put a hat on 'im, and made 'im grow hair on his shaved heathen pate."

John knew of Taddyuscung. He was the talk of Philadelphia, the Quaker's darling. "How many Indians are Christians?" John wanted to know.

"Not nearly enough to let us sleep easy," Cherry answered, and this time it was Emison's son Ash, a tall, intelligent boy of about sixteen, who guffawed. Rafe Emison, John noted, had dropped out of the conversation. He sat by the window hole looking out.

Finally, Rafe's voice echoed through the twilight darkness. "They are peaceful, I tell you. They will only be a problem if the French stir them up."

"As they will," Bard said, favoring his leg a little as he shifted the three-legged stool. He turned to John and pointed a finger, looking for all the world like a Presbyterian minister in his pulpit. "Let me go back a piece. For a hundred years or more the French, a snake-bellied bunch of bastards if you don't mind me sayin' so," he looked at Jane and smiled weakly, "anyways, the French have gone among these yere tribes from the big lakes on the north to the Ouabash River in the west. Beaver was what they wanted, or otter or ermine for the marchants of Paree. Everyone there has a beaver hat, even King Loois. The French got the furs, and the friendship of the savages. Now they claim all the land west o' the mountains."

"Don't we claim it too? What about that Pickawillany that you told me about, Emison?" McClure asked.

But Bard, pulling up his linen shirt and scratching his stomach, answered instead. "The French are goin' around puttin' out little markers sayin' all the western lands are theirs. They've sent a half-breed French sojer and some o' his Injeean friends to frighten away the English at Pickawillany."

"And if we decide to hold the Ohio lands?"

"They's jest been a war between the English and French overseas. If England moves against France in the Colonies. . ."

"War. Why not say it," Emison hissed, his patience gone. "War on this Pennsylvania frontier. And since the French have chosen to befriend the Indians and treat them fairly and we have not, they will have the Indians as allies. It will not be war with cannon and muskets, but war with tomahawks and scalpings by night. And we in these Scotch-Irish cabins stand to be attacked first. If that happens, we will have paid the price for the Old Theology, where men decide who are the loved of God and who are the lost and turn the lost into enemies. I suspect it will not be long before these Indian children of the Fallen One fall on us instead."

A thought rang in John McClure's mind like a knell in the dusky darkness. If God is a God of vengeance, the savages will fall on me and mine. For I am as fallen as they.

A long moment passed, then another. Jane rose and lit two candles. Eager to break the uncomfortable stillness she said, "Well. I've made a cake. Shall we all think of cheerier things and. . ."

Her husband wheeled to glare at her, his face a mask of conflicting emotions. "God damn it, woman, have you no sense of fitness? Take your bowls and cakes and leave us!" All eyes turned toward him for a moment as Jane set the cake down and departed, her face stricken with the unexpected rebuke.

It was only very late at night, after the window slits were covered with oiled paper against the cold and all the men and boys were snoring and grumbling in their sleep on the floor, that she at last gave in to her sadness. Tears ran from her closed eyes as she lay taut as a beech stick beside John McClure.

But it was not only in yearning for the Irish land they had left behind or for fear of the violent savages with lost souls, or even for herself, poor misunderstood wife, that she wept. It was for him, a man who had brought whatever bitter rage drove him to this new land. It was a land which now had begun to sing to her of promise, in spite of all the inconveniences of life in the wilderness.

A few weeks ago, on a large, cleared hill near Carlisle, Jane had seen hundreds of thousands of pigeons fly over, their wings flap-flapping, till they darkened the sky. And as she stood there, holding Will by the hand, she caught her breath at the beauty, the freedom of their flight. All the continuing fears and frustrations of settling dissipated for a moment, and she sensed only promise.

She felt the same emotion walking the streets of the raw settlement of Carlisle, watching men at work at different jobs. In Ireland, her laboring parents were crushed by unjust trade laws, the land hobbled by economic and religious oppression. But here a man or woman had the freedom of those birds, to ply the winds, to cry aloft to God with whatever voice he or she had, to follow the wind currents wherever they led, to work.

Surely the God of freedom had stamped his ideals in the clay and air of this new land. And if there was danger and foreboding, it was not only in the minds of the savages lurking in the woods. It was also nearer home. It was in the soul of this man of hers who could not glory in this dizzying freedom, because for some reason he was dead at heart. He came to a new land for a fresh start, but the old baggage he brought was heavy around his neck. For years she had feared it from time to time; now she firmly believed it. John McClure's heart was dead.

Chapter VII

As Bard and the Cherrys swung into their stirrups the next morning and Emison and his son prepared to drive the oxen down the road, Walter Cherry looked thoughtfully at John. "We will look forward to seeing you and your family at divine service at Big Spring tomorrow, John."

John stared over Cherry's head. "I thank you. My wife will come. I do not often worship formally any more."

After the men had departed, Jane was unusually firm in her reaction. "John, it will not be fittin' for us to go to meetin' by ourselves. And we must lead Johnny and Will in the way. Uncle would have wanted it that way, and you know it's right."

He gave her the barest suggestion of a nod and turned away.

Just after sunrise the next morning they plodded down the road through a blustery wind, Jane and little Will ahead on the gelding Orange, and John McClure and Johnny behind on Bess.

The meeting "house" at Big Spring was really a huge lean-to made of logs on a farm on Big Spring creek. The McClures had been told that the congregation was "old side," the stern, conformist side of Presbyterianism.

Scotch-Irishmen here in the valley of Conodoguinet Creek, Cumberland County Pennsylvania, for all of their independence and defiance of tradition, were conservatives when it came to religion. They wanted their ministers to talk about predestination, the belief that man is either saved or damned by God from the beginning of time, as John Calvin had taught. They wanted these ministers trained in Scotland. Bard and most of the other Scots in the valley scorned the emotionalism of the "new style" Presbyterian rebels who claimed a man could tell the very hour of his "conversion to Christ."

"I found grace in a flash of light as I sat in the necessary Sunday last," Bard would mimic in an effeminate voice, prancing about. Then he would fall down on the floor, to the amusement of all, convulsively moving "before the power of the Spirit."

We would probably have been thought new-style in Ireland, Jane thought. Our own uncle preaching to the Catholics—the horse gave a sudden jolt and stepped in a hole the size of a saucepan, then found his footing and went on. She sighed. After the rains finished, Sally Bard had said, the holes would be the size of lard kettles. In spite of the road, they travelled the six miles easily and tethered the horses in time to watch neighbors arrive.

It was the first time Jane had seen women since Carlisle. Young Ash Emison stepped forward, pulling off his slouch hat with sweeping bow. "I'd like to present my ma, Mrs. McClure," he said, respectfully. The ma was a pretty blonde woman, Alice.

"Pleased, I'm sure," Jane McClure said, smiling. "That's sartainly a lovely blue cape and bonnet." All the women were surprisingly "prettified." They might be at an English service in a parish near Dublin.

" 'Tis dyed merino," Alice Emison said. Amanda Cherry, a fluttery little woman with absent-looking eyes and hair all ratty, sat with Jane on the second bench. Their children took the bench behind. John headed for the rear of the lean-to, where the Emisons also sat near the group of grazing horses, two-wheeled carts and farm carriages. Before long a group of about forty men, women, and children were crowded under the shelter. Most of them had been in America for less than ten years.

"Are there always this many people?" Jane whispered to Amanda.

"In good weather. But nobody comes much in Janerry." She smiled as she said it and patted Jane's hand. Jane decided to ignore the gravy stains on her skirt. Amanda went on, "We meet twict a month in the warm season." She wheeled about. "Sit down, Moses. I'm a-gonna have to knock ye." Her third son was crawling under the bench and she rapped him on the head with her knuckle.

Jane shifted her weight on the bench. The children would somehow have to endure three-and-a-half hours of preaching, singing and exhortation this morning and keep reasonably quiet. Even the Cherrys, bedraggled as they were, believed in "spare the rod and spoil the child."

Walter Cherry turned on the bench to look toward the back of the tent. "The preacher," he said, gesturing with his thumb at a young man talking with Rafe Emison. "He's a good un on the covenant of works. Makes us all examine ourselves fully." The sincere-looking young man stood up, smoothed his walnut-brown frock coat, patted his tie-wig, and walked toward the log pulpit.

Once ensconced, the preacher nodded his head to an older man with a mane of white hair who sat on a bench facing the congregation, and this man rose and announced the hymn. After the congregation had risen, the old man proceeded to read the first line out loud. The congregation sang this line, then the "speller" read another and so on, until line by line, the congregation lurched its way through the psalm, singing after him.

As the group settled shufflingly back onto the benches with much coughing and clearing of throats, Jane asked Amanda Cherry, "Dinna any of them know that hymn?"

"They do. But there hain't no hymnbooks out here, so we line out all the hymns. They've gotten to like the linin' out even when they know the words."

The preacher, grasping the edge of the pulpit with his delicate hands, announced himself as the Reverend Mr. Thomas Ebley Clark, late of Glasgow, Scotland, "sent by Presbytery to supply sermon for Big Spring for the next year." There were nods of pleased affirmation. "The scripture," he said, "is from Romans: 7. 'I am carnal, sold under sin.' " He read most of the chapter.

John McClure, aloof in his back pew, watched a gray squirrel with some sort of large nut in its mouth. Would he ever learn all the types of trees in this woodsman's paradise?

Will squirmed and fussed in his mother's arms and then fell asleep. The Cherry children pinched each other quietly, then, finally lulled by the mellifluous voice reading the scripture, slumped over like limp bolsters.

Reverend Thomas Ebley Clark led more psalming and singing leading to the twice-a-Sunday main event, the sermon. "Who shall deliver me from the body of this death?" he asked in a resonant voice. "I will answer that question, which I know all of us are most seriously pondering, indeed involving our immortal souls, with several distinct theological answers."

He said, in substance, that we are delivered from the body of this death by the covenant written on Adam's heart. That as Adam was told to till the soil by the sweat of his brow, we must by good works subdue sin in our hearts through hard work. He allowed as how coming into this wild and untamed wilderness, with its rushing cataracts and forests and frightening denizens of the woods, put him in mind of all unredeemed nature. How like the valley of death is the uncut forest. How much the snarling bear resembleth behemoth charging about wreaking havoc among the very Elect.

Bige Cherry thought about this. He reckoned to himself that if wrestling with unredeemed nature delivered us, if struggling over rocks as big as cows in the ground, and broken axe handles and early frosts and flood waters around the corn roots was good for one's spirit, than indeed, a good deal of him must have been improved.

"That, secondly," the earnest young preacher went on, "we are delivered by the very depravity of the original parents' fall." There was much more.

"Thirdly, we are enabled by our own closet meditations to draw nearer to the Throne of Grace." The minister wondered how often we have allocated proper time daily for religious thought. We should do it daily! Hourly! Concerns of home or the world of business must not distract us! Amanda Cherry thought about the salt pork and beans she had left simmering on the banked fire. Would it be done? Underdone? Overdone? Walt did not like beans that had turned to mush. She wondered if the weather would be bitingly cold tonight. The pig would have to sleep inside. . .

Johnny McClure cast sideways glances at the bench across the way, at a strange-looking boy in a too-tight waistcoat. He had a harelip. Father always said it did not do to stare, but it was so odd. The lip jutted out over his teeth like a piece of fatback and he looked constantly surprised. What if you had to go around like that all the time, he asked himself, shifting his weight uncomfortably at the thought. Or with a hunchback? Or like the woman on the street in Philadelphia with scrofula? Why didn't preachers say somethin' about harelip or scrofula? That would be interestin'. Well, Ma had said there would be some of the walnut cake in the basket for dinner. He had wanted another piece last night when Mr. Bard passed it out, but he daren't ask, 'cause

Dada had been so angry.

"Fifthly," Mr. Thomas Ebley Clark went on.

"I have to fart bad," thought nine-year-old Moses Cherry, on the bench by Johnny. "Efn I don't try to hold it I may let go and Ma'll skin me. But it may be a spell before the preacher shets up and I can go to the woods. 'Twould be embarrassin' to run out right now. Damn, he does run on, don't he. I don't guess the sinners with God's wrath on 'em in the pit got any more torture'n I do this minute."

"In short. . ." the minister said.

Rafe Emison paced towards the spring. He was taking the accepted option on these long Sabbaths of stretching his legs for a few moments. In short, Rafe thought, he cannot be short. None of these conformist ministers can get to the point in less than a fortnight. So long as he was trained in Scotland or at the College of New Jersey, and so long as he was duly licensed by the Pharisees in session in Philadelphia, he can represent the gospel of Jesus Christ in the backwoods. And I can't. No matter if he be as carnal as a baboon and as graceless as an East Indian, only those chosen by Them may preach. And I, as an alumnus of the Log College of the great and sainted William Tennent in Philadelphia, am an outsider.

He knelt to drink from the creek, and as he walked back he thought of the spirit that was among them all in Philadelphia, the Tennents, father and son, and of course George Whitefield. They wanted to represent the religion of the heart, warmed and full of charity, instead of always the cold Covenant. And people listened. They really did. All over the city, families began singing hymns nightly and reading aloud from religious books. But the religion of the heart preachers were all driven from the ranks as emotional rebels and forbidden to preach the gospel of Jesus. He, tired and bitter, took up farming first at Easton and now here, where he sat on the back bench with gloomy McClure (what devil plagued him anyhow?) and prayed to his God in secret—for dinnertime to hurry up and come.

Mr. Thomas Ebley Clark, having got to his last point, "The sacrifice of Jesus on the Cross," decided to close. It had been close to two hours, and his voice was beginning to crack. And he did have to preach this afternoon. After all, as they had taught him in Glasgow, it wasn't necessary to send men to Heaven in one sermon. He smiled and started the prayer.

Chapter VIII

The road along the Susquehanna was treacherous with mud during the week before Christmas. John McClure, from his seat in the wagon, guided Bess through ankle-deep troughs of standing water, steering around gray piles of rock which had tumbled off the cliffs above the western bank of the road. Then, avoiding the little settlement at John Harris's, he determined to ford north of the ferry. Although it had been raining and spitting snow steadily for over a week, the river was not yet swollen full. In the early spring it would be a mile-wide torrent that overran the islands and threatened to go over the banks into the bottomland.

Seeking a shallow stretch, John's eyes scanned the stream, with tufted gray-green isles and the uneven currents which made it a boatman's nightmare. He turned Bess into the stream and they splashed the wagon through, having to swim it for only a moment or two. Then he looked upstream to see if there were any visible signs of the settlement he sought, Hunter's Mill. He found none. Bard had told him to hug the east shore road until he came to Fishing Creek, where the Hunter family would welcome him and sell him as many bags of grain as he wanted. He also told him to guard his purse.

It was not unpleasant to be away from the confinement of the cabin. The new fireplaces did not draw as well as they might have, in spite of the care they had all taken to see the chimneys up free and fair. The simple preparations the family was making for Christmas, the plum duff with suet and raisins, the knitting of socks and mittens, did not interest him. Not all Presbyterians out here observed Christmas, and he, too, was suspicious of the pagan frippery his wife loved.

He was displeased that he would have to ask for credit at the mill. By spring, he would have crafted and put by a supply of wooden tubs, dough boxes, and milk keelers to trade for the candles, flax, and iron tools they needed and to pay this debt and others. But until then. . .

Through the oak and ash which thinly lined the shoreline, glimpses of the smooth surface of the river appeared, like prospect paintings in the weak light of the December day, only to disappear as Bess trotted forward. He could take some pride, he reflected, in the progress made on his land in these few months. The two-room cabin was finished. Recently he hung its double door on wooden hinges, complete with latch string.

He would order expensive real windows as soon as he could. A house was not a house without blown, or at least bottle, glass windows. It would be worth it to pay whatever tax the government might charge for them. And just last week he stabled the animals in a six-foot high shelter of chestnut saplings and had Johnny stuff straw and leaves in its wide cracks.

A soap bin at the corner of the cabin for collecting grease scraps and fireplace ashes, a small outhouse, a handmill for corn—the foundations of an estate were laid. It was not Gentry Row, he thought with a smile, but it was all theirs. Or it would be after he had applied to have it patented after a year or so.

Bess's hoofs clomped free now as the road became drier near Hunter's Mill. The place had the reputation of being a hideaway for brawlers and "no good Injeeans," according to Bard and Cherry. John saw it boasted a tumbledown stockade, and a huge mill had been built on a pond up the hill from the stockade on Fishing Creek. As he drew near, he noticed the mill stood on more than a dozen oak pilings. Only a wisp of smoke rose from its chimney. Obviously the fire was not being well tended.

He reined the horse near the mill and looked around. Outbuildings were a-tumble, as if the original energy poured into the construction of the main building died before it could finish kitchens, spring houses, and barns. A woman chased a screaming, dirty boy of about three from one of the shacks. "Jonas, you brat, come to yer ma or I'll beat the stuffin' out o' you." She pulled a shawl about her shoulders, but her feet were bare on the frozen ground. Forlorn remains of cabbage leaves and fish and animal bones mingled with the dish slop around the shack's door.

She caught the squalling child and cuffed it about the head. A man with uncombed hair peered blearily out the open door. "Be a-comin' in, Betty, or you'll catch your death." Tankard in hand, he began pulling her in, and John asked him where the proprietors were.

"Off hunting. Simon and Tom Girty help run the place but they're gone too. Turner'll take care of ya." He went inside and slammed the door. And where would Turner be? John wondered. He turned down the slight incline toward the mill, curious about a caterwauling coming from behind one of its outbuildings, a curious blend of snarling, yelping, and roaring belly laughs.

He soon discovered the cause of the noise. A shaggy brown bear paced on ground worn bare under a pine tree. It was the first bear John had ever seen. He guessed it could not have been more than a year old. Tongue lolling, it paced the length of its chain in one direction, then pulled up short, walked until it was stopped in the other, then began the process all over again. A bearded man in a dirty linen shirt and worn leggings, and three boys watched delightedly. The snarling that John heard came from a mastiff cur the bearded man kept on a leash just out of the bear's reach.

"Simon, watch the son-of-a-bitch lunge," he said to the wide-eyed oldest boy, who must have been about ten. The dog strained at the rawhide loop about his neck and tried to nip at the feet of the beleaguered bear. "He's so essited I can't tell if he's gonna puke or shit." The man directed this half to the boys, half to John, whom he saw approaching. Staking the dog to a strong sapling on the edge of the clearing, he strode toward the visitor.

"We're gonna 'ave us some sport with this yere crittur," he said, hiking up his leggings.

John grunted. He needed to maintain enough civility to get the grain he needed. Pity it was too late in the day to start for home again when he had loaded up. "Where did you find him?" he asked.

"Up to the blacksmith's cabin, thataway." Turner gestured up the hill. "They's hardly any of 'em around anymore. This one come down to get at the fish offal outback and the Swede shot 'im. Din't kill 'im though, just addled his wits. While he was stunned, we drug him down 'ere and staked him up for the boys." He looked lovingly at the slightly-built, dark-haired older child who stood with his eyes fixed in fascination on the pacing animal, and at his eight-year-old brother, a younger replica. The littlest child stared unmoved. He had a dirty piece of coverlet and was stroking it and sucking his thumb.

"My name is John Turner," the bearded man said, striding forward. "I'm a trading partner to Simon Girty. These yere younguns are his. We live in that place yonder by the mill." He searched John's face. "I reckon you're here for grain."

He honked and turned his face to spit a clot of green phlegm politely out of company's range.

John nodded. "How many bushels of cornmeal could you spare? Our need is great."

"You from Shearman's Valley?" Turner asked, referring to the area directly west of them.

"No, Conodoguinet Creek."

"Lots of 'em is comin' in this year from over thar. Spring's a ways off, ain't it? Anyways, you new folk always come in too late to plant. All you brang was the shirts off your backs an' a axe. Burn yourself off a few trees, chop holes in the ground and throw in a fish or two and a corn kernel and call it a farm."

John was irritated. "Do you sell corn meal and flour here, man, or not?"

Turner was unruffled. "Waal, let's go inside and I'll get you some bags. I reckon we can spare. . ." He calculated mentally. He had forgotten the bear, and the boys drifted off to play somewhere else.

Inside the mill the sound was deafening. Wheat was being relentlessly ground by wheels driven by a perpendicular shaft attached to the overshot wheel on the stream. They ground all winter here. Nodding to the mill attendant, Turner hefted two large bags onto his shoulder and indicated two more for John to carry. "You'll be staying the night with us, I reckon, so I'll put these in the corner of the best room." He pushed open a door beyond the wheel with his boot.

"Them boys ain't mine, although they might as well be," he confided to John, offering him a bench before the smoking remains of the fire. "Simon ain't around as much as he should be—always off huntin' or tradin' with the Delawares. Damn fire's gone out. Mary," he called, "get your arse in here and put some logs on this yere fire.''

John looked up expecting to see a servant girl, but when a gap-toothed, buxom woman appeared with a load of pine logs, Turner said, with a wink, ''Simon's wife. I try to keep 'er busy while he's gone.'' John stared at him, while the woman stirred the fire, pretending not to hear.

''Hell, you think he gives a shit, man? He found 'er in Philadelphia after she'd kep' house for several men already—brought her here and found the preacher later. Then. . .''

''You shut your blabbin' mouth, John Turner, or I'll split your head. You talk too much for comfort,'' the woman said. McClure sighed and looked into the fire. Turner was obviously Mere Irish; his accent betrayed him. John's thoughts turned to the wild O'Donnell clan and others like them, both the native and Scotch Irish. Lazy, shallow, conniving—many of them seemed to have been uprooted right in the middle of their curses and whining and transplanted to Pennsylvania. He decided to change the subject.

''Who lives in this settlement, Turner?'' The other man was pulling off his boots. A smothering, yeasty odor drifted from his knitted socks, which had holes the size of silver dollars.

''Traders comin' and goin' to Pickawillany, Injeeans on their way to camp, men from Connecticut lookin' for land. They pay gold and ask no questions. Or mebbe sluts that got their arses kicked out of better places. . .'' He pounded his boot upside down, and dirt and twigs floated onto the puncheons. John noticed it was a French officer's boot, worn but ornate. He had seen one like it in Derry. First quality, purchased from some civilian supplier getting rich from war. He wondered how Turner had come by it. John drank sweet cider from a pitcher while Turner quaffed ale, and they both watched the healthily-burning fire for long moments.

Turner announced he was going out to stable John's horses. After a minute, the noise of the grindstone stopped; evidently the tender had finished for the day. Instead of silence, however, John heard another wild commotion and headed out the door, curiosity aroused. Laughing malevolently, the older boy had unleashed the mastiff on the bear. The animal, still obviously suffering from the gunshot wound to its head, lurched crazily as the mastiff snapped at it, staying just out of the reach of its paws.

Turner came from the lean-to which passed for a stable and stopped to enjoy the scene before him. ''I got a good idee,'' he said to the elder Girty boy, and whispering something to him, sent him inside the mill. Turner himself went behind the mill and returned with a wooden bucket of tar just as Simon Girty, Jr. emerged with a flaming brand from the fireplace. McClure watched as Turner leaned first with a tar stick, then with the torch, towards the bear's hind quarters. He had set the beast on fire.

Bellows of agony rent the air, adding to the general din, and slatternly people came running down the hill. On the bear's flank embers smoldered, smoked white, and spread into flames like a grass fire. The smell of burning bear grease and fur was nauseating.

John, simmering with anger at Turner and all his kind, slipped away. In a moment, standing at the edge of the crowd, as the bear continued to bellow in agony, he loaded and aimed the long muzzle of the musket. He had a clear, safe shot from the left side, and the bear fell, as the crowd jumped at the echoing explosions. The ball had obviously entered some vital organ, thank God. The beast's legs thrashed once or twice and then were still.

Hostile eyes turned to John. Soon Turner was roughly shouldering people aside to get to him. "What did you want to do that for, anyways?" he demanded, his eyes flinty.

"I don't hold to tormentin' creatures," John said, and that was true. But he also felt a deep sense of satisfaction that he had thwarted this ignorant ass's plans.

Turner grabbed him and pushed him back by the shoulders. "Come meddlin' with our business, will ye. Eh? Eh?" He pushed him again and again. It was one of the great insults in these parts, intended to unman an opponent, and it had the proper effect on John. He lunged forward and caught Turner by the shoulders and knocked him to his knees, but the Irishman was soon up, closing on him, fists up.

"We'll see what kind of balls you got, neighbor," he growled and surged at him, fists flying. John defended himself and landed a blow to the Irishman's head. His own head rang as Turner's fist connected with his jaw.

The crowd formed a circle around them. "Beat the hell out of 'im," they urged. John realized, surprisingly, some of the shouts were for him.

McClure moved forward quickly and landed a blow to Turner's head. Then his own head rang as Turner's fist connected with his jaw. "Watch 'is knees," the spectators commanded.

Good advice, John thought as he avoided them, jammed his fist joltingly into Turner's jaw—and had the gratification of hearing teeth rattle. Now the trapper was off-guard. Catching his opponent behind the knee, John threw him to the ground. He tried to grab the man's shoulders to beat his head up and down against the hard dirt ("Whump him against the ground," they were shouting) but as soon as Turner felt his shoulders leave the earth, he roared like a wild pig and, throwing his weight around, pinned John. The man had the strength of ten. He seemed to have been husbanding it until he could make this decisive move.

In the ten seconds that just passed, John realized, the tables had turned, and he was now thrashing about unsuccessfully, struggling to regain the topmost position. Through jolts of pain, as his enraged opponent bounced on his stomach and delivered blow after blow to his face, John tried to swing over. He felt his septum crack and blood began to pour from his nose.

The crowd surged in and their shouts became a thudding roar. Turner was "whomping him against the ground" according to instructions. "Go for the eyes. Gouge them right out." Turner paused for a fraction of a second, looked with a twisted smile at McClure's swollen sockets, then at the clawlike nails on his own hand. I will be blind, thought John dully. Then the face of the angry man dimmed before him, his ears roared, and the crowd rushed away to be replaced by a curtain of black which wrapped around him and lifted him out of the scene.

He stood on a track on the desert. All about him stretched undulating, lifeless hills, like the ones in his uncle's books about Araby. He had seen all this before, he knew, in some dream or another. But this scene was a little different. Now the sky glowed eerily, like the town of Derry seen from the hills above it at night.

Apprehensively, he looked behind him; whatever had been chasing him was no longer near. Not far ahead were rectangular shapes standing beside the road. They seemed to beckon to him, and he tried to walk quickly toward them. Sand clung tightly to his shoes as if each grain were a suction cup. Somehow, legs moving heavily, he came to stand before the shapes. Only now they were oval, long, colored portraits as on a castle wall, but mounted to stand free. He looked at the first one; it was his wife. Beside it, a few paces off, were portraits of his two sons.

These likenesses did not look like portraits of kings or country lords, with lapdogs and ribbons and breezes blowing the draped clothing. Instead, his wife looked puzzled as her hand tried to lift a teakettle from the fire. The lid, about to fall in the ashes, was halfway between the pot and the andirons, caught in midair. She, the fire, and the teapot were all frozen in the middle of the experience. Her hair was escaping its cap and falling over her forehead, as steam from the pot clouded about her face. The steam, too, seemed frozen, like breath on a cold morning.

Johnny was pulling a little top away from the grasp of a hand that had to be his brother's, and the last oval showed William, with frozen tears coming out of his eyes, standing on tiptoe, reaching for the top his brother had taken away from him.

As John watched, the portraits and the entire desert scene began to fade and the light at the edge of the sky seemed to rise a bit. Then he drifted into oblivion, with time for one waking thought to ring through his pained mind. That was of the babe that he had heard this morning would be born to his wife in summer. "I will never see its face, for I shall be either dead or blind," he thought.

He awoke to a world in which there was no reality but pain. At least he was not dead. The babe to be born would indeed know its father, for whatever that would be worth. With infinitely painful care, John opened his eyes to see the light of the dying fire in the room inside the mill. He had heard that fights in the valley rarely ended in death, but eye-gougings were common. His sigh was one of relief. A blind man on the frontier would be better off dead.

His face felt as if it were one excruciating nose, throbbing and enormous. The scars of his old McClure the Fist boxing bouts and the O'Donnell fight throbbed. Somebody had stanched his bleeding at least, before they tossed him onto the heavy grain bags in the corner. He gingerly shifted his weight to lessen the pain in his joints and forced open his swollen eyelids again at the sound of heavy boots on the planks. It was Turner. "I see yer awake. I don't feel so good neither. They stopped me from killin' you. Mary, 'twas. She yelled at me that it wouldn't do for folks in the valley to think we was nuthin' but a bunch of murderers. Mebbe hurt the trade. You kin stay here tonight."

His eyes narrowed. "But don't you git the idee that I've forgave and forgot. Nobody that messes with me and mine the way you messed with that b'ar has lived to tell it. We'll settle 'er up another time." He stalked out, walking stiffly, John noted with a tiny degree of satisfaction.

He slept fitfully for an hour, then awoke to find a bowl of soup beside him. He drank it, forcing the meat and barley past his swollen lips. People came and went in the huge room, flopping on the floor, throwing pine logs onto the fire to make it blaze and pop, and drinking what must have been gallons of rum and whiskey. Cadences of sound rose and fell; drunken outbursts merged into his own half-delirious sleep. He was again a boy. His father was vomiting on his birthday shirt, the one John's mother had made him before she died. The magistrate was bringing his father in, telling John his father had died under the wheels of the whiskey cart. The embarrassed, poignant tones of the magistrate's voice became the droning monotone in the room as someone or another told a rambling frontier tale. "Copperheads twined round each other,". . ."one of the Shawnees was goin' for Croghan's Gap."

He awoke at what must have been three in the morning. The only sound was the distant splash of Fishing Creek nearby, as it rushed over rocks and poured into the pond behind the log dam. The thought of the stream, clear and cold in the winter night, gave John direction. Picking himself up, inch-by-inch he dragged out the door.

Slowly, as John climbed the hill behind the pond, and as the frosty air hit his lungs and face, his head began to clear. Pain would not allow him to kneel to drink, so he lowered himself carefully to a sitting position and brought handsful of the clear water to his mouth. He drank for over a minute, then went to relieve himself.

Returning, John walked silently by Girty's cabin, where he knew Turner lodged with Mary Girty, with the three boys probably up in the loft. A wan moon came from behind scattered clouds, and as he passed the sole window in Girty's cabin, he heard sounds that could be only one thing. To judge from the gutteral moans coming from within, Mary Girty must like making the beast-with-two-backs with someone who was a beast himself. No accounting for taste, he thought ruefully through his pain, as the lady said when she kissed a cow. Obviously Turner's wounds were already beginning to heal.

The next morning John McClure proceeded deliberately along the west side of the Susquehanna with a half-full wagon and a thousand aches torturing his body. The mud on the trail was frozen almost solid. At first light, as he was harnessing the horse, Mary Girty had come out. She looked pleasant enough in the December light, pushing back her dishevelled hair. "Sir, please," she said with obvious embarrassment. "He don't know I'm out here. I'm sorry about whut happened. I'd be beholden to you if you'd accept somethin' from me. To kind of square us." That can never be, he thought, but he watched as she slipped into one of the sheds and brought out a small but perfectly made maple spinning wheel and a matching linen winder.

"We buried Ma Welty here last month, and her man went back to Virginny. Their son died o' gangrene a few weeks before when a axe head cut his leg deep. Welty left me the woman's linen machines to pay the meal bill. I ain't much good at linen. Would you accept it and try to unnerstand about John? When he—or Simon—have got rum or ale in 'em they ain't human."

Woman, you are right, thought McClure vehemently, but he nodded and packed the handsome wheel and winder as best he could into the wagon to head home.

And so it was that the first thing Jane McClure ever received from her husband, the one gift that could brighten her day in the darkness of the forest, was the bequest of a man who had lost all to that forest. The Indians believed that if spirit forces answer our wishes, there had been or would be a price paid somewhere, even if it were not necessarily by us. And so, if Jane McClure's happiness at being able to create comfort and art in the wilderness came from another woman's struggle and failure on the same ground, so be it. Someone gained, someone paid the price. It was only the law of Manitto, the Indians' God, and the law of the frontier.

The week after Christmas, word flashed around the settlements in Cumberland County that Simon Girty, Sr., returning from a week's hunting and trading jaunt in Allegheny River country with the Indian known as Captain Jacobs, got into a drunken argument with Turner. Turner ended up killing Girty on the spot before the outraged eyes of his Indian friend and had to flee for his life. The settlement was closed down for a while, and John McClure felt a dark sense of satisfaction in that fact. Another kind of price had been paid, that of the evening of scores. The Indians believed Mannito did that, too.

Except that the retribution was not complete. The one who died was Girty, not Turner. For Turner, for the beast, John would not wait for Divine retribution to operate. He would, in some way and at some point, seek it himself. Truly, he told himself, it was no easier to live in the New World than in the Old. Men hated as much, justice was bought and sold, animal nature ruled reason. God seemed to be just as absent in Pennsylvania as He had been in northern Ireland. That was the long and short of it. Why had he wasted his time thinking there could be anything different here?

Chapter IX

And so, Jane was to have another child. As snows and silence drifted over the small cabin sitting in deep groves of oak and maple trees, as Jane made the corn meal mush and fried the rabbit and swept the puncheons, she forgot about the promise she had felt so keenly when she saw the birds soar in the fall. She drifted in a state of indifference as dreary as the winter weather.

Her eyes were always on her children as they played, wrestled, and sometimes fought before the fire. Surely, she thought, she could gain some pleasure, some hope in the new child, by watching these boys she loved so strongly.

Young Johnny, reddish hair long from lack of cutting, had learned to shoot from his father. He also had learned to read the story of Dick Whittington's cat from the chapbook bought from a wandering bookseller. Johnny was still strong and serious, but his English was developing an odd twang, as he spent more time with the Bards and other neighbors. Will was passing from babyhood to childhood with a restlessness and irritability that concerned Jane. His usual style of play was to throw his corncob baby in the little wagon made by their father, then immediately pick it up and dump it out, usually on his brother's head. Winter days were long and tempers were short for all in the closed-in cabin.

The thought of summer held no promise for Jane either. June would bring festive gatherings, as the McClures cleared more land and helped others clear theirs, at the same time planting and enjoying a huge garden. July would bring roasting ears and raspberries to preserve, so they said. But August would bring. . .

A huge body she must drag around as she washed summer ginghams in the spring, cramped legs, low spirits, exhaustion, and then, the birthing itself. They said that once a woman holds her baby in her arms, she forgets the "travail" of the birth. Whoever wrote that was not a woman.

As far as she was concerned, that kind of fear and pain stayed with you always. The way you recalled birthing was the way you saw Blue Mountain. Sometimes when your sight was clear, it was almost upon you, and you could put out your hand and touch a tree on its slope. At other times it was hazy, farther away. Sometimes for brief moments or days you lost sight of it, but it was always there.

Time and time again, while Jane spoke with Sally Bard or Amanda Cherry at church, while she planted beans or Sweet William in the newly-turned, red earth, she relived her past, difficult birthings. They replayed like a dumb-show play as she sat seemingly helpless, living again the long hours of pain, when the calm, skilled care of the midwife was all that stood between her and disaster.

Weary with child care, carrying water for new plants, cooking spidersful of hot bread and stew for crews that built sheds and cleared land and harvested hay, she looked blamingly at her husband. He could offer her no comfort, so wrapped was he in his own concerns and thoughts. She forgot the bonds of trust and congeniality they had formed and thought only of his faults. He says nothing consoling to me, she complained to herself. Never, not anything. It is too much, too much, that he is as silent and cold as an owl in a tree. Surely he does not love!

And of course that was not the worst, because the one thing she would not allow herself to focus on was that she might die in the birthing, like so many others did out here, far from help. In Ireland, there had been experienced old women who knew midwifery as a science and art, and physicians nearby. But here there were only neighbor women, often ignorant of anything but the basic process. If she thought of the worst—the childbed fever, the weakening and wasting away, or the hemorrhaging of one's life blood until unconsciousness came, the pale corpse at the wake with the babe sometimes beside it—she could not have survived.

She knew she should be better. It was awful to dwell on pain and death. It could mark the child. Sally would not be so. Sally, whose skirt was always starched, whose cap was clean, who spoke gently to her children and was never ruffled, believed it was a woman's destiny to conceive and bear and rear and die, if necessary, to fulfil God's preordained plan. Clenching her fists, Jane told herself she must love the child that was expected. But try as she would, the love would not come.

When the time arrived, the birthing play unfolded as in the past, just as Jane had seen it in her mind. There were, however, some few changes. The babe decided to come two weeks early in the middle of the harvest, when no women at all were around to help. So instead of Sally, who had at least assisted at a few births, puttering and directing, readying the knife to cut the cord and taking out swaddling clothes, there was only John. He was as inscrutable as ever in this new duty, and yet for all that, as efficient and effective as he was at the time of her mother's death.

And instead of a healthy child, born lustily squalling and ready to take up the journey, rewarding Jane with many years of life, there was instead a dead babe, strangled by the cord. John could not get it to breathe, try as he would.

And so, two things were left to Jane for all her labor. First was a memory which would never leave her till the day she died, of John looking at the dead child. Exhausted and stricken, when she realized the child was not crying, Jane boosted herself to her elbows to see John slap its rear, apply cold water to the little blue face, breathe in its mouth. But cold as a doll it lay on the table, and he pulled back, bewildered, to look at it as the seconds passed.

He turned to her and his eyes sought hers, and for a brief moment, agony was written on all his features. She thought he might weep. Then he turned back to the motionless babe and began to wash and dress it. Finally, he brought it to Jane to see. It was a beautiful girl child, now creamy-skinned with a light fluff of hair. Her eyes were serenely closed as if she slept.

Too numb to react, Jane watched her husband look down at the child he held in his arms. He was far away, perhaps walking down a path with a prattling toddler, taking her to church, seeing her as the bride she would never be. For the moment no pain was mixed in his expression, and she thought she had never seen on any face such an expression of pure love. He turned and for a fraction of an instant, their eyes met in understanding. And for Jane, at that moment, a marriage made of convenience, respect, and sexual passion also became one of love.

There was a second and sobering residue from the experience—the guilty suspicion that she had killed her own baby with her troubled thoughts. Cooly she thought about it through the weeks that followed. She came to believe that if she had willed the little girl dead, it was because the wilderness had gotten to her. The woods, after all, had two faces. She had seen the bright side people talked about all the time, the chance to succeed, the seventy-five bushels of corn to an acre, the good dirt, the land for the taking. She had felt the promise.

But from the beginning she should have seen the dark side too. The forests frightened her, but she did not learn their lesson: of savage eyes within the groves, torrential floods, racing wildfire. The mark of the beast was on all these forests, along with the promise of God. And the forest had the power to turn them, all of them out here, into beasts or gods. It depended. On what? On what you let the forest do to you.

When they were in Carlisle waiting to come to the new land, Jane had seen a sorry-looking group. Tumbled together with butter churns and handplows in two-wheeled carts pulled by emaciated oxen, the women and children rode through the streets of town as their men walked ahead with heads hung low. When they stopped to get a drink at one of the cabins along the road, Jane approached a man wearing a worn hat, rough tow trousers and an English greatcoat. He said his name was Scott.

"You're going back," she said.

"Yes. But it 'twaren't because we didn't try. Three of us determined to settle as fur out as we cud go. Come from the Chesapeake, we did. M' brother's family, m'self and wife and three little uns and my nephew and his bride. We be poor folk and came with jest a few bags of meal and grain and seed corn. Some'ers we heerd that the land would provide. Anyways, the winter were harder'n usual and the snows deep as the cabin doors. We was all together, twelve in one cabin and two dogs. Tried to share things. Couldn't hunt much and the woods was wet. We didn't have no furniture 'cept log stumps.

"Then, in Janerry, the food got low. I thought mebby we could go buy some, but the thaw nivver come. We was down to gruel and a bit of venison, kids sick of the croup and stitches. My bebby wouldn't eat. That night three savages came to the door and said they was hungry. We gave 'em the last of the deer meat, what else could we do?

"After they left, the bebby squalled and squalled. Guess the wife's milk was a-dryin' up. About dawn the wife got a strange look in 'er eye and picked up the bebby and stared at 'im hard. Then she took 'im by the legs and threw 'im against the wall and dashed out his brains." Jane looked at him in horror. His eyes were fixed on the ground.

"She didn't know nuthin' after that, she still don't. That's her in the cart. We waited to plant the crop to see if she'd be better, but she ain't." In the cart sat a gaunt woman without a bonnet. Her face was wrinkled and her eyes were dull and unfixed. She looked about fifty.

Her husband said, "She were twenty-eight last month." He picked up the bucket and tin cups he had borrowed from the log house and turned to go. "We hope she'll be better back East. We got relatives in Baltimore. I guess settlin' ain't fer us."

"There are lots of 'em like that," Sally had told her sadly, after the forlorn group left. "But Janie, you can win from the woods if you put your mind to 't." Sally's mouth was firmly set. Sure she had won from the woods.

So now Jane understood. There was a choice to be made. You could either let the woods get you or not. And now, with one babe dead and many winters to face, it was about time she decided.

Chapter X

Spring came gloriously in 1755, with an unbroken succession of skunk cabbages, bluets, violets, and mayapples that unfolded their delicate beauty into June, without a cold snap to retard them. Years later, all who were in the Cumberland Valley that spring would remember the special quality it had. In the groves where nature had felled trees when "land hurricanes" came through, thumbnail-sized wild strawberries grew. Young girls gathered lapsful of dandelion greens to cook with ham hocks from the pigs in the log pens, and men returned from hunting trips laden with venison, turkey, and quail to put in the bergoo pies. There were field-clearings, and cabin-raisings and weddings from one end of the Scotch-Irish settlement to the other.

Had they only known, the peace and prosperity that seemed to pour out of the horn of plenty at the foot of the mountain ranges was really a deceptive illusion. What the Cumberland County pioneers were experiencing was really the calm before a different kind of terrible hurricane.

The sound of musket fire echoed about a clearing near Conodoguinet Creek, as it had off and on all that July morning. Laughter and the sound of horses pawing the ground followed. Twenty-year-old Ash Emison, wearing a wine-colored frock coat bought in Philadelphia, was today a bridegroom, and his friends were meeting the male relatives of the bride not far from the Emisons' home.

Ash's father, Rafe listened indulgently to the discharge of the muskets by both parties. This silly custom had started in Ireland, he knew, when the Ulstermen flaunted their guns in the face of the Irish, who were forbidden by law to have muskets after the wars. Now the Pennsylvania Scotch-Irish shot them at dances and at each house they passed during a wedding, at Christmas, and sometimes even at wakes.

Rafe Emison had begun to grow bald in the last four years, but his cool, blue eyes looked out of an unlined face, and his spare form suggested a man younger than forty-two years. He still mused on meanings. Life continued to be a Socratic logic problem to him.

There was unmistakable pride in Rafe's eyes, though, when he looked at Ash.

Ash, who could conjugate Latin and even some Greek out here at the edge of the world, Ash who knew no stranger and welcomed all, including savages when he met them, as gentlemen. Not every father was blessed with a son like Ash. Nor a daughter-in-law like Charity Hale, whose father owned the store in Carlisle, and who seemed to be as unselfish as she was beautiful. She had cared for her six younger brothers and sisters from the time she could carry them around.

Charity's father, uncles, and friends were trying to decide who would represent them in the traditional "run for the bottle," a horse race for a whiskey prize. The lucky man was a rotund cousin in a snug-fitting shirt who seemed to be eager to try his mettle. The amused Ash had nominated his best man, Bige Cherry, as irrepressible as ever, to race to the bride's house and get the bottle.

Other, mostly younger, men would gallop behind. For the first time Johnny McClure would be allowed to race with Bess at the rear of the group.

Horses grazed on the grass, which was lush and green from the abundance of rain through June and July. The older men, with nothing else to do but wait for the return of the winner, sat on a little knoll in the clearing and talked. John McClure had not seen Sam Bard for over a month. Both of them had been busy with cultivating corn and tending stock and, finally, the hay harvest.

Now, as they waited here to go into Carlisle on their way to the bride's house, John thought about the ominous events in this area since they had all come fresh from Ulster to the Bard's log home.

First, the French and Indians had destroyed the English trading post Pickawillany, in the beginning salvo of a struggle that was sure to widen. After that, the settlers at Carlisle talked of arming the town. After all, who could feel safe in western Pennsylvania? The French had seized the strategic forks of the Ohio not far away, and a young Virginian named Washington who had gone to protest the French action was forced to retreat, ignominiously. Who knew what to expect from the Indian allies of the French? Soon the English general Edward Braddock began to plan a campaign to attack the French. He set up Carlisle as a supply base for a march west that was almost nearing completion this very day.

"Bard, what do you hear in Carlisle about General Braddock today? Has he got Fort Duquesne back from the French?" John asked his friend. Bard lounged on the ground eating gingerbread from a pouch Sally had packed him. His face was as leathery as the pouch. He spent every moment he could spare from his wheel and cart business in town hunting with Ardry as far from "civilization" as he could get, beyond Shippensburg and Chambersburg in the virgin forests.

"No news is good news, John. He has two thousand good troops and he crossed the Monongahela last week. He might be whuppin' them at this moment. I hope to God it's so, because in Carlisle folks is pretty worried 'bout French or Injeean attacks."

Ash Emison drifted over, eager for anything to take his mind off the upcoming wedding festivities, which promised to be loaded with doting aunts and embarrassing moments. "People are getting hysterical. I never have believed all this talk about Indians rising up here, no matter what the French do. Our Indians have always been friendly. Big Feet and The Muskrat, for instance, are always at the store in Carlisle. They don't have anything to gain by turning against us. . ."

But his father put in from behind him, "Don't they?" He smiled enigmatically.

John raised his eyebrows and looked at Emison. Rafe was always deep as a well. Some said he was an Indian-lover, but who could tell? Probably just too smart for his own britches.

Rafe Emison continued, "Former friendship with a few individuals is not going to mean a thing once the Indians get riled enough. And they're riled at the Susquehanna Company. That bunch of mule traders finally bought the land we have here and tricked the yellow men in the process. The Indians have about come to the conclusion that the white man breaks every agreement he ever makes anyway. They are saying that if one more sour apple goes on this pile, the whole thing will fall down."

"How did you hear that?" Bard demanded. Sometimes Emison's open-minded ways irritated him. Give him a good Injeean-cussing, Injeean-hating settler every time over one of these milk-and-water Christians.

"I have Quaker friends in Philadelphia," Emison went on. "They tell me the assembly is worried about how fractious we are out here. They think we are bringing an Indian war on the frontier ourselves, and they refuse to do anything."

"I'll bet they do," Bard murmured disparagingly. "All those nice folk in Philadelphia aren't goin' to raise even an eyebrow to help us out here in the woods and the mountains. That's because the frontier is Scotch-Irish, a word that makes a Quaker turn blue."

John remained silent. He wanted the Indian troubles to go away, so he could be free to clear more fields, to build the spring house he had in mind. He took as much dry barrel business as he wanted. With the six cows he now had and the third horse he hoped he could soon afford, he would be needing a permanent barn, a German one, with the fine wood workshop he planned. And then, perhaps, even a stone house. No dream was too large in Pennsylvania.

A commotion up the path interrupted them. "Hey, ho, the bottle!" someone shouted. Bige Cherry, riding a coal-black stallion, charged into the clearing, panting, with of all people, ten-year-old Johnny McClure hot on his trail. Charity Hale's round-faced, perspiring cousin came in tiredly a few minutes later. The dapple gray mare he rode had thrown him. He managed a smile. "That shore is a fur piece down the road."

Cherry carried a jug and presented it to Ash. "Let's drink to the bride," he said. They passed the whiskey bottle around, wiping its mouth out of courtesy before they drank. John, as usual, waved the jug by without drinking. Long ago his neighbors had learned of his odd opinion about strong drink. They accepted it just as they did the fact that the Quakers used "thees and thous," or that some of the mountain people drew pictures of old women they suspected of being witches on tree stumps and shot at them.

It was a place where idiosyncrasies could be tolerated as long as they didn't touch two sacred subjects—politics and religion. Here the words were "local rights," and "Presbyterian," and woe betide the dissenter.

"Time to go find our pretty little miss," Rafe Emison said, smiling, and they mounted up for the trip to the large barn and warehouse Charity's folks owned near the Susquehanna outside Carlisle.

"They had usta lived in the store, but since they went into outfittin' they bought up land outside and built a reg'lar stone home," Bard told everyone. As they passed log houses near and through Carlisle, settlers fired muskets and hallooed; those in the party who had pistols fired back.

The two-story house, finished just this spring, was aglow with candles and branches for the ceremony. John McClure joined Ash Emison and the groom's party in the huge barn; they must not see the bride. Jane was on the lawn with the ladies. She had come in the wagon with Will and little Dan'l. Daniel McClure had been born in the spring two years ago, after a surprisingly easy birth. That day she had just finished a linsey tablecloth of small brown squares alternating with blue ones. On the light brown squares she had embroidered wool yarn designs of airy Queen Anne's lace, the beautiful wildflower she had first found in Pennsylvania. She sat at her mother's small loom almost until the very end. Then Sally Bard, who happened to be visiting, helped deliver a five-pound, squalling boy in less than an hour, thus restoring Jane's faith in motherhood.

Forever after, she associated the Queen Anne's lace tablecloth with her sunny-natured child. Using the tablecloth as a little quilt, Jane put it around her shoulders as she nursed him and later, he pulled at its fringe as he crawled about under the new cherrywood table John had made.

Now Dan'l, whose straight brown hair was coming in unevenly, giving him the look of a startled rooster, ran from person to person in the yard.

"Beetle, beetle," he shouted, holding up a fat bug he had dragged out from under a rose bush.

On a signal from the bride's father, the guests entered the house and went into the best room to await the ceremony. Jane held Dan'l on her lap and sat next to Sally Bard, plumper but ever charming. In a few moments a formal and somewhat embarrassed Bige Cherry entered the house with Ash. They approached the fireplace, where the black-clad minister waited. Bige then went up the stairs and brought down Charity, a revelation in a white linen dress and pink shawl, with a circlet of flowers in her hair. Her "best maid," Caroline Bard, pale and shaky as ever, walked by her side. "She looks lovely," Jane lied gallantly to Sally, who nodded with motherly affection.

"Let us pray," the minister began, and asked God's blessings on the new couple and home. Charity and Ash were asked to join hands. They put their gloved hands behind their backs and the best man and best maid removed the couple's right gloves so flesh could touch flesh as they made their vows.

The minister spoke. "The marriage covenant is formed," he said, looking solemnly at Ash Emison, "to provide for a defense against immorality and to regulate the passions which go unchecked by reason and religion in the lower animals. I instruct you, sir, in the name of the Lord, to head your household with the authority God has given to you, but use your authority kindly and love your wife with a whole and tender heart." Ash smiled tender-heartedly at the blooming Charity.

"Madam," he said to Charity, "it is your position to acknowledge the authority of your husband. Raise your children in the love of God and take care you practice economy." She nodded. Rings were exchanged, and after a final prayer, Ash kissed his bride long and sweetly. A huzza went up from the men in the room, who immediately formed a line to kiss the bride, as their wives gathered to kiss Ash.

It was not yet noon. Weddings in the woods of Cumberland County were conducted early, so a whopping dinner could be provided for friends and relatives who might not have seen each other for "a spell." Fried and fricasseed chicken, cabbage slaw, hot bread and muffins, apple pies with every slice arranged in "apple pie order," spoon bread, fritters, conserves, Indian succotash and beef pies all beckoned on the tables under the trees. Guests drifted out to pick up a plate and "dig in."

There were races for the young men and hopping contests in heavy meal bags for the children. Babies slept inside while their mothers sat on the long grass and talked about the itinerant candle maker who had started coming about, with his big pot and dipping wicks, and the latest scandals in the church, and how to set dye for wool.

Finally, about four o'clock, the dancing started, followed by supper under the trees and more dancing, this time in the barn. The father of the groom was the fiddler. Rafe Emison played spritely Irish and English tunes. An old man with lank, snow-white hair, whom John McClure recognized as a weaver from Dunleigh, one of Uncle's parishioners who had shipped in the famine Forties, played the reedy notes of the tin whistle. It was odd how far away Ireland seemed. All of them, washed up by life's circumstances on the shores of this forested island, shared a lifetime of experiences. But they spoke of them no more. Best not look back. When the fairies stole a child, you could never speak of it again lest both you and it turn to stone.

John McClure watched his wife, hands on her waist, dancing an Irish jig Moira taught her eons ago, oceans away. Her eyes lit up like candles. The penny whistle and the fiddle skipped and tootled along, bubbling like springs in the nearby mountains. Jane's feet, shod in Indian moccasins made at home from deerskin, flew, stamping and tapping to the rapid music. Her ruffled petticoat flipped high as she leaped to the left and to the right. She was clearly the most beautiful, exciting woman at the party; vitality and joy exuded from her like a perfumed scent. Her husband yearned to gather her up in his arms and shower kisses all over her face. But that he adored her at that moment and at many moments in his life he could not admit, especially to her. He did not know why, but it was part of a gnawing feeling inside him even in these days of plenty. Still, she "cut a fine figger," as they said out here, and everybody knew it.

It was nine o'clock. Quietly the best man and best maid and a few other friends tucked the bride and groom in bed upstairs in the loft, where they could be alone. In an hour or two friends would take up "Black Betty" the bottle and some food from the midnight supper.

The children were put down on pallets before the fire in the big house. Their parents would dance in the barn until dawn, swinging each other around to the jig-like, rolling cadences of the fiddle and whistle until they fell exhausted, collapsing into the barn stalls.

John and Jane McClure and their three sons finally returned to the cabin on the creek late the next afternoon. The party continued at the Emisons, with more feasting, drinking and dancing; but they left after noon dinner. A Scotch-Irish wedding was an exhausting business.

Less than a week later, John McClure bundled his family into the wagon to go to Shearman's Valley. He was buying a new piece of land in Johnny's name, and he needed to walk about the strip of land to prepare for the surveyor's visit. They would stay in a tent, he said, and in the wagon itself, and have a sort of a midsummer picnic time.

After her husband's work was done and she and the children had strolled the woods and meadows, Jane McClure cooked sausages and apples in a spider, and they ate off wooden trenchers in their laps, under elm trees. Then she and John put Johnny, Will, and little Dan'l under a cover in the wagon. The parents themselves stretched out in a sailcloth tent.

Later, John awakened to see an eerie three-quarters moon shining through a crack in the tent flap, throwing leafy shadows on his wife's back. As he rustled about, Jane wakened and pushed herself up on one elbow, shaking out her auburn hair. "I would walk outside a bit," she whispered.

"Canna we walk together?" he asked, struck with her beauty in the shadowy light.

She nodded. "The children will sleep. We can leave them for a while."

The two made their trips to the temporary necessary he had dug and then walked around the wagon, half-dazed in the moonlight. "It must be one in the morning," Jane murmured. She looked up at her husband and felt his happiness at being on this new land. This trip was pledge of the future, an investment. His eyes were proud as he gazed in the moonlight at the woods he would clear in a year or so. She knew he was also thinking of the sturdy house built back home, the neatly fenced fields, the cattle pens. He had turned out to be more of a farmer than most of the folk out here.

Bess and Orange whinnied gently behind the wagon, sensing that their master was near. He went briefly to reassure them. Across the road was a cultivated wheat field. The winter wheat harvest would begin any day now; for all of these valleys, it would guarantee a more bountiful winter food supply than they had ever known.

John reappeared. He took her hand, the closest he ever came to outright affection and looked into her face. Her breath was sweet, familiar. The languor he felt was replaced by desire. His hand went to her breast and her breath quickened in response. He turned and worldlessly led her down the path toward a little meadow they had seen earlier in the day. Its wild grasses and butterfly weed bent in the dappling moonlight. Now, as they walked toward it, Jane squeezed her husband's hand in anticipation.

The continuing passion she had felt for John since the earliest days, the language they learned to speak together, had grown into a late-blooming love which still surprised her. True, this man would always keep part of himself hidden. He sheltered a sensitive layer which she could not pierce, but that did not matter. She loved him now, this man who had been a stranger. The trust that began to develop when they had shared grief and which was now wrapped in a million small things, from sharing pride in Dan'l's first word to solving debt problems together, was rooting in as deeply and firmly as this grassland sod. Jane firmly believed that God had sent them that rare gift, a trustful joining. In such a joining, all pretense was gone, and the sexual expression of such trust in marriage was marvelous. Newlyweds could have no idea what it meant, Jane told herself; casual lovers were never even within reach of it.

John pulled her to him on the path and kissed her long, deeply, several times. Their steps quickened as they neared the end of the meadow overlooking the creek. His eyes quickly surveyed the grassy area beneath his feet for animals and then he sat down, pulled off his breeches, and tugged at her hand. She slipped from skirt and petticoat in an instant and lay beside him, white in the moonlight against the background of oak and laurel.

Jane's joy in the moment was heightened by the illuminated darkness, the eager, rapid breathing of the man beside her, the sweet-smelling meadow grass which was all around them. From where she lay she could see the bending branches of trees and catch glimpses of the creek below. As she turned to John's arms, she noticed that the moon shone transparently through a wisp of cloud. She kept her eyes open, on the moon, without really seeing, as she gave herself to the experience. Then, at the height of their loving, she shut her eyes tightly as her voice rose, panting like a cat's in the night. Her husband covered her mouth with his hand and exploded into his own release.

The few minutes that passed seemed an eternity. She lay almost without breathing, then slowly opened her eyes. The moon was now covered with an odd haze. But it was her husband who startled her out of her post-love stupor. His hand was still on her mouth as he lay above her, but his eyes were turned intently upwards toward the creek. Very slowly she turned her head slightly so she could see. Through the parting oak leaves, in the bright, odd light, a line of men was passing silently along the old spur path by the creek. Their bodies, glistening with oil and clad in leather leggings, were painted red with black bars and zigzags on arms and chests. Their faces were blackened, and their eyes were hollowed, black, making them look like ghouls from the grave. Her heart leapt. Her husband remained motionless for five minutes until the last of the group of about twelve had passed, then pulled himself away and silently gestured for her to get up.

In single file the husband and wife made their way back to their wagon and children, sober and without speaking. Jane's thoughts rambled aimlessly between images of fear and somewhat guilty memories of physical satisfaction. But John was able to analyze the situation coldly. He realized that at the moment of greatest human vulnerability, when his body was helpless with the fulfillment of desire, he had exposed himself and his family's future to a painted party of Delawares on the way to fight the English at Dusquesne. It was only through the grace of God that his property had not been the scene of the first massacre in the neighborhood in the Indian uprising of 1755.

The next day, after a late breakfast, John prepared to walk the premises one more time with Johnny to chart the boundary lines. Then, without warning, a horseman thundered down the road. It was Will Lytle, the Indian trader. "I ben ridin' express," he said, "to let everyone know the news. Can I have one of them donuts, young un?" He pointed at a plate Will McClure was putting back into the hamper in the wagon. Speechless with admiration, the boy turned to offer a donut to the legendary scout.

Lytle, whom the McClures had not seen since he left Carlisle three years ago, had just returned from serving as an assistant Indian agent for Pennsylvania with William Johnson in New York. As he came toward Shearman's valley, he met an express messenger who had told him a terrible story.

General Braddock had been defeated by French and Indians near Duquesne. The two armies had collided, and confusion and panic in the English ranks had caused the destruction of the British force. "Wouldn't let the men bushwhack and fight like Injeeans do, the way he orter have. Then he was wounded too. They carried him away in a litter and he died a week ago, now, I guess."

"There'll be trouble, that is for sure, and it will spread all through the Colonies. When I left Albany, Johnson was puttin' together Iroquois and mililtiamen to attack the French fort at Crown Point.

"But how could a King's general like Braddock lose?" wondered John.

"Up north they say Braddock was as weak and undecided as a new possum baby. 'Tweren't fit for fightin' out in the bush." And now, thought John, the colonists' worst fears were confirmed. The crucial Forks of the Ohio were still in French hands and the Indians thought that the English were weaklings.

Lytle was interested in the war party the McClures had seen, although John had a little trouble explaining why they had been out in the woods at such an odd hour. "Just heard or sensed something, I guess," he had muttered, avoiding his wife's embarrassed eyes.

"Probably staying away from the reg'lar paths because of the rains," Lytle said. The French, he told them, would set the Delawares, Shawnees and even the Miamis on the settlements here. The tribes would gladly "set to" to get back their hunting lands. The peace that the Cumberland Valley had known for so long was over.

Johnny and Will, who had begun packing up the tent, turned at Lytle's deadly serious tone. Young John had passed through his initial fascination with Indians and Indian fighters, but in the process had transmitted it all, magnified, to his younger brother. William thought of nothing but Shawnee warriors, tomahawks, and Delawares ominously dancing before the firelight with scalps hanging nearby on a tree.

Will was a precocious boy who constantly questioned Sam Bard and his son

Ardry for information on Indian trailmaking, legends, and fighting methods. He had inherited his mother's curly, auburn hair and the large-boned stockiness of her ancestors, but his stubborn-minded fearlessness was all McClure. He would give anything to see real Indians.

"McClure," the Indian trader was saying, directing his gaze at their father, "you ought to be thinking about joining the new regiment that's bein' formed to protect the area."

"I don't want to go to war."

"Who does? Nobody around here it seems." Lytle shook his head in disgust. "I've been around to scores of cabins and everybody is lily-livered."

"That's not the way I see it. . ." John looked at him, defiantly. "Some folks would say you're overestimatin' the danger. These few incidents aren't a war."

"I'm tellin' the truth as I see it. War is on us, and these people out here are so afraid of the government and anybody tellin' them anything, they won't even defend their own families. You've built up a fine place on the crick south and now you have this new land too. If you want some of us to defend your land, you'd better throw your lot in with the regiment. Besides, I hear you were quite a fighter in the other days. We hain't seen nothin' of that out here." Will looked at his father, wondering how he would take the taunting, but John remained calm.

"I'll think on it, long and steady. I don't have the inclination right now."

Lytle went on to tell him of preparations up near Harrisburg, where they were turning some of the houses into stockades, of plans to harvest the wheat in groups of farmers, with armed men guarding them in the rear. "We need more help from Philadelphia," he said. "Two regiments wouldn't hurt anything atall. But the damned Quakers up there won't do enough." He took tobacco out of his pocket and deposited a lump in his cheek. "The man on the land next to you here is a Quaker. Do you know him?"

John nodded. He had stopped to ask directions to the new land at the farm of Eckbert Doane, one of the few "Friends" in the area. Doane said he had moved in only a year ago and put up his cabin in two days with the help of his three strapping, adolescent sons.

"When I stopped in to give the alarm to Doane a while ago, do you know what he said to me? Do you?" Lytle seemed to grow agitated. 'Never fear, my friend,' this Quaker said. 'We can gain more by loving the Indian brethren into peace. I am having a peace feast at noon today and have asked part of a Shawnee clan to come.' Said he had been a peace commissioner in Philadelphia and knew 'em."

Jane had been trying to keep track of Dan'l, who was crawling under the wagon. "Will we be safe?" she asked.

Lytle's voice was heavy with scorn. "No Injeeans are going to come to a peace feast today. They are all powwowing up at Duquesne with the new commander, I reckon. Still, it would be wise to get on the road soon and finish up here with your gun loaded, jest in case." He got up to go, hoping to reach Shippensburg by afternoon and spend the night there.

"I'll pack a bit of lunch for you," Jane said. Her husband went to help Lytle water his horse.

In the bustle of the trader's departure and the hurried packing up, no one noticed as young Will slipped away from the wagon. No one saw him run out to the road, and swiftly, in the manner Ardry Bard had described to him as "Injeean style," steal along the edge of the path, to the farm his father had stopped at yesterday.

By the time they noticed he was missing and started a search, Will was hidden in a hollow beech tree in the woods just beyond the house, watching the Quaker sons set up sawhorse tables in the yard and their mother carry out venison pies and bowls of yellow summer squash.

Here he saw with mounting excitement four Shawnees, wearing breech cloths and with only a tuft of hair on the crowns of their heads, come into the clearing around the newly-built cabin, silently surveying the preparations for a feast. With surprise he saw the Quaker and his sons come out to welcome them, only to be rudely pushed aside.

And from his vantage point, sitting on his haunches on the rotted bark of the tree's interior he heard it all, the harsh voices of the savages saying "My brother cannot come to your love meal today. Instead he has sent me to give you a feast of hate." He heard the arrogant laughter which followed, the screams of the daughter and the mother running into the cabin, pursued by two young, painted braves, followed by sounds of furniture being overturned, a bloodcurdling wail and then silence. Then the grunts of satisfaction as scalping knives met blood and flesh and the tresses of what had been, only minutes ago two living women.

And he felt it deeply, in the pit of his stomach, as the Quaker begged for mercy on his knees (or was he praying, William did not know) and then had his skull cut in two, spilling out his brains and blood. And as the Quaker's older son ran to get the gun he kept hidden from his family in the woods, and was felled in his steps by a flying tomahawk. Unable to take his eyes off the scene, wetting his breeches, Will McClure saw the remaining sons, tall, blonde youths of thirteen and fourteen, attempting to flee and being pursued by yipping, screaming Indians, who caught them and dragged them back angrily to the clearing.

Plastering himself as tightly as he could into the hollow of the tree but still looking out of his knothole, Will could not help but see the two younger Indians finish their grisly work in the cabin. He saw them come out to help the older Indians quickly strip and stake the terrified blonde boys to trees and throw tomahawks at them until they had cut off of the hideously screaming young men, in order, their noses, parts of their cheeks, their male parts and chunks of their kneecaps, buttocks and toes, before finishing them off by burying axes deep into their skulls.

Shaking with the fear that the Indians would retreat by his tree, he watched them disappear into the woods toward the spur road, carrying the venison pies and five bloody scalps.

But when an hour later his distracted parents, drawn by the sound of far-off screams, came onto the scene and finally got around to finding him, his eyes did not see anything. It was almost a full day before he awoke from his shock and told the story they already knew from the bloody carnage in the Quaker clearing.

Chapter XI

Dust puffed from the ground inside the ramparts of Carlisle Fort as the new soldiers, carrying muskets and wearing the uniforms of the Pennsylvania regiment—green wool coat, red wool waistcoat and buckskin breeches—marched and wheeled in the sunlight in July, 1756. Lieutenant Colonel John Armstrong watched the troops drill, then beckoned to the line for John McClure to come to him.

Picking his way past a stonemason carrying mortar for a fireplace in one of the unfinished buildings, John came forward, and Armstrong told him he would meet him in a few minutes at the hickory grove beyond the gate.

McClure had come to know Armstrong well in the several months since he had joined the provincial forces. This most prominent Scotch-Irishman in the area deserved the confidence of all the settlers (and the proprietors, for that matter) who had made him a commanding officer for the forts west of the Susquehanna.

John looked up to see Armstrong come into the silent hickory grove. The colonel did not speak immediately. Instead he sat down beside John on a log and idly kicked at green hickory nuts.

"McClure, I think I've come to know you pretty well in the three months since you joined the regiment. But what I don't know is why you joined. When I first asked Lytle for prospects from the local gentry to help lead this regiment, he told me you were not a warrin' man."

"I am a beastly fightin' man when roused. I wish 'twere not so," John said with rueful honesty. "But as for goin' to war, mebbe I just wanted to wait to see if it was really important."

"You know Braddock scorned us Pennsylvania men, saying we're content to stay in our forts and let others do our fighting. But then Braddock wasn't any better in his ideas," Armstrong mused. The French and Indians raged still, in spite of all the English government and Pennsylvania could do.

"Maybe some are afraid or indifferent," John told him, "But most of us feel it's the proprietors' war. Or did feel that way. Look, we came into Carlisle for protection last summer. And things did seem to get better without our fightin'."

"So everyone came out of the forts like mice at night."

"Of course. Livin' here, in this wretched village with fifty other families, sleeping on the floors of other peoples' homes, with the fear of attacks that never come hangin' on everybody's backs, that's misery."

"But I never could understand why folk just went back out into the country, to become targets for the Indians. . ."

"I know why I went. I knew that if I didn't plant in the spring, I wouldn't eat. And the others were like me. The voice of your own land callin' you is a strong one, John."

"You knew what Contrecoeur told the Indians when he took over Fort Duquesne. To kill the settlers in any way they wanted, to torture and burn and destroy houses and cattle, until they drove us back to the sea. And they have been doing that, threatening your own wife and children and everyone in your neighborhood."

John looked up sharply at him, but Armstrong went on.

"I hope you forgive my rudeness in pressing, but this is important to me. I have a mission in mind for you, and I must know your motives."

"For truth's sake I must tell you that something within me is comin' to dislike the fighting I've done, the fighting the Scotch-Irish and all the rest of us out here seem to favor so much. And yet, there must be a time to fight, too, a day when the toes of your boots have been stomped on once too often. My day came when twenty-seven of my neighbors were killed or captured within one of these forts the government says should protect us."

"At Conococheague. We all thought it was secure," Armstrong murmured. With a look of concern he turned and scanned the slight rise beyond the hickory grove, where Carlisle's new fort was taking shape. Such as they were, the string of forts stretching from the Susquehanna west and south were the only defense posts against the marauding French and their Indian allies on this frontier.

"It was the day after Conococheague," John went on, "that I came to you and put my name on the regimental roll. If homes are to mean anything, if family life is to go on, someone must finally stand up and join the line, I guess."

"And you have been a fine soldier, John. Out here ranks have nothing to do with the English military way of doing things, you know that. They have to do with canniness and trustworthiness in dangerous circumstances." John looked into the other man's piercing black eyes and wondered what Armstrong had in mind.

The commander went on. "We may have a problem at Granville."

Fort Granville, John thought. A Government fort up north, near his land in Shearman's Valley. From the reports he had heard, it was probably not the best of the forts. But it was not as poor as the smallest ones, which were private log homes with fences built around them and possibly a lookout tower in the corner.

"I am sending you to the fort there as a special headquarters messenger. You'll have your own personal guard. The fort is commanded by Captain Edward Ward, a fine soldier. My wife Rebecca's brother, Edward Armstrong, is second-in-command. But it's the lieutenant who would be next in command that I worry about. In case of attack, should those officers be killed, he would be in charge.

At one time he was a friend of the Indians.''

"Who is it?" John asked. Armstrong looked at him, his even features thoughtful.

"John Turner. Do you know him?"

McClure started visibly. In the five years that had passed, he had not allowed himself to think of the night at Fishing Creek when he was beaten and humiliated. His response was quick and heated. "Everybody knows—of him. Why has a degenerate wastrel like Turner been made an officer?"

"Because we need him. He knows the whole area from the Juniata to Kittanning and the mountains. If anybody can tell what the Indians will do, it's Turner. And because," the man looked grim, "because I may have listened to poor counsel." Armstrong reported directly to the governor's council, which had about as much knowledge of the necessities of Indian fighting as a nest of field mice.

"I want you to stay at the fort, sending me special dispatches daily. We'll officially call you headquarters messenger, and your first message will be that I'm trying to improve communications through you. What you will really be is my eyes. Watch Turner. See how he handles himself, what he says, how he thinks and moves. I don't want to have to replace him, but if he can't handle it, I will. The situation there is unusual with the top officers often gone. There are sixty settlers in that place now, and more are coming in from the Juniata Valley and Shearman's creek every day. Their lives depend on the decisions these men make. Keep your breeches on and your powder dry." Armstrong rose from the log. "Now I have to return to training that bunch of antlerless bucks we're turning into government issue." McClure stood and the two men shook hands.

"Take a couple of hours to say goodbye to Jane and the boys," the colonel instructed him. "You march tomorrow morning. Now walk with me back up the hill and I'll tell you more about the famed Fort Granville and its officers."

The next day, McClure and three of the new soldiers brought their horses over the rutted road to Granville. Lytle is somewhere here in these mountains, John thought. Lytle had been assigned to command Fort Tuscaroras near here, but there would be no time for John to see him.

The small military party forded creeks and worked their way over hills through steamy July heat, finally reaching Fort Granville just after noon. It was as Armstrong had described it, with a square shape, a stockade wall and log buildings surrounding a small center parade square. Now its log door loomed before them. John shouted and the heavy, hinged door opened.

As they rode inside, John's thoughts centered on Turner. He dreaded confronting him, not only because the man once promised to kill him, but because he himself had also vowed revenge. The trader represented all of the ugliness he hoped to leave behind in his life. Turner was his nemesis.

Armstrong had discussed the disposition of the officers at the fort and thus given John knowledge of his enemy. Turner, it seemed, had lost no time taking care of himself and had constructed a two-roomed cabin with an upstairs for his family.

Now, outside of this "mansion," on a log long bench, sat Mary, and the three Girty boys John remembered from the bear-baiting afternoon. They looked seedier and more jaundiced than the last time he had seen them. Simon was now a stripling of fifteen, with canny eyes and dark, almost Indian-like hair. Eager for any sort of distraction in the dull routine, the three watched as the Carlisle escort party came into the compound, dismounted, and reported.

John McClure as ranking officer lined them up. He noticed out of the corner of his eye three or four little boys playing among the sacks of cornmeal and salt in front of the rude shelters that rimmed the stockade. One of them had to be Turner and Mary's two-and-a-half-year-old son, the one Armstrong had told John about in his summary.

Ward and Edward Armstrong were out of the fort, leading parties to protect settlers harvesting hay in Shearman's valley; so it was up to Turner, now sauntering out of his house, to walk the ranks and greet the headquarters messenger. His face was more pock-marked and ruddy than John remembered, and his girth had expanded like a pregnant woman's above the belted sash he wore.

A look of scornful recognition passed his face when he saw John at the rear of the slightly-crooked column. "Waal, if it ain't the b'ar's best friend Paddy Weakjaw," he drawled. "The army must be dragging its arse all over the Great Road if you're its best recruit." He laughed and slapped his side.

John looked at him stonily. "I have orders from Lieutenant Colonel Armstrong for you, Sir," he said with only the slightest emphasis on the last word. Turner perused the contents of the letter.

Glancing about at the escort party and the women and children who had ringed about to watch, the trader apparently decided to adopt a military posture. "Well, men, stow your goods in the barracks." He pointed vacantly to the long log building against the back wall of the stockade.

"As for you, McClure, step lively. You're supposed to be a soldier ain't you? I'm in command while Ward and Armstong are gone, and what I want you to do is—let me see, form a fatigue party and dig a new latrine in the far corner, thar." John glared at him, the feelings of that long-gone night returning. How could such a swine have been put in command here? Typical of all government actions, that decision was ridiculous. He hated, and always would hate, governments.

John spent the afternoon supervising the building of the outhouse and then helped two new families settle in the log shanty area. Turner had apparently told Mary of his old enemy's presence here. She found a way, when Turner was busy, to greet John civilly and ask about the spinning wheel and winder. He told her of the bedcovers and tablecloths Jane made with it, and she nodded solemnly to hear that her gift was well used. He noticed blue marks on her arms, as if a harsh handful of fingers had grasped her in anger.

At four o'clock Ward returned with his party, tired and nervous from having spent the night with an armed watch against savages. Edward Armstrong would be in tomorrow with his party, he said. It had taken longer to bring in the hay than the settlers had expected.

Having satisfactorily completed his other work for a while, John sat with a tin cup of coffee and watched the people in the fort. Although the Juniata valley lay north of his home neighborhood at Conodoguinet Creek, he knew some of these families. He recognized Tom Barlow, the farmer from the ship's crossing, who had returned with Ward's group and who now strode across the fort's yard to clap him on the shoulder. Putting out of his mind the memories of the sea trip, John listened to Barlow's story of success in wheat farming in Shearman's Valley and the birth of twin daughters. His family was settled in one of the shanties.

John briefly spoke with a few other Ulsterites and new acquaintances he had met at weddings and Presbyterian communion seasons. One of these was Ellie Randall, Sally Bard's sister. He walked over to the tripod where she was searing ox for a stew and supervising a team of women who cut up turnips and carrots. Food would be plentiful for a while, now that the harvesters had returned with vegetables and grains.

"Are you the quartermaster's assistant?" he asked her, smiling. She was at least ten years younger than Sally, less freckled and more reserved.

Steam and a very savory smell came from the bottom of the huge iron pot, as Ellie stirred with a long cooking fork. "Here the garrison lets us choose our own group chores and gives us army names. I'm Mess Captain Eleanor. I know your family is at Sally and Sam's. God save them there," she said a little sadly, "and all of us."

She poured water from a bucket into the kettle. As she added the vegetables the other women prepared, rising steam clouded about her face. Her arms, extending out of puffy sleeves of a somewhat soiled muslin dress, were pink and white. Like her sister Sally she exuded a refined sensuality, and John felt compassion for her vulnerability. Her husband had died a lonely death, ambushed on the trail west as he rode express to tell of several murders by Indians at the Great Cove to the Shearman's Creek area here. They had one little boy about three, one of the tow-headed tykes John had seen playing among the salt bags.

Now this son of Ellie's was running back and forth between his mother's skirts and a five-year-old who was tormenting him with a toy soldier over by the eating benches. "He won't let me march the man, Mama. He is bad," the little boy would say and then run to try again. Finally he sat down a little way from the pot. A large tear ran down his cheek. John, going into the line to get stew and biscuits, thought of Dan'l, who had a father and was at least in a home, even if it wasn't his own.

He let his mind rove over the families of their friends. Rafe Emison and his clan had been in Philadelphia since last fall. His fields were growing buckhorn and goldenrod, and squirrels made nests in his fireplace. The Cherrys were at Carlisle with most of the people from the lower end of Conodoguinet Creek. Charity Emison's parents had closed their store in Carlisle and fled to Lancaster, Ash and Charity and their grandaughters with them. But it would not last, it could not last. Perhaps soon everyone could cook and eat by his own fireplace. If they weren't all dead first.

At nightfall Captain Edward Ward, a bald-headed giant of a man who did not speak much, strode about with his hands behind his back observing security proceedings. He had Turner assign watch, and the night passed peaceably, with only the hoot of an occasional owl and the irritating whine of mosquitoes to break the starlit silence. John, asleep in the long, low barracks on a rope cot with a straw mattress, found it hard to believe that over a hundred people rested within this stockade. They slept like babies.

Or was it sheep? If it was, Turner was a hungry, and worse than that, stupid wolf in their fold. It was not until about two o'clock in the morning that John drifted into troubled, apprehensive dreams that were, actually, no more awful than the reality he and others on the Pennsylvania frontier in 1756 were living.

"Sally, it isn't the weedy cabbages that never get harvested. It isn't the fact I can't weave, and our clothes are worn and turned twice. Or even sneaking around with your hand over a baby's mouth so your throat doesn't get cut." Sally Bard, trying to darn by the light of a candle, nodded her head as Jane spoke. They were upstairs in the new section of the house Sam had built on to the original log house when his wheelwright business had begun to prosper.

Jane went on, "I can live with fear, even this kind of fear, after a while. But what is happening to our children? I daren't even think."

Sally was making moccasins with an awl and a piece of deerskin, and she squinted her eyes to be sure the holes she was boring were straight. "We've tried to keep a school here in town," she commented, "but how can classes go on when we are in the fort one week and t' home the next? And when families decide one night they have had enough of hearing about old folks' being hacked to pieces and pick up and go to Baltimore or Philadelphia?" She muttered to herself about not really blaming them.

Jane looked up at her sadly. Sally had changed. The bubbling, optimistic young woman of only five years ago had altered into a careworn matron whose hair was turning prematurely gray. Her home, so beautiful and welcoming, was a combination hospital and inn, with families sprawling out of the great and small rooms and children sleeping everywhere.

"Ma, is there any more barley? The soup is thin as gruel." Pale, thin Caroline, her neck sticking out of her collar like a chicken's, was, as usual, asking her mother for advice on every detail of her nursing chores. Next door, Jane knew, Ardry Bard skulked about his work in his father's wheelwright shop. He was trying to find a way to convince Sam that he should be allowed to join the militia and "go kill me some Injeeans." Only little Timothy, born to Sally the same year Dan'l came, seemed carefree.

Dan'l. Jane looked out the door at him, playing shinny with Tim, whose carrot-red hair was a bright shock against the oak trees in the yard. Dan'l's own straight, brown hair tried to escape from under a red silk handkerchief like Ardry's. He was dressed like all the men out here, in linen shirt, Indian blanket, leggings, and moccasins.

Johnny McClure had gotten the two boys little crooked sticks and was teaching them to push a large walnut around. "I can get it over the line," Dan'l said, excitedly, laughing and shoving his brother's hand away from the stick. Johnny retired, a slow smile on his face at the fierce independence of this brother he adored.

Johnny had grown old before his time, an eleven-year-old who handled a musket like an expert and who had watched the burying of massacred children his own age near Harrisburg. As a child he had been unusally talkative. Now he often kept his thoughts to himself, and when he did communicate, it was in the taciturn Scotch-Irish dialect of the frontier. He was already trying to puzzle out whether it was true, as the preacher said, that it was God's will that so many die. This week he thought not.

Jane had passed all the children she knew closely through her mind and hovered over all the strange warpings the Indian wars had brought to them. Now she thought of Will, and her heart rose a bit. Surely he was better.

Almost a year had passed now. Sally had asked her about it just today. She told her, "At first, Will went about silent during the day and screamed half of the night. Then he started movin' and he didn't stop for six months. He ran all over the cabin or fields, talkin' constantly, until his brothers were so bothered they screamed too. He teased, he laughed, he tore pillows apart."

"What did you do?" Sally had asked sympathetically.

"We didn't know whether to whale him or hold him on our laps and we did a good deal of both. Sally, the worst part was that I couldn't get to him. He was stockaded by fear. But there was one word that never, ever, passed his lips. We picked him up out of his hollow tree, at the edge of the Quaker's farm and he whispered one word, 'Injeeans.' We never heard him say, or even seem to notice the word again."

Sally nodded. "I know, Janie. If I say to him, 'Stay within hailing distance of this house. We have heard Indians were seen,' Will looks like he never heard."

Jane said sadly, "When we first came into Carlisle, I saw him walkin' back through the dusk with some of the little ones after a game of blindman's bluff, and they began talkin' like children do of 'Injeeans.' He just broke right off from 'em, whistlin' his own little tune."

Recently, Jane told herself, it had been much, much better. In the last few weeks he seemed quieter, almost too quiet. But when he did speak, his conversation was more like an eight-year-old boy's should be, of fishing with bent pins, and rolling barrel hoops and walking on stilts.

Perhaps soon he would even begin to play with his toy musket at Indians and King's soldiers. When he did that, she would know he was healed. Still, today she looked at her muscular, curly-headed son with the coal-black, veiled eyes as he watched the younger boys play, and her heart ached that his own youth had been so rudely snatched from him.

July 30, 1756 was a day that would be singularly remembered in Pennsylvania history. It began like any other day in the recent past for John McClure.

Military routine still prevailed at Fort Granville, in spite of the tenseness that surrounded it. Tired men and women went about the cooking, cleaning, and soldiering duties, trying to maintain composure and discipline.

But the truth was that they feared the worst—the return of over a hundred Delawares and Shawnees bent on taking scalps. A week ago, on July 22, a group of Frenchmen and Indians from Fort Duquesne stood outside the walls of the fort demanding that its garrison come out and fight. After the fort had refused, they left in disgust. Who knew when, and if, they would return.

John was up by six o'clock. No dispatches were going out at present, and even if there were, there was nothing to say. Nevertheless, he wanted to be up early to continue his job of observing and recording for Armstrong.

He took out the travelling dispatch kit he carried and recorded: "At six o'clock, the night guard went off the continuous watch they have been holding in the blockhouse. Settlers hold guard along with militiamen. At seven a breakfast of mush and molasses from the rapidly declining stores was served in the parade area."

John put away his leather writing packet. The morning routine was beginning in the dusty yard, and he was a part of it. It had been over a week since the savages left, and some degree of security was assumed. So the few horses and cows had been taken outside the walls again to range inside the pallisado wall.

Turner had ordered John to supervise the most dangerous job in the stockade—the care of the stock outside. It was a part of his ongoing campaign of quiet torment. The second day after the Carlisle troops had arrived, as John sat cleaning his gun outside the barracks, Turner had casually come over. Out of the corner of his mouth he whispered, just loud enough for John's ears, "I tole you I would get you someday, friend o' the b'ar. While I'm pickin' my opportunity, I'm gonna be sure you get your fair share o' the best jobs. See to 't you do 'em well."

"You cur, this is a military installation, and I'm a sergeant under Lieutenant Colonel Armstrong's direct command. I'm going to register a protest," McClure said, softly. He did not want any of the troops, particularly those who knew Armstrong well, to become aware of the special relationship he had with Turner. He was ashamed of it.

"And who's to know or hear tell of what I do, dumbox. You going to tell Ward? That milksop Edward Armstrong? By the time you tell your colonel and he goes through 'military procedure' this yere crisis'll be over, and I'll be out of this man's army." And so he detailed John to supervise night guard, to head details to bury refuse and offal, to rebuild the pens the Indians destroyed on their defiant visit outside the walls. And, after the animal pen was rebuilt, to care for the stock outside the protection of the wall.

This morning John McClure exited from the fort gate, passing the entrenchment ditch. A party being led by the gaunt figure of the commander of the fort, Captain Ward, was marching out at the same time. Ward was going to harvest the wheat that was bending heavy in Shearman's valley. Armed settlers, among them Barlow, wearing blankets and leggings, marched side by side with a guard of men from the regiment, clad in green coats with bright-red facing. As John headed for the cattle pens, he watched the troops disappear in the distance down a road through the trees towards the south, leaving a small cloud of dust that gradually filtered onto the hot road.

They would be gone only a couple of days. The fourteen men left in the garrison would have to fare the best they could in defending the fort. John had a sense of unease about their leaving, and yet things could have been worse.

First, it was not Turner, but Edward Armstrong, who commanded. Armstrong was a quiet man in his early forties who was the brother of Lieutenant Colonel John Armstrong's wife Rebecca. Though he was not particularly forceful, he was brave and diligent.

Then, the possibility that the Indians would return, though frightening to the settlers, was not really strong. The settlers had over-reacted to the Indian threat from the very beginning of this crisis. Surely Neyon de Villiers, the commandant of Fort Duquesne, had better things to do than harass a group of settlers in a fairly well-set fort. He was probably back at the forks of the Ohio by now. So the talk in the fort ran, anyway.

As John watered the horses and cattle, he mulled over his own analysis of the fort's setting. It certainly commanded a good view of the main road to the southern forts, and it had stout buildings within its stockade. It could provide for more settlers than the unfinished fort at Carlisle.

But why in the name of God did they put it right on this ravine above the roiling Juniata River? It was impossible to guard. That cliff dropped straight off almost directly behind the fort's walls and provided a difficult, but possible, access from the riverbank. Even Turner had cursed the fort's vulnerability. He may have been beastly, but he wasn't always wrong.

John closed the gate of the stock pen and began to walk back toward the fort. There it was, stalwart against the cloudy sky, yet dwarfed, really, by the groves of virgin timber behind it.

This fort and the road through the hills to Carlisle represented the only tokens that civilization existed at all in these deep woods. The other farms, cabins, and forts, hundreds, perhaps thousands of them were out there; but looking at this outpost he felt no certainty of their existence. He could not see a single human soul out here.

As he strode along through the oppressive heat of early morning, John experienced the peculiar loneliness and futility he felt from time to time since he had come from Ireland. The past week had been hellish, and he was weary from the constant tension. Suddenly he thought of Uncle George, who had wanted so much for him.

What had he done with his life? His plans of finding fortune had all gone awry, scuttled by Indian troubles. Worse yet, he was still steeped in anger and bitterness. "Here I am, Uncle," he thought ironically, "your bonny boy, child of your brother and in many ways just as much of a failure as he. Feeding the cows and digging the slop pits while a man I hate eats at my heart in a savage wilderness. Followed by the curse of Cain, unable to break it no matter what I do. Oh God, if you're there, do you care at all?"

He neared the fort gate, which was now shut; he would need to go up the ladder and pull it over after him. Something—was it the sound of a branch being snapped, or the sudden silence of the birds—made him stop for a moment and turn toward the river. The sun poked its way through the clouds, and a slight breeze fanned the large poplar leaves at the edge of the clearing. But there was more. There was something out there.

It took less than ten seconds for him to get to the ladder and only a few more to scramble up it, dropping the bucket with a clatter on the hard ground below. Not twenty-five yards behind him came hallooing Indians and dirty, unshaven Frenchmen brandishing muskets in their hands high above their heads. They had returned and waited, patiently, until the soldiers left the gates.

The day and the night which followed were an excruciating mish-mash of blood, sweat and the rich, acrid smell of gunpowder. And heat: the heat of the sun which blazed down on John McClure's head as he stood and fired through holes in the fence all day. Then flashes of heat as muskets misfired toward evening just as the Indians, luckily, fell back for the night. Finally, at dawn, the heat of burning wood as the yellow men scaled the precipice directly behind the fort and set fire to the stockade.

John McClure wearily stood shooting through a crack, near Edward Armstrong. He continued the routine of opening a cartridge with his teeth, tamping a little powder into the pan, putting the rest of the contents down the muzzle and ramming the shot home, and then pulling the trigger to let the flint do its work. The taste of gunpowder was bitter in his mouth, his lips parched. Desperately he aimed his fire at the gaps developing in the burning wall to keep Indians from rushing through them. Bullets whistled beside him; Armstrong shouted to him that private Bruce, standing just on the other side of him, had taken a ball in the throat.

Sad, thought John. Luke Bruce was one of the "antlerless deer" he helped train and bring out from Carlisle. He turned his head for a fraction of a second to look at Armstrong and saw the other man's mouth grow slack and his eyes glaze. The lieutenant plummeted straight backwards and only as he lay, face up, did blood start to spurt from a hole in his forehead. With a sigh, he died.

Turner came up from the other side of the fort. "I'm in command now," he said. "Stay at the wall," he added, roughly, to McClure. The firing from the fort now grew more desperate, as the Indians and Frenchmen pressed forward around the wall. There were over a hundred of them. It would not be long. Then there was a strange lull as the Indians stopped their shooting and regrouped. A voice, heavy with the inflection of a foreigner, rang out, promising that all would be spared if the fort surrendered. They had no desire for anyone's death. It was blandishing, reasonable, and completely false in tone, John thought.

But to his surprise, Turner was striding towards the gate. He was going to surrender. "Don't do it, Turner," John and some of the others protested.

"Shut your blabbin' mouths. I'm not a-gonna git my family kilt," Turner shouted and swung open the gates. Wildly grimacing and shouting Indians and Frenchman poured in.

As he was pulled by rough hands off the wall and spun around, John's glance fell on the ground, at the corpses of Armstrong and Private Bruce. And behind them at the limp body of Sally Bard's pretty sister.

In the last volley, she must have been hit with a bullet in the chest. Now, barely alive, yet still moaning, she was being scalped of her blonde tresses by a squatting Delaware in a breechcloth. "Pretty dolly," he said, holding her still with one hand and making his knife work with the other. He grinned darkly under his war paint. Her screaming little boy was carried off by an Indian wearing a shirt of fine French cambric. Other arms roughly pushed Tom Barlow, his wife and children toward the center yard.

John McClure struggled to escape, but the hands that held him were far too many and too strong. As his senses cleared one fact stood out. He was alive, when many were dead. But he was a captive of the Indians, and now he grimly wished he had died on the wall with Armstrong. What awaited him would probably be worse than getting your thought quickly snuffed out by a bullet in the brain. Far worse.

Chapter XII

Kittanning. A cluster of Indian-made log cabins on a rise above the Allegheny River. Smoke rose slowly from fires where meat and fish were being salted for the winter. Children played games with stones and sticks by a clearing where horses grazed. But to the party of white men picking their toilsome, painful way over rocky mountain paths through the wilderness, the word Kittanning meant the prospect of hell. It was one hundred miles beyond the white man's pale, and Indians ruled it as they liked.

And what they generally liked at this fearful period in history was to enslave and mock the white race which threatened to exterminate them, particularly testing the manhood of anyone unlucky enough to fall into their hands with some of the most excruciating tortures the mind of man has ever devised.

The Delawares were not usually torturers, leaving that to their "less civilized" brothers of the North, but in the inflamed days of the French and Indian war, flaying, roasting, and impaling were only the milder forms of their cruelty. The torturing the Indians did was not much different from violence in Europe at the time, but that was small consolation to those who must face their fate here at Kittanning in a matter of hours.

John McClure, with a huge bag of cornmeal on his back, inched his way across shaling, uphill paths, forded ice-cold streams, and tripped on the roots of trees, as the captive party agonized forward through August rains. The white men stumbled and staggered but did not dare stop. A few days back one soldier, worn out from the fighting and a wound, had faltered at the top of one of the peaks and the Indians shot and scalped him before the eyes of the captives. The trip was particularly hard on the few older children who marched with the party; the Indians had sent the smallest ones to Duquesne.

One, or possibly two, John was not sure how many, soldiers had slipped away and escaped; but he himself had no energy to try. He had eaten only a little wild game, jerked beef, and blackberries each of the days since they had marched away from the devastation of Fort Granville, and his strength was enough only to get over the next mountain. Now, as the sun set, the Indians indicated they would make camp among clumps of hemlock trees and maples with leaves just beginning to show tinges of yellow and red.

John had been carrying his burden through the highest mountains he ever saw. His muscles screamed in pain and his feet were masses of blisters, but at least the strong military issue shoes were still holding up. Some in the party were marching with bloody, bare feet.

His only consolation was that Turner was worse off than he was. The Indians were forcing the former Granville lieutenant to carry one hundred fifty pounds of gunpowder up these slippery paths, and he was suffering. The burden shifted unpredictably, throwing him off balance. Now and again his eyes passed over John with cold hatred. Nothing, thought John, was too hard for the pig who had made his own life miserable for over three weeks and who had sealed their doom by opening the gates of that stockade without batting an eye.

Someone grunted at him, and John began to gather sticks for the fire. As if he did not have enough misery, there was this business of the Indian. Beside him, through all these rocky, uphill paths for almost a week now, strode the stoical figure of a Delaware Indian. His face was young but weathered. In the middle of his chin was a small, tufted beard, a thing so unusual among the yellow men that it marked him as a singular figure. At Fort Granville this Lone Stag picked John McClure out as a special captive slave, gesturing to him to pick up the cornmeal and his own small pack of ammunition and supplies. The Indian dogged his steps ever since. Or was it that John was being forced to dog his; he couldn't tell, the Indian walked so silently and smoothly beside him.

Now Lone Stag indicated how the fire was to be made, gesturing towards some cottonwood fluff and dry weeds that lay just off the path. The Indian did not speak as John dressed and cooked a squirrel he had snared in the brush.

The rain stopped. From twenty paces in front of them and up a little rise, came the clatter of cookery, the smell of smoke. Lone Stag seemed to make camp by himself. John's clothing was sopping and heavy, and he pulled his regimental coat and fine linen shirt off to hang them on a stick before the fire. The Indian looked curiously at the mane of black hair on his servant's chest. "You have much hair, too" he said. It was the first thing outside of a command he had said to John all this walk.

"I thought Indians had no body hair," John ventured.

"Little on body, some on face. But they use. . ." he groped for the word and then put his fingers together to indicate tweezers pulling out hairs on his chin.

"But I am different," he went on. "My father was from south of the Bay of the Crabs, Chesapeake, where summer stays long and snow does not visit some years. He had much hair." Some early white trapper was probably responsible for that, John thought wryly. They sat watching the fire lick the dripping carcass of the squirrel, which John was turning on the spit.

"Where did you get the name Lone Stag?" He knew Indians went through ceremonies when they reached young manhood, and the rites had something to do with their names.

"I went into the woods with no food and sat alone on a rock near Shamokin. I am supposed to see the sights the Manittos give, mysteries of the high clouds and heavens. But I could not seem to leave the earth. Day one, not in a dream, I see small animals and even a bear and they call to me as friend. By setting of the sun my stomach calls to them."

"Day two I see only hunger. It stands out like a cry of a wolf in the night. I know it is not right of me to think so much of food; it shows my spirit puny, but I cannot stop. I see maize cakes fried on hot stones before my eyes. On the clouds, I see deer in a pot with herbs. Day three I sleep a lot. It turns cold and I shake much. But at the time of the setting of the sun I wake. Before me, in the air, is a buck of eight antler prongs, aged as the stars. It speaks to me, and I listen, as to the voice of Manitto."

" 'As I,' said the stag, 'who visit the herd but to mate and warn of danger, so are you, a lone deer. You are a wanderer to the tribe of Leni Lenapi and do not think as other braves here do. Your father came from the land of the hanging moss, and you are full of the wisdom of the stranger, as full as the clouds are of rain in midsummer. You will live always at the edge of the clearing, and you will take no wife of this people. Your counsel will be valued, but it may not always be pleasant to the ears. Chiefs will honor you, war parties will march on your advice. As you have come in like the lone stag to the herd, thus some day you will go out. Wear the beard tuft as I wear the antler crown of many years, as the mark of the Chosen of Manitto—wiseman of nature.' "

John took the squirrel off the spit and gave it to Indian, and he, in turn, broke off a piece of the smoking meat and offered to share. "They say you are the enemy of the stupid officer who gave up his fort as a present to his foe. You oppose him. For this piece of wisdom and others I have chosen you for the servant of the Lone Stag." He spoke no more all evening.

The next day was the most rugged of all. They were to traverse the final slope of the Alleghenies and then camp at the pass which would lead them to the road to Kittanning. Cold, drizzling rain continued to fall; blustery winds spat it into their faces. The cornmeal was picking up moisture. Two of the younger soldiers faltered and fainted; the Indians compelled Tom Barlow and another exhausted man to sling them over their shoulders and continue stumbling along.

I canna go on, John thought around noon, choked and gasping for breath. But the picture of his wife and children, particularly Dan'l, came into his mind, and he found he could take one more step, then another. He felt Jane's eyes on him, through sixty miles of space. She knows, he thought. It is the second sight her mother always spoke of.

Numbness set in and he seemed to lift out of his body. He felt he was watching himself walk from a peak high above the ridge. Even the Indians seemed weary.

They made camp early. One more night at most would see them into Kittanning. Increasingly, John knew, the white men's thoughts were on what would await them in the Indian camp, although in the brief syllables they exchanged, they did not speak of it. The Indians had devised the ultimate punishment for those who stole their land and lives. Horrible, prolonged torture. What could be worse for men? To have to face excruciating pain, to know you would have no control over what you did, to feel your very manhood eking out not only through the blood of your veins, but also through the cowardly, whining screams of your throat, like a year-old girl baby. Must not think of it, John told himself. Perhaps they will make me a slave.

Lone Stag, he noticed, was walking with a limp, and when his breech cloth fell aside, John could see the reason, a huge, swollen carbuncle as big as a handspan on his thigh. As their campfire began to sputter with the wet wood that was all John could find, he said to the Indian, "You have a bad boil on your leg. I can rid you of it." The Indian leaned toward him menacingly.

"It causes me no pain I cannot bear. What, am I to be a cub of a child to complain of a pimple? And if it did hurt," he shrugged, "I can get the doctor to rid me of the evil when I get to the village or the old women to put a poultice on me."

With a low voice which showed more indifference than he felt, John said, "It is not an evil spirit but evil matter that causes you trouble. You dare not wait even one day with that boil. I have wisdom from the fathers to cut it out in the wink of an eye, and you will walk straight as an ash sapling." Long Stag savagely cuffed John's mouth and wrapped himself in a blanket, then turned and sat with his back to him. John noticed how much he was favoring the swollen thigh; it must feel as if a hot iron was on the leg.

As John slept fitfully on the hard ground without a cover on that chilly night, he was shaken awake. Fearful, as he had been many times in the last week, that this was his last moment, he looked up into the gleaming eyes of the Indian in the clearing, where a half moon had now risen.

"You, MacLooer. You say with your fathers' knowledge you can rid me of the hot, hard bump. Do it now."

John looked past him. "I will need the sharpest blade you have."

Lone Stag's eyes caught John's for a long moment, then seeming to decide something, the Indian went to his pack and brought out a long knife. Leaning on the ground on one elbow, he pulled up his breech cloth. As John had suspected, angry lines of red were beginning to spread out from the six-inch swelling.

"Your blood is beginning to poison," he said to the Indian. John stuck the knife in the fire before he cut, as he had seen Uncle do in Irish cottages, using the lore of Alexander McClure, his physician father. "You will feel an awful pain and then one worse as I drive the evil matter out of the leg." Lone Stag remained impassive.

Quickly John made two cross-cuts. Red-and-yellow-tinged pus shot almost three feet into the embers of the campfire. John leaned further over the head of the carbuncle and then applied pressure to purge the wound. The process took almost five minutes, but the Indian emitted no cry.

His job finished and the swelling on the leg beginning to go down, John rinsed the knife with water. Wiping it on leaves, he gave it back to Lone Stag and then stared at the Indian through the shadows as he repacked his small pack, putting the knife alongside kettle, bowl, spoons, and an extra piece of deerskin for moccasins.

"I might have put that thing through your gut. Why did you trust me?" he asked.

The Indian was sitting deliberately on the thigh that had just been cut. "Your face is as open as a cloudless day. It has trustworthiness written on it," he said. "Still. . ." He unclasped his hand to show a short, very sharp blade in the palm and bared his teeth in what John thought must be a smile. "The racoon who submits to children as a pet in the village, retains yet his fangs, lest they should test him too much," he said. Then, sighing, he stretched out to sleep.

From the slope of the foothills above the river, McClure and the other captives viewed Kittanning. Horses and women, looking like toy Indian figures in the river valley below, were bringing in corn, harvesting the nearby fields. Weary almost beyond caring and dizzy from a fever which had begun just before dawn, John watched the scene without emotion. Tom Barlow whispered, "It will be over one way or another soon."

Yes, John thought, knowing one's fate was better than not knowing. Captivity as an Indian slave, with possible rescue or exchange, or death by torture. All on a toss of the strumpet Fortune's penny.

The sight of their destination gave new tongues to the rest of the captives. Barlow wondered aloud to one of the young regimental soldiers about his wife's whereabouts at this moment. Anne Barlow and their twins were among the captives taken to Duquesne; John felt a pang for him, and for Ellie Randall's little boy, who was with them. Maybe it was better Ellie fell at the wall. The tortures women had to endure last year after Braddock's defeat were terrible indeed.

Several of the men and children in the group began to hasten to the camp, keeping up with the Indians who were heading for home stable. A few remained at the rear of the group, distant and depressed. Of these Turner was the most obvious. Lone Stag, walking as always beside John in the middle of the group, said, "The face of your cowardly chief is as the water of the dark swamp in my father's homeland. Perhaps he knows soon he will be in the land of the death island."

"And so will we all," John commented in a low voice.

"Perhaps. But he may swim over first. Kittanning is the homeland of the Indian Tewea, Captain Jacobs. Turner killed Tewea's friend Girty before his eyes, and Tewea did not see justice done. Turner has come, a murderer, to the very cooking fire of the man who owes him revenge, and Indians do not forget."

They entered the village. Women wearing shirts with shining silver brooches on them and naked children gathered around them clucking, like hens around the farmer's wife. Turner held back, but it was not long until a tall, swarthy Indian fixed his eye on him. Captain Jacobs, the most brutal and feared man on the entire frontier, came forward with an oak cudgel and began brutally whacking John Turner about the face and head.

Good, thought John, not very enthusiastically. That's just about right. One stroke for the bear, one for the thrashing, two for the privies. Several braves seized Turner, at Captain Jacobs' command and carried him away, screaming, toward an area at the center of the village. Mocking Indian youths kicked and prodded the rest of the disheartened prisoners to the front of the longhouse, and women took the young boys to the lodges to be slaves. John did not allow himself to think of what would come next. In the fever that seemed to be growing on him, he experienced that detached, light-headed sensation he felt on the path the day before, when his feelings were as numb as his feet, and he seemed to float above the scene.

He lost track of Turner as the Indians began tying the captives to young beech trees outside one of the cabins. Strong arms bound him tightly with a hempen strap. All around were mocking faces. Children and women shouted insults in shrill voices, like gobbling turkeys.

A huge Indian woman, with a fringed tablecloth over her shoulders and only two of her upper teeth, kicked his shins until he thought he must scream. Still, somehow he remained silent. His head swam. Must stay awake he thought; 'twould be a sign of weakness to faint out here on this stake.

But a strange lethargy seized him. Why bother about fainting now or later, in the torture? Nothing mattered. They would all be dead in a few hours. Good and evil. Their inmost souls would be bared, they would become instruments for the expression of pain. They would cry without a shred of dignity, forget duty and honor and church and all, except to scream their lives out. The only meaning at the end of horrible torture would be to see Turner suffer more than he did. Surely, he laughed ruefully and a little wildly, this was the true meaning of life. He had tried to be upright, to even scores with evil men, to spit in the eye of injustice and it had come to this.

He was suddenly unbound, along with Barlow and two of the older men. They were taken near the stake where now Turner was screaming shrilly, near a huge, crackling fire. They were told to sit off to the side of the clearing, each in front of a tree but not bound. Suddenly Lone Stag was by his side. "You are to watch the death at close range as a favor for enduring well on the trail." John leaned back against the trunk of his tree. He dared not look at Barlow.

Now the warriors grabbed up their muskets and went to the fire. As Turner's eyes bulged, they stuck the musket barrels into the flames until they were red hot, then, chortling, ran to the trader and plunged the barrels into his body. His agonized screams, repeated and piercing, filled the clearing, and the smell of singed flesh drifted about. Bile crept into John's mouth; he swallowed it.

There was a moment of quiet as the Indians spoke together. Turner whimpered in pain. Then a group of Indian women ran to Turner, and one of them cut off his nose. She bore this bleeding monstrosity about showing it to the assembled crowd. Indians howled in laughter, but John was aware that Lone Stag was silent, impassive. Another group of warriors approached Turner. Again the bile came into John's throat. Somehow the anticipation of what horrid thing would happen next was as bad as the thing itself.

One young Indian, taller than the rest, sauntered up and, picking up the trader's foot, cut off his big toe halfway up. In a few minutes another Indian approached and quickly sliced off a second toe, all the way this time. A grisly train of Indians came forward one at a time, timing themselves dramatically, to cut off all the white man's toes. Turner's screams became hoarse.

John's head swam; the screams seemed very far away. Suddenly he felt as if he must say something to the Indian beside him and he told him, through the haze that was enveloping him, "I cannot, will not see this, in the name of

God. Do you understand?'' Then he slumped against his tree unconscious.

Lone Stag looked at him with a long, sharp glance and said, very softly, ''For you, my friend, Manitto may have granted that mercy. And who am I to disturb the sleep sent by the god?''

John McClure stood again on a path. All about him stretched the undulating, lifeless hills of a desert like the ones in the Araby books. From the corner of his eye he saw the last of the large oval portraits he had noticed before; and he noted with a transient flash of gratitude that it was of Dan'l, asleep in Sam and Sally's house in Carlisle, with his thumb in his mouth and his fingers over his blue coverlet. Quickly John stepped off the path and headed toward the first of the range of dune-like hills. Something was over it that he should see, he was sure of it.

With the now-familiar sands tugging at his feet, he passed over the crest of the hill and stood in Dunleigh. Joy exploded like a soap bubble in him; he looked down to see he wore the breeches of a schoolboy. Yes, it was the village all right. There was Sandy's cooperage shop, Gentry Row. He made up his mind suddenly, irrationally, more in a forward movement than a conscious thought. He would go see Widow Stark in her house near the inn.

He was suddenly aware of breathing behind him. Eyes in the back of his head seemed to see a pulsating shape. It was the ghost of earlier recurring dreams, Brohgan the Dispossessed, behind him. Even before he could feel fright, it spoke.

''Sure you gave me a Divil of a time, McClure the Fist. You thought I was after ye that other time, din' ye? Say, now ye better know I'm a friendly spirit.'' He glowed like a holy light and lit up the landscape on the road to Widow Stark's. It was odd. Brohgan was speaking Gaelic. John recognized its sound; and he understood him, even though he knew only a few words of the language.

''You don't look the same,'' John mused. It was true. In the former dream Brohgan seemed to be a long, undulating dragon. Now he was a worm, with two little arms, more like flippers, emerging from near the pockets of a purple waistcoat. John, peering to see what the flippers held, discerned a title of a book. It was Uncle's copy of *Pilgrim's Progress*. But that was at home, the voice of rationality that sometimes appears in dreams said. They did not have time to get it before they left for Carlisle. Before his eyes it turned into the cooperage account book. He could see the page. Six fir barrels, herring. Twenty shillings, it said. The smell of fish hung in the air.

''Come along lad, I have somethin' to show ye.''

It seemed perfectly natural for John to trip along beside the red, worm-like form of Brohgan to Widow Stark's. Anticipation filled him as he stood before the knocker on the door.

''After ye, lad,'' Brohgan said, his little flipper opening the door.

But inside John did not see the settee, gun rack, and secretary desk of the great room he knew, rather the gloomy interior of a large open space. With a feeling of fright he turned. Both Brohgan and the door had disappeared.

An outdoor scene was before him. Lightning flashed over a lagoon with dark blue and orange waters in the stormy setting of the sun. As his eyes grew accustomed to the gloom, he picked out a wooden house with a verandah around its upper story. He was conscious of odors, decaying animal flesh and vegetation, the sharp, salty smell of seaweed on sand, heavy, sweet odors with spicy overtones. Curious, he walked toward a group of people by the lagoon.

They stood near a large shed which housed a piece of machinery with levers, cranks, and handles for pressing sugar cane. Brohgan had brought him to the Indies. Was it Jamaica? The faces of the crowd were pepper-and-salt, white and several shades of black; but the man bound to a post at the center of the crowd's circle was jet-black and naked. He was taller than any man John had ever seen. John looked into the man's dark, angry eyes and suddenly, in the instant transmogrification of a dream, he was the man.

The crowd murmured things he could not understand. He felt the harshness of the ropes cutting into his naked back and arms. "Why am I bound?" he wondered. Behind him the sugar cane machine began to work without any human hands. Whump, whump, it beat out its brutal rhythm.

"What have I done to be punished?" McClure-slave said, and the crowd responded by beginning an eerie African chant. A white man stepped forward. His face was hidden by the huge planter's hat he wore, but the skin of his arms was greenish-yellow from the ravishes of malaria. "Lay on fifteen stripes," he ordered. His voice, grim with hatred, was vaguely familiar.

John's heart leapt in fright. He looked down at the sweat on his black chest, at the huge male organ, big as a rolling pin, lying limply above his bent knees.

A meek voice came from the crowd. "MacKenzie—ah—you know it's against the laws now to flog them naked." As if in answer to this reproach the first stripe bit across McClure-slave's back with white-hot fire. He cried out as a second descended and turned his head to see his tormentor. In a flash of lightning he recognized beneath the straw hat the face of the Derry government clerk he had tried to kill when he was eighteen. Why hadn't he known him at first?

"I demand to know why I am here," he shouted, just as the third stroke was laid across his back like a strip of molten metal. The scene dissolved, the door to Widow Stark's opened, and he and Brohgan went through it onto the deserted streets of Dunleigh.

"That was horrid, you little beast," John said. "What is goin' to happen next?"

"I dunno, it's your dream." Brohgan smiled insolently. There it was again— the Gaelic.

The morning star had risen, and before them stood the cooperage shop. John ran toward it. "Sandy, Sandy, are you there? Are you still alive after all these years, old man?"

He raced to the wide, open doors at the rear of the shop, eager to see the familiar firepit where oak was charred, the piles of stave wood in the rear. But, as before, as soon as he entered some sort of curtain closed.

This time he was part of a throng standing at the side of a narrow, dirty street At the end of the street he caught glimpses of bright-blue water. It was some sort of a bay or harbor. Coffee-colored men and women were watching—what?

A military parade. Down the street marched brown men in short trousers and turbans, mounted English dragoons and horses drawing field pieces. Riding in the rear on a splendid white stallion was a general in full military uniform, with ruffled cuffs and a cocked hat.

"Lord Clive," John murmured, with that miraculous knowledge this dream seemed to provide. The troops vanished up the road in thick, orange clouds of dust. This time Brohgan had not disappeared but pulsated unseen by the others at his side. "Ah, lad, they're on their way to punish the Siraj-ud-daula for throwing sixty white men in a dungeon hole to die on a hot night in Calcutta. They will win it all from the natives and the French in a matter of months. Soon India will be ours. Think of it, yours and mine. Well, we're part of the British Empire, ain't we?"

An odd smile came to the twisted mug that was Brohgan's mouth. "All of those joowels and maharajas and Brahmins. But lad. . ." he had a look of mock concern on his wizened face ". . .you ain't yourself, now are ye?" In an instant he disappeared.

As before, a metamorphosis occurred. John looked down to see that he had breasts and the small, thin form of a girl. Soon McClure-girl found herself shoved down a street to a funeral pyre. The crowd in the street expected her to mount the pyre and be burned, along with a dead man laid out on top. In panic McClure-girl screamed as relatives lit a flaming brand to the pile of logs. Just as she felt searing heat, McClure-girl saw the shadow of Lord Clive looming above the pyre and called to him, "Shoot, I pray you, sir. Kill me now so I do not have to endure the flames."

Clive's shadow seemed to hesitate a moment, then disappeared. McClure-girl was trapped in a horrible death, which would consume her by degrees, singeing, raising blisters, then burning the skin from off her very bones while her heart continued to beat, all in the slowest and most excruciating manner. She screamed and screamed to drown out the mounting pain.

Then, suddenly, without any fading this time, John McClure stood again on the road a mile or two outside Dunleigh, with Brohgan. It was someplace he had been many times before, was it in this dream or another? It was Moira's cottage.

The morning star was setting; dawn was not far off. In the gradually increasing glow of coming light John could see the familiar sights of the Irish farm. But everything was all wrong. Instead of flax and oats in well-tended fields, ugly six-foot thistles grew. Geese, long since dead, lay about the barnyard. It was dry, and the dryness seemed to affect his throat, so he could not speak. Out of the well shades, skeletons, rose, bringing with them the smell of the grave. They flitted past him to the hills of the West. He ran for the door, humorless laughter beginning behind him.

Inside the cot, all was dark. Then, as if a sun had risen, an early morning scene brightened before his eyes. He stood on the shores of a beautiful lake, with a dune rising like a benign god at its end. All was gold about him, the calm lake, the leaves of birch trees, the wings of a kingfisher who swooped low, and the fins of a perch which jumped to evade him.

From out of a small bark lean-to overlooking this golden lake, gentle laughter beckoned him. He walked over to the lean-to and looked inside to see an Indian family, a father, a young wife, and a child in summer fishing camp. With his heart in his throat and this time wishing it to happen, he melted into the young father. The Indian woman, her hair glossy and her eyes luminous, looked up at him in adoration.

"My husband, I am thinking this bright morning that all of this world is ours. It is the gift of the Father of Life to the great earth woman, who fell to earth through a hole in the heavens and landed on the turtle's back and became the mother of us all. This little one of ours is kin to all animals great and small." She patted the black-eyed Indian child crawling about on the pine-bough bed.

He nodded, and felt that he himself was a vessel full of wisdom, a repository of ancient lore of nature. "Yes. He is brother to the hare, the squirrel, even the great bear. He can learn from each." He gazed at her red-brown beauty, in a dress with quillwork patterns on its edge. Her breasts swelled with the milk that nourished the young child. He was filled with a love so profound he thought he would die; he adored her. He took her hands and smiled. But as he looked, her own smile faded and her face began to lose its bloom, then wither and shrivel, like a lily blossom in the cold.

He stood at the foot of two graves. An ancient chief stood by the mound. The oval shapes of beech leaves fluttered down over them all, growing brown and sere as they touched the graves. He knew that his wife and child were going beyond the Milky Way, that their spirits would depart. The old chief chanted a requiem for the dead:

> *Soon you will reach him*
> *Reach him our grandfather*
> *On through the trials of death*
> *Toward final light.*
> *Our relatives from long ago*
> *You will both then see*
> *Make every effort and you will be there.*

Yearning as large as all life filled McClure-Indian and he cried out, "No, I cannot leave her." From the grave the spirit of the wife arose, child in her arms, and floated skyward. He found he too could float and tried to overtake her. She seemed not to notice, and pain of rejection filled him to mingle with the overpowering love. Soon they came to a pine-clad island in the middle of a huge blue-water lake. The Grandfather of Death, eight feet tall, stood before him. "No, you may not follow," he said.

"I must. My love is so powerful it cannot live without what it feeds upon."

The old Grandfather looked at him with compassion. "You must go. But your devotion shall not go unrewarded. I will give you the secret of life, so that when you return it will be as though you are born anew, child of the Great Hare." McClure-Indian paused, then felt a thrill of expectation. Something in him had been waiting for this for a long time.

"This love that you feel for your wife and child, now in the noon of your youth is so intense and real you feel you will burst like a ripe melon. But it is but as nothing compared to the great sea of love which surrounds us all. What fills you is as a grain of sand is to that ocean, as one pin feather to the wing of the giant hawk. This unseen ocean of love binds all living things together. It is indeed the very life they live. This Love of Manitto is perfect and unchangeable, the pearl of living which when exchanged, comes back to man as a basket of pearls. Unlike the oil of bear which is spent in the woman's cooking pot, the Love of Manitto is not used up. It is like the harvest basket of the gods which, once emptied, fills again with luscious fruits.''

Every word of the old Grandfather seemed to enter John's consciousness like a drop of water on a lake which expanded in rings sending showers of warmth through his whole being. "This Love," the old man went on, "is the power which sends the moon across the mountaintop at prescribed times each month, which tells the bear to sleep when snow falls and wake when grass springs up. It forms the heart of hearts of each man, although he may not know it.

"This Love is the answer for all the woes you face; it is the gentle rain of Eternity upon the desert of the dream of mortality. It guides the path of the wanderer, it heals the broken body and broken mind. It makes each man his brother's soulmate. And it bridges the village of the living with the island of the dead. Nothing can stop it.

"Neither is anything worthwhile without it. A man may give good gifts but unless they come from the love of brother for brother they mean nothing. You," and he seemed to look deeply into John's soul, "have felt the indignation of the honest man against the evil in the world and you have fought that evil. But your battle is nothing, as the cry of the wind echoing in the empty canyon of winter, without the Love of Manitto. It is the key to living."

The Grandfather began to glow like foxfire. He glided toward John and his hand opened, dropping into John's hands something as warm and glowing as a candle flame. It was a pearl as big as a walnut, and in John's grasp it glowed until it suffused first his hand, then his whole body, with light. He could see his veins, his skeleton. He pulsated with warmth.

As the old Indian backed away, his face and form blurred, and like clay reshaping itself became the form of Reverend George McClure. John walked a step toward his uncle's beloved figure, but the apparition raised his hand and almost without a pause went on.

"John, this pearl is your life now. But it bursts be spread abroad. And in it is the salvation you have long sought." John reached longingly for his uncle's lean, long form; but gradually, it receded to a pinpoint of light, then disappeared completely, leaving only the glowing red of the interior of the cottage. The luminescent warmth remained in him, and with great excitement, and brushing aside Brohgan, John flung open the door and ran down the path he had walked through in these dreams before, past the hills, the oval portraits. The sand no longer sucked at his feet. Ahead of him was the glow of dawn, the promise of the rising day. Firmly, with purpose and understanding, he began to walk toward the glow, which he knew would be the source of the pearl's glory.

Then there was a clamor at the side of his consciousness, and he was awake, in the living and horrible world of Kittanning. Tewea—Captain Jacobs—with a grim smile on his face, was yelling stridently at the mass of tortured pulp that was once John Turner. Yet the trader was still alive. As Captain Jacobs stalked to the rear of the crowd, John was close enough to see that Turner's eyes showed recognition.

Instantly John McClure was on his feet. Still under the spell of what he had just experienced in his own mind, he ran to the stake and covered Turner with his body. Then he began to yell. "Stop this madness. Don't any of you have a gun to put him out of his pain? You, too, have fingers, eyes and feet. Tomorrow you could be at the stake. Leave him alone. . ." he was gesturing wildly, waving his arms. He looked about him, realizing as his dream dissipated, what he had done. He smiled wryly. "Anyway, he isn't worth it." He turned to look at the pitiful wreck of a man behind him, who had stopped screaming for just a moment. Could he know?

Roughly John was pushed down, and someone had a foot on him. It was Lone Stag. He addressed a stern speech to the Indians, who after a moment of stunned silence, had begun to surge forward. He spoke for about three minutes, and to John's complete amazement, the Indians withdrew and he was allowed to return to his tree.

It was fully ten minutes before John comprehended that he was not to be killed and probably not even tortured. Without turning, he asked the bearded Indian next to him, "What did you say to them?"

Lone Stag did not look at him. "I say that you are savant, a crazy man from Manitto. Otherwise you would not risk death so recklessly. I tell them that you are a prophet. You foretell the downfall of all the white man from sea to sea and the return of corn and hunting lands if they please God. Perhaps you do. I cannot say."

The Indians were closing in on Turner for the kill; Chief Jacobs' three-year-old son was raising a tomahawk to deliver the final blow.

So what he said had worked, in a way. But he still did not understand. "What do you mean? Could they not understand what I said?" Lone Stag remained stoically silent. John spoke to the tree next to him. "Barlow, some of those Indians speak English. Why didn't they kill me on the spot for insolence for what I said?"

Barlow's voice shot across the twilight clearing to him, "Who could understand you, man? You were speaking Gaelic."

All the rest is history, of course. Lieutenant Colonel John Armstrong, marching across the Allegheny Trace with three hundred men, mounted a surprise attack on Kittanning a week-and-a-half later, killed Captain Jacobs and several other Indian leaders and freed some of the prisoners, including Tom Barlow and John McClure. That spirited engagement of settlers, in the very midst of the Indians' heartland, took the sap out of tribal pride and undermined their confidence in their French allies. The French had told them the Scotch-

Irish would not fight, but this group of Scotch-Irishmen had fought like wildcats. The Frenchmen must be liars. So even though war was formally declared and fought and Indian attacks on settlers continued, it was only a matter of time before the French and Indian War was won by England.

What history did not record, however, was the change in John McClure, noticeable only to his family and neighbors in Cumberland County. He began to sit in the front row of the log tent church, instead of lurking back with the horses. He held church office, and he began to take an interest in his children's religious education. That would have been fine, the community thought, if the rest hadn't happened.

Unexplainably, when John McClure returned from Kittanning, he told Lieutenant Armstrong he would never carry a musket again against another man, be he Indian or white, and he resigned from the regiment. Eventually, at the end of the war, as Pontiac's revolt inflamed Indians into a desperate attack against the frontier, he became a peace advocate and journeyed to Philadelphia to plead for settlement of Indian controversies.

"Crazy as a loon," said Walter Cherry and his sons as they sat on their caving-in porch and watched the corn grow.

"An odd philosophical shift," mused Rafe Emison to himself. He was raking the ground outside the store he and his son now ran and watching his granddaughters, and the nephews who had just come to the area, Young Ash and Hugh Emison, play together.

"I can find no parallel for it in classical history. Although," he ran his hand through the few remaining hairs on his finely shaped head, "the stand that Gaius and Tiberius Gracchus took in trying to gain the people's rights in Rome is somewhat similar. Of course the case was different; the Gracchus brothers died for their views. This wasn't anything like that."

Sam Bard only mentioned John's new stance once, when it was known that McClure's letter suggesting the establishment of permanent Indian homelands was read before the governor's council. He exploded all over the wheelwright's shop so that everyone in the newly rebuilt Carlisle could hear him. "God damn it, The Fist has turned tail and run. We'd best call him the Scotch Quaker from now on." The name stuck, and John McClure was known as the Scotch Quaker all over eastern Pennsylvania from then on.

How did he explain the change in his life to Jane and his family, which now included quiet little George, born 1757, and finally little Jane in 1759? The answer is that he didn't, really. When Jane and Johnny asked who the strange bearded Indian was who appeared as regularly as the Halloween moon to take him on a long hunt to Ohio country, he simply said that they "owed each other a favor or two" and liked to "keep up."

And when Will asked darkly about the story which circulated for a while that his father had run out in front of Captain Jacobs while he was torturing Turner and screamed in jibberish, he said that he "had the ague and was clean out of my head." But he knew different. John McClure knew a durn sight different, as Sam Bard would have said. Sometimes, when he was in his cabin in January lying by the side of his wife as the wind howled, or when he walked up Blue

Mountain with the older boys to test the new nine-pound rifles they all got after the Indians retreated, he thought of Saul of Tarsus. And so, he told himself, smiling a little wryly, if the Lord appeared to me on my Road to Damascus in the form of a red Irish glowworm with a cheeky mouth, who was to fault it? The Lord worked in strange mysterious ways his wonders to perform, after all.

Chapter XIII

In the fall of 1763, when the cornstalks left over in the fields began to turn gray and bend under rains of November, and apples under the trees shrivelled in the first hard frost, Lone Stag appeared with his Indian trade musket at the door of the cabin for the long hunt.

As always, when he came to renew the friendship begun on the road to Kittanning, he did not say where he had been. But he wore the blanket-coat and heavy wool leggings of winter, and he carried meal to make corn cakes on the trail, and extra powder stored in oiled, water-proof pouches.

John McClure put aside the cracker barrels he was making for Emison's store and picked up his rifle. Stowing enough salt, dried fruit, and jerky for three weeks, he saddled Orange.

"Johnny and Will can tend to the stock and continue the clearing of the barn site," he told his wife as he came back into the cabin.

"But is 't safe? Pontiac has these Indians aroused, and the massacres. . ."

"Safe for you right here, since Bouquet and his troops quieted the tribes in the western area. And for us, tolerable safe. Besides, I'll have the wise man of the tribes with me." Lone Stag's reputation was known now even among the Scotch-Irish in the Cumberland Valley; an ambassador at large, he went among the Leni Lenape from Delaware to the Ouabash as freely as the winter wind, and he brought good counsel with him.

"Mrs. McClure, I would take Dan'l with me this time," her husband said, winking towards the ten-year-old boy.

Dan'l had already been told the plans and was now excitedly preparing for his first hunting trip. He looked with pride at the rifle his brother Johnny would be loaning him and whetted his knife against his leggings. Then he laid out on the table a little pile of items to put into a leather hunting bag. "Lead, a mold to heat the lead for bullets, and a powder horn. I've got 'em all," he said, looking up at his father and the Indian.

Jane looked apprehensive. She did not really know the story of how this strange Indian and her husband had come to be bound like brothers. She only knew that John had gone off to Fort Granville, then she had heard nothing of him for almost a month, until one night in a flash she had seen John by a campfire at the top of a windy mountain, surrounded by hostile Indian faces, but alive. Then he had returned to her, chastened and somehow changed for the better by the experience, with new views about how Indians should be treated. This taciturn but intelligent Indian had something to do with it.

As she thought about it, there was something to like, almost admire about this Lone Stag: the set of the mouth, the proud shoulders. She felt she could trust John, and, yes, even Dan'l to this Delaware, or whatever he was. She watched her husband go outside to give John final instructions and sat down by the fire, where her teapot was whistling.

It would give her some time to do lessons with Georgie and little Jane. She watched the little girl, her fine long brown hair bouncing as she danced a wood dolly on a board her Dada had made her. This replacement for the lost, secretly-mourned dead baby was a laughing sprite of a child. Already she could read the Bible and the Dick Whittington chapbook. Although little Jane could not imagine how London town might look, her eyes shone when she heard Dick say the streets were paved with gold, and when she tired of spelling it out herself, she begged her mother to read to her again and again how the cat dashed over the emperor's table devouring the greedy mice.

"Ma, you are lookin' at me," Jenny (for that was how she was called to distinguish her from her mother) said. "I do not like folks' eyes on me." She looked out the window at the misting, chilly rain. "And I don't like indoor weather," she said and bounded into the other room. There she watched Dan'l stuff the pockets of his breeches with corn muffins and jerky and leave with her Dada and the savage.

Her brother Georgie was playing his fiddle in the corner.

"Georgie, are you afeard of savages?" she asked. The boy took the fiddle from his chin and looked at her gravely.

"Afraid, Jenny. Talk like Dada instead of Mr. Bard."

"John and Will talk thataway, too."

"Well, I'm not going to."

"Georgie, I think savages are bad. They come in the night, when we are asleep and we have to get up and go to Aunt Sally's house at Carlisle. I had to leave my doll behind the last time. I was afeard of this savage, although Dada often told me that he was God's child too."

George continued looking at her over the bridge of his rather large nose. He was acting so very, very grown up now that he was going over to Mr. Emison's store to take lessons on his fiddle, she thought.

"Will says they are spawn of the Devil, although Dada tells him not to," Jenny continued loftily. It frightened her when Will and Dada argued, although lately Dada did not yell at William, just looked at him with sad eyes. She came to where George was tuning his fiddle and whispered.

"Georgie, do you 'member when Dada was in Carlisle with the Quakers and we spied on Will and saw him drinkin' whiskey up by the woodpile?"

Georgie nodded. Will had made them cross their hearts and hope to die that they would never tell.

"Did you tell, Georgie?" Jenny grasped the arm of his hunting shirt.

"No," he said uncomfortably. He did not like this conversation.

"Neither did I. Still, it made me feel bad, not telling truth to Dada. Are you feard—afraid—of Will?"

His mouth curled in scorn. "Mr. Emison says we shouldn't be afraid of anybody we can out-think." He put his fiddle in its leather case. She didn't understand what he said, but the prissy tone in his voice made her want to throw her doll at him. He was no fun lately, did not like to play savage and stoop tag or pile up the shavings in Dada's shop corner. Anyways, she was tired of the squeaks he made all the time. She sighed and put her dancing dolly away in the toy chest. She would miss Dan'l. He was the nicest of the brothers. Johnny was all right, but he never talked to her. He slept now with William in the birthing room that Dada had built on the back of the cabin when George was born.

John was almost nineteen and had his own fields in Shearman's valley and was very serious about making his fortune. But Dan'l was merry. He told jokes and called her "woodchuck" and tickled her ribs when she lay on the floor. Last winter he made her a little sled and stomped down the snow on the hill, so she could whiz down it. She loved Dan'l. Well, perhaps he would have fun on his trip with the savage. She didn't really know how he could. She hoped to goodness the savage wouldn't get angry and cut Dan'l up and cook him in a pot, like Will said they did to Mrs. Hannah Jane Green's baby.

"The rifle is a wondrous thing," Long Stag told John McClure at the campfire on the other side of the Blue Mountains that night. He was slowly turning it over, looking at the silver inlay, a goose in flight, on the stock.

" 'Twas made in the Henry shop near the Juniata. I spent nigh onto a month comin' and goin' and watchin' them bend and weld and soften and rifle it to fit my arm span." It was almost four feet long; Lone Stag pushed open the patchbox, where linen was kept to oil the lead balls when the rifle was loaded.

"How much this cost?" he asked.

"Forty dollars. I had it from the sale of nail barrels in Carlisle." John sighed a little. When he came to this country, he told himself he would make only beautiful things. Eventually, however, he made what people would pay money for. As merchants set up stores, apothecaries, and provisioning shops, he condescended to make large containers and barrels again. But never wet barrels, ugly things for fish and whiskey. At least he hadn't had to do that.

Dan'l was spitting the pheasants they shot around noon, a beautiful pair that took flight as they walked through a clearing while their horses rested. His eyes shone; everything was new and exciting, and he, too, had a rifle, even if it wasn't fancy and wasn't his own.

Lone Stag, his arms about his knees, looked through the woods toward the streaked sky of the winter sunset. "My people do not understand the ways of money. But then they do not understand many of the white man's ways."

"Just as the white man does not understand the Indian's ways," said John. For both men these long hunts met an inner need to continue an unusual friendship. They did not usually talk of subjects which had thorns for them. Lately, though, John wanted to talk deeply, to touch the soul of the other man, and so he decided to venture into the brambles. "I would ask a favor of my friend. I would like him to tell me how the Indian feels about my race and the fact that we now live in the hunting grounds." He knew part of the answer— every white man did—but something compelled him to seek more.

"I will." Long Stag pushed back from the fire a little.

The smell of the roasting fowls, savory and rich, drifted over the clearing. Dan'l, taking the cornbread from his pack, grew alert. Lone Stag did not speak for long minutes; and when he did, he did not look at the white men. "We try to see through the clouds of war and changing of our homes, the meetings of the white man's councils and the laws they pass. It is not easy to see the truth. A lake is sometimes cloudy and ruffled on the surface, but below the water are pebbles we cannot see. Yet sometimes that water clears and below are the pebbles, where they have always been but for our eyesight and the waves. So is truth; yet my father and grandfather, I think, saw the pebbles clearly and this is what they told me.

"Years ago the Long Knives came to this land in the large ships. We gave them venison and showed them how to plant the corn. With their firelocks they frightened the game and made our children cry. Still we gave to all who asked. Had not the Great Spirit given to us?

"Then the Hollanders came to what you call New York, wanting a tiny, tiny parcel of land, as they said, and shooting their guns. Your Yengeese came in up north and took the best land and wanted to make agreements with us. This we did. But what is bad is that the white man did not know the meaning of the word promise. Here in this land of the Penns you say you wish the land as far as a man can walk in a day. We give it to you and you run from sunrise to sunset. You say white man will not go to Wyoming near our village of Shamokin, yet this year you do it.

"But most of all, you do not treat us as brothers, but as dogs. You look at us to laugh, you give us liquor to craze our minds. You shout at us as if we are deaf. We, whose ears were created to understand the song of the wind. Treat us as if we are stupid. We whose minds and hearts can understand the wolf and the bear and walk so no twig snaps."

John looked ashamed. Dan'l felt a little afraid at the edge and strength of the Indian's voice. "Let me tell you a story my father's people in the south have. The Great Spirit made all men, but when he made the white man, the clay he cast was bad marl; and when it was fired with water in the pit, it burst. He stuck the pieces back together again, but the pieces did not fit right, the man was all crazy. He was made with two sides to his face, one to smile, one to twist in hate. One arm was straight to pat on the back, the other crooked to shoot a gun and kill honest men.

"The buttocks were made fat to sit and let others wait on them, the private parts foul and full of pestilence. The eyes had strange blindness; they could not see the gold of the sunrise but fixed instead on pieces of eight. The mind was twisted, saying Manitto is love and killing in His name. And so this misshapen vessel, full of cracks and ugly, became the model of all white men."

A very slight smile puckered the corners of the Indian's mouth.

John began to cough toward the end of the speech and now as he tried to smile at Lone Stag's wry humor, a coughing fit began again. Lone Stag looked concerned, but John told him, "It is nothing, my friend. Now and then I feel the fever, as at Kittanning. But it passes." He decided to change the subject. "What do you tell the chiefs as you travel, a member of no tribe but given wisdom of Manitto for all?"

"I do not tell. I wait to be asked. It is the job of chief and elders to direct wisdom to each tribe, but if the chief asks of the wandering wise one, I say— We have fallen to the level of the broken vessel. We, the true people, given to know the secrets of all nature, have made a god of white man's gold and comfort. We have sold our hearts for the blanket, the cooking pot and the whiskey.

"As the deer and bison migrated, we followed, free as they, making our homes of bark and skins. But now we must be near the trading post. We want log homes; we do not wish our houses to have smoke in them but fireplaces. Our women want the wool skirts to keep warm. So we threw all away to trade the skins of animals for these trifles. The beaver, once a friend who let our children watch him build his dam, is now the instrument of our downfall. We shall die, but many white men shall die before that time."

"This land is large," John said. "Can we not live together? You know I have gone to Philadelphia to work for peace among our peoples."

"Yes. Manitto has blessed you with the sight from the mountain top instead of the inside of the fallen log."

And for it I have paid by being despised by half of the valley, John thought.

Lone Stag went on. "But we must not beg answers of the white chiefs at the seats of the council. We must find our own lands and live the life of the earth and forest again, because we know no other. Away, far away from here. For we have been as the possum's baby, carried in the pouch of the white man, sucking a teat of slavery, living at his will. For a while, the white man liked that, but now he would rip us off the teat and throw us to the wilderness. We are abomination in his sight, and he will not stop until every last one of us is gone from the land of the Penns."

Dan'l did not forget this hunt, because on it he shot his first deer, a young buck, just outside the hunter's shack on the Allegheny River. John did not forget the words of the Indian sage; he had, indeed, good cause to remember them forcibly before a month had passed.

William McClure sat sprawled on straw in the wheelwright's shed, the farthest outbuilding on Sam Bard's premises in Carlisle. Slowly stroking the earthenware jug to warm his hands in the chilly shed, he was consuming whiskey and talking to Ardry Bard.

"I feel like a hobbled cow, 'deed I do," Will said to his old friend. They were supposed to be visiting Ardry's young cousin Tom who was staying up the road, but they left early and sneaked into the shed. Will, who had just begun an apprenticeship with Sam Bard at the wheelwright shop, often found ways to be with Ardry these days, to talk about the action of the rangers, whom Ardry had recently joined.

"If I could've been with them when they surprised the savages in the barn over by the river—to git me an Injeean scalp. I can jest feel it," Will said.

"Those God-damned, so-called Christian Injeeans make me madder'n hell. They hide behind the Quakers and Moravians skirts and then, when we turn our back, take to the warpath. But we shot 'em like panthers out of the tree before they could jump us. We went in and found 'em all asleep and had us a little massacree of our own." Ardry's freckled face was red with emotion; his fists clenched and unclenched.

"Jest about even I should think," Will said sarcastically. "Four hundred white people murdered in their cabins or on the roads in the last few years to a score of Moravian Injeeans. It's fine justice."

"And yet the Quakers and even. . ." Ardry's voice was cautious ". . .your own father raised a hew and cry that the rangers was murderers. When those Moravian Injeeans came out to git revenge and ambushed our boys as they rode."

"My own father," Will said, with an indifferent look in his eyes. He often looked older than fourteen; he had matured early and his shoulders were broad. He was a head taller than his father and still growing, and the shadows that often crossed his handsome face were dark and complex. He took a long swig of the warming liquor. Sam Bard would not notice or care if he came in drunk; Sam was often drunk himself. Christmas was coming in a couple of weeks; and young and old alike among the Scotch-Irish, Presbyterian or not, were applying themselves to yuletide cheer.

"It's hard to find the Delawares nowadays. Since they couldn't defeat Colonel Bouquet, and it looks like he's gonna wipe 'em out, they're scarcer than quail teeth. But these here Christian Injeeans around Lehigh and up to Wyoming. They're still a threat as I see it."

"They ain't all Christians. Some's backslid, and it don't matter anyways. The militia had in mind to whup the ones up north, but when they rode into Wyoming what did they find?" Ardry's eyes were bright with horror mixed with a strange sort of relish.

Will knew the details and never tired of reciting them. "Ten mutilated settlers from Yankee country. Men with pitchforks stickin' in their innards and moccasin awls in their eyeballs, and the body of a woman roasted and skinned alive, her skin split like a broiled sausage. And we sit here tonight as calm as hogs in hog heaven." Anger surged in him hot and bitter, as it always did when he thought of Indians, at large, in the forests or even worse before warm, protected Quaker fires.

"The slipper is on the other foot now," Will muttered, voicing opinions he heard the older men in Carlisle uttering. "They's more of us now and we're banded together. We'll wipe every one of them from the face of Pennsylvania before we're through."

Ardry Bard looked through the gloom at William, surprised at the confident vehemence in his voice. "And jest who is 'we?' " he asked with a mild note of surprise.

*　　　　*　　　　*

John McClure went to bed with the fever. It seemed to come every few months, the chills, sometimes so severe the bed shook, then the sweating and light-headedness. After that there would be a racking cough. In a few days it generally abated, leaving him weak and wretched. Surely it would lessen as time went on. He just needed to get it out of his system. Jennie, her black eyes big with importance, was waiting on him, bringing him beef soup and hot lemonade. "It's made with real sugar," she assured her father and he smiled wanly, in spite of the weakness in his body.

"Johnny, come here," he called. His eldest son was in the work corner, shaping a hay fork to replace one that had broken toward the end of the harvest. His quiet, angular face serious, he whittled its foot-and-a-half long prongs with loving care, not because he cared for the wood itself the way his father did, but because it would make the farming easier.

The land was in his mind and in his blood, and he dreamed of clearing and improving his own acreage someday, of building a house among rolling fields of wheat stretching on toward the river, with no trees at all and herds of cows and horses, stalls of horses. Of all things on a farm, John, Jr. loved horses most. He raced whenever anyone would loan him a horse young enough to run down the road. The old nags his father had—well, they plowed all right.

Johnny went to the cherry bed and looked down with concern. He loved this often difficult man who was his father, although he did not understand him very well. His father kept his worries to himself and, since he got religion, or whatever it was at Kittanning, he was as intense in his concern for the castoffs in the world as he had been impatient with them earlier. His father was like somebody in the book he read to him when John, Jr. was a child—*Pilgrim's Progress*. Wasn't it Faithful? He was the one who was so good but got put in the cage because his beliefs caused him too much trouble. He remembered his uncle had been that way too. Must run in the fambly, he told himself. Well, if it did, it wasn't going to affect him. All he wanted to do was stay out of sight and do his job. "Dada, do you want something?" He still called him by the Irish diminuitive which accented the first syllable; most folks out here said "Pa."

"John, do you think we could use a sledge to haul the stones for the barn? That way we could start right after Christmas."

"If the snow holds and hardens," his son answered. Always it was in his father's eye, the large German barn, with rows of fieldstones in its base and fine hewn timbers reaching up to a shallow peaked roof.

"I'll have my own shop in the corner, with a fireplace. Any good cooperage Sandy Craig could do, all my barrel work, can be done in that barn without crowding. As it is now, I can only work summers on the large barrels," John said to his son.

Johnny heard his mother puttering in the corner, picking up soggy clothing and putting it on the pegs by the fireplace to dry. She was cooking Christmas pudding in the other room in a mold shaped like a plump partridge. Everything was in apple pie order in this home his parents had worked so hard to create; Johnny was proud of it. It was just that there was never quite enough, enough flour to make two cakes, enough shoes to quit wearing moccasins, enough money for him to go to the new college at Princeton. Definitely not for that, although he might have liked it. Maybe someday Georgie could go; he seemed to be the acute one.

"They're tearin' down the old store in Carlisle and I've talked to Ash Emison about our having the stone for the barn. Can you see to it?" His father's voice was a little raspy, but he seemed to be beating the fever. "I'm feeling better," he confided and asked for some of the beef soup.

About eight o'clock that night, a cold winter full moon rose above the outbuildings where the stock slept, warming themselves with the breathy heat from each other's bodies. The creek ran clear and freezing cold over the rocks, and dead weeds spilled their crowns of snow into its dark waters in a slight breeze. An express rider approached the cabin, his horse heaving and panting with exertion. The rider quickly tied it to the post near an oak tree. He banged on the door.

Jane, unable to believe that an Indian alarm would come at this time of the year, opened the door warily and asked, "Who is't?"

"It's Branson, Ma'm. I must needs speak to John." Branson—the Quaker from Harris's Ferry who had gone to Philadelphia with John to see the assembly. What could he want? She unlatched the door slowly and the man, wearing an English greatcoat over his leather breeches, came in, stamping snow.

"My husband is poorly, Mr. Branson. Perhaps. . ." But John's voice was firm behind her.

"What is it, Lige?" John had risen from bed and come to the door. The Quaker was a tall, blonde man with a badly pocked face.

"It's the addlepates from Paxton. They've jumped the gun on us. There's a gang of them headed out this evening for Conestoga. They've vowed to kill every Indian there. All twenty of them."

"I'll get my clothing. . ." John pushed aside his wife's restraining arm and reached for his leather breeches and blanket-coat.

"Neighbor, it may be too late to stop whatever bloody acts are going on there. It may not. But thou'll want to ride out anyway." John looked at him questioningly. "I'm told thy son William and Ardry Bard have just started t' join them from Carlisle on one horse. If we start with two fresh mounts, we can probably catch them before they reach Conestoga."

The horrified faces of Johnny, George, and Dan'l formed a circle behind their mother. "Dada, you can't go out there in this yere cold. . ." only Johnny would have the courage to challenge his father.

John reached under the bed for his rifle. His voice was grim.

"And are you the man who could stop me?" He looked at his son calmly.

Could is one thing, would is another, thought Johnny McClure, and let his father brush by. The wind rushed in the door after him, bringing with it whorls of snow, and Johnny slammed it shut and bolted it, feeling the cold gust bite his face for an instant. Then all was still except for the sobbing of his mother in the darkness behind him.

Hoofbeats pounded down the Lancaster road as two desperate horsemen pushed their mounts to the limit. Above, the midnight stars shifted in and out beneath clouds that dropped snowflakes, flakes that soon became bullets stinging the muffled faces and eyes of the riders. Ten miles ahead on the road, a young man of twenty and another, taller young man of fourteen, urged the horse bearing a double burden to trot, and rested it as little as possible. And not far ahead of them, the Paxton Boys, as the group of rangers now call themselves, prepared to enter the little Indian town of Conestoga where the twenty-two men, women, and children who were the last remnants of the long peaceful Conestogue tribe slept.

And finally, the galloping horsemen overtook the walking ones. The scene was unpleasant; John McClure, with his rifle at his side, demanded that his son mount up beside him and return to their home. Will McClure, surly and grumbling, obeyed. John could not convince his friend's son to turn about and sadly watched him go on. The Quaker from Harris's Ferry, unsure of which course to take, decided to return to organize a search party to determine what had happened, if anything. This occurred two miles from Conestoga. Already smoke from burning cabins was rising into the winter dawn.

Because the horse was walking, within a couple of hours it was overtaken on the road to Carlisle by a thundering group of men on horseback. John and Will McClure drew over to the side of the road at the approaching hoofbeats.

As the rowdy group galloped by, laughing and singing drunken songs, the father and son saw, mounted on the saddlebags of the lead horses, seven or eight bloody scalps. The hair, black as charcoal, was Indian.

"Dada, you're back," Dan'l said delightedly as he opened the cabin door late that afternoon. A thaw was beginning, and the sunlight streamed from a clear, blue sky. Jane dropped the clothes she was scrubbing and ran to the door. Her eyes rested gratefully on her husband for a second, then passed to the son who was down the path caring for the horse. As he came in, she spoke to him. "Will, you have come back without harm."

He flung his heavy linen jacket at the peg by the fire and looked at her indifferently. "So my father tells me," he said and slumped into a chair by the fire.

Johnny McClure looked his father in the face. "Dada, are you all right? The fever. . .?"

"Not a cough while we were on the trace. The exertion of it all must've cured me. I think that's the last we'll have of the fever." And he called for sweet cider and took up Georgie's fiddle and played squeakily on it and was more jovial than his children had seen him in all the days they recalled.

It could be said that Will did a lot of thinking after the Conestoga Massacre. The next day, as he and Dan'l milked the cows and cleaned the shed, and melting snow dripped off the roof, Will wondered aloud if he would be allowed to go back into Carlisle to apprentice. "Ain't got no signed articles. . . 'twas a fambly arrangement. How in the hell am I goin' to face Ardry?"

Dan'l said nothing, continuing to fork manure for the pile that would fertilize next spring's fields.

"How can a man have any pride?" Will persisted. "Pa come and led me like a babe on a strap, home to m' playpen."

"I hear tell Ardry might be in trouble himself," Dan'l finally said.

"Why? Bein' so late all he got to do was finish setting a few outbuildings on fire at the Indian village." What he didn't say, but thought about, was that when Mr. Branson had come to take his mare and leave off Orange early this morning, he told John and Jane McClure that the Conestogas who escaped the massacre by the Paxton boys were being held in Lancaster in the stone jailhouse. The governor had made a proclamation issuing rewards for information on the Paxton Boys.

"Hell," Will said vehemently, "they'll niver git 'em. Half the county 'll give 'em shelter and well they should. They should git a medal instead of arrested. If Dada hadn't come who knows what I might have been able to do—maybe git me a papoose scalp."

"Well," said Dan'l, "at least you wasn't drunk or Pa might have beat you silly."

Will looked at him menacingly. Why would the old man ride through the night like that to stop him and bring him back? There was no accounting for some things and the fools that'll do 'em. Still, it might not be too good to be in jail for Christmas. There was something in that.

John McClure took to his bed again in a day or two, coughing and shaking, and this time his strength failed rapidly. At about noon on a Sunday, Lone Stag appeared at the door. "Come in, friend," Jane said. Although she could not explain her feelings, she now trusted this Indian completely.

"Why've you left winter camp, Indian brother?" John said. He lay, wan-faced in the cherry bed he had made, by a roaring fire built for him by Dan'l.

Lone Stag looked down at him. "Let us say that I have come to be with you for a day or two at your important season."

"Oh, Christmas? Seems strange. But then I never did fully understand your ways, my friend."

"It is not necessary for friends to understand each thought of the other," Lone Stag replied and sat down by the fire. As the hours passed, John's condition worsened rapidly. His fever rose, his coughing became racking and he passed out of his head. "It is the lung fever, reaching a crisis," Lone Stag said. "My people have ways of treating it. I could try if you wish."

Jane hesitated, and then recalled the healing herbs that helped many in the neighborhood for everything from snakebite to miscarriage, although there was little gratitude toward the Indians when healing occurred. She nodded approval and indicated to the boys that they should aid Lone Stag in whatever way he needed.

The Indian strung leather thongs across the cabin and hung blankets and sheets over them to enclose the bed. Then he told Johnny and the reluctant Will to bring in a huge manger trough from the cowshed and put a thin shield of earth over the bottom. He went outside to carefully select rocks which had surfaced beneath the melted snow. These he put into the fireplace coals to heat slowly and evenly. When they had heated sufficiently, he shoveled them into the manger inside John's tent.

From the pack Lone Stag had stowed by the door, he took a thick root which none of them recognized. This went into a bubbling pot of water over the fire. In a few minutes he ladled out a cup or so of the water and sprinkled it over the hot rocks in the tent. Steam rose. John's hoarse, raspy breathing began to ease. Over the next two hours Lone Stag replaced cooled rocks with hot from the fire and finally, after sundown, John slept. Refusing food, Lone Stag sat before the fire.

Jane pulled up a chair beside him. Behind the tent, John's breathing continued evenly. Finally she broke the silence. "Why do you do this?" she asked the Indian.

He rose to stir the fire and put on more logs. "He is a part of my destiny. In the vision of my youth, when I put on manhood, I saw the Grandfather Stag telling me of past and future. He said that my antlers would entwine with those of a white man. That after we fought, we should be as brothers and that I should owe a life to him and he to me."

Jane looked into his long, impassive face. The flames leapt up, crackling about the split logs. "And you fought at Fort Granville and helped him at Kittanning. But do you owe your life to him?"

"I have seen the poisoning of the blood before. If the swollen evil goes beyond the knee, it is death. He cut the poison out."

Jane nodded. So that was it. "And you have come tonight to save him."

The Indian's voice was low. "Not to save him, although in friendship I try to stop his pain. I come to ease his death."

Jane felt a choking sensation. She looked frantically at him and saw the sorrow in his eyes. "Tonight is the night my friend will take his journey beyond the stars. Manitto tells me to witness and to aid it." Jane's hand went to her throat. "Surely you are wrong. . ." Large tears began to spill onto her hands.

"Manitto is not wrong. Your husband is a good man. To everyone it is not given to swim in the Father of Waters. He has lived the life given to him well, swimming with honor and decency in the small river he was set in. Not once but twice. . ." he glanced stonily at Will's sleeping form in the corner ". . .has he offered to give up the life force for another. The Grandfathers can ask no more on this earth of us." Saying no more, he drew his blanket about him and seemed to sleep.

Dawn came and then mid-day, and John's senses seemed to clear. He called Johnny to him. Through parched lips he said, "Remember—build—barn." His son nodded. The Indian was removing the tent and the December sunlight came through the bottle glass John installed last summer. "Real window," he murmured. Jennie, George, and Dan'l, wide-eyed and solemn, came forward and kissed his cheek.

His wife, then, bent near. Speech was very difficult, his breath again rasping. "Love—Jane." It was the first time, she realized, he had ever said it.

Then unexpectedly, Will, sobbing, threw himself down on the bed. His mother moved forward to restrain him, but he pushed her away. "Dada," he whispered into the ear of the dying man, "I'm sorry. It's just that they did so much to us all. I can't help it that I hate them so much."

His father's voice had a final clarity. "Will, we can always help it when we hate." And then he closed his eyes and drifted away.

John McClure stood on a familiar sandy road. Around him stretched the hills of Araby, behind him, fading fast, the shapes of past dreams. Before him to the east was the splendor of a rising sun, its beams flooding the horizon. On feet no longer hampered, he ran toward the bright light of a new day.

Chapter XIV

A late autumn wind, the precursor of cold rain, blew strongly outside a stone inn near York, Pennsylvania. It buffeted the sign which hung above the door, making its "Blue Baboon" caper in the air. Three men wearing the uniforms and cocked hats of the Pennsylvania troops of the new Continental Congress hurried up the steps and out of the violent weather.

Shutting the door against the wind, the three advanced to a table in the taproom and sat down. Their entrance seemed to cause a minor stir among the homespun-clad farmers seated about the room, and the whisper circulated that "associators" had entered.

"Very well," whispered Captain Tom Kennedy, taking off his soldier's hat and running his fingers through his curly, straw-colored hair. "Now we shall see the lay of the land." A callow-looking barman appeared like a jackrabbit to take orders for rum and hurried back in a moment with three tankards and a bowl of walnuts.

Sitting across from Kennedy was a six-foot tall, very thin young man with a freckled face and red hair. Bony arms protruded from his buff-faced, dark brown coat; his body had yet to put on the flesh of full manhood. "They don't cotton to us being here," George McClure mumbled, looking at the floor. He did not like confrontations. He had not particularly enjoyed the military training in Philadelphia he had just undergone, especially the drills. Nothing was organized yet in the fledgling army George Washington was trying to put together, seemingly with glue and horsehair.

The third man in the trio of soldiers, a bucktoothed, nervous man of almost forty, put a walnut between thumb and forefinger and attempted to crack it, unsuccessfully. He spoke in a loud whisper. "I smell Tories. Fat ones like the one we met in the barnyard 't other day." Their recruiting duty had taken them to a farm near Chambersburg, and the man passed gas at them loudly before he shut the door in their faces. "The fools say it ain't their quarrel," Bige Cherry snorted.

Bige Cherry hadn't changed much since the day he was an embarrassed best man for Ash Emison and then, a year later, married Evalina Hanna, the tiny, wistful daughter of a wandering candlemaker. Now, his only son Malford was almost grown and was as capable a farmer as his father was casual. One day in July of 1776, Bige had just left the land he had inherited from his father in Malford's care and joined the quixotic bunch of troops that were trying to oppose the king's tyranny.

George looked across the table at Bige, wondering about what was really in the depths of the well that made up his next-door neighbor's character. Some folks said Bige Cherry never grew up, that his life consisted of eating corn bread and molasses and getting into fist-flying arguments with his neighbors about hogs. Like many men in the valley, he told droll stories about frontier life as a pastime, and each story had a point that was as sharp as the end of a peach pit. No one seemed to care that he could not read.

Bige had come to the McClure homestead two months ago, "jest to get some o' the boys to come out. We need to kick the British swellheads out of Americey and run the store ourselves," he had said.

But Will was getting ready to go on a long hunt with his younger brother Dan'l, and John, Jr. said he must stay to take care of the farm. "Have enough to do," he grumbled, "without going on some consarn saber-rattlin' expedition with the rag-tag army."

That's that, thought Cherry. But it wasn't. Soft-spoken George McClure had put down his fiddle and Greek grammar and said he didn't know but what he might go to the war. He had said Cincinnatus had gone for less cause.

Cincinnatus, Bige later told his wife, "was some furriner who left his plow to go to defend his native land." George must've studied about him, Bige thought, in his lessons with Rafe Emison before the old man died.

Now Bige Cherry looked around at the men in the inn who were eyeing the military group from Cumberland County with increasingly hostile stares and whispers. Captain Kennedy decided to be brash. He rose from the table. "I see you noticing our uniforms," he said, striding toward a nearby table of four farmers. "Perhaps you're thinking of taking up your rifles for liberty."

One farmer with extremely bushy eyebrows and black fingernails that were cracked almost in two looked up. "I 'spect I have as much love of liberty as any man," he said, and quaffed the ale left in the bottom of his tankard.

"Aye, the liberty not to go to war," laughed another man uproariously. He was young and ruddy-faced and wore the leather clothing of a tanner.

Kennedy stiffened. He had, however, decided to provide an education for these obviously ill-informed bumpkins. "Gentlemen, may we buy something to warm your spirits? Boy, another round for these fine men." All four looked at him suspiciously as he pulled up a chair. George and Bige pushed back their chairs a little and turned toward the conversation.

"Many are joining the cause. We've just been recruiting in Cumberland County," Kennedy said.

"Whar are the recruits, I say, whar?" an older man with only a fluffy rim of white hair above his ears asked. There was a snicker from somewhere across the room, where other farmers sat.

Kennedy stiffened but said nothing for a moment. The ale arrived. There was an undercurrent of amusement in the room that irritated George. "About the recruits. There is a good deal of patriotism in Cumberland, but they do not feel they can leave farm chores yet. Later in the winter they may come,'' Kennedy said.

"Go to be light horse troop, eh? Wear buff-colored waistcoats and carry shiny swords.'' The man with the broken fingernails smiled a cynical smile. "Not for me. Anyways, the game, boys, seems to be just about up.''

"Up?'' asked Bige Cherry. "It ain't hardly started yet, m' friend.''

"The name o' the game is retreat. Retreat from Long Island, give up the ghost at Fort Lee and Fort Washington. The British ships sailed right past 'em so I heered, and up to Tarrytown, New York. And the forts fell last week, shot down like ducks out of a blind. Now the poor beggars are fallin' back through New Jersey—more like fallin' on their backs.''

"Well, but our army remains safe. General Cornwallis, it seems, is very slow to move.'' Kennedy remained amiable as he passed out the ale mugs. Recruiting duty had taught him the men had to be weaned, slowly. Work on the pride, independence, those sorts of things. He lived near Shippensburg, managing the lands of his well-to-do father, who instructed much of the year at the College of New Jersey at Princeton.

"What a army it is,'' the bald man scoffed to a young companion who did not talk, only made signs in the air or on the table and snickered. "Barefoot riflemen, shipmen from Maine who know how to do pret' nigh nothin' but row, runaway apprentices who caint shoot a gun.''

George looked at the speaker menancingly. "Be you Tories?'' he asked.

"Not us. We are plain workin' men with famblies and no desire for quarrels with the King, bad though he be.'' The mute man stopped snickering and looked nervous.

"You have the sound of traitors, from your talk,'' George murmured and turned his face away from the man. Bige, however, got up abruptly and without being invited, crossed to the table and pulled up a chair. Kennedy ordered another round of ale and continued putting forth persuasive arguments.

The captain likes to hear himself talk, thought George, distracted from the conversation by his observations of the officer. As he lectured the men, Kennedy held his head high, showing his profile, his flaring nostrils and full, sensual lips. George watched him absently take out his snuff box, with a gold pineapple on its top, open it, snap it shut, and then put it away without having taken snuff. Twenty-two years old and he speaks of nothing but Lord Marlborough and his tactics. He's loyal enough but he plays at war. A typical macaroni, George thought, using the common term for an affected, dandified young man.

The drinks flowed, and Kennedy spoke in smooth, even tones. Over the space of a few minutes, the discussion with the other men grew more heated. Snatches of conversation drifting over to George suddenly alarmed him. "Every man who isn't a coward. . . associators be damned.''

George stood up and called to Kennedy, "Captain, let us go at once.'' It was too late. Bige Cherry stood and hit the bald man, who had risen from his chair to defend himself. Kennedy and Cherry were no match for the group of Yorkmen, and by the time George crossed the room, the two soldiers were being held, with drinks thrown in their faces. From somewhere, arms grabbed him also. Damn, he hated these violent quarrels, had hated them ever since the days when Will used to get drunk and swear at him and thrash him out by the creek.

The man with the broken fingernails disappeared and in a moment returned with a huge pitcher of—something. "With parmission, we will show you how we feel about the army of the Continental Congress." With that, he emptied sticky molasses over the heads of McClure, Cherry, and Kennedy, who soon found themselves ejected from the tavern on the tips of men's stiff shoes and with much accompanying laughter.

They wiped the sticky stuff out of their eyes and off their faces, as they silently headed for their horses. "Knaves," Kennedy snarled, in his slightly effeminate voice. "If the army were properly organized and disciplined, we wouldn't be sent out in little groups like this to recruit. Sometimes I despair of our ever being a military unit. I shall consider recourse to law to punish these churls."

George was not listening to him. It appeared, he thought sardonically, as if York, Pennsylvania, along with a good deal of the rest of the state, was not really a hotbed of rebel sentiment. You could make that point. But all he said was, "Let's find a stream and get this stuff out of our hair."

They must hurry to join the troops protecting Philadelphia. Cornwallis was pursuing a rebel army reduced to a miserable three thousand men through New Jersey, hotly hounding them out of first one town and then the next. Every soldier was needed.

As George sloshed frigid creek water over his head and then swung into the saddle of his army-issue horse, he asked himself why he was in the army. What was the value of this wildly idealistic experience? If Howe joined Cornwallis, as well he should, the army would be lost. And Washington, nay half the officers of the Continental Congress, would have to retreat behind the Alleghenies to save their necks from stretching.

He wondered what his friend and teacher Rafe Emison would think of this futile effort. Pity, or was it blessing, that he died before he could see his favorite pupil mount his steed, leave his beautiful classical education behind, and gallop off to the War of the Roses. And that is indeed what it is, George thought, as the two sets of English fight for their noble rights, devastating the land between with no more care than if it were a chessboard.

About the war, let us see, Rafe might have said, "*Dulce et decorum est pro patria mori.*" Would he have? Probably would not have thought that it was fitting and sweet to die for your country in this case. But he would have said "*carpe diem.*" Take whatever the day brings and turn it to good. Or like Polonius in Hamlet, once in a quarrel, acquit yourself well. Good advice. He would try it, but he would rather that his enemies were redcoats or Hessians, not his countrymen from Pennsylvania.

Lone Stag continued to come every fall after the death of John McClure, and led whoever wanted to go to one of the great forests beyond the mountains for the long hunt. He considered it a tribute to his dead white brother. If William McClure was initially made very uneasy by his presence, Lone Stag seemed oblivious to it.

The Indian's very refusal to accept Will's contempt over long jaunts through the mountains and around campfires disarmed Will. He pondered why this Indian seemed to be compassionate and intelligent and eventually began to tell people back home that "there be some Injeeans who make good sense and seem like normal people. They prob'ly have white blood in 'em." It was a part of Will's newly-evolved attitude toward Indians since they had ceased to become a threat to life and limb. Will thought of them now as the conquered race and as such, worthy only of contempt. Laugh at them, he said, even hunt with them, but do not take them seriously.

He could even be patronizingly friendly with young Indians he hunted with when he stayed at Indian villages. He prided himself on the fact that he understood their brutal natures and they understood him as a white man, and he began to pick up a few Indian words and teach them to Dan'l. On this particular long hunt in 1776, he was relaxed and conversational with both this Indian and his brother. It was a good time to take to the forest. He could escape from all the war talk and the necessity to evade going to fight blackguards in New Jersey when he had other things to do. Ohio country in all its virgin beauty beckoned, plenteous with wildlife; and although the war had intruded into its territory, the section to which they were going was peaceful.

Long Stag left Will and Dan'l in late October at the Allegheny River to go to Ottawa Country. Many of the Iroquois tribes, under the influence of Sir William Johnson's Tory nephew Guy, were supporting the Crown and beginning to terrorize settlements in northern Pennsylvania and New York. Lone Stag wished to journey north by the river so he could see if the Ottawas were taking the war belt, to convince them to remain uncommitted if he could.

Now, Dan'l, astride Vixen, a burnished chestnut whose dam was his father's horse Bess, and Will, riding a skittish mare ironically named Gentle, rode into an Indian village of the Miamis in the north central part of what is now the state of Ohio.

It was Dan'l's first long hunt in about five years; only recently had John felt he could spare him from fall chores. Besides, it was just in the last year or two that he had enjoyed the company of his opinionated, hard-drinking brother enough to want to spend two months in the saddle and woods with him, and vice versa.

When Will looked at his younger brother, he often saw a softer, more genial and outgoing version of the father he had loved so desperately and understood so little. The same slight, nervous limbs, the same hank of brown hair above an honest, open, if slightly rounder, face. At times, when Will would see Dan'l looking at him reproachfully if, for instance, William irritatedly kicked his sister's cat, or swore at a tub of lard which had tripped him, he thought for an instant he was looking at the elder John McClure.

But Dan'l McClure was a child of his mother as well as his father, Will often thought when he heard the two of them laughing long and loud about some foolish thing. They both were creatures of feeling and of delight, bewitched by beautiful skies and pear orchards in full bloom, lovers of the spaniels which, since his father's death, had been welcomed into the house. Will did not care for animals except horses. Still, Dan'l was a good jesting companion, although he drank little. And he was a good shot.

Will had been instructing Dan'l about the Indian customs of this particular village, and so Dan'l was not surprised when a group of chattering Indian children gathered around, dressed in heavy blankets and woolens to keep out the cool winds. As the two McClure brothers reined their horses, a smiling Indian youth came forward to clap them on the shoulder. "Friends of the Lone Stag, welcome. We were told to expect you about now. You honor us with your visit. Through visits like this we can learn to live in friendship." Then he added, as their horses were led away, "You will not stay in my cabin this time."

"That's Hidden Panther, the son of the band chief," Will told Dan'l. "For a Injeean, he's nobody's fool." Hidden Panther, it turned out, had been Will and Lone Stag's host for the past two years. He had prepared two small lodges near the edge of the camp, by a bubbling stream. Comfortable bear and buffalo skins rested on wooden frames off the floor, and dried peaches and apples had been set out for them in bowls.

"Not staying in his house. That's jest as well; the bear-fat smell might offend your nose. Ah. So we're to have a slice of some special hospitality." Will smiled mysteriously and Dan'l looked at him questioningly, but he did not explain what he meant.

"My brother wants to know of Indian lore, Hidden Panther. Let us walk in the woods," William said to the Indian rather imperiously. Without seeming to note anything in the tone, Hidden Panther led them through a series of trails away from camp.

It was true that Dan'l was eager to know of the Indian ways. Anything about nature intrigued him. Herbs that could be used for cooking and medicinal purposes, the family lives of animals, especially the habits of the majestic and ferocious bear, long vanished from eastern Pennsylvania, fascinated Dan'l. The yellow men themselves were not a common sight to him, as they had been to his father. Indians had largely disappeared from the Susquehanna Valley during the last ten years, so the sights and ways of this village were strange, almost exotic.

The three walked through groves of oak and maple, not different from those in Pennsylvania, except that the white man's axe had not touched them. On the early part of the trip from the river, near the Great Path, they met only a few scattered homesteads, which should not have been there. One of the reasons for the Revolutionary War was that George III was angered by settlement in this incredibly rich land west of the Alleghenies, settlement which had been forbidden by law. Pioneers crowding Pennsylvania and the southern colonies were ready to pour their pent-up homesteading energies into this new land, and some were already here in Ohio country.

"What do you eat here?" Dan'l asked the young Indian. William had gone up ahead to test his own skills at finding a path in the woods.

"Of the beasts of the land we eat the deer and buffalo, the elk and bear, the panther and racoon. Of special times a porcupine."

"You eat panther meat?"

"Its meat is sweet."

"I have heard you eat dog." For an instant in his mind's eye Dan'l could see his mother's spaniel Beauregard flopping its ears about her ankles. He wondered how Beauregard would taste, and smiled wryly.

"We do not eat dog meat. White men say we do, and I know the Ojibways will eat of this camp friend. But I do not know an Indian of the small lakes who eats dogs."

Dan'l seemed somewhat disappointed. "You shoot the wild turkeys, as we do?"

"Yes, and the duck, the bittern, and the wild goose, but never loons or herons. They do not taste good." Dan'l noted that, in case he should ever shoot a loon.

"Of fish we eat as you do, but not as my father says, like the Frenchmen," here he spat, "the snail or frog. They are unclean."

Dan'l looked keenly at Hidden Panther and had the odd sensation of seeing this Indian as a human being. "You are the son of the band chief. Your father is not here, Hidden Panther?" William had told him that Rising Star was away at the headwaters of the Maumee, talking to the tribe's council about the war.

"He has gone to Kekionga, where Maumee starts to flow, to talk to our chiefs. We are a scattered people since the war."

"Isn't this Mingo and Shawnee territory?"

"All tribes are dispersed as the English and French put bad ideas in our minds. But our band left Kekionga many moons ago with a rebellious chief and it stays away now. We argue with our own people. My father does not wish to fight to save fur lords across the sea, and the others do. We have relatives among the Shawnees; they let our band stay. For now." He smiled a little, then said, "We wish to be friends of all, and end up friends of none."

Dan'l impulsively warmed to the open-hearted young Indian. "I'll be your friend, Hidden Panther."

Hidden Panther turned and slapped his tattooed arm against Dan'l's. "Good, Dan'l MacLooer. Nika! Friend! What will you give me as a gift to seal the friendship?"

A transcendent impulse flared in Dan'l. "My father's rifle. I have my own now."

"Good!" Hidden Panther said, looking at the maple stock ornamented with a silver wild goose in flight. "And I shall have something of value for you. . ." They went, arm in arm to find Will and return to the village.

There they discovered that the women had gathered late Jerusalem artichokes and put them to cook slowly in an oven made of a hole in the ground. Venison was turning on a spit. They ate in the twilight, outside the winter shelters because it was not extremely cold. The meal ended with an orange-gold fruit Dan'l had never seen, bursting with juice, very tart and tasty—a persimmon, the Indians called it.

"Good in pudding. Put in the maple sugar and cook." A young Indian girl with black hair pulled back, clubbed, and plaited had come up by his side. She smiled and surprised him by putting an arm through his.

"This is my sister, Mulberry Blossom," said Hidden Panther. Another sister, Swamp Grass, taller than the one at Dan'l's side, was standing close to Will. The girls led the way to a lodge in the center of the village, where dancing soon began.

The young Indian men danced the dance of Smoky Moon among the flickering shadows of the campfire. The pungent smell of hickory smoke rose from the huge fire and drifted over the McClures' heads. As darkness deepened, the chants intensified, resounding in the stillness of the clearing. Soon, the women seated around the circle began to answer the chants, almost, Dan'l thought, like the hymn speller at the church at Big Spring reading one line out, the congregation answering. Except two groups chanted here. On the other side of the circle, sitting with the women, Mulberry Blossom and Swamp Grass rose to dance with the other women to the rythmic song.

Enchanted, he watched the beautiful Indian girl who had put her arm in his. Her feet beat the ground in cadence, her voice rose in a chant which had an almost hypnotic effect on the young man. The moment was strongly sensual.

Will jabbed him with his elbows in the ribs. "Dan'l, we're bein' honored. The Injeeans here believe the war will end with America winnin'. They want to lay the groundwork for peace with us. Mulberry Blossom and Swamp Grass are the daughters of the chief. They're sharin' our lodges tonight. Sumpin' new for you, eh?" His lips parted in a slight smile and Dan'l winced. His brother knew his secret. At twenty-two years of age, like his father before him, he was still virgin.

"But you know I. . ." he hesitated, "pledged myself to avoid fornication."

"Tonight you forget it. It would be a gross insult to the Injeeans, make 'em very mad. It's an honor, their way of showin' friendship."

Dan'l sighed, somewhat troubled, but as he realized guiltily, a little pleased with the situation. He did like to honor his word, even if it was given in rather odd circumstances.

The monk-like pledge had came out of a McClure family meeting his brother John had called five years ago, outside the cabin, when his mother and sister were away on a visit. They had been sitting by the eating table his father had made by the creek, on a little knoll which the McClure boys called among themselves "the swill spot" because it was here that William did his secret whiskey guzzling.

There they were: George McClure, fourteen-years-old but already taller than two of his brothers, he, Dan'l, sixteen, Will twenty-two, sometime wheelwright and already well-initiated into adult habits and pleasures, and John, the serious-minded, muscular farmer who managed the McClure land on the Conodoguinet and in Shearman's Valley. They sat in one of the wooded spots remaining among cultivated fields of corn and wheat they and their father had so laboriously wrought from the forest. It was a properous farm; their wheat was shipped to Philadelphia. They had taken care of the heritage their father left them and improved it.

John, Jr. was proud of what had been accomplished, although he always hurried by the pile of stones outside the cow pen, a pile that was to have been a huge barn by now. He had finally told them why he had called them together. "Ma and Jenny are gone, and I wanted to talk to you about somethin'. You may have wondered why I haven't married, and I know Will is talkin' about it some." Will had been courting, probably not seriously, a daughter of one of the Emisons at the mill near Mechanicsburg.

The four looked up. What was he getting to? "You're all of man's estate now," he said, looking at the tall, precociously mature George. "We have two good farms, but they's four of us. Not to mention Ma and Jenny. We got a good future, but it don't lie here." The others looked up in surprise. Their brother went on. "Dada dreamed of this home place here as the whole hog of everything he could want. My dream is bigger. I see us all as lairds—" it was a term only William understood "—Ma in peace and plenty in her old age, Jenny married to someone of the gentry." Will was alert, the others interested.

"So if we want to be, as you call it, lairds, where do we get the land?" Will asked.

"Pure and simple. Sell off. But not now. In ten years there will be land, the finest land in the world, rich and black, and ours for almost nothing, hundreds of acres apiece."

"Ohio country?" Dan'l asked. He had heard the Bards, Cherrys, and others talk of it.

"The King's Proclamation Line keeps everbody out, you know that," Will said, frowning.

"I think there's goin' to be a change, a big one," his brother insisted. "I ben talkin' to Rafe Emison when George goes in for his music and book lessons. Rafe says the Virginny interests are syndicatin', tryin' to press for land beyond the mountains. He says the rush of people to fine, fair land can't be contained."

"So?"

"These colonies are pickin' quarrels. We're like gawky apprentice boys that are growin' up and gettin sick of bein' ordered about. So we're goin' to run away, I think, before much longer."

"That's treason," Dan'l said, wide-eyed.

"No, just good horse sense. There's too much here for us to let the British keep it, especially if Virginny wants the land open. And after the war is over, millions of acres will be there for the takin'."

"But what are we goin' to do until the land is opened up, if it is?"

"It will be. And it's our only chance to get enough land for all and Ma and Jenny too. We wait, we farm and keep this place in good enough shape that some German will pay us several thousand dollars when we move." Even George looked intent at that news. John's offer was generous; the land was his. The rest of the brothers stood to have nothing, and he was offering them a profitable share for a new life.

"But here's the big thing. We don't marry yet. Not for a few years." Will looked sharply at him. "We don't know what the next few years will bring, and the Injeeans are going to be unsettled. I won't divide up the farms until we sell, and when I do, equal shares for all out of the proceeds. I don't want you cumbered down with wives and younguns." His voice was firm; he had decided on what should be done.

White clouds, fat as bolls of cotton, appeared between the trees. On the surface of the creek, water bugs skittered about; Dan'l thought he would like to go down and look at them.

"Well, how about it? Can we stay together, a fambly for six, seven years? If we do, we can all be rich."

Finally Dan'l asked the question in all of their minds. "It's yours, John. Why don't you just send us packin' and sell the land yourself?"

John McClure looked out over the creek. "Dada saved and waited fifteen years in Ireland so we could live like better folk when we came. We still will be if we wait the best opportunity. But fambly we are, and fambly we will be."

Will, whose reactions were never predictable, rose from the table. "I can do it if you can, John. Land, rollin' on over the hills, a mansion, even slaves. 'Twill be worth waitin' for."

"I guess it concerns you two more'n me," Dan'l said. "You are already of marryin' age." George shrugged his shoulders. Girls were strange, distant creatures to him; it would be no sacrifice. And five or six years was as remote as the moon. The McClure boys stood and the palms of their hands slapped together in the center of the table. "No sellin' off, no marryin' until the Ohio lands are open, your word on't," John announced firmly, and all sealed the pack with a whoop of affirmation.

"Well, there are always bawds and tinker daughters," Will had whispered in Dan'l's ear as they walked back to the house.

Not for me, Dan'l thought, and then, slowly a plan formed in his mind. Wait for marriage, however long that might be. He had joined the church at Big Spring and he was a true believer; it would be good Christian discipline to "keep himself pure," just as Dada had avoided strong drink. It wouldn't be difficult. Most of the girls in the neighborhood were not light-o'-loves anyway, and he would wait for the right one. He thought of the night yearnings and dreams he was experiencing, in which a girl with bare legs and a tight bodice danced like an Arabian before him. Oh well, it was for a good cause, getting rich, and anyway he could avoid the clap William was always worried about.

So now the Indian dance was over for the night, and the fifteen-year-old, smiling Mulberry Blossom was beckoning to him. Where is your high resolve, Dan'l McClure, he thought weakly. Hidden Panther was surely right when he said something of value would be his, if only for a moment. Her beauty filled his eyes and made him stand up and follow her, longingly. The sights and sounds of the wilderness seemed to close about him, like a leather purse, shutting out the Christian world. What was it the scriptures said, "He that looketh on a woman to lust after her hath already committed adultery with her in his heart." So, the sin was already done, in a way, and he would atone for it later. He could forget about it now. And anyway, it was only a thing of a moment, a casual deed, to be done and forgotten about. He took her hand, and as they headed for the log lodge, he experienced embarrassment and curiosity, wondering what the next hour would be like.

Will smoked a pipe of Indian tobacco outside his guest lodge. Swamp Grass had not yet come to him. She was gathering some cooking utensils for the breakfast she would cook him tomorrow. He stretched his muscular frame along the ground comfortably, tasting the smoke as he puffed. He had gone to the sweat house down the hill to ease away the slight muscle aches of the hours in the saddle, and now he looked forward with anticipation to the night ahead. He had been to this camp before. Old prim Dan'l would get the surprise of his life. The Miami girls were not promiscuous, but their attitude toward sexual intercourse was as different from that of the prim women in the Scotch-Irish settlements as cream is from skim milk. The coming together of two young, healthy people was as natural to the Miamis as eating wholesome food. To the selected whites they chose to be with, they gave themselves joyously, eager to give and get pleasure.

Will sat thoughtfully, puffing for several minutes in silence. The sounds of the village, children's voices asking questions in the strange language, dogs barking, had stilled. Dan'l had been in there for fifteen minutes now. Will smiled again.

Above, in the winter sky, the stars flickered thinly. The little fires inside the lodges burned clean, their smoke emerging from holes in the tops. Voices floated out of the dome-shaped lodge covered with cattails, bark and trader's cotton; and one of the voices was very familiar.

"Miss Mulberry Blossom." Several seconds passed. A slight giggle.

"Miss Mulberry Blossom, what are you doing?"

This time a female laugh.

A sigh. "I like you, Dan'l MacLooer."

"Miss Mulberry Blossom, oh my." Then male laughter.

"Miss Mulberry Blossom, oh my God." Then silence. William McClure, still smiling, went inside his own lodge and sat down on a woven mat.

It was the first week in December. George McClure and Bige Cherry were with the battalion at Trenton, New Jersey, helping arrange to take the army across the Delaware into Bucks County.

The war, represented by advancing British general Cornwallis, was reaching desperately near the capital in Philadelphia. Captain Tom Kennedy had been ordered out from Washington's camp again post-haste, to Cumberland County, to help General Thomas Mifflin bring newly recruited troops to help defend Philadelphia.

The brash captain had begged and received permission for a one-day trip before he left, to go to Princeton and help evacuate his father, and he had asked to take George with him. The road from Trenton to Princeton was muddy and rutted at the best of times, but in this December of 1776 it was a quagmire of neighing, frightened horses, overloaded carts and families fleeing before the advance of the dreaded redcoats and Hessians.

McClure and Kennedy urged their horses around the column of struggling refugees. By mid-day they turned off the main road down a winding lane and reined at a farmhouse to refill canteens, take a rest, and perhaps buy food. A prosperous-looking farm woman, wearing a cap and buckle shoes, came to the door and gasped when she saw the uniforms of the Pennsylvania regulars. "Oh, good gentlemen, kind gentlemen, do not harm my family, preserve us, oh God." She fell on her knees before them in a dramatic position and the startled George McClure helped her to her feet.

"Good wife, we come only to get water and perhaps buy some bread and cheese of you," George said, going with her into her substantial stone home.

"Yes, bread, good sirs, and I have cheese. Yes, cheese." She set them at the table and took out bread, cheese, and a small amount of sliced beef, the best food either of them had seen for two weeks.

"The other soldiers took the better beef and fowl and the pork pies and applecake. The potatoes I hid in the cellar. . ." she looked horrified at her revelation and then lapsed into stolid silence.

"What other soldiers do you speak of?" George asked.

"British. They had red coats and sabers hanging from their sides. They spent the night t' other night. Said they was an advance guard and needed shelter from American scouts. They stabled their horses in our barn. Ate enough at night to strangle a mule. They took my poor, dead husband's peach brandy and drank until they staggered. Swore, slapped my face when I ranted at them for putting the silver in a pillow case to take as 'spoils of war,' as they called 'em."

Kennedy looked up questioningly from his meal and the woman went on. "Took my daughter's porringer she had when she was just a baby. She goes on sixteen years now. A tea service, first quality from Philadelphia, six goblets, other things too."

She was a handsome woman whose hair was still black under a cap. A wide satin ribbon was tied beneath her chin. "They took themselves off to bed laughing and loud," she said. Her hand went to her bosom, where a brooch decorated a high-necked blouse, and her mouth worked. "About one o'clock, after the commotion had died down, a strange mewing sound woke me up. I thought perhaps the cat was trapped belowstairs, and I got up to let it out. Then I began to hear choking cries. I shall never forget them as long as I live, sirs. I went to my daughter's room and there the pretty thing was, lying in her bed, her clothing tore off and one of the soldiers ravishing her while the other prepared to do the same." Tears came into her eyes, fell fast, and spilled onto the table. George could not bear to look at her.

"I went to get my husband's musket, which I always kept loaded, and returned ready to dispatch the blackguards. But they, alerted to my intent, met me at the door of the room and used the butt of the gun. . ." She untied the ribbon of her cap from under her chin, took down the first button of her high blouse and showed a bloody bruise along the side of her face and neck. She grasped the edge of the table and George rose to support her. She continued to weep silently, and George looked into her face with real pain.

Captain Tom Kennedy rose also, but his feeling seemed to be one of embarrassment. George told himself that Kennedy was probably thinking the situation bothersome, a scene out of a London domestic drama.

"So we patriots grow to know the sacrifices of war with a despicable enemy," Kennedy said stiffly.

"I am no patriot, sir," she said, regaining her composure. "I am a loyal subject of His Majesty, George III. But," she added, "I am not sure how long I shall remain so if such are his soldiers."

They nodded, and after wishing her and her recovering daughter well, bade goodbye.

They headed into the town of Princeton and Nassau Hall, where Kennedy's father was hastily assembling his goods to go across the Delaware into Pennsylvania and begin the trip to refuge in Shippensburg.

The senior Kennedy stood outside the two-story Georgian home on the road behind Nassau Hall. He shook George's hand distractedly. He was of medium height with a thick, almost curling lower lip and clustered curls which had once been yellow like his son's, but now were white, and wore work clothes, perhaps to remain unobtrusive on the road. A trunk of clothing, bags of meal, flour, and salted hams, some pieces of silver wrapped in linen, a few pieces of furniture, and two family portraits were all that he had room to take, along with his family poodle, who yapped excitedly at everybody's heels.

George and Tom Kennedy began loading the two-wheeled cart. "I had a dreadful time arranging for this," the father admittted. " 'Tis the last one in town and ready to fall apart. The students took all the rest."

Not really believing the danger at first, the senior Kennedy thought he would stay until he had reliable word that the British were within a few miles of the area. He sighed. " 'Twas a week ago, President Witherspoon called us together to tell us the enemy was too close for us to continue classes." It was all confusion from then on, he told them, students rushing about to dispose of their goods and hire transport, Whigs in town fleeing to cross the river, American advance parties raiding and looting and turning people out of bed, and everyone in distress and fear.

"When the American army came through town, I thought of the old nursery rhyme about the beggars coming to town. Some in rags and some in tags and some in velvet gowns." American troops were stationed in Princeton under General Nathanael Greene, and now they too were retreating. As George and Kennedy's son put the older man into the cart to jolt along beside his possessions, he shook his head sadly. "Shall I ever teach the calculus again in this hall?" he wondered, then kissed his son goodbye, warning him to guard his skin.

George looked back at the magnificent, four-story brick college building, said to be the largest in America, as he rode by young Kennedy's side out of town. Even now, with his mind on everything but arithmetic, he felt a yearning toward all Nassau hall represented. I could have been there. In another time or another place. It's all like an upside down Punch and Judy play, with nothing making sense. Americans fleeing the service and stealing from their own countrymen, British attacking Tories, universities closing down for guns to fire into their walls. And as always in the last few weeks, the final question, What is this all about? Why did I come? Morosely he turned his horse toward Pennsylvania. They were to ride as fast as possible to meet the troops from home.

After three days on the road they came upon the new, brown-coated militiamen marching proudly out of Lancaster—the troops from Cumberland County, inspired by urgent recruiting efforts and ready to help defend Philadelphia. "March with all possible speed to General Washington's camp at Newton," was the message Kennedy delivered to them, but all possible speed seemed to be seven days for the green troops. The final destination turned out to be Bristol, down the Delaware a bit, where Philadelphian John Cadwalader was assembling Pennsylvania troops into a fighting unit.

When the group came into camp, Bige Cherry did a mock inspection of the men from Shippensburg and Carlisle and declared them to be "dreadful good patriots." Bige was limping around. He had "camp itch" and his thighs were raw and bare, even with the ointment the physician supplied.

George had a new tentmate, John Hunter, who came from Shippensburg, from a farm not far from Kennedy's large holdings. He was a very short man with a large hawk's nose, intelligent eyes and an especially shrewd "bush" sense of humor. A natural match for Bige, George thought, and took to him at once. The first night in camp, Hunter stretched out in the chilly tent and asked George to tell him about the progress of the war.

George complied, summing up the dismal story of failure and retreat in New York by saying, "The only reason it isn't all over with us is that Howe has been staying safe and comfortable in his mistress's arms in New York and refuses to press the war too hard."

Hunter grunted. "It ain't lust but sloth that really is his problem. The English who come over here are lazy as pigs. They cain't get too far from the fireplace, their plum puddin's, and hot toddies. They hate to lift their hand to even sign a paper," he sighed.

Then he went on: "Reminds me of the farmer who was so lazy the folks in his village decided to bury him alive and then on the way out o' town giv' him another chance, and two bushels o' corn to start life over with."

Bige knew the story, everybody did. "An' he sat up in his coffin' an' asked 'Is it shelled?' They said, 'No,' and he said, 'Drive on.' " Bige gleefully pointed his finger at Hunter, then his smile faded. "I don't see what it's got to do with Howe and the British."

"They're lazier than the farmer and we're a-gonna nail their coffins shut, too," Hunter said, and Bige nodded vigorously in affirmation. Then Hunter lay back and shut his eyes to try to get some sleep.

December 20 came, with a few snow flurries in the crisp, frosty air and the hint of Christmas about. The scraggly soldiers of George Washington had little time to worry about their bare legs, scanty rations, or even the carols the folks were singing back home. In a bold and imaginative stroke, Washington was planning to hit the enemy hard by surprise, before the Delaware River froze and allowed passage for the British into the American camps. He also wanted to strike before the enlistments of his pitiful army of three thousand were up.

The first movement of the plan would be against a group of Highlanders and

Hessians near the town of Mount Holly, across the river. The Cumberland County boys were to be part of this attack, intended to divert Colonel Carl Donop's Hessians from the main business at hand—Washington's Christmas crossing of the Delaware against the Hessian stronghold at Trenton. Donop's troops couldn't reinforce Trenton if they were fighting at Mt. Holly.

Hunter chuckled when George told him that Washington was obviously planning an offensive attack. "Very smart, that," he said, biting at a bar of maple sugar he brought from home. Hunter was already introduced to the standard mess of salt beef cooked in a spider over the fire and beans, and he had found his own ways to supplement meals. The little farmer also had a bag of apples from his home orchard.

"This strategy is right from the woods." Hunter cleared his throat, the sign of the beginning of a frontier story. "The Injeeans like to eat porcupine meat ever now and then, a delicacy 'twere. Now the problem is how to corner a porcupine. Efn you fright him up head on, he shoots his quills. So the Injeeans take their time and use their heads, 'cause they are at a disadvantage with this critter. First, they find the porcupine. Then they follow him, sneaky-like, to his den when he don't see 'em. Then, when he is asleep, dreamin' his pleasant porcupine dreams, they come up and shoot 'im from behind. He can't shoot quills when he's dead."

Bige and George looked at him quizzically as they ate. Hunter smiled knowingly. "The Hessians think they invented Christmas instead of the Lord. They'll be in their cups on Christmas night, and the General will sneak up while they sleep, cozy-like across the river. We'll see how sharp their quills are when they're caught unawares." Popping the last piece of sugar into his mouth, he strode off to cook the three days' traveling rations that all the troops had been ordered to prepare.

The next day Tom Kennedy's company was part of that force of nine hundred men who crossed the river and headed down the road to find the troops of the British and Hessians around Mount Holly. The attack force brought two field pieces with them and their rifles were ready. For the first time George felt he was really about to "get to the meat o' the nut." He had to be ready to either kill a man within the next few hours or be killed himself.

Three days till Christmas, thought Jane McClure, and her family were scattered like chaff, miles apart. Will was gone into Carlisle to make Christmas cheer with his friends. Tom Bard, the genial cousin of Sam's, who said very little but never declined a round of whiskey or a card game, came in from Chambersburg, and Ardry, married but unchanged in his spit-in-the-eye-of-the-world attitude, would keep late hours. Her wayward boy Will would be home for Christmas Day.

Jane picked up the book she had ordered from a Philadelphia bookseller, stroking its binding, smiling with satisfaction. It had a leather cover, with red on the end of the pages. John Locke's *Treatise on Civil Government*. Georgie had expressed an admiration for it, and she found a way to get it for him. But she could not send it; God only knew where George was, defending the new nation and possibly catching smallpox, like others she had heard about in Washington's army.

Someone else was absent, too. The pain at the loss of her husband grabbed her heart even after nine years. Her love. What would John think of them all today? Would he think she had done right with them? And what would he think of her? He had considered her beautiful and said so once, grudgingly, when he came back from Kittanning (she smiled, again, at the recollection). He would have been surprised at how stout she was now. She was a little suprised at it herself. Sometimes she ate to conquer the loneliness that came in the night.

But Johnny, steady John was there, heading the family, and they listened to him, and Dan'l, tending to the animals and feeding the chickens in the new chicken house, and Jenny, her good girl, sensitive and lively, who wrote poems by the fire at night. Jane had bought Jenny a small book of writing paper and a new quill pen. At seventeen Jenny worried that she was homely, and it was true that her teeth were not even and her hair was fine and thin, as John's had been. But something inside Jenny glowed like the evening star. That was beauty.

Jane sat down by the fire to stir the applesauce. She thought about her boys' postponed marriages. Certainly it made sense during the war. Very few were marrying now, and it wasn't easy to "go to housekeeping" out here in the valley even in the best of times. The land was beginning to be used up, harvest yields were down. There was not enough land for all the strapping sons who had come along. So the plan to sell and move on was a good one. But John was twenty-seven. It was hard to wait; she'd be too old to rock her grandchildren when they finally came. Still, it had been John, Sr.'s idea originally to go as gentry. Even though they hadn't ended up that way, it was still right to do all in order.

Jenny came into the cabin, slamming the door. She had been taking a walk in the cold, crisp air. She snapped off her cape and hung it carefully on a chair, laughing.

"I saw some rabbits out of their holes. Followed their tracks." She frowned. "But I scared 'em and they tried to lead me away from their dens. Poor li'l things, as if I would want to hurt them or their babes."

"I am making some shortbread. Would you like to help?"

"Umm, maybe in a bit. I have a thing or two I want to write down."

Her mother began creaming butter in the wooden bowl. Jenny sat down. Pine logs in the fire spat and popped and the girl jumped back, and plopped herself onto the braided rug Mrs. Bard made for them. She liked Mrs. Bard, liked visiting her and her old maid daughter Caroline and son Tim in the big house.

Really, though, there was too much activity lately in Carlisle, which was continuing to grow, now especially with the war, Jenny thought. The settlement at Harris's Ferry was also growing into a real town, Harrisburg. Soldiers marched through Carlisle, people argued about "loyalty." Some folks said Philadelphia might be British in the new year.

She didn't care about the war much, not really, and she wasn't the only one. Out here in this valley, people seemed to go about their business and not fret themselves about battles and strategies. Sometimes she thought it was not even happening. But it was. George's letters scared her. She patted her hair, in a bun on top of her head with a sprig of holly in it for the season, put the pen and ink on the floor in front of the rug, and took out a piece of paper.

> *A rabbit went a-walking, far from his woods abode.*
> *He met a soldier of the king patrolling on the road.*
> *"Stop you stupid animal. Be you squirrel, rat or mole*
> *King Lion says you cannot pass until you pay the toll."*

Right now Georgie would be in camp. Was he washing his linen in cold water? Was there anyone to talk to—anyone who could understand the odd, clever things he said the way she did?

> *The rabbit answered "We are free, we own this very street*
> *No one can tell us where to walk, we made it with our feet."*
> *The soldier roared, "Arrest him," but the rabbit had no fear.*
> *"I'll call my friends and relatives and they will fight you here*
> *The king may be a lion, with a castle high and tower*
> *But free rabbits fighting for their homes have supernatural power. . ."*

She didn't like the word "supernatural." It sounded like a witch was going to help the rabbits, not God. But "celestial" and "omnipotent" didn't fit. She studied the poem, disappointedly. Somehow the diction wasn't elevated enough. Georgie had given her a book of English nature poems about the woods and they were so—sublime. She tossed her paper down in disgust. It was stupid anyway, a rabbit on a road in an imaginary forest while Georgie might be lying on a real road in New Jersey, bleeding, right this very moment.

But George was still hale and hearty, if a good deal thinner from poor food during the skirmishes and forced marches the brigade had endured all during the week Jenny was celebrating Christmas. Now, on December 28, he, Bige Cherry, and John Hunter were preparing to march into Bordentown, New Jersey, along with the rest of John Cadwalader's troops.

George had not as yet had to kill anyone, and he had hardly been shot at. The diversionary action against Count Donop at Mt. Holly was a confusing, indecisive skirmish near a church. Both the Hessians and the Americans had fired a few shots and then retreated. But the threat of rebel soldiers in the area, along with the presence of a beautiful doctor's widow in the house Donop had taken over, made him decide to stay where he was instead of marching the troops to Trenton to reinforce Colonel Rall there.

It was a disastrously wrong decision on Donop's part. As George and the rest of the battalion heard the day after Christmas, Washington had marched his intrepid bunch of rebels as planned through dark and early dawn hail, sleet, and snow to surprise the Hessians as they lay sleeping off the effects of a Christmas night party. The Battle of Trenton was a glorious day for the new nation, but one of the worst in Hessian military history. Rall could have used the troops that stayed at Mt. Holly.

So it all went just as John Hunter had predicted, but he refused to gloat. "Washington and his generals may have found fame," he said, "but the battle we were in, 'twere nothin' but a fizzle. If the war were an elephant, 'twould be the frizzled fuzz at the end of his tail. If 'twere the hall of the Quaker assembly house in Philadelphia, our battle would be the doormat."

Bige Cherry chimed in. "If the war were a teacup, the Battle of Mount Holly would be six piddling leaves on the bottom of the cup. If. . ."

"All right, you two," George interrupted them with a smile.

The garralous humor of Cherry and Hunter had seen them through tough times, as they lay on the floors of meeting houses, too cold to sleep, or ate congealed beans and ham around fires that burnt their faces while their posteriors froze in the snow.

Washington's forces returned with prisoners across the Delaware. But the Cumberland County troops, minus Kennedy, who had joined Washington's staff, re-crossed and began pursuing the Hessians and royal troops south along the Delaware. Always a few miles behind them, the rebel troops could find British cooking fires still smoldering and local turncoat farmers prepared to deal with the sudden reverses of war, hastily taking down red scarfs from their doors as the British departed.

When the Second Pennsylvania Battalion came into Bordentown and were ordered to find quarters in a house the King's troops had just vacated, George was shocked at the squalid state of what had been a well-to-do New Jersey townsman's house. Cherrywood chairs were broken up and burnt in the fireplace, china service broken and tossed into the corner. Straw and filth had been scattered all about, and most of the fine possessions were taken away, looted by the Hessian women.

The three comrades, along with others of the Shippensburg-area company, prepared to stretch out before the fire for their first complete night's sleep in days. Tomorrow, the commander of the polyglot forces from New England and Pennsylvania, Brigadier General Thomas Mifflin would tell them how and when their next fight was.

Early the next morning Mifflin paraded the small Bordentown group and George scrutinized him. He had not seen the well-known Philadelphian at first hand before: Mifflin was a surprisingly young man, in his early thirties, with closely-set eyes, a firm mouth, and a hairline that was already beginning to recede.

His speech was short and eloquent. "We have just completed at Trenton what history will record as a turning point in the struggle for man's rights. We have shown tyranny what free men who battle for their own country can do, even though they fight in rags, with damp powder and without bayonets. It is not powder and bayonets, after all, which win wars and liberate men, but their own spirits, which, doggedly through all adversity, hunger, discomfort and illness, fight on. By firesides, your children and grandchildren will tell the story of this struggle in a new, free land with fair laws and united spirits.''

Cherry, standing in ranks beside George, spoke from the corner of his mouth. "He's goin' to ask us to do somethin' impossible. Mark my word.''

"I want a few good volunteers. A regiment of enemy lighthorse troops is stationed at Cranbury, and I want to surprise and take them.'' John Hunter stretched his arms out behind his two comrades on either side. Temporarily off balance from the short push he gave their backs, George and Cherry stepped forward. "We'll go, sir.'' Hunter said.

Chapter XV

Cornwallis now boxed the American army in New Jersey between the Delaware, which could no longer be crossed, and a chain of British-Hessian camps in towns north of the river. While Washington was desperately trying to avoid being snared at Trenton, the "light troops" marching to distant Cranbury talked about the predicament.

"It's thisaway for Washington," Hunter told Cherry and George as they plodded down the road. Melting snow and thawing had turned it into a slithery morass. "He's like a man I knew went out to hunt with another man in the dark, and they shot at somethin' in a tree, thinkin' 'twere a coon. The one man went up into the tree to shake it down. They was a terrible scrabblin' and scratchin' from the tree. 'Twas a live wildcat. 'Do you want me to come up and help you catch that crittur?' the other man said. 'Hell, no,' the first one said, 'git up here and help me let 'im go.' Washington's tryin' to let Cornwallis go." They chuckled and marched on.

After a while George said to the others, "Let's talk about something, anything. I'm consarned sleepy."

"How bout food?" Hunter said helpfully. "Beef stew and pound cake and hot chicken broth."

"No, not that."

"Women," Cherry suggested, but the two friends protested that subject too.

"Yankees," Hunter said. "People from *Noooo* England." The three men were particularly contemptuous of the Yankees, who were now claiming they alone were responsible for the rebel army's recent successes.

"The men from Maine say we are cowards, that the Pennsylvania line ran in New York. They say the Pennsylvania militia is loud and crude," said George.

Cherry put in, "I don't know why those God-damned Bostonians say our language is foul. Hell, they don't know a rifle butt from their own arses anyways." The group marched on in discontented silence.

"Why did you come, John?" George asked Hunter. "We're a ragged joke of an army and the redcoats are as powerful as any military force in the world. We have no discipline and no bayonets. If they catch us they'll kill us or hang us as traitors. If they don't catch us it's worse—we can get holes in our chests or our ankles blown off. And we didn't even have to go."

"You're right 'bout that. I left a new home, hadn't been in't more'n a few months. And a mother and father who needed me, brethren and sisters. Came from Delaware and now I'm back here in the East, like an Injeean doublin' back to cover my trail. Why?'' Hunter stroked the stubble on his chin. "Guess it's a capital venture. I'm buyin' shares in the future.''

George pondered this. Maybe this was really what the war was all about—a hundred years from now. It was intolerable to think that the British would be making decisions about his children's land and fortunes. His father had crossed an ocean to get away from supercilious, domineering bastards who interferred with personal freedom. Did every generation have to fight the bastards to be able to live their lives?

When they arrived at Cranbury, the pigeons had flown. Doggedly, the troops returned to Bordentown and the hope of rest. The rest, however, was of short duration.

Lieutenant Tom Kennedy needed two deep-woodsmen to help scout a back road that Washington wanted clear for some new and secret movement. Kennedy chose Cherry and George. They must go on horseback at once and would plan to meet a man from the neighborhood to complete the mounted patrol. They said goodbye to Hunter, wondering if, and when, they would ever see him again.

They arrived at Trenton about five o'clock and ate dinner around the campfire with Kennedy. Cherry offered to stir at a communal pot which had six men around it. They were supplied with a new invention: soup stock cubes, boiled down, jellied and cut into squares, so they could be taken into the field. Each man put in whatever he had, an onion, some turnips, barley or corn to the "portable soup.''

Talk drifted, as it always did around these campfires, to the generals' conduct of the war. "We're not abiding by the military code of honor," Kennedy complained. "New Year's day someone shot a ramrod through a British regular's neck. We are murdering from ambush in cold blood. Soldiers should see each other before they shoot.''

George did not answer. That was the way the Duke of Marlborough did it, all right, he thought, but it seemed like pure stupidity to any frontiersman. A man didn't expect a pheasant to strut out for him and he shouldn't parade for her, not if he expected to have her in the frypan that night.

"We shoot from trees,'' Kennedy continued with contempt. "The lines aren't properly dressed.''

"War isn't a minuet ball,'' George said testily, drinking from his canteen.

Kennedy's thin lips constricted. "War is senseless butchery unless conducted by a code of honor. I most admired Washington when he invited the Hessian officers for dinner following the victory at Trenton. This was honorable behavior.''

"Or play actin','' Cherry snorted. He had found some cider royale in a Tory basement near Cranbury and was taking a little bit for his stomach before the long ride out. "Best stock up while we can,'' he said. His haversack contained only a little jerked beef and some cooked-up mush; there wasn't time for anything fancier.

Darkness came swiftly, and with it cold and a rising wind. Kennedy brought George and Bige to a rendezvous point and they waited with the horses until the regular from the neighborhood appeared to guide them. Then, after he pointed out the dark, narrow path they should take, the two Pennsylvanians swung into the saddle to sweep the road. They did not dare guess who or what was going up this winding track. Parts of it were through a thick forest. The two penetrated where they could to listen for movements and heard none. Two-inch stumps stuck up on the trace; it had not long been a road and was not now much used. Very good, George mused, if secret movements were to be made.

The breath of the panting horses stood out in pale clouds in the cold, still air as George and Cherry stopped to rest a moment. The two scouts pulled up their cloaks against the cold. "If this ooze hadn't froze we'd be up to our arses in mud," said Cherry. His voice, filtered through the wool of the cloak, came to George as if from a distance. The stars were out, but indistinct, muffled, as if the entire dome of the sky was in batting.

They reported back to Kennedy at a prearranged meeting point, then swept the road again. The New Jersey regular returned to headquarters to lead—who? down this road. By two in the morning it was obvious who. Silently a muffled army crept along the road, carrying muskets and pulling swathed cannons so as to make no noise. Orders were whispered. Washington's army was letting go of the wildcat, sneaking away from Cornwallis along a track unknown to the British patrols. Since their scouting jobs were over, McClure and Cherry fell in with Kennedy's Pennsylvania militia which was marching near the head of the troops.

Dawn came, pink and frigid. The column left the byroad and went onto a real road, still marching. The troops paused on command, then split, the Pennsylvania militia marching by a northern route to what all now knew was Princeton, the British stronghold. The sun rose, turning the ice crystals on weeds in the New Jersey fields into millions of reflecting shards. This will be no tail of the elphant, George thought, and at that very moment glimpsed the glint of metal, the flash of red uniforms, seen through the bare trunks of trees ahead. They had found the enemy.

The Pennsylvanians who led the column of troops were confused momentarily; where in God's name were the orders? They grouped and a contingent of two hundred men advanced. The battle had begun. George and Cherry, with surprising calm, tethered the horses to a tree at the side of the road. They would return for them when, and if, they could. Now was the time to be afoot with men from home.

They heard the crack of muskets ahead, and in a couple of minutes a cannon blasting. "Hurry on, men," Kennedy and the other officers commanded. They all came out, trotting, into a field, with the stark, empty branches of fruit trees about and farm houses up ahead on a little rise. The troops of—was it General Mercer?—already had met heavy enemy firing and were scattering, some firing, some falling back. Well-dressed British lines were only one hundred yards off.

Officers ordered the troops to advance and eventually to spread out behind a fence. George, with the Philadelphians, got behind a post and began to load and fire. All about him was the hot, snapping sound of muskets and the whistle of balls flying over his head. His thoughts were disjointed. Damn. Rifle takes too long to load. Spins the ball, but it has to ram home just right. No cover behind this rail. Where is Cherry? Smoke is thick as a clogged fireplace.

The First Pennsylvania Battalion formed in line of battle opposing the redcoats. Shot whistled and screamed in the air. With his heart in his throat, George saw the First Pennsylvania begin to fall back, chaotically, on each other and on the Second Battalion.

His stomach a tight knot, expecting every minute to die, George eased back from the fence just as the British began a screaming bayonet charge. The thought entered his mind that this eerie communal scream was the wail of the banshee his mother was always talking about. Mother. Jenny. Was there ever such a thing as home, a place of comfort? Through the smoke and between volleys, he could see British grenadiers stabbing, over and over, fallen American soldiers. As he moved back he could see a Britisher knocking a wounded young soldier in the side of the head.

Others were savagely turning cannons on fleeing Virginians and Pennsylvanians. He was near enough to pick out features; the redcoats were screaming bloodthirsty imprecations which chilled him almost as much as the firing and death around him. It was as if the enemy were personally angry. A lusty voice yelled, "You God-damned rebels! We'll teach you to murder from trees."

Kennedy was dashing around yelling, "Dress the line."

Gesturing towards the murderously intent British, George shouted hoarsely at the Shippensburg captain, "So this is your honorable warfare," and then turned to try to help the men make a stand. It seemed hopeless. Most of the soldiers around him were running like rabbits.

New Englanders came up among the retreating troops, and all was utmost confusion. "God, may I not die a coward," George prayed. He caught sight of Cherry, firing calmly through the smoke from behind a tree. Then he saw officers on horseback thunder up furiously in front of the fence.

He stood still a fraction of a minute as balls whistled by his head, and he heard a booming voice, saw a huge, commanding figure loom through the smoke. George Washington was shouting encouragement. "There is but a handful of them." There was more, in an inspiring tone, but he couldn't hear the rest.

The troops stopped running. They turned and began a shouting advance, George joining in, although he had no bayonet for a charge. A joyous, fierce shout behind him told him they were being supported. Fresh troops had come up. Hatred such as he had never known propelled his muscles; he seemed to be functioning by reflex, as if he were a wooden soldier doll. Across the field, through apple trees—then he felt the inexpressible joy of seeing the enemy pause, break line, and finally run in the face of the American charge.

The soldiers of the new nation continued advancing. Whispered word was passed from soldier to soldier. "They fly. The day is our own." No words, not his mother's loving comfort, not his sister's tender laugh, could ever sound as sweet as those words did to George McClure. "The day is ours." And, he thought wonderingly, perhaps the campaign.

There, watching the great general from America on horseback calmly defying the troops of the European kings, the fear of his own troops and even death itself, George finally knew. He knew why he was there. Yes, he thought as he panted to regain his breath, it could work. Maybe there could be a new land of men of courage and strength inspired by a dream of freedom. He slumped by a tree, exhausted, as helpless as a baby. Any man who could make Pennsylvanians, the most damned independent, stubborn, and even ignorant people on the face of the earth, quit running to save their skins and pull together like a team, was some sort of man. Anybody who could do that could probably even win a war. Well, at least he was pretty sure of it. They might end up killing the wildcat.

George could not restrain the cynicism he sometimes indulged in when he thought about his brothers' disinterest in the war. "So now you non-associators are going to have to do a little marching and get your pretty shoes scuffed," he said, stretching out to read the *Philadelphia Gazette* before the fire. "It says the assembly has authorized constables to enroll all able-bodied white males between the ages of eighteen and fifty-three."

"That so?" Will McClure was whittling in the corner. George was unbearable, Will thought acidly, since his return a week ago from "the wars." It wasn't enough that he read books and talked different from everybody else out here now. Since he'd been to soldiering, his head was as big as a hog's ball, and he went about playing the hero of Princeton, and Monmouth, and Sandy Hook.

"You will all be enrolled." George looked pointedly at Dan'l and John, working on harness across from him in preparation for the spring planting. "We'll see how you like sowbelly and hardtack cooked into a nice little supper mess. How you appreciate lying on cold mud and having your ears burst with mortar shell."

"Lytle was over not long ago," John said. The Indian fighter had settled down on land near Rafe Emison's old farm and now had a son who was seven years old. "He said the groups would be called in classes, which would be rotated for active service. Short term only."

"And if you cain't go, you can get you a substitute. Or pay a fine," Will said nonchalantly, kicking at a little pile of shavings at his feet. He was making a whistle as a present for a widow "lady" whom he visited on a farm outside Carlisle.

George was consulting the article. "It doesn't say anything about substitutes here," he mumbled sourly.

"Waal, I assure you 'tis so. Lytle told me he'd fall dead if most of the boys in Cumberland County saw much service atall."

George threw the paper against the wall and, grabbing at his linen jacket, strode outside. His mother and sister were doing the wash, pounding the clothes already "biled" in a tub of rinsewater before they hung them on the fence.

"And you, Brother Dan'l," Will said, back inside the cabin, watching his pleasant younger brother rub neat's foot oil into the leather which would soon pull the plow. "Are you ready an' able to go to your country's aid?"

"My time will come, and I'll go. You will too, William, if you hafta."

"I ain't inspired. There don't seem no good reason."

"Push ain't come to shove yet. I 'spect it will." His thoughts were far away. As always, when Dan'l did "settin' down chores," his thoughts roved over Blue Mountain to the Allegheny chain, green and beautiful, and past that to the winding river, with green waters that flowed past Fort Pitt, and Ohio Country.

Lone Stag would not come this year. The Ohio Indians were unsettled and even hostile, agitated by the British; they were attacking in the county which Virginia had set up in the new land of Kentucky. Hidden Panther could no longer welcome old friends. Dan'l thought of Mulberry Blossom and moved uncomfortably in his chair.

He shouldn't a-done that. He prayed about it sometimes but he didn't feel any better. God's chosen should act like the chosen, even if it was getting hard to tell who the chosen were any more, what with Presbyterians all over the Colonies startin' to preach to all the drunks and thieves and talkin' salvation for all. At least the minister at the new Big Spring church didn't preach New Side blather. He didn't even allow Isaac Watt's hymns to be sung. Too radical.

As far as Dan'l was concerned, the war made him feel like one of the Irish ghosts his mother talked about, caught in the cairns between the human and the spirit world, wandering, unfulfilled. It wasn't that he was unpatriotic; he hoped there would be a new land. But he had never been to Philadelphia, let alone New York. He couldn't conceive of Boston. He simply wanted his own virgin land, his own future, and he couldn't have them while the war was on.

John's plan to wait to marry was hardest on Dan'l. He saw the young girls at church, ready and smiling at him and he wanted to take their hands and post the banns, right that minute. Sometimes he feared he might give in to the irresistible impulse to stand up in the morning service and take some ripe young woman's hand and say, "I want to tell you all that Addie and I. . ." And he would be humiliated, because she would never have heard tell of it before.

For John it was not quite as difficult. He had the worry and responsibility of the two farms; Will simply took his pleasure and refused to worry about the future. Georgie was cold and thought too much, without feeling, at least Dan'l supposed that was the way he was. George never talked about his thoughts with Dan'l.

Colder 'n a chilled oyster. Just the opposite of me, he thought ruefully. Tears would come to his eyes sometimes, in spite of all he could do, over the sun setting. It was unmanly. Some people in Philadelphia approved of "men of feeling." George had said so. Dan'l, though, was secretly ashamed of being so womanish.

When summer came, an irony occurred, or so George wryly alleged. Will decided to go to the Cumberland County militia instead of buying off, and further, he was chosen captain of the local company of Davis's Second Battalion.

George tried to ponder out how his brother actually ended up in the militia. Maybe it was to impress his "lady friend" with the frilly cap that he was a Yankee Doodle.

Perhaps it was because Will was always over with his drinking friend the constable, helping organize the militia classes and see that he didn't get drawn, or if he was, to "pay off" a substitute to go for him. Maybe he got bit by war fever unexpectedly, like having a dog with rabies take a nip out of you from behind. Maybe he was stung by George's sarcasms and had decided to play the man. But George discounted that. True, he had always noticed that men seemed to admire William, to look to him for leadership. But that was not because he was a leader. Certainly not.

Will was in charge now, working under a Lieutenant-in-charge, drawing the lots and organizing the drilling, and most of all, as George thought ruefully, not actually having to fight unless he wanted to. The Bards, some of the Emison cousins who ran the mill, and Bige Cherry's son Malford were taking their tours of duty by drilling with Will three times a year in security. Some men from Cumberland County would be taking short two-month stints at active duty, but Will would never do that, George was sure of it. Like most of the boys in the local company, he would fight the war in the wheat fields and before the fire. Still, George marvelled that Will had gone so far as to decide to organize the company.

And what of the women, plump, placid Jane McClure and sweet-faced Jenny? They did what frontier women behind the front lines in time of war have always done—they worked. They got up at sunrise and threw wood on the fire and cooked mush and fried bacon, trying not to let the grease spatter on their hands, and swept the cabins and aired the clothing and beat rugs and chased chickens around and wrung their necks and cooked them with three vegetables and plum pie for dessert, and then they began to think what they would do for the evening meal. And they thanked God that their men were not around Philadelphia or Valley Forge, and prayed that the news which came eventually from Saratoga in New York that a great victory was won, meant that the war would finally wind to an end.

The war did end, of course, through a series of victories won by a combination of inspired shrewdness, good luck, and determination. Many of the leaders of the Revolution were Scotch-Irishmen, men like Patrick Henry and John Knox. And, especially in the Carolinas, and at the Battle of King's Mountain, many of the most determined fighters were Scotch-Irish, "God's Bulldogs." They and all the rest simply hung on until they won independence. But when those final victories came, in 1778 and '79, when George Rogers Clark fought in Illinois and Indiana to save the Old Northwest for America, in 1781 when Nathanael Greene began to reclaim the Carolinas, and finally when the American soldiers and French ships headed for the denouement at Yorktown, there wasn't much stir about it in western Pennsylvania.

For Pennsylvanians, like most of the pioneers in frontier America, were distracted. Their heads were turned by a wild, raging malady that hit. As word of impending victory for the new nation filtered through, as knowledge that rich black virgin land might therefore be opened up beyond the mountains in Ohio and Kentucky, families, neighborhoods, entire communities determined to "sell off and move on."

The whispers of hope filtered across the now firmly-established back country of the new nation, through the stone houses that had replaced the earlier cabins, across fields now beginning to show signs of overuse. The impulse that sent the Scotch-Irish across the Atlantic, strong as the urge that sends the geese into the autumn sky, stirred again. "Find a buyer to take up the good farm for cash. Cain't go to Ohio, too many Indians. Send the scouts out to Caintuck to mark the trees and throw up a cabin on good bottom land for the group of us. Put the clothin', the best bed, the pewter mugs into the wagon and head out. Get to Pittsburg. Mebbe build us a Caintucky ark and float down the Ohio. Falls of the Ohio. Harrodsburg. Fortune awaits. Caintuck."

Jane McClure sat down slowly in the wing-back chair before Sally and Sam Bard's fireplace. Tea was being served by a serving-girl, and Sally's pretty head was lowered above the tea table as she dropped lumps of sugar into china cups.

How good it is we have these ceremonies, Jane thought. How right that when couples decide to bed, we formalize it with a solemn march before the preacher. When an old man dies, we keen and mourn and drink together. And now, I am leaving and there is tea. The memories of thirty years skulk in the corners of this room, as we pour in cream, smile at each other and nibble at cucumber sandwiches. If we were to hang those memories out and look each one in the face, we should laugh too much, and weep too much. Our first firelight dinner with its smell of apples in the air, the birthing of Timothy in that bed right over there, I sitting by Sally's side as she sat by mine when Dan'l came the same year, the times of Indian fright.

"And so you leave in two weeks." Sally's smile was still as dazzling as ever. Her salt-and-pepper gray hair curled about her face; a red ribbon bound it up in back. Jane's hair was as red-brown as the day she married and would remain so the rest of her life. Only her increased bulk and the wrinkles on her neck, making it look like old parchment, revealed her fifty-five years.

"And so we do. John and the other boys left to go to the Monongahela to build the arks with Rafe's nephews, Young Ash and Hugh Emison and Bige and Moses Cherry. We're to be ready March 15." A trace of the old staccato Scottish accent remained in the voice still. Silently she stirred her tea. The Bards' prosperity kept increasing and the small silver spoon was one sign of it. "I wish some of you were a-goin'."

"No, 'tisn't to be. Sam's leg is too stiff to get about here in Carlisle, let alone where the Indians are. Ardry's wife wouldn't think of leaving her family, and Timothy is in the army. And we have Caroline to think about." Sally's eyes grew vacant. Her thin, uncommunicative daughter was not well; her mother suspected consumption. "Besides, the Bards will be well represented." Thomas

Bard's widow and her large clan of sons, daughters and cousins from Chambersburg, William's friends, would be in the large group now preparing to rendezvous at the forks of the Ohio to journey together into the new country.

They drank their tea in silence. Finally Jane said, "I can write letters. . ." Mockingly the memory came to Jane that she said that to her friend Sarah McCord so many years ago in Ireland, but somehow she never took pen to hand. There was more than an ocean between the Old and New worlds.

When Jane rose to go, tears came to Sally's eyes. "At least send word. I'll want to know when you get t' the new home." But Jane, through her own tears could only echo, forlornly the word "home." Then she kissed her friend goodbye, put on her cap, and went one last time through the door that had welcomed her to a new life so many years before.

Ever since she was a little girl, Jennie McClure had a sort of superstition, a totem. Each day, before the sun set, she must touch certain things in the cabin if she were to rest easy that night. Touching with the tip of her index finger, like a fairy waving a wand, she began at her own bed, made by her dada. She touched the rope mattress full of goose-down feathers that sometimes wafted out when you jumped on the bed, then her parents' bed, the wardrobe chest full of her mother's old things from Ireland, Great-grandmother Anderson's wool wheel. It was the last time she would see them until they were unpacked in Caintuck.

But it was the homier niches and secret places of her childhood that occupied her most as she said her goodbyes. The corner of the chimney in the second room, where she read and played and slept on cold winter days. The ladder to the loft which she and Georgie had shinnied up so many times, running splinters in their legs. A rough puncheon board that stuck up in the corner of the best room, where Lone Stag made up his tent to ease Dada's last hours. She ran her pretty, shapely hand smoothly over all of these loved objects.

She thought a moment about the Indian, Dada's friend. He had come yesterday. He told them all that Manitto now gave him permission to go home, to the land of hanging moss, and to live out his days among his own people. Dan'l and her mother embraced him; Jenny couldn't. She still didn't like savages, no matter who they were. They gave her the shivers.

Now, she swept her cape around her full, womanly shoulders and placed a cap on her brown hair, worn long to hide its thinness. Her brothers would be in soon to load the wagon. She would walk once over the farm, to see her rabbit paths and the hidden root grottos where she had written poetry. Her hand rested on the last totem, the biggest of all, the latch to the door. "God bless whoever comes next to put you up. May they be as happy as I have been here," she prayed and went out softly.

Dada, I'm sorry about sellin' off and headin' out. I know you wouldn't want it thataway. But Old Man Grimsditch come down last winter and kep' after me, and finally he offered me a thousand pounds for this farm and 't other. What could I say? It means we all, ever one of us, can have a good farm of his own and a good weddin' stake for Jenny. You wouldn't a had me turn that down now would you?

John McClure was on the hill above the creek. He knelt beside a slight rise in the ground which could only be distinguished as a grave by the fact that it was covered by the drooping heads of blue snowdrops and violets just now pushing through the leaves, transplated there by loving hands. It was a blustery day in mid-March. He went on.

Dan'l and Will finished the Ohio River boats and sent for us. Lytle, his wife and fambly, Old Tom Bard's widow and her sons and daughters, Isaac's widow Angelica Bard and several of the Emisons are a goin', Bige and Moses Cherry (but not Malford), along with we don't know how many else. A circular has been a-goin' around telling everybody who wants to go on a Caintuck adventure to assemble on a island near Pittsburg to travel as a group. We are a-goin' to do it Dada, and I think it's right, exceptin' for the fact that I feel I'm lettin' you down.

Even today all these years after you're gone, why do I always feel I'm lettin' you down when I don't do things right? Somebody leaves the door open to the shed and the cows get out and wander around down to Cherry's, and I think, 'Dada wouldn't'a let that happen.' Ever time an axe head flies off I think it's because I didn't put it on tight the way you tole me. Even things I know I can't help, I still feel guilty about. I know it's silly.

You worked so hard for this place, and somehow we're bustin' up your dream. No matter how good the new land is, no matter how much there is for all of us, I jest keep thinkin' of everything that you sacrificed to git us here. Dan'l and Georgie and Jenny don't even know about Ireland, but I can remember it, the shop you sweated in, the scrimpin' you did, the way you sang to us when we thought the ship was a-goin' down.

You built this place up by hand, stone by stone, log by log. I cain't hardly stand to think about how you used to sit night after night makin' barrels for pickles and tubs for lard as the firelight cast shadows on your face. You'd bore a hole and put green wood pegs in, and squint and squint to be sure there wasn't a hair's breadth you din't want in the joinin'. And when you made sugar chests and spice drawers, you held them up close, close to your face, so there would be a perfect match where the wood met.

John had picked one of the snowdrops and now he threw it down in disgust toward the creek. *Too close, Dada. Oh yes, I knew your secret. I don't know if anybody else did, surely Ma must have, although we never spoke of 't. I wondered why you din't shoot much the last year or two, tellin' us it was high time for us boys to bring home the game, why you had Dan'l read the Bible to you. Then that day when a letter came to you from one of your Quaker friends in Philadelphia, you waited 'till we were all alone and told me to read it aloud to you to see how good I could read. You was losin' your eyesight.*

'Twas the one thing you feared, I think, more than all else. I never knew a man more fearless, but I remember you tole me never to fight because out here

they can gouge out a man's eyes. Maybe 'twas because of that fight you got into at the mill so many years ago. Yes, I knew about that too, although you would have blistered me to know it. The Girtys knew who you were, and they did some talkin' 'fore they went off to lead the Indians in treachery against us in the war. I was the only one in the fambly found it out by accident. I met Simon Girty, Jr. once at Harris's store, and he axed about my name. He isn't a tot'lly bad sort of man, Girty isn't, although I doubt you'd think so. Anyways, you must've suffered a good deal more'n we all knew bein' sick and worried about your eyes goin' that last year.

I know a lot more'n people give me credit for. John, the quiet one. I may not read Cicero like George (though mebbe I could've if anybody'd been willing to take a turn for me in the pig pen now and then) or write any pomes like your little gal. But what I do is watch, and I store up things like a Injeean puts away parched corn and maple sugar in his pouch.

Now, Dada, about the barn. I know I've not a-done it yet, but I swear I haven't broke the promise. There's been so much for me to do. It ain't essactly like Will or George are eager to work theirselves to death—let that pass. Somebody in each fambly's got to be the one that everybody looks to and I guess I'm it. I want you to know I'm gonna keep right on a-doin' that.

He got up from his cramped position. The wind came up a bit. A few huge snowflakes, like whirligigs, were beginning to circulate in the air. Don't know why it makes me feel better to talk to him thataway. Don't make no never mind what I say anyways, he thought. Mebbe he ain't there, if what Ma says is right and he walked right off into the other world like he was goin' to a dance. Said he got a gleam in his dull eyes like he was lookin' over the mountains. Pray to God I go like that too.

Then he turned and left, this small, well-muscled man with stooped shoulders and a slightly receding hairline. In the clearing, lacy giant snowflakes drifted down silently over the flower-crowned man's grave. And since snowflakes are impartial, they sifted also over two other graves where Jenny McClure had buried spaniels, when she was about ten years old, and over a small, neglected depression off to the side, now hardly visible, which everyone else in the family had forgotten even existed, except Jane McClure.

Finally, as the wagon, now old and rickety, rambled past the now-empty cowshed for the last time, John McClure, Jr., stooped and picked up a rock and put it in his pocket. Then he clicked his tongue to the horses to start up the small train of cattle and possessions. He drove on off toward the mountains, away from the pile of fieldstones which had long since sprouted chickweek and sedum and were well into the process of settling into the earth.

PART III

KENTUCKY
1780-1803

SONG FOR GOIN' TO CAINTUCKY

A sprightly song with Shaker tempo,
to be sung with the clapping of hands

Caintucky waters clap their hands
And sing with one accord
Through mountain pass and prairie grass
To the Garden of the Lord.

Caintucky skies are fairer than
The fairest skies on earth
The winter winds laugh softer than
A gentle maiden's mirth.

Caintucky canelands beckon me,
Spread wide before my eyes
Oh, build a boat and take me to
Caintucky Paradise

Chapter XVI

In April of 1780 the waters of the Ohio River swept along at floodtide in their course from Pittsburg to what would someday be Cairo, Illinois. Ever since the last great Ice Age, the currents of this most potent river of the New West had rushed on in a wide sweep each spring to swell the even greater Mississippi, fertilizing the bottomlands, clearing out the watershed, and resurrecting life after the harsh death of winter.

The waters of the Ohio were a confluence, made up of tides and soils from all the western watershed of the Alleghenies and Blue Ridge, grains of sand from under the Natural Bridge in Virginia, tiny pebbles from the wooded shores of the Monongahela, late snow runoff from northern Pennsylvania lakes where Indians paddled canoes.

And as the waters were an amalgam, so, too, was the stream of human cargo being swept on its breast to Limestone and the new town of Louisville. Plunderers, land speculators, second sons of wealthy families, religious zealots, and poor, restless seekers of new opportunity—all were aboard the Kentucky arks heading for hope in the new Canaan. There were now less than two thousand people in Kentucky, but this dotting of boats on the Ohio was only the vanguard. The sluice gates were opening on the settlement of the land beyond the mountains.

Water sloshed beneath the Bard's Ohio River ark as its green wood planks breasted the strong current between limestone cliffs. Sixty-three boats, loaded with cattle, household possessions, women and children, and surrounded by armed men made up the huge flotila William Lytle had organized to travel to Kentucky. The Bard and McClure boats rode midway, in the family section of the little navy.

Jenny McClure and Martha Bard looked over the side at the water as it slapped against the bow of the boat, carrying with it logs, shredded rope and an occasional old shoe. "Reminds me of gingerbread, Martha, being stirred with a wooden spoon," said Jenny. The floods of April were swelling high and late because of the unusually harsh winter. In January and February of 1780 streams iced clear to the bottom and many domestic animals froze to death.

"Martha, don't you hate to leave Pennsylvania?" Jenny asked, looking at the younger girl. This "baby sister" of easy-going Tom Bard was completely unlike him. Her eyes were strong, her mouth determined.

"Hate it? Hate leaving a smoky, one-roomed cabin with one brother who drinks too much whiskey and four other brothers underfoot? Chill-blained feet and rocky soil where flowers grow spindly? And an uneven floor that no broom can ever sweep clean?" Jenny stared at her. She was tall, already a woman with a well-rounded form. She thinks a lot for a fifteen-year-old, thought Jenny.

"Waal, you know Caintuck isn't the Garden of Eden," Jenny said, smiling a little. "There're hardly any cabins, even, for folks yet, and there will probably be smokin' fireplaces and hog and hominy in Caintuck too. 'Twill make Cumberland County look like Vauxhall Gardens." Jenny was reading a little bit about London, and it amused her to sprinkle her conversation with references to things in England to see how people reacted to them.

But Martha was thinking about Caintuck and the admittedly rough life they would be undertaking in the forest wilderness. "Someday, someday, though, it will be different. I intend to make it different. I know I was born for beautiful things. Oh, I don't just mean calicos and pretty caps, although I like 'em too. I mean a house with plaster and a separate kitchen. Pitchers on the walls. I like things nice. Pa made me a bathtub and I brought it 'long." Her father had died five years ago, but she had been his special pet. That may have been the reason, Martha sometimes thought, that her mother was so hard on her, so distant to her.

"More power to you if you can keep yourself clean on this boat and up the road a piece when we get to the trail from Louisville to our land." Jenny shuddered and drew her shawl about her against the brisk wind. If it got too cold, they could always sit on the deerskin that was thrown on the deck and get out of the wind behind the four-feet high sides of the boat, designed for hiding from, and shooting at, Indians.

"Daughter, you promised to rub my feet," a complaining voice rose from below in the small cabin.

There are two of 'em alike down there, Martha thought darkly, her mother and Cousin Angelica Bard, Isaac's widow, who had desperately wanted to come even though she suffered from heart pains. At least Cousin Angelica was pleasant and did not murmur about her poor health. While her mother. . .

"Later, Ma," said Martha, hollering down the opening of the cuddy cabin. If only her mother weren't so irritable.

"Trees, trees and more trees. And cliffs of rocks. Ain't there anything else to see on this stream? I can't imagine why the French call it the Beautiful River." Martha did not answer. She hoped her mother would go to sleep down there for a while; it might improve her temper.

" 'Twas sad to see Ash and Hugh Emison go at Limestone," said Martha, returning to Jenny's side. "But a beautiful wedding, not at all like the willy-nilly ones 't home."

"Young Ash" Emison, nephew of Rafe, and Mary Mitchell had been married by the Presbyterian minister from Easton who was travelling with the group. Ash's brother Hugh stood as groomsman, and Martha's older sister Mary, Hugh's wife, was the bridesmaid. Jennie thought of the sad goodbyes Ash and

Hugh must have said to their relatives, including "Old Ash" and Charity at the store they owned so many years in Carlisle. How the families she grew up with were split by the war and the movings. Would they ever see any of these old friends again?

After the wedding, on the shore at Limestone, the settlement party had decided to rest a couple of days and see the newly married couple and several other families off to claim their land near one of the armed stations a few miles north on the trail. "Dan'l and John saddled horses and went to hunt buffaloes with Mr. Lytle. They had a pack of fun," Jenny mused.

"I know. I heard Dan'l talk," Martha said demurely. She was a part of the group that welcomed back the hunters who toted the strange hairy beast they had felled, gutted, and thrown over the saddle bags.

Dan'l, laughing and slapping his side, told his story. Unable to resist plunging into the woods to try to capture one of the beasts they had heard so much about, Dan'l and five others had charged down the path. Not more than a few miles from the river they came upon a group of the peaceful animals grazing in a meadow. Hardly believing their luck, the horsemen galloped to a rise upwind of the herd. Lytle stationed them in a semi-circle and they fired into the herd, scattering the beasts. Several ran in Dan'l's direction, as he squatted, protected from trampling by a tree. He brought down a large male with a huge hump.

He must have noticed Martha's admiring eyes as he told the story, because after the meat was roasted on a shoreside campfire, he brought her a choice piece of the hump. As he offered the plate, he smiled politely and made a deep mock bow.

He is kind to notice me, she thought. Kindness was a quality she admired above all else in men, and saw little enough of on the frontier.

As the girls gazed dreamily at the cloudy spring sky, a shout from the pilot boat ahead roused them. "Injeeans on the north shore ahead. Duck down!" A tall man from Cumberland County, James Scott, one of the guards for this family boat, was instantly by their sides. He leaned behind the cabin house to load his rifle.

"I can jest make 'em out millin' about at the mouth of the Big Miami River," he said unemotionally. "Make a good spot for a city some day, when we get 'm all cleaned out." Jenny had observed him earlier. He was as cool as mountain snow. One to be relied on in trouble. Her brothers were at least a mile back in the rear guard, her mother in the boat ahead with another family.

"Martha, what's happenin'?" demanded Mary Bard's shrill voice from within. Martha went in quickly to reassure her and insist the two women stay put. Then she came out on deck again.

The two pilot boats, followed by two more boats of armed fighters, were pulling in for shore, half a mile above where the Indians were sighted. "Head t' shore," Scott ordered the man at the helm and the oarsmen, and then blatted a signal on a tin horn to the boats in back. "The problem is how many of 'em are there?" Scott murmured to himself.

"How many fighters do we have now that the other party left at Limestone?" Jenny asked timidly.

"About three hundred, Miss McClure," he said evenly, drawing a bead on the shoreline to cover the landing. Jenny looked up at him from where she and Martha crouched on the deck. He had an uneven complexion and a slightly large nose. An incongruous dimple on the cheek seemed to go with the barest touch of a smile that played across his lips. He was beginning to appreciate the hero's posture he was striking before the girls. Playfully he struck a pose, cocking his rifle, then laughed.

"Don't be afraid, Miss," he said to Jenny, putting down the gun as the boat bumped against the sandy, shallow bottom on shore.

"Why?" Jenny asked breathlessly. "Because you will see we don't get hurt?"

"No, m'. Because I could only see about a hundred of them and we outnumber 'em five to one. That's the way we heroes like to fight. Anyway, Injeeans always run away when they're outnumbered." He chuckled and sprang onto the shore. "Sorry I can't help you ladies down, but I must be on m' way. The guard boats will take care of ye."

The Indians did high-tail it up a creek on horses, as Scott predicted; and the men gave up pursuit and returned to push the boats out again. Later, Jenny thought about the man. He angered her. He was playing the hero, laughing at her. What kind of a man would do that?

She tried to think of what she knew about him. He had come recently to the area around Newton, near the mill, from far-away. St. Louis, was it? He was in Will's militia company, she thought. But past that, what did she know? Anyway, what did it matter? She should be watching after Martha and the older women. After all, the rest of the Bard family was back on another boat. It was no time to be thinking of arrogant young men when they were running the gauntlet of hostile Shawnees who did not wish them entering Caintuck country. Time enough for thinking when they landed.

They called the settlement Beargrass, after the creek that entered the Ohio not far from the Ohio's rapid-like Falls. Thomas Jefferson had recently decided that the new makeshift cabin city should be named Louisville, in honor of the King of France, who was aiding the American Revolution. But the name seemed to stick in the throats of the rabble who called the place home, and Beargrass it remained, at least for a while.

Around a cluster of small cabins on shore and on an island in the river, George Rogers Clark was setting up a permanent military post. Why here, the inhabitants wondered?

The Indians called this man Long Knife. Under orders from Virginia, he had sloshed through the flooded Illinois territory last year with a small group of frontiersmen to take the British outpost at Vincennes. Perhaps this new fortified town was a place from which he could supply his personal conquest, and even arrange to make a private fortune in the bargain.

Very early in the morning of April 15, 1780, William Lytle directed the people in his "settlement party" ashore and supervised the landing of their cattle, wagons, and household goods. He and his wife and son gathered their butter churns, bedboards, and other paraphernalia on pack horses and said their goodbyes, eager to get to land they held a few miles out of Beargrass.

John and Will McClure strode the streets of the little settlement, trying to decide what their next step would be. William had drawn town lots here for the McClures last year. Ash Emison and some of the other Cumberland County men had also braved the river to "be first," as the promising new town was laid out.

But Will also had put up small "pig shack" cabins and planted a small plot of corn fifty miles south along a creekbed, in a section already burnt off by prairie fire. The McClures now held this too, by "cabin right." It was a relatively small plot, but it was excellent land. So there would be a choice.

As they walked the muddy lane, John scornfully kicked aside a hardened piece of pig excrement. "Ain't much of a town, is it?" he commented. Slatternly women emerged from the doors of cabins without windows and men lounged in the doorway of a tavern, already open, although it was only breakfast time.

Will approached a man wearing a shredded linen shirt, without shoes on his feet. "Doesn't seem to be much work gettin' done here, friend," Will said. "Things seem to have gone right downhill."

Last year when he had come to draw the lots, the mood was still high over the taking of Fort Sackville in Vincennes. A blacksmith's shop was in operation and land was being cleared and cabins built around a strong fort.

"The winter, 'bout kilt us," the man said. His jaw hung open after he said it and John wondered if he were an idiot, or only driven to look like one through hopelessness.

Will nodded his head to agree with him about the winter. "Bad enough in Pennsylvania," he said. "Couldn't run the sawmill on the Monongahela where I was at, and so we couldn't build our Caintucky arks, or we might have been here in the fall. Jist as well, I guess."

"Turkeys fell frozen right offa trees," the man said. Now he was standing up a little taller, and his mouth was closed. John decided the man wasn't an idiot. He probably just hadn't had many lively people to talk to lately. The man continued, "You could hear the buffaloes out in the woods snortin' and pawin' and trying to survive. We et horses and dogs in Febyouary."

"I thought winters in Caintuck were s'posed to be milder than in Pennsylvania," John murmured. "That's what the circular said. Garden of Eden—"

The man ignored him, and pulling on a few hairs on his scruffly chin, went on. "People hain't recovered yet. Then the floodin' came and the fluxes and ague-yoos. Half the settlement has the chills and fever."

Will thanked him and withdrew. "Let's push on," John said, as they walked down the muddy lane. "We don't want our folk to get an ague. Those things hang on like a cockle burr on a horse's tail." They both were silent, remembering their father's futile struggle. "Tell Ma. She's sure to agree." These days they scrupulously referred all decisions to their mother. She tactfully refrained from disagreeing with them on most occasions.

A woman leaching out lye in a crude wooden box turned her head to give them some of the ready advice that was always available on the frontier. "Go back up this yere road a few miles and you'll find a brand-new station. They's a big house in it where the lady runs a kinda inn. You can decide there. Not here. Taint' a good spot." She gestured with her head toward the foul water standing about in pools near her feet. "I'm a-goin as soon as my younguns can stand the trip."

John conferred with his mother and the widow Mary Bard, and the widow and Martha rounded up the numerous Bard sons: Samuel and Tom, and his wife, teenaged John, Willie, Roy and Joseph. Soon they were all on the road south. Bige Cherry decided to remain at Beargrass for a while, agues or not. Since his wife Evalina had died in change-of-life childbirth last year, and Malford had decided to stay in Pennsylvania, Bige was really alone. He and his brother Moses came to Caintuck as "adventurers" to survey the passing scene, kill a few buffaloes, chase a few Shawnees, and "mebbe buy and sell us a piece of land." Beargrass probably suited them, George thought with a wry smile. Still, he would miss Bige Cherry's good humor on the trail.

None of them would really be separated for long, since these Kentucky settlements were all within easy riding distance of each other and as close as kin. They had to be. They were two thousand people alone in a wilderness of panthers and savage attacks.

In mid-afternoon the party rounded a bend in the road to see the station, with its typical stockaded walls, obviously brand new, and with cattle grazing peacefully outside. A sprinkling of dwellings sat defiantly outside the walls, including a large log house which seemed to be the inn.

The fort's wide-open gates indicated that Indians had not been very active here recently. Jane McClure breathed a sigh of relief as she stiffly got her bulk out of the cart. The Indian troubles along the river had sapped her energy. There had been so many years of all that in the past. How could she face a new place with continuing murder along lonely roads and the sudden threat of tomahawking, just at a time in her life when she wanted some peace?

The group made their way toward the inn, which had some sort of crude sign painted above its door. Dan'l McClure squinted and made out the words *El Doubloon*. Beneath them was a round object that was supposed to be a huge gold coin, but looked more like a slipped custard tart. As the party drew nearer, they became aware of a commotion in the yard by the inn; a woman was screaming in consternation at somebody or something.

The author of the screams, they saw as they drew nearer, was a short woman with very light brown skin and frizzled black hair. Her waist was pulled thin with some sort of cinching, but her upper body was thick. The lower arms, which emerged from a flower-patterned calico dress, were like twin sausages, as she waved them in the air at a servant girl standing over a wooden washing tub in the yard.

"So you will wash the deeshes in three inches of greasy water," she screamed. Dan'l, leading one of the horses and drawing up to the scene, could see the young girl's face now. She was pretty and young, with brown hair tumbling on her forehead. Her eyes looked into the face of her mistress with distress, as if trying to read which direction the storm was going to move next. She must have been used to this kind of tirade.

"Look at deese *vasos*," the sausage-woman said, holding up some tankards before she dashed them to the ground. "*Mira!* The slime in the bottom, you slut. I am going to pound the sense into your *cabeza estupida*, lazy Irish one." The woman began to beat her about the head and the girl started to cry frantically.

The entire group approaching the log inn stopped, transfixed by the scene. Before anyone could stop him, Dan'l sauntered over to the tree, hands before him in greeting.

"Sure you don't have distaste for the Irish now, do you, Ma'm? Particularly those who have the cash to pay for a night of your finest lodging?" He put his arm around her waist, whirled her around and headed her toward the door of the inn.

Astonished, she looked up into his ruddy, cheerful face. Her mouth was wide open. "How do you call yourself, sir?" she asked. Where was this woman's accent from, he wondered. The West Indies? New Orleans?

"McClure and company, a gentleman travellin' with fambly and companions," he answered, and smiled again as he escorted her on. "We'll be keepin' you busy for the next hour or so preparin' rooms. Now let's see, we'll need two women's rooms and two men's—we'll sup early. Our women'll be wantin' to see your, er, bill of fare." As if she were the mistress of the Lion and Crown in London town he danced her up to the door. The girl whose ears she boxed ran to empty the discredited dishwater and get fresh, sending a look of gratitude towards Dan'l.

"Did you see that mulatto lady's dress?" Mary Bard said to Jenny McClure and Martha as they entered the inn. "Her waist was pinched in and her bosom raised up shockingly." Mary Bard had definite ideas of what was "proper" even on the frontier.

"She looks like a joking version of something Marie Antoe-nitt and the Queen of Spain might wear at a party at Versayles," Jenny said. Reading the Philadelphia newspapers might give one knowledge of affairs of the great. It didn't tell one how to pronounce their names and palaces.

"That poor inn woman is trying to be fashionable. She gets the French fashion dolls and doesn't know how to use 'em way out here," Jane said. On the inn's porch woodsmen from the fort were tilting crudely-made ladder-back chairs and passing around a bottle of whiskey. They showered the group of Bards and McClures with questions.

"Who be ye?" "Where air ye comin' from? Air ye related to the Bards in Christiana Hunnerd on the Delaware?" The visitors were obviously a diversion in a dull existence, and the newcomers, particularly Tom Bard, answered the questions with amusement and patience.

There were two large rooms upstairs for the five women and ten men, and they would have to lodge with other visitors who were already there. Still, the inn was larger than most in the wilderness, where folk slept together in one room before the fire. It was also cleaner. Jane's eyes roved over the great room.

The hearth was well-swept, the table washed and pumiced. They said these overnight villages were going up in Caintuck now. At one end of the village, a huge log cabin could be thrown together in a couple of weeks and, as if a sorcerer had conjured, presto, an inn.

Jane heard a cacophony of squawking from the yard as someone chased a chicken that would obviously end up in their dinner pot.

She was not surprised that the new inn was well-kept. Sometimes in the most remote places there were decent accommodations, while she had stayed at places in cities which seemed owned and managed by the vermin who inhabited them. Pittsburg was the worst. She thought of the joke Will told about inns, where an innkeeper assured guests that there "waren't a single bedbug in the place," and a wit in the background replied, "No, they're all married." She hoped for a verminless night, and there was promise it might happen here. She hated asking George, who had the best eyes, to part her hair and look minutely for crawling things and then crack 'em between his fingernails.

The deerskin valises and travelling trunks were brought in by an olive-skinned young man with popping eyes, who bumped and hauled them up crooked stairs. After a brief wash, the women appeared downstairs and gathered before the roaring fire built to ward off the vapors on this spring night. Still, Jane thought, the land was higher and the climate healthier than at Beargrass, by a long shot. Lytle's land was not far from here, and John told her there would be many families soon. "Better stay in these yere parts," one of the men from the porch had advised. "Nothin' but stones and Shawnees further east."

Will and Young Sam Bard put up their feet on stools before the fire and were talking to a grizzled man chewing on a plug of tobacco. He was a trader who had travelled from Virginia to Tennessee, and he wanted to talk about the Revolution, which was by no means over yet. "The British are in the South, that's for sartain. Clinton were prob'ly goin' for Charleston last we heerd."

John came in after seeing to the horses. There was no stable. He took his seat in the circle of listeners sitting on the stools listening to the trader tell his war tales. Charleston, thought John rather indifferently, would be a prize for the British.

He gestured for the pretty little Irish girl, who also served as barmaid, to bring him a rum punch. Tonight his insides needed some strengthening. Perhaps it was just the unrelenting responsibility he felt ever since they had left Pittsburg. The McClures and Bards weren't bringing much, but even these things were difficult to get down this muddy track. They sledged the larger pieces behind the horse, but his mother had insisted on bringing several huge bedsteads and bureaus. Then there was that damned bathtub of Martha Bard's. And that wasn't all. Like a hunting shirt, this responsibility had a fringe of fear to it. The fear was of savages in hiding, who waited around bends in the river or behind three-feet-thick oak or butternut trees in the forests and sprang out with terrifying cries. Lately John noticed a pain in his lower stomach, especially when he hadn't eaten for a while. He thought it had something to do with his constant irritable nerves.

The colonists' struggle against Great Britain seemed more remote out here than it was in Pennsylvania. It had to, when your own scalp was at stake every hour. The trader continued talking. "Our garrison in Charleston is unmanned—sparse as flies in December. They say that the countryside has good fellows—weak patriots."

"The story of the war," George said, staring moodily into the coals of the fire. Then, looking up, he added thoughtfully, "I served at Trenton and my brothers were all in the militia in Pennsylvania."

"I wish they'd get all the fightin' in the East over with," said the trader. "Oh, I ain't no Tory, mark you. But mebbe we could get a few Virginia militiamen to help us keep the savages off the walls of the forts in Caintuck."

Jane was quietly eyeing the planks which were set up on sawhorses for their supper. Her admiration for the Spanish fashion-doll was growing. Cloth napkins, clean wooden spoons and noggins were all being set on courteously. And there were knives and clean-burning candles. The woman did run a decent place even if she beat her help.

Then, the hungry horde—McClures, Bards, and two other families—settled like deerflies around the victuals. The door opened and a swarthy-looking man in a tie wig and frock coat came in and stood by the table. He was the innkeeper, fresh from meeting supply boats at Beargrass. Dan'l was interested in seeing what kind of man the Spanish mistress of the house had married.

"I was originally a Virginian," the inkeeper said, in a rather dandified way, in answer to a question from Angelica Bard. They waited, but he did not comment further. One did not ask too much in Caintuck about folks' origins. "Actually, I'm rather proud of the *Doubloon* and the trade it is already getting," he told them. "We have served fifty customers in the first month we've been open."

The man took off his frock coat, sat down, and began to eat voraciously, cutting his food with a pearl-handled knife he took out of his waistcoat pocket. "The first supplies came down the river last week and we have been indulging ourselves like gluttons at a feast. My wife is a good cook. She is a daughter of one of the monied creole families in Ciudad de Mexico, and they enjoy good tables," he said. It was a proverb in these places that if the innkeeper's wife liked to eat, the guests ate well too.

First a planked fish, a pickerel served by the Irish girl. Her brown hair was neatly combed and tied back with a green ribbon. Dan'l watched her move in a sprightly way around the table; his mother in turn watched him unobtrusively. There were bowls of asparagus and the first dandelion greens and rounds of coarse Sally Lunn bread. The main dish was something they had never seen. Chicken and ham were cooked together in a spicy sauce that was delicious. "I no have *arroz* yet," the former creole nobielady explained. "It is better with the rice."

To end, a rhubarb tart. A real feast in the wilderness. They were told that out here it was either this or famine. When supplies came in, there was white bread. When they didn't, it was parched corn. The innkeeper said his garden was already producing leeks and lettuce and would grow every vegetable imaginable by July.

"Crops grow here like it's a manure pile," the Tennessee trader ventured. "Scratch the soil and corn shoots up. Eight feet high." Jane sighed. It all sounded familiar.

They left the table. The ladies in the two other families, two blonde German sisters who came from near Lancaster, retired upstairs to put their small children to bed. Jennie McClure, the Widow Mary, and Angelica Bard, panting as she climbed the steps, went to lie down.

"Still only the shank of the evenin'," Jane said to herself. She went to look for her embroidery and then sat near the window, which had a piece of cheesecloth over it to keep out the swarming gnats. She watched the shadows settling about this woodland place. Sounds of cleaning up clattered faintly out of the kitchen. The settlers from the porch, who went home for supper, now seemed to have returned and were laughing and spitting tobacco juice again.

In the great room, the men found a deck of cards. George, looking around, noted that the inn seemed well-supplied with equipment of gambling and mild dissipation, with gaming boards, dice, and trophies from horse races in Carolina. Other people besides pioneering families were obviously frequenting this inn.

On the wall was a picture, an engraving of a scene of a great many people at what seemed to be a fair. George looked at it carefully. Really, he had never seen anything like it. Actors, a high-rope artist, well-dressed gentlemen, monkeys, contortionists, skeletons, and Adam and Eve were all jumbled together doing riotous things. Their faces showed disorder and decadence. Underneath a rotting bridge, a pig was eating a copy of the *Magna Charta*. George turned from the engraving, took out his fiddle and began to tune it. Softly he played and sang:

> *Where are you goin' Lord Randall, my son*
> *Where are you goin' my bonnie lad,*
> *I'm goin' a courtin' mother,*
> *Goin a courtin' mother*
> *Make my bed soft for I fain would lie down*

Martha Bard had not gone upstairs with the other women. She stood now in the shadows near the front door of the inn. The ancient song, plaintive and low, made her pensive. She leaned on her hand at the door of the great room, watching the men, listening to the snatches of their conversation which wafted over to her as if from a great distance. "Daniel Boone a Tory. . . thirty families at Harrodsburg. . . bones of a elephant not far from here. . ." she sighed and went to sit on the porch.

The sad song also affected Dan'l, coming down the back stairs after a brief meeting with Will and John to plan tomorrow's trip. The three of them decided to press on to Harrodsburg to talk to other settlers and "get the lay of the land." At the foot of the stairs, listening to the music and feeling cramped in spirit, Dan'l decided to slip out the back kitchen door of the log house.

He emerged into an unusually balmy April evening. Curiously he walked about among the raw, new outbuildings surrounding the inn, watching the scene in the evening light. The gates of the station south of the inn were closed, leaving just a crack open. A jumble of indistinct noises came over the walls: iron pots banging, a horse neighing, a child's voice crying "Maaaa," the raucous quack of ducks. He walked by the farmyard of the inn, where chickens were settling themselves haughtily on their perches, rising up, fluttering their wings to get in the best positions for the night. Dan'l ran a quick hand through his hair. It was a gesture of irritation. He was tired of travel, tired of herding people as if they were cattle. Will and even George seemed stimulated by this life, but he awoke in his strange bed always with an odd pain, a disorientation, as if somebody in his life were dead and he missed them terribly. He chided himself for having womanish feelings again. Why must he be analyzing everything, taking everything into himself? And truly he did love the woods, if they could get to them again. Why not a walk? "Worry not for the morrow, enjoy this evenin'," he told himself.

He walked across a wide field, a grassy natural meadow that the Indians probably burned off decades ago to trap game, and that the innkeeper now used for grazing. After walking for about a quarter of a mile across the field, he entered a woods. He walked through young beech and balsam for a while, then clambered down a slight incline to what he knew must be the bank of a winding stream.

He stopped a moment to listen for its waters and heard their gentle, consistent gurgle. The lowering rays of the evening sun slanted obliquely through poplars ahead. He heard a noise. Trained to the wilderness from his trips to Ohio, he stopped short to listen. Should he be worried about Indians? They did not live in Caintuck, shunned it in fact, and no hostile ones had been seen for months in this particular area. Possibly the noise was a deer. He paused again to let silence settle. He heard evening warblers on branches nearby, a dog barking back at the settlement. Otherwise, all was still.

Then, he heard the rustling noise again and walked slowly through the high grass and nettles toward it.

Back on the porch, Martha Bard stretched her limbs and sighed contentedly. It was a warm night and, thank heavens, it was too early in the spring for mosquitoes. The gnats never bothered her. Her mother always said it was because she didn't have enough sugar in her. Mary Bard always smiled when she said this, but Martha knew she meant it.

Martha turned her cane-bottom stool away from the chair-tilters. Didn't these men ever stay with their families in the fort? Three older ones and a couple of young ones, all wearing black slouch hats, had taken up their positions on the other side of the porch. They were chortling and slapping their knees and bragging and telling stories fit to kill. Whiskey breath drifted over to her. She puckered her mouth disapprovingly.

She soon forgot about them and went into a world of her own making, enjoying a luxury she allowed herself lately—long, meandering thoughts about Dan'l McClure. He sat by her at dinner. Perhaps it meant something, perhaps it didn't. Dan'l. He was handsome enough certainly, with his bright, very dark eyes like an intelligent squirrel's. She smiled at the thought. Yes, he was like that, playful and cute. His round face shone in her mind, like the picture of a Catholic saint she saw in a shop in Pittsburg. That Dan'l was at least ten years older than she only enhanced the delicious aura she felt radiating out from the portrait gallery in her mind.

Dan'l was gentle and good. That was what she liked. He had played games with the children on the flatboat to pass the time as they travelled. And the way he had helped that wench, though she probably didn't deserve it. Slopping through her work. A Papist she was, not Scotch-Irish. That would account for it.

But Dan'l. When she said his name, a feeling as sweet as warm honeycake seemed to seep through her. It was like when the fire is burning cheerfully while the wind howls outside on a particularly sleety night and you feel it can never get through the chinks in your cabin. Or when you unexpectedly find a bird's nest on a low branch in the woods, and the baby birds are there, all fluffed up and hungry. And you tiptoe away without disturbing them. Dan'l. Dan'l. She said the name over and over, letting its associations embrace her.

He was a good Presbyterian, and that was important to her. She had experienced grace and conviction. She and Dan'l had sat in the same bench at the Shippensburg church when the group gathered to travel together to the rivers. She watched him on the long journey. He cared about good works, did not swear as most of the other men, even his brothers, did casually. Feeling a little wicked she allowed herself a daydream. It took shape and became almost a living reality. She let her mind savor the vision.

In the center of a clearing is a well-built cabin. There are flowers blooming in a garden outside the door, larkspur and bleeding heart, probably. Inside, before the hearth, Dan'l sits playing with a little girl in immaculate white clothes, starched and ironed by Martha. On the mantel is a pewter teapot. A curtain modestly screens the family clothing. Dan'l turns to his beloved wife, clasps her hand, and looks adoringly into her eyes. Then he rises and kisses her lips. . . Martha, unable to contain herself anymore, rose and pirouetted down the two steps of the plank porch and along a little path that went beside the inn. Behind her floated the braying laughter of the grizzled men. She was glad to leave that certain male smell, composed of tobacco, spirits, and unclean linen that irritated her nostrils. "They sound," she thought scornfully, "and really are, like mules."

In the dying light, by the rapidly moving stream, Dan'l sat watching the inn servant girl pinch off bits of grass and throw them into the water. She did it furiously, as if there were some satisfaction in ripping off the living thing and seeing it carried rapidly out of sight.

"I would run away if I could," she said to him.

Dan'l smiled indulgently, willing to be kind for a few moments now that he had found this child like a doe in the woods. Really, he was rather amused by her. The women around him did not often bare their hearts the way she did, and it might help raise his dejected feelings. He offered a little jest. "Dishwater, was it? Greasy, she said?"

"And how else should it be, I ask you, young gent'man, when she gives me soft soap, and that only half a pennysworth? An' the trenchers soak up the greasy mutton clean into the wood." She reached a bit for a dandelion head and threw it in too. "But if not the dishwater, young man, then th' carpets." She went on in a mimicking voice. " 'Do not sweep s' hard with the broom the rug. It will wear,' or 'the vinegar, it is too weak, the peeckles will not be firm.' She has more commandments than the Book of Dooterhominey."

"Yes," he smiled again. "Are you indentured?"

"Of a sartain I am and through no doin' of my own." She pulled the petals of a daisy out and her eyes, very large and violet, went beyond him, beyond the stream bank even. "Father was a tailor in Dublin, of the poorest sort. He had come in out of the county to make his way. He had heerd acourse of the shippin' out to Americey, and so when I were twelve, he left all behind and took us to port to ship."

She stopped her idle motion and for the first time looked at him seriously, and he was aware that her eyes were intelligent as well as beautiful.

"Father was one of those people who never knew what to think. If a watchman was a-chasin' him and he had three roads to go into, he'd choose the dead end. So when he arrived and had to choose where to go, he talked carefully to all who was a-shippin' and decided to pick Jamaica—the worst choice. On our miserable trip, smallpox struck and thirty died, but not us. We was spared to care for the others. They say country folk don't get it, and my parents were that for sartain.

"We was worn out, though, nursin' the sick and lost our health. And worse misfortune, m' father's leg was wounded deeply when a runaway keg of rum smashed into it. Well, the long and short of it 'twas, the weather was foul and the voyage long. Food ran low and we bought from a sailor's contraband supply to keep ourselves from starvin'."

Her voice was low. "When we came into Jamaica Bay, finally, as if to Heaven or Hell, our money was gone and we were bought as redemptioners at Kingston. Wondrous strange 'twas there, with murky air you could almost drink, spiders as big as hens' eggs. For food, souse of pigs' feet and native peas and sour oranges. An ugly Spaniard bought the three of us for a pittance because m' father's leg was festerin'. The poor man died before we could get to the Spaniard's plantation. A blessing 'twere though, I think. He could not have survived the cotton fields, the fevers and fluxes.

"M' mither was installed as the mistress of the house and," her eyes filled with disgust, "of that man too. But, at last, he took to playin' faro at the port, and he lost me in a game of chance to a sea captain. I thanked the Holy Mither of God for that day. In Charleston, I was bought by these people"—she clenched her fist helplessly, as if she could not describe how she felt about them. "M' new master was in trouble with the Spanish at New Orleans for smugglin'. We travelled the river to come and build this inn here. And I am a slave, though not black in skin." Dan'l's heart filled with sympathy for the poor waif who did not even have the freedom of the smallest animal in the forest.

"Next year m' term will be up. I shall take m' shillings and buy ginghams and lace and ribbons and go do millinery. And be a decent woman too.''

The sun had finally set. She looked up again, two tears on her cheeks, and it was as if she saw Dan'l for the first time. She took his hands and scanned his face. "You are a fine young gent'man." He was becoming more aware of her vital presence by the moment.

"My name is Dan'l."

"Your face is true. But your hair is as lank as a Indian's." She smiled slowly, puzzlingly. "Come put your head in my lap and I will sing you a song."

For a brief moment Dan'l examined this odd but tempting idea. Then he stretched himself out with his head in the broad lap of her homespun dress. She put her face near his and sang a snatch of a song in a beautiful, low voice. It reminded him of a cradle song he used to hear his mother sing.

Then she leaned over and kissed him for a long moment, and he was acutely aware that it was a woman's lap he was lying in. Nettles of feeling spread from his fingertips to his toes. Her lips were slightly parted as she bent to kiss him again. Then before he knew what was happening, she slipped out of the awkward position and lay beside him on the stream bank, with the smell of crushed grass about them and the dusk humming with the noise of first cicadas.

A bloodroot flower caught his eye, its creamy petals shadowed with twilight. Her body pressed itself against him, and he felt her racing heartbeat. He kissed her lips, tasting them. On them he found the sweet taste of youth mixed with the effects of coarse bread, cabbage, and ale. She loosened her bodice and took his hand to her breast. He was overcome with the wish to take her, quickly, in the fullness of this April moment, but his Presbyterian conscience yapped at the back of his mind like an irritated terrier.

"I have pledged myself to avoid casual love. I have known only one woman. . ." he murmured weakly.

"Kind, fair, young gent'man," she whispered. She was unrelenting, in several specific ways that were hard to resist.

Ah, it's too much to ask, he thought. I am only flesh and blood.

"My name is Dan'l," he said emphatically, undoing his breeches, "and I'm not all that young." But when, his temples pounding, he reached the moment of release, he pulled back from her. I'll not add to your trouble my girl, he thought, by leavin' you with a bastard in this dark and bloody land. Then he lay on his back, staring at the gray, amber-streaked sky, breathing a little heavily.

Sobbing in huge, wrenching spasms, Martha Bard hurried away from the creek. She had witnessed something she had no business seeing, something she hated. Why did I stay there on that other side, lurkin' in the shadows like some kind of Iroquois spy. It was disgustin', disgustin', she told herself vehemently. She felt as if she might vomit; shock made her forehead and hands ice cold. "Dan'l, oh Dan'l, is this the way you act when eyes are not upon you?" She was speaking aloud. "But it is you who are disgusting," a small voice inside her said. "No," she told it, " 'twas a sincere desire on my part to avoid the stifling interior of the inn, to feel the beauties o' the evening."

And so, of course, she followed this little road behind the inn quite a ways, then across a footbridge and into a wood beside the creek. Brush and newly leafed-out trees hid the creek, but she could hear its bubbling. Thinking of home at sunset, of home to come, she had pursued the sound through the trees. She had spread out her skirts under a huge sycamore.

"But when you heard the voices," the teasing voice said, "why did you not leave? Any honest woman has no use for busybodyin', particularly when men and women are trysting." The truth is, Martha was transfixed, utterly unable to move, when she recognized Dan'l's voice. She had moved forward slightly, parted the linden and sassafras branches, so she could watch them unobserved. She could not, it is true, distinguish many words.

At first there was no alarm in her mind. It was the Irish girl. She was probably tellin' him how grateful she was. No sense in makin' a fuss, trampin' up the brush. They are sittin' but a moment and Dan'l will leave.

And when the girl's voice murmured on, telling her story, Martha said to herself that she, Martha, had just as much right to walk at sunset as they. But in the back of her mind the joyous picture she had painted for herself, of a home with a husband, began to run, like a slate picture in the rain, its neat furniture and pretty child in a starchy white dress weeping away, losing their form.

She peered harder through the trees, ignoring the catch in her throat and the pain in her breast when Dan'l put his head in the girl's lap and girl lay down. Then, wholly and suddenly, Martha realized the trap she was in. She could not move or leave or she would certainly disclose her own shame and his also.

"But you watched," the little, mocking voice continued. "You did what no Christian woman should have done, you uncovered your brother's sin." It was true. Her hand glued to that sassafras sapling, she watched the two hotly rolling by the creek. She heard the girl's moan (is there pain in the act?) as he lunged upon her. She saw the wench's skirts heaving, the thrash of legs wrapped around his bare limbs. Yet, she thought fascinated, 'tis like a strange and movin' dance, in rhythm, the girl heavin', the head and loins of the man bobbin'. A rockin', she thought through her own emotion, kin to that in a child, goin' to sleep. Finally, with a strange strangled sound, the girl released her legs, while Dan'l's motions continued for a few seconds.

At the girl's cry Martha too was finally released from her immobility. She buried her head in her hands, crying silently. An agony of embarrassment and self-reproach possessed her. She would at least look no more, saving a shred of her pride and conscience. She stayed that way for long moments, finally realizing that the voices were still. Only the bullfrogs, croaking lustily in the spring night, broke the silence of the woods.

Jane McClure, sewing by firelight in the other room in the inn's downstairs, saw Dan'l come in the door and go into the great room and flop down at a table, sullenly. Through the open door, in the flickering light of an outside lantern, she saw the servant girl, straightening her bodice ribbon, slip in the side door. Jane cut her thread with her teeth. 'Tis time these McClure boys were married, she thought.

She understood the ways of a man's heart and a man's body. Well she should, she thought tenderly. What she did not understand was what she next saw. The door of the inn opened slowly again and a distraught Martha Bard, twisting a wet linen handkerchief, came in. Then, looking furtively about as if to avoid all eyes, she hurried up the stairs. What was Martha Bard doing out at such an odd time? None of this went together, but it did not bode for good, Jane thought. And putting her mending away, she headed up the stairs for her first night in Kentucky, shaking her head sadly.

Chapter XVII

Jane McClure's mood had not improved a month later, as she sat idle in the corner of the blockhouse at Harrodsburg. "Nobody asked me if I wanted to go," she thought. "But then, nobody asked me if I wanted to leave Dunleigh." Dunleigh was on her mind lately. Just before she left Pennsylvania, word came that her Aunt Hepzibah had finally died at eighty-five, leaving her a modest sum.

She thought of herself laughing in her aunt's arms as a child and the latter-day Hepzibah with a drawn, painted face, estranged from the family because she ran off to Derry with a soldier. I never told her what she meant to my childhood, in spite of all the things I said about her, she thought. We never mended things, and we should have. That was the trouble with all the leaving. You pulled up the stakes that tethered your own heart.

No, they never asked, these men, when they up and moved, west, always west in their restless pilgrimages. But, she chided herself, what would you have said if they had asked? (I mean really asked, not just the polite what-do-you-think, Ma?)

Oh, no, son, you go on without me. Dinna give it any thought. No worries about me. After all the land is legally John's, not mine. I, as widow, get a life estate in the farmhouse, isn't that the way it works? My husband was my lord and master, now my son is. That bargain was made quite a bit ago. The young maid, with the wedding band on her hand, is to provide comforts of various sorts and the man will build her a beautiful home.

Which my sons bartered for this—her eyes darted about the cabin deprecatingly. Harrodsburg. A few hundred square feet of living space in a fort with a strong "curtain" fence. Well, you have to be reasonable. The Shawnees have begun their raids again, and it's safe in here, my dear. Except, of course, for the man who went outside a piece to graze his horse not too long ago and got decapitated by a tomahawk. Several lean-to cabins, two blockhouses, a spring, and a blacksmith's shop. But don't forget the amenities, dearing. Be fair. We do have a schoolhouse where the children will read and write. And a sort of woman's circle, with a leader to organize our spinning and dyeing. Or is it dying—

Obviously we can't live outside just now. That, of course, wasn't part of the bargain when I said goodbye to what was left of my home, a cabin the mice were getting ready to move into and a pile of discards that we couldn't sell or give away. My broken loom and Uncle's sad, forgotten harp were on the top of that pile, and I'd give all of Harrodsburg to have them back. A better life, everybody said. Rich land, plenty of it. And when we got here, all we could do was look at the lands and come into the forts. But certainly I understand what an Indian massacre is. I think I should. Pray God the rest of our friends are safe in those stockaded forts they call stations. The Emisons, especially, at Ruddell's station.

If we could go outside, what would there be anyway? Cane stalks twenty feet tall that whip in your face as you go by, dark, foul-smelling lowland woods, and a river flowing through a canyon as tall as a ship's mast. Jane McClure, you're fifty-five, stout, you have no grandchildren and no opinions that anyone wants to listen to. Well, I do have desires. And I will have a life of my own, thank you.

"George, come here." He came. Her voice was not usually so harshly commanding.

She fished in a knitted purse. "Here is money. Find a way to order one of those new fly shuttle looms from Virginia or Philadelphia. I know how to weave and I'm a good weaver. I'm going into business."

There's something I don't like out there, Jenny McClure thought. She was surpised at herself. Her mother always said she herself was afraid of the woods in Pennsylvania when she first came to America. But that was the reaction of a girl who grew up with the sea breeze and windswept hills in her life. The woods never frightened Jenny. She had always believed that nature doesn't finally terrify. It simply is, better and worse.

But there was something strange in this place. She sensed it as she and George and Will and some of the other Cumberland County settlers went up north to see Lytle's lands and rode as an armed party along that dark, dark river. She looked over the side of the canyon through which it flowed. It fell off so steeply between rugged limestone cliffs that it made her dizzy.

They said the Indians from the north and south had fought and died here since earliest times.The tribes called it the Middle Ground—Caintuck— and did not live here any more. Part of their bloody struggle survived yet in that canyon and in this land, Jenny knew it somehow. It lived in the odd smells that rose off the murky waters of the Kentucky River, in the trees that hovered about its banks in bug-infested pools, their warped roots pulling at the soil like arthritic hands.

That night, the party made camp not far from the river. The light of the campfire gleamed off the men's rifles as they sat, eyes fixed on the river and the woods, spelling each other on guard. Hunting shirts and extra blankets were on the bushes nearby to frighten off wolves, but the creatures howled sadly in the woods, making Jenny shiver. And in her fitful sleep and under the spell of the canyon river, she dreamed.

In her dream she stood on one of these high cliffs over the river, but no, it wasn't this one but another one like it. She saw women and children hoeing cabbages and onions inside the walls of a stockade not unlike Harrodsburg. Suddenly time telescoped; it was sunset, then daybreak with hardly a pause. Through the woods, almost noislessly, crept men, some in war paint, some in British regimental coats.

Fighting began. She could see puffs of smoke from firing holes in the stockade, hear those inside shout encouragement to each other. But there were many, many Indians and Englishmen; and when they fired a cannon it was all over. The blockhouse was smashed. She could see the grimaces on the Indian faces, hear their grunts of satisfaction. Slowly they advanced as the door of the stockade swung open. A man came out to parley with the officer in the British uniform and after talking, nodded his head in agreement. Then the Indians charged forward, without warning. And she was in the stockade itself.

Children were running about in terror as Indians chased them and pushed them down. She tried to pull at an Indian who was intent on killing a wounded man, but her hands went through his back. She could not be seen. The glint of knives, the vengeful blood screams terrified her; she turned to see a babe of only a few months, squalling, torn from its mother's arms and flung into the fire. The baby's agonized mother attempted to pull him out and was tomahawked and thrown on top of the babe.

Then, time again compressed. She stood outside the gates, weeping as a group of women and children were marched, prodded by curses and kicks, south. An angry, arrogant Indian slammed at a tow-headed child's head with a rifle butt. The child sank to the ground. Was he dead? Jenny moaned in her sleep and turned over to see her brother's eyes, questioning, in the firelight.

"Will, I hate this place. It's evil. Why did we ever sell out in Pennsylvania?"

"This land'll all be the white man's someday. But not before all these rivers. . ." he gestured with his head toward the Kentucky, "have turned to blood."

She shuddered and slept no more that night. Not only because of the howling of animals in the hills and the fear in her own thoughts, but because when she turned to speak to him, Will hurriedly hid a bottle. His breath was saturated with whiskey, and it was not the first time she had found him alone and drinking since they came to Harrodsburg. Will was drinking heavily, and now there was no longer any place to hide it.

Every night for a week after she returned to Harrodsburg from the dark gorge of the Kentucky River, Jenny dreamed the dream of the Indian attack. She could never see where the captives went or what happened to them; she awoke just as the child was thrown on the fire. She told no one about the dream. It was not something to talk about.

But when the news came three weeks later that Ruddell's Station had been destroyed just as she had seen in the dream, with the Emisons, who had gone there, barely escaped across the river, she cried half the night. She damned the second sight she always suspected she might have, and now knew for certain was her questionable inheritance from her mother.

Jenny decided to talk to her mother about Will's drinking. A sultry July sun blazed down on the clearing around the fort, and dust settled almost visibly on the leaves of the sycamore trees by the stream. They were sitting a bit off from the other women with a couple of armed guards, shelling peas near the garden outside the walls. Soon, they hoped, the McClure men would erect a temporary cabin within running distance of the fort, like some of the others had ventured to do. But for now, with the Indians lurking about, the garden provided safe enough respite from the closeness of the stockade.

"Ma, somethin's the matter with Will."

Jane's heart jumped. She always expected, or dreaded, bad news about her second son. It was as if anytime Will was away, and news came of him, or he sent one of his infrequent, notoriously misspelled letters, she waited for the worst. He would be beaten half to death in a barroom brawl. He had fallen into a river drunk, and drowned. Why was it this way? When good news came of Will, as it certainly had, that he did a distinguished job as militia commander, that he served well for several months in the force defending Pittsburg with Lytle, she was, against her will surprised. And often defensive.

"What do you mean, somethin's the matter?" she said in a guarded voice. Defiantly she popped open a full, green pod with her first two fingers, dropped the peas into a pan and reached for another pod.

"Whiskey seems to have got him hog-tied." There. Jenny had said it.

"Oh, pshaw. You're as bad as your Dada. He couldn't stand to see people drink a dram, and I never really understood it all. It's a civilized, friendly thing to do when you're with friends."

"Not the way Will does it. He takes one drink, then right away his hand reaches for another. Once a week, at least, he's very drunk."

"It's the Irish way. When we get together, we lift our glasses and toast our friends and scorn our enemies." Jane refused to look at her daughter, smiling instead over Jenny's shoulder at one of the guards.

"Waal, I do admit gettin' drunk is as universal as death or taxes with us all," Jenny conceded.

"Lots of men are like that out here. And even in Ireland. . ."

"Tell me about my grandpa's drinking."

" 'Twas different. Well, I don't know from seein' it, but your father always said he was a drunkard. Drank every night to stupefaction. Will's certainly not like that. He doesn't have to drink." Her hand stopped above the mound of peas, hesitating, as if to pick a fat one, and she finally looked up into Jenny's eyes.

"Doesn't he?" Jenny asked, with more indifference than she felt. Then, rising from the stool, she kissed her mother and strode back among the stumps of the open area to the stockade gate.

Martha Bard set her teeth as she pushed the birch broom around the little cabin that the Bards were sharing with another widow in the row at Harrodsburg. She, three widow women including the now bed-ridden Cousin Angelica, Tom, his wife, and the other boys ate, slept and sometimes read the Bible in this one small cabin. Straw mattresses were everywhere; the loft was a solid barracks. But she would not live like a sloven. Wherever you are, she told herself, you can have order.

"James, come help me," she shouted out the door. Her shy, thin, fourteen-year-old brother came in to help her stack up the mattresses and air the bed quilts on bushes outside.

Martha Bard believed that one could achieve order in the inner life in exact proportion to the determination one went about ablutionary ministrations carried on in the outer world. She scrubbed the greasy hearth, scraped the bacon sloppings off the bottom of the spider, put the food under covers away from the swarms of flies at this time of the year, and each job she completed bought her a little peace of mind.

One of the few compliments Mary Bard ever paid her daughter was to say was there could never be too much work for Martha to polish off in one day's time, and Martha liked to feel that way about herself too. Especially here. Bring it on, churning the butter, making the shirts, carrying the water from the spring. They had no flax? Very well, she would card and spin buffalo hair and use it with filling made of nettles to make cloth or knit stockings. There was little pork here? All right, she would learn to smoke and salt buffalo meat. The cabins stank and seemed unhealthy? She would bring in summer primroses, savory, wild roses, each with a specific purpose to purify the cabin.

It was only for a short time. There would be better things. There would be wheat for bread. Sometimes she thought she was would scream if she had to look at fried possum one more time, without bread. And salt, enough salt sometime. She knew it, princess held in woodland bondage that she was. Well, anyways, she told herself, all this work kept her from thinking about what was going on outside. About white men in breech cloths like Indians, drunk in the streets of Harrodsburg in the morning. About gamblers and land speculators and murderers from Baltimore who watched her from between the cabin buildings. About split skulls in the night. And about Dan'l.

But it was difficult not to think about him; he and his good mother were always around, neighborly and helpful to the widows, especially silver-haired Angelica Bard lying on her pallet in the corner. Of course, it wasn't just them he favored. He made himself a great favorite of everyone in the settlement, offering good morning to the old folks whenever he saw them in a way that wasn't customary in these rough parts and cutting wooden whistles for the children.

At first she tried to avoid him, but it was difficult to avoid anyone in Harrodsburg. There he was, offering to help repair the guns, setting up his workbench outside their cabin to make a butter churn that rocked and worked with iron parts the blacksmith made for him and saying, with a wink, " 'Twill be for both the famblies." Clever, kind Dan'l! And she felt, everytime she spoke to him, that her face was a hot griddle with her feelings hopping about on it like drops of grease.

She finally sat down and had a good talk with herself. "Now it is true," she said, "that somethin' dreadful happened for you back by that creek near the falls. But Dan'l did not ask to have you come into the inmost part of his life, for better or worse. It's as if you came on someone in the necessary, and the door was open and they didn't know it. You'd have to find a way to carry on with that person the next day, even though you blundered by and saw him squattin' and helpless, poor thing. After all, he didn't know you saw him, there's that." So she tried to look at it that way, and she set her jaw another time, and she found that she could speak civilly to Dan'l McClure and talk to him about the supper-and-will-it-rain-businesses of life. And like an unpleasant passage in a book, the incident by the creek was firmly turned over, made to stay hidden behind more acceptable pages that had been leafed through since. Then Martha Bard slammed the book shut.

George McClure stood outside the porch of the log cabin which served Harrodsburg as land office, as the July sun beat down on the fort's dry-baked road. He had just left the schoolhouse within its walls, where he was assisting the young woman who taught with older students. Harrodsburg, in spite of the fear of Indian attack, was carrying on with its life. It was beginning to boast of many things, and one of them was being the only settlement in Kentucky where students learned Latin, thanks to Rafe Emison's old student.

Radix malorum est cupiditas. Who knows what evils this greed over buffalo wallows will breed in Kentucky, he thought with mild amusement as he watched men, some in stained, filthy linen hunting shirts, some in dandified frock coats, jostle each other to get in the land office door. Land fever was hitting Kentucky, and he watched and wondered. At St. Asaph's, at Boonesboro, so he had heard, with settlers arriving daily over the Cumberland Road, and now at Harrodsburg on the Salt River, the same thing was happening. Immigrants who seriously wanted to farm vied with pikers who wished to get rich on speculation. They all were cursing, pushing and fist-fighting to get land nobody could even live on yet because of the Indians.

He knew that a lot of the land claiming was done as the Cumberland County men had done it—by tomahawk. Whoever got there first chopped initials in butternut or oak trees and threw together a little cabin, planted corn, and said the plot was his. That was the way the old Transylvania Company set it up, to encourage settlement in the early days; and Virginia decided to honor this in its newly-formed county when it could. Sometimes that worked—the would-be farmer went and claimed his "improvements" and paid the land commissioner for the land and a warrant to have it surveyed. But sometimes that very piece of Caintuck land had been sold back in Virginia, and he found his initials were in trees that didn't belong to him, and never would.

And contrariwise, the Virginians got gypped too. Some folks, arriving over the Cumberland Road, having somehow survived its ambushes, mountain snows, and quicksand pits, found other folks on the land they'd bought, and had to move or to buy the land the second time before they'd even set a plow to it.

Kentucky in 1780, it seemed to George, was speculator's heaven and often as not settler's hell. But then it was a hell in other ways too, a brutalizing place where refinement and compassion, and even common courtesy were subordinated to one need only—day-to-day survival in a world that seemed bent on annihilation. Men forgot about the Continental Congress, the laws of Virginia, and even God in these wild outposts in the wilderness.

Today, the business in the windowless land office cabin seemed particularly hot to him. A man named Robert Patterson had opened up a new station in an area of rich grass and timberland. He was calling it Lexington, after the opening skirmish in the war, and men were fighting to buy into its future.

Suddenly George saw the men reluctantly part ranks. A red-haired man with a lean, determined face and the uniform of a colonel in the Virginia State Forces strode across the porch.

The colonel, whom George recognized from his last week here at the fort, turned to the group of land buyers who stood in a throng waiting for the agent of the colony of Viriginia. First he clapped his hands above his head, then waited determinedly for the crowd's curiosity to build as to what he had to say. He was obviously a man who expected to be listened to.

"I've seen many old friends here, since I returned to Harrodsburg after the recent tragedies at Ruddell's and Martin's stations. And if any of you know George Rogers Clark, you know he doesn't forget a friend." A murmur went through the crowd of burly men, and they stopped chewing and spitting tobacco and laughing. "I've sent express riders to all the stations in Kentucky, and we've had more than one meeting here in the last few days to see what should be done. I don't think I've seen many of you there." A sort of grumbling undercurrent began, with an edge of hostility.

"Kentucky needs friends now. You all know about the murdering and pillaging as well as I do. The British have set the Shawnees on us. The representatives of His Majesty George III have left the comfort of the fort at Detroit and come to us, determined to get Kentucky and all the Ohio country for the British fur interests. But we are not going to let them do it."

A rather scattered cheer went up and Clark took a minute to say something to one of his aides. A good share of the men turned back to what they were doing, as if Clark was finished, as far as they were concerned. George was interested in hearing what Clark had to say. He had been to the "emergency" meetings and was impressed with this gifted, energetic Virginian. He had heard about him before, of course; Will knew him at Pittsburg and believed him to be courageous as well as reliable. Of course he was controversial. But he was a man who used his wits to get things done. Hadn't he captured Kaskaskia, Will argued, by his wits, first frightening the inhabitants out of their skins by threats and then suddenly reversing himself, showing mercy to bring them to their knees? Hadn't he surprised the British Colonel Henry Hamilton, at Vincennes, and taken the whole Northwest for America? Damn the military issue men who said Clark was a reckless, unpredictable egotist. That wasn't the McClure opinion.

"I'm not finished," Clark said, clearing his throat loudly. In spite of themselves, the land-buyers turned again to listen to him. His eyes were riveting; the line of his mouth curled slightly downward with the slightest suggestion of contempt. "I have called in all the Kentucky militiamen. I'll be taking a force to show the Shawnees who owns this country. We will plunge deep into Ohio territory. Ben Linn and James Logan will be with us. I am going to need every man here. How many of you can I count on to go?"

Since most of the men did not really plan to settle in Kentucky, George wondered how many of them would respond to Clark's "request." He himself had signed on at a meeting last night. Now, eight or ten volunteers came forward. Clark suddenly grew very angry. "What is the matter with the rest of you?"

The men in the front of the group were no longer looking at Clark, but around him, at a group of settlers who came out of the land office door. The waiting crowd was counting the minutes till they could get in, salivating at the thought of thousands of acres to be chopped up and sold off to waiting immigrants in Virginia.

The shadow of a frown crossed Clark's face. "This land will be no good at all if we don't defend it now. Women and children were taken prisoners at Ruddell's station. The Indians split their skulls with tomahawks only one day out and left them for the crows to pick. Now, while the spoor is fresh, we should follow hard and show them such barbarism won't be tolerated. . ."

A man with a huge wart on his face stood up from the step of the porch and ambled up to where Clark stood. "Waal, now, sir, there may be some difference of opinion 'bout all this. Some of us don't yet have lands to fight fer. Let them that has the lands fight fer 'em. And anyways," he looked into the dark face of the commander, "seems to me the state of Virginia pays you sojers to take care o' folks yerselves."

Clark gave a signal with his head to his aides, turned on his heel and walked into the land office. George wondered what the scene would be in there. Soon he could hear the sound of angry voices filtering out from behind the hinged door. After a while Clark emerged, coolly collected, but still very angry.

"Under the authority given me by the State of Virginia to defend Kentucky, I hereby declare this land office closed indefinitely for all transactions until safety can be promised in the area. All able-bodied men are expected to bear arms in Ohio against the Shawnees. See my officers to sign up for short term militia service."

Silently, many of them nodding affirmation, the men moved off the porch and went to sign up. But others stole away, and George knew they would be trying to saddle horses as fast as they could to go back East.

"Speculators. Cutpurses and adventurers. They're not going anywhere. I've had their horses and rifles 'requisitioned for the service'." Clark leaned forward with a self-satisfied smile as he talked to the group at James Harrod's house that night. He was drinking rum and scooping up venison and new peas with a small knife and a fork. Will McClure, repairing his lead shot bag with an awl, was one of those who sat at the table with Clark. His brothers John, Dan'l, and George were part of a larger group sprawled on the floor of this roomy log home.

"They'd be halfway to Cumberland Gap by now," Will said, "if you hadn'ta done what you did at the meeting this afternoon." He watched the big, handsome man attack victuals as he must have attacked the fort at Vincennes.

"My men are manning every exit out of this place and the Kentucky country itself. I think I've stomped down every mole hill they could have used for escape." He looked shrewdly around the table and saw faces he trusted: tall, energetic Ben Logan, the founder of Standing Fort, earnest Jim Harrod who had started this fort of Harrodsburg, Ben Linn.

"Not everybody's going to like the proclamation you issued, but thank God you did it," said Logan.

Clark looked up at Logan. "What's the size of the force we're going to have, Ben?"

"We aren't having to use strangle holds to get the local men to go after the Indians. They're hot for revenge and they're afraid for their families. The buryin' detail at Ruddell's Station saw a pile of bodies three foot tall, women, children, all mixed in with animals. I expect we'll have one thousand men at the Licking River in about two days. Then we'll rendezvous, get the enlisted men together, and we'll name the best men we can get as captains." Logan reached toward the fire for a straw to light his pipe. "Captain is the key post in an army going against Indians because you've got to be able to act 'n react quickly, at the unit level."

Logan was one of the most respected men on the frontier. George was pleased to find that he would be marching with him. He speculated that the captain's position in the Harrodsburg group would go to Benjamin Linn, another local man he respected.

That night, frightened but stoic women bustled in and out of the well-guarded gates of Harrodsburg, making preparations for their men's departure. At the tub mill, a fine, thin stream of coarsely ground corn fell on Jenny McClure's upturned palm. She stopped in the midst of her hurried thoughts to recall how much she loved the feel of warm, ground grain on her hand, the sweet, nut-like taste on her tongue.

The grinding job completed, she removed her bin to make room for the others waiting in line even at this night-time hour. Filled canteens lay by the stream. She picked up her bucket of meal and then tried to determine how she would carry the leather straps of five filled canteens, when a voice behind her said, "Pardon me, Miss McClure. May I help?"

She turned to look up into the honest, homely face of James Scott. She was momentarily suprised; she had not seen him since they had arrived at the Falls of the Ohio.

"Mr. Scott, you startled me. You've come to town for the march north to Ohio Country." They walked back toward the fort gate.

She asked him where he had settled, and he said he was in the new fort at

Lexington. A sudden pang hit her as she thought of the lonely buffalo trace between Harrodsburg and Lexington, the stark cliffs and moaning winds of her dream.

"What is it?" he asked, seeing her disturbed.

"You jest so much. All say you are a master of raillery. My thoughts are too serious to tell."

"None of us are joking tonight, Miss McClure," he said softly.

"It's just that. . . I had a terrible dream a month ago. It came more than once. It was," she could hardly continue, "of the massacre at the station. The baby thrown into the fire, the scalpings, the screams of old women—I saw it all before it happened."

He turned and looked long at her, full in the face. All about them soldiers cleaned and oiled guns, children ran and leapt, dogs chased each other, drunk men lurched about.

"I have heard tell of such things before. My mother does believe in them. I do not know," he finally said. "A woman by Cumberland Gap dreamt their camp would be set upon by the savages. Three times she dreamt it. . ."

"And?"

"The third time they came down even as she was dreaming. Kilt her husband."

Jenny turned away so he would not see the tears in her eyes. "I sometimes think we are living in a nightmare. I will wake up soon in my peaceful bed in Pennsylvania."

"We will all sleep peaceful sometime, Miss Jenny," Scott said, He cupped her chin in his big hand, as if she were a child and met her weeping eyes with his own kind ones. "But I doubt 'twill be soon. There's many a moon between us and peace in Caintuck. But there's no time like now to get started on it."

Chapter XVIII

August 1. Rendezvous at the mouth of the Licking River. Clark had gone quickly overland to the Falls and procured a small body of regulars who were sent to Louisville by the State of Virginia. Now his uniformed men beached canoes and unloaded supplies. Gnats swarmed about their arms and faces in the sweltering heat of the riverbottom.

Close behind Clark came Harrod, with a force of two hundred men from the western settlements, in canoes and patched-up floatboats. He swung his portly frame out of the canoe and immediately went away to take stock of the over one thousand men assembling to go on the expedition. Before long, to a chorus of halloos, Ben Logan thundered up and splashed into the shallow waters with a force enlisted at Boonesborough and Harrodsburg and the forts near the Kentucky. With him were the McClure brothers, Tom Bard, and James Scott.

Later, the hazy summer sun set as a giant ball of fire over the river's calm waters. On its brazen surface, insects landed and skittered about; huge river bass occasionally broke water and leapt in strangely beautiful arcs. Logan spoke to the men sitting crosslegged on the muddy southern shore. "Men, tomorrow we cross this river and march for Chillicothe and the camps of the savages who stole our Caintucky women and children, who want to kill every woman's son of us in this new land. It's us or them and you know it.

"Now, men, the rations are short. All we can give you is a pound and a half of meal, nine quarts of parched corn and a bit of buffalo." He looked into their faces. "Hell, a lot of you have lived on grilled squirrel and fried Indian bread when you could get it out here. This isn't the Raleigh Tavern at Williamsburg."

There were guffaws among the troops squatting around small campfires. George McClure looked up at the familiar, weathered face of Bige Cherry, his comrade in many other camps. Not far from the fire, Hugh and Ash Emison cleaned their guns and readied their ammunition. Honest, handsome faces they have, George thought. Good men, kin of my old friend. How time and events circle about. We are like children playing fox-and-geese, chasing our own footsteps, crossing the tracks of familiar friends, as long as we live. But who will be the geese, he wondered, tomorrow when we ride to Chillicothe?

George dreaded dashing down trails to find savages. Fighting the British was one thing; you could be in readiness and knew what to expect. They grouped, they reconnoitered, they laid out battle plans on tables and ordered men to march in them. But in Indian warfare your heart was constantly in your throat. Indians had only one tactic, and that was surprise; they did not beseige, unless forced to it. They did not fight pitched battles.

You had to send scouts ahead, scouts who could travel silently, watch the owl hoots and turkey calls in the woods, notice every blade of crushed grass, fade into the trees. As the cavalcade progressed through woodland paths, every man's ears and eyes must be constantly alert for snapping twigs, birds fluttering into flight. In each man's thought was the unspoken fear of ambush, the most dreaded word in frontier warfare. For who could say at what moment might come the sudden hideous attack cry, the sight of dark, greasy faces, grotesquely distorted by hatred. Then, through the air, the swish of a tomahawk that could cleave a skull. Indian warfare made George's nerves as taut as strings. Will, of course, was stimulated by it. Hand him a rifle, put him in a saddle and give him a few savages to hone in on; but then Will was a law unto himself anyway, a savage of sorts in his own way.

George spoke under his breath to Cherry. "What do you think Captain Kennedy would make of this campaign?" His lips curled in a slight smile as he thought about the golden Mars of Washington's command. Kennedy was now with the general, serving as an aide.

"Hell, he'd say the Injeeans don't fight fair," Bige told him. "An' we ain't dressin' our lines right. Need regulation drummer boys and—hey, George, ain't you got a tin whistle someplace? Mebbe you could play 'Yankee Doodle' as we rush in from the woods. That'd sure help the element of surprise."

Soon Logan came to speak directly to the group from Harrodsburg. "Under the press of time we've talked to as many from your neighborhood as we could to select officers." George looked up with interest. "We've decided to make James Linn a company commander for this campaign and for captain, someone Colonel Clark personally recommended and you all supported whole hog." He walked over to within a stone's throw of the McClure boys—"William McClure"—and clapped Will on the shoulder in a comradely way.

George felt his features turn to marble in the flickering light of the fire. Hugh Emison, Tom Bard, all his neighbors were stamping their feet in the mud and cheering; Will was looking genuinely pleased and modest. "Why has this happened?" George asked himself, infuriated. He rose instantly to seek out Dan'l and John, down the shore a hundred yards or so.

He found them tending the horses in a clearing in the woods near the mouth of the Licking, and he got to the point at once. Telling them the news, he said between clenched teeth, "I cannot fight for Will." He did not know he could be so angry.

"Why not?" John asked evenly.

"You know that as well as I. Surely we know too much, have seen too much through too many years to have an ounce of respect for Will. I don't want to put my life in the hands of a fool, brother or not. Do you?"

"I have seen a good bit, 'tis true, but I also know what I know. Will is foolish, but he is also brave. He fought like a panther with Lytle at Fort North." Two years ago Lytle had commanded a small fort in the wilderness north of Pittsburg. Will, assigned with him, volunteered to bring out two families held hostage by the Delawares and had done it when no one believed he could.

When George first came up, Dan'l had turned from the chestnut horse he was tethering for the night to listen to him. Now he stroked the horse's sleek sides, reassuring it. "George, there's always been hot blood between you and Will. You couldn't even believe he'd go off to fight in the war. You ain't got a good reason for opposin' him as captain. He's earned it. Now I suggest you calm yerself a bit, maybe take a drink of that punch you like, that some o' the men got bubblin' over the fire. . ."

"Have you two taken leave of your senses? This is the boy who is known in every ale house in Cumberland County! Who never did a lick of work to help you, John. Who avoided the militia until he had a sudden flash of grace. It's not a fair selection. . ."

Dan'l came over and put his hand on George's shoulder. His face was calm and concerned; he looked surprisingly like their father. Suddenly George saw white. All of the discomfort, the brutality, the confinement and danger of life in Kentucky among barbarous men washed in on him and his temper snapped. He snarled angrily into Dan'l's face. "Oh yes, you, butter-wouldn't-melt-in-your-mouth. Dan'l the golden boy, the saint whom fortune always smiles on! You can do no wrong and must advise me, Big Brother." He pushed Dan'l into the mud and Dan'l arose, fists flying, his own good temper gone. John and the other men around the horses soon separated them, but not before Dan'l had given his taller brother a black eye.

Looking at George, Dan'l was suddenly remorseful. "Georgie, I'm sorry—I didn't mean to. . ." Panting, George fought to regain composure. This was not a dignified way to act, not correct demeanor for one trained to admire reason above all. Drat, to make it worse, there was William now.

"What's this about?" Will asked, with an edge to his voice. He didn't understand why his brothers were fighting. He had details to organize before the river crossing tomorrow. Besides, it was detracting from his moment of glory.

"Nothing, nothing at all," George said quickly, wheeling around and turning the injured side of his face toward the shadows of the woods. "Just an insult about my soldiering ability. I reacted too quickly. You go back and we'll come after you in a bit."

And as Will gave them all an incredulous look and turned on his heel, George said, under his breath after him, "Lead on, Hannibal." And he tried to recall an Indian proverb he once heard. What was it? "He who has a fool at the head of his war party, has death for a riding mate beside him." Yes, that was it. He nodded his head, feeling a little better for remembering the proverb.

But John, watching his younger brother slowly make his way back up the shore, had another way of looking at what just happened. "George is scared shitless of the Injeeans. And he's jealous to boot," he said to Dan'l.

Clark's army carved its way along the east shore of the Little Miami River, hacking through timberland and mucky riverbottom criss-crossed with fallen timbers, creating an artillery road. Clark believed that the cannon captured in Illinois could mean the difference between victory and defeat against the Indians. He delayed his march only long enough to safeguard his stores by building a small stockade opposite the mouth of the Licking River, then he drove the men onward.

It was an agonizing pace through hot, sodden air and stinging insects which settled into the eyes of horse and man alike. On the second night in camp one man who chose to bathe in the river counted fifty-six mosquito bites on his back alone, accumulated in just five minutes.

They arrived at the Shawnee's Chillicothe Town to find only scattered pieces of broken pottery, forgotten moccasins, and doused campfires. There was no sign of life except for a few dogs baying mournfully about empty doors. The Indians were warned, word had it by a deserter, and had fled north to Piqua Town. And so, nearly a week after they started from the Ohio, Clark's army of Kentuckians approached what would surely, finally, be battle with a large group of Indians at Piqua on the Mad River.

Dan'l McClure descended to the river to fill his canteen in the green-brown swirl of its waters. The air was heavy from recent, drenching thunderstorms. He looked about for a moment. A robin, flushed by the noise of Dan'l's movement, flew out of a white oak which bent low branches over the water. A duck and her babies were swimming by little rapids up toward the Indian village, and cabbage butterflies flitted on blossoms of weeds.

The column stopped, as it had to do frequently this day, to pull the six-pound cannon over the uneven road. Dan'l's thoughts were on the approaching battle. He had watched the Virginia State Regulars prepare for battle this morning. First, the men put on the small clothes of the uniform, with the linen shirt and overalls, then the white waistcoat. Next, they put on a dark blue wool coat with white facing, surprisingly cool even in this heat. Spanish cartridge boxes with the royal cipher of Castille and Leon were strapped about the waist, and Spanish Muskets, primed and loaded, with fixed bayonets were slung over one shoulder.

What are their warriors doing this moment, Dan'l wondered. Painting vermilion and black? Oiling their guns, testing the bows they still used in close contact, listening to the war drums beginning to beat their slow, deadly rhythm. And the women and children? They would be weary, frightened from the rapid retreat from Chillicothe. Would they be crying? He steeled himself by thinking of the swollen, flyblown bodies of tomahawked white children, some of the Ruddell's Station captives who were found last week at the Ohio. Then he sighed and struggled up the bank to the ranks. The cavalcade was moving forward.

Will was making a splendid captain, Dan'l thought. He was up earlier than anyone, seeing to supplies efficiently, maintaining tight order and discipline, even if it meant thrashing some of the rougher types who questioned an order. To see so many kinds of frontier individualists, a good many of them drafted, and some almost boys, come together into an army, was remarkable. It spoke of the leadership skill of George Rogers Clark, as well as the captains he chose.

Will revered Clark and was eager to obey him implicitly in everything. Will seemed to believe that only as he followed Linn, and Linn followed Logan and Clark as closely as possible, would destruction of these Indian homelands be guaranteed. Thus the future of Caintuck, and possibly this whole new western territory, rode with him and the other captains. And Will was sober. Dan'l had been near his brother and knew there was water only in his canteen on this campaign.

So George was wrong, terribly wrong about Will's ability to lead men. George didn't say so to Dan'l; in fact, George remained detatched and surly through the entire trip along the river, even though Will named him ensign and gave him special duties.

But what of the other things George said as he had pummelled him with such emotion by the Ohio that night? That he, Dan'l, was the favored one, that everything was given to him easily. Didn't that imply that he had never worked? Somehow the picture George had painted of him made Dan'l think of a child, simpering and sucking its thumb. There was something not quite grown up in the goody-two-shoes Dan'l George talked about. But he did admit that life had dealt easily with him; he really was untested. Could he help that? Maybe he was just lucky. He never thought about himself this way before. He didn't like to do so now, especially when he was facing the prospect of doing battle with several hundred Indians bent on killing him. Piqua Town couldn't be more than a few miles away. They would need to find a ford for the river, cross, and meet the enemy.

Once across the river, Linn reined to talk to his captains. "Colonel Clark says the Indians have been riding far and wide calling Shawnees, Wyandots, Mingoes, Delawares, possibly even a few Miamis. They're holed up in woods in front of the fort and village they have built, which is across the big field you see up there. Our cannons, particularly the six-pounder, will stand us in good stead. Spread across the field. McClure, you're to the left, by the woods."

Will McClure, according to command, brought his troops opposite the woods which ran along cleared land to the left. He and his brothers and Cherry, Bard, Scott, and the rest of the men in Linn's command, then prepared to advance northeast across the plain toward Piqua village. The village, behind the Indian line, had a triangular-shaped fort in its middle. This would be the spot the Indians would make a last stand if they had to. The soldiers knew Logan was taking his men upriver behind the village to cut off the Indians' retreat, so the army could eventually corner them in the village-fort area.

George McClure crouched in the grass, waiting for the signal to fire. He looked over his shoulder to see Harrod's troops, in the center, encountering sharp fire already from the Indians hidden in weeds and by a fence along the river. The drummer boy began his ominous rat-ta-ta-tat. A sudden image of Princeton and George Washington came and went in George's mind; how far away all that seemed. He had not overcome his fear of fighting Indians, but at least now he could face them as men, not wait for them to spring from hiding. They were there to aim at.

Now Indian musket fire intensified from the weeds and began from the woods along the prairie. Crouching, McClure's company advanced.

They fired, knelt and reloaded, then repeated the process as heavy, crackling fire came from the Indians among the trees on the left.

The concentrated fire was effective; it soon became too much for the Indians in the weeds. They began to retire as fast as they could toward the woods to re-load. Will, on foot, raised his rifle in his right hand above his head. "Caintuckians, forward! Charge 'em before they can rally!" He scrambled forward, closely followed by his brothers and the company of Pennsylvania Caintuckians. Other captains on the left also thundered forward. The McClure boys, as they would later be called in accounts, yelled fiercely, dashing among the tall weeds to crush the Indians there.

George Rogers Clark rode up behind the advance across the prairie and from a distance watched it with his spyglass. "That's it, forward! Don't let them load among those weeds. If we can overcome them here, we can send 'em scurrying. The day must be ours," he urged, as if the troops could hear him. He sent a messenger to Linn to press the advantage.

The men did not need exhortation. With bloodthirsty screams issuing from their throats, Linn's regiment advanced across the prairie, chasing the Indians not only out of the weeds, but also into the woods itself. And at the head of the entire pack of Kentucky jackals hot for revenge and wanting to confirm peace for the homes they would soon build, were four men.

"What unit is leading that pursuit?" Clark asked an aide as he viewed the scene with his spyglass.

"That's McClure and his three brothers. Fair to middlin' fighters, ain't they?"

"Damn right," Clark said, "but they're a bit too hot about it. They're too far ahead. Order Linn to stop and regroup." As this messenger spurred off, he turned to another aide. "Go find out why Logan's flank movement hasn't happened. We need it now."

Night fell on the darkened field of battle. The sounds of crows in the trees above Mad river and the croaking of frogs in the mud of its banks blended with the clatter of cutlery and the jingle of horse livery. Tired men spoke in low tones around campfires at the edge of the Indian village.

The battle had ended in a victory of sorts in the late afternoon. Still, many of the Indians had escaped. Defeated and driven back through their village, they headed for a rocky pass. Logan, unable to get his mounted troops through high palisade cliffs east of the village, did not come to protect the rear until too late, so most of the Shawnees were able to slip away into the hill country to the north. Clark's men fell back to the edge of the village to nurse the wounded, bury the twenty dead men and rest their bone-tired bodies. John and Dan'l McClure were cooking rations into a stew with, ironically, crushed corn from the stalks which grew on the battlefield.

George was posted as guard near the far edge of the shattered village. Just as well, he thought, I don't want idle chatter after that. He was near nervous exhaustion. Feelings of great relief mingled with horror in a way they never had for him in the equally awful, but more orderly, battles of the war in the East. Today he saw Indians scalped alive before his eyes by the troops, their genitals shot off as they lay in the woods behind the cornfield. Toward the end of the battle, he witnessed their outnumbered braves form a single, defiant, hopeless line facing the army of Colonel George Rogers Clark and a six-pound cannon. Defending the pitiful, shattered village behind them and the future of their wives and children, they had charged, only to be mowed down by the astonished troops like wheat before the scythe. They had been forced into a pitched battle, and they died horribly.

The pictures of this, and of the drunken recruits who disobeyed their officers at the end and rushed forward to loot and caper about the bodies, shattered George's composure and disturbed his concentration. But through all the cacophony of noise and after-battle shock that played in his mind, through all the jangled impressions that brought him almost to the point of nausea, was one recurring motif: the indisputable bravery of his brother Will.

The images were vivid: Will leaping like a stag over the fallen logs of a fence, Will, ludicrously yelling "Hey, ho the bottle," as he rallied the tired group to pursue the savages from hillock to hillock and finally through the miserable ruins of the town. Will, behind a tree with Tom Bard, firing at puffs of smoke from across the woods, then violently pulling his friend back as Tom foolishly leaned out to fire, so that instead of Tom's being buried tonight, he lay with the surgeon, who was setting his broken leg.

Clearly, Will was one of the finest men on the field. Clark specifically commended him back in camp. This Will loomed larger than life in George's thoughts, floating like a giant before-Lent parade figure in his mind's eye, his handsome face with its auburn curls smiling mockingly at George. This Will was someone he did not know. Or had never acknowledged. This new Will fascinated and frustrated him almost intolerably at this moment, and he wondered how he could live with this man day-to-day in the future. That Will could be honestly good and heroic was almost beyond his comprehension, and yet it was so. He had seen it before his eyes. A brother he always considered a bibulous, unreliable, lazy, no-good was an honest hero in a battle that would go down in history. He had strength and stature. And, his own brother thought wonderingly, he did not even know it 'till now.

A day later, the McClures were back in the woods. Catbirds called from their stolen nests and deer startled along the path that stretched on through giant, light-filtering beechwoods, fallen-timber clearings rimmed with blackberry bushes, and swampy grasslands. The appeal of the natural beauty of the woods was as real to Dan'l as it was the first time Lone Stag and his father had taken him on a long hunt.

As the rest of the troops prepared to head back to Kentucky, George Rogers Clark himself asked the "McClure boys" to take the trace north on this breathtakingly beautiful, but dangerous mission. On horseback, staying on the rim of the woods, Will and his brothers were engaging in a quick reconaissance among the bountiful Indian cornfields along the Auglaize River. Clark heard they were planted for use of the British force at Detroit in case it should come south again, and he needed information on the extent of the fields.

The McClures were to be gone only three days, travelling with the greatest care. Most of the Indians had retreated back along the Greater Miami anyway and were in hiding from the white men. A Frenchman Clark had captured told him the savages were humiliated and dispirited by the destruction of their villages at Piqua and Chillicothe. But not so dispirited, he said, that they turned down the opportunity to burn a Caintuckian they had captured at the stake, to appease the Manittos of the cornfield the Americans destroyed.

At mid-day of this second day, Will signalled that they should stop their single-file progress and rein their horses in at a clearing next to the river for a rest.

"I want a deep drink," Dan'l said, taking off his beaten hat and tossing it on the grass. He headed toward the river, which ran rapidly, about two-feet deep, over rocks near the surface here. He knelt, as did George, to drink dog-style directly from the clear water. John filled the canteens. Perhaps, John said, they should have lunch here; the horses were hidden from the path by thick brush.

At that moment, around the bend in the river came an Indian canoe. John shouted and they dove for cover, grabbing for their rifles. "Don't shoot until you see what they do," Will hoarsely whispered to his brothers. It was a tense moment, because the horses were exposed; they whinnied nervously and pawed the ground. The Indians saw them and disembarked from the canoe. The party consisted of a young brave, a lithe girl, and a small child. The Indian man beckoned the other two in his protection to stand behind him and aimed a Pennsylvania long rifle at the brush.

"You, white men. Come out or I will shoot your horses."

"At least he's got courage. One Injeean alone against us," Will growled. "We'll try to get the woman and child to take to cover and then we'll shoot 'im. We can't take no chances—he may bring others and we'll be finished." He rammed home a charge and prepared to shoot. John and George loaded their rifles grimly.

But to their astonishment Dan'l arose, white in the face as a piece of parchment, and moved out of the brush.

"What are you doin', you fool?" John whispered. He reached out, trying to catch hold of Dan'l's hunting shirt, but his brother gained the edge of the brush clump and went out on the shore, without a gun, his hands in the air.

"Hidden Panther, don't you know me? It's Dan'l McClure. Niwa! I'm not armed." The Indian gave him a long look which reflected hostility, anger and finally, recognition. He lowered the gun. Dan'l's brothers watched him wade and splash across the river. Will grunted to his astonished brothers to put down their guns, walked out of the brush, and stood on the shore too, looking wonderingly across the river, amazed that he had not recognized their old hunting companion.

Dan'l talked quietly to the three Indians for a moment or two. Then John, Will, and George watched their brother re-cross the river to them, leaving the Indian man and the stately, beautiful Indian girl silent on the shore. Tears streamed down Dan'l's face. In his arms he carried a three-year-old boy. The boy had dark Indian eyes, golden, freckled skin, and curly red hair that looked a good deal like Jane McClure's.

They sat and shared food on the shore of the river, a little group out of time and space, beyond the mutual hatred and warring of their races, Mulberry Blossom and her brother, Dan'l, and William McClure. The beautiful child played with sticks and pebbles in the edge of the water. Will spoke a few words to John and George and, trying to subdue their surprise over the Indian who carried their father's rifle, and the child who was their nephew, they took food to the woods near the road to stand guard.

"We are camped nearby, with others of our band. Swamp Grass is there," Hidden Panther told them. His face seemed older, his eyes sad. "We journey to the settlement near where the Maumee begins, to rejoin our people."

William asked about the chief. "My father died at Ruddell's Station," Hidden Panther answered. The white men's eyes looked questioning. They knew he had opposed fighting alongside the British.

"The Ottawas and Shawnees claimed my father's manhood was gone, that our people were weak as kittens. Finally he responded to the taunts and took five braves. I would not go. Manhood is not proven by fighting to protect evil people's gold."

"Where are the captives from Ruddell's?" Will asked.

"They should be now at Detroit, if any of them are yet alive." His voice was almost a whisper.

Dan'l tried to listen to the conversation, but he could not keep his eyes off the child. Three years old, and yet this little one who looked so much like him showed real cleverness. His small face was a study in childish concentration, as he popped open a mussel shell with a stick and curiously looked at the slimy creature within.

"What is his name?" Dan'l asked Mulberry Blossom, who sat, not eating, staring at the river. He realized that for her, too, their meeting was difficult, even painful.

"Asondaki. Smiling morning sun. He came to me as the sun rose." English traders had visited often with her tribe; she seemed to have a better command of the intricacies of the white man's tongue than when he saw her last, and her brother was absolutely fluent. Now she turned to Dan'l and smiled very softly, and the smile went to his heart. The coy, playful young girl with whom he shared an evening was gone; a dignified, serene young woman stood in her place.

"Mulberry Blossom, I'm sorry," Dan'l said looking into her eyes.

"Do not think I did not want the child," she said, looking equally hard at him, her smile now gone. "Indian women do not bear children they do not want, Dan'l Mac Looer. I knew life would be hard for the child who has our blood mixed in him. Yet I wanted him."

"Why did you want to bear him? It would have been easier not to."

"When you came, it was a happy time. White man and Indian lived like brothers. The woods were full of fat porcupine and deer, the pots spilled over with meal and meat, the children and maidens danced and sang. Now it is all gone, forever I think. Only hatred and killing remain."

She went on. "I wished to have something of that night, when you and I, Indian girl and white man, stayed together in peace beneath the stars of the home village. For just one night, one beautiful night, we were one people." She smiled, this time broadly, and turning, she picked up his hand and put the palm of her own warm brown palm against his palm for a moment. The impulsive, meaningful gesture filled him with aching, not for the beautiful woman she now was, but for the far-away time she spoke of, the time of youth for them and the land itself.

They sat silently for a few long moments, watching the child pad about in the shallows. William and Hidden Panther continued an earnest conversation about the recent Indian troubles.

"Come here, Smiling Sun," Dan'l said, struck as he spoke with the double meaning of his words. His son! How he had wanted a child. The naked three-year-old came over and looked up trustingly into his face. He put his hand on Dan'l's cheek curiously.

"He has never seen a white man close. I keep him from the traders."

Dan'l took out a bit of honey comb that he had carried all the way from Kentucky and offered it to the boy, who ate it greedily. "What will he have in life?" Dan'l said slowly, without looking at Mulberry Blossom.

"He will have me and his uncle, the band chief's son," she said with dignity.

He suddenly picked up the child, who resisted a little, kicking laughingly. "And now he will have me. I will send money for him to go to school, for visits. . ."

Hidden Panther turned suddenly from his conversation. His voice was cold. "No. It cannot be. It is not clear what the next moons will bring to the Miamis, but whatever that is, he must be with us. Life will be hard enough for him, lost between two peoples, but it would be impossible as an Indian half-breed child among the whites."

"But I must see him, know how he grows," Dan'l insisted. The child squirmed and laughed and snuggled into his arms.

Hidden Panther rose and took his sister by the hands to raise her from the ground. "No. Listen to me, Dan'l Mac Looer," he said, facing him. "You must never see him again as long as you live. Never. It will ruin his life if you do."

Gently Dan'l set the child on his feet. A great sadness clutched his heart like a cold hand. "I know you're right." The few half-breeds he had ever known in the East were outcasts, among white men at least. Especially as children. It was difficult to promise he would never see Asondaki, but he knew he must.

Dan'l and Will helped the Indian family cross to the canoe. Dan'l clasped arms with Hidden Panther and brushed Mulberry Blossom's cheek. Then he picked up Asondaki and kissed his red curls. The child said something he did not understand in Miami, but smiled goodbye to him. Soon the three were gliding down the stream. Mulberry Blossom turned to wave before the canoe went around a bend.

Dan'l felt a sense of panic. Could the turn of a canoe's prow around a bend take these people he yearned for out of his life forever? It was too final, too decisive. He could not let them go. Yet John was back. The horses were ready. They must be about their business and hasten back before the Shawnees were active on the roads again.

So that is the way it is, Dan'l thought as he rode along, remembering what George said of him in anger back at the Ohio. There are no golden ones, no children of fortune. And perhaps there shouldn't be anyway. We aren't complete if we live only in the sunshine, as he had. He thought of the serenity of Mulberry Blossom's face in this time of war. Sadness does not leave us where it finds us, Dan'l thought. Like the Kentucky River Jenny hated so much, suffering gouged and tore and carved and wore down until no line of us was the same. In the case of Mulberry Blossom, at least, it had chiselled a soul of deep beauty.

Still, dullness of heart settled about him like a huge, black military cloak. He could not eat, he did not want to speak through all the difficult trip back to Kentucky. His brothers worried about him as they tried to forage for food and hunt in an Ohio where the game was driven away.

Dan'l had never hated anyone, and now he hated himself. Almost casually, he had created a life. He changed a family's very existence. And he never even knew or cared that he did it, no, not while Mulberry Blossom lay in pain on pine boughs giving birth to his child, while the child's grandfather fell in a war he hated, while the family fled by night, in fear. He had known little, cared less. Wasn't it because he had lived on the surface of life, had skittered about like the water bugs he loved to watch on Conodoguinet Creek, unwilling to dive into the depths?

And yet, he told himself, urging the frightened horse across the Ohio and heading for Harrodsburg with his brothers, he had to shake this black mood. It wouldn't do. Wasn't there something in his father's book about Christian and Hopeful, who, when they were caught in the dungeon of the Giant Despair, resolved to "pluck up the heart of a man" and try their utmost to get out of his grip? He must take up his life, must try to get at the business of planting fields and building cabins out on the new lands when the Indian raids ceased, as they must.

One thing he knew now. There are no casual acts. Each thing we do is like a seed put into the fist of God. As that hand opens in the fullness of time, the seed sprouts and flourishes and becomes a tree that casts thousands of its own seeds over all the future, changing things in little and big ways. And now, wherever he went, the tree of his own growth would cast a shadow over the path of the future. For never a day would pass from then on, that Dan'l McClure would not think: somewhere out there I have a son I will never know.

Chapter XIX

The Indians did recede from Kentucky and Ohio, as George Rogers Clark told the settlers they would, in the face of a destiny as impossible to resist as spring floods along the Ohio and Mississippi.

Not that the Shawnees, Wyandots and Miamis picked up their woven baskets and cooking pots and went quietly to the remote villages near the Wabash or beyond the Grandfather River. Quite the contrary. The Wyandots triumphed briefly in the slaughter at the disastrous battle of the Blue Licks, where overzealous frontiersmen, ignoring Daniel Boone's advice, rushed into an ambush that cost seventy-seven lives. Then Indians from all the tribes in Ohio rampaged through Kentucky in the Year of Blood, 1782.

But the truth was that the Revolutionary war was over and a new time was beginning. Even though the British peevishly refused to get out of the Ohio Valley, time was against them. Time, and the tide of settlers pouring down the Ohio River and over the Cumberland Gap like ants to spilled syrup. In 1781, only a year after Clark had trouble recruiting one thousand men to punish the Indians in Piqua, there were twenty-five thousand people in Kentucky.

It has sometimes been said by historians, particularly early ones, that Kentuckians in those first years were mostly the dregs of society; they were rough, brutal, even dull-witted people who had fled responsibility or the law. Some were, but most were the most resourceful, persistent, courageous and intelligent people America ever spawned. They had to be to survive those two or three years of blood after 1780, when to walk alone outside the stockade could mean decapitation with a tomahawk, when cornfields planted in the spring were burnt before they tasselled out, when sons and daughters tending cows were murdered before their parents' eyes.

But endurance is a wonderful quality. It must have been given to the frontier people to compensate for all the babies lost to yellow fever and wasting diarrhea, or the wives who died of childbirth, or young fathers taken in the prime of life by malaria. But somehow the people endured these tragedies, and in Kentucky, eventually, the raids eased back, the cornfields were left to produce in abundance, and people, like forest animals after a terrible winter, crept from their hiding places to live again.

The McClure family began to rise up and build individual homes in the spring of 1785 on the land they claimed between Louisville and Lexington. It was a fine piece of rich riverbottom farmland with gently rolling hills in the distance. The land was now divided into hundred-acre plots paid for with the cash from the sale of their father's land. John gave each of his brothers a plot and three hundred dollars to buy stock and farm equipment. But he had plans for the remainder, several thousand dollars.

"I've thought a fair bit about what I want to do with it." John's brothers sat around him in their one-room cabin outside the walls of the fort at Harrodsburg. They remembered that day when, by their father's grave, John told them the land would be shared and they would be lairds.

"The future's in the land. A lot of it's gone to speculation already, but I think we can get in on somethin' good. We'll double, or triple what's left from the cash on Dada's land. And we'll divide the proceeds, buy us a thousand acres apiece or more, get us some slaves."

George McClure raised his eyebrows but did not look at his brothers. There were differences of opinion about this already among them. Many Kentuckians brought slaves with them into the new territory, others acquired them as farming began. John and Will were already looking toward holding slaves, but George and Dan'l were much less inclined to own people. Their mother was dead set against it, but John and Will would probably do as they wished.

"Anyways, I'm askin' George to look into how to put the money out best. He'll need to go south, maybe into Tennessee as soon as possible, get the best deal. We should be willin' to take some risks." George nodded his head. It sounded agreeable, and it would give him something to do. The schoolteaching in the shack in the fort did not satisfy his restless mind.

John went on, "How's about the rest of us go to take another look at the land we have, build us all cabins in a stockade row together, clear the fields and plant and," here he winked, "get us some gals and git married."

There was a whoop that was probably heard in Lexington. Dan'l, Will, and John McClure laughed and clapped each other on the back and made so much noise Jenny came away from the pen where she was milking cows to see what the commotion was.

Told by her brothers that "we're in a marryin' frame o' mind," and "we're all a-gonna get rich," she thought to herself, what about me? And if you had a frame o' mind, what would it be, Jenny gal? She didn't know, but she found her mind wandering against her will to James Scott. Pshaw, who wants him anyway, she demanded of herself. Big nose and all he does is joke.

"What about you, Georgie?" she asked her brother, who was leaning against the fence. "Who's the lucky miss?"

"I didn't cotton much to being told I couldn't marry, and I don't like it much better now that I'm told I can. Maybe I'll just not marry at all." Well, think of that, mused his sister, watching him huff off like a wet hen. Whatever can that mean?

Courting was easy enough in that year of better times in Kentucky. With the wound-tight spring of Indian fear somewhat released, all was meeting and walking out and planning and getting a bondsman to swear you weren't already married in this place of no records, and hiring a fiddler. No place, no occasion was sacred and all was a-courtin' time.

The interior of the large log house was darkened, even though it was daylight on a March day. The window holes were covered over with blankets, and tall candles, the only source of light in the room, were placed around a table with a coffin on it. On the bier, dead at sixty-nine of heart disease in the wilderness lay Angelica Bard, widow of Isaac Bard of Philadelphia. She had come with her parents from Raphoe when she was a little girl and grew up to riches in America, as both her parents and husband prospered in merchandising. Jane McClure stood by the bier, thinking of the dark days after the sea voyage. My, she thought, the corn pudding and lemon pound cake and sympathy this woman poured out on me when I could not appreciate it.

She looked at Angelica's features, waxen and unnaturally pale. The blueness of her scalp under white, thin hair showed the long battle she had had with a weakening heart. Vesitages of kindness and humor showed in the slack wrinkles around eyes and mouth.

You have come far, Angelica, she thought, wondering what the dead woman had looked like as a girl in Raphoe, near Dunleigh. Angelica never spoke of her own youth. You are only ten years older than I, Jane thought. Did you play ring-a-rosie and make rock houses for doll babies the way I did? Nurse a sparrow in a cage with bits of bread? We really know so little about each other in this life. Your husband is gone these eight years and you are dead in this wild land, without children to carry on your name or even your memory.

But Jane had happy news, too, that day. Ardry Bard was one of several Bards in the new Bard settlement not far from Louisville. He had joined a new Indian campaign of George Rogers Clark in Ohio a couple of years ago and went back to Pennsylvania to gather up his unwilling wife and twin children and come to Kentucky. He told Jane his father Sam had died of apoplexy last year. Sally would have come too, he said, but regretfully, Caroline was worse with consumption; Sally could not consider moving West. Jane did not even allow herself to think of what having her friend in this wilderness might have meant to her.

Ardry and his family had floated down the river at spring tide to settle in this rapidly-growing cluster of log cabins and stores now known as Bardstown. He was practicing his father's occupation of wheelwrighting.

Another piece of good news that Ardry brought was that he carried with him the fly shuttle loom Jane had waited for so long. After a year Sally Bard secured it from Philadelphia on George's request, and had waited for someone to hand-deliver it. How long these things took out here! Shipments down the Ohio must sit for months in some storehouse, run the gauntlet of Indian sniping or seizure or come over the Wilderness road with just as many hazards. But now Jane could begin her own weaving shop!

But the months, eventually years, taken up in waiting for the valuable possession were not wasted. Jane managed to learn to operate the new type of weaving machine from an itinerant weaver's visits. First at Harrodsburg, then recently in her own cabin, with Jenny out on the McClure land, this weaver had treated her like an apprentice. Eventually she learned to weave double patterns and thick-piled tapestry pieces she was proud of. A new sense of meaning entered her life.

Ardry entered the dark room and advanced to the bier to pay his respects to the deceased. His wife, an extremely timid woman with coal-black hair worn in a bun, followed close behind him holding each of their four-year-old, twin daughters by a hand. "Waal, I never knew Aunt Angelica too well, but acourse we had spent time with them whenever we had cause to be in Philadelphia," he said, looking with proper respect at the corpse. His wife agreed with quick little birdlike nods of the head. That was how she responded to almost every statement. Ardry went on eulogizing the dead woman, as was expected of a visitor at a wake. "A good woman, very good. Did her duty by her husband and neighbors. Except acourse for bein' barren."

Jane frowned. How was Angelica supposed to help that? Everyone always thought women should feel shamed and guilty if they did not produce children. But men had some part in the generating of offspring. Suppose it had been her husband's fault! Anyway, you were supposed to say only good things about the corpse. That was as much a part of the wake as prayers and the whiskey being passed around now by Jenny McClure.

How people come to these wake-parties, Jane thought. We Scotch-Irish scorned the Mere Irish, and yet we picked up their customs as a sponge picks up spilled wine. She watched Jenny put a jug and small pewter tumblers on a pewter tray, prized possession of the dead woman. Who would get it now? Angelica no doubt had spoken to her relatives about what she wanted done with her possessions. Probably one of these Bards would get the pewter set, or it would go to her only other relative, a sister due in from the East soon.

People were beginning to ask for some of the "spiritual strengthening" Jenny was serving. She passed among familiar faces, pouring out the whiskey. As she came to each one in turn, she smiled: Mr. Lytle and his son Will, Jr., just settled in at their own station, Hugh Emison, married to Mary Bard. Next to Hugh, his brother Ash, the capable, blonde-haired bridegroom of the Ohio River trip, who was now the father of two and a successful miller.

Martha and her mother and the gaggle of other Bardlings bustled in and out, making pots of spicy bergoo stew and hot bread to serve on trestle tables outside the cabin. They were assisted by plump Margaret Mossman, a sixteen-year-old relative in an embroidered smock, who kept looking at all the McClure boys as if they dropped in through a hole in the roof and were heroes from Valhalla.

Tom Bard shook his head in the corner with Will as Jenny approached with libations. "A cat come in last night through the winder," he said, letting her pour into his cup without even looking at the action. "Leapt right up on the corpse and about scared the women out of seven years' growth."

"A bad sign," Will said, declining his sister's offer with his hand. He did not drink until afternoons these days. It was proof, he told himself, of his control over whiskey. "In Bryant's Station, a baby was found dead in its cradle with no sign on it. Had died for no 'parent reason."

"Ooh, it happens now and then thataway," said Mary Bard Emison, the pug-nosed older sister of Martha. "The cat stole the breath from the baby. You can't never allow 'em in the same room with corpses nor babies."

"I don't know why we must always be so superstitious," Hugh Emison offered in his clipped syllables. "Wakes are not Christian customs. They go back to the Celts. Uncle Rafe always said. . ."

Across the room Lytle was bragging on his son, Lytle Jr., a lank, intelligent-looking boy with straw-colored hair and a round hat which he now respectfully held in his hands.

"This yere boy of mine does all right. Yessir, he does all right. He's a real trailblazer." Lytle was balancing a glass on his knee and gesturing toward a circle of listeners. "Last year we went out to survey the land and this youngun caught the measles. Nary a place on his body that weren't covered with a spot."

Lytle, Jr. smiled wanly and rubbed the toe of his moccasin around on the floor, but he did not seem to mind being the center of conversation, Jenny McClure thought.

"We had jest spent a night in camp huntin' buffaloes. We had quite a fright, we did," Lytle went on. "Wolves howlin' all over, and some signs of Injeeans about. I posted Will here as the night guard and went to sleep at the fire when this fool. . ." he pointed with his thumb, over his shoulder at his cousin James Bard, who guffawed embarrassedly. "He'd supposedly gone off for the night huntin', and now he snuck through the brush pretending he was a Shawnee."

Lytle, Jr. took up the story. "I aimed my loaded gun and the durn thing wouldn't fire. The Injeean noises out in the brush kept right up. I loaded again and tried to fire. 'Twas a flash in the pan. That woke Pa up. Just as we were both ready to shoot again, James comes roarin' in, laughin' at the top of his lungs."

"Waal, I thought 'twould be a good joke," James conceded.

"Good joke my foot," Lytle, Jr. countered. "If that gun hadda done its job, you would'a been splattered all over the ash trees in that there clearing."

"You was talkin' about the measles, Will," said Tom Bard, coming over to listen.

"The measles. Yes. Well, I said 'twere best we start back, abandon the hunt, but the youngun insisted he could go back to Lexington by himself. So he started out—you tell it Son."

"Waal, the fever sent me clean out of my head a time or two. But I pressed on. Wanted to test myself to see if I could return the sixty some miles back with my Injeean skills. I did all the things I were taught, grazed my horse in the open, avoided killin' game when I didn't have to, forded streams when I cud to throw my trail off." Growing more intense in the telling of his tale, young Lytle stood up. His face was as red as a crabapple. Everyone in the room stopped drinking and looked at him; the candles around the corpse, burning unevenly, gave off smoke.

"Next day, still feelin' poorly, I found a b'ar in m' path. Disobeyed m' pa's instructions and shot the crittur. I thought 'twould be a good trophy, so I gutted 'er and tried to get the hide on the horse. Greasy damn thing, 'twas. I wrestled her around for nigh onto a hour. Get her up on the saddle, she slips down t' other side. I were tired by now and m' fever was bad.''

Young Lytle went on, "I were out of my head that night. Thought the b'ar was risin' up to ha'nt me, wrestlin' with me, and it were alive again. I awoke to find myself right in the middle of the carcass, greasy as a lard bucket and smellin' like a skonk. Dragged myself out of it and slept till the sun were high. The next day I got her home and tole my ma the story. 'Tis a wonder,' I said, 'that the measles or the b'ar, one or 't other, didn't kill me dead.' "

" 'Measles,' Ma said, lookin' me full in the face. 'You haven't got any measles.' 'Twere true. They were all gone and I was well. Guess it must 'a been the carcass wrestlin' and the ba'r grease.''

At that moment Widow Mary Bard came in the door. "Do we have a couple o' good hands who can help a new fambly settle in a bit?'' It was a daily occurrence. People arrived in Kentucky and needed housing and hospitality until they could go to their land. This family, however, could expect extra welcome from the Bards—the wife was Angelica Bard's sister.

"What's their names, Miz Bard?'' John McClure asked, standing up and beckoning to Will to help.

"McGuires. Comin' into town all the way from Virginny over the Gap Road,'' she said, her small face frowning as she imagined the hardships of that long journey. "Father and mother and grown daughter Jane.'' As John and Will walked onto the wagon road that ran through the midst of the settlement, Mary Bard told them that Mrs. McGuire had convinced her husband to settle in the new western lands, near to her invalid sister, but they arrived just too late. John and Will nodded their sympathy.

In the midst of the road stood one of the most imposing trains John had ever seen come into Kentucky. A man in relatively clean knee breeches and the ruffled shirt of a gentleman rode a magnificently sleek, all-black stallion with high withers. Behind him, also mounted on fine horses, one spotted, one with a white leg, were two beautiful women. The older one had straw-colored hair now going white and a face that resembled Angelica Bard's. The daughter was a tall, well-set girl muffled in a riding cape even on this balmy day. Her face was lost in the shadows of an oak tree outside Tom Bard's wheelwright shop.

Judge Andrew McGuire swung down out of the ornamental saddle to shake first John's, then Will's hand. Will went to help the ladies out of the saddle, although they did not much need his aid. They seemed to be completely comfortable on horse's backs.

As Mrs. McGuire went to see to the train of servants and slaves, the tall, diffident girl coolly surveyed Will. She passed her eyes over his dark auburn curls, the eyes which did not flinch as she looked into them, the muscular shoulders in the fine linen hunting shirt his mother had made, the multi-colored belting sash, the powder horn which always hung at his side.

She unclasped the large silver button which bound the cape about her shoulders and threw back the hood. Then she shook out long, wavy black hair, starkly set off with one yellow-white streak which ran from forehead to crown and down the back of her head. Her skin was very white, her cheeks red from the ride into town. She was the most striking woman Will had seen in a lifetime of looking.

She had scrutinized him; now she felt his eyes on her. "And who may you be?" she asked evenly.

Will, with only a suggestion of a smile on his lips, took her hand and bowing his head over it, kissed it with politeness rather than warmth. "Captain Will McClure at your service, Miss. Has your trip been pleasant?"

She turned toward the saddle, gesturing at a black boy to begin unloading packages strapped there, before she answered him. "It has been four years since we have been at home in Carolina, where both my father and I were born, near the coast. We are, I guess, refugees of the war." She smiled, to herself, it seemed. "As for the trip, the least said of it, the better. We are here, that is enough." She spoke a few words to an old black groom, and he came to lead away the tired horses.

She seemed to be still considering Will, who stood relaxed, almost nonchalant before her. This time, when she spoke to him, the smile on her generous mouth seemed to be ironic. "So we have come to Aunt Angelica's only to find. . ." she shrugged. Will noticed she did not offer the usual conventional condoling things people usually said. Probably she had not known her aunt well. She stood three or four inches under his six-foot height; the cape, trailing almost to the road, was slung carelessly over her arm. Clothing, like the social amenities, did not seem to be a major concern of hers. "Will you help me settle my things in the cabin we've been assigned? I must help my mother pay her wake visit to see my aunt as soon as possible."

Will nodded and led the girl down the muddy track to Angelica's new two-story log home, the finest in the village, which the poor woman had never been able to enjoy. The mother followed close behind, with others of the village and the servants, baggage in tow, on quarter horses almost as handsome as the lead ones.

John watched the horses as he helped from further back in the train. A real stable, he thought, with unconcealed admiration. He was startled by the small stature of these quarter horses from the East; Pennsylvania horses were large and German-bred. But these obviously had Virginia thoroughbred lines mixed with native solidness.

John helped Judge McGuire and the groom lead the weary animals into the enclosed pasture behind the log house. Once all were safely inside, Andrew McGuire loosed Impromptu, the black stallion. He trotted, whinnying, to a dust pit that stood outside the stalls, where several villagers stabled their horses. Here the stallion rolled as happy as a colt, legs thrashing in the air.

"Hmph. Clearing out his insides and refreshing himself," his owner said indulgently as the horse whinnied joyfully.

John asked the judge if he might help brush and rub down the horse. "I pride myself on knowing horseflesh, but I've never seen the likes of this un," John commented admiringly, looking at the broad head, the muscular neck and breast, the sable coat that shone from frequent brushings.

"He's a son of Janus, out of one of our black Chickasaw mares," said the judge proudly. The man's features were strong and acquiline. His hair was as dark as his daughter's, with only a few gray hairs along the temples. I wonder where that girl got the streak in her hair, John asked himself in passing. Wherever it was, it made her look like a fairy sprite.

The judge was in a confiding mood. "I knew I'd find people who knew horses here in Caintuck. I told myself it would be ideal to start a fine stable here." He looked over his shoulder at the two mares, the gelding and the other horses he had brought. "It's only a part of the lot. The rest are coming with my foreman a couple of days behind; they had some shoeing to do once we were through that horrible pass."

In a moment the negro groom brought buckets of water from the creek, and John and the judge and groom washed the horses' backs with elegant brushes from a grooming pouch McGuire carried. "All the animals have been getting fat as little ponies on the lush grass you have here," McGuire said as he curried and splashed. "Bluegrass, they call it? Lots of it in pastures in eastern Caintuck."

"Yes, some bluegrass grows around here too," John said, and added in a moment, "We didn't see many fine horses in Pennsylvania durin' the war. They was all requisitioned for one army or another. Hadn't been a race in Cumberland County for over a year when we left. And here the Injeeans stole 'em as fast as we let 'em out to pasture the first years. But now things are a little quieter, and the races are startin' up here in Caintuck. I've done catch-weight racin' since I was a boy."

John looked up into the judge's piercing black eyes, eyes that seemed to take his measure thoroughly. He felt bold. If they had been in Virginia or around Philadelphia, John would have been awed by the older man's obvious aristocratic bearing. But those who loved horses felt akin, the equine Free Masons, so to speak, especially in the wilderness. Besides, his father left him some means, and he was no illiterate; he could read and write better than many a rich man out here. "Where is your land?" he asked the judge.

"Two thousand acres north of here, bought in Virginia from a salesman and certified before the magistrate. Do you have land?"

"Five hundred acres of the best farmland in the state." Well, it was an exaggeration. Each of the McClures now had one hundred acres, but it was originally his to give. Judge McGuire nodded, impressed.

"I've travelled much in the last few years, first as a judge, then as a factor, selling rice. As I went, I bought fine horses. But when the war ravaged Carolina, we finally took the whole stable to the Shenandoah Valley. I never went back to the coast." There was a comfortable silence between the two men as they curried and brushed the horse until it became the color of dark molasses.

"Now, I'm tired," said the judge suddenly. He put down the soft brush he was applying to Impromptu. "The Cumberland Road is an execration— campsights in the mosquitoes, guards constantly watching for savages, horses jolting up mountains and through creek beds. My back feels like it's been on the rack. Starting a new life is hard on animals and men to boot." He said goodbye and stalked into the log home, leaving John to wonder at the new turn of events, and at how prosperous and civilized Caintuck was becoming.

Morning came to Kentucky. It was Angelica Bard's burying day. But two people were not thinking of the solemnities of the occasion. Shafts of sunlight pierced the morning mists shrouding cottonwood trees near the edge of the village. Will McClure and Jane McGuire turned their mounts into an open prairie field. The girl wore a green velvet riding skirt and matching green jacket and hat. She sat, unusually, astride her father's black stallion, a specially cut skirt covering her legs discreetly.

Will rode the gelding Fincastle's Dream, a stocky, spotted horse with a short neck which revealed its Indian blood. He carried breafast in a hamper prepared by a slave. Janie's father had asked him to "help her see if the mounts are fit to go to the post," because a race was planned for later in the day.

The horses trotted smartly. They seemed surprisingly well-rested from the rigors of the trip and satisfied with the oats and blackstrap which had been added to their diet for this special day.

Will stole a glance at the girl who rode by his side. That same inscrutable smile was on her lips, but her color was high. The brightness of the late March day exhilarated Will. Beads of dew glistened on the egg-yolk-yellow, fuzzy heads of dandelions beside them, sending a spectrum of color into his eyes now and then as he passed a particularly large dewdrop. Fat clumps of bright green grass and English daisies caught the corner of his eye.

But then the girl kneed her horse sharply, sending it into a canter. "Catch me, McClure. If you can, that is," she shouted behind her. The excitement of the chase caught him. Immediately he and the spotted horse began to stride forward. Pulling up, he caught her, sent her a laughing, sideways glance, and urged Fincastle's Dream on. Then he pulled ahead, but not by far.

The horses galloped only a neck apart. He could hear her talking to the black stallion, cajoling him, blending her own will for speed with his. Will dared not take his eyes off the field. A felled log was approaching; he would need to jump. Jane McGuire bent low over the horse's neck. What in the world was she saying? "Come on, my darling, ready to take this log, easy, easy, magnificent moor." Magnificent moor? Distracted by the richness of sensation that surrounded him, Will began to urge Fincastle's Dream up and over—and the horse balked at the log.

Suddenly, Will found himself sitting very unceremoniously on the ground. His hands, which broke the fall, were wet and stinging. A twig punctured the leather breeches he wore. Damn it, he thought, what a ridiculous posture for "Captain McClure of George Rogers Clark's army" to be in. He wished he hadn't bragged so.

Fincastle's Dream stood calmly where he had stopped. The girl circled the stallion around and smiled down at Will with good humor. "I suspect it wasn't your equestrian skills that carried you through the Indian Wars, Mr. McClure," she said. He wiped his smarting, scratched hands on his breeches, went to the standing horse, and swung into the saddle. Angrily he urged Janie to a race to the woods which formed the end of the pasture, and he managed to win.

They dismounted and tethered the animals on a birch tree, then went into the woods and found a grassy knoll for their breakfast. She laid her velvet jacket on the branch of a nearby tree; under it was a white linen shirt not unlike a man's, with ruffles below the throat. "The slaves packed us chicken and buttered biscuits," she said, opening the hamper. She spread a cloth; he nodded his thanks graciously for the food she handed him, but said nothing.

The incident at the fence had unhinged him, stolen his usual confidence with women. She was still smiling, her face shining with health and joy in the morning. She spoke indifferently of a variety of things, of her satisfaction with the horse's performance, of the details of the race. Will grunted and nodded affirmation when it was called for, but his attention wandered. He was caught in a fascinating web, dominated by the magnetism of the woman before him.

Feeling the need to make polite conversation, he asked her about the stallion's name. "Impromptu. Yes," she laughed. It was a hearty, rather than a musical laugh and it almost seemed incongruous with such a perfect face and form. "Janus is the founder of the line of all these horses, and indeed much of the best of the present stock in the South today. At twenty-three, he came from England, out to pasture, so his English owners believed. He ran a race or two but what he did best was stand at stud.

"It turned out that this bargain horse was amazingly potent in America. He was taken around all over Georgia and Carolina, and he sired colts everywhere he went. He was thirty-two when he covered the thoroughbred mares who foaled *Belle Ame* and your mount Fincastle's Dream." Was there whimsy in her voice as she gave all these breeding details in such a frank way? Was she trying to embarrass him? He did not know.

She went on. "One day Janus was in the pasture. He broke away when the handler's back was turned and galloped over to the trainer's own coal-black, new Chickasaw mare. The trainer had just traded for this mare from the Florida Indians; she was sturdy, high-spirited, and as swift as the wind. Before we knew it—an impromptu love affair, one would say. My father paid the stud fee and the result is this horse he worships."

As she spoke, she finished one chicken leg then another, and threw the bones back over her shoulder. Then she licked her fingers, albeit daintily, laughed, and took a small, wrinkled apple out of the hamper with relish. "I'm always famished in the morning," she said. All traces of the aloofness she showed yesterday afternoon when he first met her were gone. It struck him that she might be the first absolutely honest woman he had ever seen. But there was more, something he could not quite fathom.

She spoke no more, but kept on looking right in his eyes, the way she did last night. He tried to avoid her glance by eating a chicken breast, tearing the white, smooth meat with his teeth with a feigned indifference. This honesty in her look bothered him. Wasn't normal for a woman. It was as if she were looking at him naked. It angered him and his color rose. Very well. She seemed to know what he was thinking; he would discover what else, if anything beside horses, made this pretty little miss tick.

"You said you were a war refugee, Miss McGuire. In what way did the war pursue you?" He really didn't want to be sarcastic, it just was difficult to think of her in a battle in her green velvet skirt. To him, war meant choking smoke and surgeons cauterizing the stumps of amputated legs. What did she have to do with that?

Her mood changed instantly. The smile became almost a sneer, and she waited a brief moment before she answered. "Tarleton's raiders came through Carolina. They requisitioned horses, took them from any quarter they could get them. One blustery, dark night, as we all lay in our beds, Father and Mother and I heard the horses stamping, disturbed. A troop of disreputable Tories from the backwoods were in the barn. We dashed out in our nightclothes. The black folk came out of their quarters." Though she continued looking directly at him, her thoughts were now far away.

"The Tories dashed about with lanterns in the barn collecting the horses; two stood guard with muskets. Father raced for the house to get his own gun; while he was gone one of the Tory lanterns struck the straw and flames raced through the barn. The men fled out the open door and into the woods on their own mounts, but what they left in that barn was an inferno. The buckets we brought were as thimbles of water thrown into the wind.

"I cannot tell you what it was like if you have never seen horses in a barn fire: the neighing, the clamoring, the terror in their cries. The men tried to lead them out. One slave died and Father carries scars on his arms to this day that will never fade. My mother and two slaves had to hold me back, although I was only a girl at the time. I had two colts in there. It shattered me for months. I lost my love of God that night. Sometimes I can still hear those colts crying like babies in there in the flames."

Will looked at her, and he understood. "War is hard on animals." He remembered the horses' eyes as big as walnuts, looking at him in panic as the cannon and grapeshot fell around, sometimes on them. But war was war, and there was scant worry enough to spend on the human victims.

"Nobody ever thinks of the horses in battles," she went on with grim earnestness. "Ridden to death in pursuit of th' enemy, be it Tory or Whig, untended in miserable camps till they get the foot thrush. I was talking to your brother John about it this morning in the stables, and he said he was a wagonmaster for the militia at Brandywine for a few weeks. He saw the poor things starved or rolling with colic from moldy hay until he had to destroy them after two years of faithful service."

Yes, thought Will, John would have said that. Horses had individual personalities to him. He attributed motives, a nobility to them that Will could never see.

There was a silence as they began to clean up, to pick up biscuit crusts and apple cores and put them in the hamper. But Will would not leave off his probing. He seemed driven to do it by some compelling fascination. "You say you lost your faith in God, Miss McGuire." Odd that it had not shocked him; but then, God often seemed very distant to him in this unexplainably harsh world. "What do you have faith in?"

"What I can see. Especially what I feel. My passions are talismans to me, I trust them as I trust my family."

"My brother George says it's reason we should trust."

"So do many I know. But what I love and hate serves me better. It tells the truth about life and death in a way old men with moldering books cannot do." She stood up. Crumbs fell from her skirt; she did not notice. She looked into his eyes. "And you, Mr. McClure? What do you love?"

On impulse he took her hands in his. He formed the words of his answer slowly. "My fambly. I loved my father partic'larly, although I do not yet know in what way, if any, he loved me. A few friends and the chance to be merry with them, so I do not think too deep. I do not, could not love an animal the way you do, although I like 'em well enough." She nodded slightly, seeming to accept this. She had not taken her hands away.

"And, I s'pose, I listen to my passions ever bit as much as you do, Miss McGuire. I do not work to hold 'em in check; I couldn't even promise to try. They spill over ever act I do, for better or worse." With this he looked at her a long moment. Then he took her in his arms and kissed her, tentatively at first, then hungrily. She did not resist, indeed, put her arms about his neck and drew up to him, pressing her body in its thin shirt against him, feeling the strength of his chest against her. He kissed her more deeply, again and again. The tethered horses nosed near to them; Impromptu nuzzled his leg. He pulled back, suddenly aware of the depth of her response.

"Your Dada gives you a good deal of freedom for a young woman."

"And also a pure one, Mr. McClure," she said, her voice shaking with the same emotion he felt, "but my father has long since given me free rein." She smiled that slightly crooked, wry smile of hers. "Nothing else, I fear, would have served but total freedom for me anyway."

He kissed her again and this time could not stop himself from putting his hand on her breast. Something flamed between the two of them, something he did not recognize from the back stairs affairs he had known. It was the joining of strong, defiant fires. "I think you are a rake, Mr. McClure," she whispered as she slowly took his hand away.

"And I think we are alike, Miss McGuire," he whispered back, stroking the cheek near his own. "You are a good deal Chickasaw yourself."

"But not all, Mr. McClure." She gently undid her arm and smiled the crooked smile one last time. "Horses need a safe roof, a peaceable pasture to thrive and breed. There has been too much jolting about in my life. I am looking for a calm pasture to raise my horses and live myself."

He nodded. It was something he, too, could use in his life.

They rode back across the field, neither racing nor competing, content with each other's presence; and when they parted, the sun was high in the sky and the burial about to begin.

The casket was closed and the mourners were departing two-by-two to follow it to the cemetery. Martha Bard was left, as usual, to clean up. She picked up the extra sheets which had served as drapery for the table and headed toward the door to take them to the firepit outside, as custom decreed. Dan'l McClure's pleasant face peered around the door jam. "Kin I help, Martha?" he asked.

She went to the door, carrying her burden. "Of course, Dan'l. How like you." It was the way she really felt most of the time. If her mind harbored any other pictures of Dan'l, they were buried in a hole as deep as the corpse would be today, and there to stay, she told herself. They took the linens to the pit and Dan'l put kindling and wood over them.

"We won't burn 'em yet; 'twouldn't be seemly while the funeral's yet on," he told her, wiping his hands on his pants. It was a little spookish to be cleaning up after a wake. "Say, hadn't we best be joining the others?" He looked at her for confirmation. Martha always knew how to do things right.

"I don't want to go," she said, surprised at the thought that just came to her. What she wanted to do was walk out with Dan'l, across that field over there where she saw horses trotting this morning. Yes, and forget about the responsibilities. "Let's go sit a spell, Dan'l," she said. "Maybe walk over to that log in the field. Nobody'll know we're gone." His eyes lit up. It was the kind of minor, mischievous risk he loved to take.

They walked. Martha laughed and chattered. He did not often see her this way. Probably she was glad the wake, with all its bed-changing and food-cooking were over. Glad to be freed of the care of Cousin Angelica—even that.

"Dan'l, the thing I hate most about a wake is the smell. Oh, I don't mean the corpse; they put plenty of rose water on 'em these days and Caintuck isn't hot like I hear New Orleans is, so they last well. I mean that lineny smell. The shroud, the draping, the good shirts everybody wears. That stifley, sicky-sweet smell of new linen everywhere. I couldn't 'a stood it another hour."

Dan'l took his hand and brushed off a log in the middle of the meadow. As he did it, he realized this was the field where John and Will had been runnin' horses for the rich judge who had blown into town. Practisin' for the horse race. Puttin' on airs. Maybe he, Dan'l, should enter on one of the family nags, he told himself while Martha sat down and smoothed the skirt of her sprigged calico dress.

"Piece a crystal candy, Martha?" he asked. The Bardstown store was now carrying basic supplies: iron stew pots and calico and luxury items like horehound drops and sugar candy.

"I'm thankin' you." She sucked on the candy thoughtfully. "Dan'l, do you ever paint pictures in your mind? I do it a lot, too much I think. Sometimes I even write 'em down, send 'em on to my sister Mary in a letter. But when I go to a funeral, I can't help thinkin' of people I love and how they might look when they die."

Dan'l looked at her, his face registering mild surprise. Martha hurried on, "Oh, I know it's odd but I can't stop my mind from thinkin' about it. Like what would Tom look like if he died sudden-like and was stretched out. What hymns would we sing. Would 'Oh for a thousand tongues to sing, my great redeemer's praise' fit? What would be good to say if I was to give the eulogy?

I could say. . ." and she went on, talking as if to herself about Tom's good points.

As he listened to her spirited voice going on, "better now that he's a husband," "patient with my mother," Dan'l was thinking: now, she is one of the best goldurned women I ever did see. She never stops doin' good works. She does talk a-plenty, but she seems to know when to shet her mouth.

"But the worst, Dan'l," Martha was now saying, trying to suck on the crystal candy and talk at the same time, "is when I think of Mother's funeral. And I do it every now and again. I imagine the mourners comin' in for the wake, and how when everybody sits around and tries to say a good thing about the person, what they'd say about Mother."

I love the way Martha's lips part a little when she talks, Dan'l thought, showin' those good teeth. Good teeth are worth a lot in a woman. I hate those yeller teeth, or holes you see when they smile. Throws off the image someway.

"The worst part is the two-faced nature of what they will say. 'Miz Bard was a good wife.' Why, Dan'l, that isn't really what they think. A lot of 'em from Cumberland County days know how Mother be-shrewed my father, how she chased him out of the house and made him sit in the shed for two whole days. It was cold too—October, 'twas."

Martha's strong as a elephant. She could beat the hell out of any rug, I guess, hangin' on a line in the spring. And carry a couple of buckets full of water for washin' on a tote stick, set up bean poles, stir apple butter no matter how thick it got—like nobody's business, he observed, staring into her eyes as if with profound attention to what she was saying.

"I don't want them lyin' about Mother. There are good things to say, Dan'l. I guess I should know that better than anybody. Let them say she was a good teacher of the Bible, that the milk in her springhouse never soured from poor keepin', that she taught her children to knit garters and stockings, to make patchwork and braid straw and how the Devil stalketh about lookin' for idle hands. . ."

What is she like beneath that silly dress that looks like a flower field? Take it off, Martha. That's right, just let it drop to your feet, the voice of his imagination went on. And kick off the linen fancies—you say you hate linen anyways, and let me take a good look at ya. Very pretty you are beneath that bodice. There's quite a variety in women's bosoms, so they say. I wouldn't know, I haven't looked at many. Sturdy stomach, hips wide enough to bear a full family. And below the stomach, somethin' wonderful. Now Mulberry Blossom—don't think of that. 'Twas another time and another world. Funny how the picture of Martha naked clouds over. Mebbe I ain't meant to see it jest now.

"And the fact is I love my mother, in spite o' everything, I love her. And I don't know why my perverse mind thinks o' her funeral." Tears stood in her eyes, and Dan'l felt ashamed of his thoughts. He took her hand and pulled her up from the log. She was a good Christian woman. And that was what he really wanted, although the other things wouldn't be bad to have in the bargain.

"I understand, Martha. And I do the same thing. My mind keeps goin' to

Will's funeral. I don't know why.''

"Do you understand, Dan'l? Do you really?''

"An' I keep relivin' my Dada's wake. I were just a little 'un, but I can't get it out o' my mind. You didn't know my Dada, now, did you? You was too young to 'a known him. Let's walk back now and I'll tell you about him.''

And so they did.

The funeral observances were duly completed. The long train, led by the still unreconciled and weeping Mrs. McGuire, followed the wood box to the cemetery on the edge of town. Amid newly-carved tombstones that read, "Our beloved May, resting in the Savior,'' and "Selica Jones, Mother, 1745-1784, Gone before her time,'' Angelica Bard was laid to rest, in a grave protected from wolves by a fence. Prayers were said by an elder in lieu of a minister in this distant settlement.

The last funeral blessing had been intoned. With a "whoopee" and with whiskey bottles raised high in the air, the men dashed for their mounts. Bardstown's first quarter horse race was about to begin.

George McClure brought his mother and sister Jenny back from the cemetery. "I don't know why they can't wait at least a hour,'' Jenny said to her mother. "If they had their way, they'd race their horses right over the grave. What are you whistlin' for, Georgie?''

Out of the corner of his eye George was watching his brothers get ready for the race. John was coming out of the stableyard, riding with that new, prissy judge. John was putting on the dog, riding a spotted horse as if he were an Austrian Prince. But it was Will who took George's real notice; he was receiving jockeying instructions from the judge's daughter. She was looking intently up at Will as he checked the saddle girth on the white-legged horse that was part of that fancy train they brought into town. And Will was looking at her with an equally intent gaze.

George stopped whistling and sang a little tune.

> *Curly locks, curly locks wilt thou be mine?*
> *Thou shalt not wash dishes nor yet tend the swine*
> *But sit on a pillow and sew a seam fine*
> *And dine upon hominy, hoecake and wine.*

His sister looked at him, frowning. "That's not how it goes, Georgie.''

"Maybe it doesn't go that way and then again maybe it does. We shall have to see, won't we,'' he said noncommittaly, and began whistling again.

The racetrack was the center, the only road in Bardstown. Andrew McGuire spurred Impromptu to the starting line, which was a woman's bodice ribbon stretched across the road. Sam and Tom Bard sidled into their positions as starters. Two other townsmen were judges at the finish line a quarter mile down the road, outside the settlement's gates.

John turned and jockeyed for position behind the line. He had his hands full controlling the horse Judge McGuire had asked him to ride, Fincastle's Dream, the spirited gelding who had balked while being ridden by his brother earlier in the day.

John's nerves were as frazzled as hemp twine; the last time he had raced was in a pickup mile-dash at a wedding in Carlisle. The stakes were higher here in more ways than one. He definitely did not want to look like a fool before this man. It was obvious the judge would have no trouble. Easily, with hands long used to commanding fine, temperamental horses, Judge McGuire kept Impromptu at the proper distance behind the ribbon.

In back of Judge McGuire and John McClure, the succeeding racers assembled, as citizens of the town shuffled among them, checking who would be racing the heats and betting "shinplasters"—promissory notes on their favorites. There would be six two-horse heats in this race. In the second start Will, on Janie McGuire's favorite *Belle Ame*, would race Ash Emison on Emison's new buff-colored gelding. Others would race and then, in the last heat Dan'l, a last-minute entrant, would be riding his own new Tennessee stallion Sugartime. He was matched with Samuel Thompson, a new friend from the McClure neighborhood.

Tom Bard straightened his round hat in preparation for dropping it to signal the race's start. He spat on a chip of wood and threw it into the air. John cried "wet" and Judge McGuire called out "dry." The chip fell spit side up, so John could make his choice of pathside. He called out "right side." Then Bard threw the chip again for the right to call "ready or not."

Judge McGuire won the toss. They stood at the ribbon and he called out in a loud voice "Ready?" and John, still trying to hold back the unfamiliar horse behind the line, shouted he was ready. They shot off from a standing start, and twenty-five seconds later, at the end of the track, Judge McGuire predictably emerged as the winner. But not by much, John noted with satisfaction, as he walked the horse in a circle behind the finish line to calm it.

Andrew McGuire, bestowing a handsome, composed smile on the crowd, accepted the prize money from the finish-line judge and stepped back to see the next start. Within five minutes Will McClure and Ash Emison charged down the road in a cloud of choking dust to a neck-and-neck finish which sent the judges to arguing and eventually fighting. No winner was declared.

Four good races later, including the one Dan'l took from Sam Thompson, his new best friend, everyone was in a sufficiently amicable mood again. The finish-line judges, one with a lip swollen to twice its size and the other with a bruised cheek, declared the racing over and decreed the drinking should begin. It did not finish until after midnight. John took his usual couple of glasses and went to bed early along with most of the rest of the McClures. Their trip back to the station would begin early in the morning.

That night the rest of Judge McGuire's baggage train with the Judge's overseer arrived on the outskirts of Bardstown. The line of pack horses was met by a wagon put crosswise, blocking the road just outside of town.

McGuire's overseer dismounted and looked into two bellicose frontier faces, illuminated by the fire from a pot of oil-soaked wood chips. The men were obviously drunk.

"M' name's Tom. This yere's a toll booth, neighbor," said the older of the men in slurring tones.

"And what's the toll you're wantin'?" asked the overseer, a white-haired Scotsman whose burr was as thick as his muscular arms. He glanced at the barricade, a shoe-wagon overturned, at the two men and their tethered horses. That was all there was. On his side, there was himself, a black groom boy, and a slave farrier.

"Friend, we Caintuckians love to fight. Why, we'd ruther fight than drink. And we'd ruther fight than wrestle."

"And soooo, lad, what is your toll?" the Scotsman demanded.

The younger man staggered forward, pounding on his chest with his fist.

"Fight us. Whichever one you want. You choose. Then fight 't other if you win. Fair'n square. You don't even hafta win. Jest fight and then you can go through."

"Verrry well. I shall pay yerr toll," he said, dismounting and giving the reins of the chestnut horse he rode to the black boys.

And since, by an odd coincidence, he was the boxing champion of Edinburgh ten years before he emigrated to Carolina, he speedily dispatched the older man, knocking him into the hard, pebbly dirt at the side of the buffalo path they were on.

"And now I will take you on, Laddie," he said, to the younger man, who showed just a trace of hesitation as he closed with the overseer.

It soon became obvious that it certainly was no worthy contest for the overseer, who had even done exhibition fighting for the Prince of Wales in the prize ring in London town years before. As he held the young man up one final time, before delivering a smashing fist to the chin to finish him off, the Scotsman panted, "What might they call you, Laddie? I like to know the names of the men I knock out."

"M' name's Will McClure. Captain Will McClure at your service," and he slumped unconscious before the man could even deliver the blow.

So the marryin's did occur, as the big Bibles and county records of all these families well show. Dan'l McClure married Martha Bard the very next week, April 8, 1785. Jenny (Jane) McClure married James Scott about a month later. Jane McGuire married, not William McClure but John McClure, after a suitable courtship, on November 17, 1785. Judge McGuire stood irrefutably on the horse-breeding dictum that "no bad trait must be passed on to the next generation," and thus ruled Will out after the toll-gate incident.

And George McClure's marrying requires a little more telling.

Chapter XX

The Water Pass Trace ran south and west, beaten firm by the hoofs of bison and probably even the wooly mammoths which inhabited Kentucky before the first settlers came. Roughly following the Water Pass River, the path meandered through plains and foothills without any apparent haste. It was the road chosen by George McClure and Bige Cherry for a journey to Passwater, the rough new settlement in southern Kentucky.

Passwater was a trip of more than several days jaunt into the wilderness, with sights of dashing cataracts and black bears through the branches of tall trees. It was a journey to the ends of the earth even in Kentucky terms, to a place which made Harrodsburg and Bardstown look like Philadelphia, where there were so many outlaws and cutpurses that they roamed the streets and robbed each other.

But it was also a place where money was made. Here fine lands in Tennessee and even beyond could be picked up as bargains by the clever thinker. And George McClure considered himself to be a clever thinker.

"Bige, I've thought it out carefully," he confided to his now gray-haired friend. "The good land is almost gone around here. Seems odd but it's true. The hoards coming from Virginia and Pennsylvania have gobbled up the good bluegrass all the way from Lexington and the river to Louisville. I don't want to fool with small parcels of marginal land; what I want to get is big stakes, thousands of acres in areas just opening up. The southwest portion of the continent. Who knows? I plan to double or triple, maybe quadruple my money when I find just the right buy."

"How you goin' to do that, pray tell?" Bige asked. He was chewing a wad of tobacco he grew himself; and he spat at a bayberry bush, coating its red berries with brown fluid. It was a habit he picked up after coming to Kentucky, along with betting the mares and distilling whiskey.

"By finding the right man."

"How you goin' to know who is a charlatan and who ain't?"

"Investing money is a lot like solving any other problem. You must use the empirical method."

"How's that?" Bige looked into his friend's face. He respected McClure's knowledge, but sometimes he sounded like a Scottish preacher. Words longer than a rat's tail. And he surely looked silly with that large, heavy hat on his head. Bige felt honored that he was trusted with the knowledge of what was in the brim of that huge hat—four thousand dollars in Spanish gold pieces of McClure family money.

"Empricism is a scientific method. Observe phenomena and then come up with a conclusion, a theory. You prove your theory by further investigation of evidence. Now for the past year or so I have kept my eyes open at the land offices around Harrodsburg and the rest of the territory. I have investigated where people go wrong when they try to invest. There are several pitfalls."

"Sech as?"

"First of all, choosing hare-brained schemes. The Tontine in England is like that, and people are losing vast sums over there."

"That the idee that a group of people all puts in a sartain sum and the one that lives the longest gets it all at the end?"

"That's it."

"What can a man stick his money into, other than a mattress?" Bige wanted to know.

"Well, inventions are good investments, but you must watch out for crazy machines. Three years ago people paid money to watch hot air balloons go up in the air. I read about it in the Philadelphia paper. Now there's a boiling-water wagon, a steam machine with wheels some japester has built to carry heavy loads from one place to another."

"Waal now, that jest might work. I for one would welcome it instead of havin' to use a ox to haul timber."

George nodded and smiled a little. Bige, he mused, was no more of a farmer in Caintuck than he had been in Pennsylvania. Bige and his brother Moses, now married, had a small claim not far from Bardstown, but it was not by his own choice that he earned his bread with a hoe in his hand.

George cleared his throat and went on. "I also watched people buy land around Lexington and came up with the second conclusion. You can't look too far in the future to realize the profits. There's many a slip 'twixt the cup and the lip. Those who bought Transylvania lands here saw them slide from their hands as the property changed hands and the company was lost. The entire situation altered, and they were helpless in the face of the change.

"But the biggest thing is you have to know your man," he told his friend confidently. "Who will you invest with, not how will you invest. If you're going outside the land office system, you've got to know."

Bige looked at him sceptically. "How do you tell the saints from the sinners? I alwuz had some trouble with that myself, even in the church pews. Sometimes the women with the most sanctimonious, prissy faces were the ones that one day up and runs off with the preacher and lives in sin."

George smiled tolerantly. "I fancy myself something of a judge of men, Bige. It's in the face. If a man looks at you squarely and doesn't drop his eyes, if his lips don't twitch when he tells you something, you can be fairly sure he's on the plumb line. Besides, I've done a little reading on the subject. Plutarch talks a good deal about the fine points of character in his descriptions of Caesar and Cicero. In money matters, what you want is a shrewd, practical man with intelligence.''

"Hmmp," said Bige absently. He moved the pack around on his back; it was getting to feel heavy in the dry heat of the afternoon. The iron skillet must have shifted. It would have been good to have a horse, but a horse was an open invitation to any Chickasaws ranging in the northernmost reaches of their hunting zones. Better to be able to dart into the woods with rifle loaded if the need came up.

"A tolerable amount of our neighbors have invested in Boone land titles," George went on. "But if they knew my conclusion and observed the empirical evidence, they would recall that Daniel Boone, while a great leader and an honest man, is short on horse sense and not a good risk."

"Empirical evidence," Bige said, savoring the words. "What you mean is that he got his arse kicked in that tavern in Virginny when he let them bastards give him knock-out drops an' then steal all his money? And that of most of his friends too."

"Precisely. And I think I would not have placed my money with Boone, then or now, by observing his past proclivity to impulsive action and unreasoned behavior."

"Mebbe. But I don't think a man who can build a road into the wilderness, arm and maintain a permanent fort, make friends with the Injeeans and then stab 'em in the kidneys, and still remain friends with 'em can be all that unreasonin'."

"I wouldn't presume to criticize Boone. The settlements certainly never had a firmer friend. I just wouldn't put my money with him. And mark my word, all these people who are will rue the day. But do you want to hear my last empirical conclusion?"

"Conclude on," Bige said, spitting again. "You will anyways."

George took off his hat. It was so heavy it gave him a headache sometimes. He gave his friend a long glance, then went on. "Well, it's this. You must be willing to seize the main chance. To take a risk, carefully conceived of and thought through. Only in this way may one recognize sizable returns."

"In other words, you'll never git the hog back from the ba'r efn you don't go into the woods after him."

"Yes. And remember Washington at Trenton. We won a great victory on his ability to risk danger to gain the main chance. I don't mean being foolhardy. Some men have little to risk; I have observed that the sons of rich men do not often make wise investments."

"Nothing to lose, I guess." Bige's feet were getting tired. The road was slightly mucky, with moldy leaves drifting over it from recent rains. He wanted above all else to avoid scald foot, so he stopped to take off his moccasins for a minute and stood first on one foot, then the other, to air his feet.

"Nothin' to lose," he repeated. "Reminds me of the man went to buy a mule. The farmer brought one out, and the mule right away run down the hill and into a tree. 'That mule's blind,' the man said to the farmer. 'No, he ain't blind, he just don't give a damn,' the farmer said."

"Well, I don't want to put this McClure money with someone who doesn't give a damn," murmured George. They started up again. "What I look for most is the guiding genius of a man," he said. "In each of us is a spark of direction that is readable. We are all balances of senses and experiences, passions and thoughts. But it is intellect that figures most, and the more intellect predominates over the other propensities, the more one can trust a man."

"Pig bath," murmured Bige Cherry sardonically, just behind him.

"What did you say, Bige?" George asked.

"Never mind, George. After all, you're the one with the eddication."

George shrugged and they went on, down to the Water Pass, to prepare to make camp for the night.

Supper was corncakes in the frypan, with maple syrup from a jug, and bacon cut from the slab and fried, washed down, unusually, with rum. As the fire burned lower, George grasped the arm of his friend; eyes that glowed like glass stared at them from a tree in the shadows.

"Cat," he murmured.

Moving slowly, Bige picked up his loaded rifle and aimed it carefully. With a frightful, savage howl, the bobcat leapt toward George at the same instant Cherry's rifle sounded in the night, its reverberations echoing against the silent hills.

"Damn," George whispered, going to look at the body of the fallen animal and haul it into the bushes. "I hate the sound of that rifle. It puts every Indian within any distance on alert that someone is in the area."

He sat back down again, putting his arms about his knees. "What's this wilderness all about, Bige? There's not a man within ten miles from us, unless. . ." his ears were intent for a moment, then he relaxed again. "My sister keeps having dreams about the hills and hollows of Caintuck. Says she senses evil here, and fear." He sighed and looked into the fire.

George went on, "Married only a few months and she's had a bad dream, came to her twice. In it she sees the Kentucky River, and around it a group of women and children from the long-ago past. They have come in a boat to America and now are being taken to an Indian camp on the river from a place far away. She says she can see the boat clearly; it has a curved prow and triangular sails. From a time very long ago."

"What do the folks look like in the dream?" Bige asked, curious.

"Hair as yellow as gold, with the women's all in braids. They wear jewelry of gold, and the Indians have brought a leather sack of these people's gold cups and belt buckles with them. The children's hair is almost white, and they are strong and brave. They speak a tongue she can't understand. They draw signs on a rock, like little scratches, to leave messages for the men who will search for them."

"What kinda folk look like that?"

"Maybe Norseman. From Sweden—or Norway. I never thought much about it. But what would Norsemen from Scandanavia in the old days have to do with Caintuck? In Jenny's dream the Indians march them here, over a long, sad road from what seems to be a settlement in the Spanish territory; everything is desert. The children drop from exhaustion, the Indians force them on, with their treasure. When they arrive by the river, most have died and the rest are made slaves. Some of the women marry Indian men. But they always grieve for their lost children and the men so far away in the boats."

"Funny. I heard Simon Kenton talk onct 'bout somethin' like that," Cherry mused. George remembered Kenton, the giant-sized pioneer who had helped many people settle into Kentucky country and was a famous spy for the government. George had known him in Clark's Indian campaigns.

"Anyways, Kenton said the Injeeans have a tradition of white children's ghosts hoverin' about in Caintuck. That they were captives from some ancient time. The Shawnees won't go near sartain arears here. . ."

George did not reply, considering the probabilities of any connection. Jenny had dreamt the truth before.

"Dreams are odd, ain't they? Sometimes I dream of Evalina. She were a slip of a thing, like a fluff from a milkweed pod. Her so little, and dyin' there with a baby she wanted so much. She never quickened, only twict. Don't know why, 'twaren't from not tryin'. She were forty years old. Mebbe she were wore out." The fire flickered sideways as a breeze began in the small clearing.

Bige's voice was heavy with sadness. "I waren't home when the youngun come. Out tryin' to kill some squirrels 'cause I hadn't put in enough of a crop to git us through to April. Damn." He picked up a beechnut and threw it into the fire in disgust. "She couldn't even git to Malford's house to call him for help. All alone. I come in and found her there—I cain't git it out of my mind, I guess. That were one reason I come out here."

"They call us 'The Movers' now, you know," George said a little moodily. "The Scotch-Irish. Who are we anyway and what do we want, to travel constantly, like migrating birds? There are tens of thousands of us, all with the same heritage, all restless. From Ireland, to Pennsylvania or Carolina, to Kentucky. Where next?"

"It's the puffed wigs in Philadelphia or Baltimore puts names on us like that. Prancin' about in their carriages while the Scotch-Irish 'n other poor people like 'em cut swaths through the cane of one of the finest lands in the world. While they squabble about the new laws of the country, it's us that die at the Salt Licks and in Ohio pushin' back the bloody-backed redcoats. It's us that captured and held this land, richer'n anybody dreams, from the Injeeans all the way to the Mississippi. God damn them with their silver tea sets and pewter ink wells."

George scrutinized his friend's face in the flickering firelight. Bige never revealed much of the sad, serious part of himself. Somehow the soft darkness of the forest, like a blotter, soaked up the surface emotion and too-easy jests, baring the stark, deep thoughts of a man. The shadows blurred the embarrassing edges of memory and made them easy to share. Bige Cherry's was a lonely, spare life; he was like a jaunty, single thistle blowing in the wind in a field. There were deep grooves in his cheeks and he wasn't yet fifty, and George McClure knew his shoulders ached from rheumatism picked up from long nights in cold, poorly-chinked cabins and out in the foggy bottomlands.

"I'll be movin' on m'self I s'pose, soon, McClure," he said in a quiet voice.

George nodded, but let Bige go on. "You say our folk are restless. Well, I am as much as the next man. More so, I guess. I don't know why. Somethin' in me can't be satisfied among well-dressed fields with fences, really. An' I hate towns. They's stores goin' up here, and smith shops and wainrights and taverns, like the one we was in in York back a piece, remember?"

George nodded and smiled, recalling the sound of the strident laughter of fools, the stickiness of molasses in his hair, the coldness of the stream water as they washed it out. They had shared a good deal, he and this older man.

"In about five years this place'll be just about like Lancaster, Pennsylvania, with a fire department and one hundred and two churches. Why, man, they got laws out here already about bettin' the mares and swearin' too much," Bige contended.

"What do you want out of life, Bige?" George asked thoughtfully, stirring the ashes and putting on fresh wood.

"A small cabin. Jest enough corn to grind with a handmill. My gun and plenty o' deer and b'ar and pheasants. In five years everthing here will be druv back into the mountains and you won't be able to find even a rabbit to kill. A track where I won't meet nobody, if I walk from sunrise to sunset. And no man jack within fifty miles to tell me what to do or how to live."

"Where will you find that?" George wondered.

"Mebbe over by the Ouabash or Illinois Rivers. They's Injeeans there, but some settlers have lived amonxt 'em for a hundred fifty years. They call themselves Hoosiers all acrost that region Clark conquered."

"What's that mean?" George wondered. He had heard the term a time or two.

"It's a bastard French word, means outsiders. They're Frenchies, at places like Vincennes and St. Louee. Married some English wives and in their mixed tongue Hous-ier means outside civilization, outside the Pale as our pa's woulda said. So I want to go outside the Pale and be a Hoosier."

Long after Bige lay, feet to the fire, breathing regularly, George thought about what he said. Cherry might be a Mover, might go on, but the McClures would not need to leave Caintuck. They could be lords of all right here, with the investment he was getting ready to make. They'd be rich, and he would owe it all to the methods of science. With a little help from Francis Bacon and Sir Isaac Newton, the McClures were destined to be landed gentry. Yes, he would think his way to being rich. He smiled a little and, turning over on his buffalo robe, went soundly to sleep.

The next day was a cloudy, cool one; they felt it about five o'clock in the morning when the wind came up with sudden chill. The equinox was not far off, George told himself, wrapping the skin closely around him. But he could not get back to sleep. The two men rose early, and after a breakfast of bread and bacon cooked on a wind-blown fire, went onto the road. The walk among the trees was not difficult as the wind decreased; but they eyed the skies uneasily, hoping rain would not come. Rain on a walking trip was a problem. By ten o'clock their worst fears were realized; black clouds began to spatter large drops about them, and a downpour began.

"We don't dare to go under the trees, Bige," George murmured. Everybody was talking about lightning these days. Electricity. He had just read in his copy of the Philadelphia newspaper how some cities in Germany were forbidding the ringing of bells in the rain because hundreds of bell ringers had been killed by lightning. Electricity used trees just as easily as bell ropes for conductors.

They tried walking down the road; water coursed off their skin breeches and the heavy caped hunting shirts they wore even in this late summer weather for protection against brambles and insects. George's coin hat felt larger than ever. "Hell, they ain't nobody outcheer," Bige said in exasperation. "These shirts and breeches weigh twenty pounds apiece. I cain't walk with 'em soakin' wet and carry my pack too. Let's take our clothes off; it ain't that cold. They'll ride easier wrung out in the pack. Then when the rain stops, we'll put 'em on and parade into the settlement."

George thought about it for a moment, then shrugged and set down his pack and began to pull the dripping, unpleasant fringed shirt over his head. The leather breeches followed. They wore no linen beneath the outer clothing. He wrung the clothing out as best he could and jammed it into the overloaded pack. "Somehow I feel odd, walking naked as a jaybird down this buffalo track," George told Cherry.

"Waal, we do have moccasins on. And you've still got your hat," said Bige cheerfully. Each step the road grew slimier as they slid along, bypassing puddles. "The damn mud is suckin' my shoes right off," said Cherry with exasperation. Soon they were both walking barefoot, carrying the moccasins.

By eleven oclock the rain began to decrease and the sun came out. "Put the clothes on top of the pack and they will be passably dry in an hour or two. 'Till then we'll proceed this way," George told Bige.

No sooner had they picked up the packs again than they heard noises over their shoulders. Indians were overtaking them on the road. George felt a sense of panic rise in his craw, but he fought it down. Meeting Indians did not always mean a fight. Anyway, their guns were wet, and to set down the packs and get out dry powder would be a hostile act sure to start the yellow men shooting.

Bige spoke to him in very low tones. "Act natural and see what they do. It's a damn disadvantage bein' nekkid. Mebbe we should stop and dress. . ."

"They'll think we're going to get out ammunition. Anyway, they are coming up fast. We'll have to bluff it out. . ."

Now the Chickasaws were at their sides. There were two of them, wearing breech cloths which dripped water, but they were without guns. They had the traditional scalplocks and five feathers in their hair. When they drew near McClure and Cherry, they threw their hands in the air to signal they approached in friendship. One was taller than George, at least six-feet-four. But they wore ear-to-ear smiles and said immediately, "We Indian friends. Teebopasheelay. We walk with you to the south."

George put his gun down on the road and also raised his hands. "Good. We will walk with you," but he thought, as he picked it up again, they'd as soon murder us as not. The Indians seemed to be enjoying the experience immensely. They laughed, slapping their sides, and made a good deal of sport with the white men about their nakedness. When George and Bige put back on the moccasins, the taller Indian said, "We teach you a word in Chickasaw." He pointed to the moccasin and said, "Shoo loosh" and got the two Kentuckians to repeat the word.

"That's Chickasaw?" George said out of the side of his mouth to Bige. "I think they're sportin' with us."

George and Bige laughed along with them, even about what they sensed were semi-insulting comments about their private areas. Damn, thought George, if only I had a fig leaf. There was something that made a man so vulnerable when he walked without clothes. He knew how Adam must have felt, but at least God didn't have a tomahawk and a huge hunting knife as he walked in the garden.

When the sun stood overhead in the sky, steaming the dripping leaves of elm and ash trees by the side of the trail, the Indians took out some parched corn and maple sugar, journeycake, and four peaches, and shared them. Things are looking up, George told himself. It may be we can reach the settlement without harm. If only Cherry doesn't say anything provacative now.

But it was too late. Bige was beginning to tell one of his stories. God help us if it has Indians in it, George thought, half-frantic. These Chickasaws understood quite a bit of English, and they were very smart. Able to detect patronizing insults.

"They was a woman," Bige was saying, making a sign to show curves of a female body. The Indians nodded eagerly. "Had many childern." They didn't know the word, so Bige showed little ones running about and patted them on their imaginary little heads. "Sons and daughters, many, many," he said, holding up ten fingers. They nodded. "Waal, this woman was lazy, let these little uns run about in the woods while she sat and smoked her pipe." He pointed at the trees. God, this story is like Cherry's own childhood, George thought.

"A man came to this woman and said, 'Your little son is a-cryin' out there in the forest.' The man was upset. 'Well, at least he ain't dead,' the woman said and went on smokin' her pipe."

One of the Indians, the tall one who weighed two hundred pounds, looked at Bige expectantly, waiting for him to go on with the story. The other one, small and sharp, who understood perfectly well, laughed a high, braying laugh. Then he explained in Chickasaw to the other one. They both laughed for fully a minute, again slapping their sides and putting their arms on the white men's shoulders in a comradely way.

But then a silence set in among them all. The story had caused a brief moment of closeness, but it was succeeded by stiffness. It was as if the the word "dead" at the end of the story hung in the air, and that word reawakened the ancient, archetypal enmities between the two races, the soul-deep hatreds and countless episodes of maiming and wounding and torturing and scalping. Chief Cornstalk and his son shot down as they came to help the white man in Dunmore's time. Bryant's Station attacked and burned. Friendly Indian Logan's family set upon and murdered. Cabins put to the torch, tribal villages destroyed, children dead on both sides.

Still they walked along in silence, drawing ever nearer to the village and safe harbor, George thought. But about two o'clock, just as George and Bige were about to signal a stop and put on their partially-dried clothing again, the two Indians fell back and began to confer in their own tongue. Apprehensively, Bige and Cherry looked at each other and began to ease their packs about to reach for ammunition. But the two Indians seized their arms and they struggled violently, just as two other Chickasaws on horseback charged around the bend ahead.

George fought with the giant Indian for a few seconds, but the man's strength was phenomenal. It took the two horseback Indians, along with the smaller one, to subdue Bige, but it was finally done. Quickly the Indians spoke among themselves, and their discussion soon became an argument. It seemed to center around who had the right to the prisoners. Finally, after much discussion and pointing at the two white men, Bige was taken off by the giant man and the younger horseman, leaving George with the others.

The short Indian who had walked with them told him to go into a clearing nearby. He loaded his pack onto the horse and picked up George's rifle, getting ammunition before he returned. Was this it? Was he to be shot with his own gun?

In the clearing the Indians were jubilant. To have captured a tall, fair-skinned white man and to have him at their mercy was a cause for gloating. "Oakla, oakla," they kept shouting, gesturing up the road towards the south. The short, clever Indian addressed George.

"Your friend gone to our brother's village. We take you back with us to our hunting camp, then to our villages. Our women and little ones will see you. Nahhooloh who walks in his birthday skin in the Indian hunting grounds."

He walked up to George and slapped his face. "Hey, you! Why you walk through our Chickasaw hunting grounds. Eh? Eh? We going to tie you onto this horse so you not escape. Then we take you with us." George asked for his clothing, the Indian threw back his head and laughed again. "We keep you like this," he said, "and we keep your good gun." He threw the Kentucky rifle to his companion, but he let George have his moccasins. "When you walk, you go better and longer with feet covered. And we let you wear the silly hat. It show white man a fool." Thank God for being a fool, George thought.

He bent to take off his moccasins to scrape the mud off, and the Indian grabbed them to inspect them, or perhaps to tease him. "Teebopasheelay. What a friend you turned out to be," George said grimly to the Indian, and the Indian slapped him again with the back of his hand, painfully, along the bridge of his nose. "What will happen to me after I finally get back to your village?" George asked, with a gesture asking for the return of his shoes.

"Maybe slave. Hoe the corn for me. Maybe test your courage. Pull out toenails one at a time. Then loowah, Burn, slowly, hot fire." He touched the bare feet with his hunting knife, causing George to pull back and flush in terror and giving both the Indians cause for great mirth. Then they tossed the moccasins at him, and he put them on, feeling humiliation through his fear. The Indians did not usually burn victims at the stake anymore, but it did happen occasionally.

Think, George, he told himself. It is thinking that can get you out of this. It had all happened so fast his thoughts spun centrifugally, refusing to center on the needs of the moment. What on earth was Bige doing now?

"How are you going to get me on that little pony?" he suddenly asked. "I may take him and run away."

"That easy. We tie your legs." The small Indian was strutting about like a bantam rooster. Perhaps he had never taken a captive before.

"That won't work. My legs are long, but they aren't long enough to tie under that fat pony."

"You see. It work." He seemed to feel George was attacking his intelligence, and he refused to be shown up. "Go to the pony," he ordered the other brave. "Get on him. I show him your legs tie under him. He see." The two marched across the road to where the pony was tethered and the younger brave got on the little horse's back. The short Indian, calling over his shoulder, began to undo thongs to wrap the other one's legs—

George bolted into the woods beyond the clearing. He ran as fast as he had ever run, through saplings, which he blessed God for and which obliterated the Indians' view. In spite of his fear and the extremity of his situation, he took care to keep the hat on his head. The Chickasaws were shouting after him, but he did not hear them crashing through the brush yet. They must be able to run like deer: were they fifteen, twenty paces behind? It had to be only a matter of time. Then he realized they were stopping to try to load the gun. He crashed on through the forest. Sticks and nettles clawed at his bare skin. He hardly noticed them. There was a crash of the rifle, but he ran on.

Sprinting until his lungs burst and expecting to be overtaken at any minute, he finally could go on no further. Whatever was that story where some simpleton at Fort Macinac ran for three, four miles to save his life? He simply could not move another inch. He lay on his face in back of a huge fallen log, his spirits dashed by the course of events of this day. Let the Chickasaws come. Whatever his fate, he would await it here.

Five minutes passed. Then ten. George sat up. He was not being followed. What was happening? He better analyze the situation. Maybe they had lost him. Perhaps they'd had their sport and did not consider him valuable enough to chase. Yes, that was logical. Particularly so far from the Chickasaw villages. But there was another possibility: they were playing with him, tracking him slowly and waiting for the right moment to come out and recapture him. Well, whatever it was, he must continue fleeing and stay out of sight until he reached white settlements.

He stood up, put his hat back on, and it was at that moment that he noticed his leg. Blood was trickling down it in a thin but steady stream from a wound in the fleshy part of his thigh. The rifle had hit him at long range. Drat. But the wound would probably not prove fatal, not if he got help for it.

He crashed through thicker underbrush and came to the river. He became aware of the wind now as he clambered down its bank and took a long drink. It was growing colder. He decided to follow the course of the river, keeping out of sight in the brush by its side.

The sun was lowering. He shivered from the chill, and in his weakened condition, his teeth began to chatter. Somewhere up here, somewhere must be Passwater Settlement. It is on the river, he told himself. Even those God-forsaken people need water and there will be houses.

George went deeper into the woods and sat down to rest by a log and, as exhaustion and loss of blood overcame him, fell asleep. When he awoke, it was dark. Ominous animal wails came at him out of the blackness around him. His wound had stopped bleeding, but it was growing hot. He crept about monkey-like in the dark to find a few branches and leaves. He was too tired to build a lean-to, but he covered himself with the branches and drifted into a troubled, feverish sleep, filled with dreams of leering, vermilion-painted Indians, bobcats, and, oddly, the picnic table overlooking Conodoguinet Creek back home.

Morning came and he dragged himself out of his den. His dull eyes did not notice the sun and the rising temperature. The equinoxial wind was over, and the skies smiled benignly at the tall, naked man with a hat on, staggering ludicrously along in full sight beside a river that was swollen with debris and swirling water from yesterday's rains. He was too tired to hide any longer.

Something to eat, anything, he told himself and went up the bank. He pulled up wild parsnips and ate them, tasting gritty dirt along with the sharp root flavor. Blackberries, shrivelled and dry now in August, were still on the bushes, and he let a handful drop into his hand and smashed them into his mouth. Juice came down his face, and for a confused moment in his fever he thought it was blood.

Heading painfully for the river, he drank and bathed his face a little. His cheeks ached from the bruising blows the Indian delivered, and they were as hot as his leg, which now throbbed relentlessly. On he went, out of his head at times, imagining Bige and the Indian giant, twenty-feet tall, were by his side. Suddenly about one o'clock his head cleared. There, on a high bluff above the river was a cabin. Smoke twisted out of its chimney. The bank was steep, and talking aloud, he pulled himself up the bank, root by root.

"Strength almost gone, God help me," he said and the sound of his voice frightened him. He thought he said the words in his head. Finally he stood at the top of the bank. Dragging his leg behind him in agony, he lurched toward the plank door of the cabin and reaching it, pounded with his fists. The door opened. There he stood, wild red hair escaping from a crushed hat, face purple from bruises and blackberry juice, eyes burning in his head, naked and unashamed, like an incarnation of the Devil. Before him stood an angel clad in white linen. By the grace of God she did not shut the door in fright, but took him in just as he tottered forward into her arms.

The delirium which followed seemed to go on for an eternity, in which he wandered with mournful feet among familiar scenes, endlessly stacking crockery, tobacco, and apothecary concoctions on shelves which never were filled at Emison's store. He observed fairy grottoes with dragons at dining tables, where he heard bells clanging and the voice of his father talking, and awakened to feel sharp pain and fight people off and then drift off the cliff of unconsciousness again. Two sights from the real earth persisted: the sight of a calm man in spectacles with a ruffled shirt who seemed to be his enemy because he held him down, and a woman with large, calm eyes always beside him, whom he decided was his friend. She was holding the largest cat he ever saw.

Finally, swimming up to the surface through fathoms of murky water, George awoke. Urgently he put his hand to his thigh; it was decently covered. His wound was cool and bandaged, though still painful. The bullet must have been removed. The young woman's eyes were on him. "Who are you? And why did you have on white?" he demanded. "Damn silly thing to have on to greet a naked man."

"I was leading the singing at our love feast church meeting," a gentle voice answered. "Seeing an unclothed man did not bother me. Your infected bullet wound did."

Accepting this, he went back to sleep.

He awakened hours later finally feeling refreshed and called for food. Broth and bread appeared, brought by the man in the ruffled shirt of his delirium. George looked at him carefully. He was extremely slight for a man, almost like a woman in stature, sprightly in his movements as he spooned beef broth into George's mouth.

"Well, now, we are going to have to get you back on your feet, Mr. McClure."

"You seem to have the advantage over me, sir. How do you know my name?"

"Your friend Mr. Cherry told it to us, along with the brief facts of your encounter with the savages." George tried to boost himself up to his elbows and, feeling razor-like pain, had to be helped back flat. The gentleman looked at him with compassionate eyes. "Told some of the villagers before—he died of his head wounds. He tried to flee and they hurled a tomahawk at him and headed out of the territory. We buried him near the road but did not mark the grave."

George groaned. Poor, poor Bige. He would never move on again. So many things were unfinished in his life. It was like a promising garden plot that was allowed to grow giant ragweeds, where roses had never really flourished. "I am the Reverend Thomas Linton Jordan. And this," said the man, referring to the nurse who had worn the white dress, "is my daughter Jean. We sent messages to your folk at McClure station. Word that you will recover."

"Lord knows how," George said, again gingerly touching his wound. "Only a spent bullet wound, but it festered. Who took it out?"

"Jean did," and, in answer to George's questioning look, "she has knowledge of surgeon's techniques. She assisted our surgeon back in New Jersey during the war."

"We are in Passwater?"

"At the edge of town. If a settlement only a year old, composed of forty thrown-together cabins and six taverns sprawling over foothills at the conjunction of two streams can be called a town. But such as it is, we are its ministery."

"What Presbytery?" George asked.

"You mistake us, Mr. McClure. We are Methodist Episcopals." Reverend Jordan put the spoon down on a bedside table. He was through feeding the broth and, handing George the bread to chew as best he could, he strode out of the room. "Jean can answer any other questions you have, although I would recommend you reserve your strength for recovery. I must preach this evening outdoors."

The young woman came near the bed and pulled up a bench to sit by him. She was as slight as her father in stature, but she seemed to have his steely strength in a more subdued form, as if a fierce fire were banked. Her face was an oval of composed beauty. She had a very small mouth, he thought, trying not to stare too much.

"Father is never still. He is the perpetual motion machine that has been conceived of, but never demonstrated. Still, there is so much to do here for us both. It is time for you to sit up, even though there will be pain." She leaned over him to pull him onto the pillow. He could smell lavender emanating from her blue-checked calico dress. Her arms easily held him up.

He frowned.

"What is the matter?"

"I was just thinking—you know me so well, and I know you not at all. What—what did I reveal while I was out of my senses?" He managed a wry smile.

She did not look directly at him. "You called for Ma and Jenny. You cursed someone named Will and 'butt-head Kennedy,' and Logan for arriving late, and the entire Shawnee nation. At one time you believed that General Washington was in the room and you said, 'The day is ours, sir. They fly.' "

"As indeed they did," he murmured, shaking his head at the erratic, fragile nature of human intelligence. He remembered none of this. Five days were gone from his life, and it was as if they had happened to another person. Suddenly something dawned on him. "You took that bullet out."

"I have helped take many out of unfortunate soldiers near New Castle, Delaware, where I was born and lived until two years ago."

She walked and ministered to those men not far from where I fought, he thought, and she is about my age, perhaps two or three years younger. Odd that such a beautiful woman never married. Best not ask why.

"What is New Castle like?" he asked, really for lack of something better to say. The skies of his mind were still not clear; clouds floated across their surface every few moments.

"Quite civilized. Cobbled streets with good frame houses and gardens of pansies and wisteria. Its citizens are known for their hospitality, if not for their tolerance." A shadow passed across her face, but she quickly covered it with a smile. She turned from the bed to pick up the cat again.

"May I be introduced?" asked George. He rather liked cats. He and Jenny always put bonnets and little aprons on them when he was small.

"This is Oberon. He came with us all the way from Delaware." The cat put a paw over his mistress's arm. Then he settled in her lap, turning his head to lick his butterscotch-colored fur. He must weigh over twenty pounds,

George thought.

He said, "I have heard of Methodists. James Harrod's wife has been having meetings lately at her home. . ."

"If you know of us at all, you are not of the majority. Odd that we have been around since early in the century and yet so few, especially out here, know of us. Our founder, John Wesley, lives in England. He founded a new church to purify the old. He found the Established church too cold and formal, never touching the heart." Her large eyes remained calm as she leaned over the cat to adjust the pillow under George's head. She had the ability, he noticed, to be earnest without suggesting the fanaticism so many zealots conveyed.

"But Wesley is himself an Establishment minister."

"Yes, and ever will be. But he was dissatisfied with ceremony and meaningless repetition of dogma. One day as he sat in Aldersgate Chapel at evensong, he felt his heart 'strangely warmed' as he said. He went out to join with others who would work for honest communion with God, a God of love, who would purify their lives for his service."

He looked at her curiously. "I was born and bred a Presbyterian."

"Then you are of the Old Religion."

He laughed a little, causing a stitch in his wound. "Why do you laugh?" she asked.

"I meant no offense. I was considering how often I have heard the Roman Church called the 'Old Religion' by Presbyterians. Now the axe has a different handle. *O tempora, o mores.*"

"We believe in salvation for all, not just for an aristocratic elect."

"New Light," he said, half-jocularly.

"Not at all." She refused to be offended; perhaps she had been through this explanation often. "But I will invite you to one of our meetings." And I will come, he thought, if you will be up at the front lining out the hymns and wearing your white dress. With your hair as light as the women in Jenny's dream. That will be heaven enough for me.

In the next days he accomplished the following things which removed him from the ranks of invalidism: took himself to the privy outside, clad in a dressing gown they provided for him, washed and bathed himself in the river with a cake of lavender soap and some of the nicest linen towelling he had seen in a long time, (he tried not to remember how he felt when he last laved in this river's waters) ate one buffalo steak and then called for another and, eventually, prepared to return to the world of men.

The minister's clothing was far too small for George's six-foot frame, so they secured for him a homespun shirt and breeches from someone in the town. Holding onto the bed, he dressed himself and combed through his hair, looking into a small quicksilver glass. What changes a week could make in a man's life. In a week, an armistice could be worked out and a peace treaty signed, a couple could be married, celebrated, and a child conceived, a man could sicken and die. Or live.

His hat, he noted when he first arose from bed, sat on a cherry table by the door. From respect for these people who took him in, he had not checked its wide band. Now, as he put on the homespun stuff, he ran his finger around the inside; yes, it was all still there. He sighed with relief. He could go on with his mission. All was not lost. Maybe he would visit Bige's grave, if someone would tell him where it was. His plan, his ideals were still intact. That was important to him; one must find consistency in life. And after all, it was his intellect, wasn't it, that had saved him? What else was it that flashed the idea about the horse into his mind just when he needed it? Tomorrow he would look for the right investment with the right man behind it. He combed the too-long red hair, tied it back with a ribbon in the style of the minister, and put on the hat.

The service for that night was to be in the meeting house, a rough structure used for county business, rare travelling theatre performances, and church meetings of various denominations. It was dark and the town was illuminated by torchlight when the minister, his daughter, and George arrived in a wagon. A handful of rough-looking men filed into the two-story log structure and seated themselves on the benches. There were also a few women, mostly barefooted and wearing soiled smocks. A few, though, were dressed respectfully with neat caps, hose and buckle shoes. Log torches fixed to the joists illuminated the face of the minister as he walked to the head of the group.

"Let us open this service to the glory of God by singing a hymn of Isaac Watts, 'From all that dwell beneath the skies.' Miss Jordan will read out the words."

His daughter rose and with dignity stood on a little box that served as the pulpit riser. She raised her voice clearly so the small group could hear:

> *From all that dwell beneath the skies*
> *Let the Creator's praise arise*
> *Let the Redeemer's name be sung*
> *Through every land, by every tongue.*

Well enough, so far, George thought, rising to sing. I know that one. But the rest of the service was far less recognizable. The minister's text was "You must be born again," and he spoke with great emotion, moving from off his small podium to walk across the front of the meeting house, pointing to heaven and wringing his hands at appropriate moments.

"The spirit worketh in us to uncover hidden sin and through this uncovering we are brought to the Throne of Grace. But we must expose the dire workings of the Evil One, we must repent and throw off the works of error," he exhorted, with great feeling. There was a noise on one of the back benches. George could not resist turning to see what it was. Two Indians had risen and were beating their breasts, crying real tears.

"They're repentin' and sartain they got a long way t' go," whispered a matronly-looking woman with a feathered hat who was sitting next to him.

As the minister spoke of the miracles of love in redeeming lost souls, as he spoke of the degeneracy of the human heart, of its resistance to change, others in the group began to weep. There was moaning all over the meeting house; two men who had climbed into the joists of the roof grew so agitated they fell down, landing on their feet, to George's relief.

The Reverend Mister Jordan asked for testimonies to the power of God, and a woman twisting a handkerchief stood up and said that she had been redeemed by the love of Christ from a life of self-indulgence. That she had been a nag to her husband but now restrained herself. The husband stood up and said, "Yes, 'twas so." That is a step forward, thought George. May all nagging wives be so redeemed. On the bench across from him sat a tall man with a wen on his forehead, crushing in his hands a beaver hat that fur traders sometimes wore. He stood up slowly and then hunched his belt up before he began.

"You all know me as Cussin' Joe. That's been me handle for I don't know how many yars. Waal, I want everone here to know that through the love of God I am a new man. God has pardoned all me sins and I am not the bad man I have been. I have joined Reverend Jordan's class and now am learning what being a Christian means. No more Cussin' Joe."

By God, that's damn good, thought George, reprimanding himself for taking all this less than seriously. But he could not help but grow serious when, after the minister completed his sermon and the congregation had dabbed the tears off their cheeks, Jean Jordan came again to the front to direct the singing of the last hymn.

"Mr. Wesley's brother Charles has written many beautiful hymns, but the one I love best we share with you tonight"

> *Peace be to this congregation*
> *Peace to every heart therein*
> *Peace the earnest of salvation*
> *Peace the fruit of conquered sin*

The group began to sing the song, but the tune was unfamiliar to George. It moved him strangely. The music was sweet and simply melodic, with tender harmonies:

> *Peace that speaks the heavenly Giver*
> *Peace, to worldly minds unknown*
> *Peace that floweth like a river*
> *From the eternal source alone.*

It would be good to have the kind of peace they sang of. He did not, had not, ever known it.

But the spell was abruptly broken. During the benediction a rock crashed through the window opening onto the floor beside the minister. When the group spilled out into the rutted street, they saw a gang of young hecklers lurking outside the tavern next door. They began to hoot at the Methodists, pulling their own countenances into long, artificial smiles.

At home Reverend Jordan did not seem deflated by the rock or the exit reception they received. "Two new souls joined the classes. And next week my brother minister will join me so we can ride missionary circuit all through these parts." He rubbed his hands together and helped George climb the ladder into the loft.

His guest was improved enough to cease being a patient and become a paying visitor. The thigh wound had stopped aching and now made itself known only through occasional throbs. As Reverend Jordan gave George quilts and a bolster, he commented on his guest's plan to go into town tomorrow. "Quite a town, quite a town. Sir, I think you have passed through an engagement with the Philistines only to come to Sodom and Gomorrah."

It was after three o'clock when George reached the village. It took him more than two hours to walk the two miles with his leg, but it was growing stiff from lack of exercise, and he wanted to make the trip alone. As he walked down the only lane in town, past the meeting house where the Reverend preached the night before, George muttered to himself that the Reverend's description was not all wrong. Although he did not see the specific sins on the street for which Sodom was castigated, he saw almost every other one known to man.

Groups of rough-looking men openly threw dice and played cards on puncheon platforms by the side of the road. A few young rakes dressed like beaux from Norfolk or New York strutted about and consulted pocket watches. A woman with a beauty mark on her cheek sauntered like some London slut down the road with her arm through an admiring man's. Under a footbridge which crossed the creek lay an unconscious black man with a bottle in his hand.

George made his way past youths who jostled by, oblivious of the strangers' presence, clapping each other on the backs and singing bawdy songs. All was not sin, of course. Women and children shopped for provisions in town and a man dressed as a Quaker walked by, escorting a Delaware Indian.

A little warily, George touched the hat on his head, with its lining securely loaded with the patriarch John McClure's hope for the future of all his sons. He took the hat off, and turning his back and looking furtively about, took out a gold carlos coin he would need to buy clothing. This drab, ill-fitting homespun would never do to close a transaction involving thousands of the new American dollars that were in the process of becoming legal tender.

Certainly there would be no tailor's shop here, but he saw the sign of a general merchandiser; perhaps there might be something ready to wear. He stepped into the dusky gloom, his eyes blinded for an instant from the glare outside. He made his way between a giant biscuit barrel and a smaller tub that held nails. Guns, axes, saws, spices, wooden bowls, and candles of various sizes sat on shelves above a counter. Jugs of whiskey, mounds of fluffy wool, and horses' harnesses crowded each other on the floor. Ropes of tobacco hung from the beams. A stout man with split knee breeches and spectacles approached him. "Cain I assist ya, sir?"

"Would you have coats and breeches ready to wear?" George asked.

"Well, now sir, usally I don't carry sech things, but m' wife is urgin' me to go more genteel, seein the town is growin' so fast. So I contracted fer a few suits of gent'mens' clothing." He reached beneath the counter for one. " 'Tis used only a slight bit."

George picked up a pair of brown breeches and a well-made linen coat and looked at them suspiciously.

"Who owned these?"

"Waal, sir, various sources. Don't put me on the spot." George continued to eye him steadfastly. Reluctantly he continued, "We buy up estates, so to speak. And we do have a fair share of mishaps in the town, men who have disagreements, an' take to fisticuffs or pistols afore they can be stopped."

"This is from a dead man, isn't it?"

"Sir, I assure you these items were absoutely not from a pestilence. . ."

"They better not be, or I'll pickle you with your own crock. I need the clothing. Get me some hose and good leather shoes and," he sighed, thinking of the expense, "I'll need a rifle. Do you have a closet I can use to put on these marvelous products of the free trade system?" The man showed him behind a curtain into his private quarters and gestured for the woman with powdered ringlets who sat on the bed to leave.

George put on the coat and breeches, shoes and hose and exited, looking every inch as much of a gentleman as the previous owner, a slave trader from Charleston, who had been shot in the head in a brawl, and who thoughtfully died without spilling blood on his clothes.

Back in the street, George scanned log signs to decide between two rude inns. He entered the Black Rose, filled already at this early hour. Here, he had been told, much of the speculative business he came for was transacted. Here, those who had pressing debts in northern Kentucky came to sell good land for a song. Here, those who had bought huge holdings in outlying territories of what is now Alabama and Mississippi, where the borders were often disputed, offered them first.

Of course, here also were murderers and thieves from the East, and those who dealt undercover with the Indians and Spanish, buying and selling boatloads of furs, naval stores, and indigo. At a far table he heard a whispered conversation in a Spanish accent about a scheme that was nosing about even at Bardstown—to disengage Kentucky as a separate state and ally it with Spain. Feeling a little unsettled, George reminded himself he would not be looking to deal with the unsavory part of the crowd. He wanted to buy a great deal of land at a very good price.

He ordered a glass of rum punch and circulated about with it. In the next two hours he had conversations with men who sold various things. A gentleman from Georgia wished to part with two thousand acres he had won in a card game; the title was likely to be good but not guaranteed. A group of three who came from South Carolina wished to build a quarter horse track near Danville and were selling shares. A man with a Spanish accent and a cage with two black-breasted red fighting cocks wished to offer them, guaranteeing the buyer a "fortune from de pits." Others told him of slaves with bad tempers but strong backs, shares in a sugar cane plantation with a water wheel planned by the coast, and the inevitable "equity" holdings in southern Kentucky claimed by several people and in dispute in the courts.

Darkness began to fall and the noise in the streets increased. George was discouraged. This was a sordid and stupid enterprise. Nothing good could come of it. All of the ventures he saw were silly; nothing fit the categories he had designed for himself. He ordered a plate of stew and biscuits and ate them disconsolately.

There was a clamor in the back of the tavern. The same group of ruffians he saw telling the stories on the street were setting something up, putting up boards to make a pen. He paid his bill and, curious, walked back to see what the noise was all about. In the pen that was set up on two tables and filled with sawdust was a small rat terrier. As he watched, two men in buckskin breeches so dirty they were stiff and black brought in a wire cage, loaded with large brown rats. A younger man with a blue-black beard and mustache followed with another cage. Most of the men in the tavern rose and crowded around the pen. Slave brokers in faded waistcoats jostled elbows with farmers to get a clear view of the action that was to come.

The entertainment plan was simple enough—let the terrier get at the rats and bet on how long it would take to kill one, then another. It was a game that was popular in establishments frequented by the vulgar throughout the new nation.

George shouldered his way through the crowd. He watched the man he now called in his mind "Bluebeard" collect the coins bet on the terrier who was struggling under his arm, yapping to be loosed. A boy in the crowd tried to put his hand over the dog's mouth and received a bite for his trouble.

"At 'er's a feisty little bastard," said the boy's dad, pouring whiskey over the wound to clean it out.

"What's feisty mean, Pa?" The son was a lad of about eleven with long legs which had grown too much for his deerskin breeches.

"Oh, it means a showin'-off, yappy crittur. Them rat dogs is aluz feisty."

Another older man, whom George took to be from the mountain country southeast of them, joined in.

"Feisty is when a youngun comes up to his pa who is cuttin' down a tree and tells him how to hold the axe. Then when the pa don't listen the kid yells at 'im and gets cuffed for it."

"It means damned ornery. Like most Caintuckians," the man with the blue-black beard stated definitively. He put the dog in the box and immediately it took off to find itself a suitable rat as the beseiged creatures huddled in the corner of the box, trying to crawl over each other.

George told the story of the fight when he got home. "Just like the Cyclops herding Odysseus's men into a corner and selecting one to eat, this feisty dog selected a rat and then brought it out to center ring and began shaking it for dear life. In no time at all he had dispatched it, everyone roaring approval, then went to select another helpless foe. . ."

Jean shivered. "Pray, Mr. McClure, do not continue this sad tale. I have heard of these matches but have not seen them in the village before. We have had other ones, with the fighting cocks matched until they peck and claw each other to death. And the bulldogs, and even the bears. . ."

"I beg you tell me, Miss Jordan, if this was Thursday, what do they do for entertainment on a Saturday night when things get really heated up?"

"You do not wish to know, Mr. McClure," and shaking her head, Jean bade him goodnight.

The next morning after breakfast Jean had something to show him. Leading him out into a fresh, bright September morning, she took him into the woods above the river bank, to a small area her father cleared for her. Wooden cages with wire fronts stood on huge rounds of logs and chirruping noises were all about. "I keep woodland animals out here for pets," she said. Two small racoons, a possum and its baby and a wounded baby bear were in the cages. Nearby, a miniature stockaded pen held two young deer with maimed legs.

"However did you assemble this menagerie?" George murmured.

She pulled her tow-colored hair back off her face with a graceful hand and reached through the hinged door of the pen to stroke one of the fawns. "Through an awful happening, Mr. McClure." She took him back to the edge of the clearing and gestured for him to sit down by her on a bench made from logs. She must often resort here, he thought, to watch her animals.

"Late last winter the men in the area decided the wild game had become a nuisance. That the squirrels and coons and deer destroyed the crops and the bears frightened and even killed folk and carried off farm animals. 'Twas true, of course."

"But we depend on them for game in the settlement area—don't you out here?"

"Of course. But I think some had greed in mind—the fur traders come through all the time."

George loftily repeated his favorite quotation: *"Radix malorum est cupiditas.* The root of evil is greed." She blinked her eyes but did not take notice of what he said.

She went on, "They organized a grand hunt. All in the area were to assemble on a certain day and form a ring and drive animals to the center where they would be shot." Her voice was still soft, but tension lay beneath the words. "My father and I begged them not to kill so many helpless creatures, but they did not listen. We went out, hoping at the last minute to dissuade them from the enterprise."

"And?"

"It was awful, Mr. McClure. They clanged cowbells, beat axes on anvils, shot guns. The frightened animals darted this way and that, not knowing what to do. They clustered at the center of the ring, much as the rats you described hid in the corners of their box last night. Then six or seven men shot at them. Bears were rousted out of their sleeping trees, young deer separated from their mothers. They shot them all in the center of that ring. I begged for some of the young ones who were only wounded, and Father and I brought them back here." She could say no more.

"Roundup hunting is a cruel way to deal with harmless creatures, almost as bad as shining torches in their eyes," George said.

"Especially in light of what the hunters did with the slain animals. They divided them up, according to the neighborhoods that participated. North Water Pass River men took their lot and sold the skins to buy whiskey, the settlement men just slung them on a sledge and dumped dead animal carcasses at each door in the town. Most people could dress only a few pounds of meat—it was a terrible waste and slaughter, for what?'' Jean raised her hands helplessly, then, apparently finished with the story, stood up and determinedly brushed bits of leaves off her skirt.

She checked the cages one last time and they walked back to the cabin. "I hope I never have to see such a thing again, Mr. McClure.''

"I share your hope, Miss Jordan,'' he said, and meant it sincerely. As he headed into town to resume his search for investment, he thought again whether any good could ever come out of this God-forsaken settlement, and wondered why the minister and his daughter were there. Could the love of God alone have caused such a self-imposed exile? He thought not.

When the Sabbath finally came and George sat on one of the benches in the Methodist meeting again, he had trouble concentrating on Reverend Jordan's exhortations to repent and confess and forsake sin. His mind would stray, as it often did in divine service, to pressing responsibilities. Yesterday's trip into the village to try to find a suitable investment had been frustrating. No large tracts of land which met the test of both security and high, quick return were available just now. New people seemed to be coming into this frontier village every day, but he did not trust any of them.

Then there was the matter of Miss Jordan. She was strangely on his mind, troubling him. It was not that she was so beautiful, as indeed she was, and so good, certainly that was true, but so complex. She was like a diamond, perfect in form, flashing many facets to the sun. But the deepest worth of the stone was unknowable, and he was no Hollander to assay it. Last night, for instance, there were earnest words between the Reverend and his daughter in hushed tones, after he went up to the loft. They were arguing about something. What could it have been? He wished Bige had been here to talk with.

His thoughts lingered sadly on his friend. He felt a pang as he thought about the unmarked grave. Was it his fault that Bige died? His scheming had brought them south, 'twas true. In spite of the difference in their ages, George had felt as close as kin to Bige. The pity of it was they had never really had time to relax together. Theirs was a wartime comradeship, cemented by facing hardships—biting cold in New Jersey, mosquito-laden heat in Ohio, poor rations, dysentary, the threat of death. Which of the classic poets said adversity was the touchstone of friendship? Well, Bige and he had their share of trouble and faced it together, and the friendship had proven true indeed. He would never find another man like him. Or woman? The idea came unbidden to his thought. One did not consider women as friends. Lovers, bearers of one's children. But who could discuss rational ideas with a member of ''the weaker sex?''

He strained his neck a little, shifted on the bench to catch sight of Miss Jordan. The calico and linsey-clad women around her were diving deeply into the message, swimming in emotion, clapping hands, nodding affirmation. Not she; only her face, enraptured and shining showed the depth of her commitment. He thought of the women around Jesus, His mother, the mother of Mark, the Magdalene. Thus they must have sat in the Galilean countryside looking up as the carpenter-rabbi spoke.

The sermon ended. Reverend Jordan was smiling and beckoning a bald-headed, hearty-looking man with a handsome face to come forward to be introduced. "My friends," he said, "the harvest fields have another worker. I wish you to know my brother in the Lord, come from Virginia to ride the missionary circuit with me and spread the gospel to Tennessee and the mountain region. Mr. Robert McClaren."

The congregation nodded approvingly. Mr. McClaren acknowledged the greetings with a friendly salute of his hand, and Jean rose to lead the final hymn.

Outside, she introduced George to the new minister and his family. The wife, an intelligent-looking woman with horse teeth, said she had heard of his recent escape from the Indians.

"My son Rob learned to be a good shot on the trip through the Gap," she said, bringing forward a gangly thirteen-year-old boy to make George's acquaintance. "We met several parties of Indians, but they did no more than steal several of the horses."

"Then you were lucky, indeed," said George.

"Why have you come to Passwater, Mr. McClure?" asked Reverend McClaren. When George told him, he seemed to hesitate a moment, then said, "You may want to meet a man who came with us on the Wilderness Road and west. He has many ideas which you will find interesting. And I believe he is a thoroughly honest man, although his disposition is—choleric. He will be staying at the Black Rose for a while. We'll be there, too."

George thanked the minister and told him he would look into the matter the next day.

Slices of corn meal mush swimming in butter and maple syrup greeted him when he arrived at the sunny breakfast table the next morning. Miss Jordan seemed to be in a mild and merry mood. She hummed a bit of a tune as she poured milk in a bowl for the huge cat, whose whiskers were growing snowy as it lapped.

> In Dublin's fair city, where girls are so pretty
> 'Twas there that I first met sweet Molly Mallone

What a beautiful soprano voice she had. George took up the song, chiming in with his baritone.

> She pushed a wheelbarrow, through streets broad and narrow
> Crying cockels and mussels, alive, alive oh.

They laughed together, stretching out the "Ohh" between them.

"Did you know I played the fiddle?" George asked her, suddenly merry himself. "Tolerably well, too, some of the ladies say." He made a mock bow.

"Do you now? I wish you had brought the instrument. We could have a real shebang, as they call the festive affairs out here."

Her father came to the table and seated himself, putting a large linen napkin in his lap. There was a cotton calico tablecloth on the table, and Queen Anne's lace and goldenrod arranged in a blue bottle. These people conduct themselves in a civilized style, George thought approvingly. One of the things he hated about Kentucky was the makeshift, mannerless state of everyday life. Wooden trenchers and licked fingers.

People should dine with pewter and china, like the set his mother sometimes brought out. Take time for ceremony. Dan'l's new wife Martha Bard and he agreed completely on this. Well, this investment, when it came, would make possible plenty of plate and pewter, and servants to clean 'em up for that matter.

"Mr. McClure, you have told us only in the vaguest way what your objectives are for finding your fortune. Can you elaborate?" The minister, forking eggs into his mouth, looked a little distant this morning. Why would that be? Yesterday's Sabbath had to rack up as a great success in the game of religious billiards. Two people found grace and decided to join his classes.

"Sir, I am looking for the right land to buy. I have done some scientific calculations in the matter and am putting my observations on economic principles to the test," George told him.

"You, sir are not rushing headlong into riches, then. Dashing off cliffs of depreciating currencies, ascending in bubbles of increased value." George looked at Reverend Jordan's smile. He tried to penetrate its meaning, but as the minister's jocularity did not seem to be at his expense, he went on.

"Actually, I have studied the Mississippi and South Sea Bubbles and found that the investors in England and France abandoned themselves to emotion. Why, the French would stand outside the door of the finance minister John Law until midnight, waiting for a word with him, begging him to let them buy a few shares in the venture, shares which would double within the week and then, ironically, be worthless within a year's time. They did not use reason."

Miss Jordan stirred sugar into a cup of tea. "And you will use reason to secure a fortune?"

"I desire to use reason to rule all the parts of my life. It is the way I was educated."

She did not look at him but stirred the tea very, very slowly. "I have found that reason is not always the most suitable guide to living."

"Surely it has its limitations, Miss Jordan." He turned toward her father. "As Horace says, '*Misce stultitiam consiliis brevem: Dulce est desipere in loco.*' "

The minister nodded slowly, seriously. "I have never been sure that saying is right. 'Mix with your wise counsels some brief follies, it is sweet to forget wisdom now and then. . .' but let us not quibble. No indeed, no indeed." Nervously he drummed a tattoo on the walnut table with his fingertips.

The drumming stopped. The minister cleared his throat. Jean sat rigid as a rod clutching her teacup as her father said, "And yet, I have not found that the heart is any better beacon to correct behavior. . ." the teacup clattered, the contents spilled, and George, caught in a cross-current of conflicting feelings he did not understand, rose to help clean up spilled tea and pieces of china.

He welcomed the walk into town. Foothills loomed on the horizon and behind them, in shadowy mist, higher mountains, reminiscent of those in Western Pennsylvania. He took out a square of linen Jean had laundered for him and put it around his brow to catch the sweat; it was a breathlessly hot day for September. On a day like this they had advanced on Piqua, and he had seen Will lead the troops like a true Lochinvar.

What would Will be doing now? Probably getting in the corn, now almost dry in the fields, with John and Dan'l. Seeing to the dairy animals they had just bought, clearing more acres. Wishing an Indian would just dare to try to steal a few horses and show his face about the blockhouse and the stockade wall they had constructed. And courting Martha Bard's cousin Margaret Mossman. Surely was odd, the way he reacted to Judge McGuire's rejection of him. Acted like it never happened, that he hadn't wanted to marry Janie. George began to feel something like sympathy for Will. It couldn't be easy seeing John happily hiring fiddlers and arranging for bondsmen for the wedding in a month or two. But then Will always courted his own catastrophes. Hell, he welcomed them with open arms.

He neared the town and strolled down the street. It was unusually quiet. In the freshness of the morning, with the road raked and the porches of the one-room cabins swept, and with the morning mists rolling off the foothills, this Sodom could as well be the Garden of the Lord. The new minister's boy Rob was out with a fishing rod, barefoot, ready to try the Water Pass. He was trying to look as if he belonged to the town but there was uncertainty in his eyes. He would probably enjoy getting to know some other young tadpoles around here. George gave him a wave of the hand.

The Black Rose was a confusion of smells when he opened its creaking, hinged double door. Spirits, of course, and fried onions, and stale body odor, and sawdust. And something worse having to do with rats or dogs, he believed. How often were they doing their rodent chases?

The innkeeper's wife was sweeping the area under the tables in the bar room, pushing them back as she went.

"Wouldn't it be easier to push them all back?" George wondered aloud and she shot him a scornful glance.

"I wonder if you have a"—he fumbled in his waistcoat pocket to take out the name given him by McClaren—"Mr. Abraham Richard Fowler staying here?"

"He's here a'right. Ain't very companionable. Come in and went right to bed last night. Called fer hot water, tea, and toast in his room this morning. But I'll call him down fer ya."

And what was he going to say to him?

Down the center stairway of the rude log inn hurried a tall, seedy man with his coat-tail flapping. He came to George and began fiercely shaking his hand. "Understand you want to see me. Young Dickie Fowler's the name. The Yankee Tinkerer, they call me."

"Well, I didn't know that. But the Reverend McClaren tells me you're an honest man with an idea or two, and I'm looking to putting a little money into something good."

The man had a two-day growth of beard. He took a thin bottle from his pocket and downed a swift drink. "Shall we sit a spell in the other room?" They went into the great room of the inn, which was deserted except for the wife-maid pouring suds over the puncheons and preparing to scrub with a brush. George indicated she should postpone her cleaning.

"Well, Mr. McClure, I'm a man of mechanisms," said Mr. Fowler, sitting down in one of the ladder back chairs. "I come from Connecticut, where I learned my trade as a mechanic. Then I developed a fond passion for the parts of watches and clocks, and I larned to do surgery on those useful machines."

George nodded.

" 'Twere about this time that I developed a passion also for an older woman, six yars my senior. We married and 'twere a dismal failure. The woman nagged, prodded, bawled, railed. She led me a merry dance, I can tell you, Mr. McClure. I left her and the squalling brat of ours, poor little cub. But that can't be mended."

"And so you came to invent things?"

"I came eventually three years ago to Maryland. On my way I stopped in New York to see a Newcomen engine work. These marvels and the newer ones they've recently shunted together in England can do things a roomful of men can't do—pump water out of mills, provide power for grinding."

"I have heard bits and pieces of them. But they are just marvels aren't they? Can they really do anything water power can't do?"

The other man's eyes glittered. His hand gripped the edge of the sticky table. "There's power aplenty in these machines. Someday they will do the work of horses, raise beams, move giant wheels."

"And have you developed any models of your own?"

Fowler lowered his voice. "McClure, last year an idea came to me. I was walking down a road in Baltimore when a carriage came by just as I was hit with a sharp pang in the knee. Rheumatiz. Why, I thought, could not a steam carriage take people from one spot to another and save them the pain of walking?"

"Not to mention the expense of keeping a horse."

"It has been tried in France—steam has been harnessed to an artillery carriage, but it can only go one way."

"So you have plans to make and sell steam carriages to take people about?"

"No, no," Fowler said impatiently, taking out his bottle again. This time he offered George a swig. Out of politeness George raised it to his lips, but suddenly put it down.

"That's not rum. Nor whiskey either. What is it?"

"Laudanum. Spirits of opium," the man said in a sneering whisper. "I take it for my nerves on physician's advice. Well, I worked on plans in the root cellar." He leaned closer to George. "The problem, McClure, is the greed in the human heart." George raised his eyebrows, not following the argument.

"I mean, in working with mechanics, beware of the thief. He lurketh about to snatch your genius, pluck the idea child from your very brain. Other devices I have invented have been pirated. Yes, stolen." He became increasingly more harried-looking. "But as I worked, I saw that the steam carriage would not serve in our cities. Do you know why?"

"No," George answered, trying to puzzle it out.

"The roads. Potholes, mud, filth. Damn things are impassable for horses, let alone a carriage that has to go without jolting. Now when all the roads are macadamized, with stone and tar—then it's possible. But little Dickie is a clever soul. Clever, yes." His face clouded. "It is just that my fortunes are bad." He pounded the table with such vehemence and wrath that George jumped.

"McClure, I am fortune's whipping boy. Let me tell you a little story. When I was but a stripling on the farm in Massachusetts I put out a roaring fire in the kitchen of the ancestral manse. One of seven children I was. Yes, seven. I was badly burned but instead of praising me, my older brother boxed my ears. Beat my arms and shoulders black and blue for my trouble. And it was the first of a long line of mischances. But let me go up to the room and get my drawings for the inventions."

While he was gone, George let the scullery woman come in again. She sloshed her rag mop about under the table, dampening his hose. He lifted first one foot, then another, off the floor and thought about this odd man. There was something almost demoniac about him. And yet, genius, clearly genius was there. Could he have anything worth investing in?

The plans, once Fowler spread them before George on the table, showed not a steam carriage, but a boat, a narrow keelboat with an intriguing powering system. Twelve paddles circled around, in and out of the water, propelled by a chain-drive and gear steam mechanism in the middle of the boat.

"Have you shown this to anybody, Mr. Fowler?"

"Little Dickie, if you will. I showed it to nobody else but. . ." he looked about to see who listened, and then gently beckoned George over to him. "Thomas Jefferson."

George could not help but be surprised.

Little Dickie Fowler continued, "I wrote the governor a letter, and to my chagrin he never answered it." He seemed to stare at the round, threadbare posterior of the scullery departing out the door with mop and bucket. Then his choler seemed to rise.

"Wanted it for himself, the mechanism. Avarice rose in his gorge at the sight of my beautiful boat, I know 't. I waylaid him on the streets of Annapolis and asked him about my plans. Did he know 'em and why hadn't he answered me? He feigned ignorance, Mr. McClure. So I shook my walkin' stick right in his face and pulled his nose."

George was almost out of his chair. "You pulled the nose of the signer of the Declaration of Independence? The governor of Virginia?"

"Later I regretted it, naturally. But it shows you how I don't get m' due. Not at all." George turned his attention to the plans, trying to make out just how the machine actually worked.

"Yes, well, these plans are certainly interesting. I think you may have something here. What would it take to put it into action?" he asked.

"I'm looking for subscribers, sir, one to three large ones. I need at least a thousand pounds for this. You can't make bricks without straw. I want enough to produce this boat once it is proven. We would rent a space in, say, Lexington and hire boiler men.''

"Why not work in someplace like Philadelphia?''

"I think the Southwest is the new territory. The old East is about played out. Problem is that in this country none of the locals know steam. Maybe we'd get us a man from England. I look to test it within a year, at most a year and a half. The profits could be immense.''

"How could it be used practically?''

"Thousands still coming into Caintuck each year. Use it to ferry 'em from Pittsburg. And freight. Could take a load o' hogs all the way to New Orleans in a few days.''

George's head was spinning. "Provided the Spanish open up the territory to trade with us. . .''

"Naturally. Well, what do you think?''

"It is—intriguing. Certainly. I must have time to ponder it, perhaps talk it over with my friends here. . .'' Fowler leaned across the table and suddenly grasped George's lapels.

"Don't talk to nobody. I don't want avarice to waylay this invention of mine.''

"Mr. Fowler, I feel I should speak to my—uh—minister. He will respect the confidence of the matter, feel assured.''

"I never feel assured of anything. Never trust anybody but myself.''

"I shall see you tomorrow.''

"Mr.McClure, it seems to me the man is a real eccentric.''

"True, Miss Jordan, but he is a genius. And he is honest.''

Reverend Jordan had excused himself from the supper table. He had no advice for George after all, except to say that if McClaren recommended the man's character he couldn't be all bad. Miss Jordan was clearing away the supper things.

"It's not his honesty or character I'm thinking of. And it sounds like the plans have real promise, although I can't imagine why someone would want to risk getting blown up by a boiler to take a boat ride. It's that. . .'' she pondered a moment.

"Yes?''

"There are things about a person that don't have to do with intellect, or even honesty or character. Things you learn to read from a face, a gesture—I don't know.'' She took the dishes to the bucket and sat down, her face in her hands. "You mentioned you were educated to love reason, Mr. McClure. What was your education? I'd be curious to hear about it.''

George hesitated. He had never really told anyone about it. The years with Rafe Emison had molded him, were indeed his core. For unknown reasons that core was tender. But he felt like telling Jean Jordan the story.

"When my father discovered I had some musical ability, he asked his friend Rafe Emison, who lived not far from us, to instruct me. I took the little fiddle that father bought in Philadelphia and walked the two miles twice a week. But soon Rafe told Father he noticed what he called 'an unusual spark' in me and contracted, business-like, to teach me as a school pupil. I was the only one, although he taught his own children and after me, at least for a while, his nephews Ash and Hugh in like manner.''

"What was he like?" Jean asked.

"Rafe was—a sage of the backwoods. A frontier Cicero. He was stranded in the backwaters of life by a church that didn't understand his efforts at reform, and he stagnated in Cumberland County among the oxen and flax fields. Somehow, I was a catalyst for a reawakening in him. All the frustrated energies, the undiscussed ideas, the lost opportunities swirled up in a cloud from him and finally settled on my head."

"Quite a lot for a young boy to have to bear."

"Oh, I was eager enough to learn, rabid even. I felt the same way he did, boxed-in where no books were read except the Bible. I taught myself to read it when I was four. We began with simple English chapbooks and then poetry and English history. I went through them in about a year of visits. Then we started Latin declensions, read Caesar, Pliny, Cicero. We would sit outside with bees humming and the plump mill going 'chunk, chunk,' grinding corn, and talk about a time two thousand years ago. He moved in to help his son Ash with the store, and I rode the horse to Carlisle and continued lessons, and sometimes stocked the shelves.

"He had a copy of Caesar's *Gallic Wars*, and he let me borrow it. I took it home just as a blizzard was starting one January, and I read it all one night. I was about twelve. I remember my mother getting out of bed, putting another blanket around me, and throwing logs on the fire so I wouldn't freeze. I think I really lived for the first time."

"But Rome is dead. What has your life to do with such a place?"

"It's long dead. But it was my mind that was coming alive. The Helvetians Caesar attacked, the British aborigines he saw wearing blue paint—it was the South Seas, the Northwest Passage, the moon to me."

Jean looked at him with tender eyes, understanding.

"After two or three years of this, he introduced me to Horace. Said I was ready. He read me the poem of the fountain of Bandusia. I can see him now, sitting on a bench with the pickle barrels, his eyes shining, running his fingers through his thinning hair '*O fons Bandusiae, splendidior vitro*. George,' he said, 'the life of the mind is all there is that has value. Everything else, youth, passion, the love of women, pales and passes, but the mind shines on like a single star in the morning sky when everything else has set. And your mind is a fine one.'

"So I came to love Horace for the same reasons I loved Emison, for wit, urbanity, and calm wisdom. Horace's writings seem to mean sense to me in a world where savage emotion and brutality ruled. My brother drank gallons of whiskey, my father died in the Indian wars, and all around us neighbors lived in fear of their lives. But Emison and I found solace in Horace. . . 'When life's path is steep, take solace in a calm mind,' Horace says.

"Following that, I had two years or so of Greek, and then Rafe grew ill. But that's enough of my education, Miss Jordan," he said, rising from the table and stretching his arms above his head. "How about the results? Do you find my education adequate for interesting conversation?"

"Certainly for that, Mr. McClure, but the needs of the moment may demand more from you. The best test of your education will be in the decisions you make in life. And now, Mr. McClure, I need your help on an entirely different subject."

"I am yours to command."

"It's the rats."

"What?"

"Young Robbie McClaren told my father that there is to be another rat-catching in the tavern tonight." She smiled secretively, even naughtily. "I have it in my mind to break it up, and I want your help in the conspiracy."

"Break it up? I do not think the young swains of the village would take to that very well, Miss Jordan."

"But I do not believe they would do more than complain if I make a scene. My father is grudgingly admired about these parts, and I believe I am too. They will do no more than loudly protest. Besides, I do not care. It is beyond bearing to torture poor creatures, even rats, for amusement."

George McClure offered his mock bow again. "I am an adventurer. Take me in on the plan."

And so at nine o'clock following a Methodist class in town, Jean Jordan and the boarder at the Jordan house, George McClure, could be seen advancing toward the Black Rose Tavern through streets lit only occasionally with tar-dipped torches. He carried a loaded rifle, she had a large linen bag under her arm.

The raspy wheeze of a tin whistle came through the tavern's open window along with the sound of drunken laughter. George McClure looked through the window into the shadowy interior. A group of men surrounded a man who was showing off the suit he wore. George could hear him telling them that " 'twas made all from the leg skins of Injeeans. Soft as a baby's belly," as he chortled and preened himself. In the corner was the rat pen, being readied for the night's entertainment. Sure enough, "Bluebeard" was there. His dog was on a leash tonight, and he was kneeling on the floor talking to it.

"Look who is here, Mr. McClure," Jean said in a low voice. She found Rob McClaren lounging outside the building.

"Since we moved from the tavern, Pa don't like me to hang around here. I don't want to drink; I just want to watch."

An inspiration hit George. "How would you like to help us?" he asked the young man. "We are part of an escapade." He took him aside and whispered for a moment. The youth smiled, spat on his fist, and stamped it with the other fist. It was his silent version of the word "whoopee."

The trio walked through the open door. The man with the Indian-skin suit walked over to the rat pen and the action began. "I give you the smallest brown one first, in, say two minutes," he was telling a gentleman who wore the blue breeches of an old Virginia continental soldier, a sailor's jacket, and a round felt hat. He must have visited the same store I did for his clothing, thought

George briefly. The man tallied the bet on a piece of paper; others clustered about, shouting their bets.

No one really noticed Jean Jordan. There were a few other women in the crowded room, travellers who were staying in the rooms above. Strange noises began in the bag she carried. It began to change shape every few seconds, lumping and jumping about.

Jean whispered in George's ear a brief second. He cleared his throat and announced, over the noise of the crowd and with his rifle obvious in his hand, "I have been deputized by the magistrate of this town to remind you that you are in violation of Virginia's gaming law. Bets may not be placed on animals within settlement limits except under certain specified conditions. I have here a written order from him."

The men glared at George but did not notice the small woman behind him or the boy waiting in the corner by the door. Snarling voices began to voice defiance to the law. "Well, we aint gonna stop it, Mr. Deputy, if that's who you are, until this pertickler match is over. And mebbe the whole evenin'." "Who's that big-headed, red-haired, son-of-a-bitch anyways. . ." Then, having made her way up to only two feet from the rat pen, Jean Jordan opened her bag. In an instant the enormous pussycat Oberon had sprung into the pen, like an angel of retribution.

Amidst tremendous yowling and yapping, the cat flashed about, boxing the small dog on the chops with sharp claws until it leapt from the box, sending the terror-stricken rats fleeing about the pen with high-pitched screeches. Men tried to fall back and "Bluebeard" shook his fist and attempted to get at George through the crowd. The little Pandora who loosed her hoard of evils slipped away after quietly putting down one of the sides of the pen.

Women shrieked and jumped for benches as rats ran under their skirts, and the barkeeper, the only man with a grain of sense in the crowd, entered with a broom and began sweeping the rodents toward the door. Some of the rats escaped upstairs. Meanwhile the dog scooted among the men's legs with Oberon hotly pursuing him, and the man with the Shawnee shirt was spilled unceremoniously onto one of the standing benches, upsetting it.

The dog now beat a retreat, with claws slipping on the grit of the floor as he careened toward the edge of the room. His pride wounded, the terrier stood, back to the wall, growling defiance and baring tiny sharp teeth. He had not covered the flank well enough, however. From the right, unseen young hands descended on him, "bagged" him, and carried him out the door. Jean picked up Oberon under his forelegs, and the cat unwillingly departed, hurling threats over his shoulder at the foe.

Hurrying up the road, Jean and George laughed uproariously, Rob McClaren joining them. Finally they reached the wagon.

"That was the most fun I've had since we left Virginia," Rob said. "They'll be gettin' rats outa people's beds all night in that place."

"Good you're not in there anymore, then. I hear your folks are settled in a cabin now," George said to Rob. "I think when we leave you off home, we'd better stop by and tell them why we recruited their son to be a dog-snatcher.

I hope they can accept the explanation. If I get tarred and feathered, I can use the assistance of the new minister in town.''

"Well, if anyone deserves to be tarred and feathered, it's me," said Jean, smiling. "I involved both of you in this. But remember, we were just the arm of the law. I think that will protect us from any problems.''

Reverend Jordan was waiting at the wagon. He had neither approved nor disapproved of the scheme, but he was mildly interested in the details. "Drove the money changers out of the temple, did you, with the whips. There's always room for that in Christianity.'' He was a tolerant man. He too, however, expressed concern about Rob's place in the evening's activities. "What will your parents say?'' he wondered.

"They'll understand, I bet,'' the boy answered. "Ma has been prayin' for me to do somethin' good for a change, and maybe she'll see this as a first step towards salvation. Riddin' the earth of a few rats and confoundin' a few more can't be all bad.''

Precocious lad, this, George thought. He has good prospects.

Before they climbed into the little wagon, George let loose the dog, who scurried in the direction of the tavern. "So much for 'The Feist,' '' he said. "We have at least cramped his fighting style for a while. But then, pride goeth before a fall for all of us. He will probably find himself *canis non gratis* among his former friends.''

The minister clucked his tongue at the horses and George looked at the girl beside him, exultant and merry. This gem indeed shone in many different lights. "We were fortunate indeed, Miss Jordan, that the magistrate is one of your father's new converts.''

"Yes, I didn't think you recognized him as the man who testified about having the shrewish wife and then changing until I told you tonight at the meeting.''

"We needed him on our side. I thought the laws would be similar to Harrodsburg's even out here. I wonder if he would have felt the same way about enforcing 'em a month ago?'' He smiled at his companion. "Maybe Methodism does have some practical value in spite of all the groaning.'' She shook her head reproachfully, but she did not stop smiling.

It was inevitable after all the excitement, with Oberon ensconced on the settee and the Reverend father at his desk in the cabin, that George should walk outside with Jean and take her hand with no little feeling.

She did not withdraw it, but when he brought it to his lips to kiss, she turned away.

"Oh no. This cannot be. Mr. McClure, it is all my fault. I have led you on.''

"Miss Jordan, Jean, I am going to ask your father for permission to court you.''

Her face turned as red as it had been in the tavern, but not from elation. "Come here and sit beside me on this bench.''

Obediently he sat beside her on the porch, not really listening. He wanted to put his arms around her as they sat on this pine log bench, to kiss her, but he sensed she would not wish it. What a sweet, small, flower-like thing she was. He wandered in a blissful heaven where birds sang. Of course she was protesting—it was common for women to protest when men declared their infatuation.

"I will never marry. Long ago my chances for that were dashed through my own mistake, and I have chosen another life now. I am sorry. You mean a good deal to me." She looked down at the ground, not really noticing the three or four bright red maple leaves lying there. George was forced to listen. His mind came out of its romantic wanderings among birds and flowers, and shifted gears gratingly.

"Let me take a little time to tell you the story. I think you deserve it, although no one here knows it." She sighed. The wind rustled in the drying leaves above their heads and a night wind came up. Her father, working on a sermon, scraped the chair and cleared his throat a little inside the house. She kept her voice low so the minister could not hear what was being said.

"During the war I often helped my uncle, a surgeon from New Castle with wounded men, there and across the Delaware. We went as far as Freehold, Mt. Holly, even Trenton, taking care of the wounded. He was a good man, and I had little else to do. I expect he would have been called, well, not a Tory, but a sympathizer, one who changed color with the shifting winds." Mt. Holly. George thought so little of those days recently. And she had been there, possibly even at the same time. Fox-and-geese, fox-and-geese, our paths paralleled but did not cross.

"Near Princeton we were engaged to wait upon a British officer who was wounded in one of the skirmishes. Colonel Hastings was his name. Tall as you, with gold hair and the largest, gold-flecked brown eyes I ever saw. A dragoon, and every bit dashing." George turned to look at her directly, his heart in his throat.

"Mr. McClure, George, I will call you, because I will always think of you as my friend, I have ever been a warm-hearted person. All of my love, the feelings which were so aroused by the scenes of suffering and want I saw that year came to the surface as I nursed that man. I fell hopelessly, passionately in love. He encouraged me in so many little ways, playing upon my sympathy. He said he loved me.

"I told my father about him. We had a violent argument and he said he wished to hear no more of this man ever. It was completely unsuitable for me to think of him seriously.

"My uncle removed me from my nursing chores, but I stole away, returning to Princeton. The troops were preparing to move; Colonel Hastings had been called upon to join Howe in New York. He must have me, he would, he said. He could not go without me. His honor, his future in the King's service were in my hands. We would start that very night, be married in New York." There was a long silence. George watched her quiet face, trying to understand what she was saying. The turbulent, passionate girl she was describing seemed as different from this one as embers are from icicles.

"I went. We travelled on horse through British-held territory along the

Hudson, staying at inns near the troops. I could see nothing but him, with that blandishing voice, those gold-flecked eyes.'' She delivered the narrative in a voice as gentle as if she were reading out the hymns. She did not speak for a long moment.

"He had a wife in Kent, in England. I awoke one morning to find him gone from beside me. He left a fellow officer to tell me the story, express his regret. I believe he did love me in a certain way.'' Oberon pushed the door open and came out, heading for the forest and a night-time hunt. Jean patted the cat's back as he walked aloofly by the bench. She turned back to George and with a very slight smile, looked honestly in his eyes. "Some people use words like ravished or ruined for girls in situations like mine. The truth is that no one forced me. I answered what I thought was my heart. I was only sixteen.'' There was a little wistfulness in her voice.

"I do not excuse myself on that ground. What I did not know was that it was not my heart that I listened to, but something else. My true heart I found in a very different way.''

"You have been cruelly used. How bitter you must have been,'' George whispered. Admiration and sadness for her struggled against other, conflicting emotions in him: surprise, shock, and disappointment. He had thought her a virgin flower.

"For at least a year I walked around town like a wraith. All knew about my plight. An abandoned woman, not much better than a harlot. . .'' the word was hard to say; she almost spat it out. Oceans of trouble lay behind the word. He tried to picture her small town as she had told him about it and could imagine the Wisteria-clad lanes, with folks holding on to little children, crossing the street to avoid meeting her.

"I know it must have been horrible on Father, the Establishment vicar in town. We had lost my mother only three years before, and now. . . One night, for want of something better to do in my fretful state, I went to a meeting with him. A Mr. Abbot, a lay evangelist, was preaching in a Presbyterian meeting house. It was a stormy night in very early spring and the wind howled about that house, but I heard nothing except what he said. He had the power to fix you with his eyes, to bore into your very soul. He spoke of the fearfulness of sin and pictured its torments. But he also spoke of the God of Love. He said that no sin, however awful, is beyond the love of God. He described a God I had never known, a Father whose care is infinite and all-Good. Mr. Abbot said God was purely spiritual, the Force of life itself, and that all we needed to do was cast ourselves on that Life and give ourselves to It as little children, and our sins would melt away, like the snows of springtime. That we could walk anew, transformed, like holy things.

"It was what I needed to hear, more than anything. I prayed, 'create a new heart within me, the old one didn't serve me very well,' and my prayer was granted. I seemed to rise right out of that church to see and feel the love of God through all space and time and it covered me so completely my past fell away. It was as if it had never happened.'' She smiled at George, but her thoughts were not on him.

"I joined the small group which eventually became the Methodist society, and to which Father was also attracted. I began to walk with my head up. I no longer felt ruined, I was proud of myself, excited in the new life to which I was called. I began helping others the way I had been helped and in that way I found love and forgiveness.

"I came to see that that would be enough. I could never in honesty and fairness marry. All that was over for me."

Her voice took on a faint edge of sadness. "God forgave, and yet New Castle would not. The time came when I grew tired of being mocked by eight-year-old boys and needed more active employment, so when Father decided to preach the gospel to the heathen in Kentucky, I eagerly came with him. But truly, although he would like to, he cannot fully forgive either. He is a fine man and he loves me, but he reproaches me, brings up my sin. I guess it is the cross I have to bear."

They sat in silence. The rustling of the leaves became louder. Rain was probably on the way. George marvelled at the composure, the honesty, the soul of this woman. And yet, he felt wrenched by the the things she told him. So much had happened tonight. He needed time to sort through the tumbled-up wash basket of his impressions and feelings.

A single tear was on her face; she brushed it away. "I do not ever weep."

"I admire that. Women who weep at every mournful thought disgust me. Tears are like coins; if they are too much in circulation, their value is debased."

She smiled a questioning smile. "One of Rafe Emison's sayings?"

"No, one of George McClure's. Thought of right now. We will talk more later of this. Goodnight." He accompanied her into the cabin and, bidding her and her father goodnight, slowly climbed the stairs to his bachelor's loft.

Chapter XXI

Two days passed before George could get into town to talk to Little Dickie Fowler again. As he finally approached the Black Rose, he wondered whether there would be an afterclap of the rat incident. He opened the door onto the usual morning scene with scrubbing and hangovers. He was getting to know this place pretty well.

A few discreet questions established that (1) "Bluebeard" had moved on, and taken "The Feist" with him to Tennessee (2) as George hoped, almost everyone seemed to think that the whole shebang Saturday night was a pretty good practical joke which livened up the scene (3) the magistrate had stopped by the tavern just last night to be sure no illegal activities were going on. George, breathing a little easier, sent a message upstairs to Little Dickie.

This time the man came bounding down enthusiastically, eating a spice bun. "Mr. McClure, I'm in high spirits. High spirits indeed. Now, have you had time to think about my proposition?"

George waited until Fowler seated himself across from him in the great room. "Yes. I have decided it is a bit too speculative for me. I had my heart set on land."

"Ah, you may be making a mistake," Fowler said. He did not seem too disappointed. Then he leaned across the table. Crumbs hung about the corners of his mouth. "Mr. McClure, I am going to let you in on something. Something unusual. The reason I am sky-high is that I have just heard from the legislature of Georgia that a land claim for three thousand acres that I have in their territory has been confirmed. It took a lot of intriguing, but 'tis legal now."

"Land? Where is it?"

"On the east bank of the river. Y' see, a few years ago I was hired to survey the area, from the Appalachians to the Father of Waters. I took a little time to claim some of what I surveyed m'self. Little else I got for it." A snarl twisted his lips; George was reminded how quickly the man's moods could change.

"Won't there be trouble if the national government doesn't find in Georgia's favor? Somebody else may own it."

"I'll have occupied the claim by then, and I'll make a strong case with whatever state gets it. And besides, it'll take years. I'll already have m' fortune. I plan to realize several thousand dollars just the first year."

George looked astonished. "Whatever will you plant to get that kind of money?"

The other man lowered his voice. "Cotton, man. The mills in England are cryin' for it. These new calicos, combined with the spinnin' machines they've set up, will make fortunes as big as a Persian satrap's. Why, soon they'll be addin' steam power to all the factories. Every woman in Kentucky'll be switchin' from hand-sewn linsey to machine-made cotton."

George thought a moment. It could be true. The new cotton dresses and smocks the women wore already were easy to wash, cool, and comfortable. "But cotton is expensive. And it only grows by the coast," he protested, thinking of the engravings he had seen of coastal cotton on large tree-like bushes, being picked by slaves. If only it could grow here! He began to get excited.

"It ain't really coastal cotton I'm thinkin of. I'm thinkin of greenseed cotton."

George had seen some of this on small plots around Lexington. "All the world knows greenseed cotton isn't a money-making crop. It takes too long to get those sticky seeds away from the fibers. . ."

The other man grabbed his collar. He had done the same thing when they last met. Then it was done in anger, but now he was positively ablaze with excitement he had to share eyeball to eyeball. "I have plans for a machine to take out the sticky seeds from greenseed cotton."

"What? A cotton-de-seeding machine you say?" George could not help but raise his voice. The possibilities were staggering. Before his eyes flashed scenes of porticoed mansions, slaves in livery waiting on his entire family in style (the uncomfortable question of whether he would own any was pushed to the back of his mind), libraries full of beautiful books. . .

"For God's sake man, keep your voice down. Remember, avarice waiting." He took out a small piece of paper and showed it to George. It was a drawing of a drum-like structure with a few movable parts and a hand crank. Little Dickie allowed him to glance at it only a brief moment; he seemed not to want close scrutiny of his discovery.

"How does it operate?"

"Cotton goes into the machine at one end and is forced against revolving fine teeth and sieved to remove the seeds."

"And it works?"

"Of a certainty. I have just completed the idea and tested it in secret yesterday. Come, let us go outside."

They walked down the street and outside town. George was bursting with curiosity and enthusiasm. This was a man of genius indeed. What part could he play?

Little Dickie would not speak until he reached a grove by the road, where large boulders formed a sort of natural croft. The day was cloudy and the sky beginning to lower. "Step inside," he commanded, his voice as gritty as creek sand.

George smiled a little and seated himself on the rock the other man indicated. It seemed as if they might be in a dwarf's lair, planning an attack on a nearby elf grotto. But the protection from the rather sharp wind was welcome anyway.

"Time is everything," Fowler said. "The time has come for this machine. Its mechanism is simple; I'm surprised someone else hasn't discovered it. If I don't manufacture some of these things, get my stamp on the idea and get a patent, then somebody else will this year, or the year after, but certainly within five years. New England has more than one inventor." Memories of misfortunes in the past caught up with him; he began to shake his fist and murmur.

George felt himself caught up in the urgency of the moment. "What will you need?"

"I must pay for the land. Four thousand dollars will get you half ownership. In all frankness I am embarrassed by lack of cash right now and will use the most part of your money to patent and survey the land, get it officially on the books. I'll reserve one thousand to set up a property, hire a few workers and begin manufacturing the machines."

"Ahh," said George emotionally, trying to think. His voice boomed out so loudly that it reverberated off the hills behind the croft. Little Dickie went on talking about his plan, to join a party of men from the inn and settlement going for further surveying, to make tentative arrangements, to have "improvement" cabins built on the acreage, to hire an overseer and some workers to begin clearing fields, and then to return to patent the land.

George listened with only one ear. This could be the opportunity he was looking for. Reason indicated that a plan to buy cheap land to raise de-seeded cotton, and to manufacture the machines that did the new process was as good an investment as he ever heard of.

There was another side to it, though. The man asked for what amounted to all the money. And George did not know how well Little Dickie's machine would work. But after all, wasn't that the nature of speculation? Certainly, everything he had tried carefully to learn about Fowler's skill pointed to the fact that he was a genius. A true genius whose past performance demonstrated he could invent practical machines. These things were what counted in a man, along with honesty. This man had a machine that would make a fortune for the family.

One could not afford to let chances slip down the stream. "You wish a partner, Little Dickie Fowler. I am applying for the job," George affirmed. Excitedly he slapped palms with the man, who capered about the croft jubilantly.

"You'll not regret it, Mr. McClure. This will be the discovery of the century. My name will go down in history as the inventor of the cotton de-seeder, and yours will be writ alongside as the financial wizard who made thousands of pounds from its development."

They discussed details and George, with only a little trepidation, ended by taking off his hat and consummating the deal. "Mr. Fowler, Little Dick, in this hatband is sewn the fortunes of my family for years to come. It represents the hope of my dead father that we be 'better folk,' the scrimping of my brothers, the future of my mother and sister. I am trusting you with it because I believe in your genius."

"Thankee, Mr. McClure," said Little Dickie. "You say it is four thousand dollars. I do not need to take it out and count. We must trust each other, trust, I say. But only the two of us. . ." He looked suspiciously over his shoulder.

"The eyes of jealous greed are ever about," he said. George glanced around also, but saw only a brown squirrel sitting up on its haunches. They shook hands and walked back to the tavern.

"And so," George triumphantly told the minister and his daughter at supper that night, "he leaves on the morrow with a party heading for the Mississippi. He will return in two weeks to give me confirmation of the arrangements, and then I will go back home to await riches." He was merry, his white, freckled face almost as red as his hair on this warm September evening. The minister nodded affirmation, playing absent-mindedly with a forkful of yam. Jean said nothing, but kept her eyes on the piece of fried chicken on her plate. Oberon the cat preened his butterscotch fur beside her chair, waiting for a morsel of chicken wing to come his way. He did not beg; it was beneath his catly dignity.

"And what will you do during the time he is gone?" asked the minister.

"I will need to keep occupied until he returns. Suppose I help you get in the corn harvest. I notice it standing in the fields."

"Why, sir, thank you. I have only two fields, but I need the corn they supply to see us through the winter and buy our few needs. I would welcome your hands. Perhaps we could arrange to pay your board that way."

"No, not at all, sir," said the gentleman-to-be expansively. "I would be happy to donate my services for the exercise and satisfaction I will receive. Or as Horace says, 'These fields themselves are just as good as wealth.' " Was what he just said amusing? Jean seemed to be smiling behind her beaten biscuit. He drew himself up with dignity. They had not spoken much since she had told him the story of her youth. He had not, and would not now allow himself to think about her. He had important fish to fry.

"One other hand will be desirable to get the corn in. A member of the congregation offered to help, but he is ill," the minister said.

"Why not ask Rob McClaren? He sees to have little enough to do. Perhaps we could give him a shilling or two. . ."

"Good idea. Will you take care of it for me, Mr. McClure?"

George nodded, and excused himself to write a long letter to McClure Station, detailing the prospects of the cotton scheme.

Time went by quickly. On the dry land, on the banks of the river which was now reduced to a trickle by long, hot days, George and Rob McClaren cut stalks of almost-cured corn with sharp corn knives and loaded the stalks into a nearby wagon. When the wagon was full, they drove the large horse to the barn.

A day consumed in cutting and loading, then a day or two for the shucking. 'Tis dry enough to shuck, thought George, in this southern climate, remembering how corn used to have to sit out in Pennsylvania before it was shucked. He sat Rob down and both put on cornshuckers the minister furnished, attaching the small leather tools with tiny sharp knives to fit inside the thumb. Starting at the top, they slit the shucks. The tools were to protect fingers which had to rub against the rough shucks; still, when they were done their thumbs were raw and torn anyway. The stalks, with only a touch of green still showing on them, were gathered and bound with hempen cord to make fodder for the cow and horse the Jordans kept.

When the corn crop was in, they began to repair the Virginia rail fence that the cow and horse had bumped down. "You're a town boy, a minister's son," said George. "I may not be the best farmer in my family, but I can show you the science of building fences. I learned it from my dada when I was a tadpole The boy was attentive; it was obvious he worshipped George.

"We're going to have to replace the whole road side of this fence. It's rotted out completely. Building a good fence is like marking out your life. I like to see the edges in life clean, the borders spelled out clear." Once a teacher, always a teacher, he thought. Using a good axe, George taught Rob how to split wood effectively.

"This place has a straight-rail fence," Rob remarked with disapproval. "I like the look of them zig-zag fences."

"Worm fences are good for decoration, but not to do the job. They waste field space with their zig-zags. And they take more time to make and fall down faster." These fall down fast enough, he murmured to himself. It seemed as if farmers spent an inordinate amount of time repairing fences, as cattle and the weather ruined the rails. "We're going to use oak here for the posts," he said, eyeing the wood pile and the rails they had already split.

They set to work early that morning. First they built a fire and charred the posts about three feet up. "That makes a barrier against bugs and rot. We'll sink the posts here and leave an inch or two above ground charred."

Two posts were placed side by side with scarcely three inches between them, then two more a rail's distance down. Later, five slat rails would be forced between the two posts and tamped down with a strong stick. Then grapevine would tie the top rail in place.

By high noon only three sets had been implanted. It would take at least three days to replace the side of fence. That did not surprise George; fencing was slow work. He looked up to see Jean coming over the hill with a basket. "Time for dinner," he said to the sweating boy, who did not need to be told twice.

They sat eating still-warm chicken pie from the basket she gave them. George asked the youth, "Are you a convinced Methodist, Rob?"

"No, sir," he said, "although Ma wants me to be so bad she can taste it. There's three parts of bein' a Methodist, and I guess I ain't done any of 'em." George looked up with interest.

"The first is conviction of sin. You have to confess that your life ain't what it should be and that you want a change for the better. Well, I guess I do have that, you could say. I know all the things I do, the cussin', the card playin', the tricks with bad companions, the gettin' drunk, ain't right. But I ain't ready to do anything about it."

"What's the second part?"

"Justification. That's when God is supposed to speak to you, to make you just, so they say, by His goodness. I ain't experienced that. Then, finally, after you have experienced salvation, you can find sanctification."

"What's that?"

"You lose the desire, and even the ability, to sin."

"Does that really happen to people?"

"Some I've seen. My father, I guess. He's a good man." Rob was quiet for a while, poking with a stick at the dry dirt under the elm where they sat, raising little puffs of dust.

"Could this justificiation happen to you? I mean, how does it happen?"

"Wouldn't mind if it did, I guess. But you can't wish it, or will-power it in, or stumble on it in the middle of a field, like water-witchin'. God sends the lovin' spirit of Christ to you so's you can leave your sinnin' behind and lead a clean, fresh life. They say it's like takin' a bath when God's grace comes. All the dirt goes off and you come out lookin' like a baby." He quit poking the ground and stared straight ahead. George McClure was strangely stirred, but he wasn't quite sure why. Religion was not something he expected to experience, to feel—it was simply something to do.

The work went on with the fence, through hot fall days. Pheasants strutted about across the field from them, their feathers jaunty, and once two wild turkeys crossed the clearing, opening and closing their fan tails. George did not take the time to get his gun from beside a tree where it stayed. There was always time to shoot turkeys, and he had work to do. Finally the new line of fence was completed; then came the repair work.

Finally, as this unusually dry September passed into October, there was a rainy day when Rob did not appear, and George worked alone in the small barn, trying to ready the minister's tools for the winter. It must be difficult not having a son, he thought.

Somehow he enjoyed the work more here than at the station. Maybe it was because he was working for himself, not at John's orders. He oiled harness with neat's foot oil; then he repaired the two axe handles on the wooden shaving horse. As he worked, again and again in spite of himself, his thoughts strayed to Jean. Consciously for the past fortnight he had told himself not to see her slight, strong form working about the house, walking through the field to feed her animals, bringing baskets out for them. He exchanged cordial words with her, she with him, but they did not really speak.

How else could it be? She had banished him from her life, made it very plain that she decided to remain a spinster after her tragic mistake. She did not invite him to church; he did not express a wish to go. He had thought he was in love with her, but she obviously did not admire him, as he thought at first. No, she was as cool and collected as a drink of milk from a springhouse. She did not need him, nor he her. It was one of those insubstantial flirtations one engaged in in life, and cobweb-like, it could be brushed from thought with a hand. Except that he did not find it as easy to brush away as she did.

Why was this, he asked himself sternly. What else could it be but a flirtation after the story she told? She was not, after all, the maid he dreamed of. Even if she cared, an odd, embarrassing thing was between them. Everyone knew you couldn't seriously consider a woman who wasn't a maid. It couldn't be done. He was pining over a vision that was no more than mountain mist.

Why then, did he rise up instantly now when she came hurrying into the shed, her hair loose about her face? Feel his heart leap when she called his name. "Mr. McClure, George, there is someone here to see you. . ." A horseman was at the house and was refreshing himself at her table. It had to be Dickie Fowler. Was it? She did not know because she had never seen him. George bounded up the slope to the cabin.

The man turned his head as George came in. It was one of the surveyors from the Black Rose, one of inn men Dickie had said would be part of the Mississippi party. "Where is Fowler?" George demanded.

"Dead," the man said calmly, rising from the table to wipe his greasy hands on a piece of cloth Jean had given him for a napkin.

George stood perfectly still, breathing a little heavily from exertion of the running climb. "What—do—you—mean, dead?" he said, his mind frozen.

The man realized there was more to the message than he had first thought, and he gravely began to unfold his story. "Our party reached the river nigh onto a week ago and began surveyin'. Little Dickie looked at his lands in a few hours, and then a spirit seemed to seize him. Said he could always hire a overseer and clear up details on his own land in a day or two. What he really wanted to see were the lands across the river. Built himself a raft and determined to cross over, with one other man."

"But that's Spanish territory."

"Shore is. Anyways, Little Dickie and the other man went inland from the river on a trail for about a mile. Stopped to rest. He had been sippin' at his opium bottle for two days straight. Who should come down the trail but a deputation from the Spanish government, a surveyin' party of creoles and Spaniards. They looked at him coolly and asked whatever he was about. Ordered him and the other man out of Spanish territory and pointed guns at 'em. Asked to see Fowler's pack."

A terrible sense of foreboding filled George. He could hardly bear to hear the story continue. "Little Dickie went berserk. He began screamin' that avarice was on the loose and went for his loaded rifle. One of the men dressed up like a foppish militiaman shot him." He shrugged, as if to say he could do nothing about it. "Never said another word."

George's voice came out in a terrible, cracked whisper. "What about his hat? His pack?"

"A hat? Don't know nuthin' about a hat. And the Spaniards have the pack. Good as gone if them treacherous bastards got it. Not that they could make too much out of it. It fell in the river and was drenched."

"Thank you for coming," George said and turned on his heel. He could not even muster enough courtesy to tell the man goodbye.

He went to the field of cut cornstalks and sat on a huge rock by its edge. The rain had stopped. Elm and oak branches beside him in the woods dripped crystalline globules onto the now-moist soil. The new fence row stood proud and clean at the edge of the field. Jean came and knelt beside him; he did not know or care if he was speaking to himself or her. "What went wrong? I thought it out so carefully. He had the gift of genius, and the plan was a good one."

The smell of wet pine was in the air. He turned distractedly to see a few large globes of water wobbling on low-growing, dark-green needles. He looked closer. His face, distorted, was reflected in one of the water drops. "Everything is gone.

John trusted me. Ma has always been so proud of me, my 'book learnin,' as she said. Now see what I have done to them all." He put his head in his hands.

He felt a touch on his shoulder and turned toward the woman beside him, his eyes anguished. "What was it, Jean? If we can't trust a man on the basis of his honesty and ideas, what else is there?"

"There is his heart."

He was silent for a long time and then found himself agreeing. "It may be true. I should have seen that while his mind was strong, it was governed by irrational passions. He seethed with anger, burned with joy, depending on the mood. He was as bitter a man as I have ever seen. And there was the laudanum. I suppose he never cared a bit about me and my family. But I would not admit it." His long arms almost touched the ground. "What is the heart you keep speaking of, anyway? Obviously I must not know it."

She looked at him searchingly. "Everybody talks about the heart. They say a man has no heart for an undertaking, that he has a change of heart, but nobody quite knows what it means. I told you once what I thought it was as a young, misguided girl. But I was wrong. I found out it isn't the feelings. It is what is in us that makes us people, the depth and height of us, the tenderness and humanity that God gives us. I suppose it is the soul."

George nodded and Jean went on. "You have a good heart, George, a kind heart that reaches out. But you have developed your mind too much. Life, after all, finally isn't a matter of reason. It's the heart that gives us hope."

George clenched his fist and said quietly, "*Vitae summa brevis spem nos vetat incohare longam.*"

She looked at him with wide eyes, and he quickly went on. "I'll translate that. 'Life's short span forbids us to enter on far-reaching hopes.'"

Her face flushed. She tightened her mouth and turned on him suddenly. "Why do you think you must translate Horace to me? At a moment like this. Well, *Naturam expellas furca, tamen usque recurret.* And *Virtus est vitium fugere, et sapientia prima stultitia caruisse.* And why only Horace? Why not Cicero? Or Pliny? I can do that, too."

He turned to her in genuine astonishment. "You know Horace? All these times I have been quoting, you have understood? I had no idea. . ."

"No idea a woman like me could know Latin? Well, I know it well and Greek also. Possibly better than you. You took great pains to tell me of your education without ever assuming I had one. As the only daughter of a fine scholar from Oxford in England, I have had years of the classics."

George's mouth flew open. For the first time in his life, he could think of nothing to say. She looked at him loftily for a full moment and then went on.

"And that education was my undoing. Why do you think I thirsted so for experience, for feeling, so that I fell at the feet of the first man I met? My mind was developed, my heart unplumbed. I was an encyclopaedia with nothing worth knowing between the pages." A few drops of rain began to fall, and they both arose, confusion and distress between them. It began to rain furiously. He pulled her back under the shelter of the pine trees and they stood, watching the water fall in sheets.

"I've been such a dolt, such a hopeless ignoramus," he said, turning to her. She looked up at him and her eyes were wide with feeling. Something like a dam seemed to break in him. Floods held back for a lifetime poured out, as he took her in his arms and kissed her deeply, eagerly. She did not back away. The rain, increasing, began to pepper through the branches of the trees and fell about them, dampening their clothing and hair. Uncaring, they stood embracing under the trees, oblivious to everything but each other.

He asked her father for her hand that evening, refusing any other consideration but their complete love and compatibility. She loved him. He knew it; he would not listen to her protests. The minister gave his blessing with some reservation; Jean was a vital part of his ministry as well as his life as a widower.

But, as George spoke again to her at sunset in the woods, as they held each other close and whispered to each other, he sensed he did not have her consent.

"What is it, Jean?" he said. "I know you love me."

"As I had never thought possible. But—I had vowed never to marry, to give my life to my faith. And now if I change, it can only be with a man who shares that faith."

"You wish me to become a Methodist?"

"It is my life and always will be. I am alive and happy today because of the transformation Wesleyism made in me. I could not marry someone who did not share the mission, I think."

He was silent. His mind and soul cried out to her, and his body clamored also, making it difficult to speak. "I must think. This is not the spending of a penny, the promise of a moment." He was making arrangements to return to the settlement area, and he wished to take her with him, to marry her back at Bardstown. The armed party left tomorrow morning. They must come to a decision.

After supper, he took her hand as they sat on the slope above the Water Pass. He looked at this river he had emerged from what seemed a millennium ago. Soon the moon rose, turning the Water Pass into a glimmering band of silver. Dark, tree-clad hills clustered against the moonlit horizon. "It would be so easy to say 'I will do anything for you. I will join your church.' But I have my own faith, and call it what you will, I cannot so easily leave it. Although I think my heart is changed, Methodism is very strange to me. It does not appeal to me. Besides, what would a faith be worth that was so easily put on, like a coat, to please another? I think we are both our own people. When and if we are to marry, it should be as a thing rare among men and women, a joining of hearts and minds as well as bodies." She nodded sadly.

"You will not change your condition?"

One of her rare tears glittered on her lashes, and she shook her head that she could not.

And so, they parted in the morning, as the party of men and women on horseback came by to pick George up, the father bewildered by the turn of events, Jean, serene as always, but sorrowful. George whispered to her, "I will live for the possibility that you will change your mind,'' and he mounted on a horse he contracted to pay for at journey's end.

She nodded her head again firmly and bade him goodbye with small waves of the hand, which continued all the way down the track until, turning, he could see her no more.

That night, as the group camped in a clearing and the women suspended cooking pots on tripods over the fire to prepare dinner, the sound of hoofbeats rang on the road. Instantly men reached for their guns. But the horse that rode into the clearing bore a beautiful woman in a long riding cape who smiled as George McClure helped her down.

"Wait no longer; I've changed my mind," she said, dismounting.

He kissed her, in front of everyone, before handing her over to the women for chaperoning for the rest of the trip. But as they clung, she whispered, "I told you that life was not finally a matter of reason. Well, I have another saying for you, and it is not from Horace. 'Marriage is not finally a matter of religion. It is a matter of love.' So, at least, my father tells me, and I think I want to believe him. He gave us his horse for a wedding present."

"What is in this bag?" George asked curiously as she unclasped a large leather saddlebag. The question answered itself as the sedate, whiskery head of Oberon Cat emerged from captivity.

"The rodents' days are numbered at McClure Station," George laughed, thinking joyfully of the surprised, happy welcome he would meet when he returned escorting his bride-to-be. It might sprinkle a little sugar on the sour news he would be bringing about the money.

They went to see to the horse, taking the cat on a ribbon leash. "What does Oberon mean? I never thought to wonder about it," George asked Jean.

"Oberon is the King of the Fairies in *Midsummer Night's Dream*," said Jean, enjoying the answer immensely. "I am a little surprised you do not know your Shakespeare better. But then, that part of your education may have been neglected. Perhaps I had better see to it."

As supper was prepared, they strolled hand in hand. George, holding back a smile, could not resist one last Latin offering to her, "With you I should love to live, with you be ready to die,—*Tecum vivere amem*—" She put her finger across his lips.

"Thank you. I know. And that's the last Horace you'll ever say around me."

And it was.

Chapter XXII

And John McClure became the father of James B., born the year after he married Jane McGuire, and, later, Mary, Margaret, Elizabeth and John Wedge. His brother William, marrying sixteen-year-old Margaret Mossman, fathered John, Elizabeth, Archibald, Charles, May, Will, Jr., Louisa, Malinda, and Caroline Jeane.

And Dan'l McClure and Martha Bard were the parents of John, Thomas, Charles, Joseph, Mary, Martha, Daniel, Elizabeth, Esther, James and Jane.

George McClure became the father of Catherine the year after he married Jane Jordan, and afterwards Polly, Margaret, Robert, Cynthia, Patsy Jane, George, Jr., William, James S. and John.

Jenny McClure and James Scott became the parents of Ishmael and John Robert.

This list, recorded so faithfully in Jane McClure's family Bible brought from Ireland, does not mention the over a dozen McClure babies who did not breathe, were born and left the world after a few days, or succumbed to fevers in their early years. These were babies like little James, whom Dan'l and Martha McClure watched one night in deep winter while his year-old life faded and flickered and died. His name was not even recorded in the Book. It was not that Dan'l and Martha did not love him enough to put in his name. It was just that there were so many living ones to think about, and parents expected to lose one of three babies born to them. Little James's face became a dim memory which eventually faded so that his parents could not even recall, try as they would, what he had even looked like. They decided to give his name to another child in the family. Life must go on, after all.

The family Bible must take a different tack with Jenny McClure, whose entries are really rather meager in comparison with the others and happened under slightly different circumstances than the usual yearly births.

James, Jenny, and Marguerite Scott had been three nights already on the road on this early October day in 1787. They were travelling from the Ohio to McClure Station and would be home tomorrow night. James Scott was setting a leisurely pace, walking the horses and stopping early in visitor stations, and Jenny was getting to know the mother-in-law she met for the first time earlier in the week.

Marguerite Scott would be making her new home in Lexington, and they had stopped there so James's mother could see the rapidly growing city and select items for her small, new home. She admired fripperies and lace within one of the new general stores along the main street and, after spending gold from her substantial purse on the basic supplies of living, she bought a length of fine cotton cloth for a new gown. Then the three of them watched sleek thoroughbred horses which were being groomed in lots on the edge of town.

Now two nights later, they were just west of Harrodsburg on their way to visit McClure Station. They had stopped at a settlement which provided a "stranger's cottage" for frequent visitors heading across the trail toward Bardstown. James built up the fire from wood stored outside the cabin; Jenny fried bacon and added beans that had been soaking in a saddlebag as they rode along. With a couple of glugs of molasses and chopped onion and the fresh bread they had bought in Lexington, it would make a decent supper.

Jenny's mother-in-law wiped off the table; she was not "handy at cooking," as she said. She was used to servants waiting on her. Jennie watched her from the corner of her eye, dignified, dressed in black wool so soft it could have cradled a baby. If they had one. Jenny's spirits, which were unusually high that day, fell.

She was barren. The thought was never far from her mind. It might recede as she worried over the family's struggle to regain prosperity since George had lost the fortune. She might momentarily forget it as she exulted over her mother's success in the weaving shop, where increasingly prosperous settlers ordered tablecloths and coverlets woven in handsome blocked patterns. But every time she ran into Dan's little Jackie, now one and precocious and John's Jim, toddling after his raven-haired mother to tend the horses, the thought returned, with almost physical pain. She and James had no children.

Lately, she could hardly bear to help her favorite among the sisters-in-law, George's wife Jean, care for flaxen-haired little Catherine, to watch her as she ran around ordering her boy cousins about in her precocious, funny prattle.

Somehow the presence of Marguerite Scott, who should have been a grandmother by now, was an unspoken reproach to Jenny. Her sisters-in-law brought forth their children each year since the marryin's, but she, Jenny, had not even quickened. Why? As she served up the beans and bacon on the trenchers they carried in the saddle bags, she thought for the fortieth time that month that if she were only more buxom in bed. . .

She called her husband in from tending to the horses. He entered, a smile of encouragement lighting up his homely face. "I'm here, Jenny girl." Gentle, hard-working James Scott was as expert at repairing the family's guns or most anything else mechanical as he was at growing garden things. He held her heart, as he had from the moment he had teased her as Indians approached on the Ohio River. But the feelings she had for him did not translate into passion. Perhaps that had something to do with it, she did not know. Other women she knew who admitted they did not care for the sexual part of marrriage had quickened many times and borne many children. She was healthy; she knew that. But for her each month was one of wild expectancy and then stormy tears.

Having a child dominated her mind night and day: a baby to hold in her arms, a little cradle to make a quilt for, to polish with lemon oil. For her, pregnancy was a ship on the horizon, receding ever as she neared it, candy held up above a child wildly jumping for it.

"The bacon is good," the woman across from her said. "I like it with lots of sweetening, as we had in Louisiana." Jenny loved Marguerite Scott's French accent. She slid liltingly into "the's" and "that's" and made the word "Louisiana" sound almost musical. French words were butchered around here; people called the city on the Ohio "Lewisvel, on B'argrass Crick." James had told Jenny before the women met that his mother never lost the tang of the French tongue she had spoken when his father had met and won her on one of the fur selling trips he had made to the plantations around New Orleans.

"I'll relish hearing her speak. Maybe she could teach me to say a few things," his wife had said. Jenny had painstakingly taken the time to correct her own pronunciations of the few French words she knew as best she could. The French fascinated her, with their citified ways and languorous, mysterious language.

"Mother is a Catholic and superstitious," James had said with an odd note in his voice, as he had read the letter from St. Louis. It had said that now that her sister was gone and her brother living in France, Marguerite had decided to come to live in Kentucky. It was surprising to Jenny. James had barely mentioned his mother. He had said they were not particularly close. Although he seemed to love her, there was some sort of strange distance between them. Perhaps it was religion; his father had been a Calvinist if he was anything at all and James went, but not often, to Presbyterian preaching at the small "meetin' " in the neighborhood. Marguerite Scott was a devout Catholic.

As Jenny cleared up the supper things, she thought about her impressions of her mother-in-law. Although Marguerite had been pampered, both in Martinique where she had been born, and in French Louisiana on the plantation where her family moved, she was not a spoiled rich woman. Restrained, strong in character, she was almost a little somber in disposition. The steel in Marguerite's character had drawn Jenny to her, and Marguerite had begun to form ties with her daughter-in-law immediately.

The wind began outside the cabin, but the older woman said she wished to go outside anyway, and Jenny unlatched the door to let her out, then followed. Outside Jenny tried to hold back her hair as it blew in the wind that began to howl down from the northwest. Marguerite went to the small privy up the back path, then stood staring into the woods. A few leaves clung to branches, and the newly fallen carpet of leaves on the forest floor stirred and swirled into the air. The wind moaned at them like a child from among the bare branches. "Let's go back," Jenny shouted.

But still Marguerite stood, dress blowing about her legs, her thin, almost masculine form outlined in shadow against the bare-branched forest. Jenny hurried to the cabin door.

She was still shaking when Marguerite Scott came in the door. "A rainstorm brews," was all her mother-in-law said.

They sat before the fire. James had gone to the bed in the loft while they were outside, exhausted from his exertions on the trail. Silence filled the cabin, but it was not uncomfortable. Finally the older woman spoke. "You are not happy," she said.

Jenny did not look up. She thought a long moment, then she said, "Well, I have my bad and good days. Of course I want a baby. Doesn't every woman? But I love James very much." Her mother-in-law seemed to relax a bit. Perhaps she had been afraid the marriage was under a cloud. Jenny's voice was urgent. "It's just that ever since we came here—I don't know. I don't think I like Caintuck very well."

"Why is that?"

"There is somethin' odd here, particularly at night. You'll think it strange—it is as if voices call to me, unhappy voices."

Marguerite was instantly alert. "Tell me about them. Perhaps I have had some experience in what you feel."

And so, as the wind howled and the night settled its wings about the cabin in the wood, Jenny told of her dreams. She told of the dream she had by the river palisades, of the Ruddell's Station massacre, and the other dream of the long-ago, when flaxen-haired women and children were brought to that very river to die.

She laughed a little as she finished the stories of the dreams. "And so, it seems, I am haunted."

Her mother-in-law did not join in the laughter. She looked at her, her handsome face and cool green eyes illuminated by the firelight. "You are a sensitive."

"What?" Jenny did not know the term. "People always say I'm sensitive, to creatures, to people's feelin's."

"No, it is not that." She sighed. "I am going to tell you a story. Can you be patient to hear it?" Jenny nodded.

"My people came to the country around New Orleans forty years ago, when I was but a small child. We came from the dark islands of the Indies to become planters. The old governor, Bienville, had just left, and the colony was beginning to thrive. We bought, really received from the crown, lands on the river near New Orleans. Here my father with many slaves set up a plantation to grow oranges and other crops.

"It was a life of mixed benefits. There was indolence and luxury, but also disease and the hardships of an insufferable climate. New Orleans was turning itself into. . ." she laughed a little ruefully, "well, they called it 'Versailles among the swamps.'

"But it was that swamp I hated most. Every night it closed in on us, breathing out its pestilential smells, its noxious gasses. I tried to stay away from the swamp, but it was not easy. My mother was dead of the yellow fever, my sister was ill of it, and my brother too small to talk to. I had few friends, little to do. I found I stayed much with the slaves, who were kind to me.

"At night, I came to enjoy going with them to meetings held in the clearings in the swamps. Here they lit kerosene torches to keep away the insects and to illuminate—their rites. 'Voodoo' it is called. At first, as I watched men with glistening, bare chests, wildly painted, dance to drums and strange songs chanted, I was terribly afraid. But gradually I came to know, to understand. They were conjuring, calling something up. But the something was out of their own brains. It existed, all right, and it was horrible, but without them and their fright, it could not live.

"I began to see that I had special powers of some sort. I was a sensitive, not a medium, but a sensitive. I saw things others did not. Especially I could recognize evil in its many forms. I went into New Orleans with my father and tested what I believed. It was as if I could see into the hearts of the people I passed. One was a procurer who was beating his unfortunate wenches, one an army officer flaunting a woman not his wife. The governor of the city walked by and I knew, somehow I knew. The money sent from France to supply that garrison was going into his pocket. Enormous sums, and I could read them.

"It was a rare gift, I think, and your gift is similar it seems, but not exactly the same. I came to believe the types of evil are related to the earth. There is the evil of the mountain, which is what people in high places practice. Here are your Mesdames de Pompadour, your governor's corruption, bribery, deceit. Then there is the error of the fields, where common people do common things, robbery, ravishing, adulteries. There is the evil of the cave, where brilliant men dupe others, lawyers, charlatans, encyclopaedists, priests." One of the shutters blew open, and Jenny rose to close it.

"Worst of all by far are the evils of the swamp. These are the elemental, murdering evils which arise with miasma to pollute and kill. The mark of the beast is on the swamp, and the dark river is its cousin, flowing like blood." Into Jenny's thought a vivid picture came of the Kentucky river roaring with the blood of the innocents for scores of generations. Tears came to her eyes.

"One night I was told not to come to the voodoo rites. I was warned not to set a foot near the clearing. A special meeting was going to be held at midnight."

Jenny felt the hair on her scalp rising. The woman's voice rose, competing with the rising of the wind outside.

"But of course I went. I went from curiosity, and from scorn of the power I felt in the clearing and now read so well.

"I crept into the trees by the light of an eerie moon. Bitterns made their odd cries somewhere far off.

"The usual songs, chants, circle dances went on. But then, from up the river, canoes came. From them stepped red men, Choctaws from somewhere north. They spoke, and a Frenchman with them translated. There was to be an Indian uprising and they were asking the slaves on our plantation to join with them, to murder all the whites in the plantation, move on with them, and take New Orleans. One of the slaves seemed to go into a trance. He pranced about in affirmation; all the rest sang a weird song. But his trance was not complete; as this slave leader came near my hiding place, the moon came out full bright and caught the glitter of my eyes.

"Without alerting the others, he came to me, catching me up and holding me by my shoulders. I looked deeply into his eyes. Lusts, blood hates and hideous ecstasies of dark evil seemed to swim there. I read them and I was not afraid." Marguerite clutched the crucifix about her neck. "God gave me the power to resist.

"I wrenched my way free and ran for the house to raise the alert. He grabbed a rifle and ran after me. He shot, but he missed, and the rest seemed immobilized. By the time they gave chase, I had roused my father and his retinue. They raced outside, and the conspiracy was unmasked.

"Never for a moment was I really afraid." Marguerite seemed to come back to the small cabin from far away, to look at the transfixed young woman before her. She leaned toward Jenny.

"You, too, have the gift, but you see it now in your night dreams. Another time you may feel your second sight differently." Neither woman spoke for a long moment, then Marguerite added, "I am disturbed because you do not yet clearly know how to read the evils portrayed to you."

Jenny was suddenly sickened, confused. "Why is't necessary to read evil? I want to know only good. . ."

The other woman's voice was harsh in the growing darkness that enshrouded them. "It is not enough to know good. We must be able to read evil also."

Jenny rose, turning her face from the dying fire, from the woman's piercing eyes. "No, no. It can't be true. I want to look only at good things. I can't make myself look at evil ones, never have been able to. . ."

The other woman rose. "You must, my dear, you must. There is no other way. You as a sensitive must know the many masks of evil to rip them off. Beneath the masks is the blank stare of nothingness, for God has all power. But as long as men's minds give evil power, it exists as a force as potent and unseen as electricity. You can win the battle over evil, but you must stare it down, face to face. Go back to the Kentucky River. Shout down its furious stream. Laugh. . ."

"I won't hear any more. I can't stand such stuff. You're making my head hurt," Jenny cried, her hands to her temples. Then she ran to climb the stairs to the loft.

The older woman put her hand again to the crucifix. "Dear God," she prayed, "give her courage. If she does not throttle it, it will end up throttling her." Then, sadly, she went to the little bed with the rope and straw mattress in the corner of the room.

The rain began, finally, pouring down in gushing torrents, snapping branches in the dark woods outside, sending limbs against the shutters. James Scott, awakened out of sleep by the storm, reached for his wife on the pallet beside him and pulled her to him. Jenny felt his arm about her, his presence, warm and alive in the storm. Suddenly rages of emotion swept her, and she lay herself over him, putting her insistent mouth on his. He was a little startled. Jenny had never responded to his embraces like this before. He pulled her closer, touched her in a way she had never cared for; she began to pant. What is happening to me, she thought, flushed with lust which turned her into a heaving, grasping cat in heat.

Moments later, the silence around the cabin was deep and complete. Outside the clouds, black and shredded as crepe, parted to reveal a wan new moon. The storm was over. She lay, scarcely breathing.

Nine months later, after a twenty-six-hour labor through which Jenny raged out of her head, a sickly, squalling boy was born. Her mother-in-law, who had finally reached in with two long fingers to draw him from the womb, named him Ishmael.

Chapter XXIII

And then there is the son not mentioned at all in the family Bible, who is not buried in Upper Indiana Cemetery, whose name does not appear on the McClure memorial.

Asondaki Caipawa, "child of the shining morning sun" in the Miami tongue, son of Dan'l McClure, was growing up with his namesake shining on many of his days, among the woods, rivers, and cornlands near what is now Ft. Wayne, Indiana.

His life was measured in small wonders and fine discriminations, wrapped 'round with the subtle changes of nature. He rose to the sound of the wind in the trees and the clatter of a few pots, and he took the time to observe the morning cooking fire as it smoked white before the flame broke through. Or later in a canoe he listened to the lapping of river water against reeds, while the tap of a red-headed woodpecker echoed around the shore. His language had thousands of words to describe such things as the blowing of grass in a meadow or waves on a lake, the different kinds and colors of squirrels and butterflies. It had only a few to describe technology as it was practiced even then.

This ten-year-old, red-haired Indian boy had an eye for minute changes on the map of Nature's face. He saw crushed grass where bear (maqua) had passed, or the imprint in mud of a porcupine's (akawita's) pawprint. His ear was attuned to the sounds about him in a world mute of the constant din of civilization, but alive with the noise of life in the wild, the boom of ice on the lake, the tiny tap of a nut dropping from a tree onto a leaf.

Asondaki's uncle, Hidden Panther (Kinozawia) spent much time with his tall, handsome nephew, and it was good that he did. The boy's mother (M'takwapiminji) Mulberry Blossom, still comely and supple now in her mid-twenties, naturally doted on her son and waited on him in their bent-branch home covered with bark. But there was a new husband, tall and taciturn, who did not much care for the mixed-blood in his house, and a new baby who hung from the rafter on a cradle board, whom Asondaki must sometimes rock outside in pleasant weather.

Asondaki avoided such women's chores when he could. At ten he was already well into the serious business of learning to hunt. Hidden Panther spent hours showing him how to strip and soak mulberry logs and branches. The ancient grandmothers had stripped and pounded these same branches to weave underskirts; he would use them to make the twanging bows needed even in this age of muskets.

In his forest schoolroom, Asondaki learned the moons of the year starting with Makonsa moon, time of the young bear. "Best time for bear is not in the spring," Hidden Panther said. "When they come from their lairs in Makonsa moon, they are confused and easy to trap, but thin and cross. Better trap a bear in midsummer, when they are fat and lazy, feasting on field mice." He told how the old ones, the Peorias, surrounded and rounded up bears and other animals in circles of smoky fires during Kiolia moon in late fall.

"We are a people of the woods," his uncle said. And he taught Asondaki the skills of the trail he must know, how to bend trees at right angles to show others a direction taken, how to make signs on standing rocks, how to judge animal scat by its smell and look to know which way an animal for the hunt may have gone, how to read the wind. "A good hunter seeking prey will walk in the dew of the morning to deaden his footsteps; one evading an enemy will walk only on rock or in the water if he can. Mask your scent with the oil of bear or with crushed spearmint," his Uncle said, "and carry the right weapons at all times. He who goes to meet the bear with only a twig meets his death instead."

Asondaki had many questions. "Is that a blue racer, Uncle?" he asked, watching one of several snakes that inhabited these boggy places.

"No, that is the father of all snakes, the black snake. He is the smartest of those who crawl on the belly, because he climbs and twines about in trees. Blue racer is frightening to see but not poisonous. But beware of Cicikwia, with rattles and spots."

"Yes. He brings death in his fangs. And he is sacred. He is a prophet." His uncle smiled and Asondaki went on. "When he sheds his skin it is the time to plant corn. I will watch for him."

Through these days in the wood, Asondaki looked on his quiet, light-limbed uncle with admiration bordering on worship. He followed Hidden Panther down a narrow trail to a chain of lakes and heard him say, "We are also a people of the water. Once, before any white man came, we were lords of all the area from the large lake, west to the Grandfather River, south to Beautiful Ohio waters. So we know the waters well. You must observe the strutting ways of sakia, the heron, the croaking of koka the frog, the differences between canvas back, mallard, summer duck."

Patiently Hidden Panther showed him how to burn a canoe out of a log a little at a time with coals of fire blown on with a fire blowpipe. Then his uncle helped the boy make a good beach fire from driftwood, using crumbled birch bark and dried cattail. On it the two of them broiled bass and pike caught with a line and hook purchased at the trading post.

Now, on a certain day in June, 1788, Asondaki waited for his uncle outside a summer fishing camp on the shore of a nearly round lake more than a day to the west of Kekionga, their home. He thought a little smugly of the scene back at his uncle's lodge, when he and Hidden Panther had prepared to leave for this lake camp. His cousins had pulled at their mother's leggings, begging to go and mewling like hungry cats. These two, born after the move to Indiana and after Aunt Swamp Grass died and went over the Milky Way, were not big enough to join in man's camp. They would have to content themselves, he thought with a smirking smile, with gathering mussel shells and crayfish at the river, helping pound corn with mortar and pestle, and playing at warrior. And they could always amuse themselves, young foxes that they were, with the ball and cup game. But Asondaki had other business.

The summer lodge, with its bark roof over poles bent and tied together at the top, and its woven cattail sides, was comfortably placed on a hill overlooking a swampy area leading to the lake. Breezes from the prairie on the hill behind them kept mosquitoes away and gave notice of approaching bear. His uncle was out checking the traps he had set for small game, leaving instructions for Asondaki to fish.

Now for a moment he looked across the marshland and was filled with a deep sense of appreciation at what the Great Spirit had given man. Cattails, their finger-like leaves moving in the cool breeze, lifted fuzzy heads over the entire sweep of marsh, to its far edge, fringed with the glory of the lowlands, purple fingers. Small yellow warblers darted among tree-of-life bushes, some of which were good for dye, others for tea, some poisonous. Asondaki held his breath as a red-winged blackbird suddenly winged its way across the swamp and lit in an aspen rippled silver by sun and wind.

"How I wish I could fly like you, blackbird, free of the earth." He heard its song in a tree. "Twee, twa twa twee, twee, twa twa twee." The early English traders called his people the "Twightwees," perhaps because of the call of a bird like this one. Its last note soared heavenward inquisitively, almost defiantly. "What does life mean, what does life *mean*?" it might have been saying.

Asondaki sighed. We are a people of the woods, a people of the lake, Uncle said, but he did not say a people of the shadow. Changed people, people of trouble. It was the Thing Not Much Discussed. White men often came among them now. Many warriors went to meet the Kentuckians in the south not long ago to try to stop their arrogance. There were sad wails of woe when the brave Miami men returned. Old Chief Moluntha of the Shawnees, smiling and trying to sue for peace, had been wantonly shot by a stupid white man.

This same man McGary, who also betrayed the white warriors at the Blue Licks by his empty-headedness, had asked Moluntha if he was at that awful battle. Moluntha, not understanding, had just smiled and repeated "Blue Licks." Then this McGary shot him dead. He had even said "I'll shoot any Indian I ever see simply for being a savage." There was no living with the white men, the beaten warriors said. Make treaties with them, they will be broken, try for peace, the white devils shoot you by your own cornfields.

Travellers as well as traders came to Kekionga now, the "Blackberry Patch" on the Maumee River near Asondaki's own home camp. They stayed in the French village the traders set up, and their eyes glinted with land-greed. The British and Americans disputed this wonderful land, which the Americans were setting up as their official "Territory." As if they could own what the Great

Spirit gave to the Old Ones, the Peorias, from earliest days.

"The white man can never have it, Manitto will never allow it," his uncle said. But he used the old-fashioned word—Kitchimanitowa, The Great Serpent, which gave what he said a strange, ominous sound. And then he looked silently out the door of the lodge to where smoke from the cooking fire curled away and vanished into nothingness.

Asondaki knew that his uncle and the other men of the council did not know how to stop the white man, who always seemed to do what he pleased. The white man's greed was so silly. There were so few of the bands of Indian peoples, divided but living in the same terrain, Ojibwas and Potawatomis by the Large Lakes, Shawnees on Auglaize and around Piqua, and Kickapoos and other smaller tribes on the Ouabash. Could they not be left alone?

All would be well yet, Hidden Panther said. Now there was one grand council of all Indian men in the riverlands forming, with the Miami chiefs at its head. The Miamis took scalps of soldiers moving supply trains; they attacked isolated white men. And often Hidden Panther was called upon to help talk to the white men about making better treaties. But still the shadow remained.

And there was the other shadow, something that hovered about Asondaki like a bat in the night. He felt it when he saw his light-skinned face reflected in calm water. He wasn't "quite right." He also seemed a little less enduring in games with the other boys, seemed to feel pain a little more quickly.

His mother had told him in the matter-of-fact way of the Indians that his father was a white man. He seemed to remember long ago a bright day on a riverbank with four giant men, one of whom held him and gave him honey to eat. It never meant much to him as a small child.

But lately he heard whispers at the running contests, the games of stick-and-ball. And the wounding blow came recently—his little cousin, repeating what older boys said, had taunted in a mocking voice, "You are American *metis*. The half-burnt stick, tainted wood." He wanted to strangle the little boy, but of course that would not do.

"Uncle, what can I do?" he asked. His eyes begged for the acceptance he did not feel in the tribe.

"You will get acceptance if you earn it," Kinozawia said. "Next springtime you will have your Moon-in-the-wild. Then we shall see what your own courage and your uncle's teaching can prove."

A letter came to George and Jean McClure from Rob McClaren:

"You will be surprised to hear from me, I 'low. I talk to your father all the time, Miz McClure, and he tells me you now have two children. How is your fat cat Oberon? We sure enough had a wild night of it in that there tavern, didn't we? I hope I am spelling this right, Pa is helping me.

"Things are going good for the Methodists down here. We got a real circuit organized now. But then you know that because your Pa visited you last year. The town is growing like a pickaninny in summer and is just as wild as it ever

was. All the talk is still of goin' off to Louisiana, forming a separate state with Spain. Some call it foresight, my pa and yours calls it treason. I helped your pa get his corn crop in and took it up, like Mr. McClure taught me. I'm still not too good at fences.

But I'm not going to be no farmer. A wonderful thing has happened to me, I've experienced grace. Happened right here on the living room floor. I had been out to my usual Sunday afternoon of card playing and fighting. When I got home I felt awful sick. I lay on the floor groaning. My ma got up and went on her knees beside me, and before I knew it, the Spirit moved and I felt changed. A new man, so to speak. The next week I got the call to begin preachin, and I been having meetings all over the area, even into Tennessee.

They are callin me the Boy Preacher. The words just comes to me when I preach, and lots have been made aware of their sins because of it, I think. Trouble is I have run into the Baptists. They are come in here like locusts to the corn crop, wanting everybody to get immersed, dunked for Christ.

I don't want to make it seem like this new religious feeling is a light-o'-love with me. I am sincerely a minister, and every day I think I do find a bit more of God's love in my life. I hope to see you sometime soon.

Yours, etc.

Rob

"Who would have thought it?" George murmured. He held the letter in one hand and read it aloud to Jean as she gave the new baby a bath. Outside the door of the cabin, little Catherine, two and frenetic, was trying to put the snarling Oberon cat onto the treadmill of an unusual dog butter-churner that Dan'l had just finished for them. It was a delayed wedding present, unusable because they had no dog as yet.

"You never know when Grace will come," said his wife. "It comes to all at some point."

"If they are elected to get it by foreordination," George said, with a very slight smile. He and his wife still belonged to different churches, but at least they differed congenially. It was almost a joke between them. George was oiling new boots; winter would soon be upon them and he must walk the premises each day to be sure all was well and fences in repair at the station; that was his winter job. Taking care of the group's stock as well as his own horses was John's, while repairing the line of cabins in the stockade and keeping the wood tools in shape was Dan'l's. Will took care of the wagons and leather and practiced a little bit of the wheelwright's trade on the side. And James Scott took care of all the supplying, going to Bardstown to get the linen yarn Jane McClure now bought instead of making, and the white sugar, salt, soap, and China tea they had come to regard as neccessities. People don't want to live in the woods, George often thought. As soon as they can, they start heading for any new town they can find and buy fancies, gimcracks, geegaws.

Jean's face flushed as she stirred the ashes of the cooking fire. Soon she would need to wash the babies' napkins, and start some hot biscuits. Pity they had to be baked twice a day in such warm weather. A tin oven, that would help. It reflected heat so much better than the spider pots in the coals. Martha in the cabin next door had one. But then Martha also had one of those new toothbrushes. And she was calling her name, the family name, Baird now. French. She said it had been that way in the first place. She was a good woman, though, and had been recently tending her ailing mother a good bit in Bardstown. Dan'l seemed to miss her when she went, and his mother moved up from the Scott cabin to stay with the children.

She picked up the dirty napkins and headed for the door to soak them outside. It was, however, necessary at that moment to rescue Oberon. His tail was being pulled from behind, strongly, and his howls blended with Catherine's laughter and little Ishmael's screams down the way at the Scott cabin. It seemed as if Ishmael never stopped squalling. As she picked up the fluffed-up cat just before it clawed Catherine, Jean looked askance at the tiny, beautiful face of her daughter drawn up in rage at being robbed of her playmate. "You have met your match, you grand feline," Jean said to Oberon.

"What did you say?" George called from inside the house.

"Nothing, nothing at all. I was talking to the cat," she answered, smiling at the silly answer and also at the odd contentment she felt at that moment, as she carried a cat under one arm and a stack of dirty nappies and a yelping, kicking daughter under another, into a home she loved. Winter was sure to pass rapidly in such a home.

The "Moon-in-the-wild" was half over. Asondaki stood, a small, naked figure against the shadows of huge tulip trees. Kekionga settlement and its nearby camps, with the plateau of what were now hundreds of bark lodges housing Miami, Delaware and Shawnee families in villages, seemed to be far away. The only reality was the woods itself, deep and alive with the activity of a May afternoon. Squirrels chirruped and darted about, their tails flashing high, bees buzzed in woodland mayapples, birds sang above clumps of white violets.

A pair of grouse strutted out, in the early stages of nesting. Asondaki quickly leaned behind a tree and reached for the crude ash bow he had made the first week. He shot an arrow he had devised at the hen. Missed! Spreading their tail feathers the family headed for the bush. Well, he would try the slingshot made of the hide of a deer he had found and skinned with a sharp stone. Killed by an animal and only half-consumed, it had been too rank to eat, but its carcass provided him with useful sinews, thongs, and a warm skin to wrap up in at night.

The first day, when he went without clothing or any tools into the wood, he was determined not to show his fear. Still, he thought the slight shaking of his limbs in the cool morning wind might be obvious to Chief Little Turtle, who stood watching as he departed from the main village. "A lam sang kati" (there would be a strong wind), was the only comment he sang out after Asondaki as rain began to fall.

One should not have to start his manhood month in the rain, Asondaki thought disgustedly. It was not a good omen; animals would be hiding in tree trunks, cedar sticks would be too damp to start a good fire. But so it had been decreed, and he was ready to meet whatever came. Well, before he left, he had seen a large spider on a tree outside the lodge when he awoke. Perhaps it was his grandmother watching over him, and that was a good-luck omen.

He did not eat the first day, making and staying in a lean-to while the storm passed through. After he grew accustomed to it, he was not cold. His people always prided themselves on their hardiness. Until the last few years, men had worn only a linen shirt, leggings, blanket and moccasins through the coldest winter weather and a breech cloth in summer, showing off the intricate tattoos they boasted of. So wearing nothing was not much different from the skimpy child's breech cloth he usually wore. His uncle had warned him that his feet would be the thing to worry about. Asondaki had toughened them by putting salt in the bottom of the moccasins. Now he could step on rocks, sticks, even a small thorn and not feel it. "If your feet are tough and warm, your body will stay warm," his Uncle had said.

The second day he set his first snare. Camouflaged with the smell of crushed catnip, he cautiously slipped into a meadow where he had seen rabbits the night before, feeding on lush grass at twilight.

With a rock he first dug a cattail root. Saving some to eat for himself (it had a good, nut-like flavor, rather like the raw potato the white man loved so much), he baited his trap. Rabbits loved cattail root. He bent over a little tree to make a trigger for the trap, tying the top down with some of the sinew. Then he broke off another little tree, and fixed it as a stake in the ground, creating a circular lasso with the bait camouflaged. The rabbit would come up, he told himself excitedly, nibble at the root, and the loop would tighten and fling him in the air, strangled.

He would have to wait, of course, about three hours for his man's scent to leave the clearing. Meanwhile, like the child of hope that he was, he went to chip a new skinning knife from the stone at the river bed. Using the oldest method, he threw one of the pieces of limestone against another, and among fragments and rock dust picked up one with a reasonably good edge. Well, it wasn't the flint that the horseback parties picked up over in the flint pits of Ohio, and it certainly wasn't the trader's knife he was really used to, but it would do.

When he returned to his snare, the sun had come out, sending shafts of misty light into the clearing. His mouth watered at the thought of the feast he would soon have, and he could barely stand to look. Sure enough, a fat, brown rabbit was in the snare. "The Manittos are good," he shouted, capering about the clearing. "I am a hunter on my own. I shall be named Wemiamiki when I return."

Now he must skin and cook the catch. The skinning he accomplished in three minutes, which was about a minute more than it would have taken with a real knife. He gathered tinder fluff from an old hornets' nest, last fall's leaves, and two cedar sticks with just the right feel. Rub, rub, in rhythmic motion, do not allow the wrists to feel fatigue, be ready to toss the tinder fluff in the air and blow at the first spark. He worked for about three minutes. No spark. He rested for perhaps two more. Then he tried again. This time the spark flew off, but the tinder did not catch fire.

Panting and fighting impatience, hunger, and insects that lighted and nipped now that he was still, he determined to try again. But this time he would use his secret weapon. From his deep-set navel he picked out a small cachet of fluff allowed to accumulate for this very purpose. Just a spreading, smoldering glow, that's all I need to be Wemiamiki, All-Beaver, member of the tribe. He kept the vision before him, Chief Little Turtle, Mishikinmoqwa, small of stature but infinitely dignified, with his straight, passive mouth and copper-colored cheeks, waiting, with members of the council.

"Wemiamiki," he breathed, almost as a prayer. He struck, and a smoldering glow appeared on the fine lint. He blew with just the right amount of breath. The fire started. Quickly he transferred it to a second pile of dry cottonwood and the tiniest of twigs.

And so, day by day, prayer by prayer, he had gotten through two weeks, half a moon. It became almost a game with him, as he successfully completed a task, to solemnly repeat one of the lessons his uncle had so carefully taught him. It always began the same way. "Being Wemiamiki means—walking in the moccasins of the Great Spirit as He looks at animals." We must think as the owl thinks. Know the racoon's tricks, how the deer heads to water when she is wounded.

"And we must love all creation as the Great Spirit loves and not be angry at the bee when he stings." This he said, through a little pain as he applied a poultice of mud and bee honey, which when fermented would draw out the final part of the poison.

"Wemiamiki and all men of the tribes do not waste as the white man does but use only what is needed." This, as he added stream moss to the poultice, and then carefully replaced what he did not use around the root of the tree where it had been growing. It was one of the most important lessons, because it had to do with the meaning of all life.

His uncle had explained how all things on the earth were interdependent, from the earliest time of creation. "Long ago in the heavens were a race of Great Beings. All lived in peace and harmony there. But the minds of some of these beings changed and they were excluded from the Sky World of the gods. Then the race of men had to be formed on earth. A flood was over all the earth. Out of a hole in the sky came tumbling the Earth Mother and fell onto an island where different animals came to her aid, particularly the Great Hare.

"The Earth Mother expanded to fill all the world and nourished all, giving every living thing its own secret, its vital magic: the beaver builds dams, bees make honey, man thinks and rules over all the world. So all comes from Earth Mother. Each creature has its own magic and we must respect that magic, else the guardian spirits of all this life will be angered and seek evil on us.

"We may pray to them, these Manittos, for help. When we pray, whether we ask a priest to do it or invoke the spirits ourselves, what we are doing is asking the Manitto to drive out evil spirits and their mischief. Then the help we need can happen." This was a great lesson, and Asondaki had listened carefully to it, as he did to all the instructions.

"Most of all, Wemiamiki, the true man, will show courage, valuing it above all other virtues. He will not yield to pain or distress, even if it is severe, and he will face death as he faces life, looking at it in the eye as a cougar does." This was said rather loudly as Asondaki faced the greatest crisis a man in the wilderness alone can face—when death did stare him in the eye even as a big cat would. This is how it happened.

A week before his moon was over, big with pride over his hunting success with snare, slingshot, and the dogwood spike he had used in the fishing creek, he decided to pray for his man's name vision. With difficulty he refrained from taking food for two days and waited. Sure enough, as he lay down on his deerskin and was almost asleep on the second day, he seemed to see a giant brown bear on his hind legs. The maqua spoke quietly and told him, "You will seek much, find little." It seemed an odd thing to say. The bear also told him there would be a great contest on the morrow, and through it he would learn his man's name.

When the morrow came, he hungrily went to break his fast, to catch and cook some lakefish. After he had done this, he boldly decided to precipitate the contest the bear spoke of. He would set a man's pit trap for the bear himself. Yes, his uncle had told him that that would be unnecessary for surival in the woods, that it was for advanced hunters. Yes, he knew that the animal he would trap would be too large for him to bring back to camp and he would have to get help; still, he wished to initiate, then conquer the challenge the name animal had sent him.

So, he dug a pit in an area of peat soft enough to scoop easily, but not so soft that water would enter his hole. For almost two days he dug, with rocks, sticks, and his own hands until the hole was six-feet long and six-feet high. As his uncle had told him, he took a tree limb in with him in the hole and clambered out when he was finished. Then, he baited it for bear. Catching a rabbit in his snare, he bound the animal about the stomach with rawhide he had kept wet. Then he tied the rabbit in the pit. As the rawhide contracted, the rabbit began to scream in pain. The bear, Asondaki told himself smugly, would not be able to resist for long. Then he covered the pit with hemlock boughs. Quickly he went to find food, in this case some more of the sturgeon he had been easily spearing and had cooked the night before. He told himself, you can get some honey, too. You can go up that honey tree where the bee bit you before.

As he hurried through the forest, he thought with pride of the accomplishments of the last two weeks and exulted in the confidence of his new-found manhood. It is true he was beginning to grow body hair, embarrassingly abundant and the source of discussion among other boys in the village, but it was truly his spirit that was growing. He had had his vision easily, not like some of the youths, who had to go to the woods two or three times. Soon he would be a man, a great one like the West Wind's son in the legends, Winonah's child, wrestling with evil spirits for his tribe. He too would do heroic things told around campfires in the dead of an autumn night, decide great issues with the council some day, be wise, helpful to his people.

A small voice inside him asked if it was the wisdom of West Wind to climb a bee tree when he should have been seeing to his pit, but he scoffed at it. The bear would wait; and as for the bee tree's inhabitants, what bee would dare bite a Wemiamiki who dug a bear pit as big as a pond?

He found the bee tree, a large, half-dead oak. He must ascend quickly and get to the honey and race down as fast as he could to avoid the bees' overwhelming him. He swung up with all caution abandoned. Up, finding branches for footage, up higher. There it was, near the top, with only a few bees about their odd, bumpy home. He did not look down. Ah, here it was. He reached his hands in with exuberant joy. It was loaded with honey; he put his hand to his mouth; honey poured out all over his hands and the branch and spilled about his feet. But what was this, the bees were about, more than he had thought, rushing at him. He must get away from them. He began to clamber rapidly down. Hands sticky with the honey, he sought hand and foot holds as fast as he could, bees still pursuing. Then, there was a sense of slipping, he heard a crack; and he felt himself fall a long, terrible moment through space. He bumped and scraped and came to a stop in the crotch of the tree. He was in excruciating pain.

Asondaki Caipawa had done the one thing no Indian alone in the woods must do—he had fallen and broken his leg.

After he recovered his wits enough to know what had happened, his temptation was to pound the branch of the tree, screaming for help. But no, he would not do that. Something in him, in spite of the agony and terror, still spoke for manhood.

"Here is what you must do, Wemiamiki. At least you did not hit the ground, which could have killed you. The Manitto of this tree has saved your life." He said these things aloud to calm the demons of pain and fear which were tearing at him. "You must lift yourself by your arms and one good leg down out of this tree, no matter what the pain. And then you know what you must do after that."

And so, sweating what seemed to him like drops of blood, this eleven-year-old son of Dan'l McClure and Mulberry Blossom of the Miami Indians did what neither one of them could probably have done at all, he heaved himself largely by his arms down fifteen more feet of the oak tree and onto the ground, where he lay panting and crawling, almost senseless, for an hour or so.

Gradually he saw his pressing need. "And so, Miamiki, you know what is next. You will prepare yourself for it." He ran a hand over his forehead to wipe away beads of sweat, and brushed back clustered curls from his forehead in a gesture that might have been Will McClure's. Then he dragged himself, crawled, and hopped, biting his lip until it almost bled to keep from crying out, to the short stump of a tree.

He touched thongs he had providentially bound around his neck this morning and reached to pick up strong sticks. He would need these things soon. "Now pray, Miamiki," his speech hissed out from between clenched teeth. "Manitto of the tree, help me. I need to set this leg so I can walk again and live. Drive out any evil spirit, if one should be nearby and keep away the bear I may have called to that foolish pit. Crippled as I am, he could kill me now."

Then, waiting no longer, he swung the leg onto the stump at a ninety-degree angle. He kicked his heel against the stump, shrieked in agony, and sank slowly to the ground on his good leg in unconsciousness. The broken leg remained on the stump, bone pieces now rejoined.

Four days later, thin from having eaten nothing, but hopping with the assistance of a club crutch, Asondaki returned to the village. His mother was grinding the last of the white corn supply by the river. She gasped to see the leg, dragging yet straight and firm, with two beech sticks on either side bound down with deer-hide thongs.

She ran to him; he pushed her aside and headed for the war chief's lodge. Standing for a moment at the opening of the dome-shaped, mat-covered wigwam, he wondered what he would say to Little Turtle. He and Le Gris (Twisted Ankle) were the two chiefs, but Little Turtle was the greater because he was the war chief.

Apparently he would not have time to plan a speech, because the chief, wearing buckskin leggings and an English greatcoat even in the warm weather, emerged. His eyes passed beyond the boy to his Uncle, Hidden Panther, who had come up behind Asondaki.

The chief's voice rose almost mockingly. "So, he has done the stupid thing. If he were my horse, I would get the musket out." Asondaki was smitten by the tone, but his face showed nothing.

"He showed bravery to bend and straighten the leg himself." His uncle was now standing by his side. Not every brave would have the courage to face Little Turtle's wolf-like eyes so directly, but then his uncle had always been different from other men in the tribe. Little Turtle did not answer.

"He is a man now, and a brave one," Hidden Panther insisted.

"He is *metis*, and the charred stick, already weakened, is broken."

"He has shown rare bravery, and I call upon you to call the council and award the sacred tokens of manhood."

Little Turtle's eyes sharpened. "You, the warrior from the far-off camp who does not care to fight, call upon me to do anything?"

"I, whose tongue has saved you at many a river conference with the whites, call upon you to do the simple justice of the Miamis. Besides," he murmured, "I have fought when there was cause."

A week later the council of the Miamis awarded Asondaki beads and medicine bag with feathers of turkey in it to signify his manhood, and the new name of Asondaki Alamelonda, Wounded Sun, or Eclipse.

"Why do I not get respect, Uncle?" Asondaki asked in his uncle's lodge later that night. "William Wells, the white captive, sits by Little Turtle's side as adopted son and has the rights and privileges of the tribe." He thought with a flash of anger of the curly-headed boy Little Turtle had taken into his own house.

"So he does." Hidden Panther turned troubled eyes from the lodge campfire into the humming thickets of the early June night.

"I ask the question. I am man now and may know."

"Partly because you have the blood of an American father, and Little Turtle hates the coming of their hosts into our fields. The French he welcomes."

"Wells is an American."

"He was. I think he will be again. Maumee waters washed off but little of his white skin. But you are mixed-blood. A little of both, not enough of either." It was not as brutal as it sounded, coming from his uncle.

Hidden Panther went on. "But there is more. We are a fair race, but we remember long. Old gashes in trees heal slowly and cover with thin bark. My father opposed Little Turtle's in years long past, but he recalls." Thunder rumbled far off, on the trail to Tippecanoe; and lightning bolts hurled by Tcingwia illuminated the lines of trees along the river.

"Still, you have your medicine bag. With time you will be a warrior. All will be well, wounded sun-child."

Asondaki nodded. It was a good sign, perhaps, that the Manittos had kept the bear away from his pit. Yet, limping away, with his burl crutch under his arm and the sky flashing purple-white in the night, he was not so sure that all would be well after all, as his uncle had said.

Chapter XXIV

Dada, thought John McClure a little nervously, *I don't know what you'd think about all this.* He was walking along a dusty road on the way to McClure Station, and ahead of him, chained together with a very light chain, were two negro men. *I know you wouldn't 'a took atall to slavery, but the situation here calls for it. At least it seems to me it does, and I'm the head of this yere fambly.*

He pulled himself up a bit. It was a hot September day in 1794, cotton shirt weather. A handkerchief tied around his forehead did not keep sweat droplets from trickling down his face. Best keep takin' salt, he told himself. Plenty of that now. The salt licks were free, along with the fields and homes, finally.

Not a month ago the Miami Indian confederation, led by Little Turtle had been beaten by Anthony Wayne at Fallen Timbers in Ohio country. Most people thought the Indians had been dealt a devastating blow. It was sure that they had quit most of their raiding parties, leaving McClure station quiet.

Dada, it's not like Pennsylvania in your day, he thought, addressing his dead parent. Every now and then he found himself talking with his father. It helped him sort things out, and John McClure, Jr. did not think it any crazier than half the other things men indulged themselves in out here. He fixed his eyes on the backs of the black men, as he had all day. Slaves did not run into the woods very often after they were bought at an estate sale. The only reason he had the little chain on them was to show his authority; that's what Hugh Emison had said to do.

Everbody out here is breakneck to get ahead, Dada. Y'see, back in Cumberland County the Cherrys and half the neighbors, the Scotch-Irish, sat around and drank whiskey and built a few stick pens to keep the cows and wanderin' hogs out. 'Taint that away here in the fertile part of Kentucky. Everybody here has to be the Duke of Cumberland himself. I alluz laugh when folks in the East visualize all o' us in the 'pioneerin' west' rootin' around like pigs in miserable shacks. Some folks does, but not most out here. I 'spect it's the women. You can't never keep a woman from fixin' up, gettin' fancy stuff when she can. Show me a woman an' I'll show you a pocketbook ready to buy a new china plate or winder curtains. Even Moses Cherry's got the improvin' bug. He got himself quite a stand now near Emison's, and his porch don't cave in no more. Can you imagine it?

They're startin' to build stone and even brick houses. You should see

Lexington—mebbe you can. It wasn't clear to John whether the spirit of his father travelled about like the Egyptian Ka and was at his side, omniscient, or whether it peeped out of a little hole in the celestial cloud cover, viewing the scene with a spy glass. Probably it didn't matter; Dada knew, some way he knew what his eldest son said, John believed.

Lexington has a seminary, newspaper, good streets. Caintuck is a real state now, official, and is struttin' around like a cow in a sunbonnet. Ever dirt farmer out here tries to git slaves. Say they're investin'. Slaves is three hundred and fifty dollars now; in ten years I figure they'll be worth five times that.

The whole South is growin' like a field of weeds after rain. Partly 'cause a man named Whitney invented a machine that filters them sticky seeds out o' cotton. Others are already copyin' it and rushin' to get lands in Tennessee and the outskirt regions. Georgie is havin' a fit. Says he had a share in a even better version of the machine, cotton gin they're callin' it. Says didn't we remember he tole us that's how he lost the fambly fortune you made for us—says he knew 'twere a good machine even at the time but he hadn't seen the plans close enough to even understand 'em and they was lost along with the money for the land. Ummm. He emitted a long sigh.

So we didn't get any land, and it sartainly is all gone, around these yere parts anyways.

It's a shore thing that the folks that did manage to get the land done right well. Will Lytle got himself a fine farm near Lexington. The Emisons are rich. Talkin' brick house, and they have slaves already. Hugh and Ash are set for life; but then they got a mill, like their fambly did in Pennsylvania, remember, and mills is always good money. Even then, they got younguns comin' along, about ten apiece, and if Hugh gives 'em the two hundred acres he keeps braggin' about, there ain't gonna be enough for everbody. Jest like at our place.

And Lytle, Jr. is gettin' ready to go to Ohio Country. Says they ain't nothin' here for him. A lot of the people without land are talkin' like that, o'goin' to Ohio or even Indianney. Young Sam Bard, Tom's brother, has already gone to Vincennes on the Wabash and is a-surveyin' there. We sometimes talk about goin' on to the Wabash country, but we ain't serious yet.

Mebbe it's my fault we ain't got much yet. I still worry about whether I'm doin' a good enough job runnin' things. They're all grown men, but I think of 'em lots o' times as little tykes. Mebbe it goes back to the wake, yours, when I saw 'em all sittin' there so solemn, Jenny and Georgie with their big scared eyes and Dan'l and even Will lookin' bewildered and not knowin' what to do; and I thought, they're mine to worry about. Mine. Not that we're poor, you understand, Dada. Not at all. We have a lot of fields cleared amongst us all. That's one of the advantages of livin' together. And we got a good crop goin' for us—hemp. Big market for it now as the navy expands. Soil grows it real well, shoots up to ten, fifteen feet tall. Problem is to break it it breaks your back. That's what we got the slaves for, partly.

There was a curious satisfaction, he was aware at the edge of his consciousness, in these new human possessions—twenty-year-old, jet-black men with even, intelligent eyes, slowly marching along together.

Prometheus and Spartacus are their names. That's what Georgie's wife Jean said we should name 'em if we were gonna get any, which she didn't want us to do. Damn crazy names, hard to pronounce. But I try to stay on the good side o' her and everbody, smooth over all the rough places o' livin in one long line o' cabins cheek to jowl. Like last week, when Georgie spanked one o' Dan'l's children for spittin' on his foot, he thought, ruefully. Then there were the fights last year among the women as to who owned which gray-and-white, spotted chickens. Jean McClure solved this; she suggested a separate breed of chicken for each family.

Dada, you'd like Jean a lot. We all do. They got real love between 'em, and Georgie's big-talkin' head has deflated a lot, although ever now and again he starts in tellin' us what to do, and Will and I think we're gonna have to whup the shit out of him—pardon me, Dada.

Anyways, you got a fine fambly. All the little ones are a-comin' on fast as pups in a litter. Held back a good bit, we did, for a long while, and now we're all makin' up for lost time. Dan'l and Martha have John, they call 'im Jack, and little Tom, and two babies. They're all over to Bardstown visitin' the relatives now—George, Jean, Dan'l, Martha and Will's wife Margaret, who's a Bard too.

Now about Margaret, Will's wife. She's turned out real well, too. Will took her on the rebound, he did, but she's real patient with him, the drinkin' and all. About that—I wouldn't say 'twere any worse, but it sure ain't any better. Sheriff come a couple of Saturday nights to Bardstown and threw 'im in jail. But hell, half o' Bardstown is in jail on Saturday nights anyways. But Will does his share, mostly, on the farm and brings some winter money in with the wheelwrightin'.

Will and Dan'l are talkin' of puttin' up a brickyard on the wide creek at the back o' the land, near where it runs into the river. Dan'l's uppity friend Thompson is goin in on it, and Will stayed behind to see to the clearin' of the land for the brickyard.

Jenny and Scott and Ma didn't go on the trip to Bardstown this time. They got their own little cabin just outside the stockade and they take care of the corn and garden for the rest of us. Scott's a good man. Takes good care o' his Ma, who's an odd old biddie. Some says she's a witch, but I like her. She lives in Lexington, but she's at the Scotts' now. Rumor is she's got a brother comin' over the ocean to live with her, the Marquis De Somebody, Frenchy fleein' from the Parree citizens who are threatenin' all the aristocrats. The French ain't no better than they were in your time, in spite of what Jenny says. In those days they got the Indians to boil people for 'em. Now they cut people's heads off with a machine that they keep sharp as a razor. Don't hack up the person too bad, they say. Anyways. . . (he was aware he was getting off the track, that his apostrophe to his dead father was beginning to sound like a combination of the *Frankfort Gazette's* "foreign" report and one of Martha Bard's letters to her sister).

John ran a finger around his clammy collar and took a drink from his canteen. One of the slaves raised a hand in the air and wiggled fingers. "Massaman, we need to go to the woods, 'deed we do." John followed his two charges into the elm trees, rifle in hand, and watched them as they turned their backs discreetly from him. They gave promise of being good servants. The man who had owned them and died without heirs had treated them well. They were born in Virginia on his plantation and had no brand or lash scars; the auctioneer had said they were tractable. But John would eventually have to get wives for them. That might prove difficult, but if the family fortunes were to prosper through slaveholding, there would have to be pickaninnies. In a year or two, they would get two strapping black girls.

The three returned to the road. John continued his mental soliloquy. It somehow relieved him to set his thoughts straight after this trip and the hectic, irritating summer to give a summary of affairs to his father, almost like a year-end report to the founder of a company.

Anyways, Dada, I went to Frankfort, didn't find what I wanted, and intended to go all the way to Danville and stay around through two sales. But a man I met on the road tole me about a feller with several slaves who had jest died on a place halfway to town. So I went to the sale and I found jest what we wanted and could afford. Now Moses Cherry, Hugh Emison, or Lytle won't be actin' uppity anymore. We McClures are slave-holders now, and when we sell these and 't others, who knows, we may be lairds yet. With stables full o' horses.

Thinking of horses made him think of his wife, and as always, when he contemplated that beautiful, complicated woman, Janie McGuire McClure, feelings of love mixed in him with strong gratitude. *Dada, he thought, I jest don't know how a man could be so lucky as I am. True, she doesn't like to spin and weave, but I can buy her calico to wear. And she is the smartest, most clever,* (here he paused, wonderingly) *most loving wife a man could want. I want to be able to buy her some good new bloodstock. We still got* Belle Ame *and* Fincastle's Dream, *the two weddin' presents from her pa, but* Belle Ame *has only partially proved out as a stud.*

That was all we got from that string o' horses Janie's family had. Her pa made it plain to me when he gave her to me that she were her own dowry. He wanted to be sure a man took her for herself, not her money. And now that her ma, Miz McGuire is dead, Judge McGuire done took him a sassy young gal from Louisville and don't worry much about the horses. Jane don't hardly see him anymore, though she went down for a while almost ever weekend to try to reconcile the bad blood amongst 'em all. One of them family things, I stayed out of it. I feel kinda sorry for the pore ole man alone there overlookin' the Ohio in a big ole drafty place with this gal, almost a child, that nobody will visit. He won't see my pore little gal, he's stubborn and has gotten mean lately, so the kids'n me gotta make it up to her. But things were prob'ly a mess sometimes in your day too, and as your uncle used to allow we have to do the best we can each day and things'll generally turn out better'n we expect. John looked at the sun, low in the sky. If he continued to make good time, he could hope to be at the station about nine o'clock.

In Bardstown as the sun set, a hoedown began with the whole town invited to help entertain the McClures, Tom and Sam Baird's visiting relatives, on their last night in town. Bonfires blazed and pigs basted with onions, molasses, and vinegar, turned on spits. The smell of succulent pork drifted over the site of the barbecue, once a meadow where horses had galloped. It now boasted a new frame house belonging to Tom Baird and his family.

Little Tom McClure, Dan'l and Martha's third child, danced and clapped his hand to the sound of the fiddle music. He was a wispy child, as slight as a fairy. "Jack Sprat cud eatna fat and his wife cud eatna lean," he sang in his piping, small voice.

His seven-year-old brother Jack, short of stature like his father and stocky, with a birthmark on the side of his neck, began to dance too, in a kind of clever, almost mocking imitation of a child's dance. "Jack Sprat, Jack Sprat," he shouted gleefully, stamping his feet hard. He, too, had just learned the verse from a little book his mother had received from Pittsburg. She had answered a newspaper advertisement, and everyone around the station was soon doing nursery rhymes from the book with a goose engraved on the cover.

George McClure was not really playing "Jack Sprat," but he smiled to see his nephews dancing to the music. He's softened down a lot, Martha McClure thought, seeing him respond so generously to requests for "Hangman," "Rose of the West," and "Rilly Reel." She observed the wink he had sent his wife. Our marriage is good too, Martha told herself. Children, companionship, working together. They had all that. Was there more? She shifted uncomfortably on the three-legged stool as she asked herself the question that sometimes troubled her. That spark that seemed to travel on a wire from eye to eye when George and Jean looked at each other, what was it? In spite of all the good things in their marriage, she and Dan'l didn't have it.

Well, sometime Dan'l would build them a bigger cabin outside the walls, with privacy—a room for the children and a separate small lean-to room for the bathtub. Maybe the paper-thin but impenetrable barrier she felt between her and Dan'l would dissolve and the spark she saw would develop. In the meantime, she would not think about it. She would concentrate on the good in the marriage, which was considerable.

Dan'l returned to show her something he carried in his pocket from the store down the road.

"What is it?" she asked, smiling at him.

"Specs. For Ma. She hasn't seen the filling in her work very well lately. It affects the weaving. She complains all the time."

"How do you know they'll help?"

"I let your mother try 'em on; they were right for her."

"Hmm. How did she seem to you when you talked to her?" Mary Baird stayed inside most days now, badly stooped over and truly ill with dowager's disease and other complications. Martha had spent her "due share" of hours this trip holding her hand, listening to her list of physical complaints.

"No worse'n usual. But a lot of the older ladies here keep talkin' about her, I heard 'em. 'Mary Baird sure do look peaked. Baad, she looks right baad.' They sound like old sheep," Dan'l answered.

"I don't know why old folks always talk like that," Martha complained.

Margaret Mossman, Will's young wife, had come up for the last part of the discussion. She was reassuring in her quiet way. "Seems as if they hope to find somebody worse off than they are. Tells 'em mebbe they ain't ready to die tomorrow after all." Both she and Martha were weary. It had been a long, hot summer, with months spent in fruit preparation. First, in late June came the red cherry season. The fruit had to be picked while you stood on a wobbly ladder and pitted until your hands puckered, then stewed with sugar and put under glass to "sweat" into preserves. Blackberries and huckleberries in July. Then August apples and peaches to pare, slice and dry, sour plums to put into conserve—all of it left you with a stickiness that the creek, or even Martha's bathtub, didn't get out very well.

Margaret had offered to watch not only her John, Elizabeth and baby Archie, but also Jenny and James's Ish, now almost six, to give Jenny and Mother Jane a rest. All the children were darting in and out of the barn chasing a terrier with large black spots and her five yapping puppies. But Ish had a long, dry stick. He was putting it into the fire, lighting it, taking it to a pile of weeds across the road to "star' a far" as he said. Then, laughing oddly, he would stamp out the fire he had started and return to the bonfire to start all over again. "Ish, be careful," Maragaret said in an even tone.

"Does she ever get angry?" Martha wondered, looking at the placid young girl. She never saw anyone so self-controlled. Only Margaret would have offered to watch Jenny's brattish boy. Sometimes Martha's heart ached at the burden Jenny must be bearing. It was difficult enough to bring up children, but when the child was as difficult as this fuzzy-haired, skinny-as-a-rail child, it took the patience of a Catholic saint. Now he was applying the brand—my goodness, she realized, Margaret wasn't looking—to his cousin Catherine's arm.

"Ish, stop that, or I'll beat you silly," Dan'l said, rushing over and upending Jenny's child and throwing away his stick. Dan'l had little patience with this nephew, and the boy knew it and behaved when he was around. Ish's constant unpredictability was one of the causes of irritation around the station. He seemed to have an odd, peevish wisdom beyond his years. In the last few weeks he had carried a hornet's nest on a stick into George's cabin and put it near the baby, let the chickens out of their pens several times, and painted his mother's dog's hindquarters with turpentine.

Now that the Indian situation had improved, the women sometimes talked secretly of splitting up the stockade and moving to separate houses. But the land was producing too richly and they were far too busy this summer to think of major changes. And anyway, Ma was too happy in her little lean-to shop outside the Scott cottage, where women of Bardstown, and even Harrodsburg, now came to barter for coverlets and tablecloths. Any change would upset her, Dan'l knew.

It was Mother Jane that John was also considering as he neared McClure Station, and his apprehensiveness grew. Even though she was not expecting him, she did not go to bed until late. She often sat by the embers of the fire in her cabin until after midnight, and she would be furious tomorrow if he did not come to tell her about Prometheus and Spartacus. It would seem as if he had deliberately evaded her. He must pay his respects to his mother, no getting out of it. And that would mean trouble. He had already explained how well these slaves would be treated. They would be served from a table near the family, almost like hired hands. He would consult their wishes as to marriage choices insofar as he could. Well, Janie his wife certainly knew how to treat slaves; she had been brought up with them. And after all, they were valuable property.

But he could just see his mother, her hands on her corpulent hips, her Irish temper high. He would get another tongue-lashing about Presbyterian belief, freedom of the spirit, and Uncle George in Ireland. Maybe she would even bring in the ominous threat of his being denied communion at church. Thinking about it almost made his stomach cramps start. God knows, he did not like to defy the Lord or his mother.

He decided to let the slaves settle into the small cabin built for them outside the walls of the stockade. He took them off the little chain. It was silly to have them on it in spite of what the Emisons said. With these new fugitive slave laws, slaves knew they had no chance, should they bolt.

He passed the gate of the stockade, still open. And now for Ma. Brace yourself, McClure, he thought. Well, stop in and tell Janie you're home, jest take a minute, he thought, then face the music. He gently opened the door of his own cabin and stepped inside, still holding the horn lantern which had lit the trail for him for the last couple of miles.

There was an odd sound from the corner. Had a rodent got in? He held the lantern up towards the far side of the room. But it was not as he expected. There, having just completed the act of love and lying in the hot night, naked and glowing with lust and perspiration, were his wife and his brother.

"Jane, Will?" John McClure managed to get out. But his voice sounded weak and sad, more like a goat's bleat than the voice of a man.

After a moment John set the lantern down. The couple, by now propped up on their elbows in the bed, were staring blankly into the night. They seemed transfixed, frozen in a moment of time. They heard John speak but they could not see him for the halo of light that emanated from the lantern. The next sound was of a gun being loaded. Janie cried out, "My God," picked up a sheet, and fled through the open shutters of the rude window in back of her. Running down the hill with the sheet wrapped around her, she got to the Scott cottage and pounded on the door and panted out her urgent, humiliating story.

By the time James and Jenny Scott, Mother Jane McClure and Marguerite Scott were at the door of John's cabin, there was silence again within. The same, strange, eerie lantern glow illuminated the face of a man with raw hatred in his eyes and a rifle trained on his brother. Will was calmly tucking in his shirt, having pulled on his breeches. There was an odd kind of bravado, or was it despair, in his manner. He whistled a little tune, ran a comb through his hair.

The rifle barrel glinted in the lantern glow. The group from the Scott cabin held their breaths in a circle behind the calm, infuriated man just inside the door. One wrong move could set him off—

Finally, Will spoke, and the bravado was gone from his voice. "She don't love me. She loves you," he said, in a calm, deep tone. "And I don't love her." The rifle cock clicked. Janie stood a little way back, detached from the group, leaning against a tree, head in hands. Jenny Scott glanced at her out of the corner of her eye with scant sympathy. She with her small airs and indolences. But naturally it was really Will's fault. And it would be his fault if his own brother killed him.

"John, no," his mother whispered and put an arm on her eldest son's shoulder. He shook it off.

"Get back, Ma. I'm going to shoot this son-of-a-bitch. I should 'a done it years ago when he sent Dada off to his death. He's no good and he don't deserve to live." A strange, strangled rumbling began in his throat, frightening those who stood behind him like the chorus of a Greek tragedy.

Then a clear voice rang out. "John, you think you are killing your brother but what you must think about is yourself. You are harming your own immortal soul. This is a great evil, and it is not worthy of you. You are a good man." It was Marguerite Scott. She came forward and firmly put her hand on his arm. "Give me the gun." He did not shake off her hand; there was authority in her voice.

Then, as everyone including Will stared wide-eyed at him, John lowered the gun and impassively handed it over to the French woman at his side. He wheeled about, pushed through the circle of his relatives, and without looking at his wife by the tree, went to the log barn in the stockade.

Here Dan'l found him the next day about noon. The Bardstown party had returned to find McClure station in a state of sad shock. The story was quickly told, and while the women helped tend to Margaret McClure and her children and see what could be done for Janie in the other cabin, Dan'l had headed for the stable.

The horses, *Belle Ame* and his son New Chance and Fincastle's Dream, were out in the pasture, and John was cleaning their stalls, forking hay into a wooden wheelbarrow. He did not look up when his brother came in. Dan'l stood for a moment watching his brother, seeing the anger and hurt pride in his strong face. Dan'l studied that face for a moment, thinking of how often he had seen it without really knowing the person behind it.

It was a good face, not quite handsome but strong. The hairline had quit receding, after leaving John with two little round spots of bare scalp on each side of his hairline above the eyes. There were minute lines around the corners of those eyes now, and the skin was dark and sun-blemished. John was almost fifty. Dan'l picked up another wood fork from a peg on the wall and began forking the refuse from the floor of the stalls.

They worked side by side for about twenty minutes and finally John spoke.

"Well, what the hell am I a-gonna do?"

"Do you want her back?"

"Acourse. Anyways, what are we supposed to do out here, livin' together like a bunch of hogs in a pen—get a divorce? Take my stuff and buy land o' my own or make Will leave? We got all our houses in common and we made that decision a long while back. But the thought of her lyin' there with Will rises in my gorge. An' havin' to smile and smirk at him and her and everybody, while we husk corn and make sugar candy around here. . ." He was silent, then voiced what was really on his mind. "Could I ever git into bed with her agin, without seein' them there sweatin' and sighin' at each other?"

"After some talk and some time you can, I 'spect."

"I don't want talk. Efn we go back to livin' together, it'll be without talk."

Dan'l shook his head. Each man would have a different idea of how to handle such a thing. He had no idea of what he would do. And if anyone could ever entice Martha into a sweating state in bed, he'd like to know how they did it.

"Listen to me, John. I got an idee that I been mullin' over. It may be a good way for us to git started after this thing and give you something to think about. We've talked about it before. . ." He told him what he was considering.

Leaving John in the stable, Dan'l went to find Will. Then he found his mother at the Scott cabin. She is still a handsome woman, he thought as he saw her there, sitting in a chair he'd made for her, one of the new rocking chairs invented by people in Pennsylvania. As in other times of trouble, she was sewing. Her new spectacles were on her nose.

Dan'l looked into her swollen, red eyes and was suddenly struck with the cumulative amount of suffering she had undergone in the seventy-some years of her life. He suspected he did not really know all of it. It was her habit when some bad news came, of a robber hanged in Frankfort, of a scoundrel fled with others' money, to murmur, "How his mother must be sufferin' now." What a terrible risk of pain-to-come women took in bringing children into the world. If a woman had many, the risk was compounded. Fathers too could suffer. How awful it must be, he knew as a father already, to see the ones on whom you pinned such hopes, around whom you wove such dreams, falter, fail, and turn out poorly, or worst of all, hurt others deeply with their sins.

Disappointments were a necessary, hurtful part of this life, like hangnails and colds. Dan'l thought that if a person could calculate in advance how many frustrated schemes, scraped knees, and splitting headaches he would have he might decide just to stay in Heaven, or wherever it was, and not come. But none of us had that choice.

"Ma," he said, sitting by the chair where she was darning. "John is doin' better."

"Where is Janie?"

"At home in bed with a sick headache. Jean is with her. Mrs. Scott, James's mother, has the children."

"And Margaret?"

"Will has been talkin' to her, and she seems to have decided to forgive him. I guess nobody's goin' to leave. We all have too much tied into the fambly's bein' together."

"For better or worse your father and I took each other, but you children didn't make that vow," his mother said. He thought about that for a moment. Yes, 'twas true. You could choose a wife and even be rid of her, but brothers and sisters and all their problems are yours for life.

"What's to be gained by anybody a-goin?" he asked her. "Casual lovin' happens often enough out here. Dan'l Boone came back home once to find he'd been gone too long. Rebecca had sinned with his own brother. Said she was lonely. But they stayed together and moved on into Caintuck."

"Stayin' with everybody here will be enough punishment for the two of them," Jane sighed. "What's awful about all this is how such a private sin is spread so amongst us all, like linen drawers on a thorn bush. They have made us all a part to somethin' obscene. What caused all this?" She was bewildered. Perhaps, she thought, she was too wrapped up in her weaving, perhaps she had just imagined the family harmony she wished for. There should have been signs.

"John has decided to believe that it all happened 'cause we was too close here in the stockade. Says its time we broke up the station."

"I suppose so," she murmured, weaving her needle back and forth over a darning egg.

"None of us 'abeen satisfied by the size of our farm here, but we balked at pullin' up stakes. But somehow this seems to have decided it. While I was in Bardstown I got a letter said we have claims as Revolutionary war soldiers in the new Northwest Territory, and the claims may be proved within three or four years. We'll git vouchers or currency certificates to apply to acres in Indianney. John thinks we should be movin' an' gettin' at least four hundred acres apiece from the land grants, then buy more with the money we can realize from selling slaves, buildin' the brickyard, and bringin' in good crops for the next few years. We're gonna start over big across the Ohio."

Jane was silent, so Dan'l went on, his voice beguiling. "George says it's a good idee. We all saw what that land north of the Ohio is like. Some of us can go scout around the Wabash, pick the best claims. They say it's truly God's country, the best farmland in the United States."

What she thought was, On, always on, over the hill. I'd like to stay right here, with my teapot and loom. Old people need comfort. You don't know that, Dan'l. What she said was, "We all have t' do what we have t' do." Well, it could be worse. Sally Bard had died last year in Carlisle, and she hadn't seen Ardry or her grandchildren for the last eight years, couldn't even come to Ardry's funeral when he drowned so tragically last year. She, Jane, at least had her grandchildren with her. The ironic thing was that Caroline had outlived her mother and had finally married a widower preacher. Sally had given up her life, her chance to move on, for nothing.

"One more thing," Dan'l said, watching her with real concern. "John says tomorrow we break up this yere station. He says for me to tell the others, 'If you want to sell out, I'll buy your land. But whoever stays builds a cabin on his own hundred acres at opposite ends of this land and divides up equal again when we sell the land.' And as far as he goes, John says he and his are headin' out for Indianney as soon as the war land claims are settled. Three, four, five years—we take our slaves" (his mother's eyes did not blink, she had heard about them from Martha and had gone personally to see to their comfort in all this confusion) "and profits and try our fortunes in Hoosier land. But till then we separate as far as we can git on this land. Fambly we are, and fambly we will be, but we don't have to do it under each other's noses."

Jane looked hard at her son. "So, why are you dawdling like a racoon around apple peelings. Go tell 'em," she said.

Alone again, she put her feet firmly on the ground and began slowly rocking in her new chair. She thought, Mother, the tollman is still collectin'. So far I have been able to pay all he asks, but my apron pockets are about empty. And yet, they're talkin' about another road. . .

As shadows deepened among the sycamore trees outside his cabin, John finally came home. He had purposely bathed long and leisurely in the wide creek, using hard soap and scrubbing himself with a towel, hoping it would relax him, would ease the pain that had gripped his stomach since last night. He dipped beneath the water's cool surface, splashed, and dipped again until he felt thoroughly clean from the dirt of the stable. The bath invigorated him as nothing had for a long time. Then he dressed in linen clothes Dan'l brought for him. And now he was finally going in to see Janie.

Her back was turned to him. His oldest son Jim, eight, aware of the tensions in the house and station in the last day but not sure of their cause, looked up at him with apprehension. The trouble was between his pa and ma, that he knew. Last night he heard voices raised in awful anger and hid under the cover, not daring to listen. Then today Mrs. Scott stayed with him and Mary, telling them stories of black men in the South, while his ma lay sicker than he had ever seen her. But now she was up, miraculously. "Jim, go take Mary some supper at the little table outside. And stay with her 'till she finishes," his mother said without looking up, as she stirred a pot at the fireplace hearth.

Wordlessly, the dark-haired boy picked up the plate of beans and ham she gave him and went to call his four-year-old sister, playing in the twilight with her dollies.

John stood for a full moment by the door, the same door he'd opened to the scene which had shocked his life into sadness and anger, and then he walked to the fireplace. His wife, hearing his footsteps, did not turn until he reached her. Then she wheeled about suddenly to face him, looking at him full in the face, standing as she did a shade taller than he.

The wide streak of white in her hair, the proud tilt of her chin, her eyes like flashing coals, affected him, as they always did after he had not seen her for a while. "You are the most God-damned beautiful woman I ever did see. That's what makes it so hard," he said, turning from her eyes.

She did not speak, but he went on anyway. "I said I didn't want to talk, but a few things should be said. The first is. . ." he faltered.

"That this can never happen again. I know that. It won't." She turned her head up even higher.

"How can we know?" His voice was anguished, almost a sob.

"It is enough that I know."

"Will is to blame," he said with deep-felt bitterness. "If I can't keep him out of my wife's bed, and he can't keep his own breeches on. . ."

"You may be blaming him too much. . ." her eyes were vague. She looked thoroughly exhausted.

"You can never blame Will too much. Should 'a named him weak-Will. He ain't his own man. And with those damned good looks, any woman has always been fair prey to my brother."

There was silence between them. They could hear the voice of little Mary, talking to her brother Jim at the table outside under the tree. "My dollie wants a crib, Jimmie," she was saying. A fair, sweet, sensitive child, she was the apple of her father's eye.

"I'm not a good woman, John," Janie said rather coldly. She was standing by the cabin's window, looking out into the cornfields.

"Well, and I have lived with your dark times."

"There's more to it." She sighed. "This is more than should be asked."

"But not more'n I can do, if I wanta. Look, Janie, I knew when I married you that your spirit was as unbroken as a wild mare's. Nobody will ever fully own you, and they shouldn't." He went to her. "I love you. I have ever since I saw you first ride into town like the Queen of Bardstown. You are a good mother. And I think you. . ." the words died before they could be spoken.

"Yes. I love you, in my own way. I told you, and Will, too, for that matter, years ago that I needed security, safe-keeping. I still need it. You love me as no one else ever has. Surely not my father. . ." her voice was bitter and John felt sorry for her in spite of himself.

Outside Mary's voice rose to a whine. "You play with me, Jimmie. Say you'll be the pa."

John McClure took his wife in his arms. His voice was low. "He said he didn't love you—and. . ." there was a strangled quality to his voice— "you didn't love him."

" 'Twas true. Absolutely."

"Very well. I guess all's to do is start again. . ."

His wife nodded, lifelessly.

"And let's try to get more horses, John," she said, looking into the fireplace.

Mary burst into the room, tears coming down her face. "I hate Jimmie, Ma. He won't be the pa in my playhouse, and now he says he's goin' off to sit by the crick." John went on his knees to comfort the overwrought child, while his wife went to seek her son. Tired of conflict he could not understand, he had run away into the woods.

Chapter XXV

The Tippecanoe Trail to the rivers and small lakes in north central Indiana was bright with summer flowers this day of 1796, and Asondaki Alamelonda (Sun with a piece out of it, or eclipse), told himself he should be in high spirits. A tandaksa, or bluejay, flitted across the path. Surely it was a good omen, perhaps even good enough to counteract the hooting of the owl, worst omen of all, that he had heard before dawn, as he prepared to leave camp.

Summer had always been a good time in the Kekionga camps, a time of games, of corn pushing tall, of campfires and dancing and the contracting of marriages. No more. Kekionga was gone, burned by General Josiah Harmar, with the Miamis now scattered about the rivers and lakes of northern Indiana. Mulberry Blossom and Hidden Panther's band had gone with Little Turtle. Asondaki himself was off on a venture quest—a Great Hunt to show his final skill as hunter and Wemiamiki.

As he made camp that night by the river, all seemed as usual in his world. An otter, (kinokca) slithered and scuttled about, and downstream bass jumped. But all was not the same. Not at all. The shadow which crossed his path when he was a youth had broadened until it now darkened his days. He was caught in a process of change that was smoldering through Indian ranks like a prairie fire, breaking out in flames here, smoking there. The heat of this change tormented him as an Indian watching something he did not understand happen to his people, and it hurt him as a half-breed who was not even accepted by the very people he mourned for.

There was supreme confidence only a few short years ago that Miamis, controllers of the rivers, could lead Indian peoples to throw out the white interlopers from the forests and waterlands. Whatever Asondaki might think of Little Turtle personally, he had shown himself to be a great leader of the tribes, at conferences at the new Fort Washington on the Ohio River and at many of the other forts the determined Americans were trying to raise in the valley of the Ohio.

And he had led in war. After the burning of Kekionga, the war totem was carried before the Miamis, and the scalps of officers, soldiers, and settlers were brought back for the French and Englishmen squatting about the campfires at the Miami villages to see. That same Harmar had finally been humiliated, defeated by repeated Indian ambush attacks.

Then there had been the brilliant victory of the combined tribes against Arthur St. Clair, who had come up Great Miami with his rag-tag army to threaten the Maumee villages. The Indians had won a great victory, thanks to the magic of their chiefs at the headwaters of the Wabash at dawn. Half-a-thousand of the white devils were killed, many more wounded.

Asondaki looked upriver, where beaver were trying to build a dam, and his look was gloomy. Did the white men not understand the magic of the Manittos? Indians, when armed, working in harmony with the spirits of all nature to do what is just and honorable, could beat any white man. That should be obvious. The Manittos had planned creation that way. The Miamis, Shawnees and others won against St. Clair because of this spiritual magic and because of their bravery.

But somehow the magic did not continue to work. And somehow the white man continued to come. The new American chief, General Anthony Wayne, was a fighting dog, or better, a snarling, wounded bear enraged by the loss of cubs. From the day of St. Clair's defeat, Wayne did not stop arming, marching and training his troops, and he did not care about magic. It was all very discouraging, Asondaki thought, as he gathered beech sticks for a fire. Morosely he ate the jerky he had brought. Too tired to think about troublesome shadows anymore, he wrapped in his blanket, turned towards the fire, and slept.

The next morning, Asondaki looked about as he headed along the western trail. Here, midway between Kekionga and Stone Lake, the trail went through narrow passes with rock crags on either side. He did not like these areas, where spirits of mischief could lurk. Manitto of the rocks, he prayed, I need to get through to the fine hunting grounds of Stone Lake, Mocksinkickee, where my uncle took me when I was a boy. Here I must find my Great Hunt. Now and then small, tribal villages appeared by the trail; he skirted them. He wished to avoid people.

His thoughts returned to the recent troubles. He could not get them out of his mind. Perhaps that was because he had been there.

On the white man's day of June 30, 1794, all of the young and old men of the village went to a great battle after the spring planting. He himself went with one thousand other warriors, Miamis, Piankashaws, Delawares, Shawnees, and Weas in the grim paint of war to attack a party of one-hundred and fifty American soldiers near what the whites called "Fort Recovery," the place where St. Clair had gone to his knees.

The Indian army he was with smashed the party outside the fort, but from his reserve position he watched in rage as the Indians had refused to pursue the fleeing Americans. And then they did what no intelligent Indian ever does— they directly stormed the fort. "No, this is foolishness," he shouted fruitlessly to the hundreds of warriors rushing toward that strong fort. Something inside his head told him the stupidity of these warriors would bring bad magic on the Miamis. But who would listen to him, a half-breed *metis* stripling who did not even get into the action? No, instead he was forced to watch the warriors throw themselves against the fort and be badly beaten by the cannon they had heard was inside and which they were seeking in this stupid attack.

The bad magic he foresaw came. Many braves left after this engagement, saying they needed to harvest crops and play summer games. Worse yet, there were more important desertions. William Wells, the adopted son of Little Turtle, left his "father" and Indian wife and went to become a scout for Wayne. Asondaki's eyes narrowed in scorn even now, walking this trail many moons afterward. Many Indians, even Little Turtle, seemed to approve Wells's desertion, saying it might bring about better ties with the whites. Asondaki did not see it that way. He had never trusted Wells's sincerity, as the adopted son of Little Turtle sat simpering around the village campfires. Wells pretended to be Indian, as children pretend to be bears or warriors.

And so, the terrible engagement of Fallen Timbers came. Little Turtle, after performing his medicine rites, said he could not see the value of continuing against such large, well-trained forces. He gave up his leadership to Blue Jacket of the Shawnees. When battle came, the poorly-led tribes, fighting on the banks of the Maumee, had been overwhelmed. Asondaki fought in the rear. He watched iron-disciplined soldiers of the United States Legion make relentless charges with bayonets until Indian bodies lay like so many sticks among the fallen trees. With a sickened heart he retreated with those who could get away.

And then he and the other Miami warriors tried to withdraw to nearby British Fort Miami and were refused, outright, admittance. His uncle was not surprised; he said the British and French, too, always used the Indians to bring coin into their own coffers and cared not at all for them, flinging them aside like bought women when they were done with them.

With tails between their legs, the one hundred or so Miamis slunk home. Bad magic! Bad magic! So he had not fully gained his warrior's scalplock and was left with gnawing fears in the middle of his gut for the future. He did not speak of it, even though it was now The Thing Much Talked About in camp. A new treaty last year seemed to buy a little time and space for the tribes-joined-together, but much land was now given to the white man. Where had the good magic gone?

Still, he had to admit this trail today was even more beautiful than yesterday. Toward evening he drew near the wooded hills and boglands where he spent summer camping days being trained for manhood by his uncle. Happy times, when Great Spirit and Manittos smiled always, pikefish grew long and were easy to spear, and all clouds were white ones, at Mocksinkickee, Lake of the Stones.

As the trail widened beside the lake, he saw something he had not seen ten years ago, a summer Potawatomi village spread on the hill to the north of his uncle's old camp. The Potawatomis, a people of the west and north, had lately been venturing up the river valleys. Their village, in the midst of small fields of peas, beans, and melons, spread down to a little bay bounded by a spit of land, where children were gathering mussel shells.

Soon he was surrounded and greeted by the Potawatomis. The doorstep of the leading lodge was swept, a cattail mat put out in welcome, and he was seated on the porch before the fire and cookpot. His eyes glanced through the door at the dusky interior of the lodge. It was a little different from Miami wigwams; wool leggings and checked linen and calico shirts hung from stick pegs on the domed sides. Elm baskets and iron cooking pots and skillets and tools rested on slab-bark shelves above the neat, raised pallet beds. It was on the whole in better order than the lodges of his home village. And it did not smell the same way.

The band chief whose lodge it was gestured for the young Miami to eat of the stew of garfish and onions, cooked French-style and the pot of turtle eggs. Asondaki, however, could not really do justice to the food. Facing him was the most beautiful maiden he had ever seen.

She was wearing a short, blue wool dress which showed very pretty, firm arms and leggings which came to her ankles. Her hair hung down her back in a single braid and she wore an elaborate set of silver brooches, looped and decorative over her shoulders. Her eyes were close-set but large. They looked into his with amusement and curiosity. He realized he had been staring at her for some time.

"You are a curious young alanya, Sun-With-A-Piece-Out-Of-It. So your eyes do not wear out and fall from your head, I will tell you about myself." She spoke her people's tongue, of which he knew a little, with a boldness he was not accustomed to. "I am not as other maidens. I come and go as I please. Only child of the band chief Brown Squirrel, I hunt as the women of the old times did." The chief, an old man with only two teeth, smiled, amused at the frankness of his daughter, whom he obviously treated with indulgence.

Asondaki looked up, surprised. "You are a huntress? Men say Indian women who hunt turn mean."

"Not Potawatomis. Before the French came, many of our women hunted. Now I too take up bow and arrow and spear. I do not use a gun. And I am not mean." She turned her head and smiled a crooked smile at him. Asondaki felt something slowly melt in him, like lead when it is being heated for shot.

After the meal she offered to show him the lake. Its waters were calm at the end of the summer day. Small, ripply waves caused by a slight wind from the west washed onto its pebbly shore.

"When we came I wondered at the rocks strewn about the shore," said Swiftly Running Feet, for that was her name. "I think the Manittos must have been in a hurry and dropped them on the way to form the hills south of here," she added.

At least he thought that was what she had said. The word "wedi". . . did it mean hills? Some of the language these Potawotamis spoke was unfamiliar to Asondaki's Miami ears, although he knew a good deal of the dialect from traders and Potawatomis he met on diplomatic missions and in the Wayne wars. Only sometimes did he need to ask a word.

She was smiling at him; there was a hollow place in her cheek that came and went. It was odd that she smelled so sweet. Potowatomis bathed daily in summer, it was said, in some villages (not in others) and did not always coat themselves with bear grease. His handsome face distorted with a frown. Would she find him unpleasant to the nose? But she was continuing to speak of the boulders, huge, yellow-orange, and some of them layered, which lay about the shore. "Perhaps these are the rocks the Great Spirit hurled at the Son of the West Wind when he stole fire from the gods," she speculated.

"Did he do so?" He did not recall the story quite that way, but then the Son of the West Wind had many tales told about him in all the tribes, and all were not the same.

"I bathe here. Not at this spot, too near the village, but back where a small stream enters the lake. I will take you there tomorrow."

His heart raced.

But the next day instead she showed him the hunting woods above the lake, with deep-earth springs flowing through them in many places. The forest was abundant with game, even as the one on the hill just south of here where he had camped with his uncle before his Man Moon. He told her of that time, and she asked to see the leg to see if it showed signs of being broken. Proudly he showed her that the magic of the bee tree had worked; his once-broken leg was straight and strong as the other one.

That night the chief invited Asondaki to see the Potawatomi custom of fire-fishing. Spear-throwing men in canoes stood, balanced on the still water of the lake, while others held huge pine-chip torches above to highlight and hypnotize the fish. There was an eeriness to the scene, with the flickering torches over dark water, the men's calls echoing, the mists rising as the stars came out. As the sound of voices from the the village floated down to Asondaki from over the hill, he stood wondering at the peace and prosperity of this small place. Surely the Manittos would grant him the boon of a wonderful Great Hunt in such a setting.

The next day dawned golden and orange above the still lake. Fresh fish were broiling over hot coals outside the chief's lodge, and as Asondaki came from the tiny visitor lodge where he spent the night, he smelled the food hungrily. The Chief's wife, a heavy, tight-lipped woman who was not the mother of Swiftly Running Feet, nodded that the food was not quite ready and he strode about, looking at the village. Women were fixing fresh beans and green corn to go with the abundance of bass, gar, and carp caught last night. There were thirty to forty cooking fires in a space more tightly grouped than his Miami village was. Other than that, it could almost have been a Miami scene, except for the glint of silver in the sunlight. These people wore a surprising amount of the precious metal, long earbobs and brooches for the women, nose-pieces and arm bands for the men. And last night he had been served from a dish of silver traded by the French for many fine animal skins. The Potawatomis were not poor.

Asondaki spent the morning talking to the chief about the Miamis and the Indian confederation; there was not much to do except shake heads and hope for better times. In the afternoon, he and Swiftly Running Feet walked in the woods, on a ridge above the lake, and came to the very prairie where as a child he watched the red-winged blackbird skit to the aspen tree. They sat down in the grass, on the strip of treeless land that overlooked the undulating sea of rushes and cattails he remembered. He told her of his birth, of the barely-remembered god of a father, whom his mother and uncle did not talk about.

"You look to be a white man, even among the light-skinned Miamis. You are well-formed," she said, putting her hand on his bare chest. There was no embarrassment in the comment. It was made in admiration of his bright, freckled copper face, the curls, the strongly muscled body the Great Spirit had seen fit to bestow. He turned and took her hand.

"I have watched the French *metis*, other half-breeds among us. I do not want what they want. Richardville, who wishes power among red men and buys it with stories of rich grandfathers in France—Fourier, who licks the white mens' feet with compliments. They pollute their magic buying waistcoats and snuff. Some *metis* run white men's stores and cheat our people."

"But you, too, know the white man's tongue," she said. He had already taught her a few phrases.

"Traders are constantly among us now. I seem to pick up tongues very easily. I know much of French also. Who knows? I may use them some day." She nodded and touched his shoulder, with its tattoos of sun and bear. He smiled at her quizzically, as if wondering what she was thinking. But suddenly the dark cloud came again.

"I know why I am not accepted in the way even these *metis* are. I am a *metis* of a different sort," he said. "My people have always traded with the English and French but not the Americans, with their pushy, graceless ways. Only my uncle and his band have been friends to Americans." The girl nodded; the Potawatomis had long welcomed the French and English, but not until lately had they approached the Long Knives, the Americans.

"Little Turtle is changing all that," Asondaki said. "He says they have won, that we must think about living with the American white men. And though that should make me happy, it does not. Little Turtle has become a man of two faces, smoking the pipe at both ends. Since the Great Battle his truth is as rotted as a piece of wood in a damp cave. And anyway, his father and mine differed in the tribe. And so, I am half a Miami." His eyes smoldered. "But perhaps not for long."

She looked at him questioningly. "I have determined," he told her. "I am set. I shall not return to my tribe unless I bring back the Great Hunt. I shall find him, the giant bear, king of bison, or rare wild Moose." His voice grew lower, and they both watched as the wind parted branches of the trees on the horizon to reveal flashes of the shining lake.

"I can see it in my mind. I shall come into camp when evening fires burn low, when the owl calls that the winds of changing weather soon will blow. The warriors will look up from smoking their kinnikinnick to see me in full dress, with honors I have won so far, painted. On a horse or on a sledge which I will borrow will be my Great Hunt. They will gasp. . ."

Excitedly she grasped his arm and whispered, "The snow deer. You must find and shoot the snow deer."

He turned to her. "What?"

"Listen to me, Asondaki, Shining Sun with the face of West Wind's Son. I have seen him—the deer as white as snows around the wigwam in deep-of-winter moon. He lives by the twin lakes not far from this camp. Others have seen him, but only I know his lair.''

"A white deer?'' Asondaki knew there were animals whom the Manittos had specially marked, or favored. Horses, porcupines, even white bears. These animals roved alone, the White Ones. The sun seemed to hurt their red eyes. But not he, nor any Miami he knew, had seen a White One among deer.

"What a real hunt that would be. I can see their eyes now—the medicine pouch I would get.''

"I will help you. I can tell you the trail he takes, his secret hideaways. He is truly beautiful.''

"As are you,'' was all he said, smiling. She spoke a few more words about the snow deer, then stopped speaking and looked wonderingly at him.

They ate a little fruit and dried meat slowly, sitting in the late afternoon sun on the hill overlooking lowlands. They touched each others' hands. Yearning grew between them, the yearning of the strong, supple young of the race for each other. Since their culture sanctioned freedom of this kind, they knew they soon would embrace in the joining of bodies. It was as it should be, as the lore of their people taught, man and woman in full prime, part of the magic of nature, joining as sky to earth, moonlight to starlight, soul to body.

But all things fittingly. First there should be the bath. She led him to a cool brook down the hill from where they sat. There were many of the ice-cold streams about, bubbling up in fields to find their way to feed Mocksinkickee. Earlier they had stopped to drink from them and splash water at each other. Now they followed this largest stream to its mouth in the lake on its east shore, a good way off from the village.

The sun was sinking in the sky, but they would wait to feast until later. A young, full willow tree spread its branches as a sort of leafy shield over the spot, and waves swirled gently about their feet as they stood without moccasins in the stream.

"This is my favorite place,'' Swiftly Running Feet told him. "Few come here. Perhaps some day my people will make a permanent village here and others will come also.''

"But for now only you, I, and the minnows,'' he laughed.

"And the Great Spirit.''

"Tell him to close His eyes for a few minutes.'' He took off her garments, one at a time, the little leggings, short skirt, calico shirt. Beneath the shirt were full, round breasts, larger than those of most Indian girls. Enchanted, he reached to touch them.

Smiling almost playfully she removed his breech cloth and led him through ice-cold stream waters to the much warmer lake, where she splashed his body with water. He picked up handsful of sand and scrubbed her shining skin, gently, to remove oil and dust, not to scrub away bad blood as Indians did with captives.

He murmured admiration of each part of her body, lovely arms, lovely neck, beautiful stomach, and whispered unashamedly in her ears admiration of hidden parts as he touched them. She returned the compliments, asking words in the Miami tongue she did not know.

And soon, as the sun began to set behind the leafy willow tree, they lay enraptured, limbs entwined on the warm sands of the lake, as a loon made his strange call behind them.

That night the band chief's wife cooked wild turkeys the men had brought back. At the feasting and the dancing that followed, Asondaki's eyes sought the eyes of the Potawatomi girl again and again, and at last she took him to the guest lodge where they loved again and again. And as rain fell, Asondaki realized they were forming a bond that could not be washed away, that years would not erode. He would ask for her when the time came to make a marriage contract. The rainstorm grew, coming out of the northwest and battering at the little lodges on the hill. "It is the lost hunters of our race, returned from the hunting grounds to earth," Swiftly Running Feet murmured. Asondaki held her more tightly. Before he slept, he knew the storm had blown over, going to howl among the caves to the south, and that their hunt of the snow deer tomorrow would be blessed with the omen of good weather.

Three days later Asondaki and Swiftly Running Feet crouched above an area of fallen timbers near two lakes the Indians called The Twins. Mosquitoes whined about them and landed on their arms, but they did not move as dusk deepened. The small creek near the lakes ran high on its banks. Branches of blooming elderberry trees hung over it, shedding their creamy pollen into the rapidly flowing waters.

Asondaki had not spoken for an hour. His muscles were leaden and strained as they waited for Snow Deer to come to the water. It was late now for deer to be drinking. He is not coming and we will be disappointed again, Asondaki thought. Perhaps the cover smell was not well done. He winced a little. Swiftly Running Feet, who preferred to smell sweet as clover, had painted herself and him with the most foul odors that can be found. He moved a fraction of an inch; a twig snapped. The girl turned toward him with warning eyes; he gave her an impatient glance. They had not even come near the Great Hunt, but it was not because they had not done the proper things to bring good magic.

The first day away from the Potawatomi camp they had shot a young buck, and Swiftly Running Feet had smeared its tallow and brains all over Asondaki. It would camouflage his man-scent, she said. For herself, to further confuse the tracking scents, she had chosen fat and oil of skunk. "The Snow Deer will not sense anything but the animals of the forest when he comes to drink from his favorite stream before dark," she explained.

"He brings his two wives with him," she had said, as they knelt over the young deer they shot, "and sometimes mock kosa." Asondaki looked at her then, for the words "wives" and "babies" had special, tender meanings for him. He had already told this love of his that he wished her for his wife. She said she wished it too, and when the time came, they would take each other before the tribe of her father. In this light, she wished especially for him to have the desire of his heart, so that he would be calm in his mind. But when they went on to set up camp here, they slept as companions only and stayed apart, so the Manittos would grant the strength of the hunt to them.

That first night in camp Swiftly Running Feet described Snow Deer's habits, how he fed on dewy plants at dawn on the hills above the lake, then retired to thickets during the day, and at sunset finally visited the creek near the largest lake. "He is of a wary mind. He has a great scar on his flank; other hunters have sought him and one almost snatched his spirit from him."

"Umph," Asondaki had snorted. "That is what I will do when we find him." But Snow Deer was not easy to track. All the next day they traced the entire creek bed, wearing deerskins, looking for hoof marks. Asondaki even blew his deer-bleat call. Finally, tired and irritable, they had returned to their camp by the larger of the two lakes last night. Asondaki checked the horse they brought to carry the hunt and their camping possessions, and then he said, "The White One does not exist." He took out flint to start the small fire over which they would stew rabbits.

"I tell you he does," Swiftly Running Feet insisted, taking from her travelling pouch good wild rice brought from the village.

"Tomorrow we will wait until evening to hunt. Then we will separate," Asondaki said. Hungrily he watched onions and herbs being added to the pot of rice. "We will cover his path by the stream, so he does not slip through. If he is there, we will find him."

And so tonight, just before sunset, they waited by the river. Thrushes sang from the thickets around them. The sun sank, sending showers of orange beams through the trees, and just as it disappeared, Asondaki caught sight of deer. They emerged like a gentle shadow spreading out from the clumps of trees above the creek. First a fawn, tentative on stick legs, who came unconcernedly to the creek and put his head down to drink. Then, two doe, ears alert. Although he was hidden, Asondaki instinctively leaned back even further into the shadows of the sassafras trees under which he sat.

There, stepping with great majesty down the sloping creek bank, was the most magnificent animal Asondaki had ever seen, a stag of about six years with marvelous many-pronged antlers, gray-white. His head was up sniffing the breeze. After a time he, too, put his head down and began to drink. Asondaki's hand sought his spear, made in the Potawatomi camp of Osage orange wood. Its point of fine Ohio flint was all the way from the camp west of Kekionga.

Asondaki rose on his haunches, making no noise and began to creep forward. He would need a closer shot. But the White One sensed something. He looked directly at the thicket where Asondaki hid, and for the first time Asondaki could see his eyes, shrewd, red, and unreadable. "Manitto, help me," he prayed, struck with the awesome force of a nature that could create such a creature, almost frightening in its beauty and power.

The stag looked about, sending signals of danger to the doe and fawns. Asondaki would have only a second or two. Running out of the thicket he threw his spear. It went over the back of the head of the stag, and the animal jumped straight up in the air. Then, he, his doe and the fawn crashed into the woods, bounding and leaping out of sight. No more than a minute had passed since they had come down to the creek to drink.

Swiftly Running Feet ran to Asondaki along the creek trail. "So he came," she said, when he briefly told her of the encounter. "You have lost your chance."

Asondaki nodded sadly. But back in camp after praying to the Manittos, he had another insight. "I think he knew of my presence before he ran," he said. "He knows we are here, and why we are here. He is the chief of the forest; it is his business to know all."

"That is children's talk," the girl said.

"No. This moswa is of the Great Spirit. He has a wisdom we do not understand. He looked at me, I am sure of it, and for a moment he was not afraid."

"Perhaps you are right."

"And what is more, he will return to that spot."

"To the place where you have sent your spear? I have hunted much, and I do not think so."

"Yes, woman, I tell you, he is curious. He wishes to know who wants his spirit. Perhaps he wants to toss me on his antlers a bit." He laughed, and she joined him. "Tomorrow we will stalk him, exactly where I was tonight. He will not resist the challenge of one warrior to another."

Smiling, she took his hand and put its palm against her face. "Manitto, may he succeed," she silently prayed.

And so, they crouched again in the sassafras thicket the next night. This time the sun went down through glaring clouds and the air was breathlessly hot. Rain was coming, and with it, the end of the hunt. "Perhaps he will not come," the girl finally breathed.

"He will come," Asondaki whispered harshly. Long moments went by. Dragon-flies settled on the water of the creek in the gray-orange glow of the evening, muskrats scuttled about near them, but otherwise the bank was quiet. Asondaki, his spirit falling, was about to stand up when—alone, coming out of the woods very slowly was the White One. He turned his proud head first to the left, then the right. Then he came, his antlers held high, to the very edge of the creek. He did not drink. Swiftly Running Feet emitted a low breath of admiration.

Asondaki did not wait this time. Springing from the thicket, he raised his arm and flung his spear, this time true and direct at the stag. It struck his antlers near the head. Stunned, he turned toward Asondaki, who stood stock still. Behind him, as silent as a serpent through grass, Swiftly Running Feet crept up, put her own spear in Asondaki's hands, and retreated.

The stag did not move. A deer whose antlers were hit hard, especially near the head, could be immobilized for as long as a minute. Adondaki looked into the eyes of the Snow Deer, the bright, odd, mysterious eyes and felt again a sense of awe.

"The Manitto has put you into my hands. It is your fate to die by my spear. You have lived a noble life as a king, a god of the forest and you will die with dignity. But I must take a life from you. . ." he whispered to the stag.

The White One's eyes cleared, but still the animal did not move. He stood, towering, enormous, over six feet tall, not four strides away from Asondaki. The youth raised his spear; the stag's eyes continued to look at him. He found himself fixated by them. Sharp, disturbing feelings that he did not understand began to pour through him. For a moment he stood with the Great Spirit before the time of Earth Mother, when He made the heavens and earth. In that instant of time he felt the stag's heart throbbing, the wonder and mystery of the God who created him, and a strange desire to spare this wondrous animal.

"I cannot do it," he cried out in anguish, not understanding why he did so.

"Strike," called out the girl in back of him with an anxious voice.

He hesitated a moment, again in a great upheaval of indecision, and then almost despairingly hurled his spear at the animal's chest with a force he did not know he had. With one last, wild look at Asondaki, the albino stag crashed to the ground. Dying, he gasped and bled out his life into the waters of the creek as the last light of day faded.

"I do not know why I faltered," Asondaki finally said, after they gutted the animal and, by the sporadic light of the full moon-behind-clouds, tied his carcass to a sledge behind the horse. "It was not cowardice."

"Perhaps an evil spirit tormented you," Swifty Running Feet suggested. Her look was anxious. She knew the man she loved was courageous; yet, to falter at killing a White One with special blessings from the Manittos on his flank was incomprehensible to her. It was the prize of a lifetime.

"Perhaps an evil spirit," said Asondaki, leading the horse to their camp to await dawn departure, "but perhaps good. I do not know. But I am disquieted by it."

That night they bathed together once more, and shared the love that deepened between them each day. He would not stay at the Lake of Stones, but would go as far down the trail toward the east river region as possible. And he would return to take her as wife when the gods decreed.

"Why do I think there is no honor in this deed?" he asked himself as he moodily led her father's horse through the passage of rocks the next day. Riding part of the way, he was well along the trail. He had passed near the Lake of the Dark Spirit the evening before, and the monster that lived in it might have affected his thoughts, he noted grimly. But he had passed well beyond the dark lake now. That could not be it. Perhaps it was the parting. Swiftly Running Feet was as stoical as any Indian woman, but it moved him to see her standing beside her father, holding the tail of the deer he had given her. He was honored as a great warrior during the brief time he was in the Potawatomi camp. But no, it was not just that.

It was the strange feeling he had at the time of the killing of this White One. It was almost as if a hand restrained his trained hunter's arm from killing the majestic father of the forest. What kind of magic was it that could cause a warrior to stay his hand at the Great Kill? He did not feel the troubling of a bad spirit. It was more the dawning of a new idea, one he did not understand. Was it that the father of the forest had his right to life too? That was not an idea of the Wemiamiki; the Miamis taught that it was just and fair to claim your prey in the hunt, whatever it was. Was the blood of his white father corrupting him?

Was it really corruption? Just how did these seemingly indestructible white men reason? He did not know. For the first time he began to think about what sort of man his white father was, what sort of people these were, who could mount such armies and with the persistence of huge, pinching ants overrun the entire world. And as he thought, he wondered at them, with their houses of slats, their fine saddles, their machines that shot balls of iron or that ground corn or told time. He grew more and more troubled, as he walked this path to the home of the great chiefs of the Miamis.

Or, and he hardly dared to think this, was it that it seemed too futile to kill this magnificent spirit of the woods in these times of fallen fortunes? Yes, that was part of it, he was certain. Right now, as he drew near the new Miami village, Little Turtle would be preparing for this afternoon's council meeting, telling the people of the lake and woodland that the white man must be obeyed. A new American fort named after the wild general Anthony Wayne was already going up at Kekionga. There could be no thought of war parties with the new treaty. They must get hoes and watering jars and plant corn. And put leather shoes on their feet. Little Turtle now wore white man's shirts, had white man's money in his pocket.

What kind of magic was that, Asondaki thought with a sneer on his face. What kind of magic was it, by the Great Spirit, when Little Turtle gave up his leadership of the tribes-joined before Fallen Timbers to the Shawnee? If he had seen a vision and he was a great chief, why was the vision not good magic? Had he been as great as men said, his magic should have helped avoid the dismal defeat they had suffered.

It began to drizzle; the heavy clouds that had hung about for days were finally giving up their rain. He passed through showers, but by the time he rode into the new Miami camp near the small lake the rain stopped. Several youths who had not reached their Man-moon were outside playing shinney on a bare field in the light of a summer campfire. A group of older warriors wearing silk turbans lay, already drunk, near the chief's hut. They laughed loudly and tried to welcome him, but rum bound their tongues. It was a sight he saw more and more lately.

Raids are forbidden now, he said to himself. With all this rum and the trading posts, there will be no more Great Hunts. There will be no more fasting. The braves now say it is too difficult. And without a way to prove themselves, soon there will be no more warriors. I am coming to a chief who can no longer claim a people.

It is not Little Turtle's fault, an inner voice told him, but he would not listen to it. The magnificent kill he brought on the back of the horse spoke in a way that blotted out all thoughts except those of his own will.

Little Turtle sat at council, smoking with white traders and French *metis*. All except the chief rose when they saw what Asondaki laboriously carried into their midst, and even Little Turtle himself was struggling to stand.

But Asondaki would not allow that to happen. He dumped the carcass of the White One at the feet of Little Turtle. Its closed eyes did not look at him. The head was turned oddly on its side and the antlers seemed to be outsized, a tremendous weight in death.

"Here is the snow deer, old one. My Great Hunt is at your feet. I hereby name myself full Wemiamiki. I have earned that title of honor and strength long ago. As for you, you will have to find your own sense of honor yourself." The firelight glinted off the knives of the French *metis*, who watched him intently. Not often did an Indian raise his voice to the chief. Especially a young one. But then, these were changing days.

"One last thing," Asondaki said, speaking quickly before the chief's impassive face clouded in anger. "I do not know what kind of magic the white man has, but I do know that yours is gone. I have lived by the magic of the Manittos for years, and it does not seem to be working. I am going to find out what the white man's power is. I have decided to see what an American *metis* may accomplish. Goodbye, old man."

And he abruptly strode out of the circle to find his mother and uncle and pack his things. He would go fish for a while with the Potawatomis, where he was, temporarily at least, a hero.

Chapter XXVI

September was one of the busiest times of the year at the small Indian trading post of Antoine Lasselle on the Mississinewa River in what is now central Indiana, and the year 1797 was no exception. Weas and Miamis from nearby villages were coming in to see new goods which had just arrived. Lasselle's nephew Hyacinthe had just unloaded a pirogue he'd brought up the river—two bales weighing ninety pounds each of prime goods.

Indian women wearing colorful cotton skirts attentively surveyed new pots and pans made of copper and tin. Many other goods, double crosses then in fashion, rings with bezel stones, traps to catch animals that the Indians would use to pay for next year's goods, all were laid out under an enormous elm tree in front of the post.

The "new clerk" of the settlement, as he was called even though this was his second summer, stared from behind the log bench where the wares were displayed. By the river four teenaged boys were bringing in a stag on a long carrying stick, bass on a string, rabbits, geese, and wild rice traded from further north. The post would eat well for a while, he thought.

Asondaki, whom his employer called Arthur Dakin, turned his head to look back toward the Indian camp wigwams behind him. Young Lasselle was striding across the grass into the fur preparation area. Obviously, this soft, jowly young man who dressed in the wool blanket and stocking cap of a French *coureur de bois* or fur runner, wished to check the process which was putting thousands of dollars into his pocket. Young Wea women had stretched out branch frames and driven them into the ground. On them, they scraped and pounded buckskin for leather. One woman, her legs tucked under her long skirt, scraped flesh and fat from animal skins on the ground. Others were carrying leather skins to a vat to be soaked before they removed the hair. Then the skins would be smoked, dried, and placed on stretching frames under the trees.

Some Indian women were scraping blood and flesh from the underskin of pieces that would eventually be fine furs. Later these furs would be cleaned, dried, and stiffened on the skin-stretchers that stood all about this clearing. There were small, arrow-shaped cedar boards for fisher and mink and larger, almost round frames for beaver, queen of furs. The furs would be carefully tied with sinew to the round willow frames, then smeared with brain oil and let dry in the sun until they were ready for the sailing ships to carry them eventually to the fashionable men and women of Paris and London. Lasselle's eyes took in the scene, apparently with satisfaction. He turned to go back to his pirogue to load for the trip downriver without speaking to the Indians.

The fur trade was up again now after the devastation of the Battle of Fallen Timbers, and the call for furs had stimulated business in all the river valleys from Baton Rouge to Hudson Bay. The newly-named Arthur had come in just at the beginning of the new period of prosperity, and he spent his last year learning the workings of the trade here on the Mississinewa River from Hyacinthe Lasselle and his manager Nicholas Fortin. Arthur learned to measure as the French did when he handed out trade goods to the Indians. Rum and whiskey went by the demijohn and *chopine* or pint; cloth, chintz, kerseymere or muslin were measured by the *verge* or yard. Lead was sold by the pound or *livre*, weighed out on small scales called the steelyard.

It was not particularly easy for Asondaki to learn all these French terms and measurements. But Fortin, the *Bourgeoise* or manager, was willing to take extra time to explain the intricacies of the fur trade from the manager's point of view. This bright young Miami understood English, French, Potawatomi and Shawnee tongues and would probably pick up Spanish and Iroquois within a matter of months too. He would be an asset to the business.

Fortin had, of course, recognized him from the Miamis. He was the nephew of the interpreter, Hidden Panther, and he was half-white. Of his father Dakin would not speak, only to say he was a Kentuckian he did not know. That was enough for Fortin. After all, mixed alliances were common enough, and French traders viewed them as a singular advantage in the mixture of cultures that made up the northern fur empires, where Indian, Anglo-American and Frenchman met for mutual profit. As an American *metis*, Asondaki was getting used to an acceptance he had never known among the Miamis.

Asondaki told himself that he wished to know what made the white man move, what his powers were, and that was easy enough to discover. The white man worshipped gold, currency. Their god came with many faces, however: pounds of the New York market, livres of Montreal, shillings and now dollars. Or it might be piastres, sous, reals, francs, even "currency of the post." Not that much of this god actually changed hands. Early on, Asondaki discovered that it was the value of the substance that counted, credit extended for furs and the products they bought, which made the wheels turn.

In the winter and spring the Potawatomis, Weas, Foxes, Miamis, and all the other tribes of the Great Northwest went to the woods to trap and hunt. Loaded with skins, they came into the posts in spring and summer, where they received "plus" marks beside their names for the fine beaver they turned in.

"Beaver, about two dollars a skin, bucks a dollar or 'buck,' smaller furs perhaps half a dollar, and for a bear three dollars' worth of credit this year," Fortin had said, explaining the going rate to Asondaki. Since he had just begun to work, the new clerk was not as yet allowed to record transactions, but he needed to understand them. Fortin, a hearty man with prematurely gray hair, was a French expatriate who had come with his friend and partner Antoine

Marchal to Vincennes. Here he joined his life and fortunes to the French trading network that had existed for a hundred and fifty years. He was courting Susanne, the daughter of the well-respected Vincennes merchant Francois Bosseron. His partner Marchal had already married her sister Rose. Partnership with the related Lasselle family was helping make both Fortin and Marchal prosperous.

The closely-knit French trading network operating in the Northwest and Canada was a spider's web of marriages and cross marriages. But, as Antoine Lasselle the patriarch always said, "One might as well give a fistful of gold to a brother-in-law as a stranger."

One night in early fall that first year, Fortin brought Asondaki inside the trading cabin by the river to teach him to keep the books. He brought out the ledgers and sat Asondaki down among furs, bolts of cloth on roller wheels, and rows of bottles, combs, and foodstuffs.

The *Bourgeoise* had assumed that Asondaki could read, else why would he have ask for a job which involved keeping fur-account records? But Asondaki sighed, "These are so many scratches to me. Teach me to read French." Fortin took off his stocking cap and stomped some of the mud off his knee-high moccasins. He looked at the young *metis* steadily. Asondaki knew he was trying to decide if it was worth the time and effort to keep and teach him.

"We will try you for four weeks, until I go back to Vincennes for the winter." And four weeks later, after hours of learning symbols of the alphabet and elementary arithmetic, this bright young Arthur had made a good start towards reading.

"I will leave you in charge here," Fortin said. "I return in early spring." Asondaki looked pleased at the confidence the *Bourgeoise* felt in him, but Fortin took the edge off it when he said, "It's the tail end of the trading network anyway, barely a post at all compared to Michilimackinac or Montreal."

It was true, but Asondaki did not like to be reminded that when he was finally successful, it was at the end of nowhere. He felt the need to flash something back at the man to prove his independence, even if Fortin was his boss.

"Only till spring, then. After that I have business of my own."

But he stayed this full year and enjoyed it, as now when he looked across the trading table at an old wrinkled-faced grandfather of the Potawatomis who had brought many beaver skins to trade.

"How is this tobacco twisted, my son?" the Potawatomi asked, looking at a twist on the bark table before him.

"In the normal way, father, by two men twisting it in Kentucky after it has dried." The old man examined it.

"It seems loose-twisted to me. Do you have the kind of the South?" Asondaki considered. Normally, South American tobacco was reserved for Indians of the far North, but a shipment had arrived at the post and the word was about.

"It will cost you many skins if you buy much. It must come from far away and go to the land of the English and then here."

"But it is aromatic and tight-twisted. Fortin has told me a twisting machine," here he rolled his hands to indicated a spindle being whirled, "spins this tight as the cocoon of the luna moth."

Asondaki smiled. "You know your trading, father."

"And why not, my carrot-haired young one? My ancestors and yours, traded with nations as far away as the Creeks, while these Frenchmen sucked their thumbs and listened to the stories of the Black Coats in their own lands." Both laughed uproariously. The conversation was carried on in Potawatomi, a tongue in which Fortin was not fluent. He stood by a fur press, compressing furs into compact packets that would fit into the pirogues, and he barely glanced up. This Arthur could be trusted; he had shown that in the last two years.

The old Potawatomi glanced at Asondaki and went on. "Fortin and his chief Lasselle do not cheat the Indians as the other traders sometimes do. They do not give us iron axe heads that fall apart and call them steel."

"I do not think you would accept iron for steel, father. 'The wise old bear avoids the trap,' it is said."

"Not I perhaps," he conceded, grateful for the compliment, "but another, less experienced. The locks of guns that freeze in the winter, coarsely-made muzzles, cloth short-measured, demijohns watered-out—pah!" He spat upon the earth.

No, Asondaki thought, tallying what the old man bought against the skins he had brought in, Hyacinthe and Fortin do not cheat the Indians, because they must deal again next year, and now the Indians have many choices. There are Detroit and Montreal traders, Illinois country *metis*, and now four trading houses at Vincennes and Ouitanon to the west. Besides, to give them their due, Hyacinthe and Fortin are not bad as traders go. But their code is not that of the Wemiamiki.

"Take the first chance you get." That was Fortin's code. "If you don't find the furs first, someone else will." Fortin did not wait for the Indians of the Mississinewa Valley to come to him. He wooed them consciously by bringing them meal, flour, and whiskey for the cold, hard times of winter moons and by playing bullet and moccasin with them.

The social kinnikinnick tobacco he brought them, the whiskey and rum they drank in comradeship, he carefully tallied up in the account books. And Fortin wished much for himself. Ambition they called it; it was something the Indians did not understand well. Fortin was trying to talk Marchal into setting up a tannery on the banks of the Wabash at Vincennes to buy up unusable skins, supply the increasing demand for leather, and make them both rich.

Asondaki helped the old man load the bags of grain, vessels of oil, and casks of whiskey into his canoe. He asked him, "You have seen the old band chief Brown Squirrel?"

The old man nodded. "They are at the lower end of Michigan Lake."

"And his daughter, Swiftly Running Feet?"

"As swift as ever." He smiled a toothless smile.

"I hope to make her my bride when grass is first green for horses again." Asondaki reached into the shirt pocket. "Please take her these," a fine set of Venetian beads in iridescent blues, golds, and reds and a decorative cross with a double bar, made of real (if adulterated) silver.

"And tell her that I will have a fine wedding suit made, unlike anything she has seen, to show honor to her as my wife and to our sacred ceremony.''

The man pushed off in his canoe, loaded to the gunwales. "Beware of Lenni Pinja the Fire Tiger," Asondaki shouted after him. Fire Tiger was supposed to live beneath Mississinewa rapids and could turn the canoe over. Asondaki smiled a little; the old man nodded very solemnly and dipped his paddle into the water.

And as he climbed the bank, Asondaki asked himself, "Do you believe what you just said about the fire cat?" The answer, he suddenly realized, was that he did not.

Chapter XXVII

"Hmm," murmured George McClure, lifting a blob of sealing wax from a letter addressed to him from Passwater, Kentucky, and scanning its contents. "As if we don't have enough to do selling off and getting the move ready, here's a letter from Rob McClaren inviting us to one of those big tent meetings."

"What's it say?" Jean asked, interested. She was transferring pork preserved in salt brine from the smokehouse barrel to crocks in the cabin.

"Well, I'll read it to you. 'Was at the Cane Ridge meeting, thousands attended, many saw the Lord's power. Kentucky is dead to its own sins, indifferent to church, bored with life now that the Indians are gone and the land used up.' That's true enough." George commented.

"Go on," his wife urged.

" 'At Cane Ridge when the spirit moved, some fainted, some jumped. Others rolled on the floor.' Hmm, hmm and so forth. 'Quite a sight to see. The Presbyterian minister who is organizing the tent meeting is one of the new revolutionaries, a Clear Light they call them. He hopes for similar manifestations at Big Bend. Minister name of Simon Brockhurst Pinckney.' Sounds like it would be worth it to go just to see the faithful roll on the floor."

Jean set the covered crocks of brined pork out of the way in a keeping cabinet and began to beat eggs and milk to pour over bread crusts for bread pudding. "Now, George, you know that isn't what it's about. The odd things are only part of the changes that occur when people go to these revivals."

It was a blustery March day. Catherine at fourteen was an excellent nursemaid to her brothers and sisters and had bundled them up to go outside for a walk.

Jean wiped her hands on a towel and came to him. "I suspect if you take everybody in McClure Station to this revival, there will be as many reasons for going as there are seats in the wagon. But who knows, somebody may get help from going." She thought of Rob McClaren, now a minister with a wide preaching reputation. She had not seen him since he had appeared at her door last year. He had ridden half the night to get her. Her father, his body worn out from riding, organizing meetings, and bringing souls to the Lord on the circuit, was suddenly ill with apoplexy. She arrived in Passwater to hold his hand as he died. Even now, tears came to her eyes thinking about him. He had lived to see eight of his grandchildren.

George put the letter on a table. He had decided. "Let's go. I don't want to miss this, whatever it is. I'll talk to the others. Dan'l and John can't go, they'll be with Thompson scouting land in Vincennes. And Scott is an 'opposer of religion.' But everybody else, and the older children. . ."

"Yes," said Jean enthusiastically. "We can take three wagons, be comfortable and sleep in them and tents. Your mother might stay with the littlest ones. We could cook over the tripod—we can all use a revival." She poked at coals in the fireplace.

"Anyone in particular in mind?" George asked, making a wry face.

The road to Harrodsburg, now widened for wagon traffic, was choked with humanity when the day for the tent meeting came in early June. Wagoners bringing loads of goods to stores, Indians going to town to trade, and three wagons of McClures jostling along in small Conestogas with two-horse teams, all vied for space on the dusty road. Ish Scott drove Jenny and his grandmother Marguerite. George and Jean McClure rode on the seat of another wagon, with some of their older children in the back. Martha and Margaret had purposely decided to drive together with the "Dan'l bunch" and a couple of the older cousins who liked to be with them.

In Martha McClure's wagon the younger children nudged each other, rolled about, and finally put thumbs in mouths and slept on bolsters and quilts. Up front, Will's wife Margaret McClure seemed distant, remote. She watched birds start from trees as the wagon approached and rabbits bounce from grass at the side of the roads into fields of neat, almost knee-high corn.

"Somethin' the matter, Margaret?" Martha asked her.

"No," she said uncertainly.

"Yes, there is. There's quite a lot wrong at your cabin, isn't there?"

Margaret became testy. "What've you heard?" she demanded.

"What we've all known for years and been avoidin'. Things are gettin' worse, much worse, with Will, aren't they?"

Stony silence.

"You're my own flesh and blood, Margaret." It was true. Margaret was her niece, the daughter of her long dead older sister.

Finally she sighed. "I hoped we had kept it inside our own doors. I tried hard. I'm so ashamed."

"No need to feel ashamed. 'Tisn't your problem, is it? 'Tis his."

"Oh it's mine all right. Isn't a husband sittin' out in the shed at a little table with a candle on it lookin' into the flame and puttin' himself out of his head night after night a wife's problem? And then comin' in to scream and swear 'till the children bawl in fright and say they wish they were dead? Isn't that my problem?"

"I s'pose so," Martha murmured. Did that happen? They heard yelling and saw Will drunk outside, but inside the doors. . . they didn't know what went on.

"Now that you've found out what's goin' on, what Jenny's been sayin' all along, I'll tell you the rest. Might as well, I b'en denying it long enough. I b'en trying to hold things together but ever day it gets harder. I feel like I'm in the middle of a spider's web and somebody keeps stompin' on first one edge, then t' other to tear it down. Now they done gone and built that tavern at the new settlement at the crossroads. Keep a dipper right next to the whiskey barrel. Ever night, almost, they's fights over there jest for the sake o'fightin', tall tales bigger 'n the Smoky Mountains and everbody drinkin' themselves blue. And Will beats everbody at it. And now he's got his own tavern, right to home."

"I'm listenin'."

"Nobody paid much attention to him all those years when I guess we should 'a. He jest went to Bardstown before we split the station up, got drunk ever Saturday, sometimes Friday too. And snitched a little in between. I don't well remember how long he's had the little table set up in the shed. Calls it his den, fox den."

" 'Tisn't normal, is it?" her aunt asked.

"Martha, it is a sickness. Deathly sickness with Will, what I'd call it. Somethin' midway between pneumonia and crazy-as-a-loon. Can't be anywhere near normal to come in and dump a pot of scalding stew on your bare feet and never even know it 'till the next day."

"Still, I don't know if it's sickness. Lots o' people drink and they aren't sick."

"But he don't want to. He hates it, hates himself, hates what he does to all of us. But he won't admit it."

"Can't you just ask him. . ."

"I have begged him. He says what am I talkin' about? He didn't do none of those things I say he did the night before. Didn't leave the barn door open, didn't break the table stumblin' against it. Didn't pee on the floor and call me names. And if he did it was 'cause I druv him to 't by always bein' so angry. Then, acourse I do get mad and scream and the children cry."

"I didn't know you ever screamed."

"Oh, I do. I'm a good playactor afore the rest of the family. All of us in our cabin are. Not too long ago we had a night was the worst of all. He come in and picked up the baby. Batted me aside. Said he was a-goin' to bathe her. First he decided it would be in the wash tub, then when I threw the water out and he couldn't find any, said he'd take her to the crick. I thought I was goin' to die. To fear dyin' from your own husband is bad enough; to fear it for your helpless chile is like—stranglin' in your own tears. He was so outa his head he could 'a put her in the water down there and she would 'a slipped off 'fore I could get 'er. But sudden-like he slumped in a chair and went to sleep with her on his lap."

"He must've been horrified to think about it the next day."

"He couldn't remember it. When I told him, he acted like he couldn't understand what I said and turned away. Martha, it's like his feelings are froze. When I beg, tell him of our anguish, the younguns even get on their knees, he seems like a stone statue. He's dyin' from the ground up. When I first knew him, he could be sad or glad; now it's nothin' but the whiskey. Mother, wife, and God to him."

"Have you prayed?"

"Till my knees are raw. I prayed the day I married him that I'd be a good influence, change him mebbe. I prayed the night Johnny was born that havin' a child might make him wake up."

"You could leave," Martha suggested.

"That'd be pretty hard. And when he's right sober he's the best man you'd want to know. And a good provider. He bought me a silk dress from Louisville when he sold a load of bricks the other day." She smoothed her skirt and looked over a cane patch to a hollow by the Kentucky River.

"I'm not lookin' forward to goin' to Indianney," Margaret went on. "Devil in a bottle will follow us." She was silent for a long while, then spoke grimly. "The worst part is the not knowin'. Wonderin'. The sun comes up, marigolds and scarlet sage bloom so purty outside in my garden and I say, will it be a drinkin' day or no? Will the children end up hiding, sobbing in the loft? Will I have to put away the knives and guns? Jest think, Martha, of livin' a whole life like that."

Martha shook her head, sincerely sorry, not knowing what to advise.

"And beyond that, seein' him kill himself dram by dram. The church has took away his membership. Out in the shed 't other night, after I tole him he almost drowned the babe, I heard him finally cryin'. 'Twas a sound to break your heart. He's done it again a couple times since."

Margaret took out a bottle of lemonade and poured them each a glass and said, stonily, "So I gave up prayin' for him. I pray for me. That I can stand it one more day."

"Maybe at the Revival you'll get the strength you need."

"Mebbe. I 'spec' all of us has somethin' to ask for."

"Well, I don't," Martha said emphatically. "My life is so good, so very good I just don't think it could be more perfect."

She smiled a tight smile and poked her finger in one of the sausage curls she had done up so carefully with her new curling iron this morning, fluffing it up a bit. "Good lemonade, Margaret," she said.

"Glad you like it, Martha," the younger woman said, and urged the horses to "git up" so they could get to Big Bend in time to set on supper.

Fourteen-year-old Jack McClure stretched his limbs on the floor of the wagon. 'Tis cramped here, he thought, looking at the legs of his cousins Jim and Catherine in the back corners. Better, though, than sittin' up front listenin' to the blather his mother Martha and Aunt Margaret were puttin' out.

What was it they was talkin' about? He strained to catch a few words. Oh, 'twas a serious discussion about Uncle Will's always bein' three sheets to the wind. Nothin' new there. He lay back, watching the sky and trying to think of all the synonyms he knew for the word drunk. Pickled. Sodden. Half shaved, grogged. Full as a tick, corned, bowzered. White summer clouds went by, and they took the shapes of animals, an elephant with three white knobs for a trunk, an anteater with a humpback. He spoke to his cousin Jim.

"I got the powders."

"Spunky. I got the yarbs."

Their cousin Catherine looked down at them from her corner. "Whut yarbs and powders?" She spoke in a soft whisper with heavy articulation of the lips to avoid being overheard.

Jack looked at her, considering. Catherine had always been a part of their escapades, but lately her high-spiritedness had transformed itself into something else, something that no longer included making mischief with boy cousins.

"Waal, I don't know. I don't think you better know. Efn you don't get ahold of a snake's tail in the first place, he ain't gonna bite you."

"Don't make me no never mind," Catherine said haughtily, patting her blonde hair, which was held up and back in a bun with a wooden pin. She was at this point both the joy and anguish of her parents, hoyden and angel by turns. Since she was seven, she had been more interested in the woods and fields than in reading the books her parents constantly presented to her. Her speech was their despair.

"I don't see why all the children who grow up in the woods have to talk the same, abandoning the rules of English grammar and syntax," George McClure said.

Her mother agreed. "I was always told that if children heard King's English spoken in their homes, they would pattern their own speech on it."

"I kin talk good efn I want to, but I like to talk like everbody else 'round here. I don't want ta stand out." There had only been two or three years of schooling for these McClure children. The needs of day-to-day survival, Indian fighting, planting and clearing absorbed their family's energy, leaving little for hiring a subscription teacher and "settin' up school reglar'." Still, Catherine's well-educated parents knew she was far above average in intelligence and mourned her lost education.

Catherine resembled her mother not only in beauty and brightness, but also in the effusive religious belief that seemed so vital to them both. Unlike her two boy cousins, Cat was interested in the "speertchul" part of the revival they would be attending.

Now she looked down over her nose at these two cousins of hers. They could never be still. Hadn't grown up atall yet. Always settin' up jokes, makin' grapevine loops for people to step in, overturnin' neighbors' privies, settin' dogs to horses' flanks. Jack, particularly, should have been whopped years ago, but Aunt Martha didn't believe in whoppin' this dazzlin', magnificent production of a boy, Catherine thought scornfully. Still, Jack was all right, he would turn out fine, in spite of all the mollycoddling. She had to be fair about it. "Tell me what you're up to," she demanded, curiosity overcoming pride. She still maintained the position of childhood queen of the group, and so Jack pulled himself up on one elbow and answered her.

"Waal, you know the yarb doctor Doc Blackenship?"

"You mean Divil Doctor Don?"

"That's what all the uneddicated calls him," Jack said. "He's a man o' true genius. You heerd of his cures."

James spoke up. "He has receipts to cure anything. Sixty-three o' 'em. Biles up spikenard, white plantain leaves, mixes the leavin's with stuff like cider 'n honey and cures whoopin' cough or anything.''

Catherine was unconvinced. "I know everbody's always talkin' bout him. He lives in that little place by Dogleg Crick. But our folks thinks he's crazy. How do you know him, anyways?"

"Shh," Jack warned her, pointing with a toss of his head toward his mother and aunt on the seat, heads together. "We snuck away several times. He's a great genius, Cat! Has had all kinds of fascinatin' experiences that turned him into a inspired doctor.''

"Sech as?"

"Waal, here's how he tells it. Grew up as a real terror, he did. Plunged a cat into a bilin' pot o' cabbage and bacon, he did. Then he buried a dog alive and drank so much he blew a hole in the roof of his cabin with his pa's gun. When he grew up, he married a Injeean lady, almost died o' bilbious dysentary,'' he frowned, "sumpin' like that. Anyways, he was cured by the famous yarb doctor from the Kanawha, Doctor Dykome, and from then on in he had found his callin'. Doctorin' people the right way.''

"Tell 'er the important thing," Jim McClure urged. He was a young man of few words, who conveyed his emotions with mysterious smiles or lifts of the eybrows.

"Waal, these sixty-three concoctions he makes up and sells to the public. Makes lots o' money. The receipts are secret, acourse." His voice took on an even more hushed, excited tone. "By a stroke o' rare luck, he has deigned to share one o' 'em with us. Receipt Number Forty-Two for pain relief. Could be very valuable." He took out a wrinkled piece of paper from the pocket of his buckskin trousers.

"So?" Catherine said coolly. Everyone knew those pain relief remedies worked only so far.

"Tell 'er the money part."

"Suppose they was a remedy fer pain. A real one. Not like laudanum, which puts people out but only half-way. Why, if you could put people asleep with a potient, operations could happen ever day. You wouldn't have to have five strappin' men hold a pachunt down while the surgeon cuts the hell out 'o him and he thrashes around to beat all git out.''

Jim put his word in, finally. "And when a man broke his leg, you could set it with the Elixir of Relief. He would jes' go to sleep.''

"Elixir of Total Relief," Jack corrected emphatically. "That's whut we're a-gonna call it. We're goin' to invent it!"

He spoke so loudly his mother turned about. "What're you up to, Jackie McClure?" she asked with a familiar edge to her voice.

"Nothin', Ma dear," he said sweetly. They had these altercations, mixtures of love and irritation at least four times daily. They were worse lately, especially with his pa gone to the Buffalo Trace into Indianney. Jack's frame had shot up until he was as tall as his mother and considerably thicker. As a child he had been shaped like a top; now, he was shaped like a giant turnip with a top that was a shock of straight, brown-black hair exactly like his father's. His favorite game was matching his very considerable wit against his mother's.

"Invent? Where?" Cat looked incredulous.

"Right out in the woods, at the revival, whilst everbody else's busy prayin' and gettin' the Spirit. You don't think we're gonna spend our time listenin' to them preachers tirade 'bout the torments o' the damned and the bliss o' the souls on the shores o' the heavenly river, do ye?"

"Hell, no," Jim piped up, profanely defiant, albeit in tones muted enough so his aunts would not hear. "Cat, you be'n noticin' Johnny McClure readin' a lot lately at your house?"

She nodded. Her Uncle Will and Aunt Margaret's oldest son, devoted slave of the two older boys, had been spending a good deal of time at the bookshelf in their cabin.

"He has been searching your pa's liberry for the works a ainchunt and modern science 'n alchemy to see the best sleepin' potients."

"Magic?"

"Not at all. Jes' ole lore. Acshually, we 'ere usin' the methods o' modern science. Esperimentation. See these yere boxes I tole Ma was huntin' and fishin' gear? A portable laboratory." Catherine poked her foot under a tarpaulin covering various books, bottles, and wooden boxes.

"Doc Blankenship giv us some o' his powders and syrups."

"Do he know what you're up to?"

"Not essactly," Jack answered uncomfortably. "But he giv us a order to fill at the apothecary's in Harrodsburg for him, and he said we could keep out some o' the powders."

Jim broke in, "Do you know that in Lexington a man has been shippin' bottles o' elixir all over the Northwest Territory at fifty cents a bottle? He got him a fortune in them there bottles. An' that's only fer liver trouble and itches." He turned onto his stomach. His mouth was in its usual straight line; he rarely smiled.

His cousin Jack continued. "We're goin' to set up the esperiment out beyond the last circle. In the woods."

"And how is your elixir goin' to be different from anybody else's?" Cat demanded. "How you gonna git people deep asleep and keep 'em there?" Her hand was on her waist, her head cocked scornfully.

"Easy, Miss Priss. Jim and me and Johnny air gonna find all the pain-killin' and sleepin' remedies we can git our li'l hands on and mix em' up together and the combined effects will revolutionize the physician's science."

"Waal, good luck. And you better stay out o' the way o' your ma and the aunts, that's all I can say."

"Believe me, I will. Hope Ma don't ast too many questions. Her nose's as sharp as a woodpecker's when it comes to pokin' into my business." He prepared to hop down in a few minutes when they would reach Harrodsburg.

Chapter XXVIII

Ish McClure Scott and his mother Jenny and grandmother Marguerite stopped only overnight at the Big Bend revival. They planned to use the opportunity of being in the neighborhood north of Harrodsburg to make a family visit, to go ten miles or so out in the country to Marguerite's brother Joseph's house. As soon, then, as Ish had tethered the horses, he disappeared, leaving his mother and grandmother to trek the overgrown path to Uncle Joseph's house alone.

I do try with Ish, Jenny thought, as she walked along the path with her mother-in-law, and God alone selects the kind of cross each livin' one of us must bear. But to see your only child so difficult and so disliked by everybody who knew him was a cross she sometimes thought was designed by devils in hell instead of the Almighty.

It is my fault, she thought hurriedly, as she always did when something trying happened with Ish. Yesterday, for instance, after they had arrived at Big Bend campgrounds, he set the tent up in the "tent circle" so poorly it collapsed on her and Marguerite in the night, and she so weary after the long trip she could hardly get up to right it again. But she hadn't told him exactly how to do it, now had she? And after all, if he was spoiled, who did she have to blame for that but herself?

It should have been easy to set up the tent, but as in the case of so many jobs that seemed easy for others, Ish could not or would not concentrate on it. Where was he when you spoke to him, she wondered? His eyes often looked far off, as if he were listening to a distant harmonica concert in the deep woods. Because of this inability to focus on anything and the restless mischief that made him all but useless on the hundred acres, his father had given up on him long ago, shrugging that he was "no good," and avoiding him when possible.

That meant that Jenny only had to work harder at being a good mother, to praise him when she could, telling him what a good shot he was. That was easy enough, because Ish could shoot anything that moved half an acre away, and the one thing he took good care of was his gun. He also loved to ride horses. The only other person who could tolerate him beyond his mother was his Aunt Janie, who sometimes let him ride and curry for her.

The other thing this strange child liked to do was read. Jenny would never forget the day she taught him. He picked it up quickly and from then on read everything in their cabin and begged books of even Uncle George, coming home eventually with such odd things as *Anatomy of Melancholy* and Aunt Jean's rare *Voyage to the Moon* by Cyrano De Bergerac.

"Bright," thought Jenny, encouraged when he read so much. She had heard that clever children were often troublesome. "I think he must be brighter than others, don't you, Mother?"

Her mother had not really answered. Jane McClure, Jenny knew, had long ago decided that if she were going to live peaceably in her daughter's home, she must hold her tongue and allow the parents to raise this child. And she also knew that she needed her own room, with a separate entrance door. It would serve as a shop for her anyway. Dan'l and James Scott obliged, and she was able to shut the door on Ish's problems. Jenny saw all this, and she understood.

Besides, Ish could be charming, even her mother admitted that. Often adopting the manners of someone older, he would usher his mother and Grandmother Jane to the supper table with a flourish of his round felt hat. Then he would regale the table for an hour with amusing stories, if he felt like it.

With his other grandmother, Ish's relationship was quite different. Marguerite Scott left her Catholic community in Lexington frequently to visit her son and his family, and her eyes were often on Ish. Gently but firmly, she commanded and he obeyed, if reluctantly. Marguerite told James Scott that she had formed a bond with the boy even before Ish's birth. It was one of her typical, incomprehensible comments, James thought. Now, just as unpredictably, she had decided to come with Jenny to the revival to see her brother, who lived up the road from Big Bend. A freed slave who took care of him had sent word that Uncle Joseph had appeared slightly ill when the black man had stopped by last.

The overgrown path back to the old man's cot seemed particularly long on this hot June day. "We're almost there," Jenny said over her shoulder to Marguerite.

"Ish. . ."

"Ish'll come in when he wants to. I told him I wanted him to meet Uncle Joseph. Ish has been reading about the French revolution."

Jenny wondered at the strength of a political system that could send this man flying across a distant sea to live for ten years as a hermit among strangers. How afraid he was the few times she had seen him, even now. He lived in panic that a rude knock at the door in the night or the visitor he did not know in town might represent the Revolutionary Committee that had put his name on the death list.

Marguerite told her that Joseph LaFrenier had been only a minor landowner when he returned to France from America to claim a family inheritance in Lyon. He became mayor of the town and conspired with the clergy in his village to try to stop the drowning and guillotining of thousands of citizens who opposed the politics of the reactionary leader Robespierre. Then one night, finally, he found out that his name appeared on the execution list. Somehow, through an awful ordeal that he did not discuss with anyone, he escaped and came to America in disguise and sought out his sister. After living with her for a while, he finally chose asylum in the woods. Here, still dapper and wearing an aristocrat's knee breeches, he raised currants for an annual money crop.

Jenny tapped at the door; there was no answer.

"I hope his illness has not grown worse," her mother-in-law said. As they waited, Jenny glanced at the basket of food his sister had fixed for him, a special fish chowder which would stay fresh for several days if kept cool, shortbread, lemon tarts.

Jenny pushed open the door, calling the old man's name softly; Marguerite followed her in. As Jenny's eyes grew accustomed to the gloom, she gasped. There in the corner, half-on, half-off his meager straw bed, lay Joseph LaFrenier, his jaw slack, his limbs rigid. He had been dead for at least two days. Marguerite, weeping, silent, went to the side of the dead man and knelt to pray. Turning her back, Jenny went to seat herself on one of the two low chairs in the cabin, her emotions in an upheaval. Must not be upset, she thought. The baby.

It was true. Jenny Scott, at the age of forty-one, was finally expecting another child. She was determined this pregnancy and birth would go well. The last and only other one, for reasons she could not explain, had been an out-of-control time of torture, days of nausea and headaches, excruciating pains in the legs, threatening signs of miscarriage. But these two months had been bliss, an interlude of joy so pure she thought each day must have been blended for her alone, like the essences of perfume. It must continue. She would do whatever was needed to see that it did continue. The last thirteen years with Ish had taught her strength of will, if nothing more.

She stood and went to Marguerite, steeling herself as she approached the pallet. No time to get anyone else to help them. This poor man needed to be buried. She heard a slight rustle as deerskin trousers flapped against each other and turned to see Ish watching her.

"Ish, I'm glad you're here. Uncle Joseph, as you can see, is dead." Ish did not answer. She had never let him go to a wake before. When Ardry Bard drowned and his wife died of fever all in the same week, the other children all went to pay their respects. Ish, though, had stayed back.

"Get a shovel," his mother told him. "It's fallin' to us to bury him."

"To you, mebbe. Not to me. It goes agin' my grain."

Marguerite's voice was firm in her ear. "No. You cannot allow him to leave us with this impossible job, to dig a hole for a corpse with rigor mortis. The baby inside you needs to be strong and rested. Tell him."

"Ish, listen to me," Jenny said. "You will get that shovel. We will all take this poor man out and bury him decently in the soft garden area. We will read a few words over him from the holy book." She glanced at his missal and picked up the crucifix which lay on top of it.

Ish began to protest. "Or. . ." his mother said, more firmly than Marguerite had ever heard her, "you will never expect anything more from me in this life. You can be apprenticed in the city."

For a long moment Ish said nothing, his face blank. Then, finally, "I will dig the hole, but," his eyes blinked just a fraction of an inch toward his grandmother, "she can read the words. It's her mumbo-jumbo anyways." Marguerite did not seem to take notice of the rude remark.

"And throw those Popish things on the dung piles," he said, gesturing toward the crucifix and missal book. "I won't go near him 'till that trash is out of the cabin." His mother gave him a hard look and complied with the demand.

It was soon arranged that Ish would dig and Marguerite prepare the body as best she could. Jenny must not, in her condition, handle a corpse who died of unknown causes, even though he did not appear to have expired from some malignant fever. Joseph could not be buried in consecrated ground. Jenny knew this would grieve Marguerite, but they must do the best they could and expect God to forgive under the circumstances.

"I've never understood why the French killed their own people," Jenny murmured as Marguerite washed the corpse.

"It was war. All Europe rose against France so the Revolution would not spread and take their own kings off the thrones." Marguerite's phrasing was formal, her accent heavy. "Joseph was a lieutenant colonel in the first days. But Robespierre began to fear enemies within France would ruin the war effort. Thousands were executed who did not agree with him. Joseph believed he had to fight to save his fellow townspeople."

Jenny walked sadly about in the cabin alone, after Marguerite and Ish went to bury Joseph down the hill, by the creek. It was all so wasteful. This man, driven out, dying so far from home in the worst, stupidest sort of war, that where brother fights brother on home ground.

She was moved by the sad touches of Joseph's hermit-like existence. The stack of *Moniteurs*, on the top one the headline, "Bonaparte Becomes First Consul," in French. A shelf with a trencher, pipe, bag of meal and two eggs. These humble traces of living made the dead man she hardly knew seem so human, so vulnerable. Her eyes fell on a tiny maple table in the shadowy corner by the bed. On it were three wig forms with old fashioned tie-wigs on them. Out here with wolves and bears Joseph still had his gentleman's pride.

She walked outside, past the forlorn currant bushes, which had never even grown right. Right now Marguerite, down the hill, would be shovelling dirt. Before too long her mother-in-law would be praying, "I am the Resurrection and the Life," holding Joseph's crucifix, with Ish standing sullenly by.

Was it necessary for Uncle Joseph to have to flee, to die in seclusion? He could have kept his mouth shut, many probably did. Perhaps he had cared too much about it all. But hadn't Marguerite told her many times in the last years that we must love enough to fight against evil for those we care about? Though Jenny had resisted the idea for a long while, wanting only to be left in peace, she now believed it was true. If one loves, one must struggle.

She smiled a bit and unconsciously patted her stomach. Love for this unborn child, pure, sweet as honey, filled her thought. "I would fight a dragon for you," she said to this child who had not even moved yet for the first time.

She reached the creek. Marguerite said she would eventually meet her here when the grim work was completed. It would not be for a while. She hoped it would not take them long to set the house in order after that; they had a two-hour drive ahead of them back to the revival camp.

Meanwhile, the air would do her good, Marguerite had said.

Probably so. A few years ago Jenny would not have had the courage to walk by this creek which flowed into the Kentucky River. But she had had no bad, prophetic dreams for many years now. Perched on a knoll by the creek as the sun passed under a cloud, she sat very still, but she did not fall asleep. Later she was to remember that very clearly; she did not sleep.

A strange mist rose from the water and seemed to envelop her very quickly, bringing with it a numbness that almost made her faint. Coming to herself, she saw with a gasp that the scene had changed before her eyes. June had passed to what looked like October, a searing, hot October. The creek trickled dirty and low; yellow sycamore leaves floated on its surface and accumulated at the rocks by its side currents.

Transfixed, almost frozen in place, she watched a drama unfold before her eyes. Two groups of men, not at first aware of each other, approached the stream. She could see their faces: hot, dusty faces of boys gone to war. These were not the dragoons she knew, with tight, ornate jackets buttoned up at the collar and skin-tight breeches. These men wore shirts, long, loose-cuffed pants, and caps. What, and where was this? A skirmish began. They shot at each other with guns which loaded in a miraculously quick way. Were they fighting for water rights in a terrible war? She would know more and stood up, fearful that the vision would fade. It did not.

She searched through the scene mentally, trying to understand it, and the vision broadened. The emotions of other people washed over her, the sounds of hundreds, no thousands of feet marching, of scores of arguing voices in the plains of Illinois and the halls of government, the cries of women and children dragging about barefoot in fields, of mothers parted from sons and wives from husbands, artillery, and the cries of the dying.

She put her hands to her head, but she would not stop looking. The vision moved beyond the creek, to a glade nearby. Before her on a farm lot some of the young men she had just seen, men wearing blue uniforms, were manning small cannon. Not one hundred yards away men in brown-gray uniforms fired hotly at the cannoneers, killing horses, driving back the blue troops. She seemed to pass into the midst of a group of blue foot soldiers who advanced to protect the cannons. The smoke choked them. Gray-suited sharpshooters climbed trees and began to aim at the blue men below them. She surveyed the faces of the blue support regiment and read feelings, as she was able to do in these visions. Odd, there was little fear here, only hatred of the other side, desire to do duty, and the wish for the whole thing to be over.

Her wandering thought rested on a group of new recruits. Here indeed was anxiety; no, it was petrifying fright. Her eye stopped at a tall, blonde young man with his hat off. She was drawn to him; an odd attraction moved her. Looking at him, she was conscious of knowing and loving this young man as deeply as she loved the new babe in her womb. The bullets flew, and a boy next to the young man was shot in the eye. Instantaneously, and excruciatingly, Jenny experienced odd details she eventually remembered better than the battle itself—the wounded boy falling face up, leaves sifting down over his young face and the shattered eye socket, blood on crushed acorns, the eerie noise of what sounded like Indian war whoops.

The blonde young man stood poised with the rest to follow a colonel on horseback who led them, ready to drive back the enemy. Suddenly, her perspective shifted and telescoped in on a tree across the field. There a brown-coated sharpshooter took careful aim at—the tall, blonde young soldier she now knew she loved.

"No, no," she shouted wordlessly at the shapshooter. She could see his keen eye, feel his breath, fetid with poor food and whiskey. Tears of frustration formed in her eyes. Suddenly Marguerite's words came into her mind. "If we love, we must sometimes fight." She reached out to feel, encounter the evil she was now determined to combat, and it came to her through the acrid smoke of battle, a loping beast, cold with the damp of the grave. It was the warring of brother against brother.

Jenny rose to combat. She stared into the frightened, unknowing eyes of the boy. Glowing with love, she knew she was stronger than the evils before her, that the kind of love that had grown in her through years of trouble was stronger than fear and the grave and even time itself. Jenny stood before the boy and cried out, pointing her finger, "Move, the sharpshooter aims at you." For an instant the proud, fierce eyes of the boy fixed on where she stood and—the scene vanished. Her head swam and she turned to see the calm, summer scene by the side of the creek.

Oh, my God, she thought numbly as she walked toward the cabin to find where Ish and Marguerite were. What was the meaning of the frightful vision she'd just had? The flag the standard bearer had carried had many stars in rows. Her flag had only sixteen stars sprinkled about a random field. She had been beyond her own time. Who was the boy she tried to save from the sharpshooter? Perhaps she would never know. Where was the place? Right here, on the farm beyond this creek. Jenny was exhausted by the time she found Marguerite by the cabin.

"What is the name of the settlement near here?" she asked, gasping for breath.

"Harbison's Fort," her mother-in-law answered. "But they are thinking of changing it now that forts aren't necessary. Who knows what it will be called in the future?"

Chapter XXIX

The sounds of "The Church's One Foundation," sung by two thousand voices were still resounding around the crofts and glens of Big Bend Church clearing when Jim, Jack, and Johnny McClure raced to the woods beyond the outer circles, where they had hidden their scientific gear the night before.

"Bastion L. E., L for Laboratory, E for elixer," Johhny read on the boxes, excitedly, proud to be included with his older cousins in the adventure.

"I got the refreshments," said Jim, spreading out the contents of a hamper—lemonade and gourd dippers and the ginger cakes his Grandmother Jane had made.

"This is a job lot o' stuff to be carryin' through the Virginia creeper," Jack mumbled, setting down another load of pots and powders. He picked burrs off his leggings. "But we're bein' thorough. That's the secret of the scientist's method. I done read a lot 'bout 'em."

He beckoned the other two to come over to him. "We got three types o' substances to mix, and we're each goin' to be responsible for one. Johnny, you're goin' to git the roots for the root pot," Jack instructed his cousin. "Be sure to dig plenty while you're at it. All these receipts calls fer tubfuls o' the stuff bilin'." He looked at his scribbles, gleaned through hours of scientific research. "Take twenty gallons o' sweet cider 'n bile it till it form a syrup. 'Waal, we ain't got cider, but we kin take these yere early apples an' stomp 'em up with crick water. Ought to give 'bout the same effect."

Johnny looked dubious but waited for more instructions.

"I wrote this down; you look at it whilst I go over 't. Now you gotta git a handful o' bark o' yaller poplar and dogwood, and be sure it's from the north side o' the tree. Yellow sarsapariller and roots o' runnin' briar."

"Briars?" Johnny protested. "That means I gotta pull 'em up. That'll smart some. Cain't I jest. . ."

"Jes' put some oak leaves on yore hands afore you pull 'em up. Ten gallons o' syrup o' spikenard root. . ."

"They ain't any spikenard out here."

"Guess not. Waal, git ground ivy. It'll prob'ly do as well. I saw plenty over by the tents. Ten gallons essence of parsley root—Johnny, you git all that stuff."

"Jim, you 'n I are goin' to assemble the powders and yarbs and liquors we brought and bile 'em down in the small pot,'' Jack continued. He read the receipts. "Hmm, opium, got that ready, three quarts whiskey, got that from Uncle Will's shed. . .''

Johnny looked stricken, and Jack, who had quite a bit of underlying compassion, went quickly on—

"Ahem, we bile all these things we brought down to a mere essence.'' He put two fingers close together to show how small the amount would be.

"It'll all go off in steam,'' Jim protested sceptically. "Anyways, shame to bile away good likker.''

"But on the bottom of our copper pot (must be copper) will be a residoo of salts. Now you know what two quarts of liquor does to any normal man. This residoo'll add a real whomp to the sop-o-rific qualities of the potient. Besides, I got us a few quarts more whiskey to put in as straight likker at the last. Yes, indeed, make it real sop-o-rific.''

"Whut's 'at mean?'' Johnny asked. Jack always used big words, almost as big as his ideas.

"Means it'll put 'em under the table afore you can say Tom Jefferson,'' his cousin Jim answered.

"We add a few extra items from ainshunt lore. You can git 'em, Jim. These books 're shore all-fired interestin','' Jack said, thumbing through one of the doctor's medical library offerings. " 'Efn you wish a member of the opposite sex to be interested in you, it is merely a matter of concentration. Think constantly of the beloved. Draw a pitcher of him or her and put it on yer drawin' room table. Run yer hand over the pitcher. He or she will think o' you at the very same moment, it is a shore thing.' ''

"Hurry up. It's hot out here,'' Jim said irritably.

But Jack continued thumbing, "Umm, horses, 'founder, heaves, bots, drench the horse with sweet milk and molasses'. . . I jest might be a doctor someday myself. Here we are. Now this is the hard part, Jimmo. I found this part, 'sleeping remedy' 'twas called, from a dusty ole book o' Uncle George's called *Ye Rare and Singular Rootes and Herbs and Their Efficacies in Physicke*. Jim, you got to get a goat's pizzle.''

"Whut? Where in catookit am I gonna git the pizzle of a goat?'' he demanded.

"I saw some goats a-standin' in that farmyard jest outside the campground,'' Jack ventured tentatively.

"But Jackie, no goat is gonna stand still for us to cut his pizzle. Anyways, it would hurt him bad.'' Jim had inherited his mother's sympathy for the beasts of the field.

"Waal, I guess a deer 'd do jest as well. Remember that dead one we saw far off by the crick on our way here?''

"Jest a suppose I'm a-goin' to go up to a bloated, stinkin' varmit half et by vultures and crawlin' with vermin. . .''

"It says pizzle and we better have one. It's goin' to take some sacrifices, we all know that. All the books say that the scientists sacrifice. Why Uncle George says Lavoseyear got his head whopped off in the Revolution—so gettin' a dead deer's pizzle ought to be nothin'. Also, umm, the feet o' a hoptoad.''

Jim sighed as he and Johnny headed for the edge of the clearing to begin to gather ingredients. Then he shouted back toward his cousin, "Whut was it agin that you was goin' to do, pray tell?"

"I'm the chemist. Lavoseyear McClure. As you bring the stuff in, I get the roots a bilin', salts a settin'." The boys stomped off.

Better put in plenty of calomel, Jack told himself. I sure enough got plenty o' that from Harrodsburg. Divil Doc Don alwuz says in the last resort, try calomel. No receipt's a receipt without it. Well, we'll bile this all day and bank her to simmer slow tonight. By tomorrow we'll have a good potful of pain-killin' sleepin' potient."

He went to check his bottles. "This here shore is better'n the Bible class most o' them miserable sinners is a-goin' to," he chuckled to himself.

The Reverend Simon Brockhurst Pinckney looked out from the log pulpit of the preachin' stand that evening. Two thousand people crowded under the roof of the open structure looked back. Babies sucked their thumbs and stretched out on quilts on benches; rough-looking men with two weeks' growth of beard sat slack-jawed and uncomfortable. They would listen tonight, Pinckney thought, and some of them would benefit in spite of themselves. But it was the women, the calico-clad, expectant-faced women of this Kentucky frontier he preached to anyway. Bored beyond bearing with their drudgery, emotionally starved, they exulted in the richness of the emotional experience he could provide.

Pinckney saw his fellow preacher Rob McClaren sitting out in the congregation with his friends George and Jean McClure. He would be a severe critic of the sermon. McClaren knew how to preach, even if he was not totally committed to the ministry of revival. Had his doubts sometimes, he said. Pinckney wondered what all of these people were thinking as he gathered his notes. What were they saying to each other as they prepared to be moved, uplifted, reformed by what he said?

Martha Bard McClure and her sister-in-law Margaret sat with Will McClure on one of the middle benches.

"Where are the boys, Marg?" Martha wondered, her eyes fixed on the entrance gate of the stand.

"Snuck off, I 'spect, to the woods to play their games."

Her sister-in-law looked apprehensive, so Margaret was reassuring. "We cain't watch them all the time. After all, they're big enough to kill buffaloes, and both of 'em have a-done it already. Them an' Jim'll be all right."

"I s'pose so. It jest worries me so much that I can't tell what Jack's thinkin'."

"Mebbe you ain't meant to," Margaret said serenely. "Will you look at Cat and Mary McClure?" she went on to ask, craning her neck around to see the side benches on the other side of the gathering. "They can hardly wait for the preacher to start." A row of younger McClure chidren wrestled and fell under the benches, but beyond them the older girls sat fixedly watching the podium.

"Emotin' is what it is," Will put in in a cold voice. He seemed morose; perhaps, Margaret thought, it was because he promised her faithfully not to drink at the revival and was trying to keep his promise. When he promised like this it made him surly. Usually promisin' didn't work anyways. Still, a revival, if anything, might cause him to keep his promise.

"Now Will, you've got to admit it was pretty impressive," Martha insisted, "just to see ten preachers at two o'clock in the afternoon conductin' services all around the first circle at their wagons, or made-up altars, or even stumps. Baptists at one side, Rob McClaren doin' the Methodist preachin' next to them, Free Light on the other side. A lot 'o good can come out o' these things."

Rob McClaren, at George McClure's side in the row ahead of them, was expressing it in a different way as the vast assembly began to quiet for the first hymn. "If somebody, even one somebody, stops sendin' himself to perdition, dyin' a little each day, ruinin' his own and his family's lives, I'll be satisfied that the revival worked. There's a lot of odd goin's-on at these things, but they do stop people in their tracks. And you know, to git a dog to stop barkin', you've got to first git his attention."

Jean McClure looked tenderly at Rob. He had changed a lot in the last year or two. The "Boy Preacher" was no longer a boy. Lines of sadness deepened his eyes and his smile was small and sad. His wife of a year left him two months ago with one of the church members and went to West Florida.

"She said she was all churched out," Rob had told Jean earlier. "Ever time the church doors opened, said we was there. Love feasts, mornin' preachin', evening testimonies and evidences. Box social, she as the preacher's wife had chicken to fry. Weddin' got up sudden, we supplied the cakes and punch. Said I never had the energy to pay her any mind. 'Twere partly true."

Jean nodded sympathetically, looking up into his earnest, strong young face.

"She said she jest didn't have anything more to give to God. But I do, I think." Jean clasped his hand now. He had much to give; he was one of the most convincing, gifted preachers she had ever heard. She felt it again at the service this afternoon. People trusted his honesty, the deepness that had developed in him during the last few years.

The hymn was beginning. After it was over, Reverend Pinckney waited for silence to fall. George watched the minister looking out with piercing eyes, like a red hawk, best of hunters of the woods. Pinckney's features were as aquiline as his gaze, his hair a mane of premature white above the rugged, ruddy face. Unlike most of the ministers here, he was dressed in homespun and buckskin. His well-cut shirt was decorated Indian fashion with scenes from the gospel. The audience waited in a hush of expectation. The minister gripped the pulpit with a strong hand and smiled. His confident smile seemed to say that he had knowledge that was hidden to others, wisdom from the beginning of the world.

"You know, friends, the Lord often talked 'bout houses. The unjust steward's place, the home built on sands. I s'pose it was somethin' everybody could understand, those who came to hear him from humble mud-brick cottages in Palestine.

"But friends o' Caintuck, the greatest and most promisin' houses the Lord talked about were the mansions in the sky. 'In my father's house are many mansions,' he said, and 'I'll receive ye as my own in 'em.'

THE MOVERS • 343

"What a vision, friends. A mansion in the sky fer you 'n me. Now I 'spect all of us who've lived in cabins know what a mansion must be. 'Tain't got a loft, 'tain't got paper greased with bear fat at the winders, and the fireplace in the heavenly mansion shore don't smoke." He paused as the audience chuckled appreciatively.

"No, instead I 'spect it looks a good bit like the mansion of the governor in Virginney, or the palace of King Loo-iss of France. Great hall with porticos made o' marble, steps o' marble too. Inside this mansion the glow of the Light o' the World illumines all, and over all the walls and ceiling are a hundred pearly showers o' light so real you can bathe your face and hands in it, jest float and clean yerself up with it."

Voices began to murmur affirmations. He went on to describe the shining costumes of cloth o' gold, the singing so sweet that you feel as if the lightest, and brightest sugar syrup showered over you but never stuck. And so on, through many more glories. George glanced at Mary and Catherine and Will's Elizabeth across the congregation. Their faces shone like that cloth o' gold the man was effusing about. Well, and good, George thought with only a little uneasiness. Involvement in religion would probably be an improvement in Catherine's life. But should it center so obviously on this man? Catherine spoke of nothing else but "The Reverend" when the family gathered for their campfire meal this morning. Still, so far it seemed purely good.

The description of the many mansions in heaven wound to a close with ringing talk of the spiritual joys and satisfactions of standing in the ranks of the just. As its eloquence rose like a wind across the prairie, the members of the congregation became as prairie grass, rippling before its gentle or forceful cadences.

"Oh Lord," "Yes, yes," "Amen," they murmured.

Then the voice stopped. The face of the man at the pulpit grew dark, the prairie wind blew a little cooler. "But, my friends, not all o' us 'll be there, now will we? The truth is hard, but I must say it. The door is shut for some of you, because sin has shut it. That door is not open for the envious."

"*Nooo*, Lord."

"Not for the adulterers."

"*Nooo, Lord, nooo.*"

As he went on to describe in detail sins that closed the doors of the Heavenly house, the prairie wind blew very cold indeed and the grass lay prostrate before the horrid vision of man depraved.

The voice of the minister was a loud, low stage whisper. "My friends. You are on a ladder to the mansion in Heaven but you are slippin' back." He had a replica of a small cherry-picking ladder and took it from the shelf under the podium. "You go up a rung, hopin' to be better Christians, and then you slip back two or three, sunk again in your sin and depravity." His fingers descended the ladder. . . "The rungs are breakin'," (they did) "you're fallin', faster and faster, farther away from God."

"No, no," the listeners almost screamed, holding their heads.

"You slip, slip, toward the sucking mud, the quicksand of sin, and beyond

it the pit without a bottom, shut out from God.'' The rungs flew by, "Until. . ."
he held up the little ladder, dropped it onto the ground. There were wails and
fearful shrieks, and a lady fell on the ground in the middle aisle.

Then he was silent, and they became silent too. Stillness. The prairie wind
had died for a moment, but a storm of unknown fury awaited. Next, next, they
knew, he will talk about. . . "The pit, the pit in all its horror." He went on
to describe it, the vultures waiting to surround you and pick your bones dry,
the seething holes of fire where, like Indian captives, you must roast eternally
screaming, and so on. Now at least half the audience was crying.

"But, my friends, there's somethin' that can stop this backslidin' rush down
the ladder of sin. Somethin' that can re-admit you to the house of the just.
Do you know what it is?''

They knew. They had all heard the message last night. He waited. Finally
a clear woman's voice rose from the side of the hall. "Confess, repent,
put the love o' Jesus in your heart.'' A sigh of deep ecstasy rippled across the
entire audience.

George knew the voice without looking; it was Catherine's.

Someone else repeated what she had said, others picked it up. The minister
allowed the repetitions, the moaning, the crying, to go on for at least two
minutes. Then he called with his hands for silence, and after he got it, ended
his message by yelling at the top of his mellifluous, ringing voice, "Confess!
Repent! Let Christ into your heart of stone. Put your first foot on the ladder
of salvation.''

As the hymn was sung, the emotional level in the tent was as taut as a piece
of rawhide strung between two trees. In a moment another minister arose and
called for "evidences of having been born anew, or finding salvation, and
confessions of the conviction of sin.''

One by one people arose and told stories of lives sunk in sin, changed and
straightened. Jean McClure almost rose from her chair at the exalted testimonies
which started the session off. But George, impressed at first, became
uncomfortably aware that little by little, confessions seemed to be receiving more
emphasis, with succulent details of particular "fallin's away" chewed over with
a good deal of relish. One woman described being caught, like the New
Testament woman in "the very act of adultery," and the very act seemed a
bit too vividly described. A man told of the excesses of drunkenness without
really coming to a point.

Margaret McClure watched her husband sitting with his eyes on the dark
woods outside. He shifted his weight from one side to the other, and his hands
trembled from time to time. He seemed ready to dart from the hall. She glanced
across the tent at her ten-year-old daughter Elizabeth. Elizabeth was part of
a group led by her cousins Mary and Catherine, who began to sway on their
benches, moving from side to side, leaning against each other. A woman ended
a testimony against smoking by taking out a pipe and stomping on it, to the
jubilation of the group. There was an interim of quiet; the girls began to clap
in cadence. Then they began a singing chant.

Confess, confess, repent,

> *Let the love of Jesus in your heart.*
> *Confess, confess, repent,*
> *Let the love of Jesus in your heart.*

The crowd took it up. It swept the tent and soon the entire grassfield swayed, seeming to writhe and move like a snake.

"Confess, confess, repent. . ." the girls rose to their feet to add emphasis to what they were saying. Others in the hall bobbed up. The Reverend Mr. Pinckney returned to the pulpit. George raised his eyebrows. The minister began clapping loudest of all and soon was shouting at the top of his considerable lungs, *"Confess, confess, repent."* The cadence rose to a roar of two thousand voices that could be heard on farms a mile away.

"They be gettin' the Lord purty strong," said a very old lady with only a few hairs papering over the top of her pink scalp, who lived on one of those farms.

"When the Spirit enters, it do shake sinners," her equally old husband observed.

And shake it did. As the clapping and singing continued, more than one person convinced of sin and "under the influence of the spirit for the new birth" rose, hands in the air. They jumped, they danced, they pranced about. As they continued, a woman in a sunbonnet arose, speaking in tongues. *"Ko-wi, seenoba pa beebotati,"* she screamed warningly. Soon whole rows were on their feet. The phenomena increased, to George's amazement, and as the minutes passed, the "outpouring of the Spirit" caused repentant sinners to display their distress by dancing into unconsciousness, crying out like babes, leaping on the ground like monkeys, or sitting and crying in the dust outside the tent.

But the "saved" were equally vociferous. Several happy men and women pushed back benches to form a circle and did a dance like the minuet, approaching each other with hands behind their backs.

> *I've got the love of Jesus in my heart,*
> *'Spandin', glowin' like a fire*
> *It makes me love you more.*

They came to each other, almost touching, body to body, then receded, stamping to repeat the dance.

Several people lay prostrate on the hard dust of the tent floor. "They call it coming through," Jean said to George. "After the conviction of sin, some believe they struggle with the Devil. I don't know what to think." George thought he did.

A man began to hop about on his haunches yapping, howling, barking. His eyes looked vacant. "Oooh, rarf, rarf, rarf," he yowled. Others took the barking up, still others lay flat, twitching, jerking with involuntary muscle spasms.

The girl cousins with other neighborhood friends were still swaying, chanting, holding on to each other. Their voices were growing hoarse. Mary, Elizabeth, and Catherine had streams of perspiration coursing down their faces, and their hair straggled into their eyes. George turned his eyes to see Martha and Margaret McClure dance by hand in hand, ecstatic expressions on their faces. These women're having the time of their lives, he thought.

Those who were not actively involved in being convinced of their sins, struggling with Satan, or witnessing the Spirit's power, continued clapping. They now turned their eyes toward the cedar pulpit. The Reverend Simon Brockhurst Pinckney was himself involved in witnessing. Chanting with the rest of the group, he sank to the floor. There he lay, seemingly almost insensible, moaning, "Jesus, Jesus, Jesus," for several moments. The congregation went to their knees with him.

A kneeling middle-aged man whose face was so sunken from toothlessness that it looked like a withered pear, told his daughter, "Shore is a good meetin'. One of the gol-durned best in the last year. That preacher-on-his-knees thing is good witnessin'."

His comment was interrupted by a call for the benediction, which did not in any way allay the testifyin', but only allowed the minister and those few others who wished, to leave the meeting.

The silent, grim sister of the minister was serving Jean and George and Rob McClaren fine oolong tea. It was almost midnight in one of the small cabins that had been built specifically for the ministers of the Big Bend meeting.

A blanket which served as a curtain parted. The Reverend Pinckney stepped into the circle, rubbing his hands enthusiastically over the nutmeg poundcake and dishes of sweetmeats.

"Riches of the East," he said, picking up a piece of sugared ginger. "Exotica from the provinces of Mandarin Cathay. I must admit I indulge the flesh just so far with these tidbits. Keep 'em with me at all times."

George's eyes coolly scanned the man's clothing. The Reverend Pinckney now had on well-fitted, sky-blue corduroy knee breeches with gilt buttons and a fashionable French "Incroyable" coat. Apparently the woodsman's garb had been retired for the evening.

So, too, it seemed, had the homespun accent. "A good house tonight," the minister said, stirring white sugar lumps into the tea with a pewter spoon. "Fully committed to postive spiritual phenomena occurring in their midst. Our cumulative total exceeds that of the April revival by. . ." he pursed his lips while tabulating "about four hundred souls." He looked at George's questioning eyes.

"I expect that you are wondering that I seem to have what might be called a 'stage personality' for the tent meetings, another demeanor for my private moments. It would surprise you to know. . ." he pulled a chain out of his pocket. At the end of it was a Phi Beta Kappa key. "I earned this at Harvard College."

He popped the candy into his mouth. Then, his hand, like the claw of a bird, poised above the dish of candied ginger, and selected another, even larger piece, heavily sugared. He signalled to his sister for more tea, then sighed. "I have found that the 'folks' in Caintuck don't like nor understand the theologian's Latinate language."

His sister Ophelia awakened from her silence and warmed to a subject she enjoyed. "They almost tarred and feathered him in western Virginny when he quoted from Donne's sermons and used Polycarp in the messages. Said he was uppity." She sat down among the circle of tea drinkers with her own cup. "They were intolerant about other things too. Made some slanderous charges. . ."

Her brother sent her just the barest hint of a warning look. "And so, we suit the language to the group," he informed them airily. "One must, after all, switch a cow with the right size stick to get her to move."

"Forgive me," George said, "but it all seems to smack of Drury Lane a bit more than Divine service." His wife's eyes showed she, too, questioned the minister's approach. As for McClaren, he seemed to be purposely absenting himself from the discussion, sipping his tea vaguely out of a saucer with his head turned away from the group.

"Drury Lane Theatre? I suppose so. I concede its drama. In fact, I suppose we consciously work for effect."

"Encourage the barking, the falling on the floor."

"We do not discourage it. These are sinful times. Kentucky is no longer a frontier. The energy of its people is drifting aimlessly into trouble."

"I can't argue that," George said.

"We in religious life must catch the people's eyes. Give them an event, something they will remember all their lives. Thought thus impressed with colorful images is readied for change."

George nodded a little. He did follow the line of thought. The minister went on. "Was not the Lord the master dramatist? A spell-binding speaker? The Roscius of his time? Did he not pick the central spot in Jerusalem to overturn the money-changers' table in what might have been a great scene from one of Shakespeare's plays? Walk across the water to his awe-struck disciples?"

"But Christ spoke gently, his followers listened quietly," George protested.

"Cannot the spirit come violently sometimes? It drove out legions of devils into hogs that rushed into the water, it made people babble in tongues with fire on their heads at Pentecost."

"True," murmured Jean, and she added, "I would not prescribe the way any man comes to Christ, so long as he comes."

"Rob, how do you feel about this?" George asked, putting him on the griddle.

Rob looked directly at George. "I can't tell you, because I don't honestly know. All we do is preach, and each of us has a different way o' doin' that. How the people react is somethin' different. One minute I think all these doin's are from God, the next from the Devil himself. Only time will tell. I can't right now."

There was a clamor at that instant at the door and Ophelia Pinckney opened it. A group of four or five eager young girls clustered about, giggling and shy.

The minister spoke to them for a moment, then came back and set down his cup.

"They seek spiritual counsel. We will give it to them," he said and left with the girls.

We, always we, thought George. Who is it that travels around with him to form the crowd? Clouds of unseen cherubin, seraphim, archangels, or perhaps the ranks of the saints? The minister did not return and with polite thanks, Rob McClaren and the McClures left.

"All right, everything has biled down to a residoo," Jack McClure said the next morning, his round face peering into the copper kettle his young cousins were stirring. " 'Bout two gallons o' potient."

"Didn't it bile down too far?" Jim asked him.

"Mebbe. But 'tis all right. Now we got to put it though a series of esperiments to see the way it works—how it conks a person out. Lessee. . ."

"Mebbe we could try it on a toad or a pig," Johnny McClure said, his eyes wide.

"Dummy. I'd like to see you hog-tie one of them monsters on the farms around here and put the potient in his mouth. An'a hoptoad ain't close enough to a person."

"Hey, I got a idee," Jim said slowly. "Suppose we give some, jest a little, to some o' the folks at this yere play party?" Jack looked up, slightly apprehensive.

"Oh, not enough to hurt 'em, jest enough to put 'em to sleep."

"It ain't dangerous nohow," his cousin said quickly. "Mebbe it would work."

"Sure thing. The Orchard Methodist Church is fixin' to put out lemingade and cakes at the break in the preachin'. We can jest put in a little of the potient, observe the results and. . ."

"Record 'em in our laboratory journal," Jack affirmed. "In fact, each of us will be makin' a record, if we do it right. When we all git rich, it'll be somethin' good to look back on. I got three paper tablets here."

He gave out the writing equipment and the three busied themselves cleaning up the mess. "Hurry up. Let's get this stuff all put away. Jim, you do the final bottlin' and clean up the copper pot," Jack told them. "I wanta git back as soon as possible. My ma is gettin' suspicious. She follered me out as I left the mornin' meeting today, but I give 'er the slip. Good thing we're done. Now we'll go act prissy and read our Bibles during afternoon meditation. Don't s'pose it'll hurt us none anyways," he said, with a sudden, brief flash of guilt.

Sure glad Ish ain't here, thought Jack as he scattered the fire. He would'a wanted to horn in, and I'd a hadta knock the crap outa him, or maybe have it happen to me. Ish is gettin' dang hard to beat up.

After Jack and Johnny did the final repacking and headed back up the path, Jim McClure looked at the gummy substance at the bottom of the pot. "Should only fill about eight bottles," he said to himself. "Ain't much profit there. Do seem a bit phlegmatic. I really think I should thin 'er down. Mebbe use some o' this calomel left over here an' some water. If a little's good for what ails ye, a lot should be better. He dumped a gob of calomel into the potion, added two quarts of water, stirred well, and began the bottling process.

Jenny Scott joined the rest of her family in the tent for the big closing "self-examination" meeting of the revival, in which people would prepare themselves for the communion on the morrow. Her thoughts were on Ish and her mother-in-law, who had driven on to McClure station this morning. Marguerite did not look well; pray God Ish would not insist on driving her at breakneck speed over hill and dale. Jenny had heard only part of the preaching last night and looked forward to these last big exhortations by all the ministers and the famous Reverend Pinckney in particular. The group assembled in the tent structure was expectant, ready to "testify and witness" at the drop of a hat.

Her brother Will was on the bench, next to his wife. He was withdrawn, gloomy. He did not sing the opening hymn, and after the reading of the text, he stalked out, his wife's pleading eyes following him.

To Jenny's surprise, young people began to clap after the next hymn was sung, but they quieted down as Rob McClaren came to the pulpit. His sermon was a short, quietly moving detailing of his own conversion. Then there was a pause as Pinckney came in, dressed again in buckskin leggings and scriptural hunting shirt.

He began to speak; his voice was hoarse, rasping, irritating to George, who, with Jean, was sitting beside Jenny. Pinckney's theme was salvation, but his text was Song of Solomon. He spoke of the love of Christ, using what seemed to George heated similies from Solomon's love song to illustrate the Lord's love. "I sat down under his shadow with great delight, and his fruit was sweet to my taste," he read.

No, the love poem of some rich King of Israel to his paramours was not the best stuff of religion, particularly for the young people.

The sermon wound itself up, then down. The air was hot and still; the minister's face glistened. This whole thing is taking a bad turn, George told himself. A shudder of a new and ominous sort passed over him when, after the sermon finished, he saw Reverend Pinckney go to the seat where Catherine and her friends sat, clasping their hands at him in adoration.

"Mr. Brockhurst Pinckney, when I hear you speak, I jest feel the love of the Lord flooding over me," he could hear his daughter say. Mary nodded affirmation and little Elizabeth just opened her mouth wordlessly.

"There's something unhealthy in these meetings," he whispered to Jenny.

"You're prob'ly readin' things into what's goin' on," she said, lost in her own concerns and prayers. Maybe so, he conceded.

As the group enthusiastically amened and sighed, Mr. Pinckney called again for order and announced that the "closin' testifyin' and witnessin' session" would follow a half-hour break for refreshments. He mentioned that the Baptist minister would deliver the testifyin' sermon and handle the meeting. He would be available in his cabin for counselling to any young people wishing individual spiritual guidance.

Martha McClure darted about apprehensively in the second circle of wagons and tents. Where can that boy be now, she asked herself. Fine thing when I can't even enjoy the preachin' for worryin' after him all the time. As if I don't have other children. She saw from the corner of her eye that her boys Tom, Charlie, and Joseph were cornering a squirrel in back of the pavilion; they would be all right. Don't he have any concern 'bout the rest of us, she wondered indignantly. 'Twas one thing for him and his cousins to sneak away early from mornin' worship, but to miss the big spiritual preparation meetin' tonight. What was it they were doin'? They said huntin', but they hadn't brought in any game. Yesterday she thought they must have been drinking whiskey off in the woods—there were peddlars going through the grounds even here, and the boys had some money—but when she smelled Jack's breath it was clean.

It was so exasperating. His pa could handle him better. Dan'l *would* take this time to go off to Vincennes. 'Twas important, of course, to get the good land secure in the family, but she felt so helpless with Jackie. He could be so good, sometimes, and other times as ornery as Old Scat himself. Old Scat, she thought suddenly. What an odd term—old privy stuff? She had never thought about it before. Well, fancy that.

She looked about. Jack wasn't here either. She had to admit she was beaten. Pshaw, she didn't like to follow her own son about like Major Andre or somebody. Wearily she returned to the tent. Her eyes brightened with relief. There was Jackie, smiling happily, standing right there beside the lemonade stand, bless his heart, with a big smile on his face as Aunt Jean and the others handed out the frothy lemonade from the punch bowl. Her fears were groundless. He was still her good little boy after all.

George had decided to clear his head with a walk through the woods. Out of the corner of his eye, passing through the second circle, he saw his brother Will sitting behind a wagon with his head in his hands. But George had scant time for Will's problems. George's thoughts were increasingly agitated. Scenes of the last two nights went through his mind with a seemingly new meaning, and he felt as though he were leering through a peephole at a distorted Bartholomew's Fair, a pageant of all the foibles and follies of mankind, displayed right here at this tent meeting.

He seated himself on a large rock off the path to think. Faugh! Pinckney was the worst of all, pandering to all the base instincts in the name of piety. The leering look on his face, the texts tonight. What a close line there was between religion and sex. These huge meetings, when you thought about it, were really transmuted bacchanalian revels. Disgusting images played through his mind: Midsummer Night fertility coupling encouraged by the priests, satyrs leering through medieval cathedral scrollwork, the Black Mass with its virgin sacrifices, supposedly stylish with London rakes now.

He left his rock and began to walk down the path again. Hadn't there been scurrilous happenings at some of the other revivals, he asked himself? He walked more rapidly to the outer circles. Time was passing, the meeting would be resuming; never mind. He walked furtively, diverging from the path into a clump of trees where there was a murmuring noise. He stopped, his eyes groping to adjust and finding what he dreaded: two couples in the grass, seeking release from overcharged emotions in the age-old way. He suspected they were not the only ones.

Anger gripped him. That idiot was to blame for inflaming the people, whatever his motives. And how could the motives be good? Leading innocent ones into the very sins he condemned—innocent lambs like. . .

Catherine. The thought struck him like cold hail. *Behold thou art fair, my love, thou hast dove's eyes within thy locks*. My God, the man has had charges brought against him. He raced to the minister's cabin, half-ashamed of the absurdity of what he was thinking.

William McClure sat on a bench in the woods just behind the tented wagon. A gourd and a small gallon barrel of whiskey stood before him on a stump. He stared at it as if it were the Holy Grail. I tole her I wouldn't tipple while we was here, he thought. Why'd she ask it, anyways? Jest like her. If I take a drink now 'n then, 'tis cause she is so God-awful harpin'. Don't unnerstan' me. I need a little warmin' of my body now 'n then. Perfectly harmless. Still, I did promise.

Sweat broke out on his forehead and his stomach churned. Quickly he grabbed the cup. He dipped it in the liquid and downed the drink. Ahhh, he told himself. That's all. Then, his hand shaking so badly he could hardly hold the cup, he poured and downed another whiskey. He sipped the next slowly, savoringly, turning the cup in his hands.

I shouldn't hafta sneak around. Think up reasons for leaving. (He had told her he was going back to check the wagons in case of rain.) She shouldn't make me promise, shouldn't cry and argue so, he told himself. It didn't matter anyways. He had learned not to listen. Best not to think when you down liquor. Make your mind as bare as the side of that tent there. Good ole tent. Nothin' there but dead whiteness.

In two hours he had drunk a good deal of the little barrel; still he stared at the tent. As he looked, dots of blood began to appear on its canvas side, then turned into huge, red splotches. The splotches spread into a jagged hemorrhage, then split up into pieces of nut brittle which became, each one, a scorpion. Giant pincers waved at him in the air.

"Ohh, God," Will cried in a strangled voice. He rose uncertainly to his feet, stumbled and fell. His eyes were fixed to the side of the tent, which now crawled with scorpions. They came down the side of the tent in squadrons to be joined by a horde of horseflies the size of crabapples, and these flew out of the woods and buzzed angrily toward him.

Quickly the scorpions advanced to his arms, their fuzzy feet raising the hair on his wrists. The flies landed on his face and crawled into his mouth, tickling his lips maddeningly; some went inside his shirt. He ran crazily down the path to the tent and, screaming and clawing, lurched inside. Through a haze he advanced toward his wife near the corner. He fell against her, screaming over and over again, brushing the horrid insects off himself. She backed away from him in horror and embarrassment and left him to fall on the ground.

Margaret McClure need not have felt embarrassed. The group was so full of the Spirit's outpourings, there was so much raving and screeching and hallooing at the imagined pains of hell, that no one could spare the least moment's time to notice one poor soul experiencing the very real hell of alcoholic hallucination, delirium tremens.

Jack McClure stood outside the pavilion as, an hour into the second part of the evening, the "testifyin' and witnessin' " meeting, people began to come out and hurry into the shadows. Edging into the entrance, he looked inside.

He began to write on his tablet. *Record of esperimint. 8 o'clock Potient goes inta lemingade. Some of it floats on the top but nobody notices cause of the froth. 9:45 subjects lookin drosy. girls sleepin. Lots yawnin.* But what were the people hurrying out for? More and more were leaving, and they had odd looks on their faces. Goin' to the woods? One man knocked over a chair and exited swearing.

Jim McClure called to him from near the lemonade stand. "Jackie, whut's goin' on here? These folks is rushin' out like ants when the nest is bothered."

Jackie quickly walked to him. His voice sounded a little frantic. "Mebbe I put too much calomel in the potient."

"You put it in, too?" Jim demanded squeakily.

"Too? How much you put in?" His voice was imperative, and his cousin meekly told him.

"You butt-head. Don't you know that calomel sends you to the privy faster'n you kin git your buckskins down? We put enough in to purge the entire state o' Caintuck. Ooh." He slapped his head, then gained control of himself.

"Waal, we must be disinterested. In the name of science, record the behavior, and tell Johnny whut's up and to keep his mouth shut about this if he wants t' live." After a moment he added, "Besides, nobody ever died of the calomel shits."

While his cousins' eyes bugged at what science had wrought, Jack sat on a bench at the back of the pavilion and wrote: *10 o'clock. Potient apears to be workin, either for puttin folks to sleep or givin them the shits. Dancers who start witnessin on their feet set back down quick. Others keep runnin out and some ain't makin it, tearin their hair, and yellin mad. Everbody bumpin into everbody else. Ain't stopped the witnessin' though, some barkin, some jerkin, one man clumb a tree to drive out the Divil and then had the poops hit there.*

10:10 Them that ain't got the shits have got the yawns or went t' sleep on the benches. All the witnesin has stopped as everybody is rushin about, pushin to get throo the crowd in time, liquid fartin, cussin, or snoring and fallin off the benches.

10:15 Minister tryin' to get everyone's attenshun to end the meetin. Jack put away his grandfather's French and Indian War writing kit, which he had found in a trunk at home and ran some old-fashioned blotting sand over the page.

James and Johnny looked anxiously at their leader as he emerged coolly from the tent. "Jehoshaphat, we overdone it," Jim said.

A man rushed by, coat-tails flying.

"Who's that?" Johnny asked.

"Baptist preacher," Jack told them coolly. "I bet that was the fastest benediction since Moses rushed the Jews into the Red Sea when the chariots was a-comin'."

A sign was on the door of Reverend Pinckney's cabin. "Gone to give private consultation. Come again." George McClure smashed his fist on the door. He couldn't find Catherine anywhere.

Now, carrying a chip lantern, he moved through the sassafras saplings, attempting to make as little noise as possible. "Just let me catch that lecherous hypocrite in the act of seducing my daughter." His hand closed on his gun. "If I Abelard him, not a tear will be shed in Kentucky." (The back of his mind saw sacrifices to the goddess Astarte.)

Where to look. He ranged through the last circle, from thence to the isolated groves by the creek. *Behold, thou art fair, my love, yea, pleasant, our bed is green.*

A fear that became more anguished as each moment passed raged through him. Catherine. Then he caught the murmur of what he thought was the minister's voice ahead in the dark. *That which is lost shall never be reclaimed.* All intellectual images faded in the face of pure primordial paternal love and fear. . .

"Cat, Cat," he cried plunging into the clearing. He held up the light. The minister's own little lantern was set in the niche of a tree, and he was reading from the Book of Acts to Catherine and her cousin Mary.

"Pa, whatever is the matter?" the startled girl asked, rising.

George's mouth flew open, then shut. "Taking a walk—wondered where you were. Sorry, go ahead," he mumbled incoherently. Then he backed out of the clearing, stumbling on large tree roots as he went.

He traversed the paths back though the several circles. He noted all the people who were rushing about in the woods and wondered in the corner of his mind what they were doing. But he was really able to focus only on what had just happened. "Fatherhood is an artifical status, an accident of nature," he said out loud. "It's unnatural, and I'm not very good at it." Morosely he kicked rocks out of his path. The lantern threw long shadows through the woods as he returned to his family's tent.

Chapter XXX

The Christians camped at Big Bend revival meeting arose in a chastened mood to greet the next morning. The plague that had fallen on the "witnessin' " session was viewed as a judgment on hysterics, and most people vowed to be less demonstrative in their religion henceforth. In short, they were embarrassed.

The last communion services held by individual denominations and churches were muted, reverent. Rob McClaren, minister for the "open communion" meeting the McClures attended, led a few quiet hymns, administered the sacrament and then announced that the rest of the meeting would be devoted to individual prayer and re-consecration. He would be available, he said, to those who wished to pray with him in his cabin.

William McClure, sleeping off the effects of his devastating drunk, awoke slumped-over and aching in the corner of the tabernacle. His stomach revolved like a butter churn, his tongue stuck to the roof of his mouth.

Where was his family now, he asked himself wretchedly. He felt like an outcast, alone, as he did so often these days. Remorse and abhorrence of his actions last night hit him, as he plodded out to wash and try to put together a face to meet the morning. His hands trembled violently. He was remembering little except the attack of the giant horseflies, the bites of the scorpions. Not killin' bites, I see, he thought with rueful humor, although I wish they had been. Better for everbody. He had gone through another fit of the shakes a couple of weeks ago. Now he wondered if he were going progressively insane.

But as he walked down the path to the wagon, his head splitting, all the old defenses that served to cushion him from reality for years rose to ease his pain and insulate his thoughts. They prob'ly been talkin' bout 'the problem,' said a cold voice inside his head. If it wasn't his own voice, it sounded remarkably like it. Typical o' how everbody's agin you. Jes' cause you was a few years older 'n her, everbody takes her side. Where is she anyways?

He reached the sleeping tent back in the second circle and opened its flap. It was redolent of the bacon which was eaten in it on this dark, dank day, and of unaired pallets. Elizabeth lay flushed and asleep, sick of a cold.

"Where's your ma?" Will demanded.

"Gone to Reverend McClaren's cabin," the girl said without turning to look at her father. She was familiar with his hangovers.

Will grew increasingly surly as he advanced down the winding path toward the last circle, picking his way past late-comers to church services who were tucking in their shirt tails or pushing curls under stiff bonnets.

The feelings of remorse seemed to be more difficult to squelch this time than before. Usually all he needed to do was rant at someone else and get another drink, and the nagging ache of guilt would go speedily away.

He cursed a string of God-defying oaths, the end of which offended a girl about Elizabeth's age who passed by with a towel around her neck, on the way to a Baptist immersion at the river.

There was McClaren's cabin. Will noticed, barely, the dark, glowering sky. "Damn it, I 'spect it's goin' to rain to boot," he said aloud. He detoured when he caught sight of the cabin, purposely circling it from the rear to come up unnoticed in the clump of trees at its back window. Just as he ascended the slight hill by its side, and was within close visual range, though still hidden, he saw his sister Jenny emerge. Her face was firmly-set, serene, and smiling in a way he had not often seen lately. Probably, he thought sardonically, if for no other reason than that Ish was not here. His sister's presence irritated him. Why couldn't she pray in her own place?

He moved a little closer, through thick young pines. Standing where he was he could see through the rude hole that served as a window into the dim interior of the makeshift shelter. Candles illuminated an altar on the back wall. Jes' like the Methodists to practice idolatry, he snorted to himself. McClaren had a bronze cross on his log altar. Next to it was a portrait of Jesus laying on hands, healing a crippled girl. William jerked his head further back; his wife, dressed in dark linsey-woolsey was walking sadly in. Ire rose in him. Here she is, spillin' out your fambly secrets, cuttin' you to ribbons, the voice inside said.

Will looked at a club-like branch that lay on the ground, and for an instant was tempted to pick it up and thrash Margaret before the minister's eyes. Wife-beating was not a crime in these circumstances; any husband would understand.

He strained to hear her, but could catch only occasional words. He was torn between rushing right up to the door and demanding that his wife come out and curiosity as to what she was saying about "the trouble."

They ain't no trouble, Will thought, except in her own mind, and I better make that young preacher friend o' George's understand it. His wife knelt. The two candles burned brightly; there was almost no wind. Rob McClaren's voice could be heard praying with Margaret, asking for strength and endurance and hope to be given her. Will broke out in a cold sweat. Seein' her there thataway, prayin'. . .

Don't worry about nuthin', the cold voice inside him said. It'll all stop botherin' you when you git that drink. Go look for it.

But Will did not move. His wife rose, and slipped away. McClaren sat for a moment on the rude bench, his head in his hands. What's the preacher want ta do that for? Will asked. He don't need to take her whinin's serious. At least go give 'im a piece o' your mind bout buttin' into yer fambly's matters—but drat, who was that a-comin' in now? Martha McClure. He hadn't seen her out there. Must a jes' come up.

He didn't much like spyin' on Martha; he respected her as a woman of energy and determination. But if he was goin' to speak to this minister, he must bide his time a bit.

Martha's voice was louder than Margaret's had been. He could pick out most of what she was telling the minister.

"Knot in my heart for years now. Can't git rid of it." Guess I know what a knot o' pain in your breast is. The thought came inadvertently to Will as he listened. Never mind, said the voice inside. Don't give it no never mind, I tole you.

"Comes between Dan'l and me. I even think it affects the children. I'm ashamed to keep m' secret and troubled over it, and it makes me boss and rave at them and Dan'l too."

"I know you've needed to tell someone this. Have you tole God?"

"I'll tell you an' I 'spect He'll listen, too." Lowering her voice she began a long story, only the outline of which floated out to Will. Her poignant, pained tones penetrated even the callused corridors of Will's mind, revealing that Dan'l had been involved in a peccadillo twenty years ago, and Martha had the misfortune to stand not fifty yards away. The story jarred Will. A maiden girl of fifteen. . .

"And so, you have not tole him," the minister said.

"I haven't been able to. I've tried, God knows, but I guess I haven't really wanted to. I guess I wanted to punish him and make me feel better. Anyways, he thinks of me as a princess, one of those Greek goddesses."

The minister's voice was deep with compassion. "Don't you want to talk to him now?"

"I can't face God 'till I do. I've got to find some peace. My feelin's towards him have been dead for too long, shrivelled up like a pickle. Besides, he deserves to know. He's the best man I ever met."

Against his will, Will's thought turned away from himself and to Dan'l, leader of the church, owner of a prosperous brickyard. What personal agonies Dan'l must've been through without knowin' why. And after the other sad thing, the Indian child. . .Will was surprised to note that he sympathized with, loved his brother at this moment.

Never mind, the cool voice inside him said more urgently. You got no feelin's to spare for anybody. Feelin's are nothin' but trouble for you anyways, you know that. A vision of a liquor canteen and cup hidden under the floorboards of the wagon appeared suddenly in his mind. He pushed it aside for the moment, attentive, drawn to the emotional scene being played out before his eyes.

"How can this burden be lifted, Reverend Rob?" Martha asked. The two inside the cabin were kneeling together on the floor.

"Martha, in the last two years of my trials and troubles, I learned some truth first hand. Havin' to remake my own life, I found out what religion teaches is really true. Love forgives and regenerates. When we seem to fall far, we're really only plants that has died back all the way to the roots. God brings out new shoots, leaves, and mebbe even blossoms."

William found himself looking at the light of the candles. Candles did have a hypnotizing glow, he admitted. He squinted his eyes together as he had as a child, and the candles' glow grew soft, enlarged, until it filled all his sight. Let's go, loudly commanded the inner voice. Martha began to weep.

"There's a little child in all of us, Martha, lost in a dark night, wantin' to go home."

"I been lyin' a long time. How can I get free, start to live honest agin?"

"Jest ask, Martha." A little startled, she looked up at him with tear-stained eyes. It had not occurred to her.

"Oh, there's more to it than that, things that go along with it, but basically it's jest as simple as that. If we want to be free, all we really need to do is ask." They prayed silently, together, holding hands.

Will was deeply moved. The voice which was raging at him to go for the hidden canteen was growing colder, more commanding, merging with the compelling urges of his body.

Will opened his eyes, left off squinting at the candles. The scene at the altar opened out before him, bathed in a halo of light.

The painting seemed to stand out. The face of The Christ was shrouded in shadow, but Will could pick out the features of the crippled girl being healed. She was turned toward the man who had his hands on her. Pain and adoration and the hope of a lifetime were mixed in those features.

And somewhere in Will McClure's soul the little child stirred. Trapped perhaps in a hollow tree he was; terrorized and afraid, he struggled. No, no, the cold voice screamed. The boy fought to climb out, to break the hold of the hand that held the man's heart in thrall.

"Mebbe I do have a problem," Will said tentatively to himself. "Mebbe it's a big one," he added.

The little boy fought to go upward and out—away from the terror in the dark. He gained a toe-hold and looked out, toward the sky. He began to climb.

"Oh, God," William wailed in his heart, for the first time recognizing the size of the lump of pain that filled his own breast, pushing against his rib cage, constricting his stomach.

"If it was that easy," Will told himself, "Why, jest think, I could ask, Oh God, I could ask to be cured of this hellish hankerin'." Yearning filled his soul.

And he was cured. The craving to drink left William McClure at the Big Bend revival and it never returned for all the days of his life. He drank no more, not ever. It was a miracle, and miracles are never easy to explain. Oddly, the people in Will's neighborhood did not recognize his new sobriety for what it was. His wife and children, naturally, rejoiced for a while and then accepted it as their due. The McClure brothers and his friends, well, they just said, grudgingly, " 'Bout time." And the neighbors—those that did notice, didn't believe it would last. But then maybe they don't count. After all, if a Scotch-Irish Caintuckian had been a witness to the ascension of the Lord, he would have turned to his neighbor and said, "Big spell o' weather we're gettin' over thar. Makin' me see things on them thar clouds. Gimme 'nother chaw 'baccy."

*　　　　*　　　　*

A long, flat prairie stretched as far as the men on horseback could see. Prairie grass and knee-high jimson weed brushed the flanks of the horses as Dan'l and John McClure, Tom Baird, and Samuel Thompson guided the animals through this eight-mile stretch on the last leg of their voyage to the new Indiana Territory.

It was soggy land, rich with peat and clay. Cranes lifted diffident feet and then winged their ways to tall trees at the edge of the stretch; grouse spread their tails in pairs and took flight.

Behind them lay White River campsite, the last stop on the Buffalo Trace from Louisville, Kentucky, to Vincennes in Indiana Territory. It had been a difficult, dangerous trip, and Dan'l McClure sighed with gratitude as he surveyed these swamplands, realizing they had made it through without catching an ague, getting lost, or being robbed. He re-traced the journey in his mind.

The first night out a howling storm had closed about them at twilight, and they stayed at the only shelter they could find, a crude cabin. A grunting, inhospitable man finally let them into a room filled with disheartened people. A little boy before the cooking fire was suffering from some sort of awful ailment. His eyes were indifferent to life and death.

"Milk sickness. Thought we was goin' to lose him, but he be some better tonight," a woman with a torn smock had told them.

"Milk sickness—what causes it, Ma'm?" Dan'l had asked with sympathy as well as curiosity as his brother John put a comforting hand on the child's head.

"Don't know. Some says it's ailin' cows. Some says it's a curse. Some says it's 'cause the water flows through the Divil Caves to the east."

"I heard it's because cows eat something poisonous and it goes through the milk," Samuel Thompson said to no one in particular.

Dan'l looked at his friend, an aristocrat's son from Virginia, wondering how he liked staying in this dirty cabin. The floor puncheons had a disgusting variety of objects in the cracks between the boards, the leavings of careless sweeping for several months, and the rain blew in through holes in the chinking.

"The cows ere poisoned? Could be so," said the woman nodding solemnly. "I know when I give suck to the baby there, if I et cabbage he gits the farts."

"How do you treat the milk sickness, Ma'm?" Dan'l asked. The complaint was present in Caintuck too, but it never seemed to come near the McClure farm.

"Waal—we tried rhubarb. That seemed to bind him up. But his stomach kept crampin'," she said.

The man finally spoke. "We got us a good healer over by the whetstone pits. Rubs his hand on the sick un's bloated stomach and says 'What I rub, decrease in the name of the Father, Son and Holy Spirit. We had him in, and it worked."

Samuel Thompson batted his eyes once. "Why don't you just quit drinking milk and eating butter during the bad months?" he offered testily. Thompson had little patience with the slovenly people along this trail. Kentuckians were already applying to them the derisive term "Hoosiers." Thompson was an interesting contrast to him, Dan'l thought, and it was odd they were such good friends. But then opposites attract in friendships as well as marriages.

"Stranger, we jest might do that 'er thing," the man said. Then they had all settled in amidst nipping fleas for a sleepless night. It was the first of several miserable nights on their two-week journey across the mucky, often impassible and mosquito-ridden trace.

Their spirits had lifted, though, as they neared the last campsite by the river. Dan'l had built a huge campfire to cook wild turkeys. As they spitted them, he considered how broad this road into the pioneer country was here near the river. It must be as wide as a bowling green. Thousands of buffaloes had trompled it bare, charging by means of the easiest watercourses toward the grazing grounds in Illinois country. But at some places, through deeper woods, it was only as wide as a wide horse path.

After they had eaten, Tom Baird spread out a map of the new lands. Firelight cast dappled shadows over the surveyor's marks his brother Young Sam Baird made when he worked for the government here in Indiana Territory recently.

"Here's the militia lands," Tom told Dan'l. He pointed eagerly at a roughly rectangular patch by the winding loops which indicated the White River. "Here, and here," he had indicated, "the river winds its way to the Wabash, and then to the Ohio and Mississippi. A flatboat loaded with grain and hogs kin git onto the big river in less than a day's time."

Dan'l, kneeling beside Baird, looked intently at the lands that were earmarked tentatively for them. John was not looking at the map. Why not, Dan'l asked himself. Instead, his brother sat by the edge of the well-beaten camp clearing eating hard crackers. Sartain, he was thinkin' about his wife, Dan'l told himself.

John had left Janie to deal with a tragedy in her family. Andrew McGuire's young wife had died suddenly and Janie was comforting her father, or rather arguing with him, if things were going as they usually did. Love and hate were equally balanced, so it seemed to Dan'l in what Janie felt for her father. John was as moody as a fourteen-year-old. He would liven up, Dan'l told himself, when they reached the village.

"What's your land like?" Samuel Thompson asked, looking over Dan'l's shoulder, his slanting eyes squinting in the dim light. He had not served in the militia and would have to get his stand another way. About that he already had an idea or two.

"Sam looked out for all of us Pennsylvania Caintuckians," Tom told them. "Picked one of the best parts of the militia lands, rich for corn. Acourse, the Baird lands're among the best of it."

"The cook never starves. I see he named a creek for himself," Thompson said, scratching his smooth-shaven chin.

"What bothers me is 'taint clear with the Injeeans yet," John had shot in from the side of the clearing.

"It will be," Baird assured them. "But it ain't the only cheap land. North, east, on the rivers, if you want it, you can get fine land for a dollar or so an acre. If you jump now."

Thompson looked through poplars at the dark ribbon that was White River and observed, dourly, "Vapors're comin' off the swamp. I hope the land we all have is higher'n this."

As Dan'l went to sleep that night at the last campsite, he thought about that. From what he had been told the land here was better, much better, than anything Kentucky had to offer now. It had better be. They were coming a long, hard way and none of the McClure Boys were boys any more.

So now they would finally see the legendary Vincennes, after all these months of talk, Dan'l told himself as the aging Sugartime trotted down this last leg of the buffalo road. Tom had told them Vincennes was full of Frenchmen, pigs, and women in short dresses and that it would be like nothing he or Samuel had ever seen. And the other thing he told them was that their future, the quality and quantity of the land they would buy and thus their chance for riches, would depend entirely on their pleasing one man. William Henry Harrison had recently come to the village on the Wabash to govern the Indiana Territory. In this new democracy called the United States, he ruled Indiana as completely as an eastern maharaja rules his brown men and elephants.

Baird was their guide as, later that afternoon, they walked the streets of Vincennes. "Acourse the Americans have been in charge of Vincennes since Clark took it in the Revolution, but none of these yere Frenchies pay the least bit of attention to a government eight hundred miles away in Washington City. It might as well be in France."

They passed a fort, palisaded, with blockhouses. "Ft. Knox," Tom Baird said, scornfully. "A handful of sojers with guns that don't shoot good." They walked along the Wabash toward their inn.

A terrible odor drifted out from a new building behind a pole fence.

"Tannery?" Dan'l asked, wrinkling his nose.

"Marchal's and Fortin's new tannery," Baird answered. "It's a new idee, to use up the skins and provide fancy leather to the town. But they's a thousand stinks in Vincennes anyways. One more don't hurt."

"Marchal is a Frenchman?" Thompson asked.

"He runs a store for the Lasselles, one of the French tradin' family fortunes. The Lasselles have their *Bourgeoise* all over Indiana and the South."

"I thought *bourgeoise* meant townsman," Thompson said.

"To the French here it means boss, manager of a tradin' operation. Marchal is a manager, although he's only been here a while. You'll meet him; he handles a lot of land sales."

He pointed out a story-and-a-half house with roses trailing over a white fence. "Pierre Roux; he makes fancy cabinets." And further on, "Antoine Lasselle, the tradin' lord I tole you 'bout, has his post here for the Injeeans. Near to the river."

Many of the houses were built like those in a European village, with raised roofs and two dormers, picket fences and more flowers about them than Dan'l had ever seen. Smokehouses and white benches gave the place a settled look that was missing in the log villages in Caintuck.

This was not to say Vincennes was a neat town. Garbage filled puddles of standing water in the muddy street and the houses seemed to be scattered haphazardly about the several streets instead of planned. Still, the little homes were pretty, and Dan'l commented on them.

"Wish the people were as comely as the houses," Baird said. "They drink wine outa blue bottles, boil up fish inta stews and fry pancakes that're too thin. Lazy as hogs."

"But then some folks think we Scotch-Irish are lazy," Thompson said. Dan'l snorted indignantly.

John McClure joined them. He had been at the river looking at men unloading bateaux, the boats the French used to transport merchandise. "Big bales o' beaver furs all packed together. They're unloadin' 'em and stockin' on pots, flour sacks, ever kind o' cloth. Say they come from Ouitanon up the river." As he spoke, several French traders strode down the street toward the tavern. They wore the traditional white blanket-capotes with indigo stripes on them, knit caps and knee-high leggings. Great knives, decorated poinards, were at their sides.

Tom Baird was escorting the two other Kentuckians to the house of Francis Vigo, the patriotic Spanish trader who aided George Rogers Clark in taking Fort Sackville in Vincennes during the war. Vigo had funded and helped support the western effort and was now a leading citizen of the town. Vigo had a prominent guest that the McClures and their friends needed to see. William Henry Harrison was temporarily living at Vigo's, waiting to build a home for his family on a large stand of virgin land he had bought on the river north of the city.

They sat admiring Vigo's parlor. The trader-patriot had built a fine home with tall ceilings, a wide mantel above the fireplace, and beautiful portraits and pewter about. The house was constructed in an odd but typically French fashion of vertical timbers alternating with attractively done mud-grass plaster. A crash reverberated through the street outside the house. "What's that shot?" Dan'l asked.

Vigo was offering wine in small Venetian glass cups. "The noise, my friends, is the soldiers. They shoot hogs in the streets."

"In the afternoons? Why?" John asked incredulously. There were pigs in the streets of Bardstown and Harrodsburg, but people impounded, rather than shot them.

"For amusement, perhaps?" Vigo shrugged. "They have little to do out here. The *ennui*—the pigs wander a bit freely, the soldiers drink a bit too much. Even in the afternoon."

"I'd think the folks'd object to that," Dan'l offered, sipping his wine and taking a little cake from a silver plate. The room was very comfortable, almost sumptuous, with chintzes, flowers in a Chinese vase, and lace hangings.

"The accosting of the women is worse. The other night there was a violation of an unmarried woman by a soldier. In Kentucky you must also see rough things sometimes." Yet his smile was forced. "I think soon we will be moving the fort out of the town. The Indians no longer threaten so much—but here is the governor." He stood up.

A tall young man in a fashionable, high-collared frock coat came into the room. Dan'l noticed at once that the man had a boyish and disarming handsomeness. His Adam's apple popped up above his stiff collar. This was the Caesar of the West?

Seeing William Henry Harrison's youth made Dan'l sadly aware of how old he was to be starting a new life. He did not like to think in this way, but he knew it was on John's mind too. But after all, life's opportunities came when they came.

After shaking the newcomers' hands and accepting a glass from Vigo, Harrison sat down. His knees stuck out at angles, a little awkwardly.

"Messers McClure, your friend Tom Baird has trumpeted your praises forth. And now you are thinking of migrating." They nodded.

"And so your group will be bringing your fine horses and babes and oxen and mill buhrs across our Vincennes trace, and you will be thinking of becoming scions of our territory and supporters of the Republic's ideals here on the new frontier."

He seemed to take a real enthusiasm in this kind of exuberant oratory, enjoying his own words, and, as far as Dan'l could tell, believing them.

"We have accumulated considerable property," Dan'l told him. "Sartain we are proposin' to come and live as gentleman here. And yes, we do have our militia warrants to show we fought to support the Republic and freedom."

Harrison rose abruptly, turned his back and stood before the lace curtains at the window, and poured from the decanter on the table. "And we can use some supporters of the Republic's ideals in this place." He seemed to be smiling at some private matter.

"Messers McClure, Mr. Thompson, we are only a year old as a territory. Already. . ." here he sat down and put his wine glass on one knee, where it balanced precariously, "already we are a small reflection of the new Washington city, seething with factionalism, bubbling with intrigues. I seem to have escaped the silly foot race for place in the army only to land in—a horse race with beneath-the-table-betting.

"But what we also have here is some of the best farmland in the world and easy access to rich markets of the future. A path straight to New Orleans. A road to all the lands of the new West which will be this Republic's some day. Gentlemen, we are all sitting on personal fortunes, and perhaps that is the reason for the corrupt horserace I've alluded to."

John looked interested. "We have our militia warrants here." He fished in the pocket of his hunting shirt.

Harrison did not take them. "Sam'l tells me you want more land."

"We want large holdin's, a thousand acres apiece. If we are to come, leave our good Kentucky farm, it will have to be for somethin' big," John answered.

Harrison arose and began to pace about. As he walked, he cracked his knuckles. "Sirs, we need good men here. Not these crass speculators, who will profit and leave. I hope we will not repeat the sad lessons of Kentucky. We need solid people here, rock-bottom ballast for the future of the state. And I," he looked up significantly, directly at John and Dan'l—"I wish supporters whose views reinforce my own. It is a lonely position where I am, an eagle's nest on the top of a mountain of sand."

They nodded. He's young enough to be my son, Dan'l thought.

"Tom Baird has told me you are Indian fighters. He has said your brother is a personal friend of George Rogers Clark and that you fought with him at Piqua."

"And would fight the Injeeans agin efn it came to that," John McClure said. Harrison smiled, but held up his hand in warning.

"We hope the days of fighting the Indian tribes are over. I have the great dream of seeing them settle on farms, their sons growing corn, going to schools, their daughters taught the art of the needle, distaff, and spindle."

"Do the Injeeans want to give up huntin'?" Dan'l asked.

"Not yet. But they must. That is the answer." He sighed and twirled his glass, watching the late afternoon sunlight glint off its surfaces. He spoke almost to himself. "It is not possible that these savages, however noble in basic character, should possess the finest land God ever put on this earth so they can trap squirrels for their own pots. It is destined for the race with the superior intellect. President Jefferson believes this and I do too. They must give up their land, and the sooner the better. But that may mean bloody warfare and even bloodier politics."

"Sir, you can count on us in all things," John boomed out enthusiastically, caught up in the dynamism of this man's personality. "I think we know how to be loyal to those who have helped us, and we have many sons, soon to be grown, who'll feel the same."

They sat in the deepening twilight for a moment, then Harrison seemed to change mood abruptly and bounding out of his chair, went to Thompson, who stood up to hear what he would say.

"Sir, I did not know your family in Virginia, but I have heard it was a prominent one. Near Richmond, wasn't it? Will you pay for your lands outright?"

Thompson smiled a small smile. "Dan'l and I, well, all the McClures, have made a good bit of money making bricks. I can pay some. . ."

"Ahh," Harrison said. He was quickly pacing about the room now, scrubbing his hands together. He returned to Thompson. "Sir, I have many dreams for this new land. One is personal—a house for my dear Anna which will serve as a headquarters for receiving the guests of the territory, a center for cordial hospitality, stately, warm, something one would see in Alexandria, perhaps, or Fredericksburg."

"Bricks," Thompson said, his intense eyes gleaming, for he had thought of it before they even began the journey. "I could remove here and burn the bricks from clay by the river."

"In return for a fine timbered stand of four hundred acres I have in mind." They settled the details. "And for the Messers McClure, I will see to your militia warrants. You may either keep or sell the land there and get whatever more you want on my personal recommendation. I will introduce you to Antoine Marchal, who handles much land here. I assure you, you will have the best land in the area."

The deal was consummated, with a good deal of hand-shaking and toasting of each other and the coming prosperity. Mrs. Harrison, a handsome, gentle woman with a self-effacing smile, was introduced.

"Mr. John, Mr. Dan'l, Mr. Tom," she nodded at each, "I understand you are Presbyterians."

"I am an elder, Ma'm, founder of our local church in Caintuck, and most of our family are deep in the faith," Dan'l told her.

"We need a Presbyterian church in Indiana. It is the great desire of my heart, as well as the need of these times here in this Romish town. As soon as you come, we will begin services for the first church. May I count on you?"

"Sartain, Ma'm it would give me great satisfaction to help you set one up," Dan'l said, looking at John and Tom Baird, who enthusiastically nodded. Vigo reappeared to help usher the group to the door.

As they walked down the street, Thompson spoke. "That man will go far. Perhaps even to Hell, and we will go with him," he chuckled, clapping Dan'l on the back until his friend coughed. Dan'l was pensive, as the musky, river-smelling darkness folded about them. The barking of dogs, the sound of French children's sing-song games, the high-pitched laughs of drunken Indians echoed softly in the streets. What had John promised for them all? Dan'l did not like sweeping guarantees that he might not be able to deliver.

He wondered about another thing. The hand he had just shaken, hand of the governor of the huge new territory which stretched from the Mississippi to Canada, had fingernails bitten to the quick.

The next day dawned cool. Rain which they heard falling on the roof of their inn refreshed the air, and a breeze blew from the northeast. Dan'l and John walked to the Wabash, down stone steps, and followed its bank a bit upstream.

What was it about a river, John asked himself, as he sat down on its grassy shore. Somethin' bout it. Mebbe it was the sweep, the surface of water like good glass, fringed with trees, with the swallows glidin' on currents of air, disappearin' around the bend. 'Twas more beautiful than any prospect paintin' in a book.

Or was it the clearness of the boundaries on a river? When you looked at a river, the sky was where it belonged, the water neat as a pin in its channel, trees in a tidy little line.

Or mebbe it was that a flowin' stream took your thoughts up, from the earth where you sat, with its trampled-down grass and slimy muck, and set you soarin', like one of those swallows, windin' round that bend to the white cliffs on the upper Wabash and far beyond.

Janie would find this a good place to raise her horses, he told himself. The younguns would not make her so nervous, mebbe, in Indianney. And here, far from Kentucky, he would finally be able to put behind him what happened that sultry night in the cabin.

Dan'l spoke. "John, this Wabash is the finest river I've ever seen. Your Monongahela is shore pretty, all blue-green like, and the Ohio is wide and sweepin', but this river rolls freerer than any o' them. 'Tis free o' snags, and it has sandy banks."

A sycamore leaf mounted on a sudden air current, spiralling skyward, up and up to the top of a tall tree before it fell to earth. "Indianney's a promisin' place," John said to his brother, "and we ain't too old atall to bring the famblies here. 'Tis a better place 'n Caintuck. Things will go better in Indianney."

Dan'l nodded. Sitting on this bank, he was forcefully, almost physically overwhelmed by the sense of promise that overtook him. A whole system of rivers spread out from here like the veins in a giant arm with the fist at New Orleans. The produce of a thousand farms would soon be coming out of that fist. Vincennes was a gateway for a nation awakening to itself. From this heartland people would go out, quickening the land, sweeping across a continent, planting trees, irrigating, growing wheat and corn and pigs to feed thousands, no, millions of people.

Until this moment he had not understood what the new land was about. On the streets of Vincennes he had seen Indians, French, Spanish and American white men engaged in talking trade. The region was really a cauldron, and the flame under it was commerce.

There is no place on earth like America, Dan'l thought, never has been. And it's here, where the heart beats for that great arm of a river system, that the issues of the nation will be fought for a while. As Indianney Territory grows, so will this land, and all of my fambly will grow with it.

Chapter XXXI

"Remember, Dakin, the business we are really in is that of banking," Hyacinthe Lasselle said, looking fixedly at his new Vincennes store clerk. "We take in furs and sell merchandise on credit. Extend credit freely! This tends to—uhh—bind our customers to us for future purchases and, we hope, payment. We can help them in a number of financial transactions, issuing notes and collecting debts, for instance. We are, thus, a bank."

Lasselle's clothing had changed with the times. He no longer wore the trader's leggings and blanket-coat that Asondaki associated with him on the Mississinewa. Now, when he came into Vincennes at least, he went to business in a vest of embroidered wool or even silk and fashionable tight-fitting breeches from New Orleans.

Asondaki was arranging merchandise on the shelves of the huge store which dominated the center of Vincennes on St. Honore Street, near the Wabash River. It was a new, and he hoped promising job in the world of the white man.

He moved from the Mississinewa post two years ago and bound himself with Antoine Lasselle, the head of the trading family, to serve as an *engagé* in the vast company network which extended from New Orleans to Canada. The senior Lasselle had given him the detail work of shipping to Montreal and Detroit; Asondaki cared for the peltry, made sure the flour and meal did not get wormy in the pirogues, and hired the *voyageurs* to travel the rivers during high water and carry their loaded canoes over the portages. It was interesting work, but the reponsibilities were constant. Antoine Lasselle did not allow his *engagés* to deal on their own or take a leave to marry. For one year of this toil Asondaki received five hundred dollars, tobacco, and shoes.

When the contract was up, Hyacinthe Lasselle decided to advance the hard-working young man to chief clerk in the family merchantile. The company would provide wages, board and room at the inn, and an opportunity for Asondaki to invest his salary in the company's enterprises.

Arthur Dakin was now recognized in Vincennes as a full-fledged *metis*, joining a unique community of mixed-blood men in the Northwest Territory and Canada who earned their way by speaking several languages and passing easily among several cultures to contract business for the French fur interests. Whatever the Miamis might think of Asondaki Alamelonda, as Arthur Dakin he had real prestige built on the ability to deliver an indispensable service.

And there were other privileges he enjoyed since he had proven himself as a half-white, half-Indian *metis* trader. After postponing his marriage for two years because of his work, he finally celebrated the sacred rites last spring with an elaborate ceremony.

He had commissioned an old Ojibwa, a master craftswoman in quillwork, to design the *metis* coat he had thought about for a long time. It was a splendid garment of buckskin tanned with deer brains. Epaulettes and medallions decorated its front, quillwork of blackbirds and cattails signifying his Miami heritage.

He wore the coat when, at the head of a train of horses carrying the men of his clan, he went to claim Swiftly Running Feet as his bride. There were two days of feasting and exchanging of fine presents. The shrewd Potawatomis fully appreciated Asondaki's trading wealth and connections, and when the new bridegroom returned in midsummer to spend two weeks with Swiftly Running Feet at the camp near Lake Mocksinkickee, he was honored with status even beyond that of the chiefs. He told himself he did not care that all in his clan of Miamis shunned him.

Now, aware that his new job as head clerk was one many a white man would envy, Asondaki took pen in hand. He was to take inventory of the stock today in the tolerably good written French he had developed since joining Fortin, Marchal, and Lasselle enterprises.

"The merchandise for trading to the savages is, of course, priced slightly above market price," Lasselle's smooth, oily voice continued. "It is noted separately, so many trade shirts, measures of salt, cauldrons, and sauce pans.

"Here in barrels and on shelves is the general line of goods for farmers and French in the area. Some perishable. . ." he waved his rather delicate hand in the direction of the barrels of salt fish, crackers, flour, and several grades of meal. "Remember the French have their own preferences. They do not cook the corn dogers or anything with meal as the Americans do, and they prefer to fry only in the best rendered lard, not bear grease or bacon fat. So we stock for both."

As an example of French buying needs, Lasselle showed Asondaki several shelves stocked with bolts of fifty kinds of cloth, from coarse linen to damask. French women in Vincennes did not spin or weave at all, any more than they made butter. Some called it sloth, but Lasselle preferred to think of it as a cultural difference.

"Then we have luxury goods. Things both the French and American women have begun to clamor for recently in Vincennes." Lasselle was courting Julie Bosseron, whose sisters were married to Marchal and Fortin. These sisters, the style-setters among the French ladies, had become quite elegant lately, Asondaki had noticed. They were wearing lawn dresses with satin streamers and fashionable be-ribboned hats in the style of the women of Napoleon's Paris. Asondaki listened as Lasselle described the various items of the jeweler's, milliner's or metalsmith's art stocked for the comfort of the citizens of the "Gateway to the West," as this capital of the huge Indiana Territory was being called.

"You have your various kinds of sugar, your coarse maple still preferred by many, your loaf, much desired by prospering farmers, your lump for the China teas. Here are sets of china, Blue Willow or Dutch as well as French, your tart plates, tureens and crystal items and silver pieces." Asondaki took note of them all, asking with typical honesty when he did not understand the use of some piece of cutlery or china.

"Those are tongs for the sugar; these are crumbers to remove the bread bits from the table, cream pots to put next to the sugared raspberries, individual salt cellars to sprinkle the shallots with, perfume vials for the toilette." Asondaki was learning a good deal, not the least of which was that the pewter and silver pieces must be put under lock and key at night.

"So many dirks and poinards," he murmured, noticing the array of pearl-handled knifes made of the finest steel.

"Many are bought by ladies," said Lasselle. "Even with American control of Vincennes, it is not always safe to walk the streets at night. Some fear the savages. . ."

Sauvage! Asondaki still stiffened when he heard the word that both French and Americans universally used here. The Hoosier culture favored it over the word "Indians." It was insulting. As if the white people of Vincennes, who dumped excrement and garbage into the streets until it ran over low doorsills, and who stuck their people in stocks and whipped them at a public whipping post, could be considered civilized.

Lasselle spent the rest of the afternoon showing Asondaki the intricacies of the merchandising, fur-trading business his relatives ran. He wanted to be sure that the new clerk, for so long a cog in a wheel, now understood how the entire cart ran.

Later, in his small room off the kitchen of Jones' Yellow Tavern around the corner from the store, Asondaki thought about what the trader said. If you looked at it in a different way, he thought a little sardonically, it could be described as the "Code of the Wemiamiki" of the French trading lord. He had seen it in the posts, too.

(1) Watch the measure. Asondaki had seen a ten gallon barrel go upriver and arrive with only seven and a half gallons in it. Evaporation? A bit. Do the men who bring it drink it? Certainly they did that, considering it part of the wages. Or did the Lasselles sometimes take advantage of the Indians and provide less than full barrels, making up the difference with river water? Asondaki always wondered.

(2) Know who you deal with all along the line, and be swift to punish those who put the poinard in your kidneys.

(3) Expand your interests. Marchal had started out making knives and now even had an interest in a confectionary in Lexington that dealt with sugar almonds, chocolate, jams and *bon-bons*. As a matter of fact, Fortin had talked Marchal into opening a branch office in the Spanish territory of Baton Rouge and had himself already gone to Baton Rouge to build a tannery and begin trading in furs. As a matter of fact, Fortin had badly wanted Asondaki to

accompany him, but Asondaki did not wish to be so far away from Swiftly Running Feet.

(4) Use the law of the land to serve you. Lasselle had told him, for instance, that Frenchmen married with a pre-nuptial contract, which kept back a sizable portion of the husband's estate from the wife until she paid all her debts. The French paid their debts quickly at Lasselle and Marchal's posts—it was to their advantage.

Well, thought Asondaki, I can live with these things as I have learned to live with the rest. My wages are growing daily with Lasselle, and some day I will be rich. He accepted the idea of riches, the part of the life of the *metis* that he wanted, although he still despised a good bit of the rest of it.

Still, nothing really assuaged the restless thirst he felt to prove himself worthy. It was this thirst, really, which sent him again among the money-minded white men in this new world. Occasionally he went inside the sixty-foot "long house" church with a small, tinny bell on the shores of the River, where many of the French traders worshipped. It was hard to understand, as it had been at Kekionga, why they paid heed to priests swinging their smoke pots and chanting in a language that nobody had spoken for fifteen hundred years. Did it all mean something to them? If there were principles to this religion, he did not see them talked about outside the church. Certainly not lived.

He did not ask himself too deeply about his own life. He was here making his way; that was all he needed. That, and the fact that no one asked him who his father was. The French *metis* bragged about their fathers, even those who had not married the mothers, but not he. Too much pain was connected with it all for him to care to talk about, let along ever look at the man who caused that pain.

He sat at a little table with one taper, writing in the account books of Lasselle's store night after night, and he thought about the little figures swirling around and coalescing into white man's magic—dollars—on the pages of Hyacinthe Lasselle's account book. Yes, he thought, he could do as the white man did. He could accept these new dollar Manittos and their magic, and let them provide the meaning in his life.

Arthur Dakin's mercantile tutoring continued for several months, as Hyacinthe Lasselle came in and out of town from the Indian camps. Then New Year's Day came, and with it a break in routine. Hyacinthe and his fiancé Julie took the new clerk Dakin on a Calling-Day visit to all the leading French citizens of Vincennes. The Noel celebration in this French town extended through several weeks, Asondaki noticed. It was like the Indian's harvest festival for sociability and prolonged festivity. Earlier, he saw Marchal's wife and others dressed in costumes going from house to house along the river gathering food for the poor, and there were dances and parties every night.

Now, as part of the traditional festivities on the first day of the year, Hyacinthe and Julie visited Uncle Antoine Lasselle, head of the family. They paid their respects to the astute old trader; he in turn cordially greeted them, asking sharp questions about the business. Before Asondaki left, Antoine Lasselle pounded him on the back.

"This Dakin I like," he said. "He knows a scoundrel from a saint." Then Asondaki, Hyacinthe, and Julie headed down the street to the small clapboard residence of the Widow Gamelin, whose husband had been a prominent Vincennes trader for years.

Inside, the old woman offered them jam cakes and persimmon beer, which Asondaki liked inordinately. He did not dare ask for more. As a hired clerk he was granted indulgent inclusion in these New Year's day festivities, but he was expected to stay within his strictly-specified station. Everyone kissed everyone else on this good day: little children, maidservants, friends. Madame Gamelin even kissed him. But it would not have been proper to kiss her back.

It was an unsually warm day for January. Asondaki stood outside near the open door, under a trellis, watching the river. Rose canes, he supposed, were heaving up from the thawing ground. On such a thawing day as this, his people would be coming out of their bark homes to stretch, to hunt over the slushy snow, perhaps to bring home a pheasant to roast slowly over the coals.

Conversation drifted out the door. ". . . Probate killing us, and all these herds of lawyers who have thundered in since Harrison came in. Suits for this, delays in settling that—we can be tied up collecting debts for two years."

". . . Condescending toward the French. Think of us as children. . ."

Asondaki went back through the door. Smiling politely, he stood at the edge of the conversational group containing round-faced Julie Bosseron, the man who would soon be her brother-in-law, Antoine Marchal, and her delicate sister, Marchal's wife Rose, who was expecting a child.

"Hundreds are starting to come across the Buffalo Trace," Marchal commented. "Many will need land; all will need setting up. We can look forward to increased prosperity in merchandising for years to come." Asondaki listened with one ear. He did not envy any parties crossing the Buffalo Trace. The Louisville to Vincennes section was dismal and unhealthy; the road to St. Louis was worse. It was so faint that if the light was poor, it was unrecognizable. Travelling it would be no problem for an Indian, but white men were ill-equipped and foolhardy on the trail.

"I know you have been dealing with the McClures, Antoine," Julie simpered to Marchal and shook her short, bouncing curls. "Are they ready to come from Kentucky?" Asondaki did not particularly like her superficial ways, but he began to listen to what she was saying.

"They are ready to come as soon as the grass greens for their horses," Marchal answered. "The land they bought from me, contracted for by M'sieur Daniel, is already being cleared. These are landed gentlemen, who can afford to hire someone to begin clearing, eh?" He raised his glass of wine in a mock toast.

Asondaki turned his face away. Could there be more than one Dan'l McClure in Kentucky? He did not know how white men's clans were spread about.

"This McClure migration is a slightly odd thing, really very nice. For the trade especially," Marchal continued. "Four brothers and their families, a sister and her husband and sons, and the widowed mother. She is in her eighties.

Among them they will have, as they now intend, some five thousand acres of our prime land. They seem to be special protégés of our governor. If so, they will prosper, and as they do, so shall we.''

"A toast to the McClures," Hyacinthe offered, pouring out a rich, red, wild grape wine.

The others nodded, smiled, and downed their glasses as they began to walk toward the kitchen room. It was time to cut the bean cake, to see who found the lucky bean. He would be the king at the Old Christmas ball next week.

Asondaki, standing stiff and unnoticed behind the rest, turned his back and walked through the door. His eyes were grim as he looked at the gray river.

At the end of the holiday, as the city went back to work over ground again frozen fast, Asondaki went in for an appointment with Hyacinthe Lasselle. He wanted, if at all possible, to be transferred immediately to Fortin's outpost at Baton Rouge. Hyacinthe, though surprised, granted the request. Fortin had been begging for the *metis* to come for months, and Dakin's honesty and experience were needed there as much, or more, than in Vincennes.

The train of horses stretched along several hundred yards where the stockade used to stand at McClure Station. The land, Jane McClure reflected sadly, was no longer theirs. It was now owned by a man from North Carolina. He bought the acreage for his son who was marrying this very week and preparing to come to the rich, settled farmland of Caintuck. It struck her to the heart to close up her little weaver's shop and pack the remaining coverlets and cloths away in trunks, alongside some of the mementos of the rest of her life: her mother's family things from Ireland, the Pennsylvania tablecloth that Dan'l had nursed beneath, her husband's cooper's adze.

She looked at the vegetable garden she and Jenny and James Scott had tended for them all, just now greening up in the early rains of spring. Parsley was sending its tiny, green tridents through the drooping brown remains of last summer's plants. Rhubarb knobs were emerging, as round and pink as babies' behinds from ground made spongy by thawing and freezing. Larkspur, foxglove, sage, and pansy were starting over again, as they had done in one garden or another for her for the sixty years since she was a bride in Dunleigh.

Threescore years and ten. Man is as grass. "You leave a little piece of your life behind each time you say goodbye, that's what I always think," she said to her son, John. He was helping her pack her clothing for the men to load on pack horses. Then they would travel the easy wagon road to Louisville and from there take the one-hundred-mile long horse trace from Clarksville across the Ohio River to Vincennes.

"Leave a little piece of your life." The words echoed in John's mind after he left her. Mebbe she's a-gittin' mawkish. Wish she hadn't 'a said it. Makes me feel funny. Like we were all blocks o' ice, gettin' chunked off a little at a time. Dunleigh, Cumberland County, Harrodsburg, the station, meltin' a chunk of our allotted days at each point.

Would she be all right on the trail, he wondered? While still heavy, she seemed to have shrunk in on herself the last year or two, like a dried-up orange. She seemed especially sad since she was forced to concede that she could not sit for long hours weaving any more, and she must sell the loom.

He shook his head. Cain't really help how she is. We hafta go on, don't we, he demanded of himself. And he went to look for his son Jim to be sure he and his mother had readied the small stable of horses for departure at dawn.

The next morning, as the March sun rose over Kentucky, the pack train bound for Indiana Territory prepared to set off. "March is one of the nicest times o' the year in Caintuck," Will McClure murmured. He glanced at Janie and wondered if she too were thinking of a day earlier in their lives when the sun rose over a spring meadow glistening with dew and dandelions.

"Ash, you've come to see us off." Will turned to shake hands with both Ash and Hugh Emison.

"Take good care of these bear cubs, McClure," Hugh Emison said, indicating his two sons, Samuel and Thomas Emison, who would be journeying with the group.

"Glad t' have you with us, " Will said to the young men, whose intelligent faces framed in gold-brown curls reminded him of another time and other Emisons long ago in Pennsylvania. His mother was particularly glad for the Emisons' presence. Bairds, Emisons, and McClures were venturing out into a hostile wilderness, again together.

John McClure checked the stirrups and saddle girths that would have to bear overloaded sledges and precious human cargo.

"How long do you think your boys'll be scouting the territory?" he asked Hugh Emison.

"As long as it takes them to find out the best sight for buildin' the mill," Hugh Emison replied. They could not immediately move. There was mill equipment to organize and stone grinding buhrs to be skillfully wrought for the mill. Sam'l and Tom were determined it would be the finest mill in Indiana Territory.

"I wish to God you were goin'," John said to Ash Emison. The more the years went along, the more he hated to part with friends.

"I know," Ash said, looking down the twisting road. "But at some point the trail has to end for everyone."

John nodded his head slowly and turned away. One more time, just one more time he could face the trail. He would barter the pain of parting, the upheaval, the risk and trouble for one more good chance.

Will watched old friends preparing to leave behind twenty years of living— Tom Baird and his family with several slaves who would help do the cooking and doin' on the trail, Joseph Baird who had already chosen land on the outskirts of Vincennes not far from the McClures. There were also three or four other Bardstown families and shirt-tale relatives. "Not too many Bards in Bardstown any more," Tom Baird admitted.

"Everybody onto the trail," John shouted, and the women went to round up children who were chattering and teasing each other and get them in their places.

Jane McClure turned laboriously in her stirrups to look one more time at the deserted station. She began counting on her fingers and in her head. Six McClures had made the migration from Pennsylvania, and now there were forty-four. Everyone from an eighty-year-old widow too silly to know she shouldn't be travelling to little Bob, James and Jenny's son. Should she count the babies of the several pregnant women, including Martha and Margaret? She decided not to do so yet. Time enough if the babes survived the rigors of this trail.

She frowned slightly. Their family was bringing ten slaves, and she had come to love all of them, the original Spartacus and Prometheus, their wives, Hettie and Agnes, and six children still owned by Will and John. So, she sighed, of the forty-four McClures, thirty-eight were the direct descendants of one man, John McClure of Ulster, Ireland. "Like Moses, you were," she said loud enough that those nearest to her were startled because she was talking to herself. "'Tis too bad, my dearing, you did not live to see your own enter like lairds o' the earth into the land of cream and honey."

Ish Scott did not go in the westward train. He was going to help his grandmother settle up her house and then pack to meet the group at the rally point in Louisville. His mother thought Ish acted even more odd than usual in the months before the move, leaving late afternoons to journey to Bardstown or Louisville where he stayed for inordinate amounts of time. From time to time mysterious letters came for him in the mail, and he read them in the woods.

Still, James Scott, in one of his rare insistent moods, told Ish he must see to his grandmother. He himself had enough to do with Bobbie and Jenny, who was not fully recovered since the birth of the child.

And so on this rainy spring day Ish rose from his hard loft bed and descended the rungs into the small, clapboard cottage in Lexington which had served as Marguerite Scott's home for the years she lived in Kentucky.

His grandmother had dressed with difficulty. The right side of her mouth hung low, paralyzed by the series of fits she had following her brother's death. The first fit, actually, had occurred at that time, as Ish drove her home through the streets of Lexington. His family had praised him for his quick thinking in finding a neighbor to help free her tongue from between clenched teeth, so she would not strangle herself.

"You're not ready, Grandmother," Ish said with the tone of cyncial reproach he often adopted towards her.

"I need more help in filling these trunks." She looked about at the piles of memorabilia of her life, of black lace mantillas and jewelry caskets and pictures of saints.

"I won't touch those disgustin' things," he said, flinging a gold-framed picture showing St. Stephen being stoned off the trunk onto the floor as if it were a worm.

His grandmother picked up the picture of the saint. She said nothing, but attempted to keep the paralyzed side of her mouth from working. As she lifted the lid of her trunk, dust flew about.

"This morning I knew you were not going to Indiana. I found this. . ." She unfolded a letter. "It is from the despicable politician, the enemy of President Jefferson. He and his scoundrel friends have been active about these parts. How are you involved with them? Ish, you have done some awful things but this man. . ."

Ish did not seem concerned that she had found his letter. "Despicable, is he?" he laughed, almost too casually. "I call him hero rather than the villain you think. Actually, friends of mine have written t' him about me. I've offered m' services to him in whatever way I be of use."

"He says that you should train in the militia for future military action. There is grave trouble here. . ."

"And as you always say, Granny, wherever there's trouble, I seem to be about."

"Yes," she said softly.

"I have no intention goin' to Indiana to dig in the dirt." His laugh was rueful. "Got better, more interestin' plans afoot." The curtains were drawn against the rain, and the one taper in the room did not dispel the deep gloom about them.

"No. This man you are writing to is evil, an egomaniac. He is unbelievably lecherous, an atheist who wishes no good to any man or to the country. I have seen him in my mind. It will break your mother's heart—I shall tell her what I have seen, the letter and the vision also."

Ish rose to his full six-foot height. " 'Tis best if I simply disappear." She shook her head firmly from side to side and went for the door. He advanced toward her. "You—we—must be sure you don't tell anyone of my plans."

A moment of disbelief and then anger crossed her face. Yes, he was capable of harming her; he had reasons far beyond this incident, she knew that. Involuntarily she reached for her crucifix, but she had not put it on yet this morning. It lay on the heap of her jewelry on top of the jewelry cask. Ish reached it first and dashed it to the floor, grabbing her hands at the same moment.

She breathed heavily, closing her eyes in prayer for a moment. His large-boned, powerful hands bent her wrists. Finally she could stand it no longer. She cried out in pain, attempting to back off. "I have known you for all these years," she cried.

"Have you now, Granny? Whatever do you mean?" Ish said, his voice strident.

"I know you, my enemy, have known you from the first moment you entered this mortal cycle in a night of confusion and fear. It was I who finally allowed you to be born, because I would not thwart the cycles of time. We are bound together. . ." The pressure on her wrists increased; she felt herself forced to her knees.

"I triumphed over you once only to have you turn up in our midst. You cannot win. . ." She sought frantically on the floor for the crucifix, but a shoe with a hard black sole kicked it out of the way and held her hand at the same time, causing her to cry out. Her head began to shake.

"You shore do say strange things, Granny," the brutal voice went on. "But then lots o' people have thought you were crazy for a long time. Still, I wouldn't get upset. Remember the last time you got upset you went into a fit right there on the seat o' the wagon, just 'cause I said a few things to you. And the doctor said we must never let you get the fallin' sickness agin if we could help it.'' Ruthless malignity gleamed in Ish's eyes.

Her eyes starting out of her head, the helpless old woman fell flat on the floor. Flecks of foam came to her lips; her head, then her whole body began to shake.

"I'm warnin' you. You might swaller your tongue," Ish said, waiting a moment. "Ah well, I should be goin'. Isn't anything I can do here." She choked, she shook until she rattled the cups on the table, she gagged for air through a throat that was blocked with her own tongue. Then after one last start she lay on her back, her face blue, her life fading in unconsciousness.

At last he kicked the crucifix back toward the dead woman. "Let the mackerel-snappin' priests bury her. She loved 'em well enough, for all the good they're doin' her now." As he left, he picked up and glanced at the letter his grandmother had found. The signature stood out, written in a crabbed, brown hand. It was that of Aaron Burr, the vice-president of the United States, whose name would soon be despised by most Americans as Alexander Hamilton's killer. Casually, Ishmael Scott stuffed the letter in his pocket and left, shutting the door behind him very softly.

"He who fights and runs away, may live to fight another day," he said to himself. "Goodbye now, Granny."

PART IV

INDIANA
1803-1811

SONG FOR THE BUFFALO TRACE
To be sung with the banjo and guitar

If the Eastern Knobs don't get you
With their mountain heights and fogs
The horsefly swarms and gnats in clouds
Will give you fever in the Western bogs.

Chorus: The Buffalo Trace, the Buffalo Trace
The Promised Land's in view
It's heaven when you get there
And hell until you do

A woman hid near the Buffalo Trace
With her hand o'er her baby's face
Indians crept about her,
To find her hiding place
"Don't cry, my babe," she whispered
"You'll soon be in your bed,"
Then she took her hand from its little mouth
It was suffocated dead.

The Buffalo Trace, etc.

The air was crisp on the Buffalo Trace
One February night
A father drove an oxcart
Through the slowly fading light
The cold wind blew, the hard ground froze
The family knew no rest
They died that night on the Buffalo Trace
With their faces still turned West.

The Buffalo Trace, etc.

SONG FOR THE BUFFALO TRACE
continued

White River sings the purtiest song
This side of Jordan's shore
But in the floods of March that song's
A fearful, rushin' roar
A family crossing at the camp
Heard the waters rise at the fall
But they heard no more, they were swep' away
And drownded, one and all.

The Buffalo Trace, etc.

The graves along the Buffalo Trace
Are marked with nary a cross
For younguns with the fever dead,
No time to suffer loss

Just press right on from light to dark
You know we cannot fail
The richest land in the country's
At the end of the Buffalo Trail.

But if fortune awaits at the end o' the trip
It better be a lot
To make up for what happened on the Buffalo Trace
The road that God forgot.

The Buffalo Trace, the Buffalo Trace
The Promised Land's in view
It's heaven when you get there
And hell until you do

Chapter XXXII

The Louisville to Vincennes Road in 1803 was one hundred sometimes beautiful, frequently exciting, and often excruciating miles through virgin wilderness. Five or six days by swift, experienced frontier horseman on the mail route. Two weeks for regular army moving from the fort at Cincinnati to help build the new Fort Knox at Vincennes. A month, at least, by plodding oxen, carrying a family's possessions with mounted women and children on pack horses behind it.

No inns were built through either the rugged eastern Knob hill country or the swampy, western prairies. Migrants stopped by the side of the road or in abandoned Indian campsights alive with snakes, malaria, typhoid, and yellow fever. Stifling heat, pouring rain and hail came down on unprotected heads. Sucking mud swallowed up the cart wheels, and the walkers' feet sank up to their knees.

The constant physical exertion demanded in fighting the hostile environment and the fear of Indians sapped the will and drained the energy of people already exposed to the elements too long. Yet they kept on, at least the McClure-Baird-Emison party did. It was the early spring of 1803, when historical record shows they made their progress across the Buffalo Trace to the capital of the new Indiana Territory.

Why do I always think of food these days at family worship, Jane McClure demanded of herself as she sat on a stool while the others knelt in the clearing among oaks at mid-trail point. "I am the Resurrection and the Life," Dan'l read from the big Anderson Bible that had accompanied them for so many miles on their treks.

The reading and praying had a joint purpose: to start this beautiful April day in the proper Presbyterian way and to memorialize the baby of young Henry Baird. The tiny premature child was born the day before but had not lived out the day. The weak young mother was being carried in a litter, and the prayers were also for her survival down the rest of this lurching, uneven track. John McClure and Tom Baird had decided to stay at least a day in camp so she could gain strength. And so they could repair broken axles and rest horses and oxen exhausted by pulling sledges through the mud.

"How is Henry's wife doin'?" Jane had asked Martha Baird McClure that morning.

"Where there's life, there's hope," Martha said without smiling.

Jane forced herself to concentrate on the scriptures, which usually brought her so much comfort. "Good master, what must I do so that I may inherit Eternal Life?" her son read. Then her mind strayed again. Fifty more miles. About three weeks, or more perhaps, dependin' on how many days they spent in each camp and how the weather progressed. Bringing sixty people through an almost trackless wilderness was like takin' the children of Israel through the desert. A desert with a lot of corn meal mush and bacon burnt over a campfire. And very little hot spoon bread with strawberry jam and pot roast and gravy. Shame on you, Jane McClure for thinking of food at a time when poor Henry's wife hovers between life and death, she reprimanded herself and forced her mind to devotions.

" 'These things have I done from my youth. What else remains?' 'Go and sell your goods and give to the poor and thou shalt have treasure in heaven.' " Why was he readin' that? The McClures certainly weren't layin up heavenly treasure; they were sacrificin' everything they had to make more money, buy big huge farms, be called lairds, gentlemen at last.

Well, be fair, Jane's thoughts continued, 'tis to make a better opportunity for all of them, especially the younguns. That was true, and it was a good thing. Even at this price. At least the diarrhea and shaking that afflicted her constantly last week had finally left. She had prayed it was not the beginning of the yellow fever that was fatal to so many travellers. So far they seem to have avoided that awful fate.

If your mind is strayin', at least lead it down a pleasant road, Jane told herself. She considered her other sons. It occurred to her how different they all were, than if they had been brought up in Ireland. She watched George, forty-six now, looking at a cardinal in the woods, listening for his call. George knew the call of every bird in the wilderness. He and all his brothers had summoned owls to the campfire, and prairie hens and flocks of turkeys for amusement during the deep, dark nights on the trace. George, with all his intellectual airs, lived with his gun by his side and wore leather trousers most of the time.

John, her first baby, fifty-eight years old now, was chewing tobacco and spitting it once a minute. He was doing his duty, she thought, as usual, listenin' to the Bible reading with his hands on his buckskin-clad knees. Next to him, her pretty feet sticking out from under her travelling skirt, was his wife Janie. She was still strikingly beautiful in her forties. Janie seemed to be rather more exhilarated by this trip's trials than anything else.

Well, they had all found some way to put their lives back together in the last ten years. Thank God for that, although Will and Janie hardly ever spoke now.

William's luxuriant eyebrows, now as gray as his hair, met in a frown line. What was he thinkin' of? You could never tell. Perhaps it was his friend Clark, George Rogers Clark.

Will had left the group to go into Clarksville near the Ohio to see his old trailmate. When he returned, he said he had passed a discouraging afternoon with the patriot. Clark spent his time these days keeping in touch with his Revolutionary war cronies in Virginia, trying to get Congress to honor the claims for reimbursement for the fortune he spent in winning the war in the Northwest. Wracked with illness and drinking far too much (as Will noted without comment) he was an embittered and disillusioned man. But he had welcomed a talk and a pipe with Will McClure. (*Roast chicken with chestnut stuffing. Artichokes, butter, and lemon*, the back of her mind said.)

" 'And the young man went away sorrowing, for he had many possessions.' "

Well, that serious young man in the Bible certainly wasn't like these youths who were her grandchildren. Look at Jim, Jack, and Johnny McClure, scratchin' out a surreptitious knife-toss circle there at the back of the group while keeping their eyes, with feigned piety, on their Uncle Dan'l as he read the Holy Word.

(*Cherry pie with fresh cream. Butter-fried new potatoes. Creamed peas.*) Did young girls always have more natural interest in religion than boys? There sat Catherine, contemplative in the cool of the morning, her head cocked a little on one side. The one way to hold sixteen-year-old Catherine's high spirits in check was with the reading of the Bible. She took it seriously, as did her cousins Mary, John's daughter, and Will's Elizabeth, who sat with Catherine. They were quite young ladies now. What would this new place offer them? Husbands, probably soon.

(*Ham and fried apples.*) Well, at least they might have a good dinner tonight, since the men would spend this "camp day" huntin' for fresh meat. Maybe there would be venison stew.

The reading would soon be over; well and good, she had things to do. She wanted to see if Charlotte, Abe, and Frank, the negro children of Pro and his wife, were well yet. They had been ailing with the same fever she'd had.

She wanted to check the pack horses to be sure her mother's china service and grandmother's wool wheel were still riding well, and the little table with the French legs, the one she had grown up with in Dunleigh. John grumbled about taking it, as his dada did before him. Well, it was no more trouble than some of the other things her daughters-in-law had brought along; for instance, two of Jean's beagle hounds, which nipped at the heels of Janie's several quarter horses. And Martha's bathtub. That old bathtub. If they could make it over the Buffalo Trace with that thing, they could make it with anything.

" 'This is the life Eternal, that they might know Thee—' " Thank heaven there was a life eternal. It was obvious that this temporal one was not goin' to last forever, or even much longer in her case. She stood up and looked about her one more time. Was there any good she could possibly do yet for anybody now that this small army of her descendents had inherited the earth?

A slave came to whisper in her ear. Tom Baird's young daughter-in-law had just breathed her last. Jane was needed to direct the preparation of her corpse.

" 'Where there's life, there's hope' is what everybody says," Jane said aloud to herself as she walked to the back of the train. But what's really true is, "Where there's life, there's work. Even at eighty."

Chapter XXXIII

Two weeks later, they broke ground from the last camp along the river, kicking the embers of campfires into the dirt and throwing scummy dishwater into the nettle bushes. At that moment it seemed as if a flock of prayers, like barnswallows, winged their way silently skyward. And though it could have been that a man or two was praying, these were distinctly women's prayers: the universal prayers of pioneer women from the earliest Pilgrims around Boston to the last Conestoga wives across the Oregon trail:

Oh Lord, send me to a house on a hill, a healthful house with a fine prospect in the fields beyond, where my children will rise up each morn to thrive and grow without the agues and plagues.

Give me clean land without stones, where the rows run straight and black and my squash grows long and golden as a maiden's arm, my cabbages plump and green, that we may gather around a dinner table of plenty.

A well of water clear and deep, oh Lord, and a bucket made of oak on a new, strong rope.

And if you could manage it, Lord, just by the door, a huge bush of lavender-pink roses that fill the June nights with their smell, that my darlin' and I, our children and grandchildren, may sit and smell them together.

May we worship you in peace, peace, oh Lord, peace, till our days are over and we lie together in the churchyard near our home.

The fully-loaded horses plodded through Vincennes, taking the road which ran north, then turned east outside the village. The sky was hot and hazy on that May day. John and Dan'l McClure and their group, which included the Emisons and Scotts, soon split off toward an area called Maria Creek. George's and William's land was a little to the south of this, so these two brothers and their families and the Bairds continued eastward along the main road. In the late afternoon William finally split off, and George led his group east, accompanied by Tom Baird and his family, including the broken-hearted son, Henry.

They passed through a patchwork of areas, some rich with prairie grass, some fully-timbered with oaks easily as huge as anything in Pennsylvania and Kentucky. There were already several cornfields roughly gouged from the timberland. A few log and clapboard homesteads perched on the crests of fine hills.

As they came over a little rise Tom Baird, studying the papers before him, told George McClure, "This has t' be your land."

"Finally!" Mother Jane McClure said, with rueful emphasis, as the others laughed and nodded. The Bairds bade goodbye and moved on down the road to their own plot.

A rude trail led through the woods to George's land. George dismounted and helped his wife down. Taking the smallest child John with them and leaving Mother Jane and the other children with Catherine, Jean and George moved down the path through tall trees, then saplings, which finally opened onto a prairie.

Jean's skirt slithered across the grass, and insects started before her feet as she climbed a slight rise to see the land. A cacophony of bird noise from nearby trees broke the silence. Haze stood over the fields and woods as the husband and wife stood at the top of a ridge admiring the fine view of fields, ponds, and natural prairie pastures which spread out like a rippling quilt toward the river. Jean drew in her breath sharply at its beauty.

Jean, George, and little John sat down crosslegged on the grass. Small birds slowly crossed the horizon in front of them, and the smell of some spicy plant was in the air. The sun behind the haze was a hot, fireless ball over their right shoulders. George looked toward the river, a few miles in front of them and then to the rise beneath their feet.

"We'll put the house here," he said, and Jean nodded.

"The serenity," she whispered, trying to put into words how she felt about this beautiful countryside. Little John, a stolid child, poked at a grasshopper with a blade of timothy.

Then they all turned their heads suddenly at the sound of a noise in the underbrush. It was Jane McClure, followed by Catherine and the other children.

"Did you think we were going to wait forever by that path, dearings? Here, I've picked some flowers. We can put them on the supper cloth and spread it on this hill." She looked about her with approval. "Good spot. Let's start the cooking fire." And she bustled about, carrying narrow stems of Queen Anne's lace in her hands, looking for sticks.

In those earliest years of our American Midwest the long, earnest prayers of women like Jean and Jane McClure travelled over many a long mile, clustered about in the hazy air, shook themselves of road dust, and then filtered peacefully down to earth, nestling into the rich valleys and peaceful lands above the wide, fair rivers of Indiana, Illinois and Ohio. The women were finally home.

Jane McClure lived to see her sons' fine homes go up. The McClure mansion houses were two-story, spreading homes made of clapboard and brick, raised with hired masons and carpenters, complete with smokehouses, and for Will and John, slave quarters. She saw her son Dan'l, now called Esquire McClure, found with Mrs. Harrison the first Presbyterian church in Indiana and become one of the most prominent men in the new territory.

Jane was present when John McClure and his wife Janie began a huge horse barn with a stone foundation. She wept to know that the first stone John laid was the one he had brought from his father's stone pile in Pennsylvania. She saw William's spacious frame home and prosperity grow as he arranged shipments of produce from thousands of acres of land down the river to New Orleans. She realized Will McClure was engineering a fortune for all his family.

And safe in the small but tight clapboard home George McClure built on the rise, she began her last project with the needle. Strangely, her eyes got better the last two years of her life. Sitting by the new fireside, she stitched together 7,200 white muslin pieces in the star pattern and then carefully appliquéd her own artwork over the completed quilt.

All around the edges of the quilt were scenes of tender remembrance: from her marriage dress she cut out the slightly faded, but still lovely, embroidered figures of her mother and father, hand in hand, her dog Byblow, her friend Sarah, smiling and wearing braids, by the lough. Of blue dyed cotton she fashioned Blue Mountain and the cabin by Condoguinet Creek with her husband and Lone Stag next to it. With green and brown she pieced together the Kentucky woods and, not quite lost in the midst of them, McClure Station, with its brave little homes in a row.

And finally the Wabash River, and near the McClure farmhouses all on the same looping road, friendly-looking cows feeding on the hills and meadows. All the names and pictures of her children, their spouses, and her grandchildren were on that quilt. And in the middle of this variety of loving scenes and people was one huge word appliquéd that applied to all the scenes and gave the word a meaning all her own: *Home.*

Jane McClure died, peacefully, in her sleep one rainy September night in 1805. She was buried in what would soon be the churchyard of the new Upper Indiana Presbyterian Chuch, on land donated by Dan'l McClure. The Widow Jane was the second person buried in that spot. She sleeps next to the Emison baby who died on the road nearby and was hurriedly put beneath ground for fear of Indians when the large Emison party finally emigrated in 1805.

Her quilt hangs on the wall of a Midwestern farm museum, an object of art by a master craftsman from a time long past. The Anderson wool wheel, Jane's mother's pride and joy, is lovingly cared for and proudly displayed in the very house in which she died one hundred and eighty some years ago by Thornton McClure, a direct descendent of George McClure. Thornton lives in George's house today.

Over eight thousand descendents of Jane McClure and her husband John live in the Midwest today. And they can rise up and call this Irishwoman blessed, as it says in the Bible, if they know the value of a virtuous woman—and a Bountiful Soul!

*   *   *

As the fine wood and brick mansion houses of the "McClure boys" and James and Jenny Scott, the Emisons, and Bairds rose out of the Wabash valley, so also did the even more imposing "great house" of Governor William Henry Harrison. Set on three hundred acres of prime land on the river, it commanded a view upriver toward the Wea and Miami homelands and, southward, toward the Ohio.

The home that Harrison built made a distinct statement. That statement was the same one that Versailles Palace made in a more complex form: the dweller of this aristocratic mansion is a man of power and of fortune. Do not take him lightly.

That message would not be lost on the humble dwellers of bark lodges who came to Grouseland Mansion, as it was being called. In this elegant parlor and council chamber, under crystal chandeliers and amidst mahogany funiture and silver urns, the Indians would soon be asked to sign away millions of acres of rich hunting grounds.

"There's something of both Monticello and Mount Vernon in this thing," Samuel Thompson murmured to his friend Dan'l McClure as they supervised the unloading of another wagonload of brick from the brickyards upriver half a mile.

"You've seen 'em I 'spect," Dan'l said. "I seen the pitchers—take your breath away. All Italian gardens and pillars and what you call 'em—rotundas."

"Yes. I was thinking of these round windows and the staircase particularly." They looked through the door opening of the almost-completed house to an entrance hall, where a curving staircase ascended gracefully to the second floor.

"They say the treads are made of cherrywood. They are set so deep into the wall the stair supports itself."

Thompson took off his high-crowned hat, wiped his forehead, and surveyed the workers. Two of them were familiar. Jack McClure, Dan'l's eldest son, no taller than his father but thicker through the shoulders, and Jim McClure. These two red-faced hod-carriers were wheelbarrowing bricks to masons at the rear of the house. Thompson thought them good workers and said so to Dan'l.

"They do all right when the notion takes 'em," his friend conceded. Dan'l signalled to the carter to return to the brick yards for the last load of the day. "But you know what the town's callin' 'em, don't you? Jim Dandy and Jackie Dude." Thompson's snorting laugh showed he understood the appelation. The two young men were often seen these days playing the parts of young gentlemen at Denny's tavern or looking at expensive rifles at John Small's gunsmith shop.

"It's the clothing, Sam'l," Dan'l McClure alleged. "They strike me as cheeky enough for boys o' nineteen who don't own any land. Tole me and John not long ago that they needed outfittin' proper-like. Tight trousers, shoes. Buckskin and moccasins don't suit any more they say." He sent word to the two by a passing workman that it was time for dinner. Samuel picked up the hamper packed by his wife.

"Little velveteen jackets that go jest to the waist, high ruffled shirts—that ain't all. Jack's been readin' all kinds o' books and papers lately. Tryin' to polish up his speech. And he says now that we're gentry, we shouldn't talk about

Caintuck, Harrodsburg 'n all that.''

"And I notice you're doing what he says," his friend offered.

"Waal, I'm not ashamed of it the way I think he is. But it's true, I feel different here. In Pennsylvania, we was the Scotch-Irish. In Caintuck the Caintuckians. But now. . .'' Dan'l hesitated.

"We're Americans. A country. Is that what you mean?"

"Shore is. And it all has happened in my lifetime. When I think about bein' here with Harrison and all. . .'' He turned from his friend to hide his emotion.

Thompson nodded, conceding the heady exuberance of the times being lived now in the Northwest Territory. Before he could express his reservations about Harrison, though, Jackie Dude and Jim Dandy bounded up ebulliently. "How do, Pater,'' said Jack, winking at his father. "Time for a hearty mid-day repast?'' Thompson took out cold meat pies and bread. His bride, one of Widower Tom Baird's daughters, was eagerly cooking him delicacies.

"How long's it goin' to take to finish this mansion up, Mr. Sam'l?'' Jim McClure asked the older man.

"Depends on what you mean. We'll be on the last courses of the dependency building next month. The molding for the parlor doors is due in any time from Pittsburg. The family will move in after that. But the grounds won't be done. The governor says he'll be planting elms, putting in walks, digging gardens, painting.''

"Harrison hasn't been about much, has he?'' Jack McClure commented. "Runnin' the affairs o' state from afar.'' His mother had sent a peach tart which he carefully took out of a dinner basket and unwrapped.

"Waal, if he has t' travel, he hasta,'' Dan'l opined. "Harrison is a great man, one who delivers on his promises. He said he would get the Injeeans to give up their land and settle down, and he's doin' it.''

"Give up ground, yes, settle down, no.'' Thompson said. The governor had just signed a treaty with the Delawares, Potawatomis, and other Indians transferring a section of land above the Ohio to the government. "The tribes are angry and restless.''

"Young Fox-eyes'll calm 'em down,'' Dan'l said confidently. "His Injeean policy is purty simple. Call the friendly chiefs together, give 'em tobacco and lots of strong speech and stronger whiskey and tell 'em what to do. Then, with guns in back o' you, see that they do it.''

"That's his attack policy. He covers his flank by appointing Indian agents who support what he wants,'' Thompson added.

"He hounded the old agent William Wells out o' town,'' Jack said.

"Waal,'' his father countered, "Wells went around among the Injeeans whinin' bout the injustice o' the treaty, gettin' their friendship and special favors that lined his pocket. No wonder Harrison is afeard o' him.''

Thompson looked thoughtful. "He fears little else. Seems to have the whole middle part of the country riding right on his own gold epaulettes.''

Dan'l munched contentedly on a juicy, brown summer pear, the first from his own orchard. "Not everbody. Not George, and not George's new friend John Badollet.''

Jim McClure spoke up. "Pa says Badollet's jest a sour apple foreigner who got a plush job 'cause he's part of President Jefferson's party." There was some truth in the statement. Badollet's best friend was fellow Switzer Albert Gallatin, Jefferson's Secretary of the Treasury. Gallatin got Jefferson to appoint Badollet land agent, so Badollet had friends in high places. And now, Thompson conceded to himself, so did George McClure.

Jack was unimpressed. "Waal, Uncle George thinks the sun rises and sets above Badollet's head. He's always down there at the office talkin' about 'pertinent issues,' as he calls 'em."

"Like slavery," his cousin put in. "Uncle George and Badollet oppose it, but they ain't goin' to get very far when the governor comes from Virginny and has slaves himself. You hear all the talk around here that he's goin' to find some way to make it legal?"

"Congress has said there will be no slaves in Indiana Territory. What's the matter with the law?" Thompson asked.

"Harrison's jest gettin' around it," Jim assured him confidently. "Indianney's goin' to have 'permanent indenture.' The slaves are bein' asked to sign papers bindin' 'em for ninety years." He chuckled. It was obvious the two young men approved of the governor's views.

Dan'l shook his head in disgust. It was one policy of the governor he did not agree with. The subject was causing deep dissension in the area and in the family, as it had since Pro and Spar first appeared in their midst. George was becoming a rabid opponent, while William and John were just as convinced that the future of the area lay in attracting slaveholders from the South to Vincennes.

Jack McClure had a sudden inspiration. "Mr. Thompson, you shall come as my invited guest sometime to a meetin' of our group. We need opposition views."

Thompson raised his white-blonde eyebrows questioningly. The sun glinted off a bald spot on his head.

"Young Patriots of the Wilderness. We meet each week t' talk about issues in the present gov'ment."

"Which you support, I trust."

"Shore do. Young Fox-eyes is the hero of the West. Our club is a society o' enterprisin' gentlemen from better famblies."

"A drinkin' club," his father corrected.

"Meets to share good viands and serious discussions on Federalist and Democratic issues, exchange convivial pleasantries. . ."

Jack's round, handsome face shone with merriment. These days he seemed to always talk like a corn-fed version of the *Richmond Examiner*, his father thought. Always laughin' with his cousins at some joke Dan'l didn't understand. Bright, but spoiled by Martha. He'd come through anyways when he grew up a bit. Problem was, as he often said to George and Will and John, there weren't many b'ars to kill or cabins to build anymore, and Harrison himself dealt with the Injeeans. The boys didn't have anything big to do.

The two young men brushed crumbs off their laps and hastened back to work so they could unload and be finished by four o'clock. They had made arrangements for a swim with soldiers from the new fort before supper at the inn and a full schedule that night. There may have been political intrigues and squabbles in Vincennes, but for the new generation like Jackie Dude and Jim Dandy McClure, they were only one more game in the rollicking new life they had found in Indianney.

Chapter XXXIV

Vincennes was not the only frontier outpost in America in 1805 dwelling on the fraying edge of tension. Questions of trading rights, slavery, and foreign threats to U.S. territory troubled many a western village in the new nation. And some boundaries were still unsettled, even after years of war and treaty negotiations. Sleeping among the olive-black waters of bayous and live oaks, surrounded by the United States, was a town of three thousand souls fought over by three great world powers. America and England were interested in Baton Rouge, but Spain still technically owned it.

America bought Louisiana in 1803 from France in one of the greatest bargains of all time, but Napoleon had been vague about the boundaries of the block of land he sold the Americans. Was West Florida, that area shaped like gun, stretching from Key West all the way around to Baton Rouge part of America too, President Jefferson wondered? Spain said not, claimed the region, and made it clear she intended to defend it. Americans resented having their new city of New Orleans split from the rest of U.S. territory. The settlers cried for the government to take West Florida and its capital of Baton Rouge from Spain.

It was into this land of seething political turmoil and new economic opportunity that Vincennes trading interests expanded in the first years of the century. Arthur Dakin, who still signed his letters to his wife as Asondaki Alamelonda, was only vaguely aware of the political controversies. He and his boss Nicholas Fortin were involved in working eighteen-hour-days to develop the tanning and merchantile headquarters they were determined to set up in Baton Rouge.

Fortin found the bayou city promising for business. American settlers were pouring into its area to take up cotton lands, build mills, and become landlords with the King of Spain's land. The opening of trade along the Mississippi made Baton Rouge, like Natchez, a booming river town, and there were plenty of customers for the new store and tannery business.

Fortin put his assistant to work making the tannery at Seven Springs settlement operational, and Asondaki spent his days securing hides from traders, both from Vincennes and New Orleans, clearing land for leather-processing, even buying slaves to peel bark and make vats.

There were constant irritations. The large shipment of hides Lasselle and

Marchal sent from Vincennes spoiled from the heat and improper packing. Supplies ordered from upriver took an interminable time to reach Baton Rouge. And the languid, mixed-blood workers in the area were unreliable.

Asondaki had no time to visit Indiana and the now-permanent Potawatomi settlement on Lake Mocksinkickee. A Quaker missionary, and later the Indian agent, sent letters from Swiftly Running Feet, but letters could not answer the yearning in his heart for the quiet wisdom and smooth-limbed beauty of his wife. Nor for the lake itself, where blackbirds sang in poplars among the gently rippling waters.

He thought of the coolness of those waters now, as he sat on the verandah of a large house in creole country to the southwest of Baton Rouge. He was on a business mission for Fortin. Heat stood like a physical presence, shimmering over the bayous, as heavy and oppressive as the moss on the live oaks.

Here in this remote river country it was as if the French still governed. No trace of either Spanish or American influence intruded. The two-story plantation home reflected the style the French established all over colonial America. It was made of clapboards outside and painted *bousillage* plaster within, as in Vincennes, only here mud was mixed with moss to make the walls. The main quarters and outbuildings were carefully placed among attractive gardens and oak groves. Graceful porches and open-shuttered windows caught the evening breezes.

Honoré LeFauvre had built the house to command over two thousand acres of fine riverbottom land. Now, as Asondaki gazed across a plank fence to fields of rice, cane, and indigo, he was aware of the power and wealth of the man who owned the lands. A negro servant touched Asondaki's elbow offering wine and cakes; he accepted a small glass. He did not often drink spirits lately. He had seen too many Indians in Vincennes wallowing in the streets, pouring liquor into each other's mouths, begging white men for demijohns of whiskey, and it affected his pleasure in drinking. In a matter of moments, his host joined him, pulling up a ladder-back chair.

"You wish several hundred livres of sugar," he said to Asondaki. "This year that be possible. I have built a mill on the river and have ten new slaves to operate it. My brother runs it, along with the grist mill and sugar cane presses."

Honoré LeFauvre was a man of medium height and age with fashionably long, twisting sideburns. His fingernails, Asondaki thought, seemed immaculate for a farmer, even a gentleman farmer. From time to time he took out a little file and groomed them. He might have been any gentleman in Napoleon's Paris or Marseilles, except that his skin was brown.

"We be a large family, M'sieur Dakin, tight-knit. My white father come from France, bought himself big holdin's along these rivers and bayous and married without the church. My mother were a free woman o' color." He said it with a smile, taking out a smoking pouch of fine, embossed leather, from which he soon lit a pipe of particularly strong tobacco. Asondaki, for whom languages were second nature, noticed that the native French LeFauvre spoke was almost as rough and ungrammatical as the English spoken by the Scotch-Irish in Vincennes.

"You be surprised that we have here rich free people of color?" said the older man.

"I know there are many here—very different from Indiana or Kentucky." Fortin had told Asondaki that these free mulattos were a class unto themselves. So many groups, the *metis* had sighed under his breath. Of all matters in the white man's world the subtle social nuances, the code of behavior, puzzled him most. He seemed to be always making social blunders.

Really, you had to be born into a race of people to fully understand how to act. Now he could see why white men coming to Kekionga had insulted the Indians without meaning to. He once thought that understanding this "how to act" code of the white man was like looking at the Northern Lights. They flashed a hundred ways and had a hundred subtle colors. But it was hard to sort out the different shades, and call them to mind later, because they flashed so fast. Turn your head away when you sneeze and use a small square of handkerchief, address married women as Madame, first cousins may marry in the South—every day there was something new to learn.

But it was important to sort out white man differences. Unless he could understand their codes of behavior, he would not be able to fully assimilate into their world. And more and more he was coming to think he wanted to do that.

"Ten children of Michelle LeFauvre now live on this river," his host went on. "We stay to ourselves and try to. . ." his delicate finger traced a line in front of his face "draw our own lines. We be a land-owning bunch, support the Church of course. We never been slaves, and we are not akin to the coffee-coloreds of LaVille New Orleans."

Asondaki looked at him for an explanation. "Ahh, you do not understand. I tell you. In New Orleans there be octoroons, mulattos, who act like slaves even though they be free. Curry the white man's favor. At balls they parade around the young girls who are then "placed" with white men. They be set up in homes with hangings, rugs—their children taken care of with money for life."

"And the white men's wives?"

"Better than having the men go to prostitutes," he said serenely. Adondaki frowned.

"Anyway, it be the French way." The pipe puffed, and smoke floated over the rail of the verandah. "My own father, he finally married, with the priest, a white woman. Provided smartly for my mother, who understood the custom."

"But you are not as the octoroons?"

"No," he laughed. "The priests, they are much among us since my father's time. Our daughters are upright and we marry carefully to make the fortunes, as the white men do."

Asondaki smiled. He understood this custom from Vincennes. He looked at the tea cake he was finishing. "Are there pecans in this cake?" he asked.

"Of course. Some of the best pecans in the South. They grow in the wilds of our land."

"I would like to see them. M'sieur Fortin particuarly likes to eat pecans."

"I hope you be staying a few days with us, M'sieur Dakin. I have more ideas for goods to trade to M'sieur Fortin with you. The supper is at seven."

That night Asondaki sat enveloped in the light of scores of wax candles reflected off a gleaming mahogany table. A servant in livery served shrimps and fish smothered in onions and okra, a vegetable he was still getting used to. Never had he been at such a table; while treated cordially in Vincennes he was not invited to sit at the tables of Hyacinthe Lasselle or Madame Gamelin. Madame LeFauvre, a light-skinned woman with frizzled, buff-colored hair, rang a little bell for the several courses to be served.

"May I introduce the children," LeFauvre said as conversation quieted a moment. "Petit," junior version of the father, about twenty, inclined his head, "Angeline and Jean" boy and girl twins, and then several younger ones with names that rhymed. Finally, LeFauvre introduced him to the girl sitting across from him. She was a shy, beautiful almost-white girl with coal-black hair piled high on her head and held with a diamond clip. Victorine was her name. All during the supper she did not speak, but her eyes followed Asondaki's every move. Was he using his fork wrong? It made him uncomfortable to have the girl stare so.

LeFauvre spoke expansively of prospects. Tomorrow he would show M'sieur Dakin a fine backwoods area that would make him eager to send in Fortin's workers and begin bark stripping, and pecan trees for his employer's best pies, even cows if he wished to increase the young Fortin infant's milk supply.

LeFauvre concluded supper by suggesting the twins and Victorine show M'sieur Dakin the garden. Asondaki nodded and, offering his arm to the young girl, as he had seen Fortin do, ventured out into the languid evening air. Somewhere a bird called, and the sound echoed oddly off the water of the bayou.

It turned out Mademoiselle Victorine did speak. Her throat was not raw, and she had not been stricken by the gods with cloven-tongue, as Asondaki had half-humorously wondered.

"There are not many mosquitoes at this height," she said. The garden was in the old-fashioned style, with planks of oak encircling beds of pinks and marguerites. The twins, laughing at some joke of their own, drifted behind a cedar hedge out of sight, and Asondaki and Mademoiselle Victorine were alone.

The land sloped down to a dovecote, and the quiet, comfortable cooing of pigeons floated out of the building's hexagonal walls as they approached. Mademoiselle Victorine began to cling tightly to his arm as the path grew rougher; now she looked up at him with large, trusting eyes. Something in that look reminded him of Swiftly Running Feet, and he felt a pang of loneliness.

As always, when he missed the tents of his wife and people, he mentally calculated the dollars now owed him on Lasselle's books. Not that he would return, ever, to the villages of either the Potawatomi or Miamis. No, all this work and separation would some day give him his own house with painted mantel, with five china teacups on it in French fashion, and chintz curtains, somewhere near Mocksinkickee. He would have his own trading post. The thought made him joyful and generous, especially with this family that was important to their interests. Now how was it the white gallants treated young women in Vincennes? He must be correct. Kiss the lady's hand and smile mysteriously. He did that, and with Mademoiselle Victorine on his arm, returned to the house.

He spent the next days with LeFauvre surveying the "stiff land" for stripping and timber possibilities. They also looked at the stunted cattle which might be herded and brought to Baton Rouge for families of settling Americans, and the sugar cane presses, now silent after harvest. Each night the girl Victorine walked with him in the garden. Behind them, also, each night, strode Aunt Eulalie, sister of the master of the house, who had come to visit in a carriage. What was her purpose on these walks? He did not understand or care. It had something to do with unmarried people walking about together, all very silly. He had not explained his marital status to the family. It was not their concern, and he would soon be gone. Just as well, he thought on the beautiful last moonlit night. The girl had become as clinging as a wild grapevine.

As they entered the house after the stroll, Asondaki and Victorine passed a formal room with velvet chairs and a virginal. Victorine took him in and played a bit on the instrument, her fingers pressing the keys firmly. She was singing some song about a lover gone over the seas to the wars and mourning for his love. Truly, she sounded a bit like a cow. He had never seen this room occupied and asked Victorine about it. "This is the white room. Whites only may come in here." He shrugged; obviously he was qualifying in their eyes. And he had no more white blood than they. Did they not see he was part Indian?

Later, as he looked in the mirror of his bedroom in the small bachelor's cottage where he slept, Asondaki asked himself who he really was. When they looked at him, what did they see? A twenty-nine-year-old man with dark auburn curls who looked younger than his years. The straight aquiline features of the Indian had softened somewhat as the years went by and he looked less like his uncle and mother and more like—someone else. He pulled off his embroidered shirt and looked at his coppery, hairy chest in the mirror. He peered around over his shoulder to see his back. Yes, he thought, among these dark-skinned people I could pass, if I chose.

He got into the high bed, with its mahogany headboard, and crawled beneath mosquito netting onto fine, soft sheets. "If I chose," he thought, and went to sleep.

"At next harvest, the shipment of sugar as you wished, price including delivery to our dock," Asondaki told Fortin when he returned to the Baton Rouge plantation.

"Delivery included? Very good, Dakin, my friend. The ladies in Vincennes are insisting on white sugar in their tea at their soirées and the price is up. We stand to make a tidy profit on this shipment." Fortin was pleased. The results of the creole trip were more than he could have anticipated.

Asondaki nodded his head joyfully. "My friend," Fortin had said. The words meant much.

Fortin was growing a small beard. As he cracked and sampled some of the pecans Asondaki had brought from LeFauvre's plantation, crumbs from the pecans settled into the beard. Three-year-old Antoine laughed to see his father shake his beard vigorously to dislodge the crumbs. "Doggie, doggie," Antoine said. His father and Asondaki smiled.

Antoine began running about like a dog on all fours. "I be doggie too," he said. "Dakin, watch me." He was such a little man, visiting every part of the grounds and factory, playing boss of the plantation. Asondaki had grown very fond of Antoine. The child made him long for the time when he would have his own child. A year or two, three at the most should see the money to buy the fine trading post. . .

"Tomorrow," Fortin was saying, "I wish you to help me with a transaction involving the sale of slaves. Two Vincennes men are here. I have long awaited their arrival."

"Who. . ."

"Luke Dugger and Tom Baird. They will sell five slaves here for some of our 'needy' Vincennes esquires. The governor of West Florida doesn't bother with scruples in such cases."

Neither did the governor of Indiana, if what Asondaki heard was true. Well, perhaps Harrison did draw the line at trafficking in slaves, although he encouraged his friends to hold them. What did it matter? Down here white men held Indian slaves, and Indians themselves had slaves on their plantations further east. What was it about a man, Asondaki wondered, that would allow him to take away another's freedom? Well, he would see the answer tomorrow, at least in this case, with the arrival of Dugger and Baird. He considered a moment. Dugger he knew, Baird he did not, although Fortin and Marchal seemed to have mentioned his name. Well, the morrow would tell what sort of fish would swim so far downstream to sell one of their own species.

Dugger and Baird were up with the first light, seeing to the five black men they had brought from Vincennes. The slaves slept in a shack on a drafty dirt floor where spiders and vermin crawled freely. The white men did not seem to notice the filth of the cabin, but Dugger did notice that one of the black men, Farleigh by name, was sick.

As Asondaki passed the slave quarters on his way to the tannery, he heard Dugger tell the man, "You got camp mouth. Now keep your mouth shet and don't show them pustules." Asondaki had a brief look at the slave through the window, and Farleigh was in no mood to smile. He seemed almost dazed from fever. During the trip downstream, no doubt, they were all exposed to wind, cold, and sleeting rain on the deck of the boat.

Dugger was a fancy-dressed man with coarse, illiterate ways which he tried to disguise with affected mannerisms. Asondaki took a strong dislike to him in the dealings they had in the next few days. Baird he saw only from afar.

Without much enthusiasm, Asondaki had arranged to show the slaves to prospective buyers. On one occasion all the slaves, including the desperately-ill Farleigh, were hauled across the bayou to show to a family settlement of Carolinians.

"Cain't sell these niggers," Dugger conceded as they sat at dinner that night. Susanne Fortin, looking drawn from the humid, hanging heat, served dishes the slave girl brought from the kitchen: braised duck, tarts, and a variety of wines. Asondaki watched Dugger fork the poultry non-stop into his cavern of a mouth, then pour coffee into his saucer, blow loudly, and slurp it up. Dugger's eye caught his; the white man frowned. He does not want me here at this table, Asondaki thought. He hates Indians as much as negroes. He was never surprised to encounter such dislike. After all, in Vincennnes it was the French, not the Americans, who fraternized with the *metis*.

"The price of slaves is down because the bottom of the cotton market has fallen out," Fortin told Dugger. "I could take them off your hands for land I yet hold in Vincennes."

"Don't want no more land in Vincennes," Dugger mumbled. Baird kept eyeing Asondaki. It was natural, Asondaki thought, that a naturally bigotted man like Dugger would hate him as an Indian without even knowing him. But Baird's attitude was harder to define. Baird had been looking off and on at him all evening, but the surreptitious glances were more inquisitive than hostile.

"There's uncertainty here in Baton Rouge," Fortin told them. From somewhere at the back of the house a slave woman's voice comforted a fretful child. It was little Antoine, Asondaki thought. He had gone upriver with his father to help Dugger sell the slaves and had developed a slight fever.

"Everybody has war mania," Fortin continued. "The Americans are coming, the Spanish are arming, there's a plot in Kentucky to seize this place—rumors flit around like deer flies. And a lot of people here would welcome the Americans. People want the *dons* driven into the sea."

"Hmph," Dugger said. "I may have just th' man to do it." Susanne Fortin got up to go to the crying Antoine, giving her husband a brief, reproachful glance. There was between them, Asondaki knew, a running argument about the unhealthful climate in the bayous. Susanne would suspect it was affecting the boy.

Dugger's voice grew low and he leaned across the table. "We have been tryin' to raise money and volunteers in Indiana for an expedition against the Spanish. Led by Aaron Burr."

Fortin seemed surprised. "The vice-president? He was in New Orleans this year."

"Well, he ain't the vice-president any more. But he has some right smart idees. Spit in the eye of the government in Washington City, maybe gain an empire in these yere parts too. Kick out the Spanish from West Florida here at Baton Rouge and go on south. Mexico is ripe as a muskmelon for revolution."

"Well, this place *is* a tinder box," Fortin murmured, his mind on other things. "It wouldn't take much for Burr, or someone like him to set it off."

The next day, the man across the bayou came to buy the slaves, except for Farleigh. He was dead. When Dugger found out, he vented more obscene and profane curses than Asondaki knew even existed in English. Frenchmen who thought Americans didn't know how to swear didn't know Dugger.

As Dugger and Baird prepared for the poling trip up to Natchez, and from there the long, dangerous trek up the Natchez Trace, Asondaki went to the dock to help them pack. Fortin sent his regards; he had gone to sign the contract with LeFauvre in creole country. Susanne was in the house with the feverish Antoine.

Earlier both the Fortins had given Asondaki last-minute messages to send with the travellers to Vincennes. Fortin was placing an order for a fine cherry armoire from Roux's cabinet shop. Susanne sent a box of almond bark candy and messages of grief to Marchal. His wife Rose, Susanne's sister, had died leaving an infant son. While the barge was being packed and these last-minute arrangements were being made, Baird lingered on the dock, inspecting ropes, being sure his canteen was full, checking his gun. He seemed to be trying to both look and not look at Asondaki. Finally he turned and searched the younger man's face in seeming bewilderment.

"You know, Dakin, I jest cain't get it out o' my mind that you look like somebody I know. Ben tormentin' me the whole time I be'n here. Cain't quite place it."

"I look like many Miamis you may have seen on your travels north in Indiana. I know you travel much."

"Acourse, acourse that's it." Baird leapt on board the barge. As its crew laboriously poled and rowed it out on the bayou, as the passengers standing on deck diminished in size until they disappeared around a bend into the river, Asondaki watched from the dock.

Then he turned and headed up the rise to the house with a small, weary smile on his face. He finally remembered what he had heard about Tom Baird. He had led the large group of people across the Buffalo Trace, the Caintucky Pennsylvanians. And the face Tom Baird recognized in Asondaki's, although he did not know it, was the face of a man he had known for thirty-five years, Dan'l McClure.

That night a child's delirious cries rose on the wind and Asondaki's heart leapt, realizing Antoine's father was not there. He dressed quickly and went to the Fortin's quarters. Susanne, her eyes hollow with sleeplessness, rocked the child on her lap. She looked up gratefully, Asondaki thought, when he came to the door.

"Dakin, he is so ill," she said, tears coming to her eyes.

"Let me relieve you. You must be weary," Asondaki suggested, and the woman reluctantly gave up her charge to the willing arms of the *metis*.

"I must get more compresses. The fever has reached the crisis," she said.

Asondaki held the limp child. Of course, he should have realized it. Antoine must have caught the terrible fever of the slave Farleigh. The child's forehead was burning, and his lips were parched and dry. A fetid odor came from between the lips, and Asondaki was apprehensive.

Antoine opened his eyes and recognized Asondaki. The light of the hurricane lamp illuminated his straw-colored curls and feverish cheeks. He looked like one of the angels in the Vincennes cathedral. "M'sieur Dakin, I will play a dog again for you. Be a poodle," he said. As Asondaki put his fingers to his lips to tell Antoine to save his strength, the boy sighed and closed his eyes. A tiny bubble formed on his lips, and he was gone.

His mother entered the room just at that moment and dropped the pitcher of water she brought. As it smashed on the floor, she ran to take the child from Asondaki. "Antoine, my babe," she cried, shaking him. But his head fell back, the form was limp.

"I was not here, not here," she cried hysterically. "My baby was held by a *stranger* when he died." Asondaki felt an acute pang, both for the child's death and his mother's grief, and because he had again somehow done the wrong thing with the white people.

Later, he stood around not knowing what to do as the women prepared the small body for burial. Susanne Fortin came out to speak to him. "Dakin, I thank you for being with me when—Antoine died. Perhaps it was best that way. Now I shall never have to relive that exact moment when he slipped away." She began to sob uncontrollably and left to return to the small room. It was kind of her to say that, Asondaki thought. Now I am truly a member of the family. He relished the feeling even in the midst of sadness.

It was a week before Fortin recovered enough from the loss of little Antoine to be able to discuss business. Fortin said that everywhere he turned, he heard the little boy's high-pitched laugh or his steps on the stairs. When a barge arrived from Vincennes with barrels for the family, they were found to contain toys for Antoine from Uncle Marchal. Susanne collapsed sobbing on the dock. Asondaki decided he could help his employer by leaving him to his grief and by handling details of the business himself, without asking intrusive questions.

Finally a morning came when Fortin returned to the office. He said only one thing about the death. "It was not the climate, as all in Vincennes think. This climate is better than the valley of the Wabash. Only a little hotter in summer. I have made a good choice and will stay." Then he went on to business. "The LeFauvres wish to have you handle the details of the sugar order. You seem to have charmed them," he smiled knowingly. "You can go next week, when the order will be ready for shipment."

Asondaki felt unsettled. Why was he needed to supervise the hauling of the goods? And what was this about charming them? He did not think he understood fully what that meant. Perhaps it had something to do with the daughter. Well, he was a married man and would find it easy enough to avoid that snare. He loved his wife. Here was one rabbit who could resist the root of the cattail plant.

As it turned out he had definitely been needed to supervise the loading of the sugar at the plantation's river dock. The slaves were ill-managed by

LeFauvre's brother, who seemed to wish he were anywhere else but in this mosquito bog ordering slaves to lug huge hempen sacks onto a barge. Asondaki personally helped haul the last few bags onto the boat before dark fell. The slaves were restless; there was a strange, flat quality to the air that frayed the nerves, and flies settled and bit unmercifully.

The candles did not seem to burn so brightly, Asondaki found, at this night's dinner. The glassy surface of the table showed water marks to his more-knowing eyes. Asondaki praised himself silently for gaining understanding of the subtleties of the situation.

It was obvious. The girl, who was again placed across the table from him, was "hankerin' '" for him, as they said in Vincennes. She would try to walk with him in the rose garden, probably throw herself at him as forwardly as a fifteen-year-old Miami strumpet. Well, he would not walk tonight, would say he needed to work over the accounts. Stay clear of her clinging arm. Should she want to kiss him—his will wavered a bit as he looked across the table at her, with her young doe eyes and full lips. She was as ripe as a peach at the end of July.

Honoré LeFauvre's voice interrupted his thoughts. "M'sieur Dakin, I have asked M'sieur Fortin if we might use your services to perform a favor for us. Victorine is to go to her aunt's tomorrow for a long visit, and since her brother Petit is gone away to school now, there is no one here I trust to take her on the road trip. The bayous be unhealthy this time of year for young women. Would you be good enough to go the ten miles with her? You might stay yourself at her Aunt Eulalie's and return the next day. Be you ready for such a trip?" He smiled broadly and seemed to wink.

Ignoring his odd behavior, Asondaki nodded that he would be happy to be of service to the family. What could happen on a one-day wagon trip? The group rose from dinner. The strange, fetid flatness was still in the air. "It's oppressive," Madame LeFauvre remarked with a shudder, and picked up a fluted fan from the sideboard. She suggested they retire early. Asondaki breathed a sigh of relief. He would not be subjected to the rose garden walk.

The next morning the wind blew from the southeast, steady and cool. Victorine was up early and ate breakfast. She stood silently, as usual, as Asondaki helped her father and slaves load the wagon with supplies and leather satchels

"You must be on your way right now. The weather's uncertain in the autumn," said LeFauvre. "Right now 't looks clear, but I've put a canvas in with you in case you should see rain the last few miles. We daren't put the trip off. My sister has been ill and needs Victorine's help. Besides, I don't expect the storm that's brewin' to come ashore; 'twill go on east." The sugar bags were covered too, he assured Asondaki.

On the road the girl unwound a bit.

"You're a Choctaw, M'sieur Dakin," she said. It was halfway between an accusation and a question.

"I am half-Miami, Mademoiselle LeFauvre," he said, more than half-irritated.

"I knew 'twas somethin' like that. My father says if you had any children, they wouldn't hardly look like Indians at all. Just a bit pink.''

"Does he now?" Asondaki went as rapidly as he could along the twisting trail. By ten o'clock the wind was blowing so strongly it took their hats off, and rain began to patter, then sluice down on them. LeFauvre was wrong. The storm had obviously come ashore here and was growing more intense by the moment. Asondaki put the canvas about them but soon the strength of the wind stopped any progress they could make.

"We must try to find shelter," Asondaki shouted, tying the horses as best he could by the side of the road. "A real storm," he yelled, louder, as rain caught and strangled the words in his throat. Unbidden, the Miami words came to his mind as Little Turtle spoke them so long ago, "A lam sang kati," —there will be strong wind.

"Hurricane preparin' to come ashore," Victorine confirmed. She seemed to know where she was going. Taking his hand, she led him through the dark oak grove, where limbs thrashed about like whips. Slashing rain blinded their eyes, tree limbs fell in their paths. But eventually a building loomed before them.

"Grandfather Michelle's chapel," Victorine shouted. It was a stone and board building with a small bell tower. The wind pulled at them, stronger by the minute, as they made their way through a yard of strange stone houses which Asondaki thought must be tombs. Exhuasted with fighting the wind, he pulled the door open and they collapsed, panting and wet on the floor.

" 'Tis on the edge of the property, between Aunt Eulalie's and Father's holdings. 'Twas built by Grandfather after he married the white woman, and she and he be buried in the mausoleums in the yard.'' It was the most she had ever said in his presence. He looked at her as she pulled her riding cloak off. Her very curly hair made wet ringlets about her face, and her dress clung to her body, which he saw was a beautiful one indeed, if large-boned.

As his eyes grew accustomed to the dim light which filtered through the one window, Asondaki could see a few rude log benches, an altar, and a statue of the Virgin and child painted in garish pink and blue. The noise of the wind rose by the minute. They sat numbly on the benches for what must have been an hour, listening to the howling which sounded like all the wolves in the world, and the crashing of branches, the slash of rain.

"Is there anything to keep us warm in here?" he asked finally. He wished for the flint he no longer carried and wondered with a sudden flash of irreverence if there was any lint in his navel.

The girl went behind the altar and came out with some damp, moldy laprobes. "We don't have many services here anymore, but these were from my father's day." They covered up and listened to the hurricane roar to its fullest fury. Toward nightfall the storm ceased, as the eye passed through. Then the meager light outside failed.

They had eaten nothing since breakfast, and both slept fitfully on pews on opposite sides of the church as the wind changed and rose again with unrestrained fury. At midnight a window broke suddenly, shattered by a tree crashing onto the roof. At least it may hold the roof on, Asondaki thought ruefully. He was afraid of a flood; such things happened in the big storms, especially in this low-lying river bottomland.

He felt something move beside him in the dark. "I am afraid." The voice of the girl came out of the night. He could feel her warm, short breaths beside him and he felt a pang of pity. She had looked so young bringing the blankets. She could not help it that she was dense and timid. He put his blanket about her and left his arm around her shoulder as, shivering she moved closer to him.

He started. She had taken off her dress and had only a thin linen shift plastered to her body. All the smart reserve he had built up over the last few days returned. Was she trying to attract him? Or was she only drying the sodden garment? Did it matter?

Her large, full breasts leaned against his chest as she turned toward him. Her shoulders were smooth, cool under his touch. His man's arrow began to stir, quickly stood. Gods! He had been living like a young Iroquois, depriving himself of women these two years. Now this live, warm, young woman put herself right in his way. Victorine was not aflame with desire; no, she sought him simply as a brother, for comfort. But she was drawn to him. It would not take much to arouse her, a long kiss on the lips, a touch here and there. He stood on the border between desire and action, and in that split second, as the wind wailed horribly, strange images flashed into his mind. He saw the lightning through the cracks of the wigwam on the shores of Lake Mocksinkickee as he and Swiftly Running Feet gave themselves to each other rapturously in the storm. Ominously, at the same instant he seemed to see the tombs in the yard outside, with Grandfather and the alien white woman cold in their beds. He kissed Victorine on the cheek and drew away reluctantly. Then he covered her gently with the blankets and went to the other side of the chapel.

For the first time in many moons Asondaki Alamelonda was aware again that being Wemiamiki gave him iron in his being that the white man knew nothing of. After the dawn broke and amidst rapidly diminishing wind, he prepared to deliver his charge to her aunt, a task that because of the the fallen trees on this road took all day.

The sugar order was destroyed, washed to the bottom of the bayou where no doubt it sweetened many alligators, and since it was loaded and signed for, the loss was to Lasselle, Marchal and Fortin. Asondaki took whatever sugar remained in the warehouse and after the river fell somewhat returned to Seven Springs at Baton Rouge.

The next week a letter came. "You are to be a bridegroom, I see," Fortin said, amused.

"What do you mean?" the astonished Asondaki asked.

"The LeFauvre family expects you will soon be coming to claim the hand of Victorine."

"Why should I do that? I gave them, or her, no sign. . ."

"You spent the night with her away from home."

"I did nothing to her. I swear." His face showed his alarm.

Fortin looked at him. "These are good people of the Church. She was with you without chaperone.''

"Still I cannot marry her. I am married.''

A long moment passed. Then Fortin spoke. "Why did I not know this?'' he demanded. Asondaki told him the story of his marriage among the Potawatomis.

"An Indian squaw!''

"My wife.'' He had been too ashamed to tell the white man about his wife; now he was ashamed to hear her scornfully described in the word that in most tribal languages meant prostitute.

"You fool. You courted Victorine, they say, on the last visit. Walked with her in the garden alone, 'encouraged her affections.' So they say. You have ruined a girl's reputation. Possibly kept her from ever marrying in this strict society. And I encouraged it, thinking it would be good for a lonely bachelor.''

Fortin wadded up the letter and threw it into the fire grate. "Anyone would have known that the trip itself implied you would marry her. To take her to a relative—it is the custom. Did you not know what you were committed to? They would have forgiven your lying with her. They expected it!'' Asondaki looked thunder-struck. Was it so? It was unfathomable.

"I did not know,'' he murmured. He had, indeed, thought he had acted nobly, resisting base instincts. Did not the white man's Church forbid adultery?

That evening, as he sat staring out over the bayou he pondered the thing. He would never understand the ways of the white man's world. Even blacks could understand them; he, only half-Indian could not. The Northern Lights might flash, but he could not sort out their colors. They must remain, it seemed, a mystery to him.

Chapter XXXV

"I do not know why I have even admitted you inside the circumference of my inner circle," Aaron Burr said with veiled amusement to the tall, thin young man who stood with him in late summer of 1806.

Below them black men and rough Ohio frontiersmen were loading one of the most elaborate keelboats ever to float the Ohio.

Burr went on, "You are ill-educated, sometimes morose, frequently cocky and irreverent. Worse than that, you are often disrespectful to the great." He grunted, took out pipes and offered one and a pouch of South American tobacco to Ish Scott.

They stood watching the river lave the muddy shores of Blennerhasset Island. It was named after the eccentric Irishman who served as Burr's chief lieutenant in the mysterious, new "patriotic endeavor" that everyone in America talked about so openly and knew so little about. The frontiersmen and slaves were carting barrels of wine, sacks of meal and flour, and pork aboard the boat, which had its own kitchen, bedroom, and dining quarters.

"You do have two important assets to me," Burr told Ish. "First, you come from a family that ranks among the first in Indiana Territory and I want nothing more than to convince Governor William Henry Harrison to support us. . ."

Ish quickly responded. "I told you I have no contact with my family now. You can expect nothin' there. . ."

"Tut, tut," Burr went on, undeterred. "Your uncle will soon be Harrison's magistrate, it is said. Your father owns a fine stand of land directly next to the new fort and militia headquarters. I am thinking seriously of asking Harrison for that militia when the uprising comes, and he may give it. Besides, I am basing my entire cause on the appeal to young men of influential families who wish to experience adventure. You know that."

Ish did know that. He had just returned from a recruiting trip around Pittsburg. There he spoke to sons of leading citizens, mostly from the conservative Federalist party. According to Burr's instructions, he was purposely vague. He told the young men only that an enterprise against Mexico was intended, and all who signed on would join an adventurous army to be led by the former vice-president of the United States. Each soldier would receive twelve dollars per month and one hundred acres of land. He was modestly successful.

"I fear you may be ill-at-ease in these surroundings," Burr said in a low voice to Ish. They were watching Margaret Blennerhasset in a lovely rose-colored morning dress circulate among the boat-loaders, looking for one of her little boys. There was a patrician air to the entire Blennerhasset estate, with its large, many-winged house, silk hangings, and extensive gardens. Blennerhasset spent most of his fortune creating the estate and now hoped to recoup it on Burr's expedition.

"Of course I'm not ill-at-ease," Ish snapped. "You figure just because I was born in Kentucky I know nothin'. The world has educated me a good deal since I've been in 't."

Burr chose to ignore the shortness in Scott's voice. This odd young man wanted to be by his side at all times and was useful in countless ways, not the least of which that he was utterly devoted to the endeavor. Or was it the leader himself? Burr did not know.

"It's just that I want to get to work," Ish said, in a calmer voice. "I don't care for all this courtin' of the great and powerful, this interminable plannin' and posturin' that you seem to enjoy so much."

"You young scamp" Burr said, continuing his posture of mock outrage. "If you weren't so valuable to me I'd have you thrashed for your constant impudence. I should thrash you myself. Why do I keep you on, pay you. . ?"

"I am one of the few you trust, that's why. I tell you the truth."

Aaron Burr's keen, bright eyes looked up at Ish, scrutinizing him carefully. Burr was a few inches shorter than this tall young man, indeed than most men, but he commanded respect. His immaculate dress and poised bearing gave him a sense of smooth control few could resist. Now he grew serious. "I feel I hardly know you, Scott. The letters you sent revealed your ires and partisanship, but nothing of you as a person. When you have been with me you advise and berate, but tell nothing of yourself. Why have you tied yourself to me like a desperate sailor to the mast? It cannot be because of my power and position. I am without office, if the vice-presidency ever was an office." He stepped forward to give a message to the helmsman of the keelboat about its position in the small line of boats that was forming.

Ish looked out at the river, sluggish in the heat of summer, and beyond it the outline of the island itself. Its shores were clad in tall oak, with odd, bare sticks beneath them, where underbrush should have been. Fallow deer from the estate had over-multiplied and stripped the brush. Swamps caused by frequent flooding spread almost back to the very rose gardens and gazebos the rich man had set up as his paradise. It was an odd-looking island, for an odd mission. Soon there would be flotilas of boats assembling here from all over the East, ready to go down the river.

"I'm asking you, Scott. Why are you here? I doubt it is because I was one of the so-called legendary heroes of the Revolution. You don't follow in my train with the other puppies who bound about my feet."

Ish snorted in contempt at the rich men, the Pennsylvania squires, who were buying their sons blue military coats to take part in Burr's expedition. "Why am I here? Let's say that I approve of the project with all my heart."

"Which part of the project?" Burr asked, bemused. "It seems, according to the Kentucky papers, that it has a hundred parts. That it is like the great dragon in the Book of Revelation, which has spawned and sent vituperative little dragons all over the West. Are you devoted to the plan to take the city of New Orleans and enthrone my daughter Theodosia as Queen of Louisiana?" His handsome mouth turned up in a sardonic grin.

Ish smiled also. "Acourse. And the paper's story isn't all untrue. You will do that if you can, and use it as a base of operations to mount the attack on Mexico."

"Perhaps." Burr was evasive. He seemed to trust no one with the full details of the plan. Was it that he was afraid of his own lieutenants? General James Wilkinson, his long-time associate, was supposedly ready to aid him by supplying an army in the Southwest. Burr swore by his loyalty, but he did not confide in him. Or was it that he didn't know what he was going to do until he saw what circumstances brought, and who came out to join him.

"You know that I plan to attack and free Mexico, if America goes to war with Spain. To rouse the Mexicans' spirit of independence and 'help' them rise against a dissolute king. We would encourage revolution, so that Mexico would become part of the United States."

"So you say. Like our Revolution." Ish smiled his odd smile again.

"Much like ours." Burr sighed. During the Revolution, as a twenty-year-old, he was involved in the heroic effort to capture and "free" Canada. This doomed attempt had failed in the bitter cold outside the walls of Quebec. Burr built his reputation by his bravery there and through brilliant political moves through thirty years. But the greatest plum of all—the presidency,—was denied him in a tied election vote in the House of Representatives, an election which Thomas Jefferson finally won. Many said it warped Burr's perspective forever.

"But no, you have not answered me," the former vice-president said. "You are not as the others. What is it that has made you bind yourself to me, so that you spent two years in the Kentucky militia training, wrote me scores of letters which followed me about the country offering to be a part of any enterprise, and finally become a chief recruiter in all the cities of the West for an expedition that many regard as extremely dangerous?"

All around them rang the voices of carters and servants from the island, readying a low-lying provision boat covered with canvas. Ish lowered his voice a bit. "The part of the enterprise that compels me, that fills all m' hopes by day and m' dreams by night, is your plan to split the United States in two, formin' a separate nation of what we conquer in the West and Mexico."

Burr lowered his eyes and moved close to Ish. "I have never said that to you. Why do you think that is the goal?"

"You know it is. Your daughter, whom you value more than life itself, is waitin' to follow you down the river, and you have in your eye somethin' very big indeed. The West will be a separate nation, if you have your way, and you'll be in charge."

Burr did not speak for a full moment. "I do not admit to this."

"Blennerhasset speaks openly of 't."

"Blennerhasset is a fool."

"Still, that is why I'm here and why I would die with you for 't."

Burr puffed his pipe, studying the young man without looking at him. "And why do you wish the United States so ill?"

"Maybe as the man says about the mountain, just 'cause it's there." Burr, not understanding, raised his eyebrows, and Ish insisted, "Maybe I didn't think formin' this country was a good idea in the first place."

"You are a latter-day Tory," Burr conceded with a chuckle.

"If you can't understand that, jest say it is 'cause I was brought up in the West and don't like the way the Easterners run the country."

"At any rate, I am glad to let you wrestle alligators for me, as you Kentuckians say, any time." His voice was very low. "But the success of the enterprise, to let the West take its natural course in the midst of all the Spanish troubles, whatever that way may be. . ." Ish nodded acquiescently, "depends completely on. . ."

"On Wilkinson."

"On General of the Army James Wilkinson. War with Spain is almost a necessity. Wilkinson is the key to that. He's in western Louisiana right now and he will incite it if he can."

"Will he? I wish I could be so sure."

"And, my young Cataline, have you met Wilkinson then?"

"No, but I heard in Caintuck from those who know 'm that he is a blustery and self-seekin' balloon-head."

Burr shrugged. "Nevertheless, he is in Louisiana now. What else could he be doing there?"

"What else indeed? If we knew that, we could all sleep a lot better as this fancified ark goes on its way."

Burr turned the pipe over. Tobacco, half-burned, floated into the mud. He ground the heel of his beautiful army boot over it, putting out the last few wisps of smoke.

That evening, servants in livery served quail in caper sauce at a huge Chippendale table that came from London. The beautiful and imperious Margaret Blennerhasset was holding court in almost medieval splendor, as the ringing laugh of Burr's aristocratic associates floated over the din and hum of a dinner for fourteen. They came from as far away as the Carolinas and Ohio to be part of Burr's enterprise to invade Mexico (or whatever it might turn out to be). Ish sat uncommunicative to the right of Burr and listened to him regaling the adoring Blennerhasset with tales of the U.S. Senate.

As Ish watched, Blennerhasset nodded vigorously, knocking off the silver-framed spectacles which sat on the end of his large nose to help his nearsightedness. He knelt down to pick them up, excusing himself and laughing with embarrassment as he brushed a lady's skirt.

Finally, the ladies exited and the gentlemen retired to the piazza outside the dining room, from which they could see the lights of boats on the Ohio. Burr spoke easily and confidently, in that style he had of honoring the person he addressed, first to one supporter and then another. Finally, he beckoned to Ish and they walked together into a grape arbor with a bench around its inside.

"I spoke to you of the newspaper in Kentucky, the *Western World*."

"Yes." It was attempting to tell the full details of Burr's "despicable plot," and was weaning some of his supporters away.

"It is not the only newspaper which is spreading malicious gossip around. There is a new paper in Indiana Territory—the *Vincennes Eagle*. Put out by anti-Harrison people. I have reason to believe they will soon print the story about the canal company we tried to have funded for our own purposes in Indiana Territory, the one we convinced Harrison and some of the legislators to support."

Ish nodded. He knew that the Burrites forced through the Indiana Legislature a project to build a canal at Louisville, but their real purpose was to start a bank in Indiana to help fund Burr's expedition.

"If the governor should be publically embarrassed by this paper's stories, he cannot afford to help us. I need him badly. Harrison and the Indiana militia could be the key to success in the entire expedition."

"What do you want me to do?"

Burr sighed. A master of intrigue, he never learned to like the darker side of plotting. "I have arranged to deal with the *World* in Kentucky. Now for the paper in Vincennes. The *Eagle's* publisher, Arlen Stringfellow, is a friend of my old enemy, Thomas Jefferson. It appears we will need to handle Stringfellow in Indiana too. You are very strong-minded, Scott, and very persuasive. I think you will know how to deal with this editor and his rag sheet."

They talked over a few details. Then, "One last word of warning," Burr told him, rising. "I want some of my other people to act on the Kentucky newspaper first, with no connections made. Go first to Tennessee and help Andrew Jackson recruit there. Then, take care of the Vincennes business." Ish nodded and left.

Burr looked at the clusters of grapes hanging from the roof of the arbor. Most were green, with a few showing pale lavender and the beginning of ripeness. When these grapes have been harvested, where will we all be, Burr asked himself. Will I return in triumph to drink wine made on this island—or not, he wondered and left to go to his luxury ark for the night.

Chapter XXXVI

The pink ruffles of Martha McClure's morning dress brushed against the carpet in the parlor of the McClure mansion house. She stooped to pick up a piece of lint from its rose-patterned surface. The hired girls would soon be here, and she liked to have the house in order when they came. Gave them a good idea of how spanking clean she expected it to be kept. She walked around the roomy downstairs, touching panelling on the walls, rearranging in little ways. She inched back the pewter teapot on the new mahogony sideboard, put the creamer and sugar at an angle, and walked away to look at the effect. Yes, 'twas good that way.

This mansion house was a dream come true. Funny, though, about dreams. After you got what you wanted, the dreamin' didn't stop, just changed shape, like a blob of glass expanding on the end of a pipe. Now she thought about large acreages for each of the children, an addition to the rear of this house. And the bathtub—she smiled to herself. After having been carted halfway to kingdom come it now sat full of little girls' toys in the upstairs bedroom. She had a bright new metal tub to bathe in.

She walked upstairs, listening to the wakeup talk drift from behind the door of the boys' room. Tom, Charles, Joseph and little Dan'l were rising late to do the list of chores that were supposed to "strengthen their characters" even though there were hired men to do most of the work. Tom directed them; he was a good boy. The girls were downstairs, breakfasting in the kitchen. Soon they would be ready to sit before the firescreen to begin their needlework, as befitted the daughters of a substantial gentleman.

Then she went to the end of the hall and looked in the deserted bedroom of her oldest son Jack. The quilt was thrown back, his clothing half-in and half-out of a bureau and strewn about the room. She heard her husband's footsteps. As he came up beside her in the door, she turned to give him a kiss.

"I declare, Dan'l, where can that boy be?" she said. She walked inside the room and then, as she did every day, carefully made the bed, pulling the beautiful quilt she herself had pieced up over the new goosedown pillows. Jackie never seemed to notice. Her husband entered and watched her fuss. "He ain't a boy any more, Martha. He's goin' into Vincennes today. Could be to the bookseller's, or to the newspaper office to drop off a letter to the editor for the Young Patriots." Then, he added half humorously, "Mebbe he's goin' to join the army."

"Oh pshaw. He isn't goin' to do anything like that. He knows how you feel."

"I wouldn't actually stop him, even though 'tis crazy." He smiled a little. "Burr is offerin' ten dollars a month in this neighborhood. At least Jack'd be bringin' in some money."

"He'll get around to the plum harvest when he gets home. Jack's bright, you know that. He just hasn't got started yet," Martha said, plumping the pillow.

"I s'pose so, " Dan'l commented absently. He reached into his pocket, drew out a letter and slit it open with his pen knife. At his wife's questioning look, he scrutinized it and said, "Looks like a invite. From John and Janie."

"Must be to the hunting breakfast."

"To what?" Dan'l demanded, incredulous.

"Ridin' to hounds, like in Virginia. Sam'l Thompson is to be Master of the Hounds."

"He didn't tell me 'bout that." But that could be explained. What with the building of his barn and other outbuildings, Dan'l hadn't had much time to see his old friend lately. "I don't know what's a-gonna be next in all this gentrifying this family is up to. Hired servants, slaves, summer kitchens, the gals all buyin' kid gloves up to their elbows and dancin'. Dada wouldn't a-known what to make o' it."

But he was not displeased. He finished the letter. "Waal, seems like we're to assemble at 'the meet field' at eight in the mornin' by Maria Church, Saturday two weeks from now. I 'spect the delay is so we can get the proper clothin'. Ridin' breeches, all that. S'posed to send our answer 'bout attendin' to the Master, Sam'l, right away."

Martha looked out the window, watching one of the hired girls, a skinny, back-country wench, come up the lane. Why does she dawdle that way? Did she leave her head back in that cabin in the bluffs? Martha asked herself. Still, nobody worked harder than this girl, and there was a-plenty to do. "Do you want to go to the fox hunt?" she asked her husband.

"Why not?" he answered, heading down the stairs to supervise the loading of a large shipment of hams going to New Orleans. "If we're rich folks now, we might as well act like it."

"Stop a minute," Martha shouted after him. "How many of the family do you think will be goin'?"

"Will and Margaret will probably be there," his voice floated back to her. Martha's eyes glazed over as they always did in considering the odd live-and-let-live arrangements "The Wills" and "The Johns" had arrived at after their bedroom debacle.

"The Scotts'll go if Jenny isn't feelin' poorly," she commented, "How about George and Jean?"

"Jean ain't goin' to wanta chase any poor little fox around. Besides, it says here that Governor and Mrs. William Henry Harrison will be honored guests. No, I definitely don't think you're goin' to see George there."

*   *   *

George McClure took off his mother's spectacles, which he had been wearing recently, and set them on the desk at the Vincennes land office. "Badollet, I need you to be more specific. Is there a scheme to buy up land at the mouth of the Wabash by paying off the poor farmers who want to bid for it?"

The land commissioner looked at him steadily. "Not that I know of personally. It may seem ridiculous that I'm in the dark, since I'm the land commissioner," he said in the clipped accents of a foreigner. "But anything is possible in this place, and with Harrison." He was smoking one of the new cigars from Cuba. Deep worry lines about his mouth, along with a cap of close-cropped, graying hair, made John Badollet look like a man older than his years.

George continued. "If Harrison and the others in the syndicate are paying off bidders to keep the price low, they'll make fortunes on this prime land when the land sale comes. You're one of the superintendents. . ."

Badollet sighed. "Yes. And Harrison is another. I do not need to say that I have no part nor interest in speculation. But I suspect Harrison is up to his collar in it. And I suppose this unsavory business has to be in the newspaper. Still, taking on the governor of the whole western territory. . ." John Badollet shook his head. "He and I have had our tangles. But this. . ."

George looked at Badollet, whom he had come to respect above all others as an ethical man in this place where ethics were as changeable as the currents of the Wabash. Badollet's cuffs had to be clean in this land mess, but it could involve others in the land office, perhaps discredit it. Word could even get to Jefferson—"When I said I'd write for Stringellow's new paper, he told me nobody would have special privileges if there was something to tell. Even you, my friend."

Badollet nodded wearily. The rich, pungent smell of his cigar filtered through the small office. He opened the window to allow fresh September air to drift through and stopped to look at someone coming down the street.

"Who is it?" George asked.

"Your brother. He appears agitated." George turned to the door to see John McClure burst through, his face grim and flushed. Looking through Badollet as if he were a cut-glass decanter, John went straight to the desk.

"George, the governor asked t' see me and Will. Seems you are involvin' yourself in matters that don't concern you."

His brother looked up with calm eyes but did not get up. "You've known I write for the paper. . ."

"Then why don't you try writin' the truth for a change. You cain't connect Harrison with any of these schemes. You ain't really findin' out, you're flingin' charges about like hog slop. And anyways if he wants to buy up land for himself, they ain't nary a thing illegal about it."

"Not illegal, immoral. Intimidating small farmers into not bidding, paying hush money to cover up what he's done. . ." He stood up.

"He ain't doin' that. You don't know the facts, I tell you." Veins in John's bald spots began to throb, and his brother was growing equally incensed.

"And I tell you, you left your own honor back in the woods of Caintuck. You and Will and Dan'l are licking this man's posteriors so the McClures can all be lords of the cornfields. Acting as lackeys, influencing legislators you know to vote his programs through like puppets. And now Dan'l is going to be his creature, a judge who decides just what the governor wants. Whatever happened to freedom in the Northwest Territory?''

"Are you accusin' Dan'l o' bein' dishonest?''

"No. He couldn't be dishonest if he tried. But he can be a fool." John advanced toward George menacingly. George rushed forward and pushed him.

"Damn you and your promises," he shouted, "I don't need 'em!"

The two brothers began to scuffle, shoving each other about the office. Badollet rose, alarmed, just at the moment the door swung opened to reveal the surprised faces of William Henry Harrison and his political associate Judge Henry Vanderburgh. They went to the brothers to separate them and amidst huffing and puffing, all parties finally left Badollet alone in his office and went out into the street.

Vanderburgh watched the McClure brothers leave in separate directions, casting scowling glances at each other. "Buckskin boys, first, last and always, even though they wear new wool suits," he said to Harrison with a cynical laugh. Harrison shrugged indulgently. He glanced down at the fine new military boots which hugged his own legs snugly, but Vanderburgh could not let the landoffice fight rest. He feared the elemental power in this new class of the governor's supporters.

"Arguing over the law—pretty soon they'll be telling everbody that they know it better than we do. You know the old story—apples and hog turds floating down the river side by side and pretty soon the turds get to feelin' pretty good about themselves and turn to the spectators on the riverbank and shout, 'How do you like all us apples?' "

Harrison smiled to himself, but did not look at the other man. "Pretty hard to tell a turd from an apple at a distance. I like to get to know a man right well before I decide which he is. So far these look like pretty good apples."

Janie and John McClure stood watching the slave Pro and his son Frankie grooming the chestnut granddaughters of *Belle Ame* in the huge stable. Janie strode over to put her hand on the withers of Wabash Annie.

"Remember, Frankie, that the real work will be when we bring them in. They'll all need warm bran mash and you'll have to feel for cuts and heat in the legs."

"Mebbe bandage the legs to stop 'em from fillin'," John suggested to the slaves.

Pro, whose handsome ebony face was dotted with perspiration already on this warm morning, nodded. "I sure hope them greenhorn riders don't run 'em through the corn stubble, Mist McClure," he said to John.

"Mr. Thompson's s'posed to give 'em instructions. Tell 'em not to gallop through the sheep, walk around the fences instead of takin' 'em." He looked across the horse's neck at his wife.

"I've asked Mary and Margaret to go with some of the new riders," she said. "Jim. . ."

"Jim'll be with Jackie. I told 'im not to leave his side."

"Mary wasn't very eager to ride with Mrs. Harrison, but I told her the governor's wife isn't much of an equestrian."

John smiled. "Mary's got her cap set for Sam'l Emison." His wife frowned. She did not want to hear about Mary's courting with the Emison youth. Mary was too young and shy to think about marriage for quite a while.

John looked with pleasure at his wife, dressed for the hunt in clothing she had had especially made, a wine-colored corduroy hunting skirt and vest and a brimmed hat with a pheasant feather on it. He himself was as dandified as his son usually was, with knee breeches of suede, long-tailed coat, and a riding crop.

"I must see to the house slaves," his wife said and headed for the summer kitchen, where the slave women and their daughters were turning huge hams and turkeys on spits, taking grape pies out of the ovens, and mixing cream, eggs, and corn for plantation pudding.

John McClure walked out of the stable and past the flat field which housed the brickyard, quiet now early on this Saturday morning. His Irish setter Red cavorted around his heels. Bending to ruffle the dog's neck, John picked up a rejected brick, a cull, and inspected it. It had remained in the kiln too long; its surface was melted into smooth, pink-red enamel. He liked to keep a close eye on the culls. You could see the quality of the general lot that way.

As he did so often these days, he looked about at his holdings: sheep on the hills, large herds of cows with slave boys switching them toward the creek on this dewy October morning, acres of wheat and corn already harvested. He sighed, satisfied, then consciously put down the niggling disquiet he felt as he watched his wife pass the slave quarters and head toward the main house, tensely slapping her riding crop against her leg like a man. Shore does have a strong streak in her, he thought for the hundredth time in his life. He never tired of watching this accomplished woman, today preparing for the biggest day since she moved to Indiana Territory and became one of its social leaders.

John watched the Master of Fox Hounds, Sam'l Thompson, stride across the lawn. He was taking his job very seriously, John thought. He had ridden over almost at dawn from the farm near the Scotts, where he and his wife and three small sons lived. Although he was officially Master of Fox Hounds, he was to act as his own huntsman and had borrowed a large horn from some Virginian or another. Thirty uncomfortably dressed men and their women riding sidesaddle were assembling at "the meet" on the crest of a hill down the road. It was time to join them.

Jim McClure brought the fine black stallion he rode to the back of the group and watched his cousin Jackie edge his skittish, buff-colored mare toward him. Jackie Dude sits a horse about as well as Grandma Jane used to, Jim thought, with a burst of affection for both of them. Well, not everybody could have the ease on the back of a horse that he had inherited from his mother Janie and the McGuires. Fleetingly his thoughts hovered around a picture of his other grandfather, Andrew McGuire. He had hardly known the old man and could remember him only as he had looked at the funeral in Louisville last year. Well, at least he could be grateful to him for having started this wonderful line of horses, the sons and daughters of Janus. Jim moved on to the pressing responsibilities before him.

"Now listen to me, Jackie Dude. Don't get these things wrong or we'll all git hell from my ma and Mr. Thompson. This thing has to be jes' so."

Jack nodded. He had never been more nervous in his life. To ride a horse in a set pattern of riders, being careful to avoid the dogs pursuing the pack, to leap fences and creeks in perfect control—he took off his flat-top hat and wiped his brow.

For all the riding he did on the farm, horses were as mysterious to Jack McClure as Dodo birds. Standing as tall as a shed, with their enormous, sensitive eyes always looking at him with contempt (as he saw it) when he stood on the ground ready to mount. . .'twas awful. He was not quite afraid of them, yet he had no mastery over them. His heart leapt when he tried to turn or rein, for horses seemed to sense his weakness and might, or might not obey. It was a terrible state of events. At any moment a horse could work its will upon the timorous, blubbering fool on its back. God, he hoped he could keep up on this unfamiliar horse his father had just bought and not disgrace himself.

And now the spotted dogs, kept together by their young, black "whippers-in" bayed on their leashes. Janie McClure, who had strictly trained the black youths in protocol of the hunt, rode next to Thompson, behind the pack. A murmur went through the group as Governor and Mrs. Harrison, splendidly clad in matching riding habits, rode up in the company of John McClure and his daughter Mary.

Dan'l, astride Sugarson, tipped his hat to Mrs. Harrison as the couple maneuvred their prancing, pawing horses directly in front of him. The governor's craggy face lit in a smile. "Howdo, Dan'l, Sam'l. How be you?" he asked, nodding to grave young Emison, who had just joined the party. This governor who lived among "down-home" people, adopted country speech when it suited.

Suddenly the group was off, with horses' hoofs cutting the straw of a harvested wheat field and then trotting smartly down a lane that ran through deep woods. "The hounds are a-casting for the scent," Jim yelled at his cousin, who nodded grimly. Jack's horse was brushing the low limbs of sugar maples, causing drifts of red-veined leaves to fly in Jack's eyes.

The distinctive tra-tara of the hunting horn echoed over the lane. Jim yelled to Jack, "I cain't see, but it sounds like the hounds are 'giving tongue', they call it, headin' a fox. If so, we'll be takin' off!"

Even as he spoke, the horsemen ahead of them spurred their mounts and galloped away at breakneck speed. They entered an open grazing field. Ahead of them the hounds could be seen, tails feathering madly from side to side, in full pursuit. "The little bastard's heading for open country," Harrison shouted to Dan'l and Martha McClure, directly in back of him. He spurred his horse and followed the houndsmaster.

"He's like a cur after a bitch in heat," James Scott, in the middle of the pack, observed to Jenny. The rest of the troop had trouble keeping up. Martha McClure and Anna Harrison fought to stay in the cumbersome side saddles.

"I swear I'm tuckered out," Martha cried. The horse Harrison rode, a dapple gray mare, flattened her ears and snorted with joy, up a rise, then toward a small creek.

"Lord, let me stay on this booger's back," Jack fervently prayed, bouncing in his saddle until his rearend smarted. But as they approached the jump at the creek, the horses ahead of him slowed down abruptly, then answered a signal to "check."

Toward the rear, Will and his children, Johnny and Elizabeth, circled their mounts with the ease of born horsemen. "Fox seems to have gone to earth," Will McClure told Elizabeth, "or at least so they say. Quite a flapdoodle, all this," he chuckled, looking around at the several McClures in elegant clothing, the fine mounts, the governor of the territory laughing with the other gentry at the head of the group.

Sam'l Thompson turned around. "Shh, no coffee-housing," he warned sternly, and the word filtered back to wait noiselessly to see whether the hounds had lost the scent altogether. Then Thompson gave the signal that he had lifted the pack to start over again, and the horses splashed through the stream and onto the woodland trail beyond it.

At the next wild gallop, Jack McClure's overwrought horse bolted away through trees at top speed and crashed up a rise. Jack hung on with the strong fear of breaking his neck. The mad dash finally spent itself and the gelding stood, heaving, along the crest of the hill. Jest as well, Jack thought, I was about played out. As he turned the horse to head back to his uncle's plantation, he heard voices ahead. There sat a group of men, drinking and looking over the prairie where the hunters now rode. He recognized one of the voices, coarse but familiar.

"Waal, if it ain't Jackie Dude McClure. Come over here and set a spell, give yourself a kiss o' Brown Betty." Jay Byrd Dugger, his father Luke, and a cousin named Beet Nose Bruce sat overlooking the hunt.

As Jack tied the horse to a young beech, Luke Dugger shouted over at him, "We didn't git no invite to your aunt's doin's. I'm a friend of the gov'nors too." It was true, Jack remembered. Even today Luke had on the militiaman's coat he wore everywhere. "Guess our sugar ain't refined enough to suit." Beet Nose guffawed and stood up. He pulled back the leaves of a small pawpaw tree to get a view of the prairie.

"They done gone inter the woods." He blew his nose on a wide, flat pawpaw leaf. "Shore ere some big trees up yere," he mumered, looking about at virgin oak whose lowest branches started forty feet off the ground.

"Hell, these ain't tall," Luke Dugger said. "We had a tree on our stand took four women holdin' hands to stand around. A six-foot saw weren't half big enough to cut it down. It took my niggers all day to cut it. I counted two thousand pigeons roostin' in the top o' it one day and it took sev'ral minutes for their dung to fall to the ground."

"Why are you boys up here?" Jackie asked suddenly, wondering what brought them to somebody else's hill to drink in broad daylight.

"Shit, we're havin' our own little fox hunt," the senior Dugger said. He gestured at the liquor jug. "This here's the fox. Say, we're listenin' to the music o' the pack, as they say in Virginny. Do you hear it, Beet Nose? Do you?"

"How can I hear your music o' the pack, Luke," he said giving the expected answer, "when those God-damned dogs is barkin' so loud?" The trio snickered and slapped each other on their backs.

They looked down in the valley. The hunters had returned and were chasing about in large circles. If the hunt was successful, they would soon be handing the tail to the governor's wife, smearing blood on the cheek of John Robert Scott, the youngest hunter in the party.

"Passel o' fools," Jay Dugger grunted. Jack, gingerly swinging his leg over the saddle and heading the sweating horse back to where the food was, could hardly disagree.

" 'Twas easier'n I thought to kill a fox," John McClure said, as Frankie knelt before him, pulling off his master's knee boots.

"Yes, in Virginia the foxes were hunted down enough so that it was hard to find one sometimes." Janie took off the pheasant-feather hat and set it on a dressing table.

He put his arms around her. "Well, an' was it a big smashin' success? Ever body et enough. . ."

She pulled away, suddenly, surprising him. "Will you please say ate?" She stalked over to the bed and sat on its side. Her husband, perplexed, looked at her. Frankie discreetly withdrew.

"Weren't it allright?" John thought to himself that he had spent enough to make it right.

She began to cry, turning her head toward the window that was faintly illuminated by a cloudy sunset. "It's not your fault. It's just not the same, someway." Sobs shook her body. She put her head on the bed like a little girl. "It's Father's fault. He had his own way in everything with me and now I'm spoiled for anything else." Odd way to say it, John noted.

Janie stood up and swept from the room, and soon he could hear her crying and pounding the wall in the little sewing room at the end of the hall.

He headed out to check the horses one last time before going to bed. Janie would not come back into the bedroom until after he had gone to sleep. She would sleep on the lying-in couch at the foot of the bed, as she always did after these strange, dark tantrums.

He sat outside, watching the last of the sunset purple fade into the far hills near the Wabash.

Dada, I'm worth close to one hundred thousand dollars now, he said in his mind. *What with the horses, the new farms, the good crop sales at New Orleans. And the others are the same, 'cept Georgie, acourse. He never did give a damn 'bout accumulating anything. He's well enough off, in spite of himself, though.*

He took a tobacco plug out of his pocket and determinedly bit off a huge piece and put it in his mouth. *Dada, are ya there or ought I t' wait a minute*? He had been thinking a lot lately about man's status in the next world. He couldn't figure whether angels stayed around your ears like mosquitoes, humming hymns and waiting for you to need 'em or whether they had to be summoned.

Well, Dada I like the money well enough. But I'll tell you this, an' only you. I shore didn't know bein' a laird would be such a God-damned pain in the arse. Sorry, know you'll pardon me 'cause I said it like I felt it.

He turned his head. He spat. Then he marched up the hill and into his big, rambling mansion house.

Chapter XXXVII

Jim McClure stared morosely at the off-kilter pumpkin which sat in the middle of the table at the Yellow Tavern. It was supposed to be a harvest decoration for the October meeting of the Young Patriots of the Wilderness, but the pumpkin head made him mumble to himself about his cousin, who was now speaking to the group around the horseshoe of the table.

Jack was runnin' on about the Northwest. They were having "extemporaneous oration." Each of the twenty young men present was given a topic and expected to speak graciously for five or ten minutes. But Jackie Dude McClure, the president of this fraternity of prominent pioneer sons, had talked for twenty. He was saying something about the Mississippi trade route, the untapped riches from the Louisiana Territory to the Stony Mountains. Jim put the droning voice on the back coals and stared at his wine. Why did the hotel insist on putting Peruvian bark in the wine this late in the season? The ague was layin' low right now, anyways. And only a handful got it this summer anyway.

"Separate nation," Jackie was saying now. Whew, he was gettin' bold, Jim told himself. Although everbody talked about Burr's plot, most people did it privately. Especially since the newspaper was writin' daily editorials about how dastardly the whole thing was. Uncle George was knee-deep in that privyhole of a newspaper that Harrison disapproved of, and Uncle John wasn't speakin' to Uncle George because of it. Why'd George want to get involved in politics at his late stage in the game? But then there never was any explaining Uncle George.

Jack sat down and the toasts began. A florid Jay Dugger stood up and leaned on the table. He had brought his own jug to the meeting and it was nearly empty. "To the Injean Treaty of Grouseland," he belched. "It took untold miles o' southeastern Indiana from the savages, it gave nary a inch."

Glasses were raised to that treaty and Thomas Emison stood. "To the gracious host of Grouseland." Glasses were refilled and raised with calls of "Harrison, Harrison! Hyar, hyar!"

Tom Emison's brother Samuel, neatly brushed and intensely serious, stood. "To the new university. May it light the torch of learning in these western lands." Other toasts were offered, to the new road which was being surveyed from St. Louis to Louisville, to the soldiers training at Ft. Knox.

Finally, Jack McClure offered the final toast of the evening. He cleared his throat and gazed dramatically at the stag head on the wall of the inn. "To the George Washington of the South and West. May his soldiers be every bit as valiant as those at Saratoga. Gentlemen, I give you Aaron Burr."

There was a stir around the table. Finally about half the young men raised their glasses; the rest declined. Thomas and Samuel Emison stared stonily into space. The meeting was dissolved, then, and Jack exited chuckling. Jim followed him out into the night, telling himself that the discomfiture of the group was exactly what Jack wanted.

"Jack, wait up there." His cousin turned his head and slowed his walk. They advanced to the hitching post where their horses waited. "Everything's set for tomorrow," Jim said. "Are you ready?"

"Assuredly, assuredly," Jack murmured, not looking at him.

"Now, we'll start at dawn. Should get to Louisville in four days. Floyd is stockin' up there on the Ohio, puttin' on pork and meal and the troops are comin' in by the scores ever day."

"So they say."

"You have shot your mouth off for Burr like a six-pound cannon for the last six months and now's your chance to make good on all the talk. We can go help throw out the Spaniards in Mexico and find who knows what in the way of fortune." Jack nodded.

"Promise you'll be there? We ride at sunrise." His cousin was insistent.

Jack nodded again vacantly and then turned and rode off, leaving Jim not at all sure whether he would make the rendezvous or not.

But when the sun rose over the unharvested tobacco fields, Jackie Dude McClure did appear, riding Sugarson. Jay Byrd Dugger and Johnny McClure were soon to meet the two cousins at this crossroads leading to the trace, but Jackie Dude was early. Why? Jim watched him laboriously swing his foot around the horse's posterior and waited until he spoke.

"I'm not going to join Burr."

Jim was silent for a minute. Then his ire broke forth. "But you were the one who praised the whole thing up. Who contacted Davis Floyd and promised to raise a group. . ."

"I can't go."

"Why not?" Jim was angrier at him than he had ever been in his life. He had gone to a lot of trouble to arrange this, get a uniform, defy his mother and father. Besides, he knew Jackie believed in Burr's announced plan to invade Mexico and even more, his unannounced plan to make a separate country of the West.

"I don't know. Somethin' in me don't want to go."

Jim was incredulous. "You afraid?"

Jackie flushed. The red splotch of a birthmark on his neck stood out.

"It's not exactly like that. You know me. Great gas bag when it comes to talkin', not much on action." His hands were shaking.

"What am I goin' to tell Johnny? And Jay Dugger?"

"Tell him—tell them I was afraid to spoil my clothes. Might ruin my reputation as a dude." He smiled a twisted, sad smile.

"Think about it anyways. You can follow. Davis Floyd is goin' to be in Louisville loading supplies and men for a week or more. . .''

"Shore. That's what I'll do. Mebbe come on later." He did not meet his cousin's eyes. But when he backed the horse around and eased down the road, he turned and waved an imaginary sombrero at his cousin. "Kill a don fer me, señor," he said and galloped off.

George McClure put his feet up on the huge desk and addressed the back of a man who stood pulling type out of fonts for the upcoming edition of the *Vincennes Eagle*.

"This letter to the editor that was in yesterday's paper—awful," George said, his bony wrists protruding from the long sleeves of his shirt. "If a pedant swallowed the pages of Johnson's dictionary, drank half a gallon of vinegar and then regurgitated the whole thing up, it would end up as this letter."

"It is obviously one of Harrison's henchmen," Arlen Stringfellow said. "It even sounds like Harrison dictated the letter. 'No person in high station in this territory ever benefitted illegally from the sales of land.' What other person in high station is there who owns a third of Knox County? As if they aren't going out before every land sale and getting the people who want to bid to sell out. Land jobbers is what they are, and that's what my original editorial proved."

"Whoever wrote the rebuttal to your editorial is so insipid. Let's see how you like my counter-answer to him." He cleared his throat.

That a pompous ninny calling himself Publius, in a defamatory state of mind, and with nefarious objects at heart, has written a letter to the Eagle, *stating that no illegal gain has been made on land sales, is obvious to anyone who can read.*

That his arguments are absolutely false may not be as obvious. In the name of common sense, my friend, you do meddle in wares before you know their value. You have ransacked the Greek and Latin languages, ruined your arguments with voluminous circumlocutions, satirized the editor of this paper with forced humor.

You are defending what is indefensible—land graft among the powerful. Come out from behind the mask of anonymity and show us who you are.

In the public interest,
Gracchus

Arlen Stringfellow picked up the page form and laboriously carried it to the press in the corner of the shop. The October daylight was fading. Squinting, he locked the page in place for tomorrow's paper. Then he came to the desk and sat down on its corner, across from George McClure.

"I don't know how you have the courage to fly in the face of the man who gave you land," Stringfellow said.

"Harrison is a nabob. His brother and I fought in the same war to free men, and now he and I are on different sides interpreting what that freedom means out here, that's all.''

"Does this anger your brothers?''

George was evasive. "We are all of differing characters and interests. My brothers are presently at work making plantations and becoming gentlemen.'' He frowned; it was not the whole truth. "But yes. Right now we are in a bitter argument. But they know I do what I wish.''

Stringfellow leaned his elbow wearily on the desk. He was an intense young man, a New England printer who came to Vincennes from Washington City only last year to set up the opposition paper. Without family or many friends, he boarded with the land commissioner John Badollet. There he had quickly discovered Badollet's friend George McClure shared his republican opinions and had writing skills he could use.

"We'll use your editorial. But I want you to look at something else. You recall the land company bill the governor pushed through the legislature to build the canal bypassing the falls at Louisville? Well, I have informaton the canal company was formed to raise money for Burr's conspiracy. It's a fraud. There's not going to be a canal and Harrison is going to be to blame.''

"Harrison does not support Burr's invasion,'' George said.

"Not lately, when it begins to lose support. But earlier he did. And I am going to print a full exposé of Burr's involvement in getting that canal bill forced through. I'll reveal Harrison's complicity. I have been going about getting depositions, facts. I have some secret sources.'' He held up a stack of papers, then put them on the desk.

"Young men are flocking to Louisville to join Burr,'' George murmured. He had heard rumors today, rumors he couldn't confirm, that the young ones in the family were joining the cause.

"This should make a large hole in the recruiting plans in Indiana and perhaps further. It may scuttle Burr's dreams.''

"I would like to read this editorial of yours and the documents you have, at my leisure. I can dine at the Yellow and should return about eight. Will you be here?''

"Fear not, my friend,'' Stringfellow smiled. "This issue of the *Eagle* will not fly until after midnight. I will get a bite in my lodgings and be back quick as a wink. I will see you at eight.''

George parted from his friend outside the office and walked toward the Yellow Tavern to order supper. He did not like staying in town so late, but the moon would be going in and out of the clouds tonight. It would light his way out of town when he finished his work.

The darkened taproom of the Yellow was about deserted. He would order a rum and slab of bear meat, which seemed to be the specialty these days. As his eyes grew accustomed to the gloom, he saw his nephew Jack McClure sitting at the corner table by a leaping fire, sipping a hot drink from a mug.

"Jackie Dude,'' his uncle said, and the young man looked up with a suggestion of a smile. When Jack was a boy, his uncle had admired his wit; lately, though, they understood each other less well. George sat at the table, sweeping suds from a former patron's ale off the table with his sleeve.

"Uncle George. Burnin' the twilight oil, I see, to protect *vox populi*," Jackie said. George nodded, a little amused. His nephew was quick these days with wise sayings.

"I heard your cousins Jim and Johnny went on the grand expedition to the Southwest, and I thought you might have gone too. Or don't you support it?"

"Indeed I do," the young man answered forthrightly. "The new West is the future o' the nation. Burr bought lands down there and he's goin' to claim 'em."

"Of course he is," George said, realizing that neither of them believed this pretext Burr offered for his schemes. "But I've had my fill of speculation." Somehow tonight this tavern, with its muddy floor and hunched-over men talking in whispered tones, reminded him of the old Black Rose, of Little Dickie Fowler. He had had plenty of miserable failures in his life.

"Speculation, a man ownin' land and as much as he wants, is the right, really the necessity, of every citizen o' this new land. We have to take it and develop it against the savages and other nations. It was the vision of those who fought the tyrants," his nephew said, his round sensitive face perfectly serious.

"Yes," George conceded. Washington and the rest of the Virginian founding fathers did have land speculations over the mountains—but wait. What Jack just said, the way he said it—recognition clicked like a clock spring. "Publius," he said, looking at his nephew.

"Astute Uncle George," his nephew smiled. "But then Publius isn't one person. Two of us in the Young Patriots 'assisted' Governor Harrison, if you want to call it that. Tom Emison looked up the Latin phrases. . ."

"Miserably executed they were. And the Greek was worse. I should have guessed. Why couldn't Harrison write his own letters?"

"It would seem to be more effective comin' from one of the young stalwarts of the community instead of the man accused."

"That, Nephew, is what we Pennsylvanian Caintuckians used to call connivin'."

"The honor of the governor was involved."

"Honor you say. You have one sense of honor about William Henry Harrison, I have another."

"That, Uncle, is what they call politics."

Shadows slowly darkened about the small clapboard printshop and the wind blew wet sycamore leaves across its front door. A figure stepped from drying clumps of ragweed and goldenrod to its back window. Long, thin fingers pushed at the top half of one of the cross-paned windows, raising it noiselessly, gradually, from the outside. The tall figure bent like a closed bellows to come quickly through the window, then slipped through the room.

He went to the desk and picked up the written documents which had been idly scattered about by George McClure. Taking them to the dark area where the press stood, he faced the corner and lit a taper, which he stood in a holder on the wall. Quickly he scanned the contents of the papers, then pulled out the editorial on Aaron Burr and the Indiana Canal Company, read it and re-

read it.

There was a click at the front door. He blew out the candle and stepped behind a stack of newsprint folios stored beside the press. Arlen Stringfellow stepped into the office, closing the door behind him against the rising wind off the river. "Where is that candle I left here?" the printer murmured, feeling his way across the room. It was not to be his destiny to locate his taper and light it. Strong hands held him from behind, a scarf was slipped about his throat, and before he could even cry out, the life was throttled out of him by hands with immense strength. Heavily he fell to the floor.

But the front door was rattling; the tall man looked up apprehensively. "Stringfellow—Arlen—are you in there? What's going on?" Someone was entering.

Quickly the assassin picked up the papers and eased toward the window, as candle glow flickered through the room and footsteps came toward him. He swung his feet into the window; there was a clamor. The man who had just come in tripped over the body of the printer, and his candle light failed momentarily. But not before George McClure could see that the dark figure, exiting with papers in his hand after assaulting the editor of the *Eagle*, was his own nephew Ish Scott.

George listened for the heartbeat of the man before him and confirmed his fears. He sank back on his knees, bobbing on an ocean of shock. The darkness in the room seemed to throb in on him, advancing menacingly out of the corners. In the light from the single sputtering candle he saw the moon, stars and planets bursting about him. My God, what am I, what are we, going to do, he thought, grasping the awfulness of it. There had been rumors that Ish was with the former vice-president. Somehow that invidious villain Burr arranged to have Ish kill this good man for expressing his own opinion in a free newspaper.

Repugnance flooded him. His own kin! What a double tragedy. So much had been won through so many hard years, so much lost in these few minutes. This wastrel boy—he put his head in his hands, thinking of "The Daniels" with their proud, deserved position in the community and the others in the family. Jackie had written provocative letters about this editor. John's son Jim, and Will's Rob had gone to join Burr—they would be suspected, implicated. And Jenny. Jenny. Her life would be over. Thank God Ma was gone.

What, what was to be done? The magistrate must be called—then a calming thought hit him. He would talk to his brothers. He had not done that recently. They would know what to do. "The Fambly" could handle it best.

"Do this right," George told himself as he and John approached Will's house. He realized that what he did, what they all did this night would influence the lives of everyone they loved, probably for years to come. They reined their horses at a hitching post outside the rambling portico of the new home and headed up the steps, George carrying a lantern. The needs of the moment seemed overwhelming—to be true to the law he had always revered and yet protect the family. My God, Rafe, where are you when I need you the most, he wondered.

Will and Margaret answered his urgent knock together in their night clothes.

His story, which had been told half an hour before to John, was quickly repeated in the parlor. George had called on the magistrate and told him he had come upon a murder and would return in the morning to tell all he knew. If he hedged, indicated he knew little when he knew a good deal, nothing would be permanently lost by his evasion. Ish Scott could have taken several roads out of the territory; hurried pursuit would not locate a murderer in these isolated lands anyway. George had bought the family a few hours.

"Do they have to know it was Ish? Will they find out other ways? We could deny everything and lay low till we see. . ." John suggested not very enthusiastically.

"Maybe. But the best thing is to tell the truth about what I saw. If we didn't have all these years of trying to live by what Ma and Pa and the Church put into us, well then we'd have to think of how impractical it is to cover up a lie like that. Every tree in this town has eyes and ears and somebody else may have seen him." His brothers nodded.

"But what then?" George's head was swimming with visions of articles in the Cincinnati papers—financial, political ruin. . .

"The worst part is they'll never git him," John McClure said despondently. "Ish is as wary as a wolf. He could be halfway to New Orleans. And if Burr was back of it and sets up his 'kingdom' in Mexico. . ."

"But it's worse if they do get 'im," Margaret put in. "All of us will stand by and watch ourselves disgraced as they dash about lookin' for 'im, draggin' him back, tryin' him, with us helpless as it all happens. We're—what do you call it—*accomplishes* jest by being born into this fambly, or marryin' into it. To say nothin' of these silly boys of ours. Everybody will think we're back o' it in some way. . ."

"Unless. . ." Will McClure's deep voice rumbled through the room and eyes turned to him. "Unless he gives himself up."

"Now why would he do that?" John demanded.

Will's voice was quiet, cold. "He would do it if we went out and brought him in to do it with rifles."

A moment of silence, then George said, with a relieved sigh, "It's the only way. Even if we can't find him."

They planned quietly, as the October wind howled about the clapboards of the new house, and finally John, Will, and George left the house to go to Dan'l's and seek his reaction to the plan.

"Why, why is it that children go wrong when you do everything you can?" Jenny McClure sobbed as her brothers sat about her later in the home on the bluffs of the Wabash. "Dan'l, you might as well have come out here to tell me he was drown-ded in the Ohio River. I wish you had. It would have been better. For him and me too."

She gave way to her grief and her brother came and held her in his arms. James Scott, numb with the sadness he had never allowed himself to feel over Ish, was upstairs with little Bob.

"I'm not just makin' conversation. I want to know," she demanded. Dan'l looked sadly at the circles around the eyes that had emptied themselves for over two hours now, the thin hands constricting around a handkerchief. His little sister was almost fifty, and yet she seemed to him for a moment to be back on the floor of the two-room cabin, calling to him that her dada was gone, that the wind frightened her. "You pat and rock 'em at midnight when they squall, and defend 'em against everybody when they aren't turnin' out right, and talk by the hour till your voice wears out and hope every day it'll be better. Then they go and ruin their lives almost as if to spite you. And hurt everybody else too. What makes it happen when you try so hard?"

"I don't know, Jenny," Dan'l said, helplessly, looking into her tear-stained, frantic face.

"Tell me, tell me. I'd rather die myself than go through this," she demanded, pounding against his arm with her fist.

"Mebbe jest because the Devil gits in 'em," he said.

"What does that mean?" she asked, irately.

Dan'l shrugged wearily. "I don't know atall. If I did, mebbe I could write a book like John Calvin or one o' them. I jest don't know."

Four McClure brothers stood before Governor William Henry Harrison in the parlor at Grouseland manor this Saturday morning. They had refused his offer of chairs and now the governor, dressed in the breeches and hunting coat of a gentleman farmer, waited for them to tell him why they were there.

John McClure spoke for the group. "Sir, we come as your ardent supporters" —the governor's eyes glanced at George— "waal, almost all of us, to ask a great favor." The governor nodded. Through the window all of them could see the Wabash, where boats swept by, loaded with the riches of the new region bound for southern markets. All of the people in the room knew that McClure interests had become an important part of the burgeoning region's prosperity.

"You've heard about the murder. 'Tis a tragedy for the town."

Harrison nodded affirmation. The paper was an opposition one, but he prided himself on defending freedom of expression in the new country.

"But it's more'n that to us. It's a fambly tragedy. We've just come from the magistrate." Harrison looked surprised.

George spoke up. "Sir, I found Arlen Stringfellow dead last night. And leaving, bearing what must have been papers about Aaron Burr's conspiracy, was our nephew Ish Scott."

"James Scott's son. They said he had run away. You think he went to Burr?" Harrison wondered.

Will now spoke. "We don't know whether he killed this man on Burr's orders or not. But what we propose t' do is t' find Ish. Dan'l and I'll leave with first light tomorrow, ride after him. And we will bring him back to turn himself in. Efn we can."

Harrison's eyes showed real sympathy. George had always given him credit for sincere interest in the welfare of his constituents, particularly if they were his political supporters. "You have been to the magistrate. What do you want me to do?"

"We are askin' for time to find Ish. Nothin' more. Ask the magistrate to deputize us, then leave the matter alone."

Harrison's eyes scanned the four of them. He made his decision quickly. "Very well. You have six weeks. I will ask the magistrate to consider him a fugitive from justice and let you pursue him. If you do not succeed in that time, we will make a public search." He understood the implications of what they were asking. A lawful, but private way to bring justice, not only to the town but to the family.

"It may be that some will wonder if you're investigatin' the matter thoroughly. We don't want to put you on the griddle. . ." Dan'l ventured.

"I will simply tell the truth. That your nephew is a suspect and you have gone to get him yourselves. Anyone out here will understand that."

As they left the mansion, Dan'l said to John, "You'll have to be in charge of all the fambly, again, like at the station. George'll help." John nodded. He and George working together again on the land—he would welcome that.

"Jenny'll at least have the satisfaction of knowin' he has come back and is tryin' to make up some for 't. He could plead he was under Burr's army orders—if we succeed in gettin' him to come of his own free will," Dan'l said hopefully.

"An' if we don't," Will growled, "we'll tie him up and bring 'im back like the hog he is. Or on his back in a box." They went home to pack.

Chapter XXXVIII

Three days later, Ish Scott stood on the docks at Louisville. He had pushed the fine horse given to him by Margaret Blennerhasset to the limit to insure that no possible word of the event in Vincennes could have gone before him to the city at the falls. It did not take long to locate the man he was looking for. Aaron Burr stood supervising the unloading of a barge of provisions from interior Kentucky.

It had been three weeks since Burr had seen his young lieutenant, Scott. After initial greetings were exchanged, Ish suggested they retire to a tavern on the docks, where they took a corner booth. Burr ordered rum. His hair, slightly longer than usual, hung in the back onto the collar of his immaculate white shirt. Always conscious of the details of his personal appearance, he seemed bothered by the hair. "Since I saw you I have been to Lexington, Frankfort, Cincinnati, twice to Nashville. Odd our paths did not cross. I have not been able to stop even to get my hair cut," he told Ish.

"And so you're a Samson unshorn."

"But I hope not blind."

"That remains t' be seen." Ish drank his glass off slowly, keeping his eye on Burr. "The matter of the *Eagle* is taken care of. Permanently."

Burr was instantly interested. "How?"

"I've closed down the rag by disposin' of its editor."

Burr's voice became an angry snarl. "You have been violent?"

"What did you expect? You told me t' handle it."

"Buy him off, threaten, even fire a few shots. . ."

"As you are doin' with the *Western World* in Kentucky. Well, it won't work in Vincennes."

"I want no trace of this to fall back on me."

"Don't give yourself pause over it. Look at these." He took out the papers and Burr shuffled quickly through them. One of the gifts of his high intelligence was the ability to read a page of script in a few seconds.

"I don't like violence. But these certainly would have looked awful in print. Harrison would have been forced to denounce me and we would lose our chance at the militia—and the recruits."

At tables around them Kentucky boatmen at the "spilin' point" were boasting about their ability to saw a pole, knock flat a greenhorn, and drink a hogshead of rotgut. Nothing could be overheard in the drunken turmoil, but Ish leaned close to Burr anyway.

"Listen to me. In Indiana I heard nothin' but going to join Burr. And Andrew Jackson has raised over one hundred young men from Tennessee."

"So he does trust me," Burr murmured.

"But the tide could turn, immediately from what I see. I have kept my eyes open in the three weeks I've been gone, and I think I have the picture. You must act now."

Burr raised lethargic eyes from his cup of rum. "To start the invasion? I have ordered Kentucky boats to be built to my specifications. The purveyors have not delivered the supplies."

"No. It won't do to wait. The men are ready to go now. If you wait to construct these"—his hand gestured scornfully towards the river—"floatin' palaces, with silken hangin's and sideboards, you will not get the expedition going until after Christmas."

"My timetable exactly. What is the matter with it? Besides there are important people to keep on our side."

Ish leaned into Burr's face, all but grabbing his lapels. "At the very moment you should be actin', you are dancin' at balls and wooin' ladies every night."

Burr nodded affirmation, smiling with no small amount of pride. It was true that he courted ladies, had always courted them and enjoyed showing a trim leg at a ball with moneyed people. But he needed their support. "What would you have me do? An expedition downriver takes time. The young men will wait."

"They will not. Already the Ohio country is inflamed against you by rumors and reports. We have bought you a little time by stillin' the newspapers—for a while. Go out today and use the money and credit you have to buy every boat, no matter how rude, that will float. Take the supplies you have and see that the rest get sent after you. Send a cry far and wide for your followers to join you and go, tonight if you can, to your estate in Washita, beyond the Mississippi. Make it a stronghold from which to conquer Mexico—or set up your kingdom, if that's your wish, far from all these enemies."

Burr smiled his unusual, enigmatic smile. "How many young men could I count on if I do that?"

"Two thousand, even three, I think. And more would come if you set up a headquarters there, in the Southwest. They'll find a way."

"And Wilkinson? He waits to join me but he demands supplies. . ."

"Don't trust Wilkinson."

"No?" His eyes were keen. Perhaps he had suspected it himself.

There was a silence. Ish rose and looked about him nervously. "Then you'll act immediately?"

Burr rose and threw down a coin to pay the bill. "No. All must be done with decorum, in good time."

Ish was growing desperate. "Decorum! With all the gifts o' intellect you received, you can't read people or the times." He turned to go. "And I have killed a man for nothing."

Burr gripped his arm and whispered, "Be still, you fool. All will yet be well. . .''

"But not for me, at least as long as I tie m' fortunes to you. Someone saw me do that deed. I do not know who. I must go West."

Burr reached into his waistcoat. "Do you need money?"

"No. Save it to buy candelabra for your boats, if they ever get here." He turned back outside the tavern to hurl one more insult at Burr in a scornful voice, "So you're a blinded Samson, truly. All of the Delilahs've robbed you of your manhood. You weren't destined to command, and I've been deceived." He walked up the crowded alley and disappeared from sight. Aaron Burr sighed, straightened his ruffled shirt, tucked his hair inside the collar of his coat and turned to the river docks again.

As Ish Scott strode to where his horse was tethered, a familiar voice accosted him from behind. He turned apprehensively; it was Jim McClure, with their younger cousin Johnny, pushing through the crowd on the docks.

"Ish, you weasel. Where have you been?" Jim demanded when he caught up. Ish took stock of him. Jim had grown tall and lean, his hair as black as his McGuire mother's. His other cousin Johnny looked like a freckled, frightened rabbit. Neither seemed to know about the killing in Vincennes.

"Don't bother yourself 'bout me," Ish shrugged indifferently.

"Yer ma's been half outa her mind the last three years. We've come to be with Burr's army. Are you with him?"

"No more." He looked haughtily into their faces. "And if you'll take my advice, cousins, you'll hitch your wagon to another pony." His mouth turned downward with scorn. "This un won't run."

"What?" Jim asked, not understanding.

Ish turned on his heel and started down the road, then hesitated. "Tell my mother. . ." His voice had softened, and his cousins looked at him expectantly. "Never mind."

"Where are you going?" Johnny wanted to know.

"Let's jest say I'm goin' to find a hole and pull the hole in after me." And he disappeared into the crowd and was gone, like a sprite in the night.

Dan'l and Will McClure, their horses loaded with provisions, came off the Buffalo Trace three days later. They had traded their gentlemen's coats and breeches for their old caped hunting shirts and rough linen trousers. But the trail was cold. Not at Louisville, where Burr's agents lounged about waiting for their boats and would tell them nothing, nor at Blennerhasset's Island or Cincinnati, could they pick it up. He had not gone East.

When the two brothers re-traced their steps to Louisville, they encountered Jim and Johnny McClure, who told them they were looking in the wrong direction. Will ordered his son home. Jim said he "were ready to throw it up anyhow, 'twere a half-assed affair anyway with no hope o' gain in' it." So Ish accomplished one good thing after all.

During the month of November, the older McClures travelled from Kentucky to the Tennessee border and asked information of travellers from as far away as New Orleans, but they found no word of Ish Scott.

As snow fell silently over the Wabash valley, melting on the leaves of the newly planted raintrees in Jenny Scott's yard, her brothers returned to tell her they had failed. She would have to go through Christmas knowing that her son, a wanted murderer, was still at large. Later, Will McClure was able to give her one meager crumb of encouragement. As Wilkinson betrayed Burr, and his expedition finally fell apart in Mississippi and as he and Blennerhasset were arrested and tried for treason, Will asked Harrison to commission him on behalf of the president to bring in the traitor Ish Scott, should word of him turn up. Thus Ish would be in the hands of the family before he was in anyone else's.

Chapter XXXIX

About 1808 the Indians, after a long period of quiet in the Northwest Territory, rose and shook themselves as if from the slumber of the Death-Isle. They were led by two dynamic brothers, Shawnees named Tecumseh and the Prophet, who urged them not to sign any more treaties.

As the campfires blazed and the drums beat, outlying cabins from the Mississippi to the Great Lakes experienced the fear of night-time attack and tomahawking that had made life hell for earlier generations in Pennsylvania and Kentucky. To protect the frontiers, William Henry Harrison called out the militia and prepared for war against the Indians.

Farmers around Vincennes became suddenly cautious. People built blockhouses and told their children not to walk the paths to the next farms alone. Catherine McClure, who was teaching blabschool to a few children three miles away, came home breathless one night and drew near to her father, who was walking a horse in a circle to grind corn outside their home. A young man was with her.

"Pa, this is John Hogue. He jest built a cabin up the road in the bluffs. He walked me home and we ran into. . .''

"Indians?" George McClure interjected anxiously.

"No, a bear," Catherine said and then laughed at her father's incredulous face. There were not many bears in the settled area.

"Big un too, sir," Hogue said. He was a Scandanavian giant of a man, blonde, clad in buckskin head to ankle. No linen at all. George had never seen anything like it.

"Were in a bee tree that was uprooted by the storm, hidin' in the roots, and as we sat down on t'other end, this bruin stood straight up'n stared at us as if he was the preacher gittin' ready to read us Leviticus." Well, at least the golden Thor could tell a story well, George conceded.

Catherine went on. "It had jest rained and Mr. Hogue's powder was wet, but he had his knife. He rassled the bear. . ." she took note of her father's astonishment and looked up at the young man in admiration "an' he won."

"Thank God for that," George murmured sincerely. They were in an inhabited pocket here. Twenty miles beyond Vincennes in any direction a savage wilderness howled, stretching on for hundreds, even thousands of miles in some directions. At any moment wolves, bears, or Kickapoos could push against the fragile walls of civilization they had constructed, knocking them down as if they were oiled paper.

"We brought back the feet. John is going back to gut the crittur, but he's givin' the feet to us."

"Thank you very much, Mr. Hogue. Nothing better than roasted bear paw," George managed to murmur, but he thought, stay away from my daughter, you cretin. She's just beginning to discover herself intellectually, and I don't want her within a mile of a man who (and he coolly surveyed John Hogue) goes barefooted in the woods and has an Indian tattoo.

But that night, as Catherine stood before the fire, spinning with her great-grandmother's wool wheel, she told her sisters Polly and Margit, "He was stolen from Caintuck when he was just a little tyke by the Ojibwas and taken to Michigan. He lived in a village near Macinac and migrated every summer to the Illinois river. Two years ago he slipped away. Went to find his white fambly, but they had been massacred." Her eyes were shining as she drew out the fluffy wool from her mother's sheep onto the turning distaff.

"A child o' nature," her sister Polly breathed, impressed. "Mebbe he'll come courtin'." She was thinking of marriage herself, had made a little chest of embroidered tea towels and chemises and hoped that her skills at cookery and the needle would make up for the fact that she was extremely homely. There were ten children in this house; most of the younger ones were playing in what used to be their grandmother Jane's room upstairs and their thumps and bumps could be heard plainly by the grownups.

Jean and George exchanged glances as pine logs popped and snapped before them. "Courting? Not if I have anything to say about it," George said out of the corner of his mouth to his wife. "What's the matter with some of the boys in town. Badollet's son, for instance. . ." But he spoke too loudly, and the heads of his three daughters turned toward him.

"Would anybody like some sweet cider?" Jean said, rising with a smile. But her husband stood up and, letting the stool he was sitting on overturn with a clatter, strode to the front door. He raised the latch unceremoniously, and went out into the fall night.

Later that same week Jack McClure concentrated on keeping the wheels of his father's small farm wagon out of the holes on a remote path north of John Hogue's cabin.

" 'Tis dangerous these days to live in the river bluffs. Tecumseh's Injeeans live upriver at the mouth of the Tippecanoe, and it's easy enough for 'em to bring their canoes down here." He was speaking to his mother's hired girl, Adahbelle Granger. Every night for the last week, at his mother's insistence, he had driven the girl home.

"Yessir, Mr. Jack, but my granddaddy's not afeard," the girl said, looking up at him. She had grown taller and rounder since the day three years ago when Martha McClure watched her amble up the lane toward the big house, but she was still slow-moving, dreamily deliberate in her ways.

"Call me Jackie Dee. Everybody else does." The town had shortened his nickname, along with that of his cousin Jim's, to an initial. "Why isn't your granddaddy 'afeard'?" He knew very well that her grandfather was a remote hermit who specialized in charm cures, but he wanted her to tell him about the strange stuff. Why not? It would pass the half-hour it took to get her over the bumpy excuse for a road.

"We come from Virginny mountain country, y' know," the girl said looking straight into his eyes. "Gran'daddy's a witch master. Ain't afrighted o' ary in the creation, not the lightnin' that strikes nor the sojer in that there fort." Fort Knox was not far from the bluffs where Granger and his granddaughter lived. The fort was arming now against both the Indians and the British in Canada, who were said to be looking for war.

"What's a witch master do, Adahbelle?" he asked, scrutinizing her curiously. Only a few months ago he began noticing her, really, as something more than a hovering background presence, beating rugs, emptying slops, changing sheets. She was thin, but somehow did not look scrawny. She had a strong, long neck, and her head of rather lanky blond hair was tied back in a bun with a ring of daisies about it.

"Of all the generation, he has been given most o' the gift o' white magic. He can undo the spells of the mischief witches."

Many around here feared witches, Jackie Dee knew, and resorted to wizards, who were supposed to practice good magic instead of mischief.

"Witch master does spells to heal body and mind," she went on. "And undoes bad uns. Learnt hit from his own ma. You can pass spells down from man to woman, woman to man, but hit breaks the spell if you tell your own sex."

They drew up to the cabin, deep in a woods. All around it grapevine and creeper held in fatal embrace the oak trees they were strangling. A blustery wind blew a branch at their feet as Jackie Dee halted the horses to help her down.

"I'll take you to the door," he said. Usually he left her at the lane, but this afternoon he wished to see the cabin. He had heard vague rumors about it. It was odd how many illustrious citizens from Vincennes seemed to know about this remote place. They resorted here almost as often as they did to the Indian yarb doctor or the physician who recently put out his shingle.

The couple made their way through the oddest assortment of items Jackie Dee had ever seen. Every inch of space about the cabin was occupied with something, smashed-in butter churns, leather sea trunks, huge wooden gears, even a small, rusting cannon. "Gran'daddy be a collector," Adahbelle explained, quickly. The head of a huge cat was stuck on a spike by the front door, its lips drawn back in a macabre smile over small fangs.

She pushed the door open and gestured for Jackie Dee to come inside. Odd spicy smells drifted out, and the acrid smoke of a fire gone out.

"Gran'daddy's gone. Mebbe birthin' the Chenoweth baby. They call him if the midwife is from home." Jackie Dee knelt to help her stir the fire and went out to get more wood. His mother had told him to pick up some lemon balm from the old man, who had bunches of blue clover, dog fennel and dusty miller drying on the beams of his ceiling.

"Tell me about his cures," Jackie Dee asked the girl as they threw round, white beech logs on the fire. "I used to be interested some in doctorin'."

"They come out hyar for ever complaint known to man. Or woman. If they got a burn, he puts ointment on 'em from the peppermint plant and to keep 'em from scarrin', boils three live toads in olive oil and puts 'em on the burn."

"I think Sam'l Thompson was out here for his rheumatism. . ."

"Gran'daddy writ up a charm for him." She drew in the ashes on the hearth:

Abracadabra

Abracadab

Abraca

Abra

A

As she finished drawing, she turned and again looked at him with her pale blue eyes and said, "For heartburn, eat a fishin' worm alive, fried mouse pie for bedwetting." She was silent for a moment and then licked her lips. "Jackie Dee, don't put your mind on that no more. I'm declarin' to you. I love you."

It was as if thunder clapped out of a bright July sky. Jackie Dee was astonished. "Whaa. . ." he began.

She put her hand on his arm. "I say I love you. I have all these months. Haint you seen me followin' you around? I'm so crazy mad fer you, I look fer ways t' touch the dishes you et from, pick up yer pants from the floor. I cain't do without the sight o' you onct a hour. You air the finest thing God has created on this earth, I do swear it."

After the initial shock, Jackie Dee found he wanted to hear more. No girl ever declared for him, none even looked much at him, except, of course for Bessie Elliott, the prissy minister's daughter, and he didn't give her the time of day. If truth were known, he couldn't muster the courage. He told his cousin Jim Dee, who was cutting a good swath with the ladies nowadays, that the Young Patriots took up all his time.

"I jes' do admire you so much, Jackie Dee. I heerd you tellin' your pa about Mr. Harrison's Injeean treaties. I declare you were so clever I thought I would bust. An' the way you joke with your sisters, tickle 'em. I wisht you would tickle me."

Her face was close to his. He moved closer, closer, feeling the warmth of the fire, the electricity of the moment. He kissed her, and tasted cloves. She put her arms about him and they kissed again and again. He pulled her down on the hearth.

"Jackie Dee," she whispered in his ear finally, "ha' you ever done 't?" He started. Images of the "prairie chicks" upstairs at the new inn and himself strutting around nervously with a pinch of snuff in his cheek to give himself the spunk to get in bed with them darted through his mind.

She did not wait for an answer. "I want to do 't with you." He pulled closer, agreeable. "Not here, not t'night. Gran'daddy cud come in any time n' spile it. No. Sides, it orter be perfect. Us alone, besides a fire like this un, with shadders comin' over yer purty, purty face."

His head was swimming. Nothing in his life had prepared him for this. Her lips, her heaving breast, her hips, molding themselves to him. She seemed to be temporarily insane, and over him. Why not?

"Where, when?" he murmured, touching her lips in a series of little kisses.

"Tomorry. Tell yer ma you need more time t' drive me home. They's a trapper's cabin back up the hill hyar. We can build a fire."

Suddenly he hesitated. "What's a matter?" she asked.

"Its jest that—how old are you, Adahbelle. . ."

"Goin' on fifteen," she said proudly.

"My God," he said, pulling back a little.

"Don't make no nivver mind. An' I know how to take care o' myself so there won't be no trouble, if that's whut you mean." Still he hesitated, a hundred objections in his mind. "Jackie Dee, I wan' tell you somepin'." Her voice was low and had an air of sureness about it that surprised him. "Jackie Dee, I seen you aroun' the house, and you're alwuz avoidin', hesitatin'. If you air that affrighted to face the daily things o' life, what're you goin' t' do when you haf t' face a Injeean?"

Good question, he thought, but only for a moment. For an answer, he kissed her deeply, this time with his tongue touching hers and lingering a moment.

The next day was an exquisite agony for Jackie Dee McClure. In the morning, as he passed through the parlor where she was vigorously applying a broom to the rose rug, he felt Adahbelle's eyes on him. Shivers of anticipation tore through him. His body seemed to have a will of its own; he flushed, paled, pulsated embarrassedly, so that he had to go outside.

He and Tom cut hay in one of the first fields his father had put under cultivation on the farm. It was lying fallow this year, having grown corn for three years and wheat for two more. Holding the curved, wooden scythe, he rolled his shoulders slightly with each cut as he advanced down the side of the field, trying to swing as little as possible with his arms. As the hay swished on the blade and fell rythmically with each step, Jackie Dee could see his lean, slight brother paralleling him on the other side of the field. He thought, Tom knows how to do everything right. He don't talk his mouth off, don't brag, don't flusterpate the way I do. Respect and honor're two words people use when they think of Tom. Why does she dote on me so? He swung the scythe with new determination. But perspiration coursed over him even on this mild September day, and he still glanced at the sun every few minutes to see when it would be time to head down the road to take Adahbelle home.

A magnficent dogwood tree almost enshrouded the porch of the trapper's shack, and fat, gray birds clustered in its branches, pecking its bright red berries. As Adahbelle and Jackie Dee pushed open the door of the cabin, a musty smell rushed out at them and mice skittered away. Adahbelle had brought in a small, stiff broom. "Won't take no time atall to sweep up," she said and made dust fly while he built a fire. She brought out a little hamper she had stowed in the wagon all day and spread a quilt on the floor.

Doesn't anything ever go right, he asked himself peevishly? This should be a moment of romance, but instead he felt, oddly, as if he were in a London playhouse, watching himself play the caddish seducer on stage. Or a character in a London backstreet book, the one with the "huge machine" that enthralled women. *Fanny Hill*, that was the one Jim showed him snitches of. That thought made him even more nervous.

"Elderberry wine, Jackie Dee, and English weddin' cakes my ma used to make." Her voice was dreamy. "I want it all to be so good for you." As he drank the purple-red wine, its heat seemed to course down his throat and from there all through his body, warming, comforting, relaxing.

Finally, she took the cup from his hands and lay beside him, putting her lips on his. The fire that he first felt with the wine sprang into flame, as if she were blowing on it with the sweet breath from her lips.

She undid his buttons and watched him put aside shirt and trousers. Oddly enough, he turned from her to fold and put his clothes on the floor beside him, to cover his embarrassment.

Then, without noise she rose and holding her arms up twisted her shoulders a bit and dropped her shift to the floor. In the firelight he looked hungrily at her body, thin like a little girl's but not a little girl's at all. She lay beside him on the thick quilt and began to touch him in a way none of the casual whores he had known before did. He moaned as she explored his body with hand, eyes, then tongue. Enchanted, he pulled her on top of him. She let her hair out of its pin and it swept about his chest as she settled down on him. Slowly, slowly, she began to move up and down, and firelight danced on the tips of her hair as she moved. He reached to touch her small, firm breasts and she bent ecstatically to kiss his lips. Then, again, she rose and sank on him, rose and sank. But finally, in a feverish rush of feeling he turned her over and with her panting beneath him strongly ended what she had begun. His hoarse cry, her long sigh, mingled with the chattering of birds in the dogwood trees outside the trapper's cabin.

In a moment she began to cry and he turned to her, alarmed. "What is it?" he asked, propping himself up on one elbow.

"I jest care for ye so much, so very much," she said. His apprehension ebbed away, replaced by a sense of wonder. And a smile lit his round, flaccid face.

For the next two weeks Jackie Dee McClure and Adahbelle Granger lived in a perfect frenzy, their bodies awakening to each other with an uncommon harmony. They sought each other out behind doors or in the barn for wet kisses and hot probings. Once, downstairs in the root cellar among the turnips and onions, they accomplished a vigrous set of vertical contortions which would have done credit to the "Double Jointed Man of Liverpool."

Mostly, though, they lived for the afternoons when Sugarson, with whom Jack now had an unsteady truce, would wait by the side of the obscure road while down the path they made idyllic love among the autumn leaves. "I jest want to do 't, and do 't, and do 't with you, Jackie Dee McClure," Adahbelle Granger would tell him as they lay, restoring themselves for the return to the wagon. "M' heart jest pours out like cream thataway 'cause you are so uncommon purty and clever."

And Jackie Dee could only ask himself how such a thing had come to pass. To all other questions that persisted in coming to his mind, he refused to listen.

At the end of October, after he had been gone for several afternoons to help Tom see to some salt pork shipping at the river in Vincennes, he brought Adahbelle home by wagon to her door. They had made a long stop at the trapper's cabin and both were languid, almost asleep on this still Indian summer afternoon.

Someone was with the old man. Voices could be clearly heard inside. Adahbelle did not move to get down from the wagon but sat with her head on his shoulder a moment.

"I know bad magic when I see it." The voice was young and strong. Jack had heard it somewhere before.

"For lovesickness I say swaller the heart of a rattler or sleep in the loft o' the cowshed." That was the voice of the witchmaster.

"Tain't lovesickness what has hornswaggled me. 'Tis witchcraft. She took to me from the first day and now she's resistin'. Won't see me, though I know she wants ter." Yes. It was John Hogue, who had been showing up at the Presbyterian meetings, settin' next to cousin Cat.

"Perhaps she don't cotton to ye. If ye was a gel, I'd say to take a drop o' yo' moon blood and put it in the loved one's tea. For you though—take a rabbit's foot and scratch her arm."

"Old un, I say she does love me. But someun has set upon her with black art. An' I want you to remove the spell."

There was a long silence. Adahbelle was gathering her lunch hamper to get down. The old man's voice, very low, emerged finally from the door. "Who is 't that is witchin' you?"

"Has to be Buzzard Woman."

"An Indian witch?"

"Or her husband Captain Elmer. Live in Vincennes on the backstreet. She is Ojibwa, part of the clan of m' Indian fambly, the one I run from." Adahbelle, uninterested in the conversation, waved goodbye to Jack and went inside. Jack sat, and after a moment John Hogue came out. He looked at Jack in surprise, then apprehension.

"You heerd."

"None of my business, but I did. What'd he tell you to do?"

"McClure, if your cousin or her father ever git wind o' this I'll beat you till your head's as wrinkly as a baboon's." A pained look crossed his face, and he lifted his head proudly. "You think I'm daft. But I got to trust the ways of magic when I were stolen by the Injeans. I was with the Prophet,

Tenskwatawa, for a while, and I saw strange things. I'd rather trust a witch master to take care o'me than one of them surgeons that puts hot irons on yer body so ye blister and the fever humors will leak out.''

Jackie Dee's face had just the hint of a smile on it. This was a true Caintucky giant. The truth, that Uncle George had put his foot down about his daughter's going around with a "half-bear, three-quarters lion" was something Hogue could not conceive of. "All right, I swear as a gentleman, I won't tell.''

"Ole witch master tole me to git a suit o' the witch's clothes. Skirt, hose, hat. Like that. I should set it on a stump in the dark o' the moon and put cuttings from the ear o' a black cat on 't. Then shoot the clothin' with a silver bullet. Whatever part is shot will hurt on her and the curse'll be lifted.''

Jackie Dee nodded politely. They exchanged a few more words and then Jackie Dee made a clicking noise to Sugarson to start back up the road toward home.

Hogue was right. The witch master stuff was no sillier than administering little bugs to wounds to "puss 'em up." If he had any gumption he'd be a doctor himself and try his hand at really attempting to cure people. Except that, like everything else he thought of to do with his life, it was too much trouble.

Once a week Jean McClure rode into Vincennes with George and did her Christian "outreach" work to the heathen. She visited the poor Piankashaws and Miamis who lived in sheds along the pest-ridden back streets of the town.

Husband and wife walked along the river, watching gray November clouds above its sluggish, dark green waters. "Whose house is that?" Jane asked about a handsome new story-and-a-half French house not far from Marchal's tannery.

"Michel Brouillet. The fur traders are expanding west and north and he's making money hand over fist. He now has a *metis* son, who'll probably join that elite corps of French *metis* and make a lot of money too. And it isn't only French *metis*. No. American half-breeds are beginning to make their fortunes too, and all of these new traders are moving into English territory. That's why the English are threatening war, over this fur trade.''

"May it be settled by the diplomats. You and I have known enough of war,'' Jean murmured, thinking of the past.

He looked at her, remembering something he had wished to tell her. "Last time I was in town I saw a ghost. John Hunter, my friend from the war in New Jersey.''

She nodded, interested. He spoke often of the cocky frontiersman from Shippensburg.

"His brother moved here, to the far end of the French lands east of here.''

"Is John going to come?" Her husband did not have many friends; an old one like this would be welcome in their circle.

"No, he says he has a good farm in Pennsylvania. But he laughed about Vincennes. Said, 'It's a reglar barnyard, with its nervous thoroughbreds prancin' for office, hogs in the trough, ducks quackin' that the sky is goin' to fall and everbody wantin' to be cock o' the walk.' Says Louisville and Cincinnati are the same way.''

"He doesn't like it?"

"He does. Says the old East is like an old lady, her days over, thinking about her comforts and counting her coins, but the Northwest is a pretty girl who doesn't know yet whether she's a strumpet or a Sunday School teacher, but when she up and decides—watch out. She'll rule the world."

Jean smiled, then frowned. They had come to the door of a particularly squalid one-room shack made of slabs from the sawmill. A peg had been pounded into one corner of a blanket, and this served as the door.

"Buzzard Woman, it's Mrs. McClure," Jean said, wondering how she could tap on a blanket. An anxious, copper-colored face peered around its edge.

"You come in. I be'n scared."

Jean and George McClure pulled aside the blanket and came into the room. In the corner, by a fire with smoke escaping through a hole in the roof, lay a huge drunk Piankashaw, his shirt off, his dirty turban still on lank, black hair. The smell was overpowering, but Jean McClure managed not to raise her handkerchief to her nose.

"Elmer, he got whipped at the whipping post for—no decency. But he was drunk, not lewd." George looked at the stupified man with a pang of sympathy. He had never been an Indian lover, but these Vincennes "civilized" Indians were the most pitiful things in the creation, wanderers between two worlds, living on the white man's rum, while little boys pointed at them and the rest of the village mocked.

"Somebody trin' to witch us," Buzzard woman said gathering her huge brown skirts about incongruously tiny ankles. She was clean and neat in spite of the squalor of the cabin and wore pendant shell earrings. "Last week while we gone somebody come, took my clothes. I not know why." Sadness creased her already-lined cheeks.

"Then people start to call me witch. Say I put spells on their cows, milkin' a towel here in my house to get their cream. I don't got no towels." Jean McClure opened her basket, took out soup bones, blankets, meal.

"Mis McClure, you like a saint. When I go borry blanket 'gainst the cold last week, nobody loan. They say witches always borry things, relieve their pain when a witch master is undoin' a spell on 'em."

"Preposterous," George broke his silence. "Who is spreading this about you?"

"I doan know. I a Christian, Mist McClure. Father confirmed me when I twelve." George mumbled that he would make a few inquiries, Jean comforted the woman and gave her a missionary Bible, and they left again, as November rain began to fall through the hole in the roof and ran dirtily off the drunken man's face.

In the next few weeks, ignorant, fearful folk in Vincennes would not let the "witchie woman" alone. Pots of hot scum were emptied on her doorstep, hog entrails tossed on the thin, wood slab which had replaced the blanket as a door for the winter. All this as her husband's liver wore out and he lay in constant stupor until finally, near Christmas, he died and was carried to the potter's field. Buzzard Woman tried to return to his Piankashaw tribe, but she was refused admittance. Some of the young warriors had been at the Delaware village where the Prophet had identified four so-called witches for burning at the stake, and witch fever still gripped the Piankashaws.

Only kind Mrs. McClure continued to visit. All else shunned "the witch." Finally, one bitterly cold January morning, a boatman found Buzzard Woman lying face down in the Wabash not too far from the ferryboat landing. Around her neck were both the turtle talisman of her clan and the silver cross of Christ.

And the next week John Hogue stood without being summoned before the elders of Upper Indiana church and confessed that he was sorely sorry for having caused this woman's death. Although he did not explain why he was visiting the witch master in the first place, he asked forgiveness of God and his fellow church members.

Elder George McClure was not impressed. "I was right about Hogue. The ban is still on," he told Catherine as she and her sister Polly met him at the door. "I haven't brought you up so carefully to go off with a Visigoth from the Dark Ages. Do you hear?"

Catherine's eyes flicked at her sister, but she said to her father, "I thought you brought me up t' praise the man who has the courage to admit he was wrong," and her father turned away. He hated it when his children threw back in his face what he had taught them. Especially if they were right.

Chapter XL

Beneath the Midwestern prairies in that year of 1810 an impulse began to stir, kin to the impulse the earth has to regenerate itself after a harsh winter. Out of sight of the white man this impulse budded, put out roots, and spread, so that eventually it reached all the Indian tribes from Lake Erie to the Mississippi.

Tecumseh, the forceful Shawnee endowed with both genius and a one hundred-proof hatred of whites distilled through a long chain of odious experiences, rode about to Wyandots, Kickapoos, Miamis, and Foxes spreading rage over the latest, enormous land cessions of the Treaty of Fort Wayne. "The bear has finally awakened in his cave, my brothers, to find what happened while he slept! This newest treaty stole whole ranges of the land of our fathers and gave us in return stew pots, a yearly pittance and a few bags of salt," he said.

Tribal elders sitting in council nodded and sent messages to chiefs of other bands. "One too many twigs has been put on the firepile, brothers. We must not think of ourselves as tribes anymore," the elders said, agreeing with Tecumseh, "but as Indian peoples together, united. We must drive the white demons out of all this western land."

And young warriors, who had grown up as a generation of despair, listened intently, and a dark hope budded in them too. Perhaps it is not too late, they told each other. Silently paddling their canoes down the rivers or slipping along the warrior trails, they moved to join Tecumseh and his visionary brother the Prophet at the new Indian city, where the Tippecanoe River flows into the Wabash in northern Indiana Territory.

In Vincennes, William Henry Harrison penned a letter that reflected his grave concern. "The English are sending boatloads of supplies to Prophetstown on the upper Wabash," he wrote the secretary of war, "and encouraging the tribes to attack our settlements all along the frontier. War cannot be far off, and when it does come, Tecumseh can call up a thousand warriors, maybe more against us here."

Harrison commanded Tecumseh to come to Vincennes and explain himself, bringing "only a few warriors" with him. Defiant, the Shawnee appeared in August with more than seventy-five warriors at the very door of Grouseland itself.

Dan'l, George, Will, and John McClure sat with most of their sons beneath great walnut and oak trees by the Wabash river. They came to hear the Shawnee chief and the American governor speak of their grievances. As the Indians stolidly took their places, tomahawks in their belts, George McClure noted Tecumseh's features: close-set, slightly uneven eyes which were impossible to read, a hawk's beak of a nose, and a sharp, jutting chin.

You had to admire him, George told himself ruefully, for seeing through Harrison's posturing. Tecumseh refused to go sit on the white man's chairs in the governor's intimidating mansion. From his place on what he called "the earth, his mother" he would address this council fire, he said, and he now held up his hand for quiet.

He began by outlining, accurately, the dealings of the French and British with the Indians. Then he said: "Listen! White men! Since the Battle at the Fallen Timbers you have broken every part of the peace, killing Shawnees, Winnebagos, Delawares and Miamis. You attempt to split the Indian tribes apart, to cause war amongst us all, taking all our lands until you drive us into the great lake, where we cannot live. Why do you do this?"

Harrison, almost slouching on the rude bench that was brought for him, picked at a piece of lint on the breeches of his blue and gold dress uniform and shifted his sword. With a face as stony as limestone, he listened to the harsh complaints of the Indian.

"You tell us we are under the protection of the Great Father in Washington. That if we hold up the flag of the Americans, we will be safe from all harm. Yet when men came to our village and we held up the flag, the very Indian carrying it was slaughtered by whites."

He began to speak of the Treaty of Ft. Wayne, and the corners of his proud, strong mouth turned down in scorn. "That land was sold by only a few of our nation," he said. George noticed that his eyes fell on the Potawatomi Winamac, who was sitting by the governor. Winamac, who was a friend of the Americans, began to shift his weight uncomfortably. Well he should, George thought. This Winamac was an Indian turncoat who had bartered his tribe's independence so he could sit drooling at Harrison's feet like an Irish setter.

"We will have a great council and decide what to do with these false chiefs— indeed, we will execute them!" Before Tecumseh's words could even be translated, Winamac rose in consternation, mumbling something in his native tongue and pulling out a pistol hidden in his coat.

"Black dog, liar" Tecumseh spat out, indicating the Potawatomi, and Harrison rose to intercede between the two, finally succeeding in calming the tension enough for Tecumseh to go on. For a brief moment, trying to interpret something in the governor's eye, George wondered nervously if Harrison would have welcomed the pistol shot as an easy way to be rid of Tecumseh.

"Oh, that I had the power to make the fortunes of my people as great as the visions of my mind from the Great Spirit of the Universe. Then I would say to Governor Harrison, not that he should tear up this treaty, but 'Sir, you have permission to return to your own country.' This Universal Spirit gave all these lands to the red men, His children, and we will soon hold it all in unity and sell no more."

My God, thought George, he is forecasting a bloodbath for the entire Northwest Territory. He can never win, and yet with an Indian confederation, he can hold the entire United States hostage for years to come if he wishes. Moved, and a little afraid, he glanced at his sons. Rob, George, and Willie, growing tall and full of the hope for the future, stood soberly watching the Indian from behind a group of regular army men in uniform.

Now Tecumseh's urgent, strident voice poured out in the clipped syllables of the Shawnee tongue and the interpreter raced to keep up with the words. "Sell a country? Why not sell the air, the clouds and the great sea? You have formed a union of your separate states, why should not we? And why should we trust you? You even killed Jesus Christ. And, my friends, you thought he was dead, but you were mistaken."

As Tecumseh went on, boldly demanding that Harrison revoke the Treaty of Ft. Wayne, George glanced at his brothers and could see that they too were filled with conflicting emotions: naked fear at what this savage represented and admiration for the truth and brilliance of his presentation. George thought of the thousands of tribes roaming the wild regions from the Mississippi to the Rocky Mountains and beyond to the ocean and wondered what hell would be conceived for the nation if they rode under this leader.

Harrison rose slowly, his face as doughey as a half-done biscuit, George thought. He seemed not to know what to say in the face of an Indian whose intellect and command of the facts equalled or surpassed his own. Manipulating the pride of this Indian, bribing him with the promise of a few trinkets, was unthinkable. He cleared his throat and said something about the Shawnees' coming from Georgia originally and having no claim to these lands of the northern tribes. His voice droned on, and George's eyes filled with contempt. Even the sycophants gathered around Harrison were embarrassed, George saw. He watched Vanderburgh and the others known to him through years of political sparring, turn away to spit tobacco juice or watch the river through the trees.

The Indian, with his warriors sitting at his feet, did not move, and Harrison would not look him in the eye. "The United States has treated Indian tribes in the territory fairly," the governor offered lamely. Tecumseh leapt up and sprang forward, shouting something in the Shawnee language which everyone at the council fire knew to be a denial.

As Tecumseh boomed abuse at Harrison, Harrison glowered at him and drew the dress sword at his side in direct confrontation. George rose, his heart thumping. Dan'l and the rest scrambled hastily to their feet and closed ranks about the governor. Tom Emison and Jim and Will McClure and others seized cudgels as the Indian warriors likewise stood and brought out tomahawks. At a signal, the guard of regulars from Fort Knox advanced and ominously cocked their weapons. George, plastered against one of the elm trees, held his breath expecting a hurled hatchet or shot at any moment.

But it did not come. The governor took a long breath and ordered the soldiers to lower their weapons. After a few moments, Tecumseh gave a similar order and the Indians turned on their heels to go to their camp outside town. But as George watched his brother Will McClure leave the council trees cursing vehemently, George knew that Will reflected the sentiments and frustrations of all the white men present, including himself. Not one of the settlers in these territories would be able to sleep soundly again until this Indian leader with his dangerous ideas was stopped—almost certainly by war. He left to find his sons.

Dan'l McClure stayed alone in the glen beside the river to calm his distraught thoughts. Last night Harrison spoke to him in confidence. "Dan'l, President Madison agrees with me. Tecumseh must be defeated, and soon. He must understand decisively that the days of Indian lands and hunting times are over forever. Indians must take up farming, must be assimilated and it must happen overnight. It is imperative."

Dan'l turned to him with a questioning look.

"There are new forces abroad, more hateful than those of us who would merely take the tribal lands," the governor had said with a sigh. "A whole new generation is about to come to power who wish the Indians removed from the very face of the earth. All killed, or if that is not possible, moved far west. It would be a great tragedy to do that."

Dan'l stooped to pick up a fuzzy, withered elm leaf and ran a finger over it, feeling the roughness. Mulberry Blossom had hoped that white and red men (as everyone around here now called them) could live in this garden of the gods in peace. But it was not to be. And, as he often did, he thought of Asondaki. He had never broken his promise to Hidden Panther, had never sought to see his Indian son. Was he still alive? And if he was, where was he as these ominous drums of war began to throb?

As it turned out, at the very moment Tecumseh and his braves were returning to the Shawnee camps outside of Vincennes, Asondaki was walking disconsolately along the sweltering Natchez Trace. Eight-foot tall cliffs of dirt loomed about him, tree roots poking through them to point ugly, protruding fingers at him as he bore his pack along the woeful, sunken path. It would take him several days to reach the brawling town of Nashville, and from there take the river system north, if a desperado did not rob him first. He was bringing a final shipment of fine silver north for Fortin, whose employ he would soon be leaving. Asondaki was going home.

Home? Home was not really Vincennes, although he could certainly stay there for a while without being recognized by those he did not wish to encounter. Even if he might have been recognized for his likeness to the McClure clan before, he had completely changed his look now. With a shred of satisfaction he scratched his chin with a fingernail through the curls of the luxurious new red sideburns he had grown in the last days in Natchez.

The last days. His mind stopped at the edge of remembering them, and skirted great, murky pools composed of abhorrence of himself and repulsion for—someone else.

Home was not the Miami camps of Little Turtle, either. There, listless old braves, including his once-defiant uncle, Hidden Panther, attempted to plant and harvest wheat under the shadow of the Federal fort and indifferently accepted their "annuity" pittances—salt meat, stale bread, cloth and whiskey, always whiskey. Young men like his two cousins, the sons of Hidden Panther, whispered about joining the new Shawnee prophets at their town at Tippecanoe, and some had already gone. He must and would see Mulberry Blossom sometime, but nothing else in the Miami camps mattered to him.

Mocksinkickee? When he thought of it, it was as if the boulders on its shores were converging on him, rolling down off the hills to bury him with accusation. The quicksand pools of self-hatred sucked at him, calling to him with the soft, devilish voice of a woman.

West Wind's Son, he stridently called himself, and the name conveyed a subtle, stinging pain. He said it again, savoring the mockery, the torture the heroic words inflicted on him, akin to what must be felt by those poor western Indians he had heard of who beat themselves with sharp switches after they came in contact with the Christians. The Christians. He spat on the ground.

He stopped, distracted, to see where his spittle fell. There it lay on the surface of the trail, which was entirely covered this morning with black, slimy bodies of winged insects. They had come yesterday in a buzzing horde, blotting out the very mistletoe on the trees, infesting the brown grass, swarming into his eyes and even his mouth as he batted them off. Love bugs, the natives called them. They rose from whatever lost crevices of the earth they inhabited once a year, flew in clouds that darkened these southern skies and died soon after mating, leaving a strange, sharp stink hanging in the air. Many did not survive the mating process.

His string of saliva lay glistening on at least a dozen of these strange creatures that had expired at the moment of ecstacy.

"Swiftly Running Feet, what have I done?"

And try as he would, he could not keep his mind from slipping toward the pools of despair. Weary of fighting, he allowed the memories of the last few days to rise again like fetid miasma and wrap themselves around him.

He remembered the woman as he had first seen her in the beautiful home in Natchez, her skin white as only an Englishwoman's can be, wearing a suit like a man's and smoking a thin, long cigar. He thought her the oddest woman he had ever seen. He had gone to deliver an order for Fortin; after she had asked a few questions of him about the merchandise, she lifted her eyebrows in half-humorous surprise, almost as if she did not intend that such a one as he would enter her life.

She was the temporary mistress of this rambling mansion, commanding the servants while the brother she had come to visit was gone to Canada. She invited him to stay the night and he had nodded grave acceptance out of politeness, and, he had to admit, from the strange, obsequious attraction that possessed him since he first saw the amused shadows in her gray-blue eyes.

And after the dinner, served among the heavy, sweet odor of a thousand flowers outside the open doors, and a walk to a cliff along the river, she spoke of knowing poets in London, as her eyes devoured him like an exotic, sugared comfit. Then the rich, pulsatingly alive southern night descended on the beautiful house.

And later, the polished boards of the floor creaked as she came to him in the midnight silence. He sat up to see her dressed in a flowing blue organdy wrapper.. As the moon threw shapes of shadowy oak branches and loops of hanging moss through the large panes of the windows, there was a soft rustle as she loosed the ribbon of her night robe and it fell to her feet.

And he remembered how she slipped into the large, spindled bed beside him and lay there looking at the ceiling, curiously still. She hummed a little song, her voice rising and falling tantalizingly until he thought he must burst with the long frustrated desire that washed over him. Still humming her mocking song, she turned to him and cupped his face, ran long fingers through his curls, kissed his lips, laughed and pulled back, kissed him again.

What did she want, toying with him like this? Cursing a desperate oath in the Miami language, he turned to her and covered her mouth, her face with hard kisses. She laughed in a low, throaty way, touched, tickled him. He was a bomb of exploding desire. He thought if her hand, her lips did not stop, his composure would disintegrate, and shards of his desperate loneliness would fly through the musky darkness like shell fragments. Suddenly she turned from him, leaving him to look at her back. He pulled her about and staring down into her still amused face, held her shoulders and thrust himself into her body with more violence than he ever thought he could express toward a woman. Then, in what was more like a rape than an act of love, he took her, and then took her again. For her part, she expressed no emotion except soft, almost cynical laughter.

The next morning in the dining room, as the black slave woman in aproned dress and cap served ham and hominy, the white woman glanced at the birds out the window with casually evasive eyes. She talked of her life in England among intellectuals who played practical jokes on each other, ate quail-egg soup and blancmange, and spent weekends with the Prince at his exotic palaces. Asondaki did not understand any of it. He only knew he had done what no decent man should do, particularly no man who knew the proud tradition of tribal culture. Indian men never, ever brutalized a woman in the act of love and did not even do the act of love with white women.

But as he prepared to leave, to spend the next month of his business visit in a hotel, she came to his bedroom and stood before him silently. The man-cut suit she wore was of bright blue velvet, but her hair hung long down her back. "Stay," she had said, and the mocking laugh was gone. He looked at her fearfully, pleadingly, but she came to him and put her hand inside his hunting shirt, touched his chest with the tips of her long fingernails, put her arms about his neck, took him to the bed again, in the lemony-white light of that Mississippi morning.

And the pictures trotted hard and fast through his tormented mind. Gradually she weaned him to her ways, and there were strange days when they slept till noon and spent afternoons in smoky gambling dens in Natchez-Under-the-Hill. And he remembered the details of odd parties, where the wind from the river blew the smoky tapers in the huge candelabra almost flat. She introduced him to her hard-faced, smirking friends as the Cherokee Chief and fed him goose liver. He had laughed in a troubled way and told himself he did enjoy all this, that these were the richest, most powerful people he had ever known, that perhaps by turning his back completely on the other life, and immersing himself without thought in the ways of these white gods and goddesses, he could finally know who he was. He would himself be white.

One afternoon in the garden, while heat shimmered on the paving stones and pressed down on them like the suffocating hot towels barbers use, he told her about his Indian life. His words were edged with embarrassed flippancy, but she did not mock when she heard about the Moon in the Wild and Little Turtle. He thought, she may be a true woman in spite of her odd ways. She may care for me. Truly he wanted to believe it, because she was seeping into his blood, and he thought of little else, not his business for Fortin, not the money he made, certainly not Swiftly Running Feet.

The time he spent with her in the shadowy bedroom with the French doors became everything for him. He lived in a heightened reality in which the sights, smells, the strange, piercing pleasures she taught him, combined into an exquisite addiction like the rum his tribe members doted on. He could not get enough, he must have more. And if he sensed, through it all, that this island of sexuality had a dark beach leading to deep waters, it only enhanced the desperate pleasure, the obsession.

The most awful pictures of all, which rose from the wispy smoke of his memory like shaman's dreams, were of the nights toward the end of the month when, turning back on him what he had told her of his life, she said she was giving him new initiation rites. He abandoned himself to whatever it was that she and her friends wanted, and the dark stagnant waters seeped toward the French doors of that upstairs bedroom, and he did the strange things he had never heard or thought of with others too, with her women friends, with slave girls, and finally, with a silent coal-black man from the slave's quarters.

When they were all gone, he laid on his back looking out those double doors. He thought, numbly, that the flowers did not shed their perfume tonight and the oak leaves on the shadow trees were oval, cloven, like a woman's part, not webbed like a man's hand, as they were in the Land of the Lakes.

The next day, looking like a little girl with shadowed, bleary eyes, she cried and said she regretted the night before, always did after times like that, hated it and herself and loved him, truly loved him as clean and good, someone to help her be better. And hope dawned in him as it always did, and he believed her tears and said he loved her too.

Later he knelt in the gloomy church where she and her brother sometimes worshipped, next to a large marble coffin he dare not look at, while she confessed to a priest. He gazed at the marble Manittos on the crumbling wooden walls, the snow-white woman in fluted robes holding a fat white baby who raised his hand in alabaster blessing. When they left, he told her his other marriage was not legal and he wished to become a Catholic Christian, to enter the white man's world completely, to marry her. She had nodded a very tiny nod; he did not know what it meant.

But that night, as he sat in the strange, stiff woolen suit she had bought him, he again asked her to marry him. She turned from him. Then she recovered herself and smiled at him more kindly than he had ever known; yet the kindness was that of an aunt for a child who had asked a difficult question and with whom one must be patient.

She had said simply that it could not be, that although she was what her friends called a scape-grace, her father was an earl. There could be no question of marrying a savage—she had not meant to say it and covered her mouth. Then something froze, the old hardness came into her face, and she put on the false, empty gaiety with which she iced over the cracks in her crumbling life. She said, "Just imagine you in your feathers and leather coat shaking hands with the the Prince, the First Gentleman of Europe."

He turned on his heel, reality breaking around him like the fragments of a pot that has hit the ground. He galloped up the stairs to throw his few things in his pack. Her voice floated after him. "You extend your hand and he sees the tattoo of the blackbird. This is my husband. He's named 'Eclipse of the Moon.' " Taunting laughter followed. He flung himself down the stairs two at a time, throwing off the wool coat as he went. "I had never had a red Indian, you know. Barbados blacks, Arabians, and even a young girl from Calcutta, but never. . ." Her voice floated out the door after him and hung in the air, like the smell of the odd, sweet flowers.

He arranged to go downriver to Baton Rouge that very night, on a barge with Ohioans who were sleeping off a binge in Natchez-Under-The-Hill among bags of flour and grindstones. As he sat on the prow of the boat, the stars came out. His eye traced them into shapes—warrior, tent, seven maidens, just as his uncle had taught him.

And now, having said goodbye to Fortin and taken his bitter path down the Natchez trace to return to Vincennes and claim his earnings from Lasselle, he remembered another thing Hidden Panther had taught him, on the eve of his physical manhoood.

"The wipimi, manhood's arrow, is to be used cleanly, as a symbol of the cleanness at the fertile heart of nature." He wondered if he could ever face his uncle again.

There was one more thought, and that was that the color of white skin was the color of the purifying snow. It was an odd joke. The white men feared to be with Miami maidens for fear of getting the loathsome foul-part sickness. But he had learned what true foulness was from a white woman. He could only hope that the rottenness of soul which he now felt would not last until his days were over.

Chapter XLI

"Uncle Dan'l, do you think that Tecumseh will jump out at us if we go s' far out in the country? He could come down the Wabash. . ." John McClure's daughter Mary was apprehensive. She sat beside her uncle on the seat of the wagon lurching out of the Upper Indiana churchyard after early services. It was a color-washed September day about a month after Harrison's angry confrontation with the Shawnee.

"Tecumseh told Harrison he wants peace, Mary. And b'sides, t' git to us where we're goin', he'll have to go through a whole gaggle o' Shakers first. It ain't dangerous. After all, we cain't jest sit around and wait quiverin' in our houses for Injeeans to come. We got t' go on with life." Samuel Emison, sitting behind Dan'l in the wagon with Dan'l's second son Tom, nodded. They were going to see the public church services of the new Shaker community called West Union, north of Vincennes on the Wabash. Dan'l turned his head slightly to be sure his brother George's wagon was following. A cloud of dust and the happy singing of Catherine, Polly, and Margit McClure confirmed that George's wagon was on the road too.

" 'Tis difficult makin' arrangements for family outings when George is hardly speakin' to me," Dan'l mumbled and Emison looked up questioningly at him. "Or is it that I am hardly speaking to George. Don't matter, Harrison and Tecumseh and all that has come in and finally split us up."

Sam exchanged looks with Tom McClure. Both shared concern for this political schism which saddened Dan'l McClure's heart. "I'm sorry," Sam said.

Dan'l eased the horses over to the right of the road as they met a family on the way to the later service. "I keep wonderin' what Grandma Jane would have said," Tom murmured.

"She would 'a clucked like a hen and shook her head so hard her hair tumbled about and said, 'This family has survived famine in Ireland, a hurricane at sea, Indian massacres, the Revolutionary war, and life in a stockade in Caintuck, and now are splittin' up over politics—whether men crop their hair or still wear it tied back. Shame, shame.' "

" 'Twas over the letter to President Madison, wasn't it?" Mary McClure ventured. Her father John had managed to evade getting drafted into this war, and she really did not know its details.

"Shore as a toad has spots," Dan'l told her. "You know the governor asked me and some of the rest o' the so-called leadin' lights of the territory to have a meetin' to write to President Madison askin' for Federal troops to deal with the Injeean emergency. Your Uncle George was there. . ." He shrugged and Tom in his quiet way took up the rest of the story as his cousin turned to hear him.

"After the official meeting, Uncle George's and Badollet's splinter group met in the land office for George to write a separate letter to the president, and it criticized Harrison's handlin' of the Indian agency. The governor found out and was plenty angry, said as usual they cared more about causin' trouble for him than saving the settlers' lives. Badollet and Uncle George said there wouldn't have been any crisis if he hadn't been so high-handed with the Indians. They also said the fancy-tailed, hand-picked militia Harrison's friend Ben Parke set up is just a palace guard for Harrison and would high-tail it and run for the nearest tree if they ever caught sight of a feather or heard a whoop in a real battle." Tom was not amused by this, since he, Sam, and Tom Emison had been asked to be in the Parke Dragoons.

Dan'l leaned over the lines so the young people would not see his face. For nine years this sort of stuff was all he'd heard and it was about to tear this territory apart. Angry little arguments buzzing like a swarm of deerflies about the personality of William Henry Harrison and whether you were "fer 'im er agin' 'im." Harrison rigged and bought the territorial elections. Harrison outraged the people of Illinois. Harrison controlled the newspaper. The angry rumor flies buzzed and nipped, and eventually Dan'l and Will McClure, staunch supporters of the governor, had it out with George about the letter and all the rest, and George wasn't talking to his two brothers.

"Now we have to make arrangements through the womenfolk." Dan'l's voice grew uncharacteristically bitter. " 'Martha, will you please tell Dan'l that George says they have to sign these yere papers'—silly flapdoodle." Mary looked at him earnestly, wishing she could put a little balm on the smart for him. He was, after all, her favorite uncle. Well, she was pleased there was a temporary truce, anyway, for going to see the Shakers. It was too good a show to miss; the whole town was talkin' of it. An Ohio Shaker group had sent missionaries out to Indianney and they were bustlin' about buildin' meeting houses and plantin' fields to beat all get out. They separated women and men in all the things they did and held odd dancing worship services just like all the rest of the Shaker villages. You had to see it, so Mr. Sam'l Thompson had said.

"Just to think, Uncle Dan'l," Mary enthused, "being able to live your whole life for God—to take yourself out of this evil world of tears and live among the Elect, like the Shakers do." She clasped her hands in front of her chest, and Samuel Emison, who thought the very breath she exhaled was made of cinnamon candy, smiled a little.

But he could not resist putting in his own opinion. "If God wanted us to be out of the world, why'd he put us in it?" he asked.

Mary ignored him. They had had this discussion before. The Shaker ways attracted more women than men.

"I hear they kneel before every meal and start religious service with a deep silence. Isn't that wonderful?" She was thinking of the meals at her house, where her mother Janie and father John chatted about horses and occasionally shot each other sharp glances, her brother Jim Dee still talked about Aaron Burr, and the slaves chimed in as if they were members of the family. At least that was the way it was until lately. Just of late John McClure had been poorly, taking gruel in his room for his sick stomach.

"Well, the Shakers have a good sayin'," Dan'l allowed. "Give your hands to work and your heart to God."

"You've always tried to do that, Sir," Sam Emison said, and Dan'l smiled at the sincere compliment. He liked this young man who, with his older brother Thomas, ran the mill that was beginning to be successful on Maria Creek and was an elder in the church before he was thirty.

Mary sighed. "To consecrate every action, the ironing of a shirt, the tending of the rosebushes, to God. What higher witness could there be?"

"Mebbe you should have been a nun, Mary," her uncle suggested. She looked up and smiled when she saw he was joshing. She twisted her pale hands, putting the fingers together to make a little church and steeple and waved it playfully at Sam. Her hair was as red-gold, her coloring more like George's than her parents'. Mary McClure was what she seemed on the surface, open, loving, ingenuous as the butter-and-egg flowers on Indiana hillsides. Too ingenuous, her uncle suddenly thought.

"Their real name isn't Shakers, you know," Emison said after a while from his rear seat. "They are the 'United Society of Believers in the Second Coming of Christ.' "

"When is that s'posed t' be?" Mary asked. They had reached the Bruceville Road where wagon traffic was thick. Dust drifted over everything and she quickly took off her new bonnet, stuck it under the seat, and pulled an old sheet about her.

"It's here," Emison said earnestly, trying to be fair to their views. He had done some investigating. "Well, it was. Sister Ann Lee, who started it all, was supposed to be the Second Incarnation of Jesus. She came over to America from England during the War of Independence with a little group of followers. Said she'd had a vision in jail."

"She was persecuted?" Mary said excitedly. Nothing seemed to happen around here. Her father was always telling stories about Ireland where Catholics murdered her Uncle, suffering for righteousness' sake. Not that she wanted that; she loved her uncles far too much, all of them. But just a mild amount of persecution, perhaps, in the name of the cross—She sighed.

"The vision said man could only be saved by giving up foul lusts. Live separately from the world. No more marriage," Sam Emison said. There was a frown on the keen-eyed face framed in tight, almost childish, light-brown curls. Obviously Sam Emison thought it was the worst idea he ever heard of. He could hardly wait to be self-sufficient enough to take Mary to the altar.

They spoke more of the Shakers and the ominous rumblings in Vincennes about their odd ways. They jolted along, bumping half off the seat at every rough spot in the road, ate from box lunches prepared by Jean McClure, dozed, and finally arrived at the Busseron Creek village for the late afternoon services.

George got down from his wagon and with Tom McClure's help, saw to the horses as the girls hurried excitedly up the road. "These people seem to thrive on swamps," he said to Tom, looking at the low bogs filled with cattails and reeds. Beyond the swamps, though, were neatly cultivated wheat and cornfields, alternating like squares on a chessboard. A little sadly George watched Catherine stride down the road. She shook her shoulders just slightly as she walked ahead of him, and he recalled that she had had that same walk, part defiant, part carefree, since she was a small girl herding chickens about with a stick.

Since he had forbidden her to see Hogue, she had retreated from him, putting her true feelings neatly away from his sight, like a thimble in a sewing basket. She answered his questions with measured, painful politeness, and her eyes looked at the clock on the mantel instead of his. Two weeks ago she told the parents in the neighborhood she would not conduct the little primary school, as she had last year. The families would have to look elsewhere for someone to have the children say aloud the rivers and continents of the world and learn their nines. He suspected she was still seeing the forbidden sage of the woods, but he dare not pursue it. He did not have the strength to pull the thin-stretched love between them to the snapping point, for fear it would slap back in his face.

Now, along the horseshoe of the Shaker road they passed log cabin buildings, and beside them clusters of well-kept orchards of apples and pears, with branches bending to the ground, loaded for harvest. These people know how to manure, thought George a little enviously. The group walked down the main street of what was now a settlement of sixty or more people. On their left seemed to be a log headquarters or office.

A sister dressed in a blue-and-white striped, short-sleeved gown with a white scarf over her shoulders appeared at the door of the office. She came forward to welcome Catherine, Polly, their younger sister Margit and Mary McClure. Dan'l followed closely enough behind to hear what this middle-aged Shaker woman was saying.

"Good day to thee, young ladies. I am Sister Elsbeth, Head Eldress here. I welcome thee to the home of God's people."

Catherine seemed to come alive. She began exuberantly to ask questions, but the sister put her arm around her and steered all the girls towards the woman's entrance of the log meeting hall. "Ask thy questions after the service," she suggested.

Inside they went, Dan'l and George walking five paces apart, Tom, and Sam Emison waving goodbye to Mary for the duration of the service.

Tom was called "The Spectator" by his friends because he watched the passing scene in Indiana Territory with a sharp, critically judicious eye. He commented, "Is this the army? Ever'one seems to have a uniform on." It was true. The Shaker men wore vests of blue fulled cloth, blue shirts with sleeve strings, long hose buckled above the knee and beautifully cobbled leather shoes. They took off the long coats they wore for Sabbath service even in this warm weather and stacked them onto a bench. Then the men clustered in one end of the large log room, while the Shaker women stood quietly in the other end. The visitors sat on benches along the side or stood near the door.

The men started making lines across one of the short ends of the log building; the women formed across the other. First, they knelt, and as Mary had heard, prayed silently for perhaps two minutes. They sang a hymn, and Tom McClure shook his head at his father in bewilderment. "I can't understand the words. But the harmonies are as sweet as birds twitterin' at dusk."

The Shaker men and women began little mincing steps forward and backward, their heads raised up and down to the beat of their clapping hands. This time they sang a ringing, anthem-like hymn whose words could be heard clearly:

> In Union we are One
> With Father-Mother One
> Take brothers, sisters by the hand
> And lead them to the Throne

"What's that 'bout Mother?" Dan'l asked Sam Emison loudly enough that a lady in an elongated bonnet shushed him with a look of disapproval.

"They believe that God is as much feminine as masculine," Emison said in a very low whisper. Now the shuffle's tempo increased into a sort of skipping. The new song, while lively, had the same kind of sweet harmony as the earlier one:

> We're marching to Jerusalem
> A rocky road and long
> Made lighter by our unity
> And lifted with our song
>
> Behold the Holy Zion
> Amidst the desert flowers
> With Mother Ann and Christ to lead
> Millennium is ours

The stamping feet shuffled on and the strains rose, filling the small building, reverberating from the virgin oak rafters. Dan'l McClure's eyes were on his son Tom and Sam Emison, as they gazed and listened, completely captured by the religious spectacle. There was a thrill of something like horror in the young men's eyes as they watched other young men and young women their own ages, a few from Vincennes and known to them personally, who had given up their families and daily occupations for a life of chastity and obedience among the Shaker nuns. They would never know the love of a wife, never hear children call them father, as long as they lived. . .

The women faced the wall now and shuffled and skipped toward it in perfect lines exact from end to end, their starchy, immaculate neck scarves staying in place even though the women were in rapid motion. Beside them, the men performed the same toward-the-wall and backward shuffle, back and forth, their hands outstretched palms up to "share grace" as Emison told them, their faces intent, drawn. Then abruptly the dance was over and the Shakers sat down on benches, laughing a little among themselves.

A Shaker elder, a large man with a benign, jowled face and a wide girth spoke to the visitors and the faithful alike on "We are all of one body, Christ." He went on to explain that the community here at West Union was a unity of the brethren who lived only for the service of God and that the dancing was part of that service.

"Make no mistake," he said seriously, looking straight at the visitors. "You think you see dancing, but what you see is joy in the Lord's bounty, a physical expression of thanks for food and care and inexpressible love. What seems to be turning about is really the symbolizing of a life turned to the world of the spirit." He told the group of outsiders that this outlet for spiritual enery was a good, clean activity. Shaker dancing was the spiritual substitute for the foul devilish sin of "propagation" which ensnares all in the world to hell. It was easier, he said, to exist only for Heaven here, pure and free of temptation, among the Co-elect living the Millennium. He made a specific invitation to anyone in the Vincennes area who felt moved to join the community to come, be a novitiate, learn the ways of the Shakers, live in common with all. He led a hymn to close the service.

George McClure had been silent throughout the service. As he emerged from the log building into the hazy fall twilight, he was grabbed by the arm. He turned to see Luke Dugger and his wife Delva. They must have come late, he thought, while he pulled away as politely as he could from Dugger's clasp.

"McClure, we got to do somethin' bout this thing out yere. It ain't decent," he said. His wife's small purse of a mouth was strongly disapproving.

"What's not decent about it?"

"The people that started this yere West Union Shaker settlement ere come from the East to stir us up, take our young folk away to their crazy ways."

"Sister Ann and Christ indeed! How dare they link 'em like a pair o' mules," Mrs. Dugger said, swatting at a big, ornery September fly that had landed on her husband's arm. Slap!

"An' that ain't all." Luke Dugger lowered his voice. "They say that when they have private worship, sometimes when they git dancin' all heated up thataway they blow out the candles and have a orgy o' their propagatin' all over the meetin' house—say it's allowed if you've advanced enough. . ."

"There's no proof of that," George said with more tolerance for the odd rites than he himself felt.

"Well, if you're willin' to put up with 'em, there be some about that won't. We ain't gonna stand by and let these antichrists take over the county." George watched Dugger and his wife huff off toward the campground the Shakers had provided for the visitors, where they all would spend the night.

Catherine and Mary had found Sister Elsbeth. She took them to see the immaculate broom manufactory, with its neat bundles of broom corn the Shakers themselves had developed hanging from the log rafters, its binding tools, and the strong sticks that would soon be handles. "Here the men work together, side by side and," now the eldress laughed, "here they work up appetites the size of prize hogs to come in and eat the evening meal the sisters have prepared for them."

Catherine was mildly surprised at the humor the woman showed. She listened absently to Mary chattering with the sister about theological subjects, about "gifts from God" and crucifixion of the natural man's desires, and living in common as the early Christians had done. Mary had been impressed at the service, at its sincerity and joyous piety, no doubt about that, and Catherine had to admit she was impressed too. But Catherine had only one question for the lively little woman with the tinkling laugh and the cap-shrouded face.

"Who runs the community?" Catherine wanted to know, admiring the quality of a newly made broom, turning it in her hand to see the neat stiches which bound its middle.

"Elder Lorenzo, whom thou heard speak, is the man's elder. I manage all women's affairs."

"All?" The idea was revolutionary to Catherine. She knew mothers superior ran convents, and had since the Middle Ages, but the women she lived among did not manage institutions, or anything except their husbands, for that matter.

"Yes. I keep all books, pay bills, plan supplies, and with the other eldresses organize discipline and train new converts. I am responsible to God and the group for all women's activities here."

"You have full power?"

"Within those boundaries, yes. Shakers believe in equality among men and women."

Catherine raised her eyebrows slightly and nodding, put down the broom.

That night, as the rich, slightly foul smells of the Wabash crept beneath the cover in the wagon, Sam Emison spoke to Tom McClure in a whisper. " 'Tis another sect. As if we don't have enough of 'em already."

"We all started out as sects," Tom McClure admitted thoughtfully. George McClure, lying on his back, could see the stars emerge from flitting clouds, though a lacing of tulip poplar leaves waving very slowly in the slight breeze.

It was true, he told himself. The sects, first noted for weird behavior patterns and differences, persecuted, fighting for their lives, eventually became respectable. And then they persecuted other sects.

"What bothers me," said Dan'l into the soft, equalizing darkness, "is how you cain't pin any of the groups down. They change their clothes like a actor changes his costume. John Wesley lined up his disciples 'n tole 'em to pray, n' wash at a certain time and said that was Methodism. In Caintuck the folks had the jerks and lay on the groun' writhin' and they said that was Methodism. Out here the Methodists have gone milk-and-water-go-to-meetin' and frown on the jerks. So which is the real Methodist?"

George also spoke to no one in particular (certainly not Dan'l). "Well, we're not the Presbyterians John Knox invented. We don't go to war with Catholics and hide in root cellars. Most of our preachers are preaching the religion of the heart now and are finding ways now to say everybody is saved." George had lived to see Rafe Emison's instincts vindicated by the church that cast him out.

"Bilin' down all these denominations is like bilin' down maple syrup in the spring," Dan'l said, his voice reverberating against the hollow darkness. "When you git rid o' the impurities and excess sweetenin', you got somethin' good at the bottom."

"What's that?" young Emison wondered.

"Love. Pure and simple love o' the Father for the children in the creation. All the crusadin' and killin' and arguin' and even the box socializin' and bad preachin' don't kill that Love. Keeps on comin' like a syrup pitcher that has no bottom. 'Tis the central fact o' creation. Pa used to say that, towards the end. Come to think of it, I wonder where he got all that? Indian version of the Bible, did he say?" The words came to the others as if from an odd distance, through the heavy, cool air.

Well, there better be a good stock in the pitcher, thought George McClure. Because if Luke Dugger and his crew of good hard-shell, old-time religioners had their way there was going to be a small war between the "pious Elect" and the Shakers and somebody might have to end up hiding in a root cellar again, this time in Vincennes, Indiana.

Chapter XLII

"Why do you defy yer ma so much, Jackie Dee?" Adahbelle Granger asked the young man beside her on the front porch of the witch master's cabin.

"I don't exactly defy. I jest ignore—to whatever extent I can." They were cracking walnuts on this late November day. Yellow-green juice stained their hands. Jackie went on.

"She pushed me out into the world a month before m' time and ever since she's been draggin', haulin' and pushin' me. Both of 'em, really. I feel like I'm ridin' a mule up the Knobs day and night when I'm with them."

"You argue like three mad crows."

"It's always about what I'm goin to make o' myself. The more they harp, the lazier I feel."

" 'Tis too bad," Adahbelle murmured, looking up at him with her very pale blue eyes. "You should make somethin' o' yourself. You are as fine as you are fair." Whenever she said something like that, showing the unashamed adoration she felt for him, he still wondered at the artesian springs which seemed to feed her love.

She had stopped working for his mother at the end of the summer. "I don't wanta hurt yer ma," she had said. They had long since stopped stealing time at the farm to be with each other, but still, both Dan'l and Martha seemed to know where he went and why. Jackie didn't know why they did not speak. He was of age, that was sure, but that did not keep them from trying to run the rest of his life.

Adahbelle took a job at Beckes's Tavern, advanced to chief barmaid, and had a room which Jack sometimes discreetly visited. Other times he came to the cabin. Now, pushing the thick shells off the porch, they went inside and took the walnuts to a copper kettle by the hearth.

The door creaked on its hinges as Retreat Granger plodded in. It surprised Jackie McClure that this huge old man with baggy overalls, looking like a hired hand at his father's farm, was a witch master. He had no sorcerer's cap, no long robe with stars on it. It also surprised him that the witch master tolerated their seeing each other.

" 'Twas foreordained," the old man had said when he found them in each other's arms behind the house one day last spring.

Now he was mumbling to himself about one of Tom Baird's daughters, an ethereal eighteen-year-old who had the "hypo." One day in August after a bout of fever, she came to the conclusion that she was dead, that she was being allowed to stay on earth in her body only for a short time. She lay on her bed as if in a casket; she refused to eat. Baird believed she might be "witched" and wanted relief, and the witch master was searching among his remedies.

"Gold filings in honey, about as much as would lay on the point of a penknife." If it cured her, she was only ill in her brain; if it didn't, she was witched.

"What makes these receipts work for one person, not for another?" Jackie asked him.

"The people's faith in 'em. That's what makes any medicine or charm work anyways," the old man grunted.

Early twilight was lowering and Jackie prepared to leave. As he walked with Adahbelle to the tethered horse they rode, he felt the same worries niggling at him that woke him up lately in the cold, early hours of the morning. Where could any of this go? She was thoroughly good, thought only of him. The warmth of her love, which he had first perceived largely as woman's sexuality, he lately began to see as directed sincerely and unselfishly at him. At first he had barely understood the depth of her feeling, immersing himself only in the excruciatingly sweet sexual pairing. But now he was gradually testing the love, and the responsibility of it was like a warm, restraining yoke. He was uncertain about how he felt about that yoke.

"What do you want from life?" he asked her suddenly.

"To be with you. . ." her face tilted a little, wistfully, then straightened. "And someday, I opine I'll have my own inn. Mr. Beckes says I have a tolerable hand for it and lets me work up the accounts."

She probably would, he thought admiringly. But could she read, figure that well? He had not known it. He was surprised at how little he really knew about her, and wondered that he was caring now.

When Jackie Dee reached home, his Aunt Jean, mother, father, and Tom were sitting in the parlor on the new pink chintz chairs.

"Catherine and Mary have gone to join the Shakers," Aunt Jean said through the first tears he had ever seen her shed. "They sent a note saying it was what they wanted and that they were of age, so nothing could be done to stop them."

"It took all of us," Aunt Jean said, clasping Jackie's hands and looking into his eyes, "to stop your Uncle George from going out there right away."

Shouting "freedom of religion be damned," he had gone to get his rifle right away, to shoot Shakers like turkeys in a turkeyshoot, and only Uncle John, getting out of his sickbed, had been able to convince him otherwise.

Others were not to be so easily restrained. The people of Indiana Territory, already in a state of alarm over the gathered Indian forces now wintering over at Tippecanoe on the Wabash, had to worry about their family members pledging to give up their lives to the Shakers. It was one thing to grudgingly admire the Shakers' sanctified way of life, the cleanness of line and execution of the sparse buildings they raised, the chairs they made. But to have your only child pledge to live the rest of his or her life as one of a group without faces or futures (as they saw it) was intolerable.

Groups of farmers with cudgels began to waylay parties of Shaker men on the way to market, scuffling and cursing them as home-breakers. One of the "missionaries" the colonizing settlement in Ohio sent to inspect the community was beaten insensible by a masked man. Some said the face under the dark bag with holes in it was that of Jay Byrd Dugger, Luke Dugger's son, and some also said that Jim McClure, Mary's brother, stood right behind him and held his coat.

Jean McClure, after spending several sleepless nights in prayer, wrote a letter.

> *Dear Rob:*
>
> *Please come help us. Several families here are in despair as their children, wives, or husbands go to the Shakers. There seems to be a spell on the countryside. I can't believe the converts have a sincere religious calling. I think if the famous Boy Preacher could debate the Shakers on even ground, and Catherine could hear it, their spell might be broken.*
>
> *Affectionately in Christ,*
> *Jean Jordan McClure*

Would Rob McClaren come? She could only hope, and pray.

The fire inside the Potawatomi winter home on the hill above Lake Mocksinkickee burned brightly with oak coals and the bones of animals. Swiftly Running Feet sat cross-legged before the fire, stirring beans and corn flavored with venison. Others in the tribe put fat pork supplied by the government into their pots now, but the taste of it made her stomach turn. Why would one feast on this slovenly beast, raised on the white man's slops and acorns, instead of the king of the forest, killed in a fair hunt? Somehow the thought of the penned pigs, snuffling among the garbage listlessly and without purpose in life made her cast her eyes out to the village on the hillside. The agent came, he delivered the annuities. He tried to help the Indians raise swine and corn and wheat. He told them exactly what skins to take, exactly where they could hunt. And the Indians did what they were told in exchange for being fed, like the animals in the pens.

Her husband would soon be in, coming to skewer the fish over the fire to broil. He went to the lake on this day in the smoky month, when clouds rolled overhead rapidly, like pregnant women holding their burdens ready to deliver. She smiled a little at the thought. Perhaps now that Asondaki Alamelonda was back there would be a child. She had waited so long for him, considering it her duty as a huntress, daughter of the chief. She waited when the letters stopped coming, while her father died and was buried with tribute, sitting up, in a grave on the hill, his body surrounded by a miniature log cabin fence.

And now Sun In Eclipse had returned, full *metis*, and it suprised her that he was as handsome as the picture her memory painted. She was without the sight of him so long that he was unreal, a gigantic presence in her mind, like the huge war totem the braves carried—used to carry—into battle. In her thinking she had turned him into one of the strong ones of the older days, and yet he lived up to the vision she had created of him.

She looked idly at the small bubbles of heat percolating up from the bottom of the pot of corn and beans. The smell of venison filled the little bark hut. He was so changed, yet not changed. He spoke of things she did not understand at all, of ledgers and accounts and swamp country where huge reptiles with long noses and sharp teeth hid in the water.

Still, the sight of him, with his head held high and his proud eyes looking out the door, filled her with joy. She was glad she had remained true to him.

She sighed. There was so much to understand. These times were so altered that she felt as if the mad Manitto with big bat wings had come down to spoil everything she ever loved, turning it unrecognizable and crazy. So many were ill with the fever, and the rest did not hunt or make war. The young braves had gone to winter with Tecumseh, to listen to the odd ravings of the brother-prophet. A noise interrupted her thought, and her husband came in. Her eyes roved over his strong form yearningly, as if she would never be able to see him come in that door enough.

"Bawkawtay, my husband?" She used the Potawatomi word for hunger. "The food is ready. Will you take off your coat?"

He did, but he did not watch where he set it, the beautiful *metis* coat with the shining epaulettes. He was troubled, as he was so often in this moon he had been home.

"My wife, I must talk to you." As he, too, used the Potawatomi tongue, his voice had the rusty ring of one who has not spoken a language for a long while. She raised her eyes expectantly.

"I found myself changed while I was in the Southland. Like one of the lizards they grow there, I put on the colors of the land."

"But you speak with so many voices my husband, so many sides to you. . ."

"It is not that," he said sharply; then, as if he could wait no longer to deliver himself of the burden, said, "I was not faithful to you."

She stared into the pot, her face sober, unmoving. She did not look at him. The story he began to tell her then was like one the mad bat Manitto himself would tell. None of it made sense—strange white man's homes alight with multitudes of candles where black men served and were beaten sometimes, witchery, women mad with lust—she covered her ears and would hear no more. Then she began to mourn within herself, rocking on her knees, as the pot continued to bubble on the grill above the fire.

He looked at her silently before he spoke. His voice was as harsh as a crow's caw, "Lasselle told me he would have my account ready when I returned. I shall get my money and we shall decide what to do then. The moons of the past have gone over the hill. I cannot call them back now." He took food from the pot and ate. Then he spread his mat by the fire, turned his face away, and went to sleep without speaking further to her.

Hyacinthe Lasselle was very busy when Asondaki appeared to collect his long-due wages, the pay of ten years of toil. "Dakin," Hyacinthe said, his eyes fixed on the red sideburns, which he still could not get used to, "you can be of help to me. Will you serve a week or two more during the rush-time? Then I can fully address myself to your sums, with interest. . ." he added temptingly. Asondaki barely nodded. What would two more weeks mean after all these years? He took a room at the Old Yellow, as it was now called, the best room in the house, and told them to send supper up to his room. He was feeling strangely bold, uncaring.

He no longer worried about who recognized him. The time was soon coming when he would pass among all these people in Vincennes as a rich man himself. He would set himself up as a trader, have a huge storehouse, get himself an agency. Perhaps even reveal himself at the proper moment to his relatives. As an equal. Well and good. He had paid for every comfortable moment he would have with the work of his arms and alienation from his own people.

His visit to the Miami home village near the northern river had left him anguished. Mulberry Blossom's beautiful bronze face was shrivelled like a persimmon after frost with the fever following smallpox. She told him his uncle died during the epidemic which claimed so many Miamis. And he had not been able to make his farewells. She was so weak she could barely lift her arm to indicate in the corner of the lodge the mementos his uncle had wished him to have. As he left the lodge, he saw braves lingering around the porches of the log stores, out of their heads with drunkenness and fever. They would probably not have spoken to him anyway; too much was unresolved between him and Little Turtle's band. There was no one among the people of his youth to care whether he ever came again except his mother, and so he would not come unless she called him.

That night, in Vincennes, he tossed and turned and dreamed of the White One. The magnificent stag stood on the hill above the cattail bog at Mocksinkickee and Asondaki, dressed only in the breech cloth of his boyhood, trembled near his feet. Through the midnight sky flashed the light spears of the great Thunder-thrower. The albino stag looked toward Asondaki and then spoke, and human tears flowed from his stag's eyes. "Patilongi," he intoned, one word—rainstorm, but the word reverberated against the hillsides about the Lake of Boulders, as the wind lashed stingingly. "Patilongi," the stag repeated as the bolts crashed. There was such deep sadness about him that Asondaki felt he must weep in his sleep, and he sat up stark awake. Someone was pounding on the door of his room.

His eyes blurred, as he snatched the nearest covering, his *metis* coat, and stumbled to answer. There in the darkness stood Lasselle with a lantern. "Dakin, I need you at once. Marchal is dying."

"I am sorry," Asondaki muttered, remembering Marchal was Lasselle and Fortin's brother-in-law, that he was a kind old man, with a young son Antoine who would soon be an orphan.

"Save your condolences for the funeral. I'm thinking of business now. Marchal owes a great sum to Lasselle interests and there is only one way we can get it. I must be made executor of the estate and pay his debt to us first. We must find a way to have him change his will. Go at once to the lawyer, Johnston, and meet me at Marchal's. There is not a moment to waste.''

Asondaki threw on his breeches and shirt and dashed out into the night. General Washington Johnston was the attorney who knew how to shave a legal point like a Miami barber shaves a pate. He lived on the riverfront street. The morning star winked at Asondaki, frosty and aloof, above the leafless trees along the river. The church spire was silouetted against the rising gray-green of the dawn. He delivered the message and hurried down the street to Marchal's.

Inside the room pale light began to filter through the windows. It was Antoine Marchal's last morning. In the old-fashioned canopy bed he lay, breathing feverishly in short, barking gasps. Asondaki hardly recognized this old, best friend of Fortin's. He seemed as ancient as the Death Grandfather, his skin hanging on his bones in great loops, his bones almost visible in his arms. Failure seemed stamped on his face as clearly as the imprint on a talisman. He came to the land of promise from France and the promise teased, then eluded him. The tannery was bankrupt, the Indian trade, even land sales had fallen off in the wave of Indian fear and political warfare that was strangling Indiana Territory. Still, there was a small estate remaining, and it was this that Lasselle intended to manage.

General Washington Johnston came in abruptly, spoke with Lasselle, and returned to stand with Asondaki near a candlestick at the back of the bedchamber. Lasselle stood by the bed; no one else was present. Marchal opened and closed his dry lips and in a quaking whisper asked for his son.

"He is with his aunt," Hyacinthe said. Hyacinthe's sister had cared for the boy for a year now.

Johnston pulled Lasselle back. "I've written the will as you told me. You've got to get him to sign it. We don't have much time. Do what you must and be sure to get the signature witnessed. I have to leave." He strode out and Lasselle advanced to the head of the bed.

"See here, Antoine, you must sign this new will. We have spoken of it, dear friend." His voice was soft, coaxing.

"I have a will," the croaking voice answered.

"But young Antoine's future is in question. They may make him a ward of the court." Marchal, obviously in pain, attempted to nod that that was what he wished.

"Give the use of the house and garden to my sister and she will raise him. Put me in charge of your estate. Otherwise the boy will be left alone."

Agitated, the old man clawed the blanket under his chin with his bony hand and shook his head from side to side. He could no longer speak.

Asondaki had come forward. "He will not agree," he whispered to Lasselle.

"We will see about that," Hyacinthe Lasselle's voice rasped like a file drawn across metal. He looked at the gaunt hand. It gave three hopeless flops, like a chicken without a neck in its death throes. Lasselle picked it up and put a pen in it.

"Dakin," he commanded, "come witness this signature as I help him sign."

Asondaki waited a few seconds before answering. Then, "Bear your own false witness, *mon ami*," he said with a surprisingly clear voice. "As of this moment my services with Lasselle, Marchal, and Fortin are terminated. Have my wages ready at two o'clock. And may your God have mercy on this poor old man's soul since you will not."

The first rays of the sun turned the Wabash into a sea of beaten gold as Asondaki returned to the inn to pack this things. Gold, the color of the white man's heart, the white man's god.

"I have forgiven your rudeness, Dakin," Lasselle said when his former employee appeared before him that afternoon, leather satchel in hand and wearing the *metis* coat. A fire sputtered in the grate of the company's small counting house. These white men never learn, Asondaki thought wearily, smelling the acrid smoke of green applewood.

Lasselle continued. "I am afraid there is a small problem. There have been some sizable reverses in the company's fortunes. The American laws, the customs—Americans do not honor debts, and I have extended credit very freely. Lasselle, Marchal, and Fortin is taking many debt cases to law."

Asondaki looked into the jowly, flaccid face, as apprehension fluttered its small wings in the back of his mind.

"You left your money with me," Lasselle said, "and we agreed to put it out and earn interest for you in the expansion of the company. The British and Indian troubles have destroyed our trade. I deeply regret that. . ." apprehension became a bird in flight, pushing against Asondaki's chest, "there is no money. I do not have enough to pay my own agents' salaries here."

Asondaki, astonished, did not doubt the truth of what Lasselle had said. But there was something wrong here. "There were other investors," he said. "Men who reinvested their wages. You have found ways to pay them?"

Lasselle ran his tongue over his lips and drummed rapidly on the desk with his ring finger. "Ahh, I was able to do that in some cases."

"Most cases, I expect."

Silence.

"I understand. If there was not enough to go around, or even to conveniently spare, let the *sauvage* wait. Is that it?"

Lasselle arose from his leather chair and put up a defensive hand. "Perhaps next year, after the lawsuits are settled. Wait! Perhaps I could squeeze out of ready cash one year of your wages. . ."

"And if I should bring a lawsuit myself?" He knew the answer to his own question. When had an Indian won a case in an Indiana territorial court? "Give me the money."

Lasselle stood up and took it out of the drawer, as if it had been prepared in advance to "settle the affair." Asondaki pocketed it. Then he turned to Lasselle and before the other man could offer any resistance, delivered a strong, decisive punch to his flabby chin.

It was a very un-Indian gesture. He had never, of course, heard of his McClure grandfather, but some gene in him must have transmitted ancestral memory, because he experienced as much satisfaction in knocking Hyacinthe Lasselle unconscious on that floor as ever McClure the Fist had in any village boxing ring in the north of Ireland. Asondaki smiled broadly as he left the counting house.

"I did not know myself for a long time," Asondaki told Swiftly Running Feet as he held her in his arms in the winter lodge. "In Baton Rouge there was an idiot boy, a sad white child who constantly tore at his own flesh, who had to be kept in restraints because he would gash at his arms, bite his legs, crying all the while. I was as that one, ripping at my true self. I was two people, and I thought it was my red man's self I hated, my white being I craved to realize. But the white man's creed of loving gold is as false and empty and full of vermin as last year's birdnest. Fortin tried always for the first chance, Lasselle took the main chance. But I must now find the Indian way, of the righteous chance."

And Swiftly Running Feet was glad to have the West Wind's Child beneath her roof and in her arms again. She was, nevertheless, not surprised to see him blow away from her at the time of freezing water to the camp of the Son of the Future, War-chief Tecumseh.

A group of young, tattooed Miamis with colorful turbans, Shawnees in wool shirts and leggings and even Menominee in buffalo robes from far-away Wisconsin sat around the campfire of Tenskwatawa at Tippecanoe. Asondaki, clean shaven again, sat next to the sons of his uncle Hidden Panther in the "House of the Stranger," with its beams carved with the great bears and hawks of Indian religion.

"The great horned serpent lives in the waters about us," said the Prophet Tenskwatawa, leaning toward the fire. "We know he was killed by our ancestors, but his pieces have come together and threaten our existence today. A little of him is in every white man." He squinted in the firelight. Some evil had befallen one of his eyes, Asondaki noted. Asondaki was seeing for the first time this remarkable man. Five years ago, the story was, on the point of death the Prophet had experienced a vision. In it he was carried to a mountain top and allowed to view the wide, fertile hunting fields of heaven, reserved only for those who lived clean lives of Indian purity. Since then he had preached to all tribes to forsake the evil white men's ways and return to the habits of their fathers.

"The evil serpent lived in the east and from his vomit one night emerged the white men, hatched like maggots in its foulness. They came to us and brought this foulness with them, teaching us their promiscuity, the drinking of their vile poison liquor. Because they were selfish we too, the brothers of the sun and wind, began to hoard our goods, to hide our gunpowder and food. They sowed dissension among us so brother spends his time in argument with brother instead of in the noble hunt." The aromatic smell of kinnikinnick herbs, sumac and dogwood bark, floated in the air.

"The Father of Life condemns the white man's ways. Give up your trade goods. Eat your beans and pumpkins only. And purify yourselves spiritually. You must all forsake your harlots, quit giving your daughters in prostitution. And the children of your mixed unions must be driven out." He looked up and his good eye surveyed each face about the campfire. Suddenly his eyes fixed on Asondaki. Ah, so his cousins, always jealous of Hidden Panther's love, had sung their sad song about him upon the wind and its sighing had reached the Prophet.

But Asondaki remained calm. He knew that his actions were dangerous, that the Prophet had executed Indians who had lived with whites, yet he felt strong and sure. "I have forsaken the white man's ways. Denied my own father. And as for the life of the *metis*. . ." he took his coat off and flung it out of the door of the council house. He pulled a buffalo robe about him. "Say on," he said to the Prophet, and all about the fire, even his cousins, nodded in affirmation.

That night, as he slept in the winter hut, he thought of the Prophet's message. Much that he saw earlier in the day was ridiculous, the joy-dancing, the "confessing of sins" and ritual handshaking with the Prophet-pope, the long strings of rosary-like beans he made them pull through their fingers like the priest in Vicennes did. But much was not silly. Tenskwatawa said that in the purity of Indian manhood there was spiritual strength, and Asondaki had rediscovered that truth. And that the way of the white man was as rotten as a bad turkey egg—that, surely, he if anybody should know. Was anything to be gained by staying with these leaders? Tomorrow he would test the validity of the new Indian movement when he met the Prophet's brother, Tecumseh.

Snow fell silently on a windless afternoon onto low-bending pine branches outside the House of the Stranger. Inside keen eyes were intently fastened on the tall, craggy-faced Shawnee some came hundreds of miles to hear.

"Brothers! Governor Harrison is preparing to survey the lands where our fathers hunted to give them to the white settlers. When he first took these lands in the Ft. Wayne Treaty, we challenged him at Vincennes, telling him to step no farther along this path. He sent us messages with fair words but did nothing, no more than the child whose grandmother calls him when he does not wish to come in from play. Alone, we are few. Around our meager campfires, we mourn and murmur. The hunting land of this great land of lakes has now been swallowed into the craw of the white man and slowly, slowly he digests it, leaving us nothing. The sun will rise one day soon and all will be gone."

Fox looked at Sac, Piankashaw at Miami, and heads nodded. The Indian leader continued. "We are in a good position here. The British send their supply trains to us. Our own cornfields loaded our laps this winter with good store of corn. No one need go hungry who comes to join the united tribes. Soon I think we will rise and come together, from all the areas of the Northern Lakes to Father of Waters and even beyond, to the Missouri. Like the ashes of a scattered campfire, we will jump together to rebuild the sacred fires for ourselves." Loud grunts punctuated the last words. "I see a great battle, fought by all the northern tribes. And, from the South, the Creeks, the Choctaws,

Chickasaws, all the sons of the Great Father will rise and throw the white man's yoke off. Our guns, our drums, our war cries will sound as one voice which must be listened to. No further! Keep your promises! Leave the rest of these lands to us. The Indian people are strong and deadly and will not be flung aside like children's toy babies. It is a lesson they will learn with the blood of their young men."

But after the others left, satisfaction written on their faces, Asondaki Alamelonda remained. Years of dealing with all varieties of men made him bold. "I have lived in many white men's cities. They are as the mice of the field the wolf hunts after a mild winter. Hundreds, no thousands, the wolf may eat and when he thinks all are gone, a thousand more come into that one field as if from nowhere."

"Well then, there are only more to eat," Tecumseh said without smiling. "And yet my Miami brother, for so you call yourself, you have some reason. Perhaps," his voice grew very low, "we may never drive them back. The water that flows over Niagara of the Six Nations does not climb back up again; neither may we dam it. But if we fight and show ourselves men, we may keep a large quiet pool to ourselves. We may draw a line with our lives that may preserve our way of life. Otherwise. . ." with his feet he kicked sand onto the campfire.

"You may die."

"If the Master of Life decrees. But what I say will never die because it is truth. We must have our due. If we win a victory, the drums will carry the message all across the desert to the shining sea of the West. Never again can a white governor, or even the Great White Father in Washington steal without recompensing us fairly." Tecumseh turned and left abruptly. A small flicker of the fire was left. Asondaki fixed it to burn all night to symbolize the "eternal fire" the Prophet wished always to burn to show the Indian life force. Then he left the council lodge into the soft, heavy silence of a world clad in a thick robe of snow.

Chapter XLIII

Catherine McClure watched that same heavy snowfall finally melt as she looked from the window of the Orchard Family dwelling at the Shaker village in late February. Water peppered off the roof and dripped onto the ground, melting a little line through the ice under her window. It would be a slippery day, she thought, grateful that her "gift" called for her to work a treadle loom in the weaving room instead of milking cows or working in the herb shop down the road.

The bespectacled eyes of Sister Aspasia Bunting were on her, gently reproving. "Morning silence" was supposed to be for prayer only, not for wool-gathering or looking outside. Mary McClure sat across the room on her straight-backed chair with her eyes closed, clearly walking the shores of Gennesaret, as she should be. Catherine closed her eyes, and eased into the mellow, comforting silence. Her mind reached out to contact the Father-Mother, as the Shakers called God, and the satisfaction and joy she felt ever since she came here settled over her. She prayed in silence.

A bell rang. It was time to change the beds. The four women in the "retiring room" rose as one, and almost like dancers glided forward to pull off bottom and top sheets from their sparse cots and fold them, arms outstretched, before placing them at the foot of the bed. They would remake the beds with fresh, impeccably woven linen and then go to the men's family home next door to make their beds.

This was a favorite time of the day for Catherine. She admired the cleanness, the spareness of the useful, lovingly wrought pedestal tables and ladder-back chairs, the simple, exquisite coverlets. It was this neatness that attracted her the most, the order, the denial of confusing clutter and extraneous detail which could be seen in the finely-joined floor and hewn log walls. In the simplicity and surrender of the Shaker village she found the security she had sought for so long, and she felt oddly akin to those chairs—straight, upright, undemanding, and undemanded of.

As Catherine walked down the steps she smiled a little. Her mood shifted slightly, and she wondered if perhaps she would see one of the brothers and could give him just the hint of a disconcerting smile, one she would later deny if asked about it by the eldress. Smiling at the men wasn't allowed, any more than passing them on the stair or talking to them without a sister present. What was it about her that wanted to provoke this system even though she respected, no, loved the piety and tranquillity it brought her?

Mary felt no need to go in one minute late to the evening meeting, or to cough in the fifteen minute "broad grace" before the morning meal. It was as if, frozen in the peace and order of the place, Catherine sometimes wondered if she even existed. Breaking some tiny rule nobody else broke somehow made her know she was still alive as an individual, as well as a communal soul.

Through the cornmeal-mush snow, the little troupe of Shaker women, led by middle-aged, anemic Sister Aspasia Bunting, marched to the West Family home for men. No sign of the brothers, of course. They had gone to empty the slops, make the fires, shovel the paths, and care for the animals. The women would tidy the men's beds, hanging their clothing and chairs on the high rails about the room so they could sweep. As they flipped sheets high in the air to shake out any wrinkle that dared to appear, Catherine thought of the day's routine, which she now knew well. First was this symbolic sweeping time. Mother Ann had once said to a girl wielding a broom, "I say, sweep clean." The sisters believed that they must sweep every atom of dust away, not only from the scrubbed boards of the room, but from the bottom of the heart as well.

Next was a silent meditation and breakfast with the sexes separated. All food must be consumed, crumbs swept up, and knife and fork crossed neatly when you were done. Then, the daily, holy work, each giving to the Lord and the community from his own "gift." Dinner, more work, and a six o'clock supper followed, with all the brethren and sisters sitting straight as beech saplings. The day finished with a retiring time for silent prayer, and finally the evening meeting.

Which tonight would be—Catherine's heart fell as she fought demons of confusion which threatened to intrude on her peace. Reverend Rob McClaren was coming out with a large group from Vincennes. He would be debating Elder McNutt, and her parents would be in the crowd.

Mary was living in dread of this night. She suspected her father and mother and Jim would be here, pleading and crying. Catherine was merely angry. Why was she not being allowed to choose her own way? Her mouth tightened in a frown. She had selected this "narrow road" and it pleased her. Every day she watched Eldress Elsbeth in admiration. She saw her respected by men, exerting temporal and spiritual leadership, admitting young orphans left to the group, handling the contracts by which those who sought the final affiliation gave up all temporal property to the community. The head eldress made and enforced laws, bought and sold and judged as well, better really, than William Henry Harrison. And there were other women with power here—the deaconesses and trustees who made judgments for the group. It had been the women who decided recently to welcome Indian visitors and who treated them fairly and fed them. It was they who would be responsible for organizing the debate with Rob McClaren.

Why should she care whether Reverend Rob came or not, Catherine thought, as she set the last chair on its proper wall peg with some vehemence and finished the cleanup in this men's sector. Neither Rob, nor her parents would make her change her mind. There was nothing for her at the farm, nothing real. She had found the Pearl of Great Price and was following the Lord's injunction to sell all for it. Wasn't that what she had been taught by them all anyway? She turned to join the line of marchers from the room and against her will found herself wondering exactly what Rob McClaren would actually say now that he had come all the way from Kentucky to drive out "the antichrist."

There must have been fifty or sixty visitors from Vincennes who, when the evening meeting began, stomped slush from their feet and seated themselves along the narrow benches in the meeting hall. They had given the Devil his due to traverse the almost impassable roads, but they were willing to start early and pull wagon wheels out of the muck. Many had lost relatives to the "gathering family" and were hoping to reclaim them with this new ploy.

Most of the new novitiates, unlike Catherine and Mary, still lived at home but were preparing to leave and give over all to the community of the faithful, the saved in the Second Appearing of Christ on Earth. The cousins followed the rest of the women into the meeting hall, this time behind Eldress Elsbeth.

During the first Shaker hymn Catherine allowed her eyes to stray to the crowd. Sure enough, there were her Uncle James Scott, Aunt Jenny, young John Robert and Mary's family just as she had feared. And beyond them. . . Catherine gasped involuntarily. Mary looked sideways at her, then her eyes followed Catherine's to the crowd.

There, Catherine saw, were her parents and sisters Polly and Margit, but who were the two men beside them? Samuel Emison and John Hogue. Seeing them all there jerked her, as if she had just awakened into an unpleasant world of glaring morning light, filled with strangers staring down at her. She felt as if she were standing in her chemise before them, particularly the huge, blonde woodsman. She was suddenly glad that the hymn called for some Shaker hand movements so she could cover her confusion.

Elder Lorenzo made a long, patient speech to these visitors from "the world." He spoke about the tenets of the church, Mother Ann's visions and the founding of a celibate community which was witnessing Christ's coming now. The Shakers nodded in satisfaction when he sat down and the Methodist minister stood up.

Reverend Rob's broad, decent face looked out at the crowd, and Catherine's memory transported her to Big Bend, when she had found her faith in the first place, in spite of all the people jerking on the ground and frothing at the mouth. "My friends, I have been asked tonight to tell you why I think Shakerism is an apostasy, why it does great harm to the Church and the cause of salvation," he said. Quietly, his voice at times so low one had to strain to hear it, he said that it was blasphemy to speak of Mother Ann as equal to Christ, to pretend the Second Coming was on earth when the Biblical signs were not fulfilled. He condemned the Shakers for seducing young people to leave parents and friends who loved them and whose hearts were broken. The audience from Vincennes was still; some of the younger "gathering family" members began to squirm uncomfortably. But Sister Elsbeth and Brother Lorenzo's heads were held high.

Everywhere the Church was assailed, and as it was persecuted, they knew, it grew. The Bible prophesied that they who believe would suffer for righteousness' sake.

Rob McClaren went on, cogently, clearly arguing the Shaker tenets down one by one until he came to what he most wanted to say. "Worst, though," he said, his hands reaching out to the Shakers on the benches, "is the idea of turnin' from the world. Livin' as a community of believers in retreat. Where do you think the Lord of life lived and taught? Not in his own comfortable little village, sittin' on pretty chairs, stokin' the fires and eatin' Shaker lemon pie.

"You're arguin' that you take care of the orphans and Indians and infirm who come to your doors, but I say to you that 'tisn't at our own doors that the work of salvation must be done. It is on the roadsides of life that the Christ went; it is there He lives, where the lonely and hungry are witherin' and droppin', where the slaves of sin falter and die, alone and unhelped. Go out to them where they are and put out your hand. And you will find that the Christ of the roadside will fill that hand up with blessings and healings for others, 'stead of smug satisfaction that calls itself prayer, and stay-at-home comfort that calls itself piety."

John Hogue, his lean, long frame clad in a buffalo coat against the cold, found Catherine after the meeting. She could see her father, mother, and sisters standing several paces off, watching.

"So there's a truce among all your old enemies, John," she said scornfully. "And you've all joined against me, wolves in a pack." He came to her, took her hand before she could withdraw it.

"Cathy. . ." The word, tenderly said, moved her. No one but John called her that. He had asked her name that first day by the schoolhouse. When she told him, he shortened it that way, drawing it out, as if he loved the sweetness of it.

"John, I have chosen what I want. Say no more to me. My pa is a hypocrite to preach freedom for men and deny me the right to practice it. And you a worse one to join with the man who forbids us to meet."

He still held her hand, looking down at her, intently.

She wanted to explain her need to make her own way in life, the appeal of the contentment and security here. But "It is God's will," was all she could think of to say.

"Is that it? All I know is the Indians took and kilt m' ma an' pa and preacher said 'twas the will o' God. Now the Shakers took you and you say 'twas His will. I think people are doin' a lot o' talkin' for Him these days, and sometimes they seem to get Him confused with the Devil. If Tecumseh comes down and surprises us all and takes a hunnerd scalps, I 'spect some damn fool'll say 'tis the will o' the Lord."

She slapped his face smartly and turned on her heel, regretting it even before she reached the door of her family home. His voice rang after her, and she put her hands over her ears. But even when she closed her eyes she could not shut out his pained, bewildered face. It was the face of a little boy who has loved too much and lost too often. She wondered that she could hurt him even more, and thought herself a poor Christian and a poorer Shaker yet.

Samuel Emison had requested a private interview with Mary McClure. Sister Bunting led him to a small room off the kitchen and then, bundling her shawl against the cold, went to stand under the eaves outside the building.

In the village the wind howled and freezing rain congealed on the clattering branches of the sycamore and poplar trees. Mary looked wide-eyed at Sam Emison. She had not answered his letters, had not seen him once during these long months. "It was nice of the elders to offer you folks sleepin' rooms and breakfast on the morn," she said, walking about with her back turned to him. She wore the winter blue dress of the Shakers topped with a large white collar. An unadorned cap hid hair the color of goldenrod.

"Why didn't you say goodbye?" Sam asked her, in an anguished voice.

"I couldn't," she said, standing by a small window, looking out.

"Didn't I deserve at least that?" She turned suddenly, her mouth set, and looked evenly at him.

"Yes. But something pulled me, something stronger than my feelings for you. I didn't think you'd understand. Or Ma, or Pa." She had seen John and Janie McClure earlier, told them quietly of her determination to stay with her commitment.

"I am sorry," she went on. "These people have given me salvation. . ."

He grabbed her arms, moving his head violently from side to side so hard his brown curls shook. "No!" he spat out.

She looked at him in amazement. She never heard him raise his voice, never saw him as anything but the perfect gentleman.

"Listen to me, Mary. I have loved you ever since we played together in the meadows in Kentucky. Yours was one of the first names I knew. I don't remember when I didn't love you. I can't let you go. . ." Some quiet Shaker, alarmed at the sound of his voice, opened the door a crack. Sam slammed it shut it with his foot and shouted out in desperation, "Leave us alone for God's sake for a half an hour." He wedged one of the chairs under the brass knob and walked to her again.

He put his arms around her and drew her close. "Tell me that you don't think of me in the night. That you don't wish for me, and this. . ." he kissed her lips, pulled back her Shaker cap, let her hair flow free, kissed her again. At first she was limp in his arms, then she began to return his kisses ardently, her lips alive to his.

Suddenly she pulled back. "No, no. You are tempting me. I have promised to give up the loves of the flesh. . ." He would not release her wrists, tried to pull her to him again.

"You were born to love, to bear and mother children. To deny that is to deny the life God Himself gave you."

Bursting into tears, she pulled the chair from the knob, opened the door and ran from the room. He threw a beautifully-wrought wooden candlestick against the door and then, ashamed of himself, left.

The anxious faces of Jenny and James Scott, and John and Janie McClure surrounded Sam Emison. "It is no use. If I didn't know better I'd say she was bewitched. That we should go get Old Man Granger to set us an unhexing spell or two."

"That won't help," Jenny Scott murmured, and turned from the group.

Jim McClure came up, his eyes cool. "Mebbe we should kidnap the both o' 'em. I ast the Shaker pope if they was holdin' them here by force and he said no one was kept here against their will."

" 'Tis true, I think," John McClure said sadly.

"I don't think they even know what their will is anymore," Sam Emison told them bitterly and excused himself to go to his small, prim room and sit by the spare rope bed. Finally, in utter exhaustion, he lay back. He went to sleep with his clothes on, knowing that somewhere within the same village the love of his life slept also, separated from him now by a good deal more than a pious collection of buildings sitting on a few hundred yards of Wabash valley muckland.

Chapter XLIV

In that spring after the visit to the Shaker Village, Jenny Scott often stood at the window of the farmhouse, watching storms blow their way into the Wabash valley. Already they were calling it the "year of the waters."

The bluff where the Scott home stood was high above the river, and timber had been cut in the lowland so corn could grow. Jenny watched the waters churning their yellow-brown course, inching higher and higher over last year's corn stubs and thistle tops. Each day in May a few more rows were covered as the Wabash spilled over its banks, until finally one day just before spring planting was supposed to begin, the entire bottomland was a lake.

When the Scotts first arrived in Indiana, Jenny had loved this high hill. Beneath it the placid Wabash ribboned its course like a wide, pleasant smile on the face of the countryside. But recently, the roaring waters seemed turgid, destructive.

"A swamp, that's what it is," she said. John Robert, putting firewood in the paneled firebox beside the hearth, looked up. But his mother went on staring for long moments at the river. He went out again and came in with more logs.

"Marguerite always said miasma comes out of swamps," Jenny muttered, holding the curtain back so she could see clearly. "The girls are upriver and the Shaking Quakers have them." Something in her tone made her son drop the logs at the door with a clatter and come to her.

"Ma. . ." his dark-eyed, serious face looked up at her. At ten, he was almost as tall as she was. From the time he was a baby his self-possession was remarkable. His grandmothers had both called him the "wise old soul."

"So much pain," his mother muttered, seeming not to notice him. She looked at the woven curtain, stared at its hem. "George won't speak to anybody at all, John's dyin' a little at a time. The Indian Prophet says our time has come, that our blood will wet the earth. He says the red men will walk free and take back their lands with violent hands because of what we've done to them. It is the time of reckoning, the Prophet says. See, John Robert, the waters've reached the foot of the bluff."

"They won't come up here, Ma." Only Fort Knox, across the way, stood higher. But of course his mother may have had other fears; she knew the fort was undermanned and vulnerable. Only last year a British spy had sneaked into to the fort. The Scotts were exposed like turkeys in a tree if Tecumseh came down the river and took the fort. They would be the first family to be massacred. Perhaps that was the reason for the dullness in her voice.

"Will said Mrs. Hannah Jane Green tried to run from the Delawares near Kittanning. She was nine months gone, about to start her labor. They caught her and cut her womb open. Pulled out the babe and stabbed and roasted it before her eyes. She could see it as she bled to death. . ."

"Ma, don't. . ." John Robert said, horrified. But she would not stop.

"At Gnadenhutten in Ohio country the militia came 'pon innocent Indian famblies and scalped the people live. Put stakes through their eyes. . ." Her voice was weak and odd. She went to her darning basket and picked up a large quilting needle. Suddenly she jerked down the curtain and, pulling a chair to the window, sat down with the curtain across her lap.

John Robert went to get his father, who was helping load supplies at the fort in case settlers should have to shelter in it.

"Jenny girl, are you afraid?" James Scott asked, kneeling before her chair and taking her hands in his. She shook her head imperceptibly, and did not look at him, nor at the concerned son who stood in the shadows of the firelight behind his father. "At Dada's wake, the Savage said that pain was the testing of the gods," she said.

Her eyes no longer seemed to see the flooding land. "There are torches in the swamp, and drums," she said. Her husband and son watched her bend her head over the curtains, and taking out the needle, begin to unravel the hem, pulling down the fine linen threads and dropping them onto the polished boards of the floor. "I'm tired of fighting, Marguerite," she said.

James Scott noticed a letter by her foot. He picked it up and scanned it; it was addressed to him anyway. It had come just this morning from the governor in Vincennes, with a copy to William McClure. Ish was in a jail in Missouri Territory. He had been caught gathering information for the Spanish government.

Within an hour Will McClure was at the Scott house, urgently discussing the letter with James Scott. But when Will left to continue the discussion with his brothers, Jenny did not speak to him or to anyone else. Jenny Scott had retreated from the swamps. She spoke only to herself, and the scattering of threads on the floor became a pile as she undid every piece of linen in the house her mother had ever woven.

"So he is found," George McClure remarked. He stood beside the four-foot treadle loom James Scott had crafted for Jean. It was the same loom on which Jean had taught Catherine to weave and to develop the skill she now employed for the benefit of the Shakers.

"Had been goin' and comin' along the Santa Fe trail as a trader, snoopin' into every military installation the Americans have in the west. He has took him a wife from among the Osage Indians and travelled with the tribe some." Will had come directly from the Scotts' to George's house.

"Why are you telling me?" George's voice was cold. He really had nothing to say to these brothers of his.

"Arlen Stringfellow was your friend. They will still try Ish for his murder."

"I know."

"And we said the fambly would handle him. I have a commission signed by the president, and Harrison has agreed we can go."

"Dan'l can go. . ."

William was beginning to grow irritated. "Dan'l is on the committee they're gettin' up to defend Vincennes. He's still tryin' to find out whether it's true the Injeeans are dividin' up by tribes to attack Detroit, Louisville, Cincinnati. He cain't go. . ."

George's anger rose. "It's true Tecumseh is a real enemy, but Harrison is boiling the pot of war hysteria on a hot fire. Anyone who suggests calm thinking is called a traitor! Why, he had the audacity to accuse Badollet and me of being in touch with Tecumseh, of egging Tecumseh on to get at him."

Will sighed. He was weary of politics. "John is too ill to go. So it has to be us that go get Ish. You and me."

George looked at his brother and saw how he had aged. The back of his sunburned neck was as grooved as an old hunting pouch, his waving hair almost white. The thought of journeying with him—going onto the road for one, perhaps two months, with this brother he had never learned to like, let alone respect—was awful.

"So be it. We leave the first of the week." He took Will to the door. He would need to find his young sons to arrange for them to manage the farm. Pity the older ones in his family were all daughters. This year the spring planting would have to be done without him some way or another. A sudden thought hit him.

"Why are we really going if all we will do is bring him back to stand trial?"

Will swung into his saddle. "I don't want t' be with you when you see the look in Jenny's eyes. She's like a corpse a resurrectionist brought out of a graveyard. We got to put him away so she don't wait all the time to hear of his crimes." He patted his horse to calm it. The smell of rain was in the air again. "Yet Ish may never make it back here to stand trial. If I know him, he'll try to escape first chance he gits." He patted the old white and yellow powder horn at his side. "I hope he does. I've downed many a vicious animal on the run and I wouldn't mind tryin' it again. No one ever asked to die more." He gave a slight wave of his hand and rode off through the beginnings of a drizzling rain. George watched him grow smaller and smaller until he rounded the bend by the huge German barn on John's property, and was out of sight.

All was confusion at the Shaker village as sisters and brethren packed up in a warm spell toward the end of June. They were beginning a flight from Indian troubles on the Wabash. The novitiates were being sent to Ohio, but before they left, their living unit must be carefully closed down. Women in blue work dresses scoured floors with soft soap suds and brooms, sending little lines of bubbles running across the boards. On the road, still muddy from the retreating waters, black and white cattle bellowed and bumped shoulders as they were herded on their way south. Men called to each other as they sledged bags of flour and bushels of corn to send on ahead to provide for the needs of the novitiates while they would be at the mother community.

Catherine McClure sat in the weaving room. She was supposed to be packing up the fly-shuttle loom, but instead she was hurriedly scrawling a letter. It said:

Dear John:

I did not think I would ever be writing this letter. Things have changed so much for us here, and I am afraid.

It all started with the visit a couple of months ago. After that Mary took to pondering. She could not get Sam'l's anger out of her mind and began to think she'd ruined his life. So she got confused about what her Christian duty really was.

Eldress Elsbeth was very sweet when Mary spoke to her about her spiritual quandry. She told her to pray that the Devil didn't lead her into the sin of conkoopisence—lustful thinking. Said that foulness must be turned from. But when Mary returned in two weeks to say that she still wondered if she shouldn't leave, the sister was firmer. She said of course they would not try to stay her if she wished to leave, but that she would be leaving behind her immortal soul. Leaving the community of righteousness for the life of a sinner. Betraying the Lord like Judas.

Judas, mind you. That made me angry. It went on so long, and so quietly, I began to see it as a suttile mesemerism. All the time they been at her, smiling and praying and holding "redemption" meetings for her and insisting she is damning herself. Somewhere in the midst of all that "Christian perswasion" Mary gave up. She's snared like an animal in her own little religious trap.

It's sickened me to see all the smiling, simpering, and praying to get her to stay. If you want to leave, this "Shaker love" turns cold as fast as hot maple syrup thrown on the snow.

I can't respect this any more after what I've seen and I can't leave Mary. She's as frightened and pityful as a ten-year-old. It's as if she's hipnotised. If they get us into the wagons and over into Ohio, I'm afraid she'll never be able to make a break. Please, John, forget the quarrels we've had. I didn't mean what I said in the oak grove, or out here either. We'll speak of that later. I'm too humilyatted to write to my parents. I thought I was finding independence and what I found was a form of mental slavery—well almost that. Come for us in a wagon. The Shakers won't send us away until all is in perfect order, but that can't take more than a few days.

Cathy

She stood and firmly folded the letter, addressing it boldly on the front. Then she left by a back door and walked through the woods to a farmhouse a mile away. Soon the letter was on its way to John Hogue in the hands of a boy on a large draft horse. Then and only then did Catherine return to begin packing up the loom. When she was finished, she told herself, she would put together the few small items she called her own and be ready to leave on a moment's notice.

"It don't look like anyone much is scared of the Injeean attack," Jackie McClure said to Adahbelle as they looked out the small window of her room at Beckes's Inn onto the street. Below them traders lugged heavy loads of winter wheat and apples in handcarts to the docks to put on barges, and lawyers in neat, lapelled coats and tight trousers strolled easily toward their offices.

"Tecumseh's told Harrison he's a-gonna come up and make friends, wipe away all the lies people have told the gov'nor 'bout him, so some folks are sayin' there may be peace yet," Adahbelle said.

"He's no fool. Gettin' ready to move down on us, and bringin' his women and children to make it look peaceful. They say he's got two thousand Indians, men from every tribe in the West, up there at Prophetstown ready to move." Jack McClure was in poor spirits today, his arm absently about his love, and his mind far away. Finally he said, "Adahbelle, they want me to join the militia. Maybe take up a commission."

The girl looked up into his face. "Jackie Dee, I'm jest so glad fer ye. Ye'll have to do it."

He coughed and looked away. "It's not for me. . ."

She stamped her foot. "No! 'Tis for you. 'Tis time for you to be the gent'man God intended you for. Yer pa has given you four hundred acres and you will buy more and be a rich man. And rich men go to war out here. What in the creation are ye afeard of?"

He refused to meet her angry eyes and his voice was raised to an unnaturally high pitch. "I don't know. It's jest that when my father wants me to do somethin', I hate doin' it. I've never known why. Its just that I don't want to commit myself. To take life seriously scares the britches off me. Mebbe I'm just afraid of fightin'. Mebbe I'm afraid of dyin'. Perhaps I'm a coward. It'd be an awful thing to admit. . ." He turned to her, anxious, perspiring.

"I know you ain't, Jackie Dee. An' I want you to do this. Go and be a sojer. It's the right thing to do. We cain't let these Injeeans slaughter us all in our beds and you're. . ."

Jackie turned brutally to her, grabbed her arm. The small, apple-shaped birthmark on his face showed beet-red. "Who are you to say? Will you design my life? Go on and run your bar and leave me. . ."

She turned and bolted from the room and he heard her vomiting in the basin in the closet outside. Finally she returned and sat beside him, chalky white. He was surprised and chagrined. "Adahbelle, did I do that to you? I'm so sorry. . ."

" 'Tain't nothin' Jackie Dee. You didn't do it." He took her hands and looked into her face. He hadn't really noticed her lately. She had grown more thin and pale than usual, lost weight.

"You haven't been eatin' right. I do recall that. What is it. . ."

"Nothin'. I jest don't hold my victuals down too well." The sound of children chasing each other and occasional horses neighing came in the open window. Filtering up from below were taproom noises, laughter rising and falling, and the sound of chairs scraping on the floor.

"How often have you been losin' your dinner?" he asked. But before she could answer the truth dawned on him and he said, "My God. Can it be true?"

She turned her head from him and nodded. The late afternoon sunlight shone through the window onto her strong profile, the beautiful neck that reminded him of a swan's, the strong, thin body in a faded, buff-colored calico dress and bar-girl's apron. "I tried all the herbs. This time they didn't work. Not even periwinkle. . ."

He took her in his arms. "My dearest one. . ." They kissed for a long moment.

He withdrew and kissed her neck. After a while he said, "We must be married right away." She pulled from him.

"No, no!" she all but shouted. " 'Twouldn't do. We knew that all along. Our love was enough, I never asted for more." She pleaded that he was destined for someone of the "better sort," that the marriage would never be accepted in the town, that it would break his parents' heart. But something new, firm, was growing in him, and he would not listen.

"We'll certify the marriage at the Justice's tomorrow. Then I'll pick you up the next day at your grandfather's and we will go to the preacher's."

He talked longer and kissed her more, and finally she quit protesting and put her head on his shoulder. She smiled sweetly and he knew he had pleased her. And when he left the inn, peace surrounded him like the summer twilight that was falling on the valley. Why had he held back from asking her before? Refused to think about what the outcome of their love would be? It was just what he wanted and he had not even known it. Marrying her now seemed the fulfillment of his life. Yes, he had noticed it lately, he was a better man because of her, as if gluing her strength onto his own poor, weak wood had produced one good, strong board. The thoughts about "class" were silly. This was still the frontier, although the folk of Vincennes sometimes forgot it. He would marry the woman he loved, and to the Devil with anyone who spoke against it. Fifty years from now he would still have her strength, her serenity to depend on. Let the gossipers get lost in Mammoth Cave for all he cared. For the first time in his life Jack McClure felt completely right about something he was doing.

The next day Jack picked Adahbelle up at the inn and took her to the magistrate's office. There, with what struck him as due modesty, she signed her willingness to marry him. Then he took her to her cabin and left her to prepare for the marriage.

With joy he arranged for the minister at Upper Indiana Church to marry them and hired a room for a little wedding supper at the Old Yellow. It would never do for the supper to be in the same tavern where she worked. And there must be music, he told himself, a fiddler and a flute. She would need a lovely new dress. He had never bought her much of anything but now he would make up for it. At Lasselle and Marchal's he picked out a white empire-cut gown and a hat with long yellow ribbons and put it on his bill, along with long white gloves and small, bleached leather shoes. When he emerged from the store at three o'clock, his father was waiting for him.

Dan'l McClure stood with his hat in his hand, looking shy and embarrassed. The magistrate, who now held the job Dan'l McClure had just left, must have just told him about the license, Jack thought. What would his father do? Jack was determined to go ahead and not even Dan'l McClure could stop that.

"I'm gettin' married, Pa," was all he said.

"I know."

"She is three months gone, but I love her and want to marry her anyways." There was anguish in his voice, but also the triumph of newly discovered courage and fidelity.

"I'd like to be there. Your ma won't come. She had hoped you'd marry the Elliott girl." Dan'l shrugged. He looked searchingly at Jack, trying to understand. "Let's go out and take the bride the things you've bought an'—I want to meet her granddad."

Jack continued to be surprised at his father's attitude. "You knew about us all along, didn't you, Pa."

"Yes, I knew."

"Why. . .?" He couldn't put it into words. Why didn't Elder McClure try to stop his son from living in immorality?

"Mebbe I've learned somethin' in the last few years. Mebbe people, even children, have to live their own lives and not be melted down and forced like bullet lead into molds they don't fit in. Mebbe it's God's job to mold their lives." His head hung low. " 'Sides, I can't throw any stones at you. I had my times too." His son looked at him in surprise.

Dan'l clapped him on the shoulder and they headed for their horses.

Jack drove by way of the river road on the hot July afternoon. "Posey escaped along here," Dan'l mused to himself in a voice heavy with sadness. Just two days ago a certain Captain Posey of the Fort Knox regulars had started an argument in his quarters and killed another soldier. Out of his head with drink and fear of apprehension, the murderer had come to the Scott's farm and forced them at gunpoint to feed him and stay up all night with him. Finally, he had fled when dawn came, stealing their horses. The shock of having a wild-eyed killer under her roof finally cracked Jenny's last, thin hold on reality, and she sat like a stone by her bed, knowing nothing, responding to no one. If only the matter of Ish could be brought to a close, it might bring her back. Perhaps Ish would see his mother, possibly even be repentant. Were his brothers making any progress toward finding him? Dan'l wondered.

"Stop, Pa, I want to pick Adahbelle some flowers," Jack shouted impulsively. He reined the horse and came back with his arms loaded with tiger lilies and black-eyed Susans. "There's the house, down that lane," he pointed.

The horses came to a halt by a rotting rowboat in the front yard and Jack tethered them to a locust tree. He bounded out and raced up the steps, saluting the grimacing cat's head on the doorpost. "The bridegroom cometh," he yelled.

Dan'l sat smiling. He looked about at the strange yard of the house, smelling the odors of sun-blanched sage and rosemary in the herb garden. Odd how things worked out, he thought. The girl at the inn outside Louisville so long ago had been a hired girl too. He walked about as the horses nosed for grass among the broken-down rummage of the yard, and he thought of the people in that inn and wondered where they all were now. What a long road they had all come! He visualized it as a long, fingerwoven hunting sash like he used to wear in Caintuck, stretching over mountains and hills and rivers. Each of them had had a separate quest. John and Will had wanted fortune; they had found it. George had wanted to satisfy his restless curiosity, and who knows if he had done that?

But he, Dan'l, had followed after the wilderness. He had looked so hard for it, but he had never really found it. This was, of course, because when you got to the wilderness, bringing all your settling parties, it suddenly wasn't wilderness any more. The sawyers and skidding teams, the mules and plows pushed all before them. The wilderness died so that neat fields of corn and wheat could wave in the wind, satisfying the eye of the prosperous plantation owner and the purse of the grain speculator in New Orleans. There had been a hundred, a thousand wildernesses in America and he had known many of them. They were all going, would go, as the giant Civilization shoved all the wild world into its insatiable, gaping mouth.

Yet there was a rudimentary strength in the new giant and the villages and settlements it was spawning all over the land. The Scotch-Irish, his people, Dan'l thought proudly, had midwifed so much of the civilization in America—Pennsylvania, Virginia, Kentucky, Tennessee and the South, and now the new Midwest with their restless spirit. His people had out-fought and out-connived and out-prayed all the others, and led them all into the wilderness, and their feisty individualism might, probably would, stamp the future forever.

But the Scotch-Irish were going on, heading west already. They said over the Mississippi there was wild, unknown land, soil so rich if you could break it with an axe you could put in a corn seed and it would shoot up higher'n a house. . . Oh yes. He laughed and thought of what his mother would say about that.

He became aware that Jack had been in the house a long time. That young whelp was supposed to have brought out Adahbelle and introduced her, but he had forgotten about his father. The two of them were billing and cooing inside—but no. Jackie Dee was suddenly at the door, pale and distraught, and his father bolted to his side.

"Pa." He was shaking.

"Jack, for God's sake, what is it?"

"She's gone."

"Gone? She ran away?" Why would she Adahbelle do that? The marriage was a good one for her.

Jack's voice was barely audible. "She's dead, Pa." Dan'l could not believe his ears. Behind Jack appeared the hulk of an old man whom Dan'l remembered seeing a time or two in town. The witch master, Retreat Granger. His voice was hollow and sad.

"She took to herself with a knitting needle whilst I was away. Hoped to be done with the babe thataway. Felt she'd done a bad thing. . ."

Jack sat on the wooden stoop, his head in his hands. He was in shock and

Dan'l looked searchingly, agonizingly at the old man.

"She bled to death. Nothin' I could do, for all my powers. 'Tweren't more'n a hour ago. . ."

Jackie Dee looked straight ahead. "Her face was white, bleached like no livin' thing I ever saw." He looked down painfully at the small slippers he still held in his hand.

The witch master stared at the back of Jack's head. "Like her ma, got herself in trouble. 'Twere writ in the heavens, like I said. She were a sweet youngun. Alwuz took good care o' me, saw to it m' clothes were washed, jowl 'n greens on the table, and put her head on m' knee if I got to pinin' too much."

Jack did not look at either one of them. "She did this for me. She was afraid she'd spoil my life, afraid I didn't want to be married to her. . ."

The old man, looking down at Jack, confronted his eyes squarely. "Don't be too sure o' that, young fella. Did you ever think she might not o' wanted to be married to you? She had fears and dreams o' her own, you know."

"I don't believe it," Jack McClure mumbled in a pained tone as he and his father headed back down the lane, but his voice had more of questioning than of assurance in it.

Chapter XLV

At Prophetstown, Asondaki watched a train of Indian families breaking camp. Potawatomi and Miami women with cradle boards on their backs loaded sledges with cooking pots and travelling tents. Dashing about their skirts, naked little children chased fat dogs or watched their brothers play with the hurling baskets and balls they loved. At the river, warriors loaded canoes. Tecumseh was preparing to travel south.

"Will he then attack the white men at Vincennes and the other towns?" Swiftly Running Feet asked her husband.

"By no means. He cannot do so even if he would. His confederation must include the Indians of the south to be successful, the Choctaws, Chickasaws, all those south of the Ohio. It is a great dream, and he must spend a few weeks in the land of the magnolia flowers." He thought briefly of that life, and all that he had gratefully left behind there.

"So why does he go?"

"Harrison has demanded that the Great Chief come to show his intent. But Tecumseh will go, not because the governor has demanded it, but to show the strength of the Indians in the Northwest before he goes to the southlands. Three, perhaps four hundred Indians will come into the streets of Vincennes. It will frighten the Frenchmen, I can tell you, as they lounge in their gardens, and startle the Americans in the gun and candy shops." He laughed a little, ruefully.

Swiftly Running Feet looked at the tomahawks, muskets, and ammunition that was going into the canoes. She shook her head uncertainly and walked with Asondaki toward the wigwams of the camp. There was new joy and hope in her movements these days. She and Asondaki awaited the child of their resurrected love, due when the pale winter moon shone.

"Then there will not be war at Vincennes," she ventured.

"Not unless the Great One sends home the women and children. No, he will wait, I think, until the tribes of the southern lands take up the war belt. Should they all respond, nothing is to stop a great battle that will shake the earth. This chief, these people, are angry, and their anger stretches across two hundred years."

The tall chief Tecumseh came from the woods, walking with dignity to take leave of his brother. The Prophet stood outside the Stranger's Lodge with some of his followers. Asondaki was struck by the difference in their looks as they stood talking, Tecumseh with his aquiline features and even dignity, the Prophet shorter in stature and unhandsome, at times quiet, at other times chattery and frenetic as a chipmunk.

"My husband, what if Harrison should not believe the strength the chieftain shows and he comes to us here?"

"That will not happen. Tenskwatawa the Prophet will not provoke it. He is not as much a fool as he sometimes looks. And Tecumseh is leaving many warriors here, too. Nevertheless, I am sending you to wait for the coming of the child back among the Potawatomis, beyond these conflicts. I have decided that I have given my help to Tecumseh, told him all I knew of the white men's ways and intents. I will wait until early winter when he returns with the great force of Indians, and then I will leave and come to you. My debt will be paid to my people and what happens then is in the hands of fate."

"Where will we go then?"

Asondaki's eyes seemed to look into the distance. "Beyond the Mississippi, where traders are finding furs and opening posts. I have contracted to buy some land in Missouri Territory. I will ask Lasselle again to give me what is mine. If he does not, we will take what we have and build it into much again."

They came to the door of the bark hut and bent to enter its dark interior. Swiftly Running Feet sat down carefully on a rug of white bear, very rare, from the far north, that her husband had obtained for her by trading. Asondaki touched her arm above the narrow bracelets that ringed it, stroked her smooth, brown cheek. "The vision bear told me long ago that I would seek long, find little, but he did not know," Asondaki told her. "Perhaps he was a lying Devil Bear. I found you. What greater could I find? I tried to discover which of my two sides, white or red was greatest and saw finally that the question was wrong. Does one ask which hand is strongest? Which foot runs fastest? A man is a whole. So the bear was wrong. I have found much, much indeed. I shall live as myself, learned of both people, a trader who can deal with both in perfect peace."

And he kissed her and put his hand on her stomach as she sat. "You have said the child moves now," he said seriously. "I will feel the young hunter's thrashings."

"He does not thrash so hard yet," she told him, laughing. They sat silent for a long moment, seeping in their contentment.

"There is one more trail I must follow before we turn our heads to the west," Asondaki said finally. "I must go and meet my father."

The group of Indian warriors floated down the Wabash, speaking peace and carrying muskets. They made a leisurely trip, stopping to camp with their women and children and allowing news of the journey to precede them to the white settlements. Word reached southern Indiana that ten thousand warriors might be on the way to join Tecumseh as he travelled, and nervousness akin to panic spread through villages and outlying areas of Indiana and Illinois. Harrison summoned the militia and called in the Fort Knox regulars to meet the threat. The regulars paraded through the streets of Vincennes sporting tight white trousers, snappy blue coatees, and tall shako hats with trim on them; the militiamen followed in linen trousers and military hunting shirts.

Fort Knox on the banks of the river was undermanned and open to attack. All of Indiana now knew that it was built in the wrong spot. James Scott took John Robert and Jenny, who knew neither day nor night, from the bluffs of the Wabash to join the Emison women in the "Fort Petticoat" stockade on Maria Creek. The McClures rebuilt an old fort from former Indian times on John Hogue's property and Hogue spent almost every waking moment for a week helping them stockade it.

As the Indians advanced toward Busseron Creek settlement on the Wabash, the Shakers launched their novitiates onto the road. Late afternoon skies darkened to clotted gray. Catherine McClure, brushing past sisters and brethren loading wagons sent by the Ohio community, went to find Mary, who sat weeping and reading the Bible in the end cart in the small train. As Catherine walked, she turned her head to glance up the road. Why had John Hogue not come? She had just about abandoned hope of a rescue, had even sent a begging, humiliating note to her father. But he had not arrived either. All had forgotten her. It was what she deserved.

She came to stand beside the wagon, looking up at her cousin. "Mary, we must leave. Now! We'll ride a ways with the train and then slip away."

"The Indians. . ." Mary protested, looking toward the woods. They would be two women alone in forests dotted with Shawnees and Potawatomis bent on blood revenge.

"We will be ahead of them."

"Sister Elsbeth. . ."

"None of the sisters and brothers have time to argue about the two lowliest novitiates leaving. They are absorbed in thinking about converting the Indians when they come. Let's leave *now*!"

Crying softly, Mary shook her head from side to side. "The wrath of the Lord is comin' on the community because of us who thought to fall away. The Injeeans are jest a few miles off and we must remain stalwart. 'Tis no time to desert the Elect. . ." Catherine climbed up beside Mary on the wagon seat and looked at her in exasperation. She had been this way for the last week, wracked with religious anxiety and guilt. God, you can't mean for faith to tie people in knots this way, Catherine raged. Mary was as fixed as a hitchin' post and just as wooden-headed.

Shaker men, grunting and sweating and not worrying now that they were brushing near the women, slung barrels of molasses and pickled pork into the back of the wagon, hurrying to complete the final loading before the never-ending rains should begin again.

"Get down I tell you," Catherine said with growing irritation. "I have our things in this little satchel. . ."

She stood up and began to pull her cousin by the arm. A few big drops of rain spattered the dust of the road; lightning rent the clouds just over the river.

"Let me go. This is a trial and temptation to prove my faith. Cat, you're Satan's tool." Catherine, frustrated beyond endurance, slapped Mary's face smartly. Then she too began to cry and they clung to each other.

"Go by yourself, Cat," Mary said.

"I can't leave you. I won't."

"I can't make m'self go, even though part o' me thinks I should. It'd be like turnin' against God. I'm afraid."

The horses were hitched. The wagon jolted to a start and moved down the road. But as the skies opened and drops fell all around like small piercing arrows, Catherine heard hoofbeats coming on the road behind. Before she had time to turn around, she was scooped up by the powerful arms of John Hogue, as Sam Emison leaped into the wagon and carried away the feebly protesting Mary to his horse. The rain pelted down, deadening all voices and shrouding the departing Shaker wagon train. Lightning split a tree nearby. Catherine, wrapped round with a blanket and holding on to the strong back of her lover, was aware that behind these two furiously dashing horses were two more shadowy riders. Her cousins Jim and Tom were bringing up the rear guard of this rescue party.

Sam Emison, taking no chance, held Mary tightly in front of him and covered her with his military cloak as the rain drenched them both. As they passed along the Bruceville Road the rain eased into a steady drizzle, and the thunder rumbled its way off toward the Ohio River. Sam's arms were tender as he held her, and finally she relaxed against him. The pewter buttons on his military hunting shirt felt cold and hard against her back, and she murmured a little, putting up her hand to move them and caress him at the same time.

Someday soon Sam Emison would explain the turmoil they went through to get to her. George McClure could not come for his daughter because he was in Missouri territory, Hogue had had to fortify the stockades for panicked settlers, and he, Jim, and Tom had to get passes to leave the Benjamin Parke Dragoons in the apprehensive city. But the other thing that he had to tell her could not wait.

"Mary, the reason your father did not come out to bring you home was that—he's lying ill, awfully ill in the house. His stomach is bleeding inside. We're going there now."

The girl cried out desperately and buried her face in the cloak as gentle rain fell around them both.

Tecumseh finally camped his warriors outside Vincennes and came into the town, where dragoon militiamen and U.S. army regulars bristled with muskets. The Shawnee chief appeared in the city, telling Harrison he would parley with him, but both sides must leave their weapons in camp, and so it was arranged.

Even as the fear of Tecumseh sent most of the settlers into terrified hiding, the McClures defied all the Indian danger to leave the stockades. They went to the bedside of the man who had headed the family through thirty years of troubles and who was now dying.

Mary was inconsolable. "Pa, I added to your pain 'cause I couldn't see what to do. Forgive me, Pa," she sobbed, her pretty face streaked and swollen with crying. Sam Emison took her from the room.

Margaret McClure brought her older children to say goodbye to their uncle. Robert was growing into a less-timid, red-haired man. He was in the Parke Dragoons, along with his brother Archibald. Elizabeth, newly married but still fiery-tempered was with them. They stood looking down at their uncle. John McClure, whose eyes had grown as dim as his father's in his last days, mistook this second son of Will's, Archy, for his own brother.

"Nice uniform, Will," John McClure said in a whisper, through his pain. "You fight Tecumseh." Curly-haired young Archy, who did look like a taller version of his father at nineteen, looked questioningly at his mother. "You alwuz did hate the Injeeans. Captain Jacobs. . ." John could manage no more. The young soldier nodded to the dying man just as if he himself were Will McClure.

Janie McClure knelt by her husband's side. For the past few days he had seemed to wander the many roads he had been on. He lived in his dazed way simultaneously as a young child in the garden with his mother in Dunleigh, as a young man racing down the roads with long-dead comrades in Cumberland County and as a slave-holder in Kentucky. Worst was the sea voyage, which he seemed to experience again last night. Janie and Jim McClure literally had to hold him in his bed. The wailing of the wind in the summer thunderstorm outside, the very one through which the young folk had ridden away from the Shakers, seemed to become for him the hurricane. His favorite dog Red howled at the clashing thunder and Janie had thoughts of banshees.

But now he lay quietly, the firelight shining on the scalp of his bald spots, his nose prominent above hollow, sunken cheeks. Dan'l held his hand. He had come alone, leaving Martha and his children who were not in the dragoons to help defend Hogue's fort, with Jean McClure and her children. It was awful to see your brothers and sisters grow old, Dan'l thought, with loved family traits etched upon their eroding faces. It was worse yet to see one of them die. They took with them a chunk of your life, of tenderness and pain and shared childhood and left a hollowness no one else could quite fill.

John began to moan and through the next hour drifted between pain and unconsciousness until he knew them no more. Red could not be restained, jumping toward the bed, whining, until finally Jim took him from the room. Gradually, as the night wore on, everyone except Janie and Dan'l drifted away to sleep a few hours in the beds upstairs or on the floor of the parlor.

Dan'l watched his sister-in-law as she sat in a small chair by the bed. She now held John's hand herself, would allow no one else to touch him. Her yet-handsome face was ravaged with complex emotions. Dan'l tried to read them: love, regret for lost opportunity, probably, and most certainly guilt. But stamped on her face and obvious in her hunched shoulders, and racked, sobbing body was real grief. If any of them in the family had ever doubted her love for his brother, they could not now. Mary, completely composed, returned with Sam Emison and sat on a little needlepoint chair in the corner of the room with her Bible open.

On the landing of the stairs, the grandmother clock John had bought Janie chimed four o'clock, in long, solemn notes which reverberated through the house. John McClure tried to sit up, and his lips moved. "He's trying to say something," Janie said, turning to Dan'l. She motioned to Mary to quickly find Jim and the other children.

Dan'l bent his head over his brother's face. John's children appeared and clustered about behind their mother and uncle at the bedside. Dan'l leaned closer still.

John McClure opened his eyes. "Dada, is it you?" John said quite loudly, and then added, with an odd, sure note in his voice, "I knew you was there all the time." And then he died.

Tecumseh conferred for about a week with Harrison, promising he would go to see the Great White Father in Washington when he returned from the South. He asked the governor to maintain the present state of affairs until he got back. Then, sending most of his warriors and the women and children home, he took a group of his men and travelled downriver into the Ohio and south, to gather support for a confederation of Indians that now reached from Canada to Missouri Territory.

It was in that very Missouri Territory, among tribes of Osages made restless by the influx of settlers from the Midwest and Tecumseh's militancy, that Will and George McClure sat around a campfire near the Mississippi River. While George roasted quail over the fire, his brother aimed a pistol at Ish Scott, tied up for the night.

"Well, Uncles, this is rare sport indeed, ain't it," Ish said, scraping at the dirt irritatedly with the hand which stuck out of the ropes. A sardonic smile was painted on his mouth, which was as small and bow-like as Jenny's.

"We like it almost as much as you," George McClure said, adding maple sugar to mush. "I'm a landed gentleman now, you know, and I thought I had put my days of long-hunting animals behind me." What he did not say was there was a secret satisfaction in knowing he could still track a coon, still evade a Shawnee. Fifty-four wasn't so old after all. Still, it was an outrage to have to come and get this wastrel sprig of the McClure tree who should have been cut down long ago.

"But then you all always did enjoy kickin' shit out of me back at the station," Ish said.

"No more'n you deserved," Will said, lighting up a cigar and stretching his feet, clad in expensive Spanish boots, toward the fire.

"There was always a conspiracy against me," Ish said. "There were all the good little boys and girls, Jackie and Jimmie and Cat and the rest who wore starchy little shirts and petticoats and knew their catechism, and scraped their trenchers in the bucket the way they should. Then there was Ish."

His uncle Will puffed three smoke rings at Ish through his teeth and looked at him hard. The federal magistrate in New Madrid had been a little sad to part with Ish. He had relieved the boredom in the fallen-down little town which perched on the flood plain of the Mississippi, telling his stories of Burr and the Santa Fe Trail and Mexico. But Will was not sad to leave New Madrid with its drunken keelboatmen and miserable store and inn. They had been there, waiting for the extradition papers to come, for almost a month.

"I remember once I was supposed to be stackin' a pile of wood," Ish reminisced, curling his lip. "I had built the woodshed m'self with a slantin' roof and even a cupola on the top. Took me the best part of a month to construct the damn thing, and I did it alone."

Will grunted, summoning recognition. That woodshed had been a surpassingly good one. Strange he did not take more notice of it back then.

"I was s'posed to pile the wood the uncles cut and I decided to make a creation of it. Carefully cut the pine, smellin' sweet as a woods in summer, into kindlin' and laid it end to end, perfect. Then the cordwood. Made it into a design alternatin' hardwoods, oak 'n others so the dark was against the white and it made pretty lines runnin' diagonal across the pile. Took me all afternoon.

"Jackie 'n Jim were supposed to help me, but they were off in the woods chasin' squirrels. They came in and knocked the end off the pile on purpose and I took at the both o' 'em and knocked 'em down, but finally they ended up beatin' me purple. And then they stacked about ten logs up just as Uncle Dan'l came along, and he praised 'em for the fine job of cordwood stacking. On what I did!"

George dished up the quail and mush and began frying apples in a skillet with sugar and cinnamon. Was it so with Ish? Had there been helpful, decent things he did they had not noticed? Perhaps there were a few.

"Born bad, that's what everybody at the station thought," Ish said, looking into the woods, which was beginning to come alive with the sounds of dusk. "Mostly it was jest that I wasn't willin' to be a good Presbyterian. An atheist in a Kentucky stockade is as welcome as a snake at a quiltin' bee."

George kept the fire built high and smeared pennyroyal on all their clothing against the mosquitoes. The smell of the loamy earth, rich and mysterious, of wood burning to ashes, of the sassafras and peppermint they had crushed as they made camp, and the trace odor of skunk coming in from about a mile away tantalized him. It spoke of the many camps he had made, and of his youth, which had died slowly like the embers of this fire, so that he had not even missed it until only the warm ashes remained.

Ish fell asleep in his ropes a few yards away. Will lit another cigar, and George thought about this trip which he had dreaded so much. They were two weeks late getting off, and even then they combined business with the rueful necessity of getting Ish into custody. Will was now brokering hogs and corn for merchants in both Illinois and Indiana, so they had gone through St. Louis to arrange for shipment of the goods and would go to Natchez to settle details of the sale.

It surprised George that his brother was deferential across the Kaskaskias Trace. They had developed a comfortable relationship, and one night even crossed the line into companionableness. In an inn at the bustling river town of St. Louis they had sat up late one night as sweat poured off their faces in the humid heat, and as the lights burned low, they began to talk and eventually got to exchanging grudging confidences.

"You're the cause of me bein' Captain Will McClure, y' know," Will admitted.

"What d' you mean?" George asked, staring into a glass of sherry.

"When y' come back from the wars and bragged so much about Washington and goaded us all on, I decided I was a-goin' to show you. Be a bigger hero 'n you. No matter what it took."

George laughed a little. "And the first night I really got roaring, senseless drunk it was your fault," he confided. His brother looked up at him questioningly.

"After the Battle at Piqua. I knew I had to admire you, but I was so jealous I couldn't face it." He turned his face away and said no more. He had never fully admitted the intensity of what he had felt at Piqua, even to himself.

After that night in St. Louis George was aware some sort of line had been crossed. And he was glad. It was wrong almost to the point of indecency for old men to fight.

"You're smoking too much since you got rich," George now told his brother as he stared at him across the campfire. "Lytle always said tobacco was bad for the stomach."

"You could be right. Certainly chawin' ain't helped John. Pray God he is better now."

"Yes. But Janie doesn't think he'll last the summer out." At that moment their brother was lying surrounded by tapers in the parlor he had proudly built and furnished.

The sound of Janie's name brought the spectre of the past before them; her dark, haughty face seemed to materialize in the smoke of the fire.

"You didn't understand that, y' know," Will said quietly.

"Janie and you?" George said more casually than he felt. It was always there, a banked anger both he and Dan'l still felt, he knew. Once Will seduced his brother's wife it was never possible to face him again with any degree of real respect.

"I have to take m' blame. I should never have let it happen to us out there. Should have been wiser. Poor thing." Did he mean Janie?

"She went along for about a year after the marriage without sayin' much t' me. I was sick from the drinkin', sometimes sick for her too. We was cut from the same piece of cloth, patterns matchin'. Same pride, cantankerousness, and both randy as hound dogs. But I had mostly put that aside when I found Meg. Janie, I yearned for with m' worst side, Margaret, I loved with m' better."

George was silent, looking at the odd, half-sunken mounds in the woods just beyond them. Indian graves, heaped up with leaves and dirt from a hundred years ago, they were. Northern woodland Indians did that—Ottawas or Ojibwas. So what kind of squabble did they have with these southern Indians to get themselves killed and buried so far from home? What were the people like who had fleshed out the bones down there? Did they know the same scorching pain he and his family knew? "What did happen that week we were all gone?" he asked.

"Don't know if you'll believe me. Don't know why I should ask you to—it'll sound like I'm justifyin' myself now. She come after me at the brickyard site where I were workin' alone. Brought m' lunch out t' me. Teased at me the first day and kept at me all week. Then, the last day, she took her dress over her head and stood there lookin' at me, nekkid and proud. She pulled me down into the grass by that crick. Don't know how but I couldn't do it to John there and then. It almost killed me. I begged her but I were only flesh and blood. I came to her that night John came back. I wanted to be with her in that bed more than I ever wanted anything in life.''

"The old story of adultery," George said, still cool.

"Acourse, and I take the blame, finally.''

"After that did you ever. . .''

"No. Never. Although we still were bound soul to soul. Will be 'till the day one of us dies. She talked to me a lot, depended on me through all these years, though.''

George raised his eyebrows. What was this? All of them thought Janie and Will loathed each other after the adultery.

"She were sick, so sick. And so alone. She loved John but couldn't tell him about—''

"About what?''

Will sighed, long and hard, and stubbed out his cigar, throwing the butt into the fire. "About her daddy. She and he—were lovers.'' George looked at him with an uncomprehending expression on his face.

"Well, it is awful. I guess it does happen in the South sometimes, incest, prob'ly other places too. Anyways, he started with her when she was jest a little tyke hardly old enough to know the difference. She had hated it but couldn't let go. When she were about eighteen she threw herself at a man, to escape, I s'pose, and he married her. McClintock by name. A horse tradin' scoundrel as it turned out. Her pa had it annulled.''

"Good God, so she was married before she ever came to Kentucky,'' George said, shaken.

"And divorced. She were attracted to both John and me. Guess we were the older men she had come to prefer. And, truly, she did want security and decency in her life. She found that with John. But her dada couldn't let go of her, nor she of him. After his wife, who he hadn't lived with for years anyways, died, he tried marryin' a young gal from Louisville and you know 'bout that.''

"All that trouble—the town wouldn't accept her as the wife of an aristocrat— she grew despondent, didn't she?''

"Janie were drawn, like by some awful drug, to the house there on the Ohio. Kept goin' down, sayin' her Pa were in trouble—the trouble was her daddy was after her again and the new wife knew it. Must 'a been hell, for all o' 'em.''

"And his wife died,'' George said slowly, apprehensively.

"Threw herself off the cliffs there one night in the dark.''

George nodded grimly. So that was it. He half-wondered about it at the time.

"After that, the spell was broke for Janie. She finally could be free o' that obsession and she tole me then she were goin' to make it right for John if it took her the rest of her life. Give her credit, I think she's tried.''

"Yes. And he never knew at all.''

"Mebbe he half-guessed somethin' was wrong between Janie and her dada.

But no, he never knew. Some things are best kept down cellar in famblies, and this is shore one o' 'em.''

Suddenly, there was a flash of light and activity and confusion around the fire; Ish had awakened without their knowing it. He had got hold of one of the knives in the cooking pack and cut the bonds on his hands. He was in the last stages of freeing his arms when George had turned his head and seen him. His feet kicked fire toward his uncles, his huge strong frame thrashed about at them. The knife in his hands slashed at the two men who were trying to confine him. Finally, George found himself holding Ish down while Will bound up his own severely cut wrist.

"You God-damned fiend," George said through clenched teeth. It was all he could do to hold Ish's wrists down and get the rope around them again. "We're—taking you home—to see your mother, maybe return her sanity—we told you that," he panted.

Will was sitting on Ish's feet. Beneath him, Ish's eyes glowed with the rage of a trapped panther. "You have a good chance of justice miscarryin' and you not gettin' hung," Will growled at him. "After all these years it's going to be difficult to prove anything on the murder charge, anyways."

"And traitorin' and spying for the Spanish? How about those charges, dear uncles?"

"They won't try them in Indiana," George answered "and it doesn't matter what happens, you deserve it. But you have to see your mother, make some peace, apologize."

"For what? For bein' myself? For hatin' the United States Government and hopin' the Spanish could win back the West? What I did would be considered patriotism if it happened against the British in the Revolution. Nevertheless I may get off Scot-free." He laughed at his pun as his eyes grew narrow and malign. "I'm a professional spy, and I didn't work just for the Spanish. The British may give me a medal if they win the war that's comin' up." George, finished tying the knots and looked warily at him.

"Oh, you don't know all, my dear uncles do you? Certainly I'll go back and tell dotin' Mama and Papa that I was in their backyard last year. I stayed around Fort Knox in disguise for over a week and then reported to the British in Quebec." He lay back his head and laughed at the irony of his visit on his parents' doorstep.

"You were the British spy. . ." George began to bang Ish's head against the dirt, swearing at him with every oath he had ever heard until Will, weak from loss of blood, stopped him.

They stayed up the rest of the night with guns aimed at Ish's head. Toward dawn, Will cleared his throat and said to George, " 'Twas you that got that knife. I might have been finished after he gashed me so deep—you took it from him. I never thought. . ." he did not finish what he intended to say.

"Never thought I could do something physically brave? What did you think I was doing at Princeton? And how about Piqua? I was right behind you in that meadow when we went after the Shawnees. Or were you too busy being the frontier hero to notice who followed when you led?"

"Mebbe I was," Will said and scowled. But when he reached out and gruffly patted his brother on the back with his good hand, it was obvious he was reconsidering the matter.

"We cain't hold him by ourselves, George," Will said, holding up his cut left hand as a murky dawn finally came over the ridge above the Mississippi.

"No. But I think we can hire a raft downriver a piece. We'll get him to Natchez. We were going to go up the trace anyway. Let's hire horses and a guide to keep a gun on him the whole way to Nashville. We can afford it now, by God. If your hand isn't better by then, we'll keep the guard all the way to Indiana Territory."

Later that morning George and Will marched Ish Scott slowly down the overgrown river trail toward a lean-to on the riverbank. "Muskrat's Raft Shack," the crudely lettered sign on the eaves said.

A huge, coal-black man came out of the lean-to. "You Muskrat?" Will asked, reaching into his pocket with his unwounded right hand for his money purse.

"Yessuh," he said. Was he a freeman? Will thought so.

"The wood in these yere rafts looks like 'twas cut before George Washington was born," Will murmured, kicking the side of the largest of the three rafts and caving it in with the toe of his boot.

The black man shrugged indifferently. "Them're are all I got now," he said and returned to the shack, where he was dividing bait into small crockery pots. Crawdads wiggled their feelers between his fingers as he took them from a metal bait trap.

"I know jest how they feel," Ish said sardonically. He was in high spirits this morning, evidently stimulated by the knowledge that he had kept his captors up all night and exhausted them.

"Well, we'll take the biggest raft," Will said and paid the price with a gold coin. The man in the lean-to looked at the purse with large eyes.

"You're going to have to watch that purse, Will, from here on in," George said as Muskrat turned his back. "And when we get to the trace. . ."

"I got eyes in my head and a brain too, George," his brother said, irritatedly.

They put Ish, hands tied at the wrists, between them on the raft, with Will holding a pistol directly behind him. George poled down the river.

"Listen to me, you bastard," Will said, prodding Ish with the pistol. "I'd rather kill you than take you back; I've tole you that a'ready. An' what you said last night finished it off for me. You was a spy for the English right in your ma's backyard, and you left her to sit like a potato out o' her mind there. So jest give me the chance to blow your ass off, I dare you." Ish said nothing, but he did not seem inclined to escape. Instead, he warily watched the strong, churning waters of the Mississippi, unusually high for late summer because of the renewed flooding in the Ohio valley.

After a while the brothers relaxed a little, watching the shore line go by, even waving at barges loaded with early harvest goods heading to New Orleans. Occasionally villages came into sight with wooden buildings spread out on the lowlands by the river or clinging to the cliffs above.

"Why'd you have to order me around 'bout the money purse? I don't know why you and Dan'l and John alwuz have to tell me how to run the details of m' life," Will said glumly. His hand was beginning to throb, although the cut had closed.

"Do we?" George asked from his position at the back of the raft.

"Acourse. But I do know, really. 'Tis because you still think o' me as a drunkard." George was silent. He hadn't thought of it before.

Will began to chuckle, ruefully. " 'Tis the price all us reformed drunks have to pay to society for all the trouble we caused. Even though we change, nobody notices. They still expect nothin' from us, trust us with nothin'."

A huge pile of sawyer trees sticking up in a narrow passage in the river caused George to crane his neck and narrow his eyes as he steered the raft through. Then he asked, "What was it like being a drunk?"

"Like being two people at once and not able to do a damn thing about it. You never have a waking moment that in the back of your mind you don't know you're a sot and at the same time you deny it with all you have. The worst part is you lose your hope. Did you ever worry sometimes that when you die you'll be awake and jest lyin' in the box in the cemetery unable to move but able to think? Fer a hunnerd or thousand years trapped in that box? Well, that's the way bein' a drunk is, and you think you gotta face it for thirty, forty years."

"God. It must have been awful."

"That's what makes bein' sober so good." There was a long silence as they stared at the currents eddying, swirling into little circles around them. Even though the river was moderately flooded, the tips of branches were visible over by the shore and George watched them, concerned. Ish slumped over, seemingly asleep again.

"Do you remember Pa's wake, Will?"

"Yes. Do you?"

"Only a little. I remember Jenny crying because there were Indians. Rafe Emison preached the sermon. . ."

"I can see it like it was yesterday. 'Twas colder'n a witch's tit that month, but we'd had a thaw so they could put 'im in the ground."

"I'll never forget the Indians."

"Nor can I! Shawnees, Delawares, an' I was the one who had tried to go to the Conestoga Massacre to kill me some papooses." Will shook his head. "I was scared out of m' moccasins. 'Twas impressive, though. Even though it was Pontiac's rebellion, even though white men and Injeeans were killin' each other all along the frontier, the tribes come to honor Pa for what he did tryin' to give 'em a fair share."

"I do remember they each brought something to place on the casket."

"The feathers of an eagle and of the red hawk for his bravery. White wampum beads and a clay pipe for what he did with the Quaker assembly for peace. They sat there on the cold ground, those faces painted for mourning, long winter robes on, throwin' certain herbs, I don't know for what on the casket. Then Lone Stag spoke."

"What did he say. I hardly remember any of it. . ."

"I don't think I understood it all. It was about how sacrificing for another person is the highest bravery. That all nature teaches 'bout it. When the quail puts herself out to lead away the hunter and save her chicks, when a mother bear fights off a whole pack o' wolves, it shows us unselfishness in Nature. But when a man fights, dies for those who're not even his kin, it shows us—the Great Spirit." His voice was low. The memories must have been painful as a boil, George knew. Debris clunked against the ancient logs of the raft but the two men hardly seemed to notice it. They stood again in the fullness of their youth on the bank of Conodoguinet Creek and forty years were as a day.

"Then Rafe spoke," George said softly.

"He said that knowin' Pa had made him sure that life had meanin'. That one good man could alter things, for time and eternity. That none of us would be the same in years to come because of what Pa had been." George nodded affirmation. The charged memories caused an emotional silence between the two middle-aged men. The strains of the trip and the pain of disappointments recently felt began to tell. They were close to tears.

Finally Will spoke. "Was it right? What Pa said?"

"When?" George asked, not daring to look at him. Ish stirred in his sleep.

"When he died. He said to me, 'We can always help it when we hate.' "

"I don't know," George said sadly. "I've hated too much in my life." He looked up into his brother's weather-worn face and met his eyes. "But I think I'm about ready to give it up in my old age. Yes, Pa was right." He smiled a wry smile and looked away at the shoreline. Will, realizing that what George was saying was about as much of an apology as his brother could ever muster, was moved.

They rounded a bend. Suddenly, before Will could collect his senses and stop him, Ish sat up and shifted his weight to the edge of the raft. Whether he did it on purpose or by accident, the two brothers never knew, but George, looking on shore and unprepared, was thrown to the side.

"Pole, pole, we're headin' for a sawyer," Will shouted, looking dead ahead. But it was too late. The raft hit a huge underwater tree with teeth-jarring force, throwing George into the water.

Ish was swept off the raft, too and began to cry with real terror.

"What do I care, you worthless scum?" Will shouted above the river waters. "You threw us into the sawyer apurpose. Die, drown like a rat!"

The current tore at the remnants of the raft that were holding together precariously in the snag. The pull of the river threw the raft's logs about and caused one to graze Will's forehead. George had all he could do with his heavy, soaked clothing to swim to shore.

Ish clung to another branch of the submerged tree which protruded above the water. It was shifting frighteningly underwater with his weight. He reached out for the raft, as the strong current tore at him. "Uncle, cut my bonds so I can at least try to hold on to the raft. Please, please. I'll stay with you. Anyway, you have the pistol." Will's eyes were cold, and a second that seemed like an hour went by. Then he fumbled for the hunting knife he always carried and reaching as far as he could, cut the ropes that bound Ish's wrists. As he did so, the tree shifted once more and Ish's branch went completely beneath the surface, leaving Ish thrashing in the dark river.

"I can't swim, he shouted hoarsely." God, it was true, thought Will, still leaning toward him from the bit of raft that was left. How convenient, to have this wasted life claimed by the Missisippi river, the blight washed away. . .

Ish started to sink. He went under and rose in a brief second, thrashing and sputtering in terror as water entered his lungs. As he faced Will, Will could see a light in his eyes that frightened him, a devilish light that shone through human terror. Then the roar of Ish's voice and the water rushing about the raft combined and became a voice from the past Will had loved, imperative, compelling, and he put out his good hand and took hold of Ish's hand to pull him onto the raft. But the raft at that instant broke apart completely and Will was thrown under the water for a long moment. When he surfaced and cleared his eyes, the last of the sawyer was gone. So too, was Ish Scott.

The new leather trader's coat was grander than the old one had been, Asondaki told himself. This coat, which the Ojibwas had just sent down from their village in Michigan, was as soft as a dog's underbelly, but it was not decorated as the *metis* coat was. It would suit well for the man who would be the owner of a lucrative trading post in Missouri Territory or beyond and would offend neither Indian nor white.

Some of the French *metis* in Vincennes had admired the coat. He had gone there to settle his accounts finally, had reached a settlement with Hyacinthe Lasselle for partial payment of the sum owed him and now was heading out of town. As he walked the road which led northeast, he thought that Vincennes at the moment did not seem to be a very safe place for anyone with Indian blood. Dragoons were everywhere. More army regulars had arrived in Kentucky boats and were quartered in the inns of the town. The steel of swords and muskets glinted in the sunlight. Was some movement intended? Or were they just drilling? Tecumseh must return soon if he intended to seize the moment. Of course it could not change Asondaki's course. He had met his obligation and would go back just to await the chief's return and say goodbye.

He had asked the way he needed to go from someone in Lasselle's and as he framed the question, his heart had leapt. He came now to the church road the man in the store had described to him. It seemed to be a good road to live on. The one brother now dead had lived on the farm he was passing, with the huge barn and horses grazing in the fields in the lush September afternoon. And now, on the left, the cemetery where they said the grandmother—his grandmother—was buried, with its rounded, light-brown stones. He went on past mellow fields spiked with wheat stubble from the crop just harvested. The winey smell of crushed apples was in the air. Finally a wide house of red brick loomed before him, set on a slight rise. The home of Dan'l McClure. His father.

Inside, that father was presiding at a sort of a family ceremony. Jack McClure, smiling with tight lips, entered the parlor.

"Come over here, Jackie, and stand by me," Martha said to her oldest son, patting at her skirt as she had done when he was six. She was standing by the new piano.

"I was asleep," he admitted, and then looked around. "What's this? A surprise?" Cake and lemonade and little punch cups stood on the table beneath the lace curtains. His brothers Tom and Charlie, handsome in their dragoon uniforms, and his younger brothers Joe and Danny stood near the table. Four of his sisters crowded onto the sofa and little Jane sat at their feet.

Well, Pa must be going to have Bible reading in the evening as well as the morning, and serve lemonade, too, after he dispenses Deuteronomy, Jack McClure thought with nervous amusement. "Is it my birthday?" he asked.

Dan'l McClure smiled proudly. "John," he said. Just the one word, and it seemed to echo strangely about the room. " 'Tis a name all my brothers and sisters have chosen for one of their children, to honor the finest man we ever knew, our father. And I chose it for my firstborn son." There was silence. The clock on the mantel ticked officiously. Martha Bard's nervous breathing could be heard. Little Jane, a miniature of her mother, shifted her feet out from under her and slapped them. They were going to sleep.

"Son John, you have had a melancholy summer. For a while we was worried about you." Melancholy, I guess that was it, Jack thought. It had been almost two months since Adahbelle died and only recently did he feel like even getting up in the morning. The memory of her white, blood-drained face had become a permanent fixture of his daytime thoughts, a haunting presence in his nightmares.

"Now that you are better, we have good news." What can this be, Jack thought warily. He had hardly enough energy to listen to what his family was saying. His mother was carrying something. A long sword. "Jack—John—we have a surprise for you." His father spoke.

Jack felt the eyes of his mother and his brother Tom on him, drilling holes through his exposed head. "Governor Harrison will be makin' a campaign against the Injeeans at Prophetstown while Tecumseh is away. Destroy their power. The Parke Company will be the select unit involved in the campaign and Harrison has jest made a few changes in its top command. You are to be sergeant."

Thunder boomed above Jack's head. He flushed, then felt as if he were clasping icicles he couldn't let go of. He had never thought to be in the dragoons; it was not his way. They knew that. What sort of plot was this? He was Jackie Dee the japester, never serious, avoiding responsibility. Or at least he had been until Adahbelle. . . His mother was advancing with the sword, her eyes bright, sausage curls bouncing. At that moment he saw the hired woman Artesia slip into the room and wait to be recognized by his mother.

Martha handed the sword to Jack, then turned not too pleasantly on the woman. "Well?" she demanded.

"A man to see Mister McClure. Best come now." Dan'l excused himself and went to the door.

Jack McClure nodded to his mother and breathed a sigh of relief that this ridiculous farce had been interrupted. Holding onto the sword, he led Martha to the refreshment table. He could not meet the eyes of his brother Tom, who, handsome in his private's uniform, stood aloofly toying with a spyglass in the corner of the room. If anybody should have been named sergeant. . .

The sun was beginning to set, through tall virgin cottonwoods around the house. A strong breeze tousled the wavy hair of the man who stood before Dan'l McClure and flip-flopped the tails of the fine leather coat he wore. He did not speak; he simply stepped forward and smiled a wistful smile, extending his hand. "So I finally see you," he said.

Dan'l looked into his face. About thirty, he guessed, with a strong honest face, slightly slanting eyes and the look of—his own mother. My God. "Do I know you?" he said, still holding onto the man's hand.

"I am Asondaki Alamelonda—McClure." There was an edge of pride in the last word. "I have come with a message from M'takwapiminji. Mulberry Blossom, my mother." Dan'l felt himself reeling. The sun coming through the cottonwoods seemed to glare directly into his eyes. He was distracted by the wind, which buffeted their voices.

Asondaki withdrew his hand slowly and turned his head a little on the side as he smiled into Dan'l's face. A smile as bright as the morning sun, Dan'l thought and was reminded of a morning by the bend of the Auglaize river, where a radiant child played with mussel shells. "Mulberry Blossom?" he asked quietly.

The smile faded. "She is dead. She could not survive the winter after the smallpox. She wished me to give you a message, one I do not understand myself. She said that I was the pledge of something between the two of you and that as long as I am alive that pledge survives. She prayed God to bless you." His eyes flicked. "She had become a Christian."

Dan'l nodded sadly. He scanned the handsome, unusual face of his son. He had hungered for the sight of him for so many years. But a voice calling his own name drifted from inside the house. Martha was wondering where he was.

"I wanted to meet you so often. There is so much to tell you," Dan'l hesitated only the slightest fraction of a moment. . ."Son."

Asondaki nodded and smiled again. A figure materialized in the door. "Miz McClure says could you tell her when you'll be in for the cereymony." Dan'l hesitated. Confusion, or was it fear, clouded his eyes.

"Yes, yes. Son, wait here. I'll be back in jest a moment. . ." Flustered, he went into the house. But when he returned, in only a few minutes, no one was there. He stood, a hand above his eyes, squinting into the setting sun.

Asondaki walked through the cottonwood grove. He thought to himself, she did not know. For all Dan'l McClure's honesty, he had never told his wife. He struck out cross-country toward the river to return to Prophetstown.

What was cowardice anyway? Jack McClure asked himself. The party was over and he stood by his bed, alone, with the door shut and locked. The quilt, stitched by his mother in shades of rose and green, was drawn across the feather mattress.

Discretion was supposed to be the best part of valor, wasn't it? All the old men told stories of how they survived battles by indulging their fears and getting behind trees at the right times, running or hiding at others. Wasn't that cowardice? And why did a man like him, who thought the issues meaningless and who hated confrontations, especially physical, have to don a sword and epaulettes and lead in battle to please his parents or his neighborhood?

An honor, they said. John McClure he was now. Oldest of the clan to bear the great man's name. He hated it. A family was like a vise, holding you firm, as you bend, bend, slowly until you conformed to the pattern of the past. Or snapped. He stared at the shapes in the quilt. Huge stylized curving rose petals with green leaves repeated themselves across its surface. Rose of Sharon pattern, they called it. "I am the Rose of Sharon, the bright and morning star." Leave it to his mother to preach at him even while he slept.

He began to perspire, his heart to palpitate, as it always did when he faced a challenge he felt pushed into. The despondency which he had fought daily since Adahbelle's death crept upon him again, and he felt faint, so great was the sickness in his heart. He sat upon the bed.

There was no meaning in anything he did, and this was simply the last in a life of insipid, regrettable missteps. One could not turn down William Henry Harrison's appointment. He was now set up, like a bowling pin on a green, to fall, irretrievably. To disgrace everyone, especially himself.

He picked up the sword, looking at its fine curved steel handle, the tooled, intricate scrollwork on its scabbard. He could not go into battle, never. On a horse? He would run, as he had from Burr's expedition, and it would be the end of his life in Vincennes, where such stories lingered forever.

Harrison had written to the President of the United States that the men who were in this select unit were the bravest in the Northwest, from the finest families. "Not needing money," the paper quoted him, "gallant, patriotic, and the officers are the flower of the frontier," he had said. The lump of despair he recognized lately at the pit of his stomach seemed to grow, opening up, swallowing everything in him inside its blackness.

Beside his bed was a copy of a book which his father had given him. It sat there decoratively, unthumbed since he had moved into the bedroom. Idly, looking for something tangible to put his hands on in his desperation, he picked it up. *Pilgrim's Progress*—his grandmother had carried the damn thing across the buffalo wallows. He opened the cover, turned to the first leaf, which was dotted with brown water spots and what seemed to be tiny scales of salt. "This book given to George McClure, January 15, 1710 by his father, Alexander McClure, Physician, Dunleigh, Ireland" in one crabbed hand and in another, the notation, *Pilgrim, see page 36, G.M.* A twinge of curiosity pierced the blackness. Jack McClure turned to the page and read *Pluck up a good heart, O Christian, for Greater is He that is in thee, than he that is in the world.* With numb indifference, he tossed the book against the wall.

The black hole inside him could not swallow all his will. He picked up the dragoon's pistol his father had given him. Coldly he loaded it with a lead ball. He was trembling all over, he could hardly breathe and was nauseously sick.

He put the pistol to his head, but his legs were shaking so he had to sit down on the bed with it. The hand that did not hold the pistol pushed against the bed for stability, touched one of the huge, raised roses. He looked at it. It became Adahbelle's face, wan, but smiling.

She was the Rose of Sharon to me, he thought suddenly, the bright morning star. She looked at him and saw something very different from all this. Why? Was any of it there? He thought at one time it might be. Maybe he owed it to her to find out. It might be the one thing he could do for her now. The shaking in his knees stopped. He sat for a long time staring at the quilt. Then he stood up and walked over to the bureau. He put the pistol down on it, carefully, and took up the sword. Then, still carrying it, he stooped down and picked up the copy of *Pilgrim's Progress* and gently laid it on the bedside table. He went to the door and unlocked it with a click.

Chapter XLVI

A great comet appeared in the sky over the United States in September and October of 1811, and its globular head and sweeping tail were clearly visible in the night sky over Indiana.

Jenny Scott began to speak again, one night, as her husband and son came in from looking at the comet over the river. "Portents are abroad. Even the animals of the forest are unsettled," she said. John Robert hurried over to her, startled that she finally spoke, and also realizing that what she said was true. Deer and bear had been seen in Vincennes streets; great flocks of birds seemed to crowd the skies.

From her chair near the fire, Jenny went on in an ominous voice. "Soon even the land will shake, fire will rise from the bowels of the earth and spew forth. The great river will flow backwards and many will die." She spoke no more, although her brothers soon came home to tell her Ish was dead and that at least she need not worry about him constantly, that there might be some grain of joy for her in the times ahead. Catherine and John Hogue, Mary and Samuel Emison and others of Jane and John McClure's grandchildren were planning marriages as soon as the Indian campaign was over.

Jenny never spoke again. And in the family, it was always remembered that like Cassandra, Jenny forecast the waste and destruction of the terrible year when the War of 1812 began.

The Indians saw the comet too. "You see the Fire Dragon flies across the skies," Tenskwatawa the Prophet told them. "He tells us we at the camp of the Prophet are under his protection. Do not fear the white man. The time of retribution is not far off." And they listened, believing he truly spoke the word of God.

What strange tentfellows war makes of us, George McClure thought as he watched the Benjamin Parke Dragoons ride smartly up First street on their way out of town. We have fought claw and fang, like panthers here in the territory and now we all ride off together to fight the common danger.

One of Luke Dugger's boys rode next to the son of John Badollet, and General Washington Johnston followed private Sam Emison, as if they hadn't been on opposite sides of at least twenty territorial issues in the last year. Lieutenant Thomas Emison, his white horse prancing spiritedly, led the non-commissioned officers including First Sergeant Jack McClure, whose face flushed bright red above his high-collared greatcoat. George counted on his fingers, and nudged his wife in the ribs. "Seven Baird grandsons, two Emisons and—Dan'l's Jack, Tom and Charlie, John's Jim, Will's John and Archie, and Willie," their own sixteen-year-old, sitting stiffly in a new saddle. "One tenth of the brigade is McClures." Jean nodded. On the other side of the road bobbed the bonnets of Cat, Polly, and Margit, Elizabeth, and Mary and the younger McClure maidens who had come to see the cousins off to war.

Bairds, Emisons, McClures, George thought. They had lived and suffered in the same land of Ireland a hundred and fifty years ago. And they had come over ocean, mountain pass, great river, and dangerous trail together. Fox and geese. . . Now the new generation must go to war to put its own stamp upon the land. It was as if the Battle of the Boyne, Kittanning, Trenton, Piqua had never been fought. Each generation must buy its heritage, often with blood. He had known it at Princeton. It was not pleasant, it was not even rational, but it was the truth.

But so the Indians thought also, for they had been at Kittanning, Piqua too. They had the same wish and need to stamp the land themselves, if you looked at it from a different end of the spyglass.

Dan'l McClure stood with Martha and the numerous cousins across the street, near the Territorial Capital building.

"What a loss if they should not come back," Martha said in a soft voice. "A whole generation in the territory. . ."

"They'll come back. McClures are like that. So are all the Scotch-Irish. They know how t' survive."

" 'Twould be a high price to pay. . ."

"Oh, Ma used to talk about the tolls folks who take off on untried roads have to pay. But if we'd been countin' the costs, Pa and Ma 'd never got on that boat in Derry, and we'd never built the Caintucky arks. And I would never 'a come here and gone inta politics when I was fifty years old." He was silent for a minute then added, "Takin' the new roads is what livin' is, ain't it? Stayin' behind is dyin'. Why, you jest look at England and Ireland a hunnerd years from now, Martha, and see what they're like, made up of all the stay-at-homes."

"So you say," his wife murmured.

"Yes, I do. I say the tolls life asks ain't a nickel more than we're prepared to pay."

But Martha McClure could not help looking across the street at Jenny Scott's frozen face and thinking about her and all the other people the McClures had buried somewhere along the new roads. Many of them were women. Taking the new road was always hardest on them.

"Kill the redskins. Bring back a scalp on each bayonet," John Robert Scott shouted as he jumped up and down beside his father and his Aunt Janie and her children. Other citizens were also yelling imprecations. "Slaughter the Shawnees, decapitate the Delawares."

"It takes a lot of hating to get a war in gear," George McClure said to Jean.

"That sounds like one of the things Will has been saying lately," she smiled faintly. Will was ill, very ill. He had never recovered from the malaria he had contracted in the Mississippi bottomlands and could not see his sons go off so proudly this September morning. It was a day as clear as chandelier crystal. Yesterday's drenching rains had washed the dust from the air.

"Rafe Emison used to call this holy hate, this thing we feel about the Indians. Said the frontier bred it into the young ones with their mother's milk," George mused.

His wife turned her head to him. " 'Tis true, but this is a two-way cart road. Right now I expect they are generating just as much hatred toward us."

He nodded and they watched in silence as the last of the dragoons that Harrison had assembled headed out on the muddy road north, through the radiant autumn afternoon.

Jack McClure sat looking at his journal on the bare-cut new escarpment around Fort Harrison up the Wabash from Vincennes. He looked at the script inside the cracked leather cover. "Sergeant John A. McClure, Cumberland County, Pennsylvania." So the old man was a sergeant too. The crumbling blotter pad still retained imprints of a dispatch. He tried to make them out from the backwards writing. Ft. Granville. Indians. He had heard about that too.

He flipped a couple of pages to scan his own writings during the last three weeks:

September 24—Left Vincennes and camped at Busseron Creek Shaker settlement. Shakers avoided us like we were the Smallpox.

October 1—We are marching according to general orders with dragoons on the outside of the column for protection. Riflemen from Kentucky, Indiana militia and the Fourth United States Regiment are with us. Du Bois's Scouts precede us, filtering through the woods as reports of the Prophet's Indians about increase. Hunting parties brought in quail, racoons, pheasants.

October 18—Some men want to go home, tired of cold weather and boredom. Harrison spoke to them and they have agreed to stay. We are building a strong fort with blockhouses, storage space to command the Wabash here.

He looked up. Thomas Emison was before him with a paper in his hand. "I have just been to a staff meeting. Harrison has strictly prohibited shooting at marks. Says we won't have enough ammunition to meet the Indians."

"That's reasonable, but the men's morale is going to suffer. They're as jumpy as kittens. They're imaginin' thousands of Indians gatherin' upriver. I don't see why recreation is going to hurt. . ."

"And no card playing or dice-throwing. Except for backgammon. He's stepping up inspection on arms. Says the condition of the muskets is deplorable."

"Anything more?" Jack was resigned to his duties as sergeant, helping manage the company at Parade and drill, calling the roll after the adjutant put the company through the paces of drawing swords and dressing the ranks, and supervising passing out the rations while the fife and drum played the lively strains of "Roast Beef."

"The contractors have not appeared with the food we need," Emison said.

"What will rations be 'till they come?" his cousin asked him with a sigh.

"Three fourths of a pound of flour, a bit more beef. Maybe the hunters will bring in more venison. And they could get to the Indian corn fields before long. The provision boats'll be here soon."

"I hope so. I hate chasin' deserters through the woods. And I dread the court martials that Harrison's ordered."

Thomas Emison was silent. Bringing a group of individualistic Scotch-Irish farmers who were not efficient soldiers through savage-infested woodlands in November was not easy.

"What'll happen at the court martials?" Jack asked Thomas.

"I don't know how the militia will be treated. The regular army orders fifty lashes on the naked back."

"Harrison'll never dare that with these local units. . ."

"No, they'd high-tail it back to Bruceville or Corydon. He'll order a few lashes. Or drum 'em out of camp, heads shaved and powdered. Whatever the punishment, it is less than they deserve," Tom said calmly. His disposition was as serene as his brother Samuel's was intense.

"At least the Injeeans seem to be lettin' us alone."

"Only when you are on guard duty do they seem to come out of the trees." His cousin smiled. A week or so ago when Jack was on cavalry guard, sentinels near him were fired on by lurking Indians and one man was wounded. McClure led three men crashing through the underbrush in pursuit, but the Indians evaporated. Still, Thomas Emison and the other officers commented, the army back at the camp had turned out in good order for a bunch of raw militiamen.

"I think your part in that skirmish was satisfactory. It would have been very difficult to bag an Indian in that confusion."

Jack nodded, thanking him with a faint smile, then shrugged. At least he had been able to stay on the horse.

That night Harrison paraded the troops. As they stood at ease, he told them, "You will have to fight. There is no pulling back now. Having come so far toward the Prophet's lair, we must not give the impression that we are weak or will retreat. Every cabin in these territories would then be bait for attack, to say nothing of Vincennes itself. Yes, we will fight sooner or later."

And so the troops marched closer to where the confederated Indian tribes on the Wabash congregated in a village with their wives and children, where they waited for Tecumseh to return with enough strength from the South to mount a mighty campaign against the whites.

In the Indian camp on the Tippecanoe and Wabash Rivers, on October 31, Potawatomi scouts told the Prophet that close to one thousand troops had crossed the Wabash. Harrison's force had taken three hours to splash the wagons, now loaded with supplies, through. They were advancing ten of their miles a day.

"Will they have cannon?" Tenskwatawa asked Asondaki as they sat in council in the November night.

"I think not. Bringing artillery causes the white man great trouble over trackless waste."

"I do not wish to fight, and my brother has forbidden it until he returns with many braves. Will the white men seek to fight us?"

"I do not know. Perhaps this march is only a threat, to keep you in the camp."

"You say so, and I think so too. But some here wish to go out and fight the whites even as they march."

"Winnamac does." Asondaki's voice revealed the indifference he felt to these details of Indian confederation politics. Swiftly Running Feet awaited the birth of the baby at Lake Mocksinkickee, and his thoughts were ever on her and the trading post he would soon build across the Mississippi. A phase of his life was ending, and what was happening here did not really involve him. He had done his duty. Word had been brought that Tecumseh was heading north again and would soon seek out Harrison for a fight. He would stay a week more to await the great chief's return. Before he left, in honor's name and in memory of his uncle whose sons were here, he must bid goodbye. If Tecumseh did not come within the week, he would leave for the Lake of Rocks anyway.

In the meantime, he spoke to Miami warriors, like his uncle's sons. They accompanied Stone-eater, trained by Little Turtle himself in that chief's former war-chief days, and Loon, two strong leaders who would be indispensible to Tecumseh when he arrived.

A negro attendant from Harrison's army wandered into the camp and readily spoke to the Indians. He confirmed that there was no artillery and Tenskwatawa nodded his head in a satisfied way. There were no cannons to blow up the Indian village. "The white men are making a show of strength, as deer at rutting season do, pawing the ground, flashing their antlers about," the Prophet said to those about him.

Yet when a wan sun shown behind heavy clouds the morning of November 6, the army was at Tippecanoe, and Asondaki realized that the decision of whether to fight or not had come to the very doormat of Tecumseh's confederacy. Tenskwatawa sent scouts out to parley, then spoke to the council. "The white man wishes to talk to us of how we can have peace, tomorrow morning." He snorted and a bitter smile twisted his already misshapen features. "Still, we need not be afraid. The Great Spirit has sent these white men into our hands."

"You will fight?" Asondaki asked apprehensively.

"Or we will kill the Great Chief Harrison. When he is gone, the weak white troops who have never fought will flee. Two Winnebagos have volunteered to go to the parley tomorrow acting as guard. On signal they could attack the white chief. . ."

"It is not a good idea," Stone-eater said, his lean face intent. "Let us attack tonight, while fires are bright, illuminating the white men as our targets."

Two men in the uniforms of the British army settled like fat hens into the council circle. They had come into camp a few days before. Asondaki disliked their haughtiness, the patronizing tone of their broad, nasal syllables as they gave advice from "His Majesty's command." But their presence showed how near war with England really was for the Americans. The Americans would fight over trade on the high seas and in the fur empires, the Indians would again be in the middle here. But he would not have to see it. He and his family would be among the rich forest patches and broad plains of Missouri, where the war would not reach.

The decision of how, or how not to fight the imposing army with its tents pitched beyond the swampland went on into the night in the Prophet's camp, and the tenseness grew. Winnamac made it plain he and his tribe would leave if there was not battle on the morrow, and Tenskwatawa finally told the council he would go into a trance and get the instructions of the Great Spirit.

Asondaki watched from his place beside his cousins around the fire. Mialanaqua, Catfish, the older of the sons of Hidden Panther, was now a bandchief and had a place of honor. The Prophet danced around with a bowl of firecoals, fingering his strange pope's beads, bending his head back and forth and wailing a fierce, otherworldly chant.

Watching the odd scene in the blazing firelight, Asondaki again experienced the alienation he so often felt in his early years. These fools would fight without Tecumseh. He knew it now. They would risk the chance to make the statement of united Indians, secure fair compensation for the future, even win separate lands which would be forever theirs by a great victory.

The Prophet's wails grew in intensity, filling the council house. Winnebagos, Kickapoos, Sauks, Miamis sat in rapt awe. I should not have stayed, Asondaki thought with growing alarm. I will have to watch them throw themselves against Harrison, who has prepared to win a battle that should not be happening now. Either that or leave immediately. My cousins, son of my uncle—many others of my clan, will rush out to be squashed like June beetles—

The Prophet came out of his trance. "The Great Spirit has decreed the white men's doom. They sleep tonight on their arms and they will never awake. A spell will settle, like the fog of the lakes, about them. They may shoot with their muskets, but we will feel no pain. Bullets, bayonets will have no power against us. We will go into their very midst tonight and kill them as they sleep, my brothers!"

A shout of affirmation went around the circle.

One of the red-coated soldiers cleared his throat, and the Indians turned toward him. His cheeks puckered in from the smoke of the pungent herbs he was puffing in his pipe. He had a thin, effeminate face. "I say do not attack at night. At dawn, when you can finish the job and pursue the troops in the light."

His companion, a flabby man with almost black shirt cuffs, stood behind him, nodding quickly in approval. He, too, had the look of a girl. It was said these two men were "camp-mates" like the men his ancestors used to dress in women's clothing and use for amusement in depraved moods.

It was decided after an hour of discussion that the attack would be at dawn, through the willow swamp to the northwest of the American camp.

Asondaki, still wearing the nondescript homespun shirt and buckskin breeches which could identify him as neither Indian or white man, began to gather his trail pack for departure.

The trail east would be congested. Indians, particularly Miamis, would be entering into the Prophet's camp as news of the coming battle spread. Asondaki should be on his way. That it was a cold night without light of the moon did not bother him—he would build a fire up the trail. He stopped, looking at his few mementos, the medicine bag with the turkey feathers in it he had carried with him all these years, a silver brooch his mother had tied her beautiful hair back with, and the Pennsylvania rifle. Hidden Panther had given it to Mulberry Blossom, and it had been the only thing she had to remember Dan'l McClure by. Except for him, of course, he thought with a pang.

Asondaki thought of what would be happening tomorrow and his thoughts began to choke him. The futility, the senseless, mind-deadening stupidity of such a fight. Was there a righteous side? Harrison said he had his own reasons, maybe he did. But what the pot boiled down to was that the white men had lied, cheated, and stolen from every Indian tribe they met. They were bent on completely destroying an entire race of people to get land. His uncle had told him of the legendary wise man of the Delawares, Lone Stag, who used to come to the Ohio camps. "The main fault of the white man," he had said, "is that he thinks of us as no better than his dogs or hogs." This stung the most all along. The lack of respect. The Americans were hunting a bunch of troublesome, stupid animals with the purpose of wiping them out. While the Indians thought of each man as the individual child of the Great Spirit, given the freedom of the land by Him. And they treated each man with respect.

And so, the Indians were right after all. To die here, with dignity, defending that idea would be worthy for these tribes. Still the pain in his heart for them all had not lessened as his cousins approached.

"And so, Wounded Sun, you prepare to go from the camp of war," said Mialanaqua, evenly. The controversies of other days had lessened, Asondaki conceded, and his cousin had grown into the stature of Hidden Panther, his father. And so, his words stung.

"Akimawita, this burnt stick has never known his people," the younger, unreconciled brother said scornfully.

All about them the tribes prepared hastily for battle, cleaning rifles, readying bows, painting eyes, taking emetics to purify themselves for battle. "I challenge you, my kinsman," said Mialanaqua. Asondaki returned his gaze inquiringly.

"Shall you go back to grub for gold in the white man's world while we fight here? Will you not stand with us for these women and children and our freedom? The way of my father Hidden Panther was never to fight unless there was cause. The destruction of a people is cause. Will you fight in my father's name?"

Asondaki mind seemed suspended in a void, poised on the edge of nothing. He could not speak.

"He taught you the greatest lesson of the Wemiamiki, did he not?"

Asondaki's voice was barely a whisper. "To face death as we face life, looking it in the eye as a couger does. . ."

"But there is more, Asondaki Alamelonda."

"To face it together, with the All-Beaver. For as many cattail leaves have only one root, so Wemiamiki are one plant, one people."

Mialanaqua turned and walked away without speaking further. Asondaki stood silent in the confusion for a long time. Then, very sadly he set down the trail pack and went to look for the paint pot and feathers of war.

Jack McClure stuck his head out from under the greatcoat that served as his only tent in the pre-dawn darkness. A clammy drizzle was filtering over the sleeping cavalry, militia, and U.S. army regulars who surrounded the dying campfires of Harrison's camp. He got up and threw logs on the fire, watching the prostrate, sleeping lumps that were his brothers Tom and Charlie and his cousin Sam Emison.

His eyes fell on Emison's long rifle, lying just beyond reach of his arm. It had belonged to Sam's father Hugh in Kentucky. Sam groaned, obviously having a troubled dream and turned quickly over. Jack could see, showing under Emison's coat, the fine powder horn he had made, a twin to the one Thomas Emison carried. Sam had such a fanciful nature. Unicorns, griffins, smiling bears, all executed in skillful scrimshaw.

Jack hung the greatcoat before the fire on a stick. He took the butt of his rifle and gently prodded Charlie, but before he could do the same thing to Tom, his younger brother sat up, wide awake and staring at him with eyes impossible to read.

"Let's go to the horses, before the rest of the camp is up," Jack said to Tom. His brother shrugged his thin shoulders. Tom was proving to be a conscientious soldier, as everyone expected, but he could not bring himself to acknowledge that Jackie Dee McClure was giving him an order.

Jack turned to find Jim and Johnny McClure behind him. "The horses are skittish this mornin'," Jim McClure said, as they walked toward the tethering ground. "Harrison's white has broken its tether and. . ."

At that moment a shot rang out. Then a weird, frightening scream pierced the air from the throat of someone who had to be in agonizing pain.

The three turned as if they were the ones shot and stared off to the west, where Barton and Geiger's militia troops were stationed. Soon other shots followed, other screams. The Indians had broken faith and were attacking. Jack, Jim, and Johnny McClure raced for their rifles and ran to fire into the dark swamp wherever they saw a flash of light, heard a noise.

"So this is what battle is," Jack McClure told himself, trying to keep his stomach from discharging its contents a few minutes later. "Fear and confusion." Ashes from the campfires were kicked about as men doused them so they would not become illuminated targets, horses neighed in the rear in terror, units hurried hither and yon seemingly without orders, drums rattled. He had just come from the side of a man shot repulsing a savage among the very campfires, and had himself shot after the fleeing Indian. In the rainy darkness a force of unknown size was encircling the American camp, forcing the threat of annihilation down their very throats.

Only Harrison seemed calm, here toward the center of the camp. He must at all costs prevent the Indians from encircling and destroying this small army which represented the destiny of the American Midwest.

Crisply he issued a series of commands, ordering two units to the rear to anticipate a thrust from the southwest, putting other units into the angle where the savages first broke through.

A messenger from Jo Daviess of Kentucky, who led the cavalry units, rushed up to him.

"Colonel Daviess requests that he be allowed to pursue the savages," the messenger announced, breathless.

"He has asked twice. I have said it is not a propitious time," the commander said, frowning.

"He asks for his chance at glory."

"He will get that soon enough," Harrison growled, but added, "Let him proceed as circumstances allow and his own will determines." In a few moments he began to spur his horse toward the angle of hottest fire. Thomas Emison put his hand on the bridle.

"Sir, in no wise go into that part of the battle. The Indians are purposely looking to shoot you. They have already killed Colonel Owen because he was on a horse like yours."

Barely sparing him a glance, Harrison spurred his gray and shot off. In a few moments Harrison was back at the center of the camp, the horse rearing and neighing. Daviess's messenger appeared again.

"Sir, I have the sad duty of reporting that Colonel Daviess is mortally wounded."

Harrison shook his head. "And so now perhaps he has enough of glory." He turned to Benjamin Parke. "Colonel, take command of the cavalry. That means Emison commands the Parke Dragoons." He nodded his head at the young man.

And Emison looked at Jack McClure. "Take on my responsibilties, McClure," he said shortly.

"Take—on—my—responsibilties." Jack repeated the words to himself slowly.

"I want to get out there," Tom McClure said shortly to his cousin Archie, as they stood among the Parke Dragoons in their reserve position in the center of camp.

"They'll kill 'em all before we git into 't. And us afoot," Archie snorted. "Why do we have t' stand and watch? I feel 'bout as useful as a hog in a waistcoat."

He sounded like Uncle Will as he said that, thought Jack, who stood nearby, and in a flash remembered that word had come his uncle was dead. He had survived all those battles and died in his bed. But here—lead balls and arrows were flying all around. Commanding officers were being borne into the center of the camp, their blood spilling from stomach or head wounds. Indians with gaping bayonet, saber, and rifle wounds were lying face down on the outskirts of the camp. Young men with arrows in them, surprised before they could even pick up their rifles, were being carried to aid stations.

All about them hot fire continued to crackle as the first rays of dawn streaked along the ridge above the Indian camp. The Indians were no longer breaking into the camp, but reports of devastating losses along the left flank filtered among the waiting reserves. "Spencer of the Corydon Yellowjackets and Warrick of the militia were killed, along with many of their officers, by a savage force coming strongly through the rear of the swamp. An ensign is commanding, but the gap has been filled," a panting officer raced up to report.

After moments that passed like hours, Tom Emison appeared from nowhere, and McClure wheeled about to face him. "The savages may be beginning to pull back, perhaps to re-group. Mount thirty of the Parke Dragoons. Prepare to charge." In as much haste as he could muster and selecting his cousins first, McClure followed the order.

The Parke Dragoons were in the saddle, sabers drawn, when Harrison gave Emison his command, "Follow the militiamen who lead the attack on foot. Pursue the savages retreating there into the swamp and annihilate them." Soon, Emison and McClure leading, the dragoons were picking their way through scenes of hand-to-hand combat as militiamen fought Winnebagos with bayonets, sabers, and bare hands, on trampled mucky oak leaves.

"Quickly, we must reach the ones beyond this ground," Emison shouted, indicating with his head the direction the charge should take. As McClure paused, ready for the charge, the bay gelding reared in fright.

"Charge," Emison roared. Beside Jack, Sam Emison, Jim, Archie, Tom and the rest tried to control their mounts, frenzied with the noise of musket fire.

For a moment the old horse panic washed over Jack, incongruous among the overriding distractions and sentiments of the battle.

In that split second, as he fought his own personal battle, a strange, cold calm possessed Jack and he said, bending over the horse's mane, "Hold, my friend. 'Tis our moment." The horse calmed and stood, pawing the ground a little. "Courage is only makin' yourself do somethin' dangerous that you don't want to do atall. That goes for all of us, including you. Let's go."

He spurred, harder than he had intended and the surprised horse took off like a streak. The dragoons followed, yelling, flashing swords. Indians all across the field, hearing the charge, immediately disengaged and ran into the concealing willow mucklands, where the panting horses could not follow. Jack McClure, Thomas Emison, the other cousins and members of the Parke Dragoons reined their mounts on the crest of the hill. Raising their sabres above their heads, they yelled oaths and imprecations to the departing savages as they watched the grasses part and the last of the dark bodies slip into the woods.

The Battle of Tippecanoe was finished, and when the Parke Dragoons returned to camp the green militiamen hoisted Thomas Emison and Jack McClure to their shoulders.

vicClure had been overheard saying "Courage is only making yourself something dangerous you don't want to do at all," and the saying became famous around Vincennes, along with other sayings from the battle (some overblown and misquoted) and the bravest deeds of the dragoons and militiamen.

George McClure and John Badollet added their own private observations to the list of aphorisms later in Vincennes as they watched the very ordinary battle become a myth in a week's time. "Heroism is only having somebody see what you do and put it in the paper," was what George said.

No one seemed to know that Sergeant Jack McClure had uttered his stirring words before the final charge to a horse. He was a hero. The hurrahing soldiers nominated him to be one of the men who painted Governor Harrison's name on a big rock as the conquering army returned to southern Indiana.

As the Indians retreated that morning of the battle, they bore off most of their dead. But two or three bodies lay concealed among high, bending swamp grass and were not discovered until late afternoon, when the militiamen swept the ground on their way to scout the village. They bent over the body of one brave who had fallen face down near the creek, and turning him over, puzzled over him. He had dark-red, wavy hair, and his features, showing traces of mixed blood, were remarkably composed in death. Most of all they wondered at the handsome Pennsylvania rifle beside him, with a goose in flight on its stock. In honor of that fine rifle, which a Kentucky militiaman took for his own, they did not scalp or mutilate this Indian, as they did the other savages that day of the Battle of Tippecanoe.

Epilogue

In the giving-birth hut at the edge of the Winter Camp of Potawatomis at Lake Mocksinkickee, a baby's cries pierced the December darkness. The mother, who had an easy birth, even though she was an older woman as Indians go, sat up and quickly cut the cord with a hunting knife and tied it off. She cleaned the child with spring water and wrapped it in doeskin swaddling clothes.

"You are beautiful" she said, marvelling at the light pinkness of the little girl. "I will name you Dawn Yet To Come, and we will go to find the new life in the West, as he wanted. I swear it to you, my babe."

The earth trembled and shook, spilling what was left of the water pot.

"Nanamamkickiee," she whispered, using the Miami word for earthquake her husband taught her. She had felt the shocks all night as she awaited the birth of the child, sensed their portentousness for the troubled world in which the new babe would live. "Never mind, I will protect you, daughter of the West Wind." She put her nose against the red fuzz on the baby's scalp.

Then, wearily, she placed the babe beside her, put logs on the heating fire, and turned over to sleep. Thus mother and babe lay sleeping peacefully until the sun rose, sending brazen rays across the surface of the Lake of the Boulders, all frozen now except where the stream entered on the east shore beneath the low-bending weeping willow tree.